the
Unofficial
Guide® to

Walt Disney World 2003

Other *Unofficial Guides*

the Unofficial Guide® to Walt Disney World 2003

Bob Sehlinger

WILEY

Wiley Publishing, Inc.

Please note that prices fluctuate in the course of time, and travel information changes under the impact of many factors that influence the travel industry. We therefore suggest that you write or call ahead for confirmation when making your travel plans. Every effort has been made to ensure the accuracy of information throughout this book, and the contents of this publication are believed correct at the time of printing. Nevertheless, the publishers cannot accept responsibility for errors or omissions or for changes in details given in this guide or for the consequences of any reliance on the information provided by the same. Assessments of attractions and so forth are based upon the author's own experience, and therefore, descriptions given in this guide necessarily contain an element of subjective opinion, which may not reflect the publisher's opinion or dictate a reader's own experience on another occasion. Readers are invited to write the publisher with ideas, comments, and suggestions for future editions.

Published by:

Wiley Publishing, Inc.

909 Third Ave.

New York, NY 10022

Produced by Menasha Ridge Press
Cover design by Michael J. Freeland
Interior design by Michele Laseau

For information on our other products and services or to obtain technical support, please contact our Customer Care Department within the U.S. at (800) 762-2974, outside the U.S. at (317) 572-3993 or fax (317) 572-4002

Wiley also publishes its books in a variety of electronic formats. Some content that appears in print may not be available in electronic formats.

ISBN 0-7645-6604-0

ISSN 1059-3578

Manufactured in the United States of America
10 9 8 7 6 5 4 3

Contents

Part Six   Special Tips for Special People   283

List of Maps

Acknowledgments

Special thanks to our field-research team, who rendered a Herculean effort in what must have seemed like a fantasy version of Sartre's No Exit to the tune of "It's a Small World." We hope you all recover to tour another day.

Lynne Bachleda	Madeline O'Bryan
Molly Merkle	Taylor O'Bryan
Holly Cross	(the Human Probe)
Leslie Cummins	Tiffany Prewitt-McClain
Shannon Dobbs	Len Testa
Georgia Goff	Grace Walton
Chris Mohney	Barbara Williams
Nathan Lott	

Peals of laughter and much appreciation to nationally renowned cartoonist Tami Knight for her brilliant and insightful work.

Many thanks to Pam Brandon, who braved mountains of Disney merchandise and scoured countless central Florida shopping venues to provide us with our new comprehensive shopping chapter.

Psychologists Dr. Karen Turnbow, Dr. Gayle Janzen, and Dr. Joan Burns provided much insight concerning the experiences of young children at Walt Disney World. "Hotel Woman" Georgia Goff and Nathan Lott inspected many dozens of hotels. *Unofficial Guide to Cruises* author Kay Showker assisted with our coverage of the Disney Cruise Line.

Many thanks also to Molly Merkle, Chris Mohney, Gabbie Oates, and Marie Hillin for production and editorial work on this book. Steve Jones and Annie Long earned our appreciation for their fine work and for keeping tight deadlines in providing the typography. Cartography was provided by Steve Jones, Tim Krasnansky, Brian Taylor, and Gary Antonetti, and the index was prepared by Ann Cassar. Finally, thanks to Lee Wiseman, who tallied survey results and handled reader-mail.

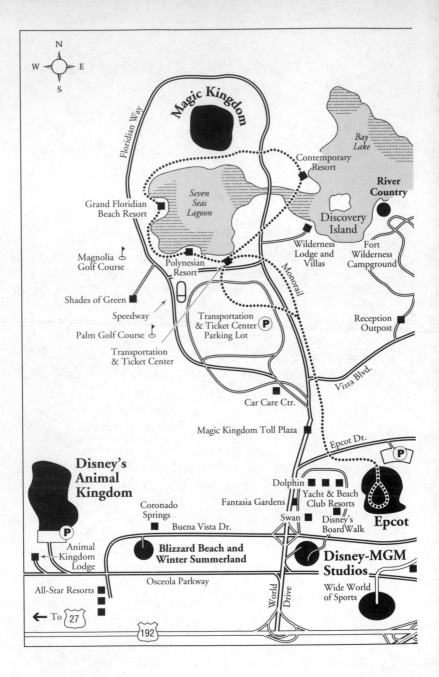

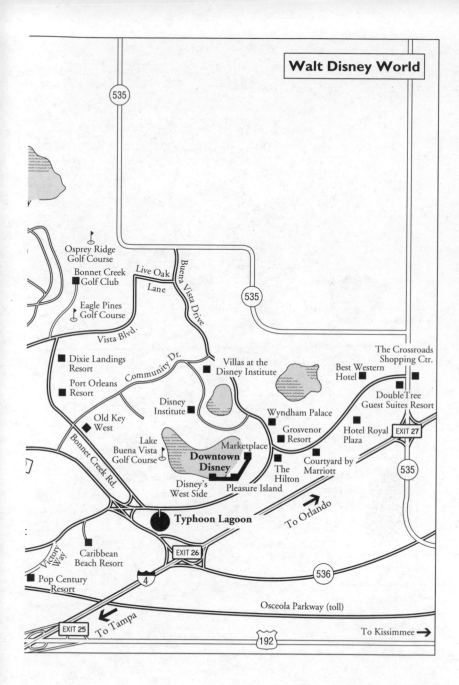

Walt Disney World

535

Osprey Ridge
Golf Course

Bonnet Creek
Golf Club

Live Oak
Lane

Buena Vista Drive

535

Eagle Pines
Golf Course

Vista Blvd.

Community Dr.

The Crossroads
Shopping Ctr.

Dixie Landings
Resort

Port Orleans
Resort

Villas at the
Disney Institute

Best Western
Hotel

DoubleTree
Guest Suites Resort

Disney
Institute

Wyndham Palace

Hotel Royal
Plaza

EXIT 27

Old Key
West

Grosvenor
Resort

Lake
Buena Vista
Golf Course

Marketplace

**Downtown
Disney**

Courtyard by
Marriott

535

The Hilton

Bonnet Creek Rd.

Disney's
West Side

Pleasure Island

Typhoon Lagoon

To Orlando

Victory Way

EXIT 26

Caribbean
Beach Resort

4

536

Pop Century
Resort

Osceola Parkway (toll)

EXIT 25

To Tampa

192

To Kissimmee →

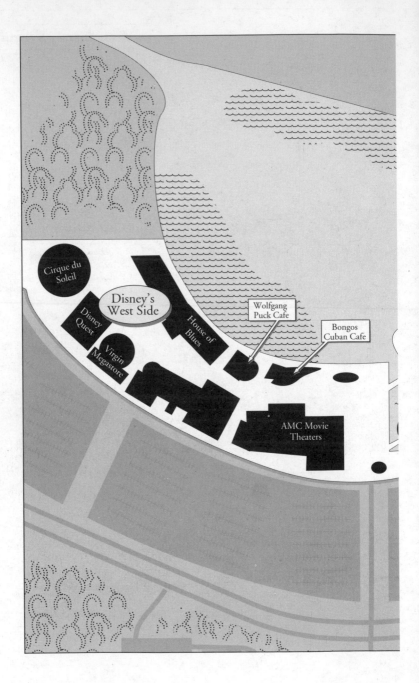

Cirque du Soleil

Disney's West Side

Disney Quest

Virgin Megastore

House of Blues

Wolfgang Puck Cafe

Bongos Cuban Cafe

AMC Movie Theaters

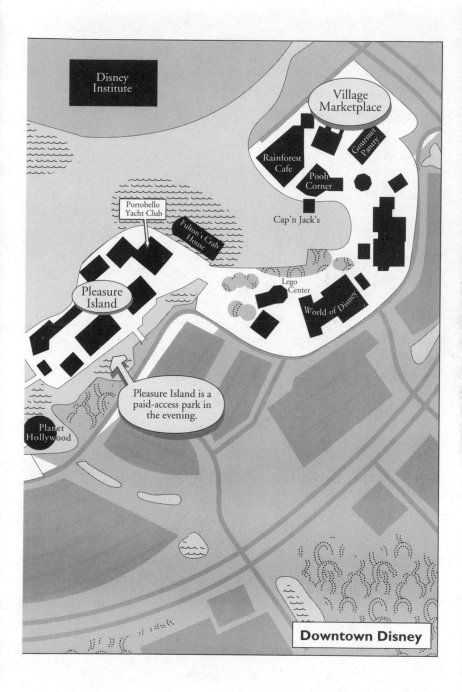

Disney
Institute

Village
Marketplace

Rainforest
Cafe

Gourmet
Pantry

Pooh
Corner

Cap'n Jack's

Portobello
Yacht Club

Fulton's Crab
House

Lego
Center

Pleasure
Island

World of Disney

Pleasure Island is a
paid-access park in
the evening.

Planet
Hollywood

Downtown Disney

Introduction

How Come "Unofficial"?

Declaration of Independence

The author and researchers of this guide specifically and categorically declare that they are and always have been totally independent of the Walt Disney Company, Inc.; of Disneyland, Inc.; of Walt Disney World, Inc.; and of any and all other members of the Disney corporate family not listed.

The material in this guide originated with the author and researchers and has not been reviewed, edited, or in any way approved by the Walt Disney Company, Inc.; Disneyland, Inc.; or Walt Disney World, Inc.

This guidebook represents the first comprehensive *critical* appraisal of Walt Disney World. Its purpose is to provide the reader with the information necessary to tour Walt Disney World with the greatest efficiency and economy and with the least hassle. The authors believe in the wondrous variety, joy, and excitement of the Disney attractions. At the same time, we recognize that Walt Disney World is a business, with the same profit motivations as businesses all over the world.

In this guide we represent and serve you, the consumer. If a restaurant serves bad food, or a gift item is overpriced, or a certain ride isn't worth the wait, we can say so, and in the process we hope to make your visit more fun, efficient, and economical.

The Importance of Being Goofy

Disney's chief financial officer leaned forward on his desk, thumping his pencil against a small plastic statue of St. Jude.

"Harold, get in here!"

"Yes, sir. What's the matter?"

"The recession, and people afraid to travel, for starters, and you Harold . . . yes, you . . . you are the matter! What have you done about those cost cuts I told you to make?"

"Boss, I've done every thing you asked. Pluto's on dry dog food, we've cut Michael Eisner's salary by $13.98 a month, made cast members wash their own underwear, eliminated early entry, and laid off 4,248 employees."

"You let Eisner off easy, you weenie!" rumbled the CFO, whacking St. Jude off the desk. "Plus, you were supposed to lay off 4,250 employees. You're two layoffs short!"

"Honestly boss, we axed . . . er, laid off . . . everyone not absolutely essential. But we've compensated for missing our layoff goal by making changes in other areas.

"Like what?" the CFO inquired, clearly skeptical.

"Well," Harold responded, "at Epcot, in the World Showcase part, we've re-themed Morocco as Branson, Missouri, to make the guests feel safer."

"You, idiot! Branson's not a country. All the pavilions at the World Showcase are supposed to represent countries. What did you do with the Moroccans?"

"Let'em all go, boss, except the belly dancer. She fit right in with the new theme. We've got her clogging to Rocky Top at the God Bless America First Saloon."

"Good grief, man . . . Walt would pop right out of the freezer if he knew about this! What else?"

"You'll like this one. At the end of the day we collect all the unsold popcorn from the parks and use it to feed the animals at the Animal Kingdom."

"No, Harold, I don't like it one bit!" he growled, his voice rising to a pitch clearly audible to patrons at the Texaco station across the street. "But it does explain why every animal in the park has diarrhea! Look, enough is enough," the CFO said, slumping back in his chair. "Stop freelancing and just do what I tell you. Speaking of which, you've got two more employees to lay off."

Harold disappeared from the CFO's office and returned seconds later with a bulky computer printout. "This is the roster of who's left, sir. I've been over it a thousand times but can't find anyone else to cut."

"Let's see," said the CFO, spreading the printout across his desk. For several minutes his eyes wandered over the list. Finally, he checked two names with a red marking pen and handed the printout back to his assistant.

Genuine shock spread over Harold's face as he read the marked names. "Boss, you can't be serious! You want me to fire Goofy and Chip?"

"Goofy's high maintenance," the CFO countered, "and way overpaid. And he's clumsy, too... Do you know how many little kids he steps on each year? Let's can him. Get Pluto some elevator shoes and a couple of swank outfits. He can take over Goofy's gigs."

"And Chip?" Harold asked.

"Totally redundant. Who needs two characters that look exactly alike? Nobody can tell them apart anyway. Let Dale hug a few kids, pop out of sight for a minute, and then come back as Chip. Who'll know the difference?"

As Harold turns to leave the room, his boss calls him back. A glimmer of hope flicks across the assistant's face. Maybe the CFO has reconsidered. "Yes, sir?"

"After you've booted those two fuzzheads, call the Fairy Godmother and ask if she'll take early retirement."

And so it goes . . .

What really makes writing about Walt Disney World fun is that the Disney people take everything so seriously. Day to day, they debate momentous decisions with far-ranging consequences: Will Goofy look swishy in a silver cape? Have we gone too far with Little Mermaid's cleavage? At a time when the nation is concerned about the drug problem, can we afford to have a dwarf named "Dopey"?

Unofficially, we think having a sense of humor is important. This guidebook has one, and it's probably necessary that you do, too—not to use this book but, more significantly, to have fun at Walt Disney World. Walt Disney World is to tourist destinations as New York is to cities: big, complex, and intimidating. A certain amount of levity is required simply to survive. Think of the *Unofficial Guide* as a private trainer to help get your sense of humor in shape. It will help you understand the importance of being Goofy.

Honey, I Blew Up the Book!

The first edition of *The Unofficial Guide to Walt Disney World* was considerably less than 200 pages, a mere shadow of its present size. In the years since that edition, Disney World has grown tremendously, adding Disney-MGM Studios, Downtown Disney, the BoardWalk, Typhoon Lagoon, Blizzard Beach, several new attractions in Epcot and the Magic Kingdom, about 24,000 new hotel rooms, and, in summer 1998, the Animal Kingdom, Walt Disney World's fourth theme park. The *Unofficial Guide* has grown to match this expansion (and the author has put on a little weight himself).

We have no idea where it all will end. In 30 years we may be selling an alphabetized, 26-volume edition, handsomely packaged in its own imitation oak bookcase. In the meantime, we offer a qualified apology for the bulk of this edition. We know it may be too heavy to be carried comfortably without the assistance of a handcart, llama, or Sherpa, but we defend the inclusion of all the information presented. Not every diner uses catsup, A-1 Sauce, and Tabasco, but it's nice to have all three on the table.

Concerning *Unofficial Guide* content, a mom from Vallejo, California, requested that we include a map of Orlando Airport. Other reader ideas for new content included these suggestions:

I think your guide should have a list of attractions that provide 1) seats, 2) air-conditioning, and 3) at least 15 minutes off your feet.

I feel your Unofficial Guide should include a claustrophobia rating for each attraction.

I think a great idea would be to have a sturdier pull-out part, maybe a little separate booklet that would list full-service and counter-service restaurants in back of the touring plans.

I wish you would discuss rest rooms more in the next edition. I found myself constantly searching for one.

These comments are representative in that many of you would like more detailed coverage of one thing or another. Believe me, we've debated adding to the book a map of the airport, as well as hundreds of other things, but have not done so. Why? Because we don't have an infinite number of pages with which to work, and we felt that other information was more important. You'd be amazed by the wealth of good, worthwhile material that doesn't make the cut. What if we put it all in? Well . . . the book would look more at home in your hayloft than on your bookshelf.

For Those Who Desire Additional Information

As thorough as we try to make *The Unofficial Guide to Walt Disney World*, there is not sufficient space to share all the tips and information that may be important and useful to certain readers. Thus, we have developed five additional Disney World guides, each designed to work in conjunction with this book. All five guides provide specialized information tailored to specific Walt Disney World visitors. Although some tips from the big book (like arriving at the theme parks early) are echoed or elaborated in the other guides, most of the information is unique. In addition to *The Unofficial Guide to Walt Disney World*, the following titles are available:

> *Mini-Mickey: The Pocket-Sized Unofficial Guide to Walt Disney World,* by Bob Sehlinger.
>
> *Inside Disney: The Incredible Story of Walt Disney World and the Man Behind the Mouse,* by Eve Zibart.
>
> *The Unofficial Guide to Walt Disney World with Kids,* by Bob Sehlinger.
>
> *The Unofficial Guide to Walt Disney World for Grown-Ups,* by Eve Zibart.
>
> *Beyond Disney: The Unofficial Guide to Universal, SeaWorld, and the Best of Central Florida,* by Bob Sehlinger and Chris Mohney.

Mini-Mickey is a nifty, portable, *Cliffs Notes* version of *The Unofficial Guide to Walt Disney World*. It distills information from this comprehensive guide to help short-stay or last-minute visitors decide quickly how to plan their limited hours at Disney World. *Inside Disney* is a behind-the-scenes, unauthorized history of Walt Disney World, and it is loaded with all the amazing facts and great stories that we can't squeeze into this guide. *The Unofficial Guide to Walt Disney World for Grown-Ups* helps adults traveling without children make the most of their Disney vacation, while *The Unofficial Guide to Walt Disney World with Kids* presents a wealth of planning and touring tips for a successful Disney family vacation. Finally, *Beyond Disney* is a consumer guide to the non-Disney attractions, restaurants, outdoor recreation, and nightlife in Orlando and central Florida. All of the guides are available from Wiley Publishing and at most bookstores.

The Death of Spontaneity

One of our all-time favorite letters came from a man in Chapel Hill, North Carolina:

Your book reads like the operations plan for an amphibious landing.... Go here, do this, proceed to Step 15.... You must think that everyone [who visits Walt Disney World] is a hyperactive, type-A, theme-park commando. What happened to the satisfaction of self-discovery or the joy of spontaneity? Next you will be telling us when to empty our bladders.

As it happens, *Unofficial Guide* researchers are a pretty existential crew. We are big on self-discovery if the activity is walking in the woods or watching birds. Some of us are able to improvise jazz, and others can whip up a mean pot of chili without a recipe. When it comes to Walt Disney World, however, we all agree that you either need a good plan or a frontal lobotomy. The operational definition of self-discovery and spontaneity at Walt Disney World is the "pleasure" of heat prostration and the "joy" of standing in line.

It's easy to spot the free spirits at Walt Disney World, particularly at opening time. While everybody else is stampeding to Space Mountain, they are standing in a cloud of dust, puzzling over the park map. Later, they are the people running around like chickens in a thunderstorm, trying to find an attraction with less than a 40-minute wait. Face it, Walt Disney World is not a very existential place. In many ways it's the quintessential system, the ultimate in mass-produced entertainment, the most planned and programmed environment anywhere.

We aren't saying that you can't have a great time at Walt Disney World. What we *are* saying is that you need a plan. You don't have to be compulsive or inflexible; just think about what you want to do before you go. Don't delude yourself by rationalizing that the information in this guide is only for the pathological and the superorganized. Ask not for whom the tome tells, Bubba—it tells for thee.

Dance to the Music

When you dance, you hear the music and move in harmony with the rhythm. Like each day at Walt Disney World, a dance has a beginning and an end. However, your objective is not to get to the end, but rather to enjoy the dance while the music plays. You are totally in the moment and care nothing about where on the floor you stop when the dance is done.

As you begin to contemplate your Walt Disney World vacation, you may not have much patience for a philosophical discussion about dancing, but it's relevant. If you are like most travel-guide readers, you are apt to plan and organize, to anticipate and control, and you like things to go smoothly. And, truth to tell, this leads us to suspect that you are a person who looks ahead and is outcome oriented. You may even feel a bit of pressure concerning your vacation. Vacations, after all, are special events, and expensive ones to boot. So you work hard to make the most of your vacation.

As discussed in the previous section, we believe that work, planning, and organization are important, and even essential at Walt Disney World. But if they become your focus, you won't be able to hear the music and enjoy the dance. Though much dancing these days resembles highly individualized *grand mal* seizures, there was a time when each dance involved specific steps that you committed to memory. At first you were tentative and awkward, but eventually the steps became second nature and you didn't have to think about them anymore.

Metaphorically, this is what we want for you and your companions as you embark on your Walt Disney World vacation. We want you to learn the steps in advance so that when you're on vacation and the music plays, you will be able to hear it. And you will dance with effortless grace and ease.

A Word to Our Readers about Annual Revisions

Some of you who purchase each new edition of the *Unofficial Guide* have chastised us for retaining examples, comments, and descriptions from previous years' editions. This letter from a Grand Rapids, Michigan, reader is typical:

Your guidebook still has the same little example stories. When I got my [new] book I expected a true update and new stuff, not the same-old, same-old!

First, the *Unofficial Guide* is a reference work. Though we are flattered that some readers read the guide from cover to cover and that some of you find it entertaining, our objective is fairly straightforward: to provide information that will enable you to have the best possible Walt Disney World vacation.

Each year during our revision research, we check every theme park, water park, attraction, hotel, restaurant, nightspot, shop, and entertainment offering. While there are many changes (most attributable to Disney World's exponential growth), much remains the same from year to year. When we profile and critique an attraction, we try to provide the reader with the most insightful, relevant, and useful information, written in the clearest possible language. It is our opinion that if an attraction does not change, then it makes little sense to risk clarity for the sake of freshening up the prose. Walt Disney World guests who try the Mad Tea Party, the Haunted Mansion, or the *Country Bear Jamboree* today, for example, experience exactly the same presentation as guests who visited Disney World in 1997, 1990, or 1986. Moreover, according to our extensive patron surveys (several thousand each year), today's guests respond to these attractions in the same way as prior-year patrons.

The bottom line: we believe our readers are better served if we devote our time to that which is changing and new as opposed to that which remains the same. The success or failure of the *Unofficial Guide* is determined not by the style of the writing but by the accuracy of the information and, ultimately, whether you have a positive experience at Walt Disney World. Every change we make (or don't make) is evaluated in this context.

We Got Attitude

Some readers disagree about our attitude toward Disney. A woman from Winchester, Virginia, lambasted us, writing:

Do you people dislike Disney? I can appreciate your opinions, but this whole guide was dumping on Disney! After getting halfway through, I went and spent more money on the Birnbaum book. I go to Disney because it's Disney—and I know it's expensive—it's a vacation! Your book—to put it politely—pissed me off!

A reader from Little Rock, Arkansas, took us to task for the opposite prejudice, commenting:

Your book was quite complimentary of Disney, perhaps too complimentary. Maybe the free trips you travel writers get at Disney World are chipping away at your objectivity.

From an Annapolis, Maryland, mom:

On day four of our six-day trip to WDW it hit me as to the purpose of your guide. Your guide is so cynical and negative that what you actually experience is bound to seem joyful, spontaneous, and positive! I now believe that Disney does sponsor your guide to make sure everyone feels like they are having a great time in spite of your pessimism.

And from a Williamsport, Pennsylvania, mother of three:

Reading your book irritated me before we went [to Walt Disney World] because of all the warnings and cautions. I guess I'm used to having guidebooks pump me up about where I'm going. But once I arrived I found I was fully prepared and we had a great time. In retrospect, I have to admit you were right on the money. What I regarded as you being negative was just a good dose of reality.

Finally, from a Vienna, Virginia, family:

After being at Disney for three days at the height of tourist season, I laughed out loud at your "The Death of Spontaneity" section. We are definitely free-spirit types who don't like to plan our days when we are on vacation. A friend warned us, and we got your guidebook. After skimming through it before we left, I was terrified that we had made a terrible mistake booking this vacation. Thanks to your book, we had a wonderful time. If it had not been for the book, we definitely would have been trampled by all the people stampeding to Space Mountain while we were standing there with our maps.

For the record, we've always paid our own way at Walt Disney World: hotels, admissions, meals, the works. We don't dislike Disney, and we most definitely don't have an ax to grind. We're positive by nature and much prefer to praise than to criticize. Personally, we have enjoyed the Disney parks immensely over the years, both experiencing them and writing about them. Disney, however, as with all corporations (and all people, for that matter), is better at some things than others. Because our readers shell out big bucks to go to Walt Disney World, we believe they have the right to know in advance what's good and what's not. For those who think we're overly positive, please understand that the *Unofficial Guide* is a guidebook, not an exposé. Our overriding objective is for you to enjoy your visit. To that end we try to report fairly and objectively. When readers disagree with our opinions, we, in the interest of fairness and balance, publish their point of view right alongside ours. To the best of our knowledge, the *Unofficial Guides* are the only travel guides in print that do this.

Too Many Cooks in the Kitchen?

We received this query from a Manchester, Vermont, reader, and feel that it deserves a serious response:

I read a review on the Internet criticizing the Unofficial Guide because it was "written by a team of researchers." The reviewer doesn't say why he thinks the team approach is inferior, but the inference is along the lines of "too many cooks spoil the soup." Why do you use the team approach?

There are several reasons. Foremost among them is that the team approach gives us the capability to undertake much more sophisticated and extensive research projects. Collecting waiting-time data for our new touring-plan software (see page 73–78), for example, required the efforts of more than a dozen researchers visiting the Disney parks for several days at each of four different times of year. Another project, monitoring the Disney transportation system, requires riding and timing every bus, boat, and monorail route, a task that takes four researchers almost a week to complete. In covering the lodging scene, the *Unofficial Guide* reviews, rates, and ranks almost 200 Disney World–area hotels, almost four times as many as other guidebooks. On any given research trip, we have one or two teams of specialized hotel inspectors checking out hotels all day long.

No other guides do this, nor can they really, because the scope of the research and processing of data require time, experience, and resources that are beyond the capabilities of a single author or even several co-authors. An entire organization collects and compiles information for the *Unofficial Guide,* an organization guided by individuals with extensive training and experience in research design as well as primary data collection and analysis. Known and respected in both the travel industry and academe, *Unofficial Guide* researchers have served as consultants or project planners for the Busch Entertainment Corporation, H.B.J. Theme Park Division, the Utah Ski Association, the Eastern Professional River Outfitters Association, and the Boy Scouts of America, among others.

Not all of the *Unofficial Guide* research relates to the parks and resorts. We also conduct extensive research on you, the reader. From the concept up, you see, *Unofficial Guides* are different from other guidebooks. Other guides (regardless how information is formatted to fit a given series) are researched and developed by individual authors or co-authors, usually travel writers. Thus, everything is filtered through the lens of those authors' tastes, preferences, and opinions. Publishers of these guides hope that the information the author presents is compatible with the needs of the reader, but if it is, the compatibility is largely accidental. In *Unofficial Guides,* by way of contrast, it is your tastes, preferences, and opinions that dictate the content of the guides. In other words, we start with the needs of our reader, identified through exhaustive research, and build a book that specifically meets those needs.

Another reason for using a team approach is to minimize author bias. As discussed earlier, a single author incorporate his (her) own singular tastes and opinions in his work. Our research team, by way of contrast, includes individuals ranging in age from 60 to 16 and sometimes, for special assignments, we seek the assistance of children as young as 8. Thus, the opinions and advice in the *Unofficial Guide* are informed by the perspectives of a diverse group of researchers, a process that, we believe, achieves the highest level of objectivity.

A final reason for the team approach is the need for special expertise in certain areas. Face it, no individual author can possibly be qualified to write about every topic in the vast range of important subjects that make up a good guide to Walt Disney World. Thus, our chapter "Walt Disney World with Kids" was developed in consultation with three nationally respected child psychologists and an advisory group of parents. Similarly, we have professional culinary experts dedicated solely to the task of rating restaurants. Our golf coverage, likewise, is handled by professional golf writer, Larry Olmsted, and our data base and touring plan program are developed and managed by programmer and software developer, Len Testa. When you cover shopping, you want a local who lives to shop and who knows where to find every back-counter deal within 50 miles. Guess what? We've got her!

So, the bottom line is that there are more of us so that we can do more for you. Bob Sehlinger puts the fruits of our research into words, but behind Bob there is an organization unequaled, to the best of our knowledge, in all of travel publishing.

The How and the Why of It

A Dayton, Ohio, reader offered the following comment:

> I used several guides preparing for our [Disney World] trip. One of them dumped on the Unofficial Guide for referring to Dumbo as a "cycle ride." Though my kids are totally infatuated with Dumbo, I found your section about how the various types of rides work to be both interesting and useful. Dumbo's charm and appeal doesn't change the fact that it's a cycle ride. Get a life!

Most guidebooks do a reasonably good job with what and where. *Unofficial Guides* add the dimensions of how and why. Describing attractions like Dumbo, or hotels or restaurants (the what) at a given destination (the where) is the foundation of other travel guidebooks. We know from our research, however, that our readers like to know how things work. Take hotels as an example. In the *Unofficial Guide*, we not only provide the reader with abundant hotel choices (rated and ranked, of course), but also explain the economic and operational logic of the lodging industry (the why), and offer instruction (the how) that enables the reader to consistently take advantage of opportunities for hotel discounts, room upgrades, and the like. In this guide and all our other *Unofficial Guides*, whether we're discussing cruise ships, theme parks, ski resorts, casinos, or golf courses, we reveal the travel industry's inner workings and demonstrate how to use such insight in selecting and purchasing travel and for planning itineraries. For the reader, knowledge is power, which translates into informed decision making and confidence.

By way of analogy, most guides give the reader a plate of fish to choose from. An *Unofficial Guide* does this as well, but additionally points out which fish are best. More importantly, however, an *Unofficial Guide* teaches the reader how to fish. Anyone who has ever read the hotel chapter in any *Unofficial Guide* can use the information and methodology to book a great hotel room at a bargain price in any city in the world.

The *Unofficial Guide* Publishing Year

We receive many queries each year asking when the next edition of the *Unofficial Guide* will be available. Usually our new editions are published and available in the stores by late August or early September. Thus the 2004 edition will be on the shelves in August or September of 2003.

Letters and Comments from Readers

Many of those who use *The Unofficial Guide to Walt Disney World* write us to make comments or share their own strategies for visiting Walt Disney World. We appreciate all such input, both positive and critical, and encourage our readers to continue writing. Readers' comments and observations are frequently incorporated into revised editions of the *Unofficial Guide* and have contributed immeasurably to its improvement. If you write us or return our reader-survey form, you can rest assured that we won't release your name and address to any mailing-list companies, direct-mail advertisers, or other third party. Unless you instruct us otherwise, we will assume that you do not object to being quoted in the *Unofficial Guide*.

Reader Questionnaire and Restaurant Survey

At the back of this guide is a short questionnaire you can use to express opinions about your Walt Disney World visit. The questionnaire is designed to allow every member of your party, regardless of age, to tell us what he or she thinks. There is also a separate restaurant survey that you can use to describe your Disney World dining experiences. Clip the questionnaire and the restaurant survey on the dotted lines and mail them to:

Reader Survey
The *Unofficial Guide* Series
P.O. Box 43673
Birmingham, AL 35243

How to Contact the Author

Bob Sehlinger
The *Unofficial Guide to Walt Disney World*
P.O. Box 43673
Birmingham, AL 35243
E-mail: unofficialguides@menasharidge.com

When you write, put your address on both your letter and envelope; sometimes the two get separated. It is also a good idea to include your phone number. If you e-mail us, please tell us where you're from. Remember, as travel writers, we're often out of the office for long periods of time, so forgive us if our response is slow. And although *Unofficial Guide* e-mail is not forwarded to us when we're traveling, we will respond as soon as possible when we return.

Questions from Readers

Questions frequently asked by readers are answered in an appendix at the end of the *Unofficial Guide*.

Walt Disney World: An Overview

If you're choosing among tourist destinations of Florida, the question is not whether to visit Walt Disney World but how to see the best of the Disney offerings with some economy of time, effort, and finances.

What Walt Disney World Encompasses

Walt Disney World encompasses 43 square miles, an area twice as large as Manhattan Island or roughly the size of Boston. Situated strategically in this vast expanse are the Magic Kingdom, Epcot, Disney-MGM Studios, and the Animal Kingdom theme parks; three swimming theme parks; two nighttime-entertainment areas; a sports complex; several golf courses, hotels, and campgrounds; more than 100 restaurants; four large interconnected lakes; a shopping complex; three convention venues; a nature preserve; and a complete transportation system consisting of four-lane highways, elevated monorails, and a system of canals.

The Major Theme Parks

The Magic Kingdom

When people think of Walt Disney World, most think of the Magic Kingdom. It's comprised of the collection of adventures, rides, and shows symbolizing the Disney cartoon characters, and Cinderella Castle. Although the Magic Kingdom is only one element of Disney World, it remains its heart. The Magic Kingdom is divided into seven subareas or "lands," six of which are arranged around a central hub. First encountered is Main Street, U.S.A., which connects the Magic Kingdom entrance with the central hub. Clockwise around the hub are Adventureland, Frontierland, Liberty Square, Fantasyland, and Tomorrowland. Mickey's Toontown Fair (originally named Mickey's Birthdayland), the first new land added to the Magic Kingdom since the park opened, is situated along the Walt Disney Railroad on three acres between Fantasyland and Tomorrowland. Access is through Fantasyland or Tomorrowland or via the railroad. Main Street and the other six lands will be described in detail later. Three hotels (the Contemporary, Polynesian, and Grand Floridian Beach Resorts) are close to the Magic Kingdom and are directly connected to it by monorail and boat. Two additional hotels, Shades of Green and Disney's Wilderness Lodge Resort and Villas, are nearby but aren't served by the monorail.

Epcot

Epcot opened in October 1982. Divided into two major areas, Future World and World Showcase, the park is twice as big as the Magic Kingdom and comparable in scope. Future World consists of pavilions concerning human creativity and technological advancement. World Showcase, arranged around a 41-acre lagoon, presents the architectural, social, and cultural heritages of almost a dozen nations, with each country represented by replicas of famous landmarks and local settings familiar to world travelers. Epcot is more educationally oriented than the Magic Kingdom and has been repeatedly characterized as a permanent World's Fair.

The Epcot resort hotels—Disney's Beach Club, Disney's Yacht Club, Disney's BoardWalk Resort, the Walt Disney World Swan, and the Walt Disney World Dolphin—are within a 5- to 15-minute walk of the International Gateway entrance to the theme park. The hotels are also linked to the park by canal. Epcot is connected to the Magic Kingdom and its resort hotels by monorail.

Disney-MGM Studios

Opened in 1989 and about the size of the Magic Kingdom, Disney-MGM Studios is divided into two areas. The first is a theme park focused on the past, present, and future of the motion-picture and television industries. This section, containing movie-theme rides and shows, covers about half of the Disney-MGM complex. Park highlights include a re-creation of Hollywood and Sunset Boulevards from Hollywood's Golden Age, movie stunt demonstrations, a children's play area, audience-participation shows on sound effects, and four high-tech rides.

The second area is a working motion-picture and television production facility encompassing three sound stages, a backlot of streets and sets, and creative support services. Public access is limited to studio tours, which take visitors behind the scenes for crash courses on Disney animation and moviemaking, including (on occasion) the opportunity to witness the actual shooting of a feature film, television show, or commercial.

Disney-MGM Studios is connected to other Walt Disney World areas by highway and canal but not by monorail. Guests can park in the Studios' pay parking lot or commute by bus. Patrons staying in Epcot resort hotels can also reach the Studios by boat or on foot.

Disney's Animal Kingdom

More than five times the size of the Magic Kingdom, the Animal Kingdom combines zoological exhibits with rides, shows, and live entertainment. The park is arranged somewhat like the Magic Kingdom, in a hub-and-spoke configuration. A lush tropical rain forest serves as Main Street, funneling visitors to Discovery Island at the center of the park. Dominated by the park's central icon, the 14-story-tall, hand-carved Tree of Life, Discovery Island is the park's center, with services, shopping, and dining. From Discovery Island, guests can access the theme areas: Africa, Asia, DinoLand U.S.A., and Camp Minnie-Mickey. Scheduled to open in phases, Discovery Island, Africa, Camp Minnie-Mickey, and DinoLand U.S.A. came in 1998, followed by Asia in 1999, with a fifth land to be added over the next couple of years. Africa, the largest theme area at 100 acres, features free-roaming herds in a re-creation of the Serengeti Plain. Guests tour in open-air safari vehicles.

Disney's Animal Kingdom has its own pay parking lot and is connected to other Disney World destinations by the Disney bus system. Although there are no hotels at the Animal Kingdom, the All-Star, Animal Kingdom Lodge, and Coronado Springs Resorts are nearby.

The Water Theme Parks

There are three major swimming theme parks in Walt Disney World: Typhoon Lagoon, River Country, and Blizzard Beach. Typhoon Lagoon is distinguished by a wave pool capable of making six-foot waves. River Country, a pioneer among water theme parks, is much smaller but done very well. Since Typhoon Lagoon opened in 1989, River Country has catered primarily to Disney World campground and hotel guests. Blizzard Beach is the newest Disney water park and features more slides than the other two parks combined. All three parks are beautifully landscaped, and great attention is paid to atmosphere and aesthetics. Typhoon Lagoon and Blizzard Beach have their own adjacent parking lots. River Country can be reached on foot by campground guests or on Disney boat or bus by others.

Other Walt Disney World Venues

Downtown Disney (Downtown Disney Marketplace, Pleasure Island, and Disney's West Side)

Downtown Disney is a large shopping, dining, and entertainment complex encompassing the Downtown Disney Marketplace on the east, the gated (admission-required) Pleasure Island nighttime entertainment venue in the middle, and Disney's West Side on the west. Downtown Disney Marketplace is home to the largest Disney character merchandise store in the world, upscale resort-wear and specialty shops, and several restaurants, including the tacky but popular Rainforest Cafe. Pleasure Island offers, in addition to the gated attractions described below, several upscale restaurants and shops. Disney's West Side opened in 1997 and combines nightlife, shopping, dining, and entertainment. Dan Aykroyd's House of Blues serves Cajun-Creole dishes in its restaurant and electric blues in its music hall. Bongos, a Cuban nightclub and cafe created by Gloria and Emilio Estefan, offers Caribbean flavors and rhythms. Wolfgang Puck Cafe, sandwiched among pricey boutiques (including a three-level Virgin Records megastore), is the West Side's prestige eatery. In the entertainment department you'll find a 24-screen cinema; a permanent showplace for the extraordinary, 70-person cast of *Cirque du Soleil;* and DisneyQuest, a high-tech, interactive virtual reality and electronic games venue. Downtown Disney can be accessed via Disney buses from most Disney World locations.

Pleasure Island

Part of the Downtown Disney complex, Pleasure Island is a six-acre nighttime entertainment center where one cover charge gets a visitor into any of eight nightclubs. The clubs have different themes and feature a variety of shows and activities. Music ranges from pop rock to country and western to jazz. For the more sedentary (or exhausted), there is an adjacent 24-screen movie complex, and for the hungry, several restaurants exist, including a much-hyped Planet Hollywood.

Disney's BoardWalk

Located near Epcot, Disney's BoardWalk is an idealized replication of an East Coast turn-of-the-century waterfront resort. Open all day, the Board-Walk features upscale restaurants, shops and galleries, a brew pub, and an ESPN sports bar. In the evening, a nightclub with dueling pianos (New Orleans's Pat O'Brien's–style) and a swanky dance club join the lineup. While there is no admission fee for the BoardWalk per se, individual clubs may levy cover charges at night. In addition to the public facilities are a 378-room deluxe hotel and a 532-unit timeshare development. The BoardWalk is within walking distance of the Epcot resorts and the International Gateway of the Epcot theme park. Boat transportation is available from Disney-MGM Studios, while buses serve other Disney World locations.

Disney's Wide World of Sports

Covering 200 acres, Disney's Wide World of Sports is a state-of-the-art competition-and-training facility consisting of a 7,500-seat ballpark, a field house, and venues for baseball, softball, tennis, track and field, beach volleyball, and 27 other sports. In addition to being the spring-training home of the Atlanta Braves, the complex hosts a mind-boggling calendar of professional and amateur competitions. Although Walt Disney World guests are welcome at the complex as paid spectators, they can't use the facilities unless they are participants in a scheduled competition.

The Disney Institute

Until 2002, the Disney Institute offered professional development courses for private groups and corporations. The Institute, including its various lodging properties, has been closed indefinitely. Remaining open are the Institute's golf, spa, and athletic facilities.

DISNEYSPEAK POCKET TRANSLATOR

Although it may come as a surprise, Disney has its own somewhat peculiar language. Here are some terms you are likely to bump into:

DisneySpeak	English Definition
Adventure	Ride
Attraction	Ride or theater show
Attraction Host	Ride operator
Audience	Crowd
Backstage	Behind the scenes, out of view of customers
Bull Pen	Queuing area
Cast Member	Employee
Character	Disney cartoon character impersonated by an employee
Costume	Work attire or uniform
Dark Ride	Indoor ride
Day-Guest	Any customer not staying at a Disney resort
Face Character	A character that does not wear a head-covering costume (Snow White, Cinderella, Jasmine)
General Public	Same as day-guest
Greeter	Employee positioned at the entrance of an attraction
Guest	Customer
Hidden Mickeys	Frontal silhouette of Mickey's head worked subtly into the design of buildings, railings, vehicles, golf greens, attractions, and just about anything else
In Rehearsal	Operating though not officially open
Lead	Foreman or manager, the person in charge of an attraction
On Stage	In full view of customers
Preshow	Entertainment at an attraction prior to the feature presentation
Resort Guest	A customer staying at a Disney resort
Role	An employee's job
Security Host	Security guard
Soft Opening	Opening a park or attraction before its stated opening time
Transitional Experience	An element of the queuing area and/or preshow that provides a story line or information essential to understanding the attraction

Disney Cruise Line

In 1998 Disney launched (literally) its own cruise line with the 2,400-passenger *Disney Magic*. Its twin ship, the *Disney Wonder,* was launched in 1999. Cruises depart from Port Canaveral (about a 90-minute drive from Walt Disney World) on three-, four-, and seven-day itineraries and include port calls at Castaway Cay, Disney's own private island. Cruises can be packaged with a stay at Walt Disney World. Although the cruises are family oriented, extensive children's programs and elaborate childcare facilities allow parents plenty of opportunity for time away from the kids.

The Ruffled Mouse

The Walt Disney Company was having a tough year even before the terrorist attacks of September 11, 2001. For Walt Disney World, the events of 9/11 turned a bad situation into a disaster. All of the Disney theme parks were closed for a couple of days in response to the attacks. When the parks reopened, security screening stations were established in front of the entrance of each park. Since then, all packs, purses, diaper bags, and other containers are searched before guests are allowed to proceed to the turnstiles. Screening, though thorough, is done efficiently and expeditiously, with minimal inconvenience to guests. Security in the parks has been beefed up as well and is more visible.

Before September 11, and after, Disney initiated a sweeping range of cost-control measures, including the layoff of some 4,000 cast members. Among cuts that directly affect Walt Disney World guests are the following:

- Elimination of the Surprise Mornings early-entry program for Disney resort guests.
- Shortened operating hours. All the parks now open later. The Magic Kingdom and the Animal Kingdom likewise close earlier. Depending on the season, the Magic Kingdom has closed as early as 6 p.m., the Animal Kingdom as early as 5 p.m., and the Disney-MGM Studios as early as 6:30 p.m. At Epcot, once again depending on season, the World Showcase section of the park has not opened until noon and Future World has closed by 7 p.m. Coupled with the elimination of early entry, the touring time available to Disney resort guests has been reduced by as much as 30% in a given day. Admission prices have remained the same.
- Delayed opening and early closing of certain attractions in all of the parks.
- Some attractions have been removed from service, to be activated only during extremely busy periods. Among these are the *Carousel of Progress* and *The Timekeeper* in the Magic Kingdom.
- Several attractions have been permanently closed and not replaced (all before 9/11). These include 20,000 Leagues Under the Sea, the Keelboats, and the Skyway at the Magic Kingdom; the Soundstage Tour at the Disney-MGM Studios; and the riverboat attraction at the Animal Kingdom.
- Drastic cuts in the number of performances per week of live stage production in the theme parks.
- Street entertainment has been vastly scaled back.
- Several theme-park restaurants have been closed indefinitely, and a number of character meals eliminated.

- Opening of the new Pop Century Resorts was postponed (it still had not opened when we went to press). The Villas at the Disney Institute have been closed indefinitely. The French Quarter section of the Port Orleans Resort was closed until the end of May 2002.

- Room package delivery for resort guests has been largely eliminated.

All guests, including those of us at the *Unofficial Guide,* wish Walt Disney World a speedy and complete recovery. We cannot avoid mentioning, however, that the perennially successful Parks and Resorts division of the Walt Disney Company has been forced to carry a disproportionate share of the burden, not only in regard to 9/11 and the recession, but in compensation for the dismal performance of other Disney Company divisions and subsidiaries.

Part One

Planning before
You Leave Home

Visiting Walt Disney World is a bit like childbirth—you never really believe what people tell you, but once you have been through it yourself, you know exactly what they were saying!

—Hilary Wolfe, a mother and *Unofficial Guide* reader
from Swansea, United Kingdom

Your guide was a little overwhelming (like a research project to plan our vacation), but then so were all the choices at Disney.

—Mother of two from Greenfield, Indiana

Gathering Information

In addition to this guide, we recommend that you obtain:

1. The Walt Disney Travel Company Florida Vacations Brochure
This full-color booklet describes Walt Disney World in its entirety, lists rates for all Disney resort hotels and campgrounds, and describes Disney World package vacations. It's available from most travel agents or by calling the Walt Disney Travel Company at (800) 327-2996 or (407) 934-7639. Be prepared to hold; you may have a long wait. When you get a live representative on the line, tell them you want the 8 ½" × 11" vacations booklet that lists the benefits and costs of the various vacation packages. Often, if you're not specific, they'll send you a 9" × 4" Disney Resorts brochure that is a puff-piece containing lots of photos and almost no useful information.

2. The Disney Cruise Line Brochure   This elaborate color brochure will provide all the particulars on vacation packages that combine a cruise on the Disney Cruise Line with a stay at Walt Disney World. The brochure is available from travel agents, by calling the Walt Disney Travel Company at (407) 828-8101, or at **www.disneycruise.com.**

3. Orlando MagiCard   If you're considering lodging outside Walt Disney World or if you think you might patronize attractions and restaurants outside of Disney World, it's worthwhile to obtain an Orlando MagiCard, a Vacation Planner, and the Orlando Official Accommodations Guide (all free) from the Orlando Visitors Center. The MagiCard makes you eligible for discounts at hotels, restaurants, and attractions outside Disney World. To order the accommodations guide, call (800) 255-5786. For additional information and materials, call (407) 363-5872. Phones are manned during weekday business hours. Allow four weeks for delivery. On the Internet, see **www.go2orlando.com.**

4. Florida Traveler Discount Guide   Another good source of discounts on lodging, restaurants, and attractions throughout the state is the Florida Traveler Discount Guide, published by Exit Information Guide. The guide is free, but you will be charged $3 ($5 shipped to Canada) for handling. Call (352) 371-3948, Monday–Friday, 8 a.m.–5 p.m. EST. Similar guides to other states are available at the same number. It's sometimes difficult to get through on the phone, however. Also, their **www.roomsaver.com** website has hotel coupons you can print off your computer for free.

5. Kissimmee–St. Cloud Tour & Travel Sales Guide   This full-color directory of hotels and attractions is one of the most complete available and is of particular interest to those who intend to book lodging outside of Disney World. In addition to hotels and motels, the directory lists rental houses, time-shares, and condominiums. To receive a copy, call the Kissimmee–St. Cloud Convention and Visitors Bureau at (800) 327-9159 or check out **www.floridakiss.com.**

6. *The Eclectic Gourmet Guide to Orlando*   Researched and written by the same team that produces this *Unofficial Guide,* the *Eclectic Gourmet* is the best resource available for finding great restaurants outside Walt Disney World. The guide, which rates, ranks, and profiles more than 150 restaurants, is available for $11.95 plus shipping by calling (800) 243-0495 or at **www.globe-pequot.com.**

Request Information Early

Request information as far in advance as possible and allow four weeks for delivery. Make a checklist of information you have requested and follow up if you haven't received your materials within six weeks. Sometimes, as a Garland, Texas, man notes, persistence is the key:

Per your advice, I called WDW to get the Florida Vacation Guide. They never sent it. Called back two more times and finally got it the week before we left. In fact, got two.

Disney Magazine

If you're really a Disneyholic, this magazine will supply full-color hype of all developments in the Walt Disney Company, including theme parks, movies, Disney art, collectibles, and merchandise. The quarterly publication also offers glimpses of Disney behind-the-scenes history. Though there's not much useful information, the *Disney Magazine* is usually a fun read. The magazine is free to Disney Club (see page 115) members or can be purchased separately for $19.95 for a two-year subscription. Write *Disney Magazine*, P.O. Box 37265, Boone, IA 50037-0265 or call (800) 333-8734.

Gathering Information on the World Wide Web

In planning your Walt Disney World vacation, you will find all of your favorite characters on the World Wide Web. But, in addition to Mickey, Minnie, Donald, Pluto, and Goofy, you will also find Delta, American, Hertz, Hyatt, and Hilton.

The advent of the World Wide Web and its immense popularity have brought about a lot of changes in the way we seek out everyday information. In just a few short years we have gone from getting most of our travel information from printed books or magazines and our favorite travel agent to booking entire vacations online. But as wonderful as this sounds, there are pitfalls. It's no small task figuring out how to find the information you need and understanding the tricks that make navigating the web easy. Finally, even as an accomplished web user, you may be surprised to find that your most valuable travel resource is still your tried-and-true travel agent.

You may have heard that travel providers like to sell directly to consumers on the web in order to avoid paying commissions to travel agents, and that the commission savings are passed along to the buyer. While there is some truth in this, discounts (on the web or anywhere else) have much more to do with time perishability of travel products than with commissions. An empty seat on a jet, for example, cannot be sold once the plane has left the gate. As the point of perishability approaches, the travel provider (hotel, airline, cruise line, etc.) begins cutting deals to fill its rooms, cabins, and seats. Websites provide a cheap, quick, and efficient way for travel sellers to make these deals known to the public. You should understand, however, that the same deals are usually also communicated to travel agents.

We like the web as a method of window shopping for travel, for scouting deals, and for obtaining information. We do not believe that the web is necessarily the best or cheapest way of purchasing travel or that it can be substituted for the services of a good travel agent. The people who get the most out of the web are those who work in cooperation with their travel agent, using the web as a tool to help their agent help them. This is because almost any deal you locate on the web can be purchased through a travel agent, and the more business you give your travel agent, the harder your agent will work for you. It's all about relationships.

It is a bit convoluted to write about the interactive travel experience on paper without the benefit of the very medium we are discussing. We urge you to use your computer or to find a friend with a computer and an Internet connection in order to get the most out of these guidelines. We guarantee that you will discover some wonderful things along the way, many things, in all likelihood, that we haven't seen. Each person's experience on the web is unique, and you'll find many compelling distractions along the way. But bring your patience to the web, because it can take some getting used to and it is not perfect. Once you know your way around, you will save a lot of time and, occasionally, some money. When you find resources that you like, bookmark them in your browser. The more you use them, the more efficient you will be.

Walt Disney World on the Web

Searching the Internet for Disney information is like navigating an immense maze for a very small piece of cheese. There is a lot of information available on the web, but you may have to wade through list after list until you find the Internet addresses you want and need. Once you have them, finding information can again be extremely time consuming.

Disney's official website offers much of the same information as the Walt Disney Travel Company's vacation guidebook, but the guidebook has better pictures. Though the website is supposedly updated daily, we frequently find errors. Now you can purchase theme-park admissions and make resort and dining reservations on the Internet. The website also offers online shopping, weather forecasts, and information on renovations and special events. Disney's official web address is **www.disney.com.** Universal Studios Florida also offers a home page at **www.universal orlando.com.**

If you search for additional information, you will find that there are many individuals who maintain very elaborate Disney-related websites. One woman in California maintains a website through which you may access everything from official Disney pages to the "Arielholics Anonymous Home Page." Individuals also maintain Disney chat groups, which can be sources of both correct and incorrect information, depending on who is chatting. Disneyphile techies from all over the world help to maintain lists. There are lists of hidden Mickeys, lists of attractions ranked and rated by Joe Blow from Kokomo, lists of characters, and more lists of lists. You could explore the Web for weeks on end for myriad information maintained by these people.

Len Testa, Internet guru and *Unofficial Guide* researcher, has combed the web, looking for the best Disney sites. Here are Len's picks:

Best Official Theme-Park Site   The official Walt Disney World website (**www.disneyworld.com**) gets the nod over the official Universal Studios site (**www.universalorlando.com**) and the official SeaWorld website (**www.seaworld.com**). Each contains information on ticket options, park hours, and attractions. Disney's site goes one step further by providing color maps of each park, plus lists of attractions closed for maintenance.

Best General Unofficial Site   The Walt Disney World Information Guide (**www.wdwig.com**) is the first website we recommend to friends interested in going to Disney World. It contains information on virtually every hotel, restaurant, and activity in the World. Want to know what the rooms look like at the Disney resorts before you book a reservation? This site has photos of rooms at every resort—sometimes for each floor of a particular resort. Wdwig.com is updated several times per week, and includes menus from Disney restaurants, ticketing information, maps, driving directions, and more.

Best Moneysaving Site   We humbly suggest that Mary Waring's **www.mousesavers.com** is the kind of website for which the Internet is intended. The site keeps an updated list of discounts and reservation codes for use at Disney resorts. The codes are separated into categories such as "For anyone," "For residents of certain states," and so on. Anyone calling the Disney central reservations office (phone (407) W-DISNEY) can use a current code and get the discounted rate. The savings when using these codes can be considerable. On a recent trip we paid about $89 per night for a room in the Casitas at Coronado Springs, using one of the discount codes. The family two doors down paid the full rack rate of $180 per night for essentially the same room, but they probably didn't sleep as well as we did. The site also lists discount codes for rental cars and non-Disney hotels in the Orlando area.

Best Site for Breaking News and Rumors   We check **www.wdw magic.com** every few days to get the latest news and rumors on Walt Disney Worl. WdwMagic.com had satellite images of the construction of Mission: Space in 2001, two years before the ride was scheduled to debut. The site also has pages dedicated to the major rides, parades, and shows in each park, including audio and video. New user forums allow you to read and post messages to other Disney fans. Runner-up: **www.screamscape.com.**

Best "Tribute to Walt Disney World" Site   We get a kick out of Mike Lee's Widen Your World (**home.cfl.rr.com/omniluxe/wyw.htm**), a site dedicated to attractions that no longer appear in WDW. The planning, construction, and guest experience of each attraction are described in detail. The site is one good bibliography away from a thesis, in our opinion. Mike's got something special planned for the 30th anniversary of If You Had Wings ("the ex-Tomorrowland attraction that everyone loved the minute it closed"), including audio and photos. If you want to reminisce about your favorite extinct attraction, this is the place to go.

Best Orlando Weather Information   The Weather Channel's website offers printable 10-day forecasts for the Orlando area at **www.weather. com/weather/local/usfl0372.** We find this site to be especially useful in the winter and spring months, when temperatures can vary dramatically. During summer, the ultraviolet index forecasts will help you choose between a tube and a keg of sunscreen.

Best Website for Traffic, Roadwork, and Construction Information **www.expresswayauthority.com** contains the latest information on roadwork and construction in the Orlando and Orange County area. The site also contains detailed maps, driving directions, and toll-rate information to the most popular tourist destinations.

There are literally hundreds of other Disney sites, as well as sites that rate and contrast thrill rides in theme parks in the United States and all over the world. Start with those listed above and follow the links.

Information about Walt Disney World is also available at the public library, travel agencies, AAA, and by calling or writing any of the following:

IMPORTANT WALT DISNEY WORLD ADDRESSES

Walt Disney World Info/Guest
Letters/Letters to Mickey Mouse
P.O. Box 10040
Lake Buena Vista, FL 32830-0040

Walt Disney World Central
Reservations
P.O. Box 10100
Lake Buena Vista, FL 32830-0100

Convention and Banquet Information
Walt Disney World Resort South
P.O. Box 10000
Lake Buena Vista, FL 32830-1000

Walt Disney World Educational
Programs
P.O. Box 10000
Lake Buena Vista, FL 32830-1000

Merchandise Mail Order
(Guest Service Mail Order)
P.O. Box 10070
Lake Buena Vista, FL 32830-0070

Walt Disney World Ticket Mail Order
P.O. Box 10100
Lake Buena Vista, FL 32830-0140

Compliments, Complaints, and Suggestions
Walt Disney World Guest Communications
P. O. Box 10040
Lake Buena Vista, Florida 32830-1000

Important Walt Disney World Telephone Numbers

When you call the main information number, you will be offered a menu of options for recorded information on theme-park operating hours, recreation areas, shopping, entertainment complexes, tickets and admissions, resort reservations, and directions by highway and from the airport. If you are using a rotary telephone, your call will be forwarded to a Disney information representative. If you are using a Touch-Tone phone and have a question not covered by recorded information, press eight (8) at any time to speak to a Disney representative.

General Information	(407) 824-4321
Accommodations/Reservations	(407) 934-7639 or (407) 824-8000
All-Star Cafe	(407) 827-8326
All-Star Movie Resort	(407) 939-7000
All-Star Music Resort	(407) 939-6000
All-Star Sports Resort	(407) 939-5000
AMC Theaters Pleasure Island	(407) 298-4488
Animal Kingdom Lodge	(407) 938-4760
Beach Club Resort	(407) 934-8000
Blizzard Beach	(407) 560-3400
BoardWalk Resort	(407) 939-5100
Caribbean Beach Resort	(407) 934-3400
Celebration Realty Office	(407) 566-4663
Centracare	(407) 238-3000
The Crossroads	(407) 239-7777
Disney Main Gate	(407) 397-7032
Kissimmee	(407) 390-1888
Lake Buena Vista	(407) 934-2273
Cirque du Soleil	(407) 939-7600
Contemporary Resort	(407) 824-1000
Convention Information	(407) 828-3200
Coronado Springs Resort	(407) 939-1000
Dining Priority Seating	(407) 939-3463
Disabled Guests Special Requests	(407) 939-7807
Disney Institute Recreational Facilities	(407) 827-1100
DisneyQuest	(407) 828-4600

Disney's Wide World of Sports	(407) 363-6600
Disney Professional Seminars	(407) 824-7997
Downtown Disney Guest Services	(407) 934-6374
Downtown Disney Marketplace	(407) 828-3800
Fantasia Gardens Miniature Golf	(407) 560-8760
Fort Wilderness Campground	(407) 824-2900
Golf Reservations and Information	(407) WDW-GOLF
Grand Floridian Beach Resort and Spa	(407) 824-3000
Group Camping	(407) 939-7807
Guided Tour Information	(407) 939-TOUR
Guided VIP Solo Tours	(407) 560-6233
House of Blues Tickets and Information	(407) 934-2583
Lost and Found for articles lost:	
Yesterday or before (All parks)	(407) 824-4245
Today at Magic Kingdom	(407) 824-4245
Today at Epcot	(407) 560-7500
Today at Disney-MGM	(407) 560-3764
Today at Animal Kingdom	(407) 938-2265
Main Street Physicians	(407) 239-1195
Merchandise Guest Services Department	(407) 363-6200
Ocala Chamber of Commerce	(352) 629-8051
Ocala Disney Information Center	(352) 854-0770
Old Key West Resort	(407) 827-7700
Outdoor Recreation Reservations and Information	(407) WDW-PLAY
Pleasure Island Information	(407) 934-6300
Polynesian Resort	(407) 824-2000
Port Orleans Resort	(407) 934-5000
Resort Dining and Recreational Information	(407) 939-3463
River Country Information	(407) 824-2760
Shades of Green U.S. Armed Forces Hotel	(407) 824-3400
Telecommunication for the Deaf	
Reservations	(407) 939-7670
WDW Information	(407) 939-8255
Tennis Reservations/Lessons	(407) 939-7529
Typhoon Lagoon Information	(407) 560-4141
Walt Disney Travel Company	(407) 828-3232
Walt Disney World Dolphin	(407) 934-4000
Walt Disney World Speedway	(407) 939-0130
Walt Disney World Swan	(407) 934-3000
Weather Information	(407) 827-4545
Wilderness Lodge and Villas Resort	(407) 824-3200

Winter Summerland Miniature Golf	(407) 560-3000
Wrecker Service	(407) 824-0976
Yacht Club Resort	(407) 934-7000

When to Go to Walt Disney World

Why do they call it tourist season if we can't shoot them?

— Palatka, Florida, outdoorsman

Selecting the Time of Year for Your Visit

Walt Disney World is busiest Christmas Day through New Year's Day. Thanksgiving weekend, the week of Washington's birthday, Martin Luther King holiday weekend, spring break for colleges, and the two weeks around Easter are also extremely busy. What does "busy" mean? As many as 92,000 people have toured the Magic Kingdom alone on a single day in these peak times! While this level of attendance isn't typical, it is possible, and only those who absolutely cannot go at any other time should challenge the Disney parks at their peak periods.

The least busy time is from after the Thanksgiving weekend until the week before Christmas. The next slowest times are November through the weekend preceding Thanksgiving, January 4 through the first week of February, and the week after Easter through early June. Late February, March, and early April are dicey. Crowds ebb and flow according to spring-break schedules and the timing of Presidents' Day weekend. Though crowds have grown markedly in September and October as a result of special promotions aimed at locals and the international market, these months continue to be good for weekday touring at the Magic Kingdom, Disney-MGM Studios, and the Animal Kingdom, and for weekend visits to Epcot.

Many readers share their thoughts about the best time to visit Walt Disney World. These letters are representative.

From a Centerville, Ohio, family:

Catching on to the "off-season," we took the kids out of school and went to WDW in mid-May. So did a lot of other people. In fact, there were enough people there for me to think crowds must be increasing in the off-season as more people wise up about avoiding the masses. If I'm wrong, and this really was half the summer crowd, "high season" these days must be total and complete gridlock.

A mom from West Plains, Missouri, writes:

We visited WDW three times in the past eight years, each time in the second week of June. Each time the crowds were worse, and this time they were so big that we won't go at this time of year anymore.

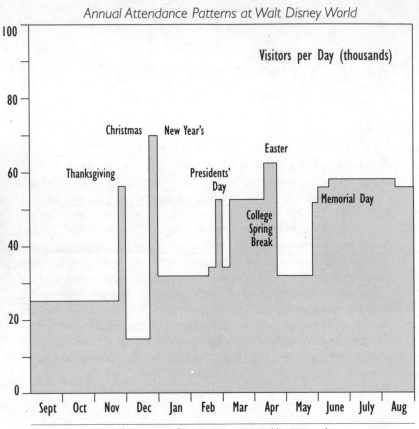

Annual Attendance Patterns at Walt Disney World

Visitors per Day (thousands)

Thanksgiving
Christmas
New Year's
Presidents' Day
College Spring Break
Easter
Memorial Day

(Attendance figures represent weekly averages)

The Downside of Off-Season Touring

Though we strongly recommend going to Walt Disney World in the fall, winter, or spring, there are trade-offs. The parks often open late and close early during the off-season. When they open as late as 9 a.m., everyone arrives about the same time, which makes it hard to beat the crowd. A late opening coupled with an early closing drastically reduces the hours available to tour. Even when crowds are small, it's difficult to see a big park like the Magic Kingdom or Epcot between 9 a.m. and 6 p.m. Early closing (before 8 p.m.) also usually means that evening parades or fireworks are eliminated. And, because these are slow times at Disney World, some rides and attractions may be closed for maintenance or renovation. Finally, central Florida temperatures fluctuate wildly during the late fall, winter, and early spring; daytime lows in the 40s and 50s are not uncommon.

Given the choice, however, we never would go to Walt Disney World in summer or during a holiday period. To us, small crowds, bargain prices, and stress-free touring are well worth risking a little cold weather or a couple of closed attractions. So much easier is touring in the fall and other "off" periods that our research team, at the risk of being blasphemous, would advise taking children out of school for a week at those times rather than battling the summer crowds.

Most readers who have tried Disney World at various times agree. A gentleman from Ottawa, Ontario, who toured in early December writes:

It was the most enjoyable trip [to Walt Disney World] I have ever had, and I can't imagine going [back] to Disney World when it is crowded. Even without the crowds, we were still very tired by afternoon. Fighting crowds certainly would have made a hellish trip. We will never go again at any other time.

A father of two from Reynoldsburg, Ohio, offers this opinion:

Taking your kids out of school. Is it worth it? Yes! Excuse my editorial comment at this point, but it used to be true that missing a week of school would place your child so far behind it could take months for him/her to regain that lost week. Not so today. With advance preparations and informing the teachers months before our departure, this was no problem. With less than an hour of homework after dinner, our kids went back to school with assignments completed and no makeup work. But it was all those other hours with no lines and no heat that were the real payoff.

There is another side to this story, however, and we have received some well-considered letters from parents and teachers who don't think taking kids out of school is such a hot idea. A Fairfax, Virginia, dad put it thus:

My wife and I are disappointed in that you seem to be encouraging families to take their children out of school to avoid the crowds at WDW during the summer months. My wife is an eighth-grade science teacher of chemistry and physics. She has parents pull their children, some honor-roll students, out of school for vacations, only to discover when they return that the students are unable to comprehend the material. Several students have been so thoroughly lost in their assignments that they ask if they can be excused from the tests. Parental suspicions [about] the quality of their children's education should be raised when children go to school for six hours a day yet supposedly can complete this same instruction with "less than an hour of homework" each night.

Likewise, a high-school teacher from Louisville, Kentucky, didn't mince words on this subject:

Teachers absolutely hate it when a kid misses school for a week, because: (a) parents expect a neat little educational packet to take with them as if every minute can be planned—not practicable; (b) when the kid returns he is going to be behind, and it is difficult to make up classroom instruction [at the time] when the kid needs it.

If a parent bothers to ask my opinion, I tell them bluntly it's their choice. If the student's grades go down, they have to accept that as part of their family decision. I have a student out this entire week, skiing in Colorado. There's no way she can make up some of the class activities (and that's exactly what I told her mom).

Dazed and Confused To present a complete picture, we must warn you that the difference between high and low seasons has blurred considerably in recent years. Even during off-season, crowd size can vary enormously. With Walt Disney World promotional hype in perpetual overdrive, huge crowds can materialize anytime, as these *Unofficial Guide* readers attest:

First, a mother from Bridgewater, New Jersey:

Although you mentioned the fact that school trips are [common] in Epcot during September and October, we were unprepared for the impact these groups had, especially since the kids are often unsupervised. From what I can see, the park can be enjoyed only on weekends during these months. Our visit was completely destroyed by unsupervised hordes of 10- to 12-year-olds.

A New York woman related this:

We planned our trip for the off-season (October) because we thought it would be less crowded, but we were sadly mistaken. The crowds were still overwhelming (especially at Magic Kingdom!).

A reader from Laureldale, Pennsylvania, agreed, writing:

Five years ago a trip to WDW in October was a pleasure. Now the crowds are getting larger. By midmorning at the Magic Kingdom, lines for Splash Mountain were 50–60 minutes long.

Ditto for a mother of two from Tallahassee, Florida:

Do not go in October; it was packed!

A Huntsville, Alabama, mom agreed, writing:

I think you should really emphasize to people: DO NOT GO TO THE MAGIC KINGDOM ON A SATURDAY IN OCTOBER. Whatever you want to see there—it's not worth it.

A Lima, Ohio, family encountered large crowds in early December:

Even though we went at the slowest time of year, it got very crowded by noon.

And an Enid, Oklahoma, woman found mid-November too crowded:

Our stay was considered the "slow" time, but we found the crowds huge.

A family from Staten Island, New York, found weekdays tranquil, but ran into a mess at the Magic Kingdom on Saturday:

Saturday (at MK) was rather horrifying. There were what seemed to be hordes of "day-trippers" (Scout troops, church groups, the Demolay Temple from Tampa, etc.). Even Tom Sawyer's Island was no idyllic oasis at 11:30 a.m. We left at about 1:30 p.m. for a swim and nap back at our motel and returned at 8 p.m. (the MK was open until midnight that night) to discover that the crowds had not thinned appreciably.

Other readers visiting during slower periods, however, report light crowds and easy touring. A Sanford, Maine, family toured during the second week of December:

It was so slow that most of the backtracking was unnecessary. The most fun came from looking at the empty, roped-off queuing areas and saying, "I'm so glad we came at the time we did!" and not having to wait.

And a West Seneca, New York, woman liked September:

The last week in September was dead. It was like we had the park to ourselves. We didn't wait longer than 15 minutes for a ride.

Finally, a Massachusetts family had good luck in late August:

Overall, the week we were at WDW was not crowded. Often there were no lines except at the Magic Kingdom "Mountains." Except for the heat, late August is a good time to go—it's not crowded and the parks are still open late.

In the final analysis, the only thing you can really count on is that, high or low season, Disney will be out beating the bushes to get people through the turnstiles. Plus, everything is relative. A busy day during off-season may catch you off guard if you had expected to have the parks to yourself. But believe us, the busiest off-season day is nothing compared to the masses you'll encounter during holidays and high season. Our advice, regardless of time of year, is to arrive at the park early and be prepared for big crowds. If attendance is light, you can kick back and forget the touring plans and our other crowd-beating strategies. On the other hand, if the place is jammed, you'll have a plan and be ready to go.

As a postscript, the likelihood of tangling with locals in September, October, and November can be significantly reduced by avoiding the Magic Kingdom on Saturday and Epcot on weekdays.

We Got Weather!   As if the crowds aren't enough, you must also consider the weather. September, October, and November are pleasant, but December and January can hit you with just about anything. And thunderstorms and pouring rain are not uncommon at any time of year.

A New Yorker who is accustomed to the vagaries of weather offers this bit of advice:

The weather when we were there was quirky. We were pepared and brought along umbrellas, ponchos, sweaters, etc. We learned quickly (the hard way) always to have these items with us, because the local weather forecasters were not to be trusted.

From a Dalton, Massachusetts, mother of two:

We visited the Magic Kingdom on a day that included about five hours of torrential downpours. We were wet, but we were also cool and got to ride multiple times any ride we wanted. Your advice about praying for rain was very sound, but maybe we prayed too hard. A few light showers would have done as well.

In addition to rain there's heat and cold. First, a letter regarding the heat from an Arlington, Texas, family:

If you are from Europe or the North, consider how hot the sun gets [in Florida]. We're from Texas, and this summer it was 110 degrees every day for about two weeks. We thought we would laugh off 90 degrees and some sun, but we had to admit it was still damn hot in the afternoons, and we got pretty wilty.

As for cold, an Owings Mills, Maryland, family braved the cruel depths of the central Florida winter:

Believe it or not, it is possible to have a good time in early January. Even with a high of 45 degrees, we were able to enjoy the Magic Kingdom one day since many attractions are indoors. Still, with young kids we braved Dumbo and other "wind chill" rides with hats and gloves. Best of all, the parks were almost empty before 11 a.m.

Selecting the Day of the Week for Your Visit

Selecting the best day to visit a Walt Disney World theme park requires analyzing several variables. Entering into the equation are:

1. The time of year of your visit (holiday, summer, or off-season).
2. Habits of people traveling to Walt Disney World from outside of Florida.
3. Attendance patterns for each day of the week at the respective parks.

A typical vacation scenario during summer would be for a family to arrive in the Orlando area on Sunday and to visit the Magic Kingdom on Monday and the Animal Kingdom on Tuesday; Epcot and Disney-MGM Studios on Wednesday and Thursday; and Typhoon Lagoon, Blizzard Beach, or a non-Disney area attraction on Friday. For those traveling by car, Friday often is reserved for heading home or to another Florida destination. If this were all we had to consider, we could recommend Fridays and Sundays as the best days all year to avoid crowds at the theme parks.

During the off-season, however, Disney initiates dozens of promotions to attract locals to Walt Disney World. Because these folks aren't on vacation, they tend to visit the theme parks on weekends. During fall, late winter, and spring, crowds might be larger on weekends than weekdays at the Magic Kingdom, the Animal Kingdom, and Disney-MGM Studios.

Crowds at Epcot, however, particularly during September and October, are almost always larger on weekdays. In addition to its promotions, Disney has a cooperative program with local schools that brings tens of thousands of children to Epcot for field trips in March, September, and October. Similarly, in late spring, high-school students on "senior days" or prom nights fill the theme parks. Many of these programs are on weekdays.

The Unexpected and Untimely Demise of Early Entry

In 2001, the early-entry program was terminated, a move that took both the media and the Disney faithful by surprise. The program, which had been in effect for almost a decade, allowed Disney resort guests to enter a designated theme park one hour before the general public ("day guests" in Disneyspeak).

Here, quoted in full from slick handout, is why Disney claims to have cancelled early entry (known officially as "Surprise Mornings"):

Many of our guests chose not to take advantage of our Surprise Mornings (early Disney Theme Park Entrance) program. They told us they wanted more of the Disney Characters. We took it as a wake-up call. So we've replaced Surprise Mornings with a new kind of magic—now the friends you've come to love are coming to you!

If Pinocchio had uttered this lame explanation, his nose would have reached all the way to Tampa. Really, what hogwash! The "wake-up call," pure and simple, was the Walt Disney Company's bottom line. And the left-field attempt to connect guests wanting more characters with pulling the plug on early entry is a stretch almost beyond comprehension. Incidentally, the "friends you've come to love are coming to you" is a bus full of characters that calls on the various resorts. According to reader mail and surveys of guests at Walt Disney World, this "Character Caravan" is so insignificant that pitching it as a substitute benefit for early entry strains credulity. As a reader from Murray, Kentucky, put it:

I can understand cutting costs as a consequence of the recession and the terrorist attacks, but trying to convince us that the character bus is a perk comparable to early entry is patronizing and insulting.

And a Worthington, Ohio, mom sized it up as follows:

[Disney] traded us a chicken for the whole farm and then told us it was our idea.

• WALT DISNEY WORLD CLIMATE •

	Average Daily Low	Average Daily High	Average Daily Temperature	Average Daily Humidity %	Average Rainfall per Month (inches)	Number of Days of Rain per Month
January	49°	72°	61°	74	2.1	6
February	50°	73°	62°	71	2.8	7
March	55°	78°	67°	71	3.2	8
April	60°	84°	72°	69	2.2	6
May	66°	88°	77°	72	3.9	9
June	71°	91°	81°	77	7.4	14
July	73°	92°	82°	79	7.8	17
August	73°	92°	82°	80	6.3	16
September	73°	90°	81°	80	5.6	14
October	65°	84°	75°	77	2.8	9
November	57°	78°	68°	76	1.8	6
December	51°	73°	62°	76	1.9	6

Hurricane Season (June–September)

Early entry, in economic terms, requires the designated park to be partially manned for the early-entry guests. It also requires special transportation-system arrangements and parking-lot staffing. All things considered, it's an expensive proposition. Moreover, because early-entry guests show up at the crack of dawn specifically to experience popular attractions, they do not spend money in the restaurants and shops. So, from Disney's perspective early entry is an all-cost-no-benefit deal.

We understand Disney's thinking and consider the elimination of early entry unfortunate, but reasonable in a business context. What we object to is Disney's disingenuous spin in asserting that early entry was expendable because nobody used it. We use early entry every year and can attest that large numbers of resort guests availed themselves of the privilege. In fact, we have long recommended that our readers avoid the park scheduled for early entry because legions of resort guests using early entry insure more crowded conditions in that park.

The early-entry program was developed as an incentive to lure guests to the Disney-owned resorts. For many guests the early-entry perk was the primary reason for lodging in a Disney-owned hotel. Clearly, the Disney folks don't think the incentive is working anymore. As Walt Disney World plowed through 2002, the French Quarter section of Port Orleans as well as all of the various accommodations at the Disney Institute remained closed. In addition, the opening of the finished half of the new Pop Century Resort was postponed indefinitely, as was the completion of the remaining half. In short, the Disney hotels were hurting. And this was the time Disney chose to eliminate the most compelling reason for staying at a Disney property. Go figure.

Do prospective Disney resort guests understand what they've lost? This letter from an irate mom suggests that the implications are crystal clear:

I am writing to express my anger that Disney has decided to get rid of the Early Entry program. Last June we spent seven days visiting Disney and every day but one we used Early Entry privilege. Now as we were planning another trip in June of 2002, I found out through a parent magazine that Disney has eliminated the Early Entry privilege. Not even my travel agent knew about these changes. After calling Disney, I found out that people being surveyed at the parks were the deciding factor in the decision to dismiss the Early Entry program. I want to know who the heck they surveyed? There are absolutely no drawbacks to the Early Entry program. Who wants to wait one to two hours for a ride on Dumbo or Space Mountain? I think it is ridiculous that Disney is taking our privileges away, especially when we pay soooooo much to stay in a Disney Resort. Now the only reason to stay in a Disney hotel is transportation that isn't all that good! What a shame!

Will Disney bring early entry back? Maybe, if (1) business returns to pre-2001 levels, and (2) occupancy at the Disney hotels fails to recover in step with park attendance. Truth to tell, early entry at Walt Disney World was a nice perk, especially in the off-seasons, when it added an hour to the shortened daily hours of operation, but it really wasn't crucial. Disneyland Park in Anaheim, however, is another story. During the busier times of year, Disneyland Park fills so full, so fast, that early entry is the only way, even with FASTPASS, to get a jump on the crowds.

Our Recommendations

1. Least Crowded Days From September through May (excluding holidays and typical spring-break weeks), Saturday and Sunday are the most crowded days, while during summer the opposite is true (because locals stay home and out-of-state guests use Friday, Saturday, and Sunday for traveling).

Magic Kingdom At the Magic Kingdom, Sunday and Friday are least crowded in summer, and Friday and Wednesday are least crowded during the rest of the year.

Disney-MGM Studios At Disney-MGM Studios, Monday and Friday are best during summer. During off-season, try Monday and Tuesday.

Epcot Monday, Wednesday, and Thursday are least crowded from January through May, as well as in November and December. During summer, crowds are smaller on Saturday and Sunday. In September and October, when school groups inundate Epcot, visit on Saturday or Sunday.

Animal Kingdom High- or low-season, visit the Animal Kingdom on Monday, Tuesday, or Sunday.

2. Early Entry If early entry is revived, avoid the park running early entry during busier times of year. If you are a Disney resort guest, take advantage of early entry if it's offered during less busy times of year. Avoid the Magic Kingdom on Saturday irrespective of the time of year.

3. E-Ride Night In 1999, Disney instituted a program called E-Ride Night, where resort guests with multiday passes can (for an extra $12) remain in the Magic Kingdom after official closing time and ride all the biggies with little or no waiting. Offered exclusively in the off-seasons, the E-Ride Night program is described in detail on pages 482–483. Needless to say, for folks who want to sleep in, E-Ride Night is the best thing since catsup on fries. Like most Disney programs, it is subject to termination at any time. Pass has to be used on the same day in which it was purchased.

The Cruelest Times of All: Summer and Holidays

A reader from Columbus, Ohio, once observed, "The main thing I learned from your book is not to go during the summer or at holiday times. Once you know that, you don't need a guidebook." While we might argue with the reader's conclusion, we certainly agree that avoiding summer and holidays is a strategy worth pursuing. That having been said, we also understand that many folks have no choice concerning the time of year they visit Walt Disney World. Much of this book, in fact, is dedicated to making sure those readers who visit during the busier times of year enjoy their Walt Disney World experience. Sure, off-season touring is preferable, but, armed with a little knowledge and some basic strategy, you can have a great time whenever you visit.

To put it in perspective, early summer (up to about June 15th) and late summer (after August 15th) are not nearly as crowded as the intervening period. And even the crowds of midsummer pale in comparison to the vast hordes that invade during holiday periods. If you visit in midsummer or during a holiday, the first thing you need to know is that the guest capacity of the theme parks is not infinite. In fact, once a park reaches capacity, only Disney resort guests arriving via the Disney transportation system are allowed to enter. If you are not a Disney resort guest, you may find yourself in a situation similar to this dad from Boise, Idaho:

This is the worst of it. The Magic Kingdom and the [Disney-] MGM Studios were so full they closed the parks. For three days we could not enter those parks, so we were forced to go to Epcot and use up two days of our four-day pass. We decided to pay for another night at our hotel to see if the crowds would let up, but no luck. All we could do was just drive around Orlando and sightsee.

The reader didn't tell us what time he arrived at the Magic Kingdom or the Studios, but we can pretty much assume he wasn't on hand for opening. If you roll out of bed early and get yourself to one of the parks an hour or so prior to official opening time, you are practically certain to be admitted.

The thought of teeming, jostling throngs jockeying for position in endless lines under the baking Fourth-of-July sun is enough to wilt the will and ears of the most ardent Mouseketeer. The Disney folks, however, feeling bad about those long, long lines and the nearly impossible touring conditions on packed holidays, compensate their patrons with a no-less-than-incredible array of first-rate live entertainment and happenings.

Shows, parades, concerts, and pageantry continue throughout the day. In the evening, particularly, so much is going on that you have to make some tough choices. Concerts, parades, light shows, laser shows, fireworks, and dance productions occur almost continually. No question about it, you can go to Walt Disney World on the Fourth of July (or on any other extended-hours, crowded day), never get on a ride, and still have a good time. Admittedly, it isn't the ideal situation for a first-timer who really wants to experience the attractions, but for anyone else it's a great party.

Disney provides colorful holiday decor for most holidays, as well as special parades and live entertainment for Christmas, New Year's, Easter, and Fourth of July, among others. Regarding Christmas, our advice is to visit in early December when you can enjoy the decorations and festivities without battling the crowds.

Disney monitors the occupancy of hotels in the area in order to project attendance. On days when huge crowds are expected, Disney will often open the parks well in advance of the official opening time. This applies to all the parks and is done to prevent parking-toll booths, ticket windows, transportation systems, and entrance plazas from being overwhelmed. When Disney puts its early-opening plan into operation, the parks do not discriminate between Disney resort guests and day-guests (those not staying at Disney hotels). In other words, when really big crowds are expected, Disney will often open all of the parks early and admit any guest.

Unfortunately, Disney does not disclose in advance that it plans to open the parks early, nor will operators at Disney's main information phone number clue you in. You basically must guess based on the time of year whether implementation of the early-opening procedure is likely. Over major holidays, the probability of Disney opening the parks early is high. For nonholiday periods during the peak summer season, it's a lot iffier.

When we visit during the summer or holidays, we sometimes make a reconnaissance run to one of the Disney transportation system information windows (located at each of the parks and at the Transportation and Ticket Center [TTC]) and ask what time the parks actually opened that morning. Make it clear that you are not inquiring about the official opening time, but rather that you want to know exactly what time guests were admitted. If the parks opened early on the day in question, there is a great likelihood that the same conditions will prevail for the next couple of days.

If you visit on a nonholiday midsummer day, arrive an hour before the stated opening. If you visit during a major holiday period, arrive 70 minutes ahead of the official opening time. Hit your favorite rides early using one of our touring plans, and then return to your hotel for lunch, a swim, and perhaps a nap. Don't forget to have your hand stamped for re-entry when you exit. If you are interested in the special parades and shows, return to the park in the late afternoon or early evening. Work under the assumption that, unless you use FASTPASS, early morning will be the only time you can experience the attractions without long waits. Finally, do not wait until the last minute in the evening to leave the park. The exodus at closing is truly mind-boggling.

Epcot is usually the least crowded park during holiday periods. Expect the other parks to be mobbed. To save time in the morning, purchase your admission in advance. Also, consider bringing your own stroller or wheelchair instead of renting one of Disney's. If you are touring Epcot or the Magic Kingdom and plan to spend the day, try exiting the park for lunch at one of the nearby resort hotels. Above all, bring your sense of humor and pay attention to the morale of your party. Bail out when it gets to be more work than fun.

The Disney Calendar

In addition to the annual events described below, Walt Disney World will probably extend its **100 Years of Magic Celebration** into 2003. A celebration of Walt Disney's 100th birthday anniversary, the event features *One Man's Dream,* a multimedia tribute to Walt Disney at the Disney-MGM Studios, a new (launched in 2002) full-scale parades at the Animal Kingdom and the Studios, and embellishments to the Magic Kingdom parade and Tapestry of Nations parade at Epcot.

Walt Disney World Marathon Usually held the first weekend after New Year's, the marathon pulls in about 20,000 runners and their families, enough people to affect crowd conditions in the parks. Additionally, the race itself disrupts both vehicular and pedestrian traffic throughout Walt Disney World and the theme parks.

Mardi Gras A special Mardi Gras party is held at Pleasure Island from the Friday before Mardi Gras through Mardi Gras Tuesday. Admission to Pleasure Island is required. Pleasure Island is mobbed, but the rest of the World is largely unaffected.

Black History Month The entire month of February, Black History Month is celebrated throughout Walt Disney World with various displays, artisans, storytellers, and entertainers. There is no extra charge to enjoy the activities, and the effect of the celebration on crowd levels is negligible.

Atlanta Braves Spring Training The Atlanta Braves hold spring training at Disney's Wide World of Sports from the middle of February through the end of March. Admission is required to watch the training. Attendance levels at the theme parks are not affected by the Braves's activities.

Epcot International Flower and Garden Festival A celebration of flowers, gardening, and landscaping, the Flower and Garden Festival is held annually from the third week in April through the first Saturday in June. Expert horticulturists showcase exotic floral displays, share gardening tips, and demonstrate the latest techniques for planting, cultivating, and pest control. Even if you don't have a green thumb, the 20 million blooms from some 1,200 species will make your eyes pop. And the best thing about the Flower and Garden Festival is that it does not noticeably impact crowd levels at Epcot.

Minor League Baseball The Orlando Rays, the AA farm club of the Tampa Bay Devil Rays, play about 70 Southern League home games at

Disney's Wide World of Sports between the first week of April and the first week of September. There is an admission charge, of course, and the presence of the Rays does not affect attendance at the theme parks.

Epcot International Food and Wine Festival   From the third week of October through the third week of November, the Food and Wine Festival celebrates food, wine, and the culinary arts. Approximately 30 nations each trot out their most famous cuisine, wine, and entertainment. Held outdoors around the World Showcase Lagoon, the festival offers culinary demonstrations, wine seminars, tastings, and opportunities to see some of the world's (i.e., the real world's) top chefs in action. Although many of the activities are included in the price of your Epcot admission, the best workshops and tastings are by reservation only and cost extra. Call (407) WDW-DINE well in advance for details and prices. Crowd conditions in the park are impacted only slightly.

Mickey's Not-So-Scary Halloween Party   Held each year on the Friday and Sunday before Halloween plus on Halloween night, the party runs from 7 p.m. to midnight at the Magic Kingdom. The event includes trick-or-treating in costume around the park, as well as parades, live music, storytelling, and a special fireworks show. Aimed primarily at younger children, the event is decidedly happy and upbeat as opposed to spooky and scary. The party is by reservation only. Admission is about $28 for adults and $23 for children ages 3–9 if purchased in advance. Tickets at the gate (assuming they are available) run $30 for adults and $25 for children. For reservations and additional information, call (407) W-DISNEY. Teens and young adults looking for a Halloween happening should check out parties at Pleasure Island, Universal CityWalk, and at the Universal theme parks.

A woman from Nokomis, Florida, reports that the only scary thing at the Not-So-Scary Halloween Party were the crowds:

I've been to Mickey's Not-So-Scary Halloween Party twice, and both times it has been an overcrowded nightmare! Don't even bother to try and ride anything.

Christmas and New Year at the Theme Parks   Our advice for touring the parks the week between Christmas and New Year is to skip the Magic Kingdom, if at all possible. We love the Magic Kingdom. Really we do. But that love is tempered by the fact that women will wait in line up to twenty minutes to use the restrooms during this week. Thirty-minute waits to get your lunch at counter-service restaurants are typical. Ask a teenager what happens in a "mosh pit" and you'll have some idea what Fantasyland looks like midafternoon, only with more strollers and peppier music.

Epcot, on the other hand, is at its best during the holidays. Touring in the evening hours will reward you with stunning displays of holiday decorations and slightly smaller crowds than during the day. Exceptional live entertainment abounds, too. The American Pavilion, for example, has two choral groups—easily over a hundred and fifty singers—performing holiday favorites simultaneously during this week.

Disney-MGM Studios is also a good choice for evening touring during the holiday period. Crowds will still be larger than normal, but the decorations make up for it. One "must see" is the Osborne Family Spectacle of Lights at the Studios Backlot. "Spectacle" is an apt description, as it contains a staggering five million Christmas lights, including 3-D images that can be viewed using special glasses. For Christmas, the Studios simulates winter weather by mounting bubble-making machines on top of the buildings in the New York Street area. At night, millions of small bubbles cascade down on park guests. The effect was striking—it took us a minute to realize it wasn't really snowing. An outstanding effect, we hope it becomes a permanent part of the holiday display.

Mickey's Very Merry Christmas Party   The party is staged from 8 p.m. to 1 a.m. (after regular park hours) on a number of evenings in December. Advance tickets cost $34 for adults and $24 for children ages 3–9, while tickets at the gate run about $40 and $29, respectively. For exact dates and prices, call (407) W-DISNEY. Included are use of all attractions during party hours, performances of Mickey's Very Merry Christmas Parade, a party memento (usually a family photo), carolers, "a magical snowfall on Main Street," and fireworks.

A reader from Pineville, Louisiana, tried the Very Merry Christmas Party and found the guest list too large for her liking, writing:

Another thing I will not do again is buy tickets and go to the Very Merry Christmas Party. The event was sold out with 20,000 actually in attendance. We went in December to avoid crowds and were taken by surprise to find wall-to-wall people at the Very Merry Christmas Party. They offered some great shows, but we could not get to them. The parade at 9 p.m. and the fireworks at 10 p.m., then fighting our way back to the parking lot was all we could muster. We spent 30 minutes on arrival just getting a stroller. We did not ride anything, and there were some things that we had wanted to go back and ride. Mickey's Very Merry Christmas Party is not the time for rides!

The reader from Nokomis, Florida, who had such a rough time at Halloween, recommends Christmas for repeat guests:

Christmas is so much better [than Halloween]! You just can't experience a more festive time, with the decor, lights, carolers, performers, and shows. If you've been to Disney before and have been on a good number of the rides, you can relax and enjoy all the Christmas festivities going on. I highly recommend a Disney Christmas vacation for repeat guests.

Note that the reader is referring to the period between Thanksgiving and Christmas, not to Mickey's Very Merry Christmas Party.

As a last comment, none of Disney's special holiday parties (Halloween, Christmas, etc.) are a good bet if you're crowd averse or are primarily interested in experiencing the attractions. And remember, during major holiday periods such as Christmas, most of the festive extras can be enjoyed in the weeks preceding the week in which the holiday falls.

Part Two

Making the Most of Your Time and Money

Allocating Money

Did Walt really intend for it to be so expensive that the average family couldn't afford it?

—*Unofficial Guide* reader and mother of one from Amarillo, Texas

How much you spend depends on how long you stay at Walt Disney World. But even if you only stop by for an afternoon, be prepared to drop a bundle. In Part Three we'll show you how to save money on lodging, and in Part Nine you'll find lots of tips for economizing on meals. This section will give you some sense of what you can expect to pay for admission, as well as which admission option will best meet your needs.

Walt Disney World Admission Options

Reviewers who complain that prices quoted in guidebooks are out of date should note that Walt Disney World ticket prices change about as often as the prime rate. In fact, since the first edition of the *Unofficial Guide* in 1985, Walt Disney World admission prices have escalated 160%! Prices quoted below are those prevailing at press time. Admission-price increases historically have been in the 3–5% range.

There are basically ten Walt Disney World admission options (many with silly names). Please note that the prices below include sales tax, whereas prices quoted in Disney literature or on the Disney information phone line do not.

Type of Pass	Adult Price w/ Tax	Child Price w/ Tax
1-Day/One-Park Only Pass	$51	$40
1-Day/One-Park Bounce-Back Pass	$45	$35
4-Day Park-Hopper Pass	$204	$161

Type of Pass	Adult Price w/ Tax	Child Price w/ Tax
5-Day Park-Hopper Pass	$230	$182
5-Day Park-Hopper Plus Pass	$262	$209
6-Day Park-Hopper Plus Pass	$294	$235
7-Day Park-Hopper Plus Pass	$325	$262
Ultimate Park-Hopper Pass	*Varies according to length of stay*	
Annual Passports*	$370	$315
Florida Resident/Seasonal	$190	$161

* More expensive Annual Passports include water parks, Pleasure Island, and Disney's Wide World of Sports.

The **1-Day/One-Park Only Pass** is good for admission and unlimited use of "attractions and experiences" at the Magic Kingdom, Epcot, the Animal Kingdom, or Disney-MGM Studios, but does not provide same-day admission to more than one of the four.

The **1-Day/One-Park Bounce-Back Pass** works as follows (we think): If you purchase a 1-Day/One-Park Pass (see above) at the regular price, you are eligible to buy a 1-Day/One Park Bounce-Back Pass at a discounted rate, *as long as you buy it on the same day you bought the original pass.* But wait, there's more: if you purchase a 1-Day/One-Park Pass and a second, discounted 1-Day/One-Park Bounce-Back Pass, you are eligible to buy a third and fourth 1-Day/One-Park Bounce-Back Pass at an even greater discount. All passes must be bought on the same day.

The 1-Day/One-Park Bounce-Back Pass, originally trotted out in 1999, is a good example of why Walt Disney World doesn't have an 800 number. When first introduced, it took a Disney information operator over 12 minutes to explain how the Bounce-Back works, and she had to consult her supervisor twice in the process. When we called to check on the Bounce-Back for this edition, we made upwards of five phone calls just to get an information operator to admit that the pass exists. Frustrated by our persistence, a Disney operator finally grudgingly acknowledged that the Bounce-Back is still available but that "Disney doesn't want anyone to know about it." Because the Bounce-Back was trumpeted to the far corners of the realm only three years ago, this prompted us to ask, "Why have it if you don't want anyone to know about it?" The answer, according to Disney info, is that park ticket sellers are instructed to try to talk guests into buying multiday Park-Hopper passes instead of 1-Day/One-Park tickets. If a guest balks at purchasing the more expensive multiday pass, the ticket seller is then authorized as a last resort to offer the Bounce-Back Pass in order to prolong the guest's Disney visit. The bottom line, evidently, is that Bounce-Backs were cannibalizing sales of multiday Park-Hoppers, so they were withdrawn, except as an incentive to keep one-day guests on property.

If you buy four days of 1-Day/One-Park admissions on a given day under the Bounce-Back arrangement, you will spend $51 for the first pass, $45 for the second, and $39 for the third and fourth, or $174 total (for adult passes; it's $141 for a child's passes). This is approximately $18 per adult and $15 per child less than you would pay for 4-Day Park-Hopper Passes (see below). For the savings, you forfeit two features of the Park-Hopper Pass. First, you give up the right to visit more than one park in a single day, and second, Bounce-Back passes expire, whereas Park-Hopper Passes are good forever. If you buy a 1-Day/One-Park Pass and then buy a 1-Day/One-Park Bounce-Back Pass, the Bounce-Back Pass expires four days from the date of purchase. If you buy two Bounce-Back passes, the first one expires in four days and the second one in six days. If you buy three, the third expires in eight days.

Though only Disney could dream up something like this, it's a pretty good deal for anyone who wants to visit the theme parks over a 3- or 4-day period and doesn't care about hopping from park to park on the same day.

The **4-Day** and **5-Day Park-Hopper Passes** provide same-day admission to the Magic Kingdom, the Animal Kingdom, Epcot, and Disney-MGM Studios. You can tour the Studios in the morning, have lunch at the Animal Kingdom and dinner at Epcot, and stop by the Magic Kingdom for the evening parades and fireworks. Unused days are good forever.

The **5-Day, 6-Day,** and **7-Day Park-Hopper Plus Passes** provide for unlimited use of the major theme parks as well as limited visits to Pleasure Island, Blizzard Beach, Typhoon Lagoon, River Country, and the Wide World of Sports for the number of the days stated on the pass. Like the Park-Hopper Pass, Park-Hopper Plus Passes are good forever and do not have to be used during one stay or on consecutive days.

Regarding the water parks, Pleasure Island, and Wide World of Sports, the 5-Day Park-Hopper Plus allows two visits to the venues of your choice. The 6- and 7-Day Park-Hopper Plus Passes come with three and four visits respectively. Any admissions you don't use are good forever, including your visits to the minor parks of your choice (water parks, Pleasure Island, and the sports complex). *Note:* You can't hop from water park to water park in the same way that you can between the major theme parks. If you buy a 5-Day Park-Hopper Plus Pass and visit Typhoon Lagoon in the morning and Blizzard Beach in the afternoon, you'll use up both of your admission options to the water parks and minor entertainment venues.

The **Ultimate Park-Hopper Pass,** for Walt Disney World lodging and campground guests, provides the same benefits as the Park-Hopper Plus Pass but can be purchased for any length of stay two days or longer. This program replaces the Unlimited Magic Passes and offers a comprehensive admission option (all major and minor parks) for stays of any length. These passes are incredibly convenient: guests are issued a card that functions as a combination park pass and credit card. The card can be used at restaurants, shops, and other facilities throughout Walt Disney World, and purchases are charged to the guest's room. On the negative side, Ultimate Park-Hopper Passes are good only for the guest's stay.

Also, because the Ultimate Park-Hopper Pass is only available to Disney resort guests, Disney does not publish the price. This makes prices subject to manipulation and increases the difficulty of comparing various admission options. We can tell you, however, that the Ultimate Park-Hopper Pass is more expensive than regular Park-Hopper passes because it includes the water parks and various entertainment venues. If you don't intend to spend much time at the water parks, Pleasure Island, or Wide World of Sports or alternatively plan to spend a day or two outside the World, you're much better off (even as a Disney hotel guest) buying a Park-Hopper pass. However, the Ultimate Park-Hopper Pass does allow you to hop from water park to water park to Pleasure Island, etc., on the same day.

The **Annual Passport** is good for unlimited use of the major theme parks for one year. An add-on is available to provide unlimited use of the minor theme parks. In addition to admission, Annual Passport holders get a number of perks, including complimentary parking and seasonal special offers such as room-rate discounts at Disney resorts. This pass is not valid for special events.

The **Florida Resident's Passport.** Walt Disney World has expanded the admission options for Florida residents, who now can select from a menu of choices, including:

Florida Resident's Seasonal Passport   This pass (about $190 for adults) allows unlimited use of the major theme parks during specified (quieter) times of year. Major holidays are excluded.

Florida Resident's Epcot   After 4 p.m. Passport. About $105 for adults, this pass allows Floridians to visit Epcot any day after 4 p.m.

Florida Resident's Annual Passport   These passports are available to residents at about 17% off the regular price.

While applicants must prove Florida residency to be eligible, it isn't necessary to have a Florida driver's license or to live in Florida year round. A utility bill in your name for a Florida address will suffice.

For Additional Information on Passes

If you have a question or concern regarding admissions that can be addressed only through a person-to-person conversation, call Disney Ticket Services at (407) 827-4166. If you need current prices or routine information, you're better off calling (407) 824-4321 for recorded admission info.

Which Admission Should You Buy?

If you have only one day at Walt Disney World, select the park that most interests you and buy the 1-Day/One-Park Only Ticket. If you have two days and don't plan to return to Disney for a couple of years, buy two 1-Day tickets, a Bounce-Back Pass, or an Ultimate Park-Hopper Pass if you're a Disney lodging guest. If you think you might pass through the area again in the next year or two, spring for a 4-, 5-, 6-, or 7-day pass. Use two days of admission to see as much as you can, and save the remaining days for another trip.

If you plan to spend three or more days at Walt Disney World, buy a 4- or 5-day pass. If you live in Florida or plan to spend seven or more days in the major theme parks, the Annual Passport is a good buy. If you live in Florida and don't mind being restricted to visiting Disney World at designated off-peak times, the Florida Resident's Seasonal Pass should be considered.

If you visit Walt Disney World every year, here's how to save big bucks. Let's say you usually take your vacation during summer. This year, plan your Disney vacation for July and buy an Annual Passport. Next year, go in June. Because Annual Passports start on the date of purchase, those you buy this year will still be good for next year's vacation if you go a month earlier! If you spend four days each year at Disney World (eight days in the two consecutive years), you'll cut your daily admission to about $46 per adult per day including tax. The longer your Disney vacation, of course,

the more you save with the Annual Passport. If you visit the theme parks seven days each year, your admission will be less than $27 per day.

Another Tip for Saving Money on Admissions

You can also save on admission prices by planning ahead and keeping an eye on the calendar, as this mom from Broomfield, Colorado, explains:

If you are planning a trip well in advance, purchase your Park-Hopper Passes before the end of the year. Our travel agent recommended this because Disney usually increases their prices in the new year. So we purchased our tickets for June back in December, and sure enough, I found out that the price for a Park-Hopper Pass had increased $20 per person. That's an $80 [savings] for our family!

And Disney doesn't guarantee that prices on some things won't increase without notice. We reserved a refrigerator for our room when making reservations in October. At that time, the charge quoted was $6 per day. Upon check-out the charge on my bill was $10.60 per day!

Discounts on Admission

Legitimate discounts for newly issued Disney admissions are more readily available than in years past. The discounts fall in one of two categories: discounts available to anyone and discounts available to certain groups. All of the discounts apply to multi-day passes to the Disney parks only. Discounts for one-day and multi-day admissions to other central Florida theme parks and attractions are also available.

Admission Discounts Available to Anyone

Surprisingly, the deals available to anyone are about the same as those offered to special groups (with the exception of military and civil service personnel).

Ticketmania offers discounts on tickets for almost all central Florida attractions, including Disney, Universal, SeaWorld, and *Cirque du Soliel,* by shopping online at Ticketmania.com. Discounts for the major theme parks are about 4%. Discounts of up to 7% are available for some Universal/SeaWorld combo passes. Tickets for other area attractions, dinner shows, and the like are more deeply discounted. The tickets sold are exactly the same as those available at the theme parks and other destinations. As of the time the *Unofficial Guide* went to press, Ticketmania offered free shipping with 5–10 day delivery. Rush shipping is available for an additional charge. After receiving your order and payment information, Ticketmania confirms the order via e-mail and specifies both when the tickets will be shipped and when you should receive them. Though Ticketmania is primarily set up to do business on the Internet, customers can reach it by phone at (877) 822-7299, 10 a.m. to 8 p.m. EST, seven days a week.

Wal-Mart on US 192 in Kissimmee has an in-house travel agency that sells Disney admissions at about 4% off retail. Passes for other area theme parks are also available. You must buy passes in person. From Walt Disney World take US 192 south. The Wal-Mart is located near mile marker 15 close to the Medieval Times dinner theater. Phone is (800) 669-0913.

Orlando Convention & Visitors Bureau Official Visitors Center If you are staying at one of the Universal Florida hotels or in the International Drive area, you can save about 2–3% off regular prices at the Visitor Center. The center is located at 8723 International Drive about a half mile south of the intersection with Sand Lake Road. If you are coming from I-4, take Exit 29A. Open 8 a.m. to 6 p.m. daily. The phone is (407) 363-5872. The Convention and Visitors Bureau also sells tickets online at www.orlandoticketsales.com.

Admission Discounts Available to Certain Groups and Individuals

Canadians Canadians purchasing their admission at a Disney Store in Canada will save about 6% by avoiding taxes.

Club Members Members of the Disney Club (see page 115), AAA, and the Disney Vacation Club can avail themselves of a 4–5% discount on admissions.

Disney Corporate Sponsors If you work for a company that has a corporate sponsorship relationship with Walt Disney World, you might be eligible for either discounted admissions or preferential treatment at the theme parks. Inquire at your personnel or employee benefits office.

Military, Department of Defense, Civil Service Active-duty and retired military, Department of Defense civilian employees, and some Civil Service employees, as well as their dependents, can buy Disney multi-day admissions at a 9–10% discount. At most military and DOD installations the passes are available from the Morale, Welfare, and Recreation (MWR) office. Civil Service employees should check with their personnel office to see if they are eligible and for instructions on how and where to purchase the tickets (usually they must be ordered in advance). Military personnel can purchase a discounted admission for non-military guests as long as the military member accompanies the non-military member. If for a group, 50% of the group must be eligible for the military discount.

Florida Residents Florida residents are eligible for a number of different discounted admissions, most of which were described on page 48 in this chapter. A valid form of identification, such as a passport, Florida drivers license, or Florida State ID card, showing a Florida address is required. Time-share owners who reside outside Florida are not eligible.

Each Florida resident must qualify individually, and passes incorporate a fingerprint scanning device that prevents passes from being transferred to another person. Because children do not usually posess any of the required identification, it's possible for grandparents to purchase Florida resident passes for out-of-state grandchildren.

Old Passports and the Animal Kingdom

Unused days on multiday passports sold before the Animal Kingdom opened in 1998 are good only for the other three parks. In other words, you can't use them for admission to the Animal Kingdom.

Partially Used Passes

Many readers ask if they can use remaining admissions on partially redeemed 4- through 7-day passes brought home by relatives. Whoever originally purchased the pass agreed to the purchase condition that "the pass must be used by the same person for all days." Because most passes sold in recent years do not bear the photograph or signature of the purchaser, guests have generally had no difficulty gaining admission with a partially used pass acquired from a friend or relative. For the past couple of years, moreover, it has been normal practice to issue passes that do not even bear the name of the purchaser. This makes the pass perfectly, though illegally, transferable.

A corollary question concerns what to do with unused admissions on 4-, 5-, 6-, or 7-day passes that you purchase legally during your vacation. Our advice is to hang onto the passes. For starters, resale of unused multiday passes is a misdemeanor. Second, because Disney raises admission prices almost every year, using an old pass during your next visit will save you money.

Recently, black-market ticket sellers have become bolder. Although it's true that most theme-park tickets offered at a deep discount involve suffering through a time-share pitch, there is now an active and open market in the buying and selling of unused admissions on multiday passes. Most of this activity is on US 192 in small stores with signs reading "We Buy Unused Days on Park Passes" or similar language. Savings on "pre-owned" passes are considerable, sometimes more than 50%, and salespersons claim that buying and reselling passes is perfectly legal. Disney, uncharacteristically silent on the matter, has yet to challenge these operations. Our advice is to buy only new, unused passes from a legitimate source. The modern plastic pass must be computer scanned to ascertain the number of unused days left on the card. When you purchase a partially used card from a stranger, you have no way of verifying how many, if any, unused days remain.

Where to Buy Your Admission at Walt Disney World

You can purchase passes at the major theme parks and at the resort hotels. Many hotels outside Walt Disney World maintain a desk or kiosk where independent brokers sell tickets to area attractions. These brokers are legitimate, but convenience is the only advantage to buying from them. Expect to pay regular Disney prices or a little more.

Where to Buy Your Admission in Advance

You can buy most multiday passes at a Disney Store before you leave home. The stores also can order 1-Day/One-Park Only tickets (allow three weeks for delivery). As discussed above , you can purchase multiday passes online, at **ticketmania.com** or **orlandoticketsales.com**. If you're driving to Disney World, you can buy your admission at the Ocala Disney Information Center at Exit 68 on I-75. If you fly, you can buy tickets at the airport Disney Store.

Tickets are also available by mail from the Walt Disney World Ticket Mail Order service (address on page 26), and you can also place an online order at **www.disney.com**.

Where Not to Buy Your Admission in Advance

Because passes to Walt Disney World aren't discounted, offers of free or cut-rate tickets should trigger caution. Anyone offering free tickets to any attraction in the Orlando/Kissimmee area is probably selling real estate or time-share condominiums. You may receive a free ticket, but you will have to endure a lengthy site inspection and/or high-pressure sales pitch.

The Time-Share Game

We get letters periodically from readers who figure they can beat the time-share game. Specifically, they intend to rake in the freebies offered by the time-share people, politely sit through the presentation, and then say, "No, thanks." Here's a report from a Texas couple traveling with four children, ages 1, 2, 11, and 14, who gave it a shot:

> On our way down south we kept seeing these signs. You can't miss them: "Florida Vacations for Less! Fifty Percent off Hotels! Discount Tickets!" Big, huge signs in red, white, and blue. We thought, "What the heck, let's see what they've got." We took the exit and pulled up next to a trailer that was totally dwarfed by its billboard. My wife went in, and a few minutes later [returned and told us that] they have this good deal for a hotel and tickets, but you have to see a presentation they have on time-shares. Voluntarily walking into a den of hungry salesmen was not my idea of a fun vacation experience. We moved on.

Going down the Florida Turnpike we saw those same types of signs again. Well, we still didn't have our Universal tickets, so [we thought] let's give these guts a try. They had a deal [that] sounded awesome. One-day Universal tickets for four people were [regularly] $205, or if you take this deal you can get four two-day tickets to Universal for $125! And, they offered us a beautiful two-bedroom suite with jacuzzi, king-sized bed, full kitchen, porch, kid's room, three TVs, and heated pools, [plus] tennis, boating, fishing, fitness center, beautiful location on the water, and right next to Disney, for $100 a night. Normal price: $350 per night. What's the catch? You have to listen to a 90-minute sales presentation on time-shares.

I hate those presentations, [but] still I felt compelled. It was beautiful, and it was in our price range. [I told them] that I hate high-pressure salesmen, [but they said] it's not like that. "They'll serve you breakfast and show you around. That's all. No pressure at all. Very nice people." "OK, I said, I'll do it. I'll suffer through 90 minutes to get a discount." Sounded like a fair deal to me.

We were pleasantly surprised when we arrived. Beautiful, huge place with all the amenities like the lady said.

After three days touring theme parks the day arrived for the scheduled time-share presentation. We sat down with a very nice gentleman, richly dressed and not intimidating at all. We had our youngest with us [the 1-year-old, while the older children watched the 2-year-old back in the room]. So we sat down, made some cordial introductions, and made our way into the buffet line for free eggs and sausage.

After breakfast their salesman shared various aspects of his personal life, including his family, past athletic achievements, and work habits. He closes, he told us, more than half of his deals, and he showed us a certificate he got recently. He also told us that the resort where we were staying was one of the best in the world [and that] everyone was going to want to stay in our time-share because everyone wants to go to Orlando. The company has resorts all over the world and they're all wonderful places like this one. It was looking like a really good deal.

The baby started getting fussy after about the first two hours, but the salesman was being so pleasant and interesting. He explained all about how, if we wanted a vacation home, we'd have to spend $500,000 and then find people to stay there when we weren't there. Then there's upkeep and taxes, and isn't this hotel better? And you can trade with anyone and stay in Alaska or Israel or Peru or California, no problems, only $129 for a whole week, you build equity, isn't this better? And if you tell someone else about it and they buy one, you get [a cash bonus], and there's this lady that's retiring early and sending her kids through college on referrals, it's so easy. "Now let me show you around our property on this nice little golf cart."

We rode on the cart. We walked around. We saw the pool and the massage room, and the exercise room, and it was very good. Then we went into *a room full of tables where [other] vacationers were sitting with their salesmen, discussing the wonderful opportunity. So our salesman finally shows us the price: $25,000.*

There's no way. He wanted a $4,900 down payment TODAY, then $450 a month for ten years! I tried to work these numbers out, and near as I can tell that's [an excessive] interest rate. We did the calculations: it works out to an interest rate of 24.49% a year not including closing costs. So I told him no way. There is no way we can squeeze that kind of money out of our budget. Forget it.

He looks hurts, but he's a gentleman and tells us to wait right there and he'll see what he can do. His manager then comes in and tells us that she has one [time-share] available for $8,800. What a break! How lucky can you get? Over half off! Unfortunately, we didn't travel to Florida with plans of making a real-estate purchase so we didn't have either the $250 down payment or the $150 a month in our budget. And unfortunately, they said, we had to make a decision that day. No buts about it, can't go home and think about it or ask your realtor if it's a good idea.

So another lady comes over. We explain to her that it sounds like a good idea, but we need to think it over and maybe we'll come back with money to put down and we can work a deal that way. OK, she says. We'll just keep this offer open until next time. So, just give me $250 now, plus $50 a month, and next January you can stay here and buy the time-share. No? How about this, you give me just $50 now, then $100 the next month, then $200 the next month...

At this point, three hours since our little no-pressure [presentation] started, the baby was crying and fussing and we were feeling like a hamburger on the grill, so my wife finally said we have to go. We're worried about the kids, this has been more than 90 minutes, we need to get back, we can't decide this right now. OK, we finally got through to her. She grabbed the paper away from us, wrote "Refused offer. Refused to come back." on the bottom and told each of us to sign it. "So, what does this mean?" we asked. "It means you refused the offer and can't come back." And with that she left. We took the crying baby to the gift shop to pick up our tickets to Universal, and vowed to never ever, ever, ever, go back to that place again.

There is no way of knowing how representative is the Texas couple's experience of time-share pitches in general, but it's a sobering example of what you might be walking into. Among other things, we found the psychological methodology of the sales presentation very interesting. It started very socially with a shared meal followed by the salesman sharing aspects of his personal life. These tactics help lower the prospects' defenses by shifting the tenor of the encounter from a business meeting to a relaxed social gathering. With the sharing of his personal life, the

salesman invited reciprocal intimacy on the part of the couple. This is calculated not only to lessen resistance, but also to establish a relationship wherein the couple cares about the salesman. If the salesman is successful in establishing this connection, it makes it more difficult for the couple to say no to the offer when the time comes.

Notice that the presentation, including the meal, is drawn out over several hours. At two hours and counting the salesman was still extolling the virtues of the time-share. He had not even gotten to the site inspection, much less any discussion of price and terms. The strategy here is twofold: first, as researchers have proven, customers who invest a lot of time in a purchase decision are less likely to walk away. Second, occupying so much of the salesman's time, in addition to accepting his extended hospitality, make the couple feel obligated to him.

The salesman buttresses his main presentation and dazzles the prospective buyers with ancillary deals, specifically the discussion of referrals and how one lady had sent her kids to college with money she had earned making referrals. This tactic distracts the couple from the real proposition on the table, makes the deal appear more affordable, and in regard to referrals, puts the prospective buyers and the salesman on the same team. As a referral source, the buyers are hypothetically joining forces with the salesman to sell time-shares. If the salesman can get the couple to actually picture doing this, they'll abandon some of the inhibitions inherent in the naturally adversarial relationship of buyer and seller.

The salesman laid a lot of track in preparation for divulging the price and terms and closing the sale. Because the Texas couple doesn't mention being offered any alternative financing, and because of the mortgage holder's legal obligation to disclose the Annual Percentage Rate (APR) of interest in the event the deal goes forward, we believe that the opening price quote and terms were a set-up. In other words, if the deal proceeded based on the price and terms initially offered, any marginally sane person would (as did the husband) figure out that the interest rate was sky high. If they didn't work it out on their own, they'd certainly have it shoved in their faces when the mortgage holder disclosed the APR as required by law. Either way, the opening offer is set up to create a deal breaker. This, in turn, sets up the little act where the manager miraculously arrives on the scene with the deal of the century.

This is the real offer, the one that the entire manipulative, carefully stage-managed drama has been leading up to. Expressed differently, the candy is dangled in front of the prospects and they want it. Then suddenly it's yanked out of reach because the initial deal is out of the question. At this point the prospects are disappointed, deflated, and emotionally wrung out. But wait, because their salesman has become so fond of them, he intervenes on their behalf, and the manager swoops onstage, offering the candy at a fraction of the original price. Disappointment turns to elation and the prospects jump hungrily on the candy. At least that's how it's scripted. For the Texas couple an intuitive sense that something was fishy, reinforced by a fussy baby, saved the day.

The appearance of the third manager on the scene gives the impression that the time-share sellers are really bending over backwards to work with the couple. This applies extra pressure in addition to making the prospects feel more obligated. If the Texas couple had continued to vacillate, there's no telling how many managers might have turned up. Because the prospects dug in their hells, however, the sellers played their last remaining cards: anger and guilt. Grabbing the offer document and demanding that the couple sign a written "refused offer" statement communicated to the prospects that they had wasted everyone's time, had abused the salesman's friendship, and had spurned management's (supposed) good-faith efforts to accommodate them in every respect. Icing on the guilt cake was the implicit message that the couple must be pretty stupid, worthless, or both (read inadequate) to walk away from such an extraordinary opportunity.

The Disney Vacation Club Time-Shares

In the interest of complete fairness, we want to state categorically that sales presentations for the Disney Vacation Club time-shares in no way resemble the pitch experienced by the Texas couple. Disney Vacation Club presentations are friendly and professional, and though there is an obvious effort to sell to you, you will not be subjected to any of the pressure or manipulations chronicled in the foregoing account. Moreover, in the decade or more that Disney has been selling time-shares, we have had not one reader complaint concerning either the Disney sales presentation or the time-shares themselves. Most readers report an experience similar to that of a mom from northern Virginia:

I'm not sure if you mentioned this anywhere, but if you are staying on Disney property and go to the Disney Vacation Club spiel you can get coupons (for free lunch or dinner at many of the moderately priced restaurants in the parks) for all who attend. Just ask. The spiel is very short, you can leave at any time, and it is not high-sales pressure. They pick you up and drop you off anywhere on [WDW] property.

There is nothing intrinsically wrong with the time-share concept, and more and more reputable firms are diversifying into this area of real estate. If you're interested in a time-share, do your homework before leaving on your vacation. Identify the sellers, check out their reputations, and make appointments to visit the properties that interest you.

How Much Does It Cost per Day at Walt Disney World?

A typical day would cost $406.40, excluding lodging and transportation, for a family of four—Mom, Dad, 12-year-old Tim, and 8-year-old Sandy—driving their own car and staying outside Disney World. They plan to be in the area for a week, so they buy 5-Day Park-Hopper Passes. Here's a breakdown:

HOW MUCH DOES A DAY COST?

Breakfast for four at Denny's with tax and tip	$26.00
Epcot parking fee	6.00
One day's admission on a 5-Day Park-Hopper Pass	
Dad: Adult 5-Day with tax = $218 divided by five (days)	46.00
Mom: Adult 5-Day with tax = $218 divided by five (days)	46.00
Tim: Adult 5-Day with tax = $218 divided by five (days)	46.00
Sandy: Child 5-Day with tax = $177 divided by five (days)	36.40
Morning break (soda or coffee)	10.00
Fast-food lunch (sandwich or burger, fries, soda), no tip	35.00
Afternoon break (soda and popcorn)	18.00
Dinner at Italy (no alcoholic beverages) with tax & tip	98.00
Souvenirs (Mickey T-shirts for Tim and Sandy) with tax*	39.00

One-Day Total (without lodging or transportation) $406.40

*Cheer up; you won't have to buy souvenirs every day.

Allocating Time

During Disney World's first decade, a family with a week's vacation could enjoy the Magic Kingdom and River Country and still have several days for the beach or other area attractions. Since Epcot opened in 1982, however, Disney World has steadily been enlarging to monopolize the family's entire week. Today, with the addition of Blizzard Beach, Typhoon Lagoon, Disney-MGM Studios, the Animal Kingdom, and Downtown Disney, you should allocate six days for a whirlwind tour (or seven to ten days if you're old-fashioned and insist on a little relaxation during your vacation). If you don't have six or more days or think you might want to venture beyond the edge of "The World," be prepared to make some hard choices.

The theme parks and swimming attractions are huge and require a lot of walking and, sometimes, a lot of waiting in lines. Moving in typically large crowds all day is exhausting. The unrelenting Florida sun often zaps the most hardy traveler, making tempers short. In our many visits to Walt Disney World, we observed, particularly on hot summer days, a dramatic transition from happy, enthusiastic tourists upon arrival to plodding zombies later in the day. Visitors who began their day enjoying the Disney wonders lapsed into an exhausted, production-line mentality. ("We've got two more rides in Fantasyland, then we can go back to the hotel.")

We recommend you approach Walt Disney World the same way you would an eight-course Italian dinner: with plenty of time between courses. The best way not to have fun is to cram too much into too little time.

Which Park to See First?

This question is less academic than it appears, especially if there are children or teenagers in your party. Children who see the Magic Kingdom first expect more of the same type of entertainment at the other parks. At Epcot, they're often disappointed by the educational orientation and more serious tone (many adults react the same way). Disney-MGM offers some pretty wild action, but the general presentation is educational and more adult. Though most children enjoy zoos, animals can't be programmed to entertain. Thus, children may not find the Animal Kingdom as exciting as the Magic Kingdom or Disney-MGM.

First-time visitors especially should see Epcot first; you will be able to enjoy it fully without having been preconditioned to think of Disney entertainment as solely fantasy or adventure.

See the Animal Kingdom second. Like Epcot, it has an educational thrust, but it provides a change of pace because it features live animals.

Next, see Disney-MGM Studios, which helps all ages make a fluid transition from the educational Epcot and Animal Kingdom to the fanciful Magic Kingdom. Also, because Disney-MGM Studios is smaller, you won't walk as much or stay as long.

Save the Magic Kingdom for last.

Operating Hours

Disney can't be accused of being inflexible regarding operating hours at the parks. They run a dozen or more schedules each year, making it advisable to call (407) 824-4321 for the *exact* hours before you arrive. In the off-season, parks may be open for as few as eight hours (from 9 a.m. to 5 p.m.). By contrast, at busy times (particularly holidays), they may be open from 8 a.m. until 2 a.m. the next morning.

Official Opening vs. Real Opening

Operating hours you're quoted when you call are "official hours." Often, the parks actually open earlier. Many visitors, relying on information disseminated by Disney Guest Relations, arrive at the official opening time and find the park packed with people. If the official hours are 9 a.m.–9 p.m., for example, Main Street in the Magic Kingdom will open at 8 or 8:30 a.m. and the remainder of the park will open at 8:30 or 9 a.m.

Disney publishes hours of operation well in advance but allows the flexibility to react daily to gate conditions. Disney traffic controllers survey local hotel reservations, estimate how many visitors to expect on a given day, and open the theme parks early to avoid bottlenecks at parking facilities and ticket windows and to absorb the crowds as they arrive.

At day's end, rides and attractions shut down at approximately the official closing time. Main Street in the Magic Kingdom remains open 30 minutes to 1 hour after the rest of the park has closed.

The Vacation that Fights Back

A vacation is what you make it, but visiting Walt Disney World requires levels of industry and stamina more often associated with running marathons. A mother from Middletown, New York, spells it out:

> A vacation at WDW is not a vacation in the usual sense—sleeping late, total relaxation, leisurely meals, etc. It is a vacation that's frankly exhausting, but definitely worth doing. WDW is a magical place, where the visitor feels welcomed from the minute they arrive at their accommodations to the last second before boarding the shuttle bus back to the airport.

A mother of two from Indianapolis, Indiana, adds:

> My main thought throughout our time at WDW was, "It's so much work to have so much fun!" I can't imagine going without your touring plans in hand—I'm sure we'd have only seen half as much and we'd have become so angry with each other over trying to decide what to see next. Even with generally careful following of the one-day plans and arriving an hour early, we missed at least one "not-to-be-missed" feature per theme park, mostly due to brain death in the heat.

A British gentleman, thinking we exaggerated about the walking required, actually measured his outings each day using a pedometer. Here's what he discovered:

> I decided to wear a pedometer for our recent visit to WDW. Our visits to the theme parks were spread over five days, during which my wife and I (ages 51 and 55) walked a total of 68 miles for an average of 13 miles per day!

The point is: at Walt Disney World, *less is more.* Take the World in small doses, with plenty of swimming, napping, reading, and relaxing in between. And here's some comforting news: Disney World isn't going to pack up and move to Mongolia. If you don't see everything this trip, you can come back!

Also, and this might come as a shock, you can prepare. An Ohio reader discovered this secret, but alas, too late:

The only thing missing from your book is more strongly worded advice about being able to walk unlimited miles and stand for an infinite amount of time. I fly a desk for a living and don't get near enough walking or standing exercise to prepare myself for the rigors of The World. My wife and I have determined that before we go to Disney World again we will be able to walk at least five miles without a rest or feeling any pain the next day. After pounding the pavement for hours on end we were so exhausted that we had no choice but to spend two of our vacation days just recovering from the previous days walking.

The reader should be thankful he wasn't touring with the British readers using the pedometer.

Hitting the Wall

As you plan your time at Walt Disney World, consider your physical limitations. It is extremely exhausting to rise at the crack of dawn and run around a theme park for 8–12 hours day after day. Sooner or later (usually sooner), you're going to hit the wall. Every Disney World vacation itinerary should include some break days (when you don't go to a theme park) and sleeping-in days (when you take the morning off). Plan your break days and sleeping-in days to follow unusually long and arduous days, particularly after days when you stay in the parks to see the evening parades or fireworks. Keep telling yourself over and over that you'll enjoy your vacation more if you are well rested.

A Suwanee, Georgia, reader makes this suggestion:

The one area that I think you can expand on in your book is preparing people for the overall pace and exhaustion level that this type of vacation warrants. Over half of the people planning to follow a rigorous touring plan will succumb to exhaustion. I was also never able to locate information on how much time you need at each part to really see it all. My initial plan for the family entailed a day at MK, one day each at Epcot, AK, Disney-MGM, Universal Studios, and Islands of Adventure, one down day, and a leftover day for a second visit to something we hadn't finished. By day two I became acutely aware that there was no way we would be able to keep up that pace.

A mom from LaGrange, Illinois, tried to sidestep our advice to stay rested:

As I was planning, I was very sure we would not be taking a swim/ nap break in the middle of the day. No way! On the very first day of touring (at the Magic Kingdom) my seven-year-old said (at 9:30 a.m.—after only two hours at the park), "I'm hot—when can we go back to the hotel and swim?" Needless to say, we took that little break every day.

If you neglect this all-important element of self-preservation and pacing, you'll be writing us letters like this one from a father of three from Unionville, Connecticut:

> It's difficult to follow your [touring plans] for more than one day in a row. The kids are too exhausted to last through the fireworks and there isn't time to return to the hotel because of the crowdedness of the [parks].

A Tolland, Connecticut, family altered their touring habits to create an "easy day":

> There is so much to do and see at WDW, we inevitably push the kids, and then pay the price. One day, when they were tired, we went to MGM and only did shows. We got there in time for Indiana Jones, then moved to the Hunchback of Notre Dame, then to lunch. Since most of the day was seated, the kids got time to rest and weren't too cranky.

A mom from Narberth, Pennsylvania, reported that it was necessary to change dinner time:

> We found that getting up as early as we did, it was important to make early dinner reservations—6:30 p.m. at the latest. The one time we tried to eat at 8 p.m., our younger son fell asleep at the table and could not be awakened.

The Practicality of Returning to Your Hotel for Rest During the Day

Many readers write about the practicality of departing the theme park for a nap and swim at the hotel. A dad from Sequim, Washington, made the following request:

> I would like to see nearness to the parks emphasized in your accommodation guide, taking traffic and hotel access into account. We tried going back to the hotel for midday breaks, but it was too time consuming. By the time you got to the car, negotiated traffic, rested, and reversed the process to get back to the park, it took two–three hours for a short rest and was not worth it! (Stayed at Quality Suites Maingate East)

In our opinion, by way of preamble, the reader was overly anxious about the time away from the parks. Two–three hours really won't cut it. If he had resigned himself to a four to five hour break, his family would have stayed rested and relaxed, and at the time of year they visited, had plenty of time to enjoy the parks.

Here's the scoop: At the Animal Kingdom, Disney-MGM Studios, and Epcot, you can get to your car in the parking lot in about 20 minutes. From the Magic Kingdom it will take you 30–35 minutes. Now, obviously, if you're at the farthest point from the park entrance when you decide to go back to the hotel, or if you barely miss a parking lot tram, it will take longer, but from most places in the parks the above times are a good approximation. Once in your car, you'll be able to commute to most US 192 hotels, all Walt Disney World hotels, all Lake Buena Vista hotels, and most I-4 corridor and south International Drive hotels in 20 minutes or less. It will take an extra 10 minutes to reach hotels on I-Drive north of Sand Lake Road and hotels in the Universal Florida area.

So, for most of you, the one-way commute will average 40 minutes. But here's what you get for your time: (1) a less expensive lunch at a restaurant of your choosing; (2) a swim; and (3) a one-and-a-half to two-hour nap. If you add up the times, you'll be away from the parks on your break about four to four-and-a-half hours, counting commuting time. If you want, you can eat dinner outside of Walt Disney World before returning to the parks. Clearly, this won't work during the times of year that the parks close early, but then again, these are not the times that most families go to Walt Disney World. If you visit when the parks close early, you'll see more attractions in less time, owing to reduced park attendance, and will be able to leave the parks earlier in the day and take your rest break in the late afternoon or early evening. Not ideal, but neither are the crowds and heat of the summer vacation season.

A corollary to this discussion is what you do the next day. If you're getting a three–five hour break each day and not keeping late hours, you'll be able to stay the course. If you elect to forego the break, you need to alternate full days with very easy, sleep-late days in order to charge your batteries. If you do neither, you'll be saying hello to the wall by your third day.

Arrival-Day Blues:
What to Do when You Have Only a Half Day

Chances are you'll have only part of a day available for touring or other recreational pursuits on the day you arrive at Walt Disney World (and perhaps on the day you depart). It's a common problem: you roll into the World at about 1 p.m., all excited and ready to go . . . but where?

The first question is this: do you feel comfortable blowing an expensive day's admission to the parks when you have less than a full day to tour? Certainly the time of your arrival and the closing times of the respective parks are considerations, but so is the touring disadvantage that you suffer by not being on hand when a park opens. FASTPASS, a sort of reservation system for popular attractions (see pages 83–90), provides some relief from long afternoon lines, but FASTPASS is not available for every attraction, nor is there an unlimited supply of passes available.

Opting for a Partial Day at the Theme Parks

If you decide to splurge and burn a pass on a half day or less, check out recommendations for least crowded days of the week (pages 34–35).

One option, but only if you can get to the park by 1 p.m., is the Animal Kingdom, which requires less time to tour than the other parks. Because guests who arrive at opening time frequently complete their tour by 2 p.m. or so, crowds tend to thin somewhat in the late afternoon. As an added bonus, FASTPASS is offered for the three most popular attractions. If you arrive much after 1 p.m., however, the daily allocation of FASTPASSes, especially for Kilimanjaro Safaris, might be exhausted. And the Animal Kingdom closes earlier than the other parks. Still, if you arrive by 1 p.m. and stay until closing (5–8 p.m. depending on the season), a fairly comprehensive tour is possible.

Whenever you arrive at a theme park (including the Universal parks) after 10 a.m., you should direct your attention to higher-capacity attractions where your waiting time is relatively brief even during the most crowded part of the day. As mentioned before, in the Disney parks you can also cut your time in line by using FASTPASS. Another time saver at Test Track in Epcot and at several Universal Studios and Islands of Adventure attractions is the "singles line." A singles line, found only at rides, is a separate line for individuals who are alone or who do not object to riding alone. The objective of the singles line is to fill those odd spaces left by groups that don't quite occupy the entire ride vehicle. Because there are not many singles and most groups are unwilling to split up, singles lines are usually much shorter than regular lines and can save you a bunch of time if you don't mind riding by yourself.

The Disney parks are better for partial-day touring than the Universal parks, simply because Disney parks operate more high-capacity attractions than the Universal parks. However, the Universal Express program currently has more perks than Disney's equivalent FASTPASS (especially if you've bought multi-day park admissions or are staying at a Universal resort). This means that those who can use Universal Express the most may end up touring more efficiently than a similar guest could at Disney. Even so, nothing is guaranteed, especially given Universal's reputation for breakdowns. We like the Universal parks and admire their cutting-edge technology, but the best way to see them is to be there at opening and follow our touring plans.

The following chart lists the attractions in each Disney park that can be enjoyed with the least amount of waiting during the most crowded part of the day. Note that although the queues for these attractions may seem humongous, they move quickly and your wait will be tolerable. In addition to the attractions, be sure to check out parades, stage shows, and other live entertainment. Attractions not listed below generally stay packed until an hour or so before closing; however, they can often be experienced with little waiting during evening parades, fireworks, or, in the case of Disney-MGM Studios, *Fantasmic!*

LEAST CROWDED ATTRACTIONS BETWEEN 11 A.M. AND 6 P.M.

Magic Kingdom

Main Street	Walt Disney World Railroad
Adventureland	Swiss Family Treehouse
	Enchanted Tiki Birds
	Pirates of the Caribbean
Frontierland	Raft to Tom Sawyer Island
Liberty Square	*The Hall of Presidents*
	Liberty Belle Riverboat
	The Haunted Mansion
Fantasyland	It's a Small World
Tomorrowland	*Carousel of Progress* (open seasonally)
	The Timekeeper (open seasonally)

Epcot

Future World	Innoventions
	The Circle of Life (The Land)
	Food Rocks (The Land)
	Universe of Energy
	The Living Seas
	Cranium Command (Wonders of Life)
	Spaceship Earth
World Showcase	El Río del Tiempo (Mexico)
	Wonders of China (China)
	The American Adventure
	O Canada! (Canada)

Disney-MGM Studios

	The Great Movie Ride
	Beauty and the Beast (go 30 minutes early)
	Disney-MGM Studios Backlot Tour
	New York Street Backlot
	Hunchback of Notre Dame (go 35 minutes early)
	MuppetVision 3D
	Walt Disney: One Man's Dream

Animal Kingdom

The Oasis	Wildlife Exhibits
Discovery Island	Discovery Island Trails
Africa	Pangani Forest Exploration Trail
	Wildlife Express
	Rafiki's Planet Watch (access via Africa)
Asia	*Flights of Wonder* (go 15 minutes early)
	Maharajah Jungle Trek
DinoLand U.S.A.	*Tarzan Rocks!* (go 30 minutes early)
	The Boneyard
Camp Minnie-Mickey	*Festival of the Lion King* (go to the latest show)

If you desire step-by-step instructions for your arrival-day touring, simply choose one of our one-day touring plans and scan down the steps until you find the first step directing you to any of the attractions listed in the chart above. Start with that step and follow the touring plan sequentially from there.

Alternatives to the Theme Parks on Arrival Day

You'll undoubtedly have a number of things to accomplish on your arrival day before you're ready to head out for some fun. You must check in, unpack, and purchase admissions at a minimum, and you'll probably make a detour to the grocery or convenience store to buy snacks, drinks, and breakfast food. At all Disney resorts as well as many non-Disney hotels, you cannot occupy your room until after 3 p.m.; however, many properties will check you in, sell you admission passes, and store your luggage.

The least expensive way to spend your arrival day is to check in, unpack, do your chores, and then relax at your hotel swimming pool. Be careful not to get too much sun: the last thing you want is a painful sunburn at the beginning of your vacation.

Other daytime options include a trip to one of the local water parks. Because the Disney water parks are so crowded (you really need to be on hand for opening, just like at the major Disney theme parks), we recommend **Water Mania** on US 192, about 10–15 minutes from most hotels in and around Walt Disney World. Water Mania has some great slides but hardly a shadow of the long lines found at Blizzard Beach or Typhoon Lagoon. Plus, it's much less expensive. **Wet 'n Wild** on International Drive is also an excellent water park. Generally it's less crowded than the Disney water parks but more packed than Water Mania, and more expensive, too. The great thing about Wet 'n Wild is that it stays open late in summer. Any water park that stays open past 5 p.m. is worth a look because crowds at all parks clear out substantially after 4 p.m. or so. If the water park is open late and you find yourself getting hungry, you won't have any trouble rustling up a fast-food dinner. No matter which water park you choose, remember to lather up with waterproof sunscreen. For more information on water parks, see Part Fourteen: The Water Theme Parks.

If you're thinking of a somewhat drier outing, we heartily recommend **Gatorland,** a quirky tourist attraction located on US 441 near Kissimmee (about 20 minutes from Walt Disney World). Gatorland, aside from being a slice of pre-Disney Florida history, is an exceptionally interesting and well-managed attraction. It's a perfect choice for a half-day outing, providing, of course, that you like alligators, snakes, and lizards. For more information, call Gatorland at (800) 393-JAWS or check their website at www.gatorland.com.

Cypress Gardens, though about 40 minutes from Walt Disney World, can also be seen in half a day if you skip the ho-hum stuff. Mature visitors will enjoy the gardens and landscaping more than kids, but the whole family will appreciate the signature water-skiing show, ice-skating revue, and various educational wildlife presentations. The bad news, other than its remote location, is that Cypress Gardens costs about as much as admission to a major Disney park. More information on Cypress Gardens is available at (800) 282-2123 or on the web at www.cypressgardens.com.

If none of the above fire your boiler, there's always miniature golf (expensive in the World; more reasonable outside it) or **DisneyQuest,** Disney's high-tech entertainment venue featuring interactive games and simulator technology. Alas, like the Disney theme parks, DisneyQuest is expensive and doesn't handle crowds particularly well. It's located at Disney's West Side. Late mornings and early afternoons are the best times to go.

In the Evening

Dinner provides a great opportunity to plan the following day's activities. If you're hungry for entertainment as well, try a dinner show or take in a show after dinner. If you go the show route, we recommend seeing *Cirque du Soleil* at Disney's West Side. *Cirque du Soleil* is expensive, but we think it's the single best thing in all of Walt Disney World. Disney also offers some dinner shows, of which the *Hoop-Dee-Doo Revue* is the pick of the litter. Both *Cirque* and *Hoop-Dee-Doo* are extremely popular, so make your reservations far in advance. In addition to *Hoop-Dee-Doo,* there are a couple of other Disney dinner shows and a dozen or so non-Disney dinner shows in the area. The latter are advertised in local visitor magazines (often with discount coupons) available for free at any non-Disney hotel.

If you don't try *Cirque du Soleil* or a dinner show, consider a night at Pleasure Island, Disney's nightclub complex, or Universal's club scene, CityWalk. Both venues are best appreciated by adults—and energetic adults at that. Whatever you do, don't wear yourself out the first day.

Departure Days

Departure days don't seem to occasion as much consternation as arrival days. If you want to visit a theme park on your departure day, get up early and be on hand when the park opens. If you have a lot of time, you can check out and store your luggage with the bell desk or in your rental car. Or if you can arrange a late check-out, you might want to return to your hotel for a shower and change of clothes before departing. Some hotels are quite liberal regarding late check-outs, but others will assess a charge for the extra time you occupy your room.

Optimum Touring Situation

We don't believe there is one ideal itinerary. Tastes, energy levels, and perspectives on what constitutes entertainment and relaxation vary. This understood, here are some considerations for developing your own ideal itinerary.

Optimum touring at Disney World requires a good itinerary, a minimum of six days on site (excluding travel time), and a fair amount of money. It also requires a prodigious appetite for Disney entertainment. The essence of optimum touring is to see the attractions in a series of shorter, less exhausting visits during the cooler, less crowded times of day, with plenty of rest and relaxation between excursions.

Since optimum touring calls for leaving and returning to the theme parks on most days, it makes sense to stay in one of the Walt Disney World resort hotels. Disney lodging guests have freer use of the bus, boat, and monorail systems and have more choices for baby-sitting and children's programs. Sound good? It is, but be prepared to pay.

If you visit Walt Disney World during busy times (see page 29), you need to get up early to beat the crowds. Short lines and stress-free touring are incompatible with sleeping in. If you want to sleep late *and* enjoy your touring, visit Disney World when attendance is lighter.

The Cardinal Rules for Successful Touring

Many visitors don't have six days to devote to Disney. Some are en route to other destinations or may wish to sample additional attractions of Orlando and central Florida. For these visitors, efficient touring is a must.

Even the most time-effective touring plan won't allow you to cover two or more major theme parks in one day. Plan to allocate at least an entire day to each park (an exception to this rule is when the parks close at different times, allowing you to tour one park until closing and then proceed to another park). If your schedule permits only one day of touring, concentrate on one theme park and save the others for another visit.

One-Day Touring

A comprehensive, one-day tour of the Magic Kingdom, the Animal Kingdom, Epcot, or Disney-MGM Studios is possible, but requires knowledge of the park, good planning, and plenty of energy and endurance. One-day touring doesn't leave much time for sit-down meals, prolonged browsing in shops, or lengthy breaks. One-day touring can be fun and rewarding, but allocating two days per park, especially for the Magic Kingdom and Epcot, is always preferable.

Successful touring of the Magic Kingdom, the Animal Kingdom, Epcot, or Disney-MGM Studios hinges on *three rules:*

1. DETERMINE IN ADVANCE WHAT YOU REALLY WANT TO SEE

What rides and attractions appeal most to you? Which additional rides and attractions would you like to experience if you have time left? What are you willing to forego?

To help you set your touring priorities, we describe the theme parks and every attraction in detail in this book. In each description, we include the author's evaluation of the attraction and the opinions of Walt Disney World guests expressed as star ratings. Five stars is the best possible rating.

Finally, because attractions range from midway-type rides and horse-drawn trolleys to colossal, high-tech extravaganzas, we have developed a hierarchy of categories to pinpoint an attraction's magnitude:

Super Headliners   The best attractions the theme park has to offer. Mind-boggling in size, scope, and imagination. Represents the cutting edge of modern attraction technology and design.

Headliners   Full blown, multimillion-dollar, full-scale, themed adventures and theater presentations. Modern in technology and design and employing a full range of special effects.

Major Attractions   Themed adventures on a more modest scale, but incorporating state-of-the-art technologies. Or, larger-scale attractions of older design.

Minor Attractions   Midway-type rides, small "dark" rides (cars on a track, zig-zagging through the dark), small theater presentations, transportation rides, and elaborate walk-through attractions.

Diversions   Exhibits, both passive and interactive. Includes playgrounds, video arcades, and street theater.

Though not every Walt Disney World attraction fits neatly into these descriptions, the categories provide a comparison of attraction size and scope. Remember that bigger and more elaborate doesn't always mean better. Peter Pan's Flight, a minor attraction in the Magic Kingdom, continues to be one of the park's most beloved rides. Likewise, for many young children, no attraction, regardless of size, surpasses Dumbo.

2. ARRIVE EARLY! ARRIVE EARLY! ARRIVE EARLY!

This is the single most important key to efficient touring and avoiding long lines. First thing in the morning, there are no lines and fewer people. The same four rides you can experience in one hour in early morning can take as long as three hours to see after 10:30 a.m. Have breakfast before you arrive so you won't waste prime touring time sitting in a restaurant.

The earlier a park opens, the greater your potential advantage. This is because most vacationers won't make the sacrifice to rise early and get to a theme park before it opens. Fewer people are willing to be on hand for an 8 a.m. opening than for a 9 a.m. opening. On those rare occasions when a park opens at 10 a.m., almost everyone arrives at the same time, so it's almost impossible to get a jump on the crowd. If you are visiting during midsummer, arrive at the parks an hour before official opening time. During holiday periods, arrive at the parks 70 minutes before official opening.

3. AVOID BOTTLENECKS

Helping you avoid bottlenecks is what this guide is about. Bottlenecks are caused by crowd concentrations and/or faulty crowd management. Avoiding bottlenecks involves being able to predict where, when, and why they occur. Concentrations of hungry people create bottlenecks at restaurants during lunch and dinner; concentrations of people moving toward the exit near closing time create bottlenecks in gift shops en route to the gate; concentrations of visitors at new and popular rides, and at rides slow to load and unload, create bottlenecks and long lines.

We provide touring plans for the Magic Kingdom, the Animal Kingdom, Epcot, Disney-MGM Studios, and Pleasure Island to help you avoid bottlenecks. In addition, we provide detailed information on all rides and performances, enabling you to estimate how long you may have to wait in line and allowing you to compare rides for their capacity to accommodate large crowds. Touring plans for the Magic Kingdom begin on page 480; Epcot, page 536; the Animal Kingdom, page 576; Disney-MGM Studios, page 610; and Pleasure Island, page 722. We have also included One-Day Touring Plans for Universal Studios Florida on page 632 and Universal's Islands of Adventure on page 650.

In response to reader requests, we have added clip-out versions of the touring plans at the end of this book.

What's a Queue?

Although it's not commonly used in the United States, "queue" is the universal English-language word for a line (such as you wait in to cash a check at the bank or to board a ride in a theme park). In fact, there is an entire mathematical area of specialization within the field of operations research called Queuing Theory that studies and models how lines work. Because the *Unofficial Guide* draws heavily on this discipline, we use some of its terminology. In addition to the noun, the verb "to queue" means to get in line, and a "queuing area" is a waiting area that accommodates a line.

Touring Plans: What They Are and How They Work

We followed your plans to the letter—which at times was troublesome to the dad in our party ... somewhat akin to testing the strength of your marriage by wallpapering together!

—Unofficial Guide reader and mother of two

See More, Do More, Wait Less

From the first edition of the *Unofficial Guide*, minimizing our readers' waiting time in attraction lines has been a top priority. We know from our research, and from that of others, that theme park patrons measure overall satisfaction based on the number of attractions they are able to experience during a given visit: the more attractions experienced, the better. Thus, from the beginning, we have developed and offered to our readers field-tested touring plans that allow them to experience as many attractions as possible with the least amount of waiting in line.

Our touring plans have always been based on theme park traffic flow, attraction capacity, the maximum time a guest is willing to wait (called a "balking constraint"), walking distance between attractions, and waiting-time data collected at specific intervals throughout the day and at various times of the year. The touring plans derived from a combinatorial model (for anyone who cares) that married the well-known assignment problem of linear programming with queuing (waiting line) theory. The model approximated the most time-efficient sequence in which to visit the attractions of a specific park. Once we derived a preliminary touring plan from the model, we field-tested it in the park, using a test group who followed our plan and a control group (that did not have our plan) who toured according to their own best judgement.

The two groups were compared, and the results were amazing. When theme park attendance exceeded 48,000, the group touring without our plans spent an average of 3½ hours more time waiting in line and experienced 37% fewer attractions than did those who used our touring plans.

Over the years, this research has been recognized by both the travel industry and academe, having been cited by such diverse publications as *USA Today, Travel Weekly, Bottom Line, Money,* and *Operations Research Forum.*

John Henry and the Nail-Driving Machine

As sophisticated as our model (described above) may sound, we recognized almost a decade ago that it was cumbersome, slow, and did not approximate the "perfect" touring plan as closely as we desired. Moreover, advances in computer technology and science, specifically in the field of genetic algorithms, demonstrated clearly that it wouldn't be long before a model, or program, was created that would leave ours in the dust.

Do you remember the story of John Henry, the fastest nail driver on the railroad? Well, one day a man appeared with a machine he claimed could drive spikes faster than any man. John Henry challenged the machine to a race, which he won, but that killed him in the process. Well, we felt a bit like John Henry. We were still very good at what we did, but knew with absolute certainty that sooner or later we'd have to confront the touring plan version of a nail-driving machine.

Our response to this immanent challenge was to build our own nail-driving machine. To that end we teamed up during the mid-1990s with Len Testa, a cutting-edge scientist and programmer who was working in the field of evolutionary algorithms and who, coincidentally, was a theme-park junkie. Bringing our many years of Walt Disney World observations and data collecting together with Len's vision and programming expertise, we developed a state-of-the-art program for creating near perfect touring plans.

Several university professors, many of them leaders in their fields, have contributed research or ideas to the new software program. Results from early versions of the software have been published in peer-reviewed academic journals. The most recent versions of the software are protected through a series of pending patent applications. Special thanks go to Dr. Albert C. Esterline of North Carolina A&T State University and Dr. Gerry V. Dozier of Auburn University. Credit is also due to Dr. Nikolas Sahinidis and his graduate students at the University of Illinois at Urbana-Champaign, who have published a number of exceptionally helpful studies. Chryssi Malandraki, Ph.D., from United Parcel Service and Robert Dial, Ph.D., from the Volpe National Transportation System Center likewise provided assistance and encouragement over the years.

It has been a process of evolution and refinement, but each year the new program came closer and closer to beating the results of our long-lived model. In 2002, at field trials conducted during the busy spring-break period, the new program beat the best touring plan generated by the traditional *Unofficial* model by 90 minutes at the Magic Kingdom. If you recall, touring plans generated by the *Unofficial* model saved an average of 3½ hours standing in line compared to guests touring without the plan. Well, the new program saved an additional 90 minutes over that. Needless to say, we were very pleased, but believe us, it wasn't easy.

The Challenge

Creating effective, dependable touring plans has always been difficult, and remains so. The main problem is that there are many different ways to see the same attractions. For example, if we wanted to visit Space

Mountain, Pirates of the Caribbean, and Splash Mountain as soon as the Magic Kingdom opens, there are six possible ways to do so:

1. First ride Space Mountain, then ride Pirates of the Caribbean, then Splash Mountain.

2. First ride Space Mountain, then ride Splash Mountain, then Pirates of the Caribbean.

3. First ride Splash Mountain, then ride Space Mountain, then ride Pirates of the Caribbean.

4. First ride Splash Mountain, the ride Pirates of the Caribbean, then ride Space Mountain.

5. First ride Pirates of the Caribbean, then ride Splash Mountain, then Space Mountain.

6. First ride Pirates of the Caribbean, then ride Space Mountain, then ride Splash Mountain.

Some of these combinations make better touring plans than others. Since the queue for Space Mountain increases very rapidly, it's best to see Space Mountain first thing in the morning. For similar reasons it would be better to see Splash Mountain before Pirates. In this example, touring plan number 2 would probably save us the most time standing in line. Touring plan 5 would probably result in the most waiting in line.

As we add more attractions to our list, the number of possible touring plans grows rapidly. Adding a fourth attraction would result in 24 possible touring plans, since there are four possible variations for each of the six touring plans listed above. In general, the number of possible touring plans for n attractions is $n \times (n-1) \times (n-2) \times \ldots \times 1$ (Don't let the mathematical notation throw you. If we plug real numbers in, it's quite simple.) For five attractions, as an example, there are $5 \times 4 \times 3 \times 2 \times 1$ possible touring plans. If you don't have a calculator handy, that adds up to 120 potential touring plans. For six attractions, there are $6 \times 5 \times 4 \times 3 \times 2 \times 1$, or 720 possible touring plans. A list of ten attractions has over three million possible touring plans. The 21 attractions in the Magic Kingdom One-Day Touring Plan for Adults have a staggering 51,090,942,171,709,440,000 possible touring plans. That's over 51 million billion combinations, or roughly six times more than the estimated number of grains of sand in the whole world. Adding in complexities such as FASTPASS, parades, meals, and breaks makes the number of combinations grow further.

Fortunately, scientists have been hard at work on similar problems for many years. Companies that deliver packages, for example, plan each driver's route carefully to minimize the distance driven, saving both time and fuel. In fact, finding good ways to visit many places with minimum effort is such a common problem that it has its own nickname: the traveling salesman problem.

For more than a small number of attractions, the number of possible touring plans is so large it would take a very long time for even a powerful computer to find the single best touring plan. A number of techniques have been proposed that give very good, but not necessarily exact, solutions to the traveling-salesman problem in a reasonable amount of time. If the words "dynamic programming," "simplex method," or the names "Lin" and "Kernighan" mean anything to you, you probably also "get" the engineering jokes in Dilbert.

The *Unofficial Guide's* new program uses a sophisticated, custom-made computer program to create its touring plans. We know of at least one other software tool that creates touring plans, RideMax™ for Disneyland. We tested an early version of the software, but found it lacked certain important features we needed, and many of the touring plans produced were significantly inferior to those derived from the original *Unofficial Guide* model. We also evaluated several commercially available software packages. Using an office spreadsheet program, for example, would have required us to omit or greatly simplify many of the conditions you're likely to encounter in the parks, and would only work for a small number of attractions. In addition, we wanted the software to work on a variety of computing platforms, from multimillion dollar supercomputers, to ordinary personal computers, as well as the World Wide Web and small personal digital assistants (PDAs) similar to the Palm Pilot™. No off-the-shelf software we examined could do all these things.

The *Unofficial Guide* Touring Plan software program contains two state-of-the-art algorithms that allow it to analyze quickly tens of millions of possible touring plans in a very short time. (An algorithm is to a computer like a recipe is to a chef. Just as there are specific steps a chef takes to make a chocolate cake, there are specific steps a computer takes to process information. Those steps, when grouped together, form what's known as an algorithm.) The software can analyze FASTPASS distribution patterns at all the attractions, for example, and suggest the best times and attractions to use FASTPASS. The software can also schedule breaks throughout the day, say, to return to your hotel for a nap. If you're going to eat lunch in the park, the software can suggest restaurants close to where you'll be around lunchtime that will minimize the time you spend looking for food. Numerous other features are available, many of which we will discuss later in the section called "Custom Touring Plans."

The new program, however, is only part of what's needed to create a good touring plan. Good data are also important. In a little more than a year, we made half a dozen weeklong trips to Walt Disney World to collect data. At the Magic Kingdom, for example, a group of researchers recorded the estimated wait time at every attraction, show, FASTPASS

booth, and restaurant in the park, every thirty minutes, from park opening to park closing. On a typical day the researchers walked about 18
miles and collected around 500 pieces of data each. A typical route
would have researchers start at the Swiss Family Treehouse in Adventureland. After collecting data on all of Adventureland, the researchers would
continue on to the attractions and restaurants in Frontierland. After that
came Liberty Square, then finally through half of Fantasyland, before
walking back to the Swiss Family Treehouse for an eight-minute break
before starting the next round of data collection. A platoon of other volunteers collect data in the other half of the park.

One data collector, conscientious to a fault, took his eight-minute
break in the same spot every day, directly under the Tomorrowland Transit Authority. He endured the same pre-recorded TTA announcement
("Paging Mr. Morrow, Mr. Tom Morrow…") every 23 seconds, for six
days. We hear his therapy is going well. All of the researchers endured
blisters, heat, and run-ins with strollers. Their persistence and determination to collect the data was truly astounding. Christine and Mike Testa,
Linda and Rob Sutton, Guy Garguilo, Mais Homsi, and Kenny Cottrell
supervised on-site data collection and did a bang-up job.

So how good are the new touring plans in the *Unofficial Guide*? The
computer program the *Unofficial Guide* uses gets typically within about
2% of the optimal touring plan. To put this in perspective, if the hypo-
thetical "perfect" Adult One-Day touring plan took about 10 hours on
average to complete, the touring plan in the *Guide* would take about 10
hours and 12 minutes. Since it would take about 30 years for a really powerful computer to find that "perfect" touring plan, the extra 12 minutes is
a reasonable trade-off.

Incidentally, the program indicates that it may be possible to see the
almost 40 attractions in the Magic Kingdom in a single day. This would
involve around 17 hours in the park, and conditions would have to be
right—a summer day with an E-Ride night would be the best time to try.
If you're in peak physical condition and would like to try this ultimate
Magic Kingdom touring plan, drop us a line and we'll provide the details.

Custom Touring Plans Are Now Available

The new *Unofficial Guide* Touring Plan program allows us for the first time
to offer our readers customized touring plans to all of the Disney theme
parks (Universal Studios and Universal Islands of Adventure custom touring plans will be available next year). If you want to arrive at the park at 11
a.m. instead of at park opening (as called for by the one-day touring plans
in this guide), or if you want to commence touring at 3 p.m., a customized
touring plan will guarantee the least time waiting in line. *If you plan to*

arrive when the park opens, as prescribed by the touring plans in the Guide, *you will not need a customized touring plan.*

Each customized plan costs $11. Here's how it works. You can download a Custom Touring Plan Questionnaire from **www.touringplans. com,** or e-mail a request to unofficialguides@menasharidge.com. On the questionnaire, you can specify the dates of your vacation; the park you intend to visit; what time you want to arrive at the park; the attractions you want to experience; whether or not you want to watch a parade, fireworks, or other live performances; when and where you'd like to have a meal (the plan can make suggestions based on where in the park you'll be at your designated mealtime); and when you want to depart from the park. Because Disney changes its park operating hours without advance notice, the best time to request your custom touring plan is 2–4 weeks before leaving home. Your customized touring plan will be e-mailed to you within two business days of receipt of your questionnaire.

General Overview of the Touring Plans

Our touring plans are step-by-step guides for seeing as much as possible with a minimum of standing in line. They're designed to help you avoid crowds and bottlenecks on days of moderate-to-heavy attendance. On days of lighter attendance (see "Selecting the Time of Year for Your Visit," page 29), the plans will still save time but won't be as critical to successful touring.

What You Can Realistically Expect from the Touring Plans

Though we present one-day touring plans for each of the theme parks, you should understand that the Magic Kingdom and Epcot have more attractions than you can see in one day, even if you never wait in line. If you must cram your visit into a single day, the one-day touring plans will allow you to see as much as is humanly possible. Under certain circumstances you may not complete the plan, and you definitely won't be able to see everything. For the Magic Kingdom and Epcot, the most comprehensive, efficient, and relaxing touring plans are the two-day plans. Although Disney-MGM Studios has grown considerably since its 1989 debut, you should have no problem seeing everything in one day. Likewise, the Animal Kingdom is a one-day outing.

Variables that Will Affect the Success of the Touring Plans

How quickly you move from one ride to another; when and how many refreshment and rest-room breaks you take; when, where, and how you eat meals; and your ability (or lack thereof) to find your way around will all have an impact on the success of the plans. Smaller groups almost always move faster than larger groups, and parties of adults generally can cover more ground than families with young children. Switching off (see pages 254–257), among other things, inhibits families with little ones from moving expeditiously among attractions. Plus, some children simply cannot conform to the "early-to-rise" conditions of the touring plans.

A mom from Nutley, New Jersey, writes:

[Although] the touring plans all advise getting to parks at opening, we just couldn't burn the candle at both ends. Our kids (10, 7, and 4) would not go to sleep early and couldn't be up at dawn and still stay sane. It worked well for us to let them sleep a little later, go out, and bring breakfast back to the room while they slept, and still get a relatively early start by not spending time on eating breakfast out. We managed to avoid long lines with an occasional early morning, and hitting popular attractions during parades, mealtimes, and late evenings.

And a family from Centerville, Ohio, says:

The toughest thing about your touring plans was getting the rest of the family to stay with them, at least to some degree. Getting them to pass by attractions in order to hit something across the park was no easy task (sometimes impossible).

Finally, if you have young children in your party, be prepared for character encounters. The appearance of a Disney character is usually sufficient to stop a touring plan dead in its tracks. What's more, while some characters continue to stroll the parks, it is becoming more the rule to assemble characters in some specific venue (like the Hall of Fame at Mickey's Toontown Fair) where families must queue up for photos and autographs. Meeting characters, posing for photos, and collecting autographs can burn hours of touring time. If your kids are into character-autograph collecting, you will need to anticipate these interruptions to the touring plan and negotiate some understanding with your children about when you will follow the plan and when you will collect autographs. Our advice is to either go with the flow or alternatively set aside a certain morning or afternoon for photos and autographs. Be aware, however, that queues for autographs, especially in Toontown at the Magic Kingdom and Camp Minnie-Mickey at the Animal Kingdom, are every bit as long as the queues for major attractions. The only time-efficient way to collect autographs is to line up at the character-greeting areas first thing in the morning. Because this is also the best time to experience the more popular attractions, you may have some tough choices to make.

While we realize that following the touring plans is not always easy, we nevertheless recommend continuous, expeditious touring until around noon. After noon, breaks and diversions won't affect the plans significantly.

Some variables that can profoundly affect the touring plans are beyond your control. Chief among these are the manner and timing of bringing a particular ride to capacity. For example, Big Thunder Mountain Railroad, a roller coaster in the Magic Kingdom, has five trains. On a given morning it may begin operation with two of the five, then add the other three if and when needed. If the waiting line builds rapidly before operators decide to go to full capacity, you could have a long wait, even in early morning.

Another variable relates to the time you arrive for a theater performance. Usually, your wait will be the length of time from your arrival to the end of the presentation in progress. Thus, if *Country Bear Jamboree* is 15 minutes long and you arrive one minute after a show has begun, your wait for the next show will be 14 minutes. Conversely, if you arrive as the show is wrapping up, your wait will be only a minute or two.

What to Do if You Lose the Thread

Anything from a blister to a broken attraction can throw off a touring plan. If unforeseen events interrupt a touring plan:

1. Skip one step on the plan for every 20 minutes you're delayed. If you lose your billfold, for example, and spend an hour finding it, skip three steps and pick up from there.

2. Forget the touring plan and organize the remainder of your day using the *Recommended Attraction Visitation Times* clip-out lists at the back of this guide. These timetables summarize the best time windows to visit each attraction.

What to Expect when You Arrive at the Parks

Because most touring plans are based on being present when the theme park opens, you need to know a little about opening procedures. Disney transportation to the parks, as well as the respective theme-park parking lots, open an hour-and-a-half to two hours before official opening time.

Each park has an entrance plaza just outside the turnstiles. Usually you will be held outside the turnstiles until 30 minutes before the official opening time. At 30 minutes prior to the official opening time you will generally be admitted through the turnstiles. What happens next depends on the season of the year and the anticipated crowds for that day.

1. Low Season At slower times of year, you will usually be confined in a small section of the park until the official opening time. At the Magic Kingdom you will be admitted to Main Street, U.S.A.; at the Animal Kingdom to The Oasis and sometimes to Discovery Island; at Epcot to the fountain area around Spaceship Earth; and at Disney-MGM Studios to Hollywood Boulevard. If you proceed farther into a park, you will encounter a rope barrier manned by Disney cast members who will keep you from entering the remainder of the park. You will remain here until the "rope drop," when the rope barrier is removed and the park and all (or most) of its attractions are opened at the official opening time.

2. High Attendance Days   When large crowds are expected, you will be admitted through the turnstiles 30 minutes prior to official opening time, just as during slower times of year, only this time the entire park will be up and running and you will not encounter any rope barriers.

3. Variations   Sometimes, Disney will run a variation of the two opening procedures described above. In this situation you will be permitted through the turnstiles and will find that one or several specific attractions are open early for your enjoyment. At Epcot, Spaceship Earth and sometimes Test Track will be operating. At Animal Kingdom you may find Kilimanjaro Safaris and *It's Tough to Be a Bug!* up and running early. At Disney-MGM Studios look for Tower of Terror and/or Rock 'n' Roller Coaster. The Magic Kingdom almost never runs a variation. At the Magic Kingdom, you'll encounter either number 1 or 2 as described above.

A Word about the Rope Drop   Until recently, at all four parks, Disney cast members would dive for cover when the rope was dropped as thousands of adrenaline-charged guests stampeded to the parks' most popular attractions. This practice occasioned the legendary Space Mountain Morning Mini-Marathon and the Splash Mountain Rapid Rampage at the Magic Kingdom, the Tower of Terror Trot at Disney-MGM Studios, and the Safari Sprint at Animal Kingdom, among others. Each morning, a huge throng would crowd the rope barriers waiting for the signal to sprint to the entrance of their favorite ride. It was each person for himself—parents against offspring, brother against sister, coeds against truck drivers, nuns against beauticians. So there you were, a dental hygienist from Toledo, thinking you'd like to ride Space Mountain and finding yourself embroiled in this ritual insanity. There was nothing to do except tie up your Reeboks and get ready to run.

Lest you think we're exaggerating, consider the words of those who have experienced it. From an Oakland, Tennessee, teen:

We waited the half hour, made new friends, and discussed the "Space Mountain Mini Marathon." I wasn't sure if I believed it or not. But when the announcement came over the loudspeaker and the rope dropped, we all took off. First walking fast, then jogging, then running. It was thousands of people trucking it as fast as their legs could take them over what felt like miles ... In that mess I lost my mom. She quit, figuring she didn't want to ride anything bad enough to fall over with a heart attack. I made it. I don't know how, but I did it. I was also one of the first 25 or 30 people in line. I let some people go on in front of me because I was waiting for my mom who never showed up. There are thousands more people involved in this than I ever imagined, and it covers what seems like the same distance as an actual marathon, with people running much faster. Even though Space Mountain wasn't as great as I had hoped, I wasn't disappointed.

Well, this scenario no longer exists—at least not in the crazed versions of years past. Disney has beefed up the number of cast members supervising the rope drop in order to suppress the mayhem. In some cases the rope is not even "dropped." Instead, it's walked back. In other words, Disney cast members lead you with the rope at a fast walk toward the attraction you're straining to reach, forcing you (and everyone else) to maintain their pace. Not until they come within close proximity of the attraction do the cast members step aside. A New Jersey mom described it thus:

You are no longer allowed to sprint to these [attractions] because of people being trampled. Now there is a phalanx of cast members lined up at the rope who instruct you in friendly but no uncertain terms that when the rope drops they will lead you to the rides at a fast walk. However, you are not allowed to pass them. (No one ever said what would happen if you did pass). To my surprise, everyone followed the rules and we were splish-splashing within five minutes after 9 a.m.

A variation of this tune was reported by a Kansasville, Wisconsin, mom:

No more Rapid Rampage/Space Mountain Mini Marathon! A helper was picked by a waiting cast member from the group of people waiting before the rope was dropped, and the cast member and helper escorted the crowd—we were given specific instructions to stay behind them—to Splash Mountain, picking up additional groups being escorted along the way. Safer, yes ... but a LOT less fun! Having experienced the "Mini Marathon," I will miss it ... it was one of the few uncontrolled things at WDW, which is probably why it was squashed!

You never know with Disney, though. The current rope-drop procedure may be abandoned and the traditional insanity allowed to resume. Because Disney likes to control everything, however, we don't think so. And while we'll miss the passion of the early-morning races, we have to admit that the new practice is probably safer.

So, here's the straight poop. If Disney persists in walking the rope back, the only way you can gain an advantage over the rest of the crowd is to arrive early enough to be one of those up front close to the rope. Be alert, though; sometimes the Disney folks will step out of the way after about fifty yards or so. If this happens you can fire up the afterburners and speed the remaining distance to your destination.

Touring Plan Clip-Out Pocket Outlines

For your convenience, we have prepared outlines of all the touring plans in this guide. These pocket versions present the same itineraries as the detailed plans, but with vastly abbreviated directions. Select the plan appropriate for your party, then familiarize yourself with the detailed version. Once you understand how the plan works, clip the pocket version from the back of this guide and carry it with you as a quick reference at the theme park.

Will the Plans Continue to Work Once the Secret Is Out?

Yes! First, all of the plans require that a patron be there when the theme parks open. Many Walt Disney World patrons simply refuse to get up early while on vacation. Second, less than 1% of any day's attendance has been exposed to the plans, too little to affect results. Last, most groups tailor the plans, skipping rides or shows according to personal taste.

How Frequently Are the Touring Plans Revised?

Because Disney is always adding new attractions and changing operations, we revise the touring plans every year. Most complaints we receive about them come from readers who are using out-of-date editions of the *Unofficial Guide*. Be prepared, however, for surprises. Opening procedures and show times, for example, may change, and you never know when an attraction might break down.

FASTPASS

In 1999, Disney launched a new system for moderating the waiting time for popular attractions. Called FASTPASS, it was originally tried at the Animal Kingdom and then subsequently expanded to cover attractions at the other parks. Here's how it works.

Your handout park map, as well as signage at respective attractions, will tell you which attractions are included. Attractions operating FAST-PASS will have a regular line and a FASTPASS line. A sign at the entrance will tell you how long the wait is in the regular line. If the wait is acceptable to you, hop in line. If the wait seems too long, you can insert your park admission pass into a special FASTPASS machine and receive an appointment time (for sometime later in the day) to come back and ride. When you return at the appointed time, you will enter the FASTPASS line and proceed directly to the attraction's preshow or boarding area with no further wait. Interestingly, this procedure was pioneered by Universal Studios Hollywood many years ago and has been pretty much ignored by major theme parks ever since. It works well, however, and can really save a lot of time standing in line. There is no extra charge to use FASTPASS.

FASTPASS is still evolving, and attractions continue to be added and deleted from the lineup. Pending changes aside, here's an example of how to use FASTPASS: Let's say you have only one day to tour the Magic Kingdom. You arrive early and ride Space Mountain and experience Alien Encounter with only minimal waits. Then you head across the park to Splash Mountain and find a substantial line. Because Splash Mountain is designated as a FASTPASS attraction, you can insert your admission pass into the machine and receive an appointment time to come back and ride, thus avoiding a long wait.

We found FASTPASS to work remarkably well, primarily because Disney provides amazingly preferential treatment for FASTPASS holders. In fact, the effort to accommodate FASTPASS holders makes anyone in the regular line feel like an illegal immigrant. As a telling indication of their status, guests in the regular lines are referred to as "standby guests." Indeed, we watched guests in the regular lines stand by and stand by, shifting despondently from foot to foot, while dozens and sometimes hundreds of FASTPASS holders were ushered into the boarding area ahead of them. Clearly Disney is sending a message here, to wit: FAST-PASS is heaven; anything else is limbo at best and probably purgatory. In any event, you'll think you've been in purgatory if you get stuck in the regular line during the hot, crowded part of the day.

Readers write to us regularly with their standby-line horror stories. Here's one from a Pequea, Pennsylvania, family:

We, a group of four 12-year-olds and five adults, decided to ride Test Track when we arrived at Epcot at 11:00 a.m. FASTPASSes were being issued for [late that night] and the singles line was not open yet, so we decided to brave the 120-minute wait (at MK and MGM many waits ended up being less than the posted time). What a disaster! Once inside the building, the FASTPASS and singles line (which opened when we were very near the building) sped ahead while the standby line barely moved. The ride broke down twice, but the delay due to that was minimal. After 3 hours and 20 minutes, we finally made it to the car! One man who was in the FASTPASS line said that he counted 12:1 ratio between FASTPASSers and standby people being let into the [boarding] area. When we neared the "Holy Grail" of the front of the line, the attendant would ask how many people were in our party and then let that number in and then fill the rest of the [boarding] area with FASTPASS and single riders. Disney needs to seriously reconsider their boarding policy!

However, FASTPASS doesn't eliminate the need to arrive at the theme park early. Because each park offers a limited number of FASTPASS attractions, you still need to get an early start if you want to see as much as possible in a single day. Plus, as we'll discuss later, there is a limited supply of FASTPASSes available for each attraction on a given day. If you don't arrive until the middle of the afternoon, you might find that all the FASTPASSes have been distributed to other guests. FASTPASS does make it possible to see more with less waiting than ever before, and it's a great benefit to those who like to sleep late or who enjoy an afternoon or evening at the theme parks on their arrival day at Walt Disney World. It also allows you to postpone wet rides, like Kali River Rapids at the Animal Kingdom or Splash Mountain at the Magic Kingdom, until the warmer part of the day.

How do guests like FASTPASS? This note from a Surrey, British Columbia, family is typical:

> Please, please do not emphasize how great FASTPASS is! It is (so far) the best-kept secret at WDW. For the popular rides, it's the only way to go during peak times. It saved us hours of waiting in lines. We couldn't believe everyone wasn't using it—but we were glad they weren't!

Understanding the FASTPASS System The basic purpose of the FASTPASS system is to reduce the waiting time for designated attractions by more equally distributing the arrival of guests at those attractions over the course of the day. This is accomplished by providing an incentive, namely a shorter wait in line, for guests who are willing to postpone experiencing the attraction until later in the day. The system also, in effect, imposes a penalty (i.e., being relegated to standby status) on those who opt not to use it. However, distributing guest arrivals more equally sometimes also decreases the waiting time for standby guests.

When you insert your admission pass into a FASTPASS time clock, the machine spits out a small slip of paper about two-thirds the size of a credit card—small enough to fit in your wallet but also small enough to lose easily. Printed on the paper is the name of the attraction and a specific one-hour time window, for example 1:15–2:15 p.m., during which you can return to enjoy the ride.

When you report back to the attraction during your one-hour window, you'll enter a line marked "FASTPASS Return" that will route you more or less directly to the boarding or preshow area. Each person in your party must have his or her own FASTPASS and be ready to show it to the Disney cast member at the entrance of the FASTPASS Return line. Before you enter the boarding area or theater, another cast member will collect your FASTPASS.

You may show up at any time during the period printed on your FAST-PASS, and from our observation, no specific time within the window is better or worse. This holds true because cast members are instructed to minimize waits for FASTPASS holders. Thus, if the FASTPASS Return line is suddenly inundated (something that occurs essentially by chance), cast members rapidly intervene to reduce the FASTPASS line. This is done by admitting as many as 25 FASTPASS holders for each single standby guest until the FASTPASS line is reduced to an acceptable length. Although FASTPASS will eliminate as much as 80% of the wait you'd experience in the regular line, you can still expect a short wait, but it's usually less than 20 minutes.

You can obtain a FASTPASS anytime after a park opens, but the FASTPASS Return lines do not begin operating until 30–45 minutes after opening. Thus, if the Magic Kingdom opens at 9 a.m., the FAST-PASS time clock machines will also be available at 9 a.m., and the FAST-PASS Return line will begin operating at about 9:30 or 9:45 a.m.

Whenever you obtain a FASTPASS, you can be assured of a period of time between when you receive your FASTPASS and the period to report back. The interval can be as short as 30 minutes or as long as 3–7 hours, depending on park attendance, the popularity of the attraction, and the attraction's hourly capacity. As a rule of thumb, the earlier in the day you secure a FASTPASS, the shorter the interval between time of issue and your one-hour return window. If the park opens at 9 a.m. and you pick up a FASTPASS for Splash Mountain at 9:25 a.m., your appointment window for returning to ride would be something like 10–11 a.m. or perhaps 10:10–11:10 a.m. The exact time of your return window will be determined by how many other guests have obtained FASTPASSes before you.

To more effectively distribute guests over the course of a day, the FAST-PASS machines bump the one-hour return period back five minutes for a set number of passes issued (usually the number is equal to about 6% of the attraction's hourly capacity). For example, when Splash Mountain opens at 9 a.m., the first 125 people to obtain a FASTPASS will get a 9:40–10:40 a.m. return window. The next 125 guests are issued FAST-PASSes with a 9:45–10:45 a.m. window, and the next 125 are assigned a 10:10–11:10 a.m. time slot. And so it goes, with the time window dropping back five minutes for every 125 guests. The fewer guests who obtain FASTPASSes for an attraction, the shorter the interval between the receipt of your pass and the return window. Conversely, the more guests issued FASTPASSes, the longer the interval. If an attraction is exceptionally popular and/or its hourly capacity is relatively small, the return window might be pushed back all the way to park closing time. When this happens the FASTPASS machines simply shut down and a sign is posted saying FASTPASSes are all gone for the day. For example, it's not unusual for Test Track at Epcot or Winnie the Pooh at the Magic Kingdom to distribute an entire day's allocation of FASTPASSes by 1 p.m.

Rides routinely exhaust their daily FASTPASS supply, but shows almost never do. FASTPASS machines at theaters try to balance attendance at each show so that the audience of any given performance is divided about evenly between standby and FASTPASS guests. Consequently, standby guests for shows are not discriminated against to the degree experienced by standby guests for rides. In practice, FASTPASS diminishes the wait for standby guests. Generally, with very few exceptions, using the standby line at theater attractions requires less time than using FASTPASS.

When to Use FASTPASS   Except as discussed below, there's no reason to use FASTPASS during the first 30–40 minutes a park is open. Lines for most attractions are quite manageable during this period, and this is the only time of day when FASTPASS attractions exclusively serve those in the regular line. Regardless of time of day, however, if the wait in the regular line at a FASTPASS attraction is 25–30 minutes or less, we recommend joining the regular line.

Think about it. Using FASTPASS requires two trips to the same attraction: one to obtain the pass and another to use it. This means you must invest time to secure the pass (sometimes there are lines at the FASTPASS machines!) and then later interrupt your touring and backtrack in order to use your FASTPASS. The additional time, effort, and touring modification required are justified only if you can save more than 30 minutes. And don't forget: even in the FASTPASS line you must endure some waiting.

Five attractions in the Disney parks build lines so quickly in the early morning that failing to queue up within the first six or so minutes of operation will mean a long wait. The attractions are Test Track at Epcot, Kilimanjaro Safaris at the Animal Kingdom, Space Mountain at the Magic Kingdom, and Tower of Terror and Rock 'n' Roller Coaster at Disney-MGM Studios. (Mission: Space will be added to this list after it opens in 2003.) With these attractions, you can either be present when the park opens and race directly to the attraction or opt for a FASTPASS. For instance, if you arrive at Rock 'n' Roller Coaster 30 minutes after opening, the line will probably be so long that you'd want to use FASTPASS.

Another four FASTPASS attractions, including Splash Mountain, Winnie the Pooh, Peter Pan's Flight, and Jungle Cruise in the Magic Kingdom, develop long lines within 30–50 minutes of park opening. If you can get to one or more of these before the wait becomes intolerable, all the better. Otherwise, your options are FASTPASS or a long wait.

If you're wondering how FASTPASS waits compare with waits in the standby line, here's what we observed at Space Mountain in the Magic Kingdom during Spring Break on a day when the park opened at 9 a.m.

From 9 to 10 a.m. both sides of Space Mountain served standby guests (there are two identical roller coasters in the Space Mountain building). Before 10 a.m. the entire right side was cleared and became dedicated to FASTPASS at 10 a.m. At 10:45 a.m. the posted standby wait time was 45 minutes, while the FASTPASS wait was only 10 minutes. At 1:45 p.m., the posted standby wait time was 60 minutes, with 10 minutes for FASTPASS. These observations, in addition to documenting the benefit of FASTPASS, also reveal shorter waits in the regular line than those observed at the same time of day prior to the advent of FASTPASS.

FASTPASS Rules   Disney stipulates that "you must use your current FASTPASS ticket or wait two hours before getting another FASTPASS ticket for a different attraction." This stipulation represents a change from the original program. Previously you could possess only one FAST-PASS at a time and could not obtain another until the first was used. Undoubtedly Disney received hundreds of letters similar to the one we received from a reader in Newport News, Virginia:

About 1 [p.m.] there was a long line at Winnie the Pooh, so we walked up and got a FASTPASS without bothering to notice what the return time was. When I looked at my [FASTPASS] ticket, it said to come back between 6:45 and 7:45 [p.m.]! I tried to get the Disney person at the FASTPASS machine to take it back, but she said there was nothing she could do. According to the rules, I was stuck and could not get another FASTPASS for the rest of the afternoon. As it worked out, we left the park before it was time to use the FASTPASS. That was our last day and I never did get to ride Winnie the Pooh.

Because situations (and complaints) like this one were legion, Disney amended the rules so that now you can obtain a second FASTPASS two hours from the time the first one was issued. Rules aside, the real lesson here is to check out the posted return time before obtaining a FAST-PASS, as a father of two from Cranston, Rhode Island, advises:

You should always check on the sign above the FASTPASS machines to see the ride [return] time that you will receive. We made the mistake of not look-ing at the time before we got our FASTPASSes for Space Mountain. The time we received was not for two hours and was at a time when we could not ride because of lunch reservations. So we couldn't take advantage of FASTPASS at Space Mountain and couldn't get any other FASTPASSes until after lunch.

If the return time is hours away (as in the case of the Newport News reader), forego the FASTPASS. Especially in the Magic Kingdom, there will be a number of other FASTPASS attractions where the return time is only an hour or so away.

There are a number of attractions where the time gap between issuance and return can be three to seven hours. If you think you might want to use FASTPASS on the following attractions, try to secure it before 11 a.m.:

Magic Kingdom	Disney-MGM Studios	Epcot
Winnie the Pooh	Rock 'n' Roller Coaster	Test Track
Peter Pan's Flight		Mission: Space (2003)
Space Mountain		
Splash Mountain		
Buzz Lightyear		

Tricks of the Trade   Although Disney stipulates that you "must use your current FASTPASS or wait two hours to get another," it's possible to acquire a second FASTPASS before using the first. Let's say you obtain a FASTPASS to Kilimanjaro Safaris at the Animal Kingdom with a return-time slot of 10:15–11:15 a.m. Any time after your FASTPASS window begins (i.e., after 10:15 a.m.), you can obtain another FASTPASS, say for Kali River Rapids. This is possible because the FASTPASS computer system only monitors the distribution of passes, ignoring whether or when an issued FASTPASS is used.

Like us, Nancy, a reader from Vienna, Virginia, enjoys testing the FASTPASS system. With little effort, she managed to hold three FAST-PASSes simultaneously. Here's what she did:

It was a lovely and quiet day at the Magic Kingdom so the return times were generally within an hour from when we got the FP. We also got all the FPs in the same general area [of the park]. Although armed with walkie-talkies, we weren't phased by the prospect of criss-crossing the park to grab an FP if it was necessary.

10:00   *get FP for Thunder Mountain RR: return time 10:50–11:50*

10:50   *get FP for Jungle Cruise: return time 11:35–12:35*

11:35   *get FP for Haunted Mansion: return time 12:40–1:40*

At this point I'm holding three FPs.

11:40   *ride Thunder Mountain RR*

12:00   *ride Jungle Cruise*

12:40   *ride Haunted Mansion*

In the meantime (between 10:00 and 11:40), we boarded Pirates of the Caribbean, visited the Tiki Room, and explored Tom Sawyer Island. We really did not need the 3 FPs at one time, as we never had to wait in excess of 10 minutes for a ride, but I wanted to know if it could be done!

When obtaining FASTPASSes, it's faster and more considerate of other guests if one person obtains passes for your entire party. This means entrusting one individual with both your valuable park-admission passes and your FASTPASSes, so choose wisely.

Don't pack too much into the time between obtaining your FAST-PASSes and the end of your return window. We interviewed a number of families who blew their FASTPASS time slot by trying to cram an extra attraction or two into their touring scheme before returning to use their FASTPASSes.

FASTPASS GUIDELINES

- Don't mess with FASTPASS unless it can save you 30 minutes or more.

- If you arrive after a park opens, obtain a FASTPASS for your preferred FASTPASS attraction first thing.

- Do not obtain a FASTPASS for a theater attraction until you have experienced all the FASTPASS rides on your itinerary (using FASTPASS at theater attractions usually requires more time than using the standby line).

- Always check the FASTPASS return period before obtaining your FASTPASS.

- Obtain FASTPASSes for Rock 'n' Roller Coaster at MGM-Studios, Test Track at Epcot, and Winnie the Pooh, Peter Pan's Flight, Space Mountain, and Splash Mountain at the Magic Kingdom as early in the day as practicable.

- Try to obtain FASTPASSes for rides not mentioned on page 89 by 1 p.m.

- Don't depend on FASTPASSes being available for rides after 2 p.m. during busier times of year.

- Make sure everyone in your party has their own FASTPASS.

- Be mindful that you can obtain a second FASTPASS as soon as you enter the return period for your first FASTPASS or after two hours from issuance, whichever comes first.

- Be mindful of your FASTPASS return-time slot and plan intervening activities accordingly.

Tour Groups from Hell

We have discovered that tour groups of up to 200 people sometimes use our plans. A lady from Memphis writes:

> When we arrived at The Land [pavilion at Epcot], a tour guide was holding your book and shouting into a bullhorn, "Step 7. Proceed to Journey into Imagination." With this, about 65 Japanese tourists in red T-shirts ran out the door.

Unless your party is as large as that tour group, this development should not alarm you. Because tour groups are big, they move slowly and have to stop periodically to collect stragglers. The tour guide also has to accommodate the unpredictability of five dozen or so bladders. In short, you should have no problem passing a group after the initial encounter.

"Bouncing Around"

Many readers object to crisscrossing a theme park as our touring plans sometimes require. A lady from Decatur, Georgia, said she "got dizzy from all the bouncing around" and that the "running back and forth reminded [her] of a scavenger hunt". We empathize, but here's the rub, park by park.

In the Magic Kingdom, the most popular attractions are positioned across the park from one another. This is no accident. It's good planning, a method of more equally distributing guests throughout the park. If you want to experience the most popular attractions in one day without long waits, you can arrive before the park fills and see those attractions first thing (requires crisscrossing the park), or you can enjoy the main attractions on one side of the park first thing in the morning then try the popular attractions on the other side during the hour or so before closing, when crowds presumably have thinned. Using FASTPASS definitely lessens the time you spend waiting in line but tends to increase the bouncing around because you must visit the same attraction twice: once to obtain your FASTPASS and then again to use it.

The best way to minimize "bouncing around" at the Magic Kingdom is to use the Magic Kingdom Two-Day Touring Plan, which spreads the more popular attractions over two mornings and works beautifully even when the park closes at 8 p.m. or earlier.

We have revised the Epcot touring plans to eliminate most of the "bouncing around" and have added special instructions to even further minimize walking.

Disney-MGM Studios is configured in a way that precludes an orderly approach to touring, or to a clockwise or counterclockwise rotation. Orderly touring is further confounded by live entertainment that prompts guests to intermittently interrupt their touring to head to whichever theater is about to crank up. At the Studios, therefore, you're stuck with "bouncing around" whether you use the touring plan or not. In our opinion, when it comes to Disney theme parks, it's best to have a plan.

The Animal Kingdom is arranged in a spoke-and-hub configuration like the Magic Kingdom, simplifying crisscrossing the park. Even so, the only way to catch various shows on the daily entertainment schedule is to stop what you're doing and troop across the park to the next performance.

Touring Plans and the Obsessive-Compulsive Reader

We suggest you follow the touring plans religiously, especially in the mornings, if you're visiting Disney World during busy, more crowded times. The consequence of touring spontaneity in peak season is hours of otherwise avoidable standing in line. During quieter times of year, there's no need to be compulsive about following the plans.

A mom in Atlanta, Georgia, suggests:

Emphasize perhaps not following [the touring plans] in off-season. There is no reason to crisscross the park when there are no lines.

A father from Marlboro, New Jersey, writes:

The time we went in November, the longest line was about a five-minute wait. [At this time of year], your readers do not have to be so neurotic about running into the park and then to various attractions.

A mother in Minneapolis expresses her opinion:

Please let your readers know to stop along the way to various attractions to appreciate what else may be going on around them. We encountered many families using the Unofficial Guide [who] became too serious about getting from one place to the next, missing the fun in between.

We realize the touring plans can contribute to some stress and fatigue. A mother from Stillwater, Maine, writes:

We were thankful for the touring plan and were able to get through the most popular rides early before the lines got long. One drawback was all the bouncing around we did backtracking through different parts of the Magic Kingdom in order to follow the touring plan. It was tiring and a bit hectic at times.

What can we say? It's a lesser-of-two-evils situation. If you visit Walt Disney World at a busy time, you can either get up early and hustle around, or you can sleep in and see less, spending a lot of time in lines or backtracking to use FASTPASS.

When using the touring plans, however, relax and always be prepared for surprises and possible setbacks. When your blood pressure rises and your Type-A brain does cartwheels, reflect on the advice of a woman from Trappe, Pennsylvania:

You cannot emphasize enough the dangers of using your touring plans that were printed in the back of the book, especially if the person using them has a compulsive personality. I have a compulsive personality. I planned for this trip for two years, researched it by use of guidebooks, computer programs, video tapes, and information received from WDW. I had a two-page itinerary for our one-week trip in addition to your touring plans of the theme parks. On night three of our trip, I ended up taking a non-scheduled trip to the emergency room of Sand Lake Hospital in Lake Buena Vista. When the doctor asked what seemed to be the problem, I responded with

"I don't know, but I can't stop shaking, and I can't stay here very long because I have to get up in a couple hours to go to MGM according to my itinerary." Diagnosis: an anxiety attack caused by my excessive itinerary. He gave me a shot of something, and I slept through the first four attractions the next morning. This was our third trip to WDW (not including one trip to Disneyland); on all previous trips I used only the Steve Birnbaum book, and I suffered no ill effects. I am not saying your book was not good. It was excellent! However, it should come with a warning label for people with compulsive personalities.

Tour Plan Rejection

We have discovered you can't implant a touring plan in certain personalities without rapid and often vehement rejection. Some folks just do not respond well to the regimentation. If you bump into this problem with someone in your party, it's best to roll with the punches as this couple from Maryland did:

The rest of the group was not receptive to the use of the touring plans. I think they all thought I was being a little too regimented about planning this vacation. Rather than argue, I left the touring plans behind as we ventured off for the parks. You can guess the outcome. We took our camcorder with us and watched the movies when we returned home. About every five minutes or so there is a shot of us all gathered around a park map trying to decide what to do next.

Finally, as a Connecticut woman alleges, the touring plans are incompatible with some readers' bladders as well as their personalities:

I want to know if next year when you write those "day" schedules you could schedule bathroom breaks in there, too. You expect us to be at a certain ride at a certain time and with no stops in between. In one of the letters in your book, a guy writes, "You expect everyone to be theme-park commandos." When I read that I thought, there is a man who really knows what a problem the schedules are if you are a laid-back, slow-moving, careful detail noticer. What were you thinking when you made these schedules?

Touring Plans for Low-Attendance Days

We receive a number of letters each year similar to this one from Lebanon, New Jersey, reader:

The guide always assumed there would be large crowds. We had no lines. An alternate tour for low traffic days would be helpful.

If attendance is low, you really don't need a touring plan. Just go where your taste and instinct directs and glory in the hassle-free touring. Having said that, however, there are attractions in each park that bottleneck even if attendance is low. These are Space Mountain, Splash Mountain, Dumbo, The Many Adventures of Winnie the Pooh, and Peter Pan's Flight in the Magic Kingdom; Test Track and Mission: Space (opens 2003) at Epcot, Kilimanjaro Safari at the Animal Kingdom; and Tower of Terror and Rock 'n' Roller Coaster at the Disney-MGM Studios. All are FASTPASS attractions. Either experience them immediately after park opening or use FASTPASS. Don't forget that crowd size is relative and that large crowds can gather at certain attractions and on certain days even during less busy times of year. Our recommendation is to follow the touring plan of your choice through the first five or six steps. If you're pretty much walking onto every attraction, feel free to scrap the remainder of the plan.

A Clamor for Customized Touring Plans

We're inundated by letters urging us to create additional touring plans. These include a plan for ninth- and tenth-graders, a plan for rainy days, a senior's plan, a plan for folks who sleep late, a plan omitting rides that "bump, jerk, and clonk," a plan for gardening enthusiasts, and a plan for single women.

The touring plans in this book are intended to be flexible. Adapt them to your preferences. If you don't like rides that bump and jerk, skip them when they come up in a touring plan. If you want to sleep in and go to the park at noon, use the afternoon part of a plan. If you're a ninth-grader and want to ride Space Mountain three times in a row, do it. Will it decrease the touring plan's effectiveness? Sure, but the plan was created only to help you have fun. It's your day. Don't let the tail wag the dog. If you feel it's impossible to adapt the touring plans in the *Unofficial Guide* to your situation, consider ordering a computer-generated custom plan as described on page 77–78.

Understanding Walt Disney World Attractions

Walt Disney World's primary appeal is in its rides and shows. Understanding how these are engineered to accommodate guests is interesting and invaluable to developing an efficient itinerary.

All attractions at Disney World, regardless of location, are affected by two overriding elements: capacity and popularity. Capacity is how many guests the attraction can serve at one time—in an hour or in a day. Popularity shows how well visitors like an attraction. Capacity can be adjusted at some attractions. It's possible, for example, to add additional trams at the Disney-MGM Studios Backlot Tour or to put extra boats on the water at the Magic Kingdom's Jungle Cruise. Generally, however, capacity remains relatively fixed.

From a designer's perspective, the idea is to match capacity and popularity as closely as possible. A high-capacity ride that isn't very popular is a failure of sorts. Lots of money, space, and equipment have been poured into the attraction, yet there are empty seats. El Río del Tiempo, a ride in Epcot, comes closest to fitting this profile.

While it's extremely unusual for a new attraction not to measure up, it is fairly common for an older ride to lose its appeal. The Magic Kingdom's *Enchanted Tiki Birds,* for example, played to half-capacity audiences until its 1998 renovation.

In general, attractions are immensely popular when they're new. Some, like Space Mountain (Magic Kingdom), have sustained great appeal years beyond their debut, while others, like Epcot's The Living Seas and El Río del Tiempo, declined in popularity after just a few years. Most attractions, however, work through the honeymoon and then settle down to handle the level of demand for which they were designed. When this happens, there are enough interested guests during peak hours to fill almost every seat, but not so many that prohibitively long lines develop.

Sometimes Disney correctly estimates an attraction's popularity but fouls the equation by mixing in a third variable such as location. Spaceship Earth, the ride inside the geosphere at Epcot, is a good example. Placing the ride squarely in the path of every person entering the park assures that it will be inundated during morning hours when the park is filling up. On the flip side, *The American Adventure,* at the extreme opposite end of Epcot, has a huge capacity but plays to a partially filled theater until about noon, when guests finally work their way into that part of the park.

If demand is high and capacity is low, large lines materialize. Dumbo the Flying Elephant in the Magic Kingdom has the smallest capacity of almost any Disney World attraction, yet it probably is the most popular ride among young children. The result of this mismatch is that children and parents often suffer long, long waits for a one-and-a-half-minute ride. Dumbo is a simple yet visually appealing midway ride. Its capacity (and that of many other attractions, including Space Mountain) is limited by the very characteristics that make it popular.

Capacity design is predicated on averages: the average number of people in the park, the normal distribution of traffic to specific areas within the park, and the average number of staff needed to operate the ride. On a holiday weekend, when all the averages are exceeded, all but a few attractions operate at maximum capacity, and even then they are overwhelmed by the huge crowds. On low-attendance autumn days, full capacity is often not even approximated and guests can walk onto most rides without wait.

The Magic Kingdom offers the greatest variety in capacity and popularity, with vastly differing rides and shows. Only the Magic Kingdom and the Animal Kingdom offer low-capacity midway rides and spookhouse-genre "dark" rides. Technologically, the mix ranges from state-of-the-art to antiquated. This diversity makes efficient touring of the Magic Kingdom much more challenging. If guests don't understand the capacity/popularity relationship and plan accordingly, they might spend most of the day waiting in line.

While Epcot, the Animal Kingdom, and Disney-MGM Studios have fewer rides and shows than the Magic Kingdom, almost all of their attractions are major features and rank on a par with the Magic Kingdom's Pirates of the Caribbean and The Haunted Mansion in scope, detail, imagination, and spectacle. All but one or two of the Epcot, Animal Kingdom, and Disney-MGM Studios rides are fast loading, and most have large capacities. Because Epcot, the Animal Kingdom, and Disney-MGM Studios attractions are on average well engineered and very efficient, lines may appear longer than those in the Magic Kingdom but usually move more quickly. There are no midway rides at Epcot or Disney-MGM Studios, and fewer attractions are specifically intended for children.

In the Magic Kingdom, crowds are more a function of the popularity and engineering of individual attractions. At Epcot and the Animal Kingdom, traffic flow and crowding is much more affected by park layout. For touring efficiency, it's important to understand how Magic Kingdom rides and shows operate. At Epcot and the Animal Kingdom, this knowledge is decidedly less important.

Crowds at Disney-MGM Studios have been larger than anticipated since the park opened. Though Disney has added new attractions, a well-considered touring plan is essential. Likewise, the Animal Kingdom is currently operating with only five of its six planned theme areas open. Lack of capacity plus the allure of a new park translates into lengthy queues.

It's necessary to understand how rides and shows are designed and function to develop an efficient touring plan. We will examine both.

Cutting Your Time in Line by Understanding the Rides

There are many types of rides at Walt Disney World. Some, like The Great Movie Ride at Disney-MGM Studios, are engineered to carry more than 3,000 people every hour. At the other extreme, rides as Dumbo the Flying Elephant can accommodate only around 400 people an hour. Most rides fall somewhere in between. Many factors figure into how long you will wait to experience a ride: its popularity; how it loads and unloads; how many persons can ride at one time; how many units (cars, rockets, boats, flying elephants, etc.) are in service at a time; and how many staff are available to operate the ride. Let's take each factor one by one.

1. How Popular Is the Ride?

Newer rides like the Rock 'n' Roller Coaster at Disney-MGM Studios, Mission: Space (opens 2003) and Test Track at Epcot attract a lot of people, as do such longtime favorites as the Jungle Cruise in the Magic Kingdom. If you know a ride is popular, you need to know how it operates in order to determine the best time to ride. But a ride need not be especially popular to form long lines; the lines can result from weak traffic engineering (i.e., it takes so long to load and unload that a line builds regardless). This is the case at the Mad Tea Party and Cinderella's Golden Carrousel in Fantasyland. Since mostly children and teens ride the Mad Tea Party, it serves only a small percentage of any day's attendance at the Magic Kingdom. Yet, because it takes so long to load and unload, long waiting lines form.

2. How Does the Ride Load and Unload?

Some rides never stop. They are like circular conveyor belts that go around and around. These are "continuous loaders." The Magic Kingdom's Haunted Mansion and Epcot's Spaceship Earth are continuous loaders. The number of people that can be moved through in an hour depends on how many cars, "doom buggies," or whatever are on the conveyor. The Haunted Mansion and Spaceship Earth have lots of cars on the conveyor belt and consequently can each move more than 2,000 people an hour.

Other rides are "interval loaders." Cars are unloaded, loaded, and dispatched at set intervals (sometimes controlled manually, sometimes by computer). Space Mountain in Tomorrowland is an interval loader. It has two tracks (the ride has been duplicated in the same facility). Each track can run as many as 14 space capsules, released at 36-, 26-, or 21-second intervals. (The bigger the crowd, the shorter the interval.)

In one kind of interval loader (Space Mountain), empty cars (space capsules) are returned to where they reload. In a second type, one group of riders enters the vehicle while the previous group departs. These are "in-and-out" interval loaders. Splash Mountain is a good example of an in-and-out loader. As a boat docks, those who have just completed their ride exit to the left. At almost the same time, those waiting to ride enter the boat from the right. The reloaded boat is released to the dispatch point a few yards down the line, where it is launched according to the interval being used.

Interval loaders of both types can be very efficient at moving people if (1) the dispatch (launch) interval is relatively short and (2) the ride can accommodate a large number of vehicles at one time. Since many boats can be floating through Pirates of the Caribbean at one time, and since the dispatch interval is short, almost 3,000 people an hour can see this attraction.

The least efficient rides, in terms of traffic engineering, are "cycle rides," also called "stop-and-go" rides. On cycle rides, those waiting to ride exchange places with those who have just ridden. Unlike in-and-out interval rides, cycle rides shut down during loading and unloading. While one boat is loading and unloading in It's a Small World (an interval loader), many other boats are advancing through the ride. But when Dumbo the Flying Elephant touches down, the whole ride is at a standstill until the next flight is launched. Likewise, with Cinderella's Golden Carrousel, all riders dismount and the Carrousel stands idle until the next group is ready.

In cycle rides, the time the ride is in motion is "ride time." The time the ride idles while loading and unloading is "load time." Load time plus ride time equals "cycle time," or the time from the start of one run of the ride until the start of the next.

The only cycle rides in Disney World are in the Magic Kingdom and the Animal Kingdom.

3. How Many Persons Can Ride at One Time?

This figure expresses "per-ride capacity" or "system capacity." Either way, it's the number of people who can ride at one time. The greater the carrying capacity of a ride (all other things being equal), the more visitors it can accommodate in an hour. Some rides can add extra units (cars, boats, etc.) as crowds build, to increase capacity, while others, like the Astro Orbiter in Tomorrowland, have a fixed capacity (it's impossible to add rockets).

4. How Many "Units" Are in Service at a Given Time?

"Unit" is our term for the vehicle in which you ride. At the Mad Tea Party the unit is a tea cup; at Peter Pan's Flight it's a pirate ship. On some rides (mostly cycle rides), the number of units operating at a given time is fixed. Thus, there are always 16 flying elephants on the Dumbo ride and 90 horses on Cinderella's Golden Carrousel. There is no way to increase the capacity of such rides by adding more units. On a busy day, the only way to carry more people each hour on a fixed-unit cycle ride is to shorten the loading time or decrease the actual ride time. The bottom line on a busy day for a cycle ride is that you will wait longer and possibly be rewarded with a shorter ride. This is why we steer you away from cycle rides unless you're willing to ride them early in the morning or late at night. The following are cycle rides:

Magic Kingdom   Dumbo the Flying Elephant, Cinderella's Golden Carrousel, Mad Tea Party, Magic Carpets of Aladdin, Astro Orbiter, Goofy's Barnstormer

Animal Kingdom   TriceraTop Spin

Many other rides throughout Walt Disney World can increase their capacity by adding units as crowds build. Big Thunder Mountain Railroad in Frontierland is a good example. If attendance is light, Big Thunder can start the day by running only one of its five mine trains from one of two available loading platforms. If lines build, the other loading platform is opened and more mine trains are placed into operation. At full capacity, the five trains can carry about 2,400 persons an hour. Likewise, Star Tours at Disney-MGM Studios can increase its capacity by using all of its simulators, and the Maelstrom boat ride at Epcot can add more Viking ships. Sometimes a long queue will disappear almost instantly when new units are brought. When an interval loader places more units into operation, it usually shortens the dispatch intervals, allowing more units to be dispatched more often.

5. How Many Staff Are Available to Operate the Ride?

Allocating additional staff to a ride can allow more units to operate or additional loading or holding areas to open. In the Magic Kingdom, Pirates of the Caribbean and It's a Small World can run two separate waiting lines and loading zones. The Haunted Mansion has a one-and-a-half-minute preshow that is staged in a "stretch room." On busy days, a second stretch room can be activated, permitting a more continuous flow of visitors to the actual loading area.

Additional staff makes a world of difference to some cycle rides. Often, the Mad Tea Party has only one attendant. This person alone must clear visitors from the ride just completed, admit and seat visitors for the upcoming ride, check that each tea cup is properly secured, return to the control panel, issue instructions to the riders, and finally activate the ride (whew!). A second attendant divides these responsibilities and cuts loading time by 25–50%.

By knowing the way a ride loads, its hourly capacity, and its popularity, we can anticipate which rides are likely to develop long lines and, more important, how long we will have to wait to ride at any given time of day.

Cutting Your Time in Line by Understanding the Shows

Many featured attractions at Walt Disney World are theater presentations. While they aren't as complex as rides from a traffic engineering standpoint, understanding their operation may save touring time.

Most theater attractions operate in three phases:

1. Guests are in the theater viewing the presentation.

2. Guests who have passed through the turnstile wait in a holding area or lobby. These people will be admitted to the theater as soon as the

show in progress concludes. Several attractions offer a preshow in their lobby to entertain guests until they're admitted to the main show. Examples include *Enchanted Tiki Birds* and *Alien Encounter* in the Magic Kingdom; The Living Seas and *Honey, I Shrunk the Audience* at Epcot; and *Sounds Dangerous* and *MuppetVision 3D* at Disney-MGM Studios.

3. A line waits outside. Guests in line will enter the lobby when there is room and will ultimately move into the theater.

Theater capacity, the presentation's popularity, and attendance level in the park determine how long lines will be at a theater attraction. Except for holidays and other days of heavy attendance, the longest wait for a show usually doesn't exceed the length of one complete performance.

Since almost all theater attractions run continuously, stopping only long enough for the previous audience to leave and the waiting audience to enter, a performance will be in progress when you arrive. *Impressions de France* in the French pavilion at Epcot is 18 minutes in duration; your longest wait under normal circumstances is about 18 minutes if you arrive just after the show has begun.

All theaters (except a few amphitheater productions) are very strict about access. Unlike a movie theater at home, you can't enter during a performance. This being the case, you will always have at least a short wait.

Most theaters hold a lot of people. When a new audience is admitted, the outside line (if there is one) usually will disappear. Exceptions are *The Making of Me* in the Wonders of Life pavilion and *Honey, I Shrunk the Audience* in the Imagination pavilion at Epcot; and *Voyage of the Little Mermaid* and *MuppetVision 3-D* at Disney-MGM Studios; and *It's Tough to Be a Bug!* and *Festival of the Lion King* at the Animal Kingdom. Because these shows are so popular (or have a small capacity, like *The Making of Me*), you may have to wait through more than one show before you're admitted (unless you go early in the morning or after 4:30 p.m.).

How to Deal with Obnoxious People

At every theater presentation at Walt Disney World, visitors in the preshow area elbow, nudge, and crowd one another to make sure they're admitted to the performance. It's unnecessary. If you are admitted through the turnstile into the preshow area, a seat has automatically been allocated for you in the theater. When it's time to enter the theater, don't rush. Relax and let other people jam the doorways. When the congestion eases, stroll in and take a seat.

Attendants at many theaters will instruct you to enter a row of seats and move completely to the far side, filling every seat. Invariably, some inconsiderate yahoo will plop down in the middle of the row, stopping traffic or forcing other visitors to climb over him. Take our word for it:

There is no such thing as a bad seat. All Disney theaters are designed to provide a near-perfect view from every seat. Our recommendation is to follow instructions and move to the far end of the row.

Visitors are also asked not to use flash photography in the theaters (the theaters are too dark for the pictures to turn out, and the flash disturbs other viewers). This admonition is routinely ignored. Flashers are more difficult to deal with than row-blockers.

A Word about Disney Thrill Rides

Readers of all ages should attempt to be open-minded about the so-called Disney "thrill rides." In comparison with rides at other theme parks, the Disney thrill attractions are quite tame, with more emphasis on sights, atmosphere, and special effects than on the motion, speed, or feel of the ride itself. While we suggest you take Disney's preride warnings seriously, we can tell you that guests of all ages report enjoying rides such as Tower of Terror, Big Thunder Mountain, and Splash Mountain. The baddest thrill rides in Florida are the Montu coaster at Busch Gardens, The Hulk coaster at Islands of Adventure, and SeaWorld's Kraken coaster.

A reader from Washington sums up the situation well:

Our boys and I are used to imagining typical amusement park rides when it comes to roller coasters. So, when we thought of Big Thunder Mountain and Space Mountain, what came to mind was gigantic hills, upside-down loops, huge vertical drops, etc. I actually hate roller coasters, especially the unpleasant sensation of a long drop, and I have never taken a ride that loops you upside down.

In fact, the Disney [thrill rides] are all tame in comparison. There are never any long and steep hills (except Splash Mountain, and it is there for anyone to see, so you have informed consent going on the ride). I was able to build up courage to go on all of them, and the more I rode them, the more I enjoyed them—the less you tense up expecting a big, long drop, the more you enjoy the special effects and even swinging around curves. Swinging around curves is really the primary motion challenge of Disney roller coasters.

Seniors who experience Disney thrill rides generally enjoy the smoother rides like Splash Mountain, Big Thunder Mountain, and Tower of Terror, and tend to dislike more jerky attractions. This letter from a Gig Harbor, Washington, woman is typical:

I am a senior woman of small stature and good health. I am writing my comments on Space Mountain, Splash Mountain, Big Thunder Mountain, and Star Tours. My experience [is that] all of the rides, with the exception of Star Tours, were wonderful rides. Star Tours is too jerky and fast, the music is too loud, and I found it to be unacceptable.

Notwithstanding the reader's comment, we receive mostly positive comments from seniors concerning Star Tours. Body Wars and the Rock 'n' Roller Coaster, however, are different stories. Body Wars has an unrivaled reputation for inducing motion sickness, and Rock 'n' Roller

Coaster is a serious coaster that shares more in common with Hulk and Montu than with Space Mountain or Big Thunder Mountain.

A Plea for Compassion and Courtesy

A complaint that our readers continue to make with regrettable frequency concerns able-bodied guests pretending to be disabled in order to receive preferential treatment. The following comments have been retained from previous editions because they describe the situation so eloquently.

An outraged Stevens Point, Wisconsin, mother writes:

As the parent of a handicapped child, I was appalled to see the blatant misuse of wheelchairs. People who loaded them with purchases and hopped in as they came to a ride. One party came in with the father in the wheelchair. At the next ride, one of the kids was in the chair. At the next, the mother was in the chair! This practice is not only unfair to nonhandicapped people [waiting in line] but also is an affront to those who really need [a wheelchair].

On the same topic, a woman from Rockford, Illinois, made a well-considered appeal for tolerance and understanding:

I read with interest readers' comments about apparently able-bodied people "abusing" wheelchairs at WDW. I am sure there are a few scoundrels, but the vast majority of people are honest. People with lupus or a number of other connective tissue diseases, people with heel spurs, hip or knee problems, heart or kidney disease, and people on chemotherapy can all look perfectly healthy—even though they would never be able to walk through WDW. Readers may ask why so many of these folks would go to Disney World. Where else can you vacation with your healthy, active spouse and young children and still keep up with them? These are families who can't go surfing or skiing or to water parks together.

And if readers find themselves resenting the fact that the children of these people don't have to wait, they might consider that these children do wait—51 weeks a year. They wait at doctors' offices. They wait until the next round of chemo is over before they can go to the zoo (if dad feels better). They wait till mom can walk better before they can go to the mall. They wait until next year and maybe dad will be able to coach soccer. They wait, and wait, and wait.

Have a heart, healthy people. Just because someone can walk a little bit or get on a ride without help or doesn't look as handicapped as your child, it doesn't mean they don't need special facilities. Limp a mile in my shoes (with the orthotics).

Part Three

Selecting Your Hotel

The Basic Considerations

Locating a suitable hotel or condo is critical to planning any Walt Disney World vacation. The basic question is whether to stay in the World. Luxury lodging can be found both in and out of Disney World. Budget lodging is another story. Room rates start at about $80 a night in the World and range to more than $500. Outside Disney World, rooms are as low as $35 a night at some independent motels.

Beyond affordability is the convenience issue. We've lodged both in and out of Walt Disney World, and there is special magic and peace of mind associated with staying inside Disney World. "I feel more a part of everything and less like a visitor," one guest writes.

There's no real hardship in staying outside Disney World and driving (or taking a hotel shuttle) to the theme parks. Meals can be less expensive, and rooming outside the World makes you more receptive toward other Orlando-area attractions and eating establishments. Universal Studios, Universal's Islands of Adventure, Kennedy Space Center, SeaWorld, Gatorland, and Cypress Gardens, among others, are well worth your attention.

Lodging prices are subject to change, but our researchers lodged in an excellent (though not plush) motel surrounded by beautiful orange groves for half the cost of staying in the least expensive Disney hotel. Our commute to the Magic Kingdom or Epcot parking lots was 17 minutes one way.

If you have young children, read Part Five: Walt Disney World with Kids (page 229) before choosing lodging. Similarly, seniors, couples on a honeymoon or romantic holiday, and disabled guests should read the applicable sections of Part Six: Special Tips for Special People (page 283) before choosing a hotel.

About Hotel Renovations

We have inspected several hundred hotels in the Walt Disney World area to compile the list of lodging choices presented in the *Unofficial Guide*. Each year we phone each hotel to verify contact information and to inquire about renovations or refurbishments. If a hotel has been renovated or has refurbished its guest rooms, we reinspect that hotel along with any new hotels for the next edition of this book. Hotels that report no improvements are checked out every two years.

We should point out that most hotels over five years old, both in and out of Walt Disney World, refurbish between 10 and 20% of their guest rooms each year. This incremental approach minimizes disruption of normal business but also makes your room assignment a crapshoot. You might luck into a newly renovated room or alternatively be assigned a threadbare room. Disney resorts will not guarantee specific rooms but will annotate your request for a recently refurbished room on your reservation record and will try to accommodate you when you arrive. Non-Disney hotels will often guarantee an updated room when you book.

Benefits of Staying in the World

Walt Disney World resort hotel and campground guests have privileges and amenities unavailable to those staying outside the World. Though some of these perks are only advertising gimmicks, others are real and potentially valuable. Early entry to the theme parks, the most useful and compelling benefit of all, was terminated by Disney after a run of almost a decade. Given the convenient proximity of non-Disney hotels, the demise of the early-entry privilege makes Disney lodging decidedly less attractive to visitors with cars.

Here are the remaining benefits and what they mean:

1. Convenience   If you don't have a car, the commute to the theme parks is short via the Disney Transportation System. This is especially advantageous if you stay in one of the hotels connected by the monorail or boat service. If you have a car, however, there are dozens of hotels outside Disney World that are within 5 to 10 minutes of theme-park parking lots.

2. Baby-sitting and Childcare Options   A number of options for baby-sitting, childcare, and children's programs are offered to Disney hotel and campground guests. Each of the resort hotels connected by the monorail, as well as several other Disney hotels, offer "clubs," or themed childcare centers, where potty-trained children ages 3–12 can stay while the adults go out.

Though somewhat expensive, the clubs do a great job and are highly regarded by children and parents. On the negative side, they're open only in the evening and not all Disney hotels have them. If you're staying at a

Disney hotel that doe not have a childcare club, you're better off using one of the private in-room baby-sitting services (pages 277–278). In-room baby-sitting is also available at hotels outside Disney World.

3. Guaranteed Theme-Park Admissions   On days of unusually heavy attendance, Disney resort guests are guaranteed admission to the theme parks. In practice, no guest is ever turned away until a theme park's parking lot is full. When this happens, that park most certainly will be packed to the point of gridlock. Under such conditions, you would have to lack the common sense of an amoeba to exercise your guaranteed-admission privilege. The privilege, by the way, doesn't extend to the swimming parks, Blizzard Beach, Typhoon Lagoon, or River Country.

4. Children Sharing a Room with Their Parents   There is no extra charge per night for children younger than 18 sharing a room with their parents. Many hotels outside Disney World also observe this practice.

5. Free Parking   Disney resort guests with cars don't have to pay for parking in the theme-park lots. This privilege saves about $6 per day.

6. Recreational Privileges   Disney resort guests get preferential treatment for tee times at the golf courses.

Removing early entry to the theme parks pretty much torpedoed the incentive package Disney has used for years to lure guests to its resorts. Location still counts, however. It's a pleasure to zip to the entrance of the Magic Kingdom on the monorail or simply walk to Epcot from your hotel. And then there are the handful of Disney resorts that are so unique that incentives really don't matter. Chief among these are the Animal Kingdom Lodge and the Wilderness Lodge. These hotels are so wonderfully exotic that the loss of early entry seems somehow inconsequential.

Staying in or out of the World: Weighing the Pros and Cons

1. Cost   If cost is a primary consideration, you'll lodge much less expensively outside Disney World. Our ratings of hotel quality and cost (pages 204–213) compare specific hotels both in and out of the World.

2. Ease of Access   Even if you stay in Disney World, you're dependent on some mode of transportation. It may be less stressful to use the Disney transportation system, but with the single exception of commuting to the Magic Kingdom, the fastest, most efficient, and most flexible way to get around is usually a car. If you're at Epcot, for example, and want to take the kids back to Disney's Grand Floridian Beach Resort for a nap, forget the monorail. You'll get back much faster in your own car.

A reader from Raynham, Massachusetts, who stayed at the Caribbean Beach Resort (and liked it very much) writes:

Even though the resort is on the Disney bus line, I recommend renting a car if
it fits one's budget. The buses do not go directly to many destinations and
often you have to switch at the Transportation and Ticket Center. Getting a
[bus] seat in the morning is no problem [because] they allow standees. Get-
ting a bus back to the hotel after a hard day can mean a long wait in line.

It must be said that the Disney transportation system, particularly the
bus system, is about as efficient as humanly possible. No matter where
you're going, you rarely wait more than 15–20 minutes for a bus, monorail, or boat. Although it is only for the use and benefit of Disney guests,
it nonetheless *is* public transportation and users must expect the incon-
veniences inherent in any transportation system: conveyances that arrive
and depart on their schedule, not yours; the occasional need to transfer;
multiple stops; time lost loading and unloading large numbers of passengers; and, generally, the challenge of understanding and using a large,
complex transportation network.

If you plan to have a car, consider this: Walt Disney World is so large
that some destinations within the World can be reached more quickly from
off-property hotels than from Disney hotels. For example, guests at hotels
and motels on US 192 (near the so-called Walt Disney World main
entrance) are closer to Disney-MGM Studios, the Animal Kingdom, and
Blizzard Beach water park than guests at many hotels inside Disney World.

A Kentucky dad overruled his family about staying at a Disney resort
and was glad he did:

My wife read in another guidebook that it can take two hours to commute to
the parks if you stay outside Walt Disney World. What nonsense! I guess it
could take two hours if you stayed in Tampa, but from our hotel on [US]
192 we could commute to any of the parks except the Magic Kingdom,
and have at least one ride under our belt in about an hour. We found out
later that the writer of the other guidebook is a writer for Disney Magazine.

3. Young Children   Although the hassle of commuting to most outside-
World hotels is only slightly (if at all) greater than that of commuting to
Disney hotels, a definite peace of mind results from staying in Walt Disney World. The salient point, regardless where you stay, is to make sure
you get your young children back to the hotel for a nap each day.

4. Splitting Up   If you're in a party that probably will split up to tour
(as frequently happens in families with children of widely varying ages),
staying in the World offers more transportation options and, thus, more
independence. Mom and Dad can take the car and return to the hotel for
a relaxed dinner and early bedtime while the teens remain in the park for
evening parades and fireworks.

5. Feeding the Army of the Potomac   If you have a large crew that chows down like cattle on a finishing lot, you may do better staying outside the World, where food is far less expensive.

6. Visiting Other Orlando-Area Attractions   If you will visit Sea-World, Kennedy Space Center, Universal Studios, or other area attractions, it may be more convenient to stay outside the World.

The Disney Resorts

Disney Resorts 101

Before making any decisions, there are a few basics to grasp regarding the Disney resorts.

1. Resort Classifications   Disney loves to categorize, so it's not surprising that they have developed a hierarchy of resort classifications. Deluxe Resorts are Disney's top-of-the-line hotels. Home Away From Home resorts offer suite accommodations, some with full kitchens. Many of these resorts equal or surpass the Deluxe Resorts in quality while others are actually attached to a Deluxe Resort. Moderate Resorts are a step down in guest room quality, amenities, and, of course, cost. Anchoring the bottom of the list are the so-called Value Resorts with smaller guest rooms, limited amenities, and the lowest rates of any Disney-owned hotels. Finally, there is the Fort Wilderness Campground, which offers, in addition to campsites, fully equipped Home Away From Home vacation cabins.

DISNEY RESORT CATEGORIES—PRICES AND AMENITIES

Value $77–$124	Moderate $133–$219	Home Away from Home $224–$990	Deluxe $194–$815
Food courts	Food courts	Food courts	Food courts
Snack bars	Snack bars	Snack bars	Snack bars
Lounges/Bars	Lounges/Bars	Lounges/Bars	Lounges/Bars
Pools	Pools	Pools	Pools
Playgrounds	Playgrounds	Playgrounds	Playgrounds
	Bell services	Bell services	Bell services
	Whirlpools	Whirlpools	Whirlpools
	Table-service dining	Table-service dining	Table-service dining
	Water sports	Water sports	Water sports
		Beach	Beach
		Fine dining	Fine dining
		Room service	Room service
		Character breakfasts	Character breakfasts

DISNEY RESORT CATEGORIES—PRICES AND AMENITIES (continued)

Value $77–$124	Moderate $133–$219	Home Away from Home $224–$990	Deluxe $194–$815
		Powerboat rental	Powerboat rental
		Fishing	Fishing
		Valet parking	Valet parking
		Kids' programs	Kids' programs
		Tennis courts	Tennis courts
		Walking/jogging paths	Walking/jogging paths
		Fitness center/spa	Fitness center/spa *
		Kitchens/kitchenettes	Concierge service
			Monorail access
			Closest to parks
			Larger rooms
			Suites

* except Polynesian Resort

2. Making Reservations Whether you book through your travel agent, online, with a tour operator, through an organization like AAA, or through Disney directly, you will save by booking the room exclusive of any vacation package. In travel industry parlance, this is called buying "room only." Though we'll scrutinize later in this chapter the advantages and disadvantages of buying a package, we'll tell you now that Walt Disney World packages almost never save you money.

In dealing directly with Disney for "room only," call Disney's Central Reservations Office (CRO) at (407) W-DISNEY instead of the Walt Disney Travel Company. Though the Walt Disney Travel Company can sell "room only," it specializes in vacation packages and offers less attractive payment and cancellation terms than the Central Reservations Office.

Understand that the CRO and Walt Disney Travel Company representatives do not possess detailed personal knowledge of the resorts. If you need information of a special nature, call the resort directly, ask for the front desk, and pose your question before phoning the CRO. If your desired dates are not available, keep calling back. Travelers change their plans all the time so something might open up.

3. A Most Confusing View Rates at Disney hotels vary from season to season (discussed in the next section) and from room to room according to view. To keep its guests guessing, each Disney resort has its own seasonal calendar. Seasons such as "Regular, Value, Peak, and Holiday" come and go and come again at the whim of the resort with little or no coordination with the other resorts or with that tired old January-to-December calendar the rest of us use. But confusing as the Disney seasons are, they're logic personified compared to the panoply of guest-room views offered by the Disney resorts. Depending on the particular resort, you can choose from among Standard Views, Water Views, Parking Lot Views, Pool Views, Lagoon Views, Garden Views, and Savanna Views, among others.

Standard View, the most ambiguous category, crops up at about three-fourths of the Disney resorts. It is usually interpreted as a view that does not fit any of the other view classifications offered by that hotel. At the Animal Kingdom Lodge, for example, you have Savanna Views, Water Views, and Standard Views. Savanna Views overlook the replicated African savanna, Water Views look out onto the swimming pool area, and Standard Views offer stunning vistas of other stuff, whatever it might be.

At least, however, with a standard view you can pinpoint what you won't be seeing. With Water Views every resort has a different definition. According to the Assistant General Manager at the Grand Floridian, for example, a Water View is a direct, unobstructed, frontal view of the Seven Seas Lagoon. Views of swimming pools don't count, nor do views of the Lagoon where you have to look sideways. If the Grand Floridian sells you a Water View room, by George, you're going to see some water.

Zip over to the Yacht Club Resort, another Deluxe property, and the definition of Water View is completely different. Like the Grand Floridian, the Yacht Club is situated on a lake, but booking a Water View room doesn't guarantee you'll ever see the lake. At the Yacht Club anything wet counts, whether it's right in front of you, or so far to the side you have to crane your neck. If somehow you can catch a glimpse of the lake, a creek, or a swimming pool, you've got a water view.

Our favorite is the Contemporary Resort. Emanating out toward Bay Lake from the giant A-frame are two "Garden Buildings." Some of the best lake views in all of Walt Disney World can be had from rooms in these three-story buildings. Many of these rooms are so close to the water you could spit a prune seed into the lake from your room. So guess what they call the views from those rooms? Garden Views.

We could go on and on, but pinning Disney down on what precisely will be outside your window is the main point. In our discussion of the individual Disney resorts later in this chapter we'll tell which rooms have the good views.

4. How to Get the Room You Want   Disney won't guarantee a specific room when you book, but will post your request on your reservations record and try to accommodate you. Our experience indicates that if you give them your first, second, and third choices, you'll probably get one of the three.

When speaking to the Disney agent, it's important to be specific. Port Orleans Resort, for example, offers either standard or water-view rooms.

Water view could mean either a view of the river or a swimming-pool view. If you want a room overlooking the river, say so, do likewise if you want a view of the pool. Similarly, be sure to clearly state such preferences as a particular floor, a corner room, a room close to restaurants, a room away from elevators and ice machines, a nonsmoking room, a room with a certain type of balcony, or any other preference. If you have a laundry list of preferences, type it up in order of importance, and e-mail, fax, or mail it to the Disney Central Reservations Office. Be sure to include your own contact information and your reservation confirmation number. If it makes you feel better, call back in a couple of days to make sure your preferences were posted to your reservations record.

We'll provide the info needed for each resort to frame your requests, including a resort layout map and our recommendations for specific rooms or buildings. When we discuss guest rooms, we'll use "to" to indicate a range of rooms. Thus "rooms 2230 to 2260" refers to the 31 rooms within that range. Sometimes we'll specify even or odd number rooms within a range, for example "odd numbered rooms 631 to 639." In this case we're referring to rooms 631, 633, 635, 637, and 639, eliminating intervening even-number rooms. For the sake of brevity, we may from time to time refer to "rooms 15-11, 22, 31, and 40." In this instance, "15-" is a numerical prefix that applies to all of the rooms listed. Thus the actual room numbers are 1511, 1522, 1531, and 1540.

How to Get Discounts on Lodging at Walt Disney World

There are so many guest rooms in and around Walt Disney World that competition is brisk, and everyone, including Disney, wheels and deals to keep them filled. This has led to a more flexible discount policy for Disney World hotels. Here are tips for getting price breaks:

1. Seasonal Savings   You can save from $15 to $50 per night on a Walt Disney World hotel room by scheduling your visit during the slower times of the year. However, Disney uses so many adjectives (regular, holiday, peak, value, etc.) to describe its seasonal calendar, that it's hard to keep up without a scorecard. To confuse matters more, the dates for each "season" vary from resort to resort. Our advice: if you're set on staying at a Disney resort, obtain a copy of the Walt Disney Travel Company Walt Disney World Vacations Brochure, described on page 21.

If you have a hard time getting a copy of the brochure, forget trying to find the various seasonal dates on the Walt Disney World website. Easier by far is to check them out on the Disney-independent **mousesavers. com** site described in Number 4 below.

Understand that Disney seasonal dates are not sequential like spring, summer, fall, and winter. That would be way too simple. For any specific resort, there is often four or more seasonal changes in a month. This is important, because your room rate per night will be determined by the season prevailing when you check in. As an example, let's say that you check into the Animal Kingdom Lodge on April 19th for a five-night stay. April 19th is in the more expensive Peak season that ends on April 20th, followed by the less pricey Regular season beginning on April 21st. Because you arrived during Peak season, the Peak season rate will be applied during your entire stay even though more than half of your stay was in Regular season. Your strategy, therefore, is to shift your dates (if possible) to arrive during a less expensive season.

2. Ask about Specials When you talk to Disney reservationists, inquire specifically about special deals. Ask, for example, "What special rates or discounts are available at Disney hotels during the time of our visit?" Being specific and assertive paid off for an Illinois reader:

I called Disney's reservations number and asked for availability and rates.... [Because] of the Unofficial Guide warning about Disney reservationists answering only the questions posed, I specifically asked, "Are there any special rates or discounts for that room during the month of October?" She replied, "Yes, we have that room available at a special price...." [For] the price of one phone call, I saved $440.

Along similar lines, a Warren, New Jersey, dad chimed in with this:

Your tip about asking Disney employees about discounts was invaluable. They will not volunteer this information, but by asking we saved almost $500 on our hotel room using a AAA discount. Also by asking, we got to ride in the front of the monorail, which thrilled our 10-year-old son (and his dad).

3. "Trade-Up" or "Upsell" Rates If you request a room at a Disney value resort and none are available, you may be offered a room in the next category up (moderate resorts, in this example) at a discounted price. Similarly, if you ask for a room in a moderate resort and none are available, Disney will usually offer a good deal at a Home-Away-From-Home rooms or a Deluxe resort. You can angle for a Trade-Up rate by asking for a resort category that is more likely to be sold out. In most of 2002, because of some hotel closings, there was a limited availability of rooms at the moderate resorts. Several readers have reported success in scoring a bargain room at a deluxe resort by requesting accommodations at the Disney Institute, which was closed in 2002 and is supposedly to remain closed for two years.

4. Know the Secret Code The folks at **www.mousesavers.com** keep an updated list of discounts and reservation codes for use at Disney resorts. The codes are separated into categories such as "For anyone," "For residents of certain states," "For annual passport holders," and so on. For example, the site listed code "CVZ," published in an ad in some Spanish-language newspapers and magazines, offering a rate of $65 per night for Disney's All-Star Resorts from April 22 through August 8 and $49 per night from August 9 through October 3. Dozens of discounts are usually listed on the site, covering almost all Disney resort hotels. Anyone calling the Disney central reservations office (call (407) W-DIS-NEY) can use a current code and get the discounted rate.

The site also features a great links page with short descriptions and URLs of the best Disney-related websites, and a current-year seasonal rates calendar for each of the Disney resorts.

5. Expedia   Online travel seller Expedia (**expedia.com**) has established an active market in discounting Disney hotels. Most discounts are in the 15–25% range but can go as deep as 45%.

6. Walt Disney World Website   Disney has become more aggressive about offering deals on its website. Go to **disneyworld.disney.go.com** and click on the brown box marked "Vacation Savings" in the upper left. Rooms in all resort categories were sold in 2002 at discounts of up to 42% off rack rates. You must click on the "Vacation Savings" box to get the discounts. If you click on "Reservations & Tickets" in the upper right corner you'll be charged full rack rate with never a mention of discounts being available. Finally, be aware that you must cancel reservations *for rooms sold at discount* 46 days prior to arrival if you want a full refund. Reservations booked on the site through "Reservations & Tickets" must be cancelled six days prior to arrival. In any event, before booking rooms on Disney's or any other site, be sure to click on "Terms and Conditions" and read the fine print before making reservations.

7. Annual Passholder Discounts   Annual Passholders are eligible for a broad range of discounts on dining, shopping, and lodging. If you visit Walt Disney World once a year or more, of if you plan on a visit of five or more days, you might save money overall by purchasing annual passes. During 2002 we saw resort discounts as deep as 35% for annual passholders. It doesn't take long to recoup the extra bucks for an annual pass when you're saving that kind of money on lodging. Discounts in the 10–15% range are more the norm.

8. Ocala Disney Information Center   The Ocala Disney Information Center off I-75 in Ocala, Florida, routinely books Disney hotel rooms at discounts of up to 43%! The discounts are offered as an incentive to walk-in travelers who may not have considered lodging at a Disney property or even going to Disney World. The number of rooms available varies according to date and season, but you almost always can count on getting a good deal. Because the program is designed to snare uncommitted travelers, you must reserve your room in person at the center. If you call in advance and tell staffers you're on your way down, however, they usually will tell you what's available and at what discount. The phone number is (352) 854-0770. You can also arrange priority seating for dining. The center is open daily from 9 a.m. to 6 p.m.

9. Travel Agents Once ineligible for commissions on Disney bookings, travel agents now are active players and particularly good sources of information on time-limited special programs and discounts. In our opinion, a good travel agent is the best friend a traveler can have. And though we at the *Unofficial Guide* know a thing or two about the travel industry, we always give our agent a chance to beat any deal we find. If our agent can't beat the deal, we let her book it anyway if it's commissionable. We create, in other words, a relationship that gives her plenty of incentive to really roll up her sleeves and work on our behalf.

10. The Disney Club The Disney Club (The Disney Club has replaced the Magic Kingdom Club) is offered as a benefit by employers, credit unions, and organizations. Membership provides periodic, time-limited discounts on Disney lodging and a 3–5% discount on theme-park tickets, among other things. Ask your personnel department if this benefit is provided. Persons not signed up through work can buy a one-year family Disney Club card for about $40, additional cards $10. Outside the US and Canada $60. For information, contact:

The Disney Club
P.O. Box 4763
Shawnee Mission, KS 66201-9273
(800) 654-6347
www.disneyclub.com

A dad from Bay Minette, Alabama, chastised us for not giving the card its due:

> You didn't say much about the [Disney Club]. We went again in late September. It was really crowded. We bought the [Disney Club] card and saved $300–400 on our rooms and tickets.

Another pleased Disney Club card holder wrote, suggesting:

> Contrive to emphasize the [Disney Club] card. Between the vacation package and rental car, I estimate I saved about $600–700.

Note that the benefits of the Disney Club card are not as good as those of its predecessor, the Magic Kingdom Club Gold Card, especially in regard to discounts at Disney hotels. With the Disney Club card, discounts are available for only about half the hotels, and then only for certain dates.

11. Organizations and Auto Clubs   Eager to sell rooms, Disney has developed time-limited programs with some auto clubs and other organizations. Recently, for example, AAA members were offered a 10–20% savings on Disney hotels, preferred parking at the theme parks, and discounts on Disney package vacations. Such deals come and go, but the market suggests there will be more in the future. If you're a member of AARP, AAA, or any travel or auto club, ask whether the group has a program before shopping elsewhere.

12. Room Upgrades   Sometimes, a room upgrade is as good as a discount. If you're visiting Disney World during a slower time, book the least expensive room your discounts will allow. Checking in, ask very politely about being upgraded to a "water-" or "pool-view" room. A fair percentage of the time, you'll get one at no additional charge.

13. Extra-Night Discounts   During slower times, book your Disney hotel for half the period you intend to stay. Often, the hotel will offer extra nights at a discounted rate to get you to stay longer.

14. Military Discounts   The Shades of Green Armed Forces Recreation Center, located near the Grand Floridian Resort, offers luxury accommodations at rates based on the serviceman's rank. Shades of Green, however, will be closed for renovation until September 2003, when it will reopen with more than double the original number of guest rooms. While Shades of Green is closed, active duty and retired military, as well as DOD personnel, can take advantage of comparable rates at Disney's Contemporary Resort. For rates and other information see **www.shadesofgreen.org** or call (888) 593-2242.

Walt Disney World Lodging

The Grand Floridian, Polynesian, Contemporary, Wilderness Lodge and Villas, and Shades of Green Resorts are near the Magic Kingdom. The Walt Disney World Swan and Dolphin Hotels, the Yacht and Beach Club Resorts, and Disney's BoardWalk Inn and Villas are near Epcot. The Villas at the Disney Institute (formerly the Disney Institute Resort) are on the far northeast side of Walt Disney World. The All-Star, Coronado Springs, and Animal Kingdom Lodge Resorts occupy a similar position on the far southwest side. Centrally located are the Caribbean Beach Resort and Disney's Pop Century Resort. Along Bonnet Creek, the Old Key West and Port Orleans Resorts also offer a central location.

WHAT IT COSTS TO STAY IN A DISNEY RESORT HOTEL	
Grand Floridian	$329–$1,690
Polynesian Resort	$304–$650
Animal Kingdom Lodge	$204–$875

Swan (Westin)	$295–$465
Dolphin (Sheraton)	$295–$465
Beach Club Resort	$289–$990
Yacht Club Resort	$289–$735
BoardWalk Inn	$289–$776
BoardWalk Villas	$289–$1,865
Contemporary Resort	$234–$650
Wilderness Lodge and Villas	$269–$920
Old Key West Resort	$254–$359 (studio)
Fort Wilderness Cabin	$224–$314
Coronado Springs Resort	$133–$418
Caribbean Beach Resort	$133–$219
Port Orleans Resort	$133–$219
All-Star Resorts	$77–$124
Pop Century Resorts	$77–$124

WHAT IT COSTS TO STAY IN THE DISNEY VILLAGE HOTEL PLAZA

DoubleTree Guest Suites Resort	$200–$300
The Hilton Resort	$195–$659
Wyndham Palace	$170–$210
Hotel Royal Plaza	$170–$210
Courtyard by Marriott	$160–$180
Grosvenor Resort	$135–$220
Best Western Hotel	$120–$140

Choosing a Walt Disney World Hotel

If you want to stay in Walt Disney World but don't know which hotel to choose, consider:

1. Cost   First, look at your budget. Rooms start at about $80 a night at the All-Star and Pop Century Resorts and top out near $775 at the Grand Floridian. Suites are more expensive.

The BoardWalk Villas, Wilderness Lodge Villas, Old Key West Resort, and Beach Club Villas offer condo-type accommodations with one-, two-, and three-bedroom units complete with kitchens, living rooms, VCRs, and washers and dryers. Prices range from about $295 per night for a one-bedroom villa at the Beach Club to more than $1,150 per night for a three-bedroom villa at the BoardWalk Villas. Fully equipped cabins at Fort Wilderness Resort and Campground cost $224–314 per night. A limited number of suites are available at the more expensive Disney resorts, but they don't have kitchens.

Also at Disney World are the seven hotels of the Disney Village Hotel Plaza. Although commodious, rooms in these hotels are sometimes more expensive than at hotels served by the monorail. We find few bargains at the Village Hotel Plaza and feel less of the excitement one has when staying inside the World. While the Village Hotel Plaza is technically part of Disney World, staying there is like visiting a colony rather than the mother country. Free parking at the theme parks isn't offered, and the hotels operate their own buses rather than use Disney transportation.

Not included in these rankings or in the following discussion is Shades of Green, formerly known as the Disney Inn. Shades of Green was purchased by the U.S. Department of Defense in 1994 for the exclusive use of active-duty and retired servicemen and women. Rates at Shades of Green, one of the nicest Disney World hotels, are based on the guest's rank: the higher the rank, the greater the cost. All rooms, however, regardless of rank, go for a fraction of what military personnel would pay at other Disney resorts. According to a serviceman from Fort Worth, Texas, Shades of Green is the way to go:

Shades of Green is the best-kept secret in Disney. It is actually a [military] resort in the Disney complex with all the benefits of being a Disney resort. It was a great deal, and military members usually look for the best deals. When my wife and I stayed there in May, we paid $58 a night. That is not per person. That was the total price. The price will vary according to your rank. The hotel was very nice. The rooms were huge. It had two double beds and a lot of room to spare. They also had VCRs in the rooms and a movie vending machine on the second floor. Shades of Green is right across the street from the Polynesian Resort. It is about a 10–15 minute walk to the Ticket and Transportation Center. The hotel does have shuttle buses that take you to the TTC (about a two-minute ride.) Our overall stay at Shades of Green was wonderful. I would highly recommend this hotel to anyone who is eligible to use it.

2. Location   Once you have determined your budget, think about what you want to do at Walt Disney World. Will you go to all four theme parks, or will you concentrate on one or two?

If you intend to use your own car, the location of your Disney hotel isn't especially important unless you plan to spend most of your time at the Magic Kingdom. (Disney transportation is always more efficient than your car in this case because it bypasses the Transportation and Ticket Center and deposits you at the theme-park entrance.) If you haven't decided whether you want a car for your Disney vacation, see "How to Travel Around the World" (page 314).

Most convenient to the Magic Kingdom are the three resorts linked by monorail: the Grand Floridian, Contemporary, and Polynesian. Commuting to the Magic Kingdom via monorail is quick and simple, allowing visitors to return to their hotel for a nap, swim, or meal.

The Contemporary Resort, in addition to being on the monorail, is only a 10–15 minute walk to the Magic Kingdom. Contemporary Resort guests reach Epcot by monorail but must transfer at the Transportation and Ticket Center. Buses connect the Contemporary to Disney-MGM Studios and the Animal Kingdom. No transfer is required, but the bus makes several stops before heading to either destination.

The Polynesian Resort is served by the Magic Kingdom monorail and is an easy walk from the Transportation and Ticket Center, Disney World's transportation hub. At the transportation center you can catch an express monorail to Epcot. This makes the Polynesian the only Disney resort with direct monorail access to both Epcot and the Magic Kingdom. To minimize your walk to the transportation center, book a room in the Pago Pago, Moorea, or Oahu guest buildings.

Most convenient to Epcot and Disney-MGM Studios are the BoardWalk Inn, BoardWalk Villas, Yacht and Beach Club Resorts, Beach Club Villas, and Swan and Dolphin. Though all are within easy walking distance of Epcot's International Gateway, boat service is also available. Vessels also connect Epcot hotels to Disney-MGM Studios. Epcot hotels are best for guests planning to spend most of their time at Epcot or Disney-MGM Studios.

If you plan to use Disney transportation and intend to visit all four major parks and one or more of the swimming theme parks, book a centrally located resort with good transportation connections. The Epcot resorts and the Polynesian, Caribbean Beach, Pop Century, and Port Orleans Resorts fit the bill. Old Key West Resort is centrally located but offers only limited bus service between noon and 6 p.m.

Though not centrally located, the All-Star, Coronado Springs, and Animal Kingdom Lodge Resorts have very good bus service to all Disney World destinations and are closest to the Animal Kingdom theme park. Wilderness Lodge and Villas and Fort Wilderness Campground have the most convoluted transportation service.

If you plan to golf, book the Villas at the Disney Institute (closed indefinitely) or the Old Key West Resort. Both resorts are built around golf courses. Shades of Green, the armed forces recreation center, is adjacent to two golf courses. Located near but not on a golf course are the Grand Floridian, Polynesian, and Port Orleans Resorts. For boating and water sports, try the Polynesian, Contemporary, or Grand Floridian Resorts or Wilderness Lodge and Villas. The Lodge is also the best hotel for hikers, bikers, and joggers.

3. Room Quality Few Walt Disney World guests spend much time in their hotel rooms, though they're among the best designed and most well appointed anywhere. Plus, they're meticulously maintained. Top of the line are the spacious and luxurious rooms of the Grand Floridian. Bringing up the rear are the small, garish rooms of the All-Star Resorts. But even these are sparkling clean and livable.

Here's how the Disney hotels (along with the Swan and the Dolphin, which are Westin and Sheraton hotels, respectively) stack up for quality:

Hotel	Room Quality Rating
1. Grand Floridian Beach Resort	96
2. BoardWalk Inn	93
3. Beach Club Resort	92
4. Yacht Club Resort	92
5. Old Key West Resort (studio)	92
6. BoardWalk Villas (studio)	91
7. Wilderness Lodge Villas (studio)	91
8. Animal Kingdom Lodge	90
9. Polynesian Resort	88
10. Contemporary Resort	87
11. Dolphin (Sheraton)	86
12. Swan (Westin)	86
13. Wilderness Lodge	86
14. Coronado Springs Resort	83
15. Port Orleans Resort	81
16. Caribbean Beach Resort	76
17. Pop Century Resorts	74
18. All-Star Resorts	73

4. The Size of Your Group   Larger families and groups may be interested in how many persons can be accommodated in a Disney resort room, but only Lilliputians would be comfortable in a room filled to capacity. Groups requiring two or more guest rooms should consider condo/villa accommodations, either in or out of Walt Disney World. The most cost-efficient lodging in Walt Disney World for groups of five or six persons are the cabins at Fort Wilderness Campground. Both sleep six adults plus a child or toddler in a crib. If there are more than six in your party, you will need either two hotel rooms, a suite, or a condo.

Hotel	Maximum Number of Persons per Room
All-Star Resorts	4 persons plus child in crib
Animal Kingdom Lodge	4 persons plus child in crib
Beach Club Resort and Villas	5 persons plus child in crib
BoardWalk Inn	4 or 5 persons plus child in crib
BoardWalk Villas	Up to 8 persons plus child in crib

Hotel	Maximum Number of Persons per Room
Caribbean Beach Resort	4 persons plus child in crib
Contemporary Resort	5 persons plus child in crib
Coronado Springs Resort	4 persons plus child in crib
Dolphin (Sheraton)	5 persons
Fort Wilderness Homes	6 persons plus child in crib
Grand Floridian Beach Resort	4 or 5 persons plus child in crib
Old Key West Resort	Up to 8 persons plus child in crib
Polynesian Resort	5 persons plus child in crib
Pop Century Resorts	4 persons plus child in crib
Port Orleans Resort	4 persons plus child in crib; 5 persons in room with child's trundle bed
Swan (Westin)	4 persons
Wilderness Lodge	4 persons plus child in crib; junior suites with bunk beds accommodate 6 persons
Wilderness Lodge Villas	Up to 8 persons plus child in crib
Yacht Club Resort	5 persons plus child in crib

5. Theme   All of the Disney hotels are themed. Each is designed to make you feel you're in a special place or period of history. Here are the themes at Disney resorts:

Hotel	Theme
All-Star Resorts	Sports, music, and movies
Animal Kingdom Lodge	African game preserve
Beach Club Resort and Villas	New England beach club of the 1870s
BoardWalk Inn	East Coast boardwalk hotel of the early 1900s
BoardWalk Villas	East Coast beach cottage of the early 1900s
Caribbean Beach Resort	Caribbean islands
Contemporary Resort	The future as perceived by past and present generations
Coronado Springs Resort	Northern Mexico and the American Southwest
Dolphin (Sheraton)	Modern Florida resort
Grand Floridian Beach Resort	Turn-of-the-century luxury hotel
Old Key West Resort	Key West
Polynesian Resort	Hawaii/South Sea islands
Pop Century Resorts	Icons from various decades of the twentieth century
Port Orleans	Turn-of-the-century New Orleans and Mardi Gras
Swan (Westin)	Modern Florida resort
Villas at the Disney Institute	Combination rustic villas and country club atmosphere
Wilderness Lodge and Villas	National park grand lodge of the early 1900s in the American northwest
Yacht Club Resort	New England seashore hotel of the 1880s

Some resorts carry off their themes better than others, and some themes are more exciting. The Wilderness Lodge and Villas, for example, is extraordinary. The lobby opens eight stories to a timbered ceiling supported by giant columns of bundled logs. One look eases you into the Northwest-wilderness theme. Romantic and isolated, the lodge is a great choice for couples and seniors, and is heaven for children.

The Animal Kingdom Lodge replicates the grand safari lodges of Kenya and Tanzania and overlooks its own private African game preserve. By far the most exotic of the Disney resorts, it's made to order for couples on a romantic getaway as well as for families with children. The Polynesian, likewise dramatic, conveys the feeling of the Pacific Islands. It's great for romantics and families. Many waterfront rooms offer a perfect view of Cinderella Castle and the Magic Kingdom fireworks across Seven Seas Lagoon.

Grandeur, nostalgia, and privilege are central to the Grand Floridian and Yacht and Beach Club Resorts and the BoardWalk Inn and Villas. Although modeled after eastern-seaboard hotels of different eras, the resorts are amazingly similar. Thematic distinctions are subtle and are lost on many guests.

The Port Orleans Resort lacks the mystery and sultriness of the New Orleans French Quarter, but it's hard to replicate the Big Easy in a sanitized Disney version. Old Key West Resort, however, hits the mark with its Florida Keys theme. The Caribbean Beach Resort's theme is much more effective at night, thanks to creative lighting. By day, the resort looks like a Miami condo development.

Coronado Springs Resort offers several styles of Mexican and Southwestern American architecture. Though the lake setting is lovely and the resort is attractive and inviting, the theme (with the exception of the main swimming area) isn't especially stimulating. Coronado Springs feels more like a Scottsdale, Arizona, country club than a Disney resort.

The All-Star Resorts encompass 30 three-story, T-shaped hotels with almost 6,000 guest rooms. There are 15 themed areas: five celebrate sports (surfing, basketball, tennis, football, and baseball), five recall Hollywood movie themes, and five have musical motifs. The resort's design, with entrances shaped like giant dalmations, Coke cups, footballs, and the like, is pretty adolescent, sacrificing grace and beauty for energy and novelty. Guest rooms are small, with decor reminiscent of your teenage son's bedroom. Despite the theme, there are no sports, music, or movies at the All-Star Resorts. The new Pop Century Resort is pretty much a clone of the All-Star Resorts, only this time the giant icons are symbolic of particular decades of the twentieth Century. Expect giant Big Wheels, 45 rpm records, silhouettes of people doing period dances, etc.

Pretense aside, the Contemporary, Swan, and Dolphin are essentially themeless though architecturally interesting. The Contemporary is a 15-

story, A-frame building with monorails running through the middle. Views from guest rooms in the Contemporary Tower are among the best at Disney World. The Swan and Dolphin Resorts are massive yet whimsical. Designed by Michael Graves, they're excellent examples of "entertainment architecture." Unfortunately, a little too much whimsy and entertainment worked their way into the guest rooms, which are "busy," bordering on garish.

6. Dining   The best resorts for quality and selection in dining are the Epcot resorts: Swan, Dolphin, Yacht, and Beach Club Resorts, Beach Club Villas, and BoardWalk Inn and Villas. Each has good restaurants and is within easy walking distance of the others and of the ten ethnic restaurants in the World Show-case section of Epcot. If you stay at an Epcot resort, you have 21 of Walt Disney World's finest restaurants within a 5- to 12-minute walk.

The only other place in Disney World where restaurants and hotels are similarly concentrated is at the Disney Village Hotel Plaza. In addition to restaurants in the hotels themselves, the Hilton, Courtyard by Marriott, Grosvenor Resort, and Wyndham Palace are within walking distance of restaurants at Downtown Disney.

Guests at the Contemporary, Polynesian, and Grand Floridian can eat in their hotel, or they can commute to restaurants in the Magic Kingdom (not recommended) or in other monorail-linked hotels. Riding the monorail to another hotel or to the Magic Kingdom takes about ten minutes each way, not counting the wait for the train.

All of the other Disney resorts are somewhat isolated. This means you're stuck dining at your hotel unless (1) you have a car and can go anywhere you like or (2) you eat your meals at the theme parks or Downtown Disney.

Here's the deal. Disney transportation works fine for commuting from hotels to the theme parks and Downtown Disney, but it's hopeless for getting from one hotel to another. If you're staying at Port Orleans and want to dine at the Swan, forget it. It can take you up to an hour and a half each way by bus. You could take a bus to the Magic Kingdom and catch a train to one of the monorail-served hotels for dinner. That would take "only" 45 minutes each way.

Of the more isolated resorts, the Wilderness Lodge and Villas and Animal Kingdom Lodge serve the best food and offer the most varied selection. The Coronado Springs, Port Orleans, Old Key West, and Caribbean Beach Resorts each have a full-service restaurant of acceptable quality, a food court, and in-room pizza delivery. None of the isolated resorts, however, offer enough variety for the average person to be happy eating in his/her hotel every day. The Pop Century Resorts and the All-Star Resorts (Disney's most isolated hotel) have nearly 6,000 guest rooms but no full-service restaurant. There are three food courts, but you have to get to them before 11 p.m.

DISNEY RESORT AMENITIES AND RECREATION

Resort	Suites	Concierge	Number of Rooms	Room Service
All-Star Resorts			5,760	
Animal Kingdom Lodge	✓	✓	1,307	✓
BoardWalk Inn	✓	✓	375	✓
BoardWalk Villas	✓		517	✓
Caribbean Beach Resort			2,112	
Contemporary Resort	✓	✓	1,041	✓
Coronado Springs Resort	✓		1,965	
Fort Wilderness Homes			410	
Grand Floridian Beach Resort	✓	✓	900	✓
Old Key West Resort	✓		709	
Polynesian Resort	✓	✓	853	✓
Pop Century Resort			5,760	
Port Orleans Resort			3,056	
Wilderness Lodge and Villas	✓		728	✓
Yacht and Beach Club Resorts	✓	✓	1,213	✓
Shades of Green		✓	287	✓
Walt Disney World Dolphin	✓	✓	1,466	✓
Walt Disney World Swan		✓	758	✓

7. Amenities and Recreation   Disney resorts offer a staggering variety of amenities and recreational opportunities. All provide elaborate swimming pools, themed shops, restaurants or food courts, bars or lounges, and access to the five Disney golf courses. Predictably, the more you pay for your lodging, the more amenities and opportunities you have. The Grand Floridian, Animal Kingdom Lodge, Yacht and Beach Club Resorts, and Swan and Dolphin, for example, offer concierge floors.

For sunning and swimming, the Contemporary, Polynesian, Wilderness Lodge and Villas, and Grand Floridian offer both pools and white-sand beaches on Bay Lake or Seven Seas Lagoon. The Caribbean Beach Resort also provides both pools and beaches. Though lacking a beach, the Animal Kingdom Lodge, Yacht and Beach Club, Port Orleans, and Coronado Springs Resorts and the BoardWalk Inn and Villas have exceptionally creative pools. Below we rate and rank the swimming facilities at each of the Disney resorts as well as for the Westin-owned Swan and Sheraton-owned Dolphin Resorts.

Fitness Center	Water Sports	Marina	Beach	Tennis	Biking
✓					
✓		✓		✓	✓
✓		✓		✓	✓
	✓	✓	✓		✓
✓	✓	✓	✓	✓	
✓	✓	✓			✓
	✓	✓	✓	✓	✓
✓		✓	✓	✓	
✓	✓	✓		✓	✓
	✓	✓	✓		
	✓	✓			✓
✓	✓	✓	✓		✓
✓	✓	✓	✓	✓	
✓				✓	
✓	✓	✓	✓	✓	
✓		✓	✓	✓	

Hotel	Pool Rating
1. Yacht and Beach Club Resorts (shared complex)	★★★★★
2. Port Orleans	★★★★½
3. Animal Kingdom Lodge	★★★★
4. BoardWalk Inn and Villas	★★★★
5. Coronado Springs Resort	★★★★
6. Polynesian Resort (renovated 2001)	★★★★
7. Wilderness Lodge and Villas	★★★★
8. Contemporary Resort	★★★½
9. Dolphin Resort	★★★½
10. Grand Floridian Resort	★★★½
11. Swan Resort	★★★½
12. All-Star Resorts	★★★
13. Caribbean Beach Resort	★★★
14. Fort Wilderness Campground	★★★
15. Old Key West Resort	★★★
16. Pop Century Resorts	★★★
17. Shades of Green	★★½

Bay Lake and the Seven Seas Lagoon are the best venues for boating. Resorts fronting these lakes are the Contemporary, Polynesian, Wilderness Lodge and Villas, Grand Floridian, and Fort Wilderness Campground. Though situated on smaller bodies of water, the Caribbean Beach, Old Key West, Port Orleans, Coronado Springs, Villas at the Disney Institute, Yacht and Beach Club, and Swan and Dolphin Resorts also rent watercraft.

Most convenient for golf and are the Shades of Green, Old Key West, Contemporary, Polynesian, Grand Floridian, and Port Orleans Resorts. Tennis is available at all of the deluxe and Home-Away-From-Home resorts, as well as at the Swan and Dolphin Resorts. Disney resorts with good fitness and weight-training facilities are rated and ranked as follows:

Hotel	Fitness Center Rating
1. Villas at the Disney Institute	★★★★★
2. Grand Floridian Resort	★★★★½
3. Animal Kingdom Lodge	★★★★
4. BoardWalk Inn and Villas	★★★★
5. Yacht and Beach Club Resorts (shared facility)	★★★★
6. Contemporary Resort	★★★½
7. Coronado Springs Resort	★★★½
8. Wilderness Lodge and Villas	★★★½
9. Dolphin Resort	★★★
10. Swan Resort	★★★
11. Old Key West Resort	★½

Resorts not listed above do not have fitness and weight-training facilities.

While there are many places you can bike or jog at Disney World (including golf-cart paths), the best biking and jogging is at the Fort Wilderness Resort and Campground and the adjacent Wilderness Lodge and Villas. Also good for biking and jogging is the area along Bonnet Creek extending through Port Orleans and the Old Key West Resorts toward Downtown Disney. The Epcot resorts offer a lakefront promenade and bike path, as well as a roadside walkway suitable for jogging.

Eight Disney resorts offer evening childcare programs on-site: the Grand Floridian, Animal Kingdom Lodge, Yacht and Beach Club, Polynesian, Wilderness Lodge and Villas, and BoardWalk Inn and Villas. All others offer in-room baby-sitting. Baby-sitting options are discussed in detail on pages 276–280

In the table nearby, we've outlined the amenities and recreational opportunities at each of the Disney resorts. Note that each resort listed also offers restaurants or snack bars, lounges/bars, pools, children's activities, baby-sitting, and shopping.

8. Nightlife The boardwalk at BoardWalk Inn and Villas has an upscale dance club, a New Orleans Pat O'Brien's–type club with dueling pianos and sing-alongs, a brew pub, and a sports bar. BoardWalk clubs are within easy walking distance of all the Epcot resorts. Similarly, some of the Villas at the Disney Institute are within walking distance of the nightlife at Downtown Disney. Nightlife at other Disney resorts is limited to lounges that stay open late. The best are Mizner's Lounge at the Grand Floridian, Kimono's at the Swan, and the California Grill Lounge on the 15th floor of the Contemporary Resort. At the California Grill Lounge, you can relax with a drink and watch the fireworks at the nearby Magic Kingdom.

9. Reader Reports Many readers share with us their experiences and criticisms regarding the Disney hotels. Some copy us on letters of complaint made directly to Disney. If you wrote or copied us about a bad experience, you might be surprised that we did not quote your letter. Any business can have a bad day, even a Disney hotel, and a single incident might not be indicative of the hotel's general level of quality and service. In our experience, if a problem is truly endemic the same complaint will usually surface in a number of letters. But even with our voluminous Disney mail, reader comments often paint a mixed picture. For example, for every letter critical of Disney's Grand Floridian, it's not unusual to receive another letter telling us it's the best place the reader ever stayed. Finally, remember that we tend to hear more often from readers when things go badly than when everything is fine. Whether your experience was positive or negative, we encourage you to write and share it with us. The more comments we receive, the more accurate and complete a picture we can provide you.

Readers' 2002 Disney Resort Report Card

Each year, several thousand readers mail or e-mail us their responses to the survey at the end of the guide. The "Report Card" below documents their opinion of the respective Disney resorts, as well as of the Swan, Dolphin, and Shades of Green Resorts. Room Quality reflects their overall level of satisfaction with their guest room. Quiet is a measure of how well their room is insulated from external noise. The Transportation Service grade rates the Disney bus, boat, and/or monorail service at their hotel. Overall Value indicates the reader's opinion of how the hotel stacks up in terms of value for the dollar. The Check-In Efficiency grade rates the speed and efficiency of the check-in process. Finally, the Overall Grade represents an average of all five grades. The new Beach Club Villas and the Pop Century Resort were not open when we went to press, hence no grades.

We would point out that the readers were pretty tough on the resorts, especially in the grades awarded for room quality. In this category, readers generally rate the guest rooms at the respective resorts lower than do the *Unofficial Guide* hotel inspectors. In assessing this difference, remember that readers are rating one guest room during a specific visit, while the *Unofficial Guide* inspectors provide a comparative rating of almost 200 Disney and non-Disney hotels in and around Walt Disney World. For *Unofficial Guide* hotel ratings see "How the Hotels Compare" on pages 203–213.

READERS' DISNEY RESORT REPORT CARD

Resort	Overall Room Quality	Transportation Efficiency	Check-In	Quiet	Service	Overall Value
All Star Movies	B	C	B	B	B	B–
All Star Music	C	B	B	C	C	C
All Star Sports	C	B	B	B	B	B–
Animal Kingdom Lodge	A	A	A	B	B	A–
Beach Club	B	B	A	C	A	B
Boardwalk Inn	B	A	A	B	B	B+
Boardwalk Villas	B	B	C	C	B	B–
Caribbean Beach Resort	B	B	A	C	C	B–
Contemporary	B	A	B	D	A	B
Coronado Springs Resort	D	C	C	D	B	C–
Dolphin	C	B	C	D	B	C
Grand Floridian	B	B	C	D	C	C
Old Key West	A	B	C	B	B	B
Polynesian	B	B	A	C	B	B
Port Orleans	C	B	B	C	B	C+
Shades of Green	A	D	B	A	A	B+
Swan	C	C	B	D	A	C+
Wilderness Lodge	C	C	C	B	B	C+
Yacht Club	B	A	A	C	A	B+

Walt Disney World Hotel Profiles

For those of you who have plowed though the foregoing and remain undecided, we provide profiles of each of the Walt Disney World resorts.

The Magic Kingdom Resorts

Disney's Grand Floridian Resort & Spa　Walt Disney World's flagship resort is inspired by the grand Victorian seaside resorts of Florida at the turn of the century. A complex of four- and five-story white frame buildings, the Grand Floridian integrates verandas, intricate laticework, dormers, and turrets beneath a red shingle roof to capture the most memorable elements of 19th-century ocean-resort architecture. A five-story domed lobby encircled by enameled balustrades and overhung by crystal chandaliers establishes the resort's tone of understated opulence. Covering 40 acres along the Seven Seas Lagoon, the resort offers lovely pools, white-sand beaches, and a multifaceted marina. The spa at the Grand Floridian is equaled only by that of the Disney Institute.

The 900 guest rooms, while luxurious with Victorian wood trim and soft-colored-print wall coverings, are warm and inviting without being stuffy or overly feminine. Armoires, marble-topped sinks, and ceiling fans maintain the Victorian theme. The typical room is 440 square feet (dormer rooms are smaller), large by any standard, and furnished with two queen beds, a daybed, a reading chair, and a table with two side chairs. Many rooms have a balcony.

With a high ratio of staff to guests, service is outstanding. There are several full-service restaurants at the Grand Floridian, with a number of

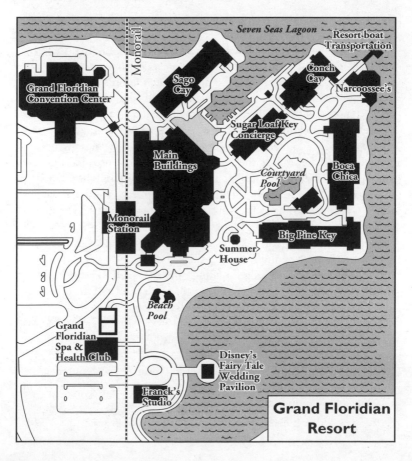

others a short monorail ride away. The resort is connected directly to the Magic Kingdom by monorail and to other Walt Disney World destinations by bus. Walking time to the monorail and bus loading areas from the most remote guest rooms is about seven to ten minutes.

GRAND FLORIDIAN BEACH RESORT

Strengths	Weaknesses
Beautiful guest rooms	Distant guest self-parking
Outstanding public areas	
On Magic Kingdom monorail	
Restaurant selection via monorail	
Excellent lounge	
Recreational options	
Fitness center and spa	
Child-care facility on site	

Good Rooms and Not So Good Rooms at the Grand Floridian   The Grand Floridian resort is spread over a peninsula jutting into the Seven Sea Lagoon. In addition to guest rooms in the main building, there are five dispersed guest room lodges. Most guest rooms have a balcony, and most of the balconies are enclosed by a rail that affords good visibility. Rooms just beneath the roof in each building, called dormer rooms, have smaller, inset, solidly enclosed balconies, which limit visibility when you are seated. Most dormer rooms, however, have vaulted ceilings and a certain coziness that compensates for the less desirable balconies.

If you want to be near the bus and monorail stations, most of the restaurants, and shopping, ask for a room in the main building. The best rooms are 4322 to 4329 and 4422 to 4429, which have full balconies and overlook the lagoon in the direction of the beach and the Polynesian Resort. Other excellent main-building rooms are 4401 to 4409, with full balconies overlooking the marina and an unobstructed view of Cinderella Castle on the opposite side of the lagoon.

Of the five rectangular lodge buildings, three (Conch Key, Boca Chica, and Big Pine Key) have one long side facing the lagoon and the other facing inner courtyards and swimming pools. At Conch Key, full-balcony rooms 7228 to 7231, 7328 to 7321, and 7425 to 7431 offer vistas across the lagoon to the Magic Kingdom and the castle. Less expensive rooms in the same building that offer good views are 72-, 73-, 74-11, 13, 15, 17, 19, 21, and 72-, 73-, 74-12 and 14 (Grand Floridian room numbers are coded: Take room 7213—7 is the building number, 2 is the floor, and 13 is the room number). In Boca Chita and Big Pine Key ask for a lagoon view room on the first, second, or third floor. Many garden-view rooms in Big Pine Key, and a few in Boca Chica, have views obstructed by a poolside building. These are the worst views of any Grand Floridian guest room.

The two remaining buildings, Sugar Loaf Key and Sago Cay, face each other across the marina. The other side of Sugar Loaf Key faces a court-yard while the opposite side of Sago Cay faces a fingerling of the lagoon and a forested area. All of these views are pleasant enough, but not in the same league as those of the rooms recommended above. Exceptions are end rooms in Sago Cay (rooms 5139, 5144, 5145, 5242 to 5245, 5342 to 5345) that have a view of the lagoon and Cinderella Castle.

Disney's Polynesian Resort The tropics of the South Pacific are re-created at this deluxe Walt Disney World resort. The Polynesian is composed of 11 two- and three-story Hawaiian "longhouses" situated around the four-story "Great Ceremonial House." The buildings at the Polynesian feature natural wood tones, with exposed-beam roofs and tribal-inspired geometric inlays in the cornices. The Great Ceremonial House contains restaurants, shops, and a rain-forest atrium lobby. With a rocky waterfall and over 70 species of tropical plants, the lobby reinforces the lush, verdant image of the South Seas. Spread over many acres along the Seven Seas Lagoon, the resort has a white-sand beach with volleyball courts. The Poly-nesian's landscaped pool complex was completely redesigned in 2001.

POLYNESIAN RESORT STRENGTHS & WEAKNESSES

Strengths	Weaknesses
On Magic Kingdom monorail	On-site dining
Adjacent to Epcot monorail	Confusing layout
Restaurant selection via monorail	Noise from nearby motor speedway
Recreational options	No fitness center
Child-care facility on site	
Exotic theme	
Swimming complex	

Many of the 853 guest rooms at the Polynesian offer views of the Seven Seas Lagoon. Typical rooms measure 409 square feet. While the guest rooms are smaller than most of Disney's deluxe rooms, they are quite comfortable. The rooms are furnished with two queen-size beds, a daybed, an armoire, and a table and chairs. With batik-design bedspreads and curtains and bamboo furniture, guest rooms maintain the island theme and are visually interesting. Bathrooms are somewhat small, although well designed. Many rooms have balconies.

A problem unique to the Polynesian is the proximity of the Walt Disney World Speedway. A number of guests have written complaining

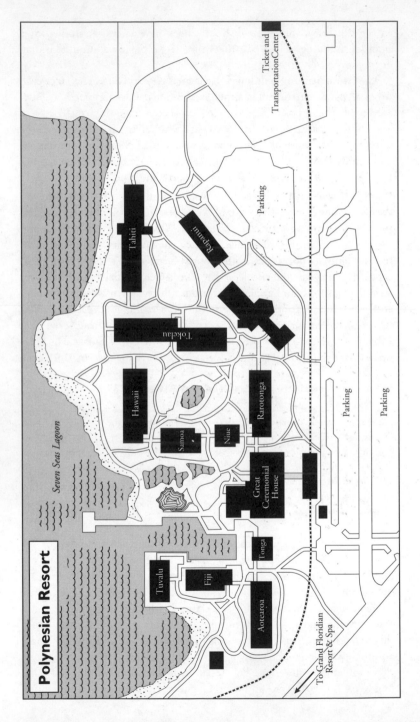

Polynesian Resort

Seven Seas Lagoon

Tahiti

Rapanui

Tokelau

Hawaii

Samoa

Niue

Rarotonga

Tuvalu

Fiji

Tonga

Great Ceremonial House

Aotearoa

Parking

Parking

Parking

Ticket and Transportation Center

To Grand Floridian Resort & Spa

132

about the noise of roaring racecars while they were trying to nap. Rooms with parking-lot views are most likely to be affected.

Service at the Polynesian is excellent. There are two full-service restaurants with easy access to others in the Magic Kingdom area via monorail. The Polynesian has a monorail station on-site and is within easy walking distance of the Transportation and Ticket Center. Bus service is available to other Walt Disney World destinations. Walking time to the bus and monorail loading areas from the most remote rooms is 8–11 minutes.

Good Rooms and Not So Good Rooms at the Polynesian Resort   The Polynesian's eleven guest-room buildings, called "longhouses," are spread over a long strip of land bordered by the monorail on one side and the Seven Seas Lagoon on the other. Though periodically refurbished, all of the buildings except the more recently added Tahiti, Rapa Nui, Tonga, and Tokelau were part of the original hotel, which opened along with the Magic Kingdom in 1971. All of the buildings offer first-floor patios and third-floor balconies. The older buildings have fake balconies on their second floors and a goodly number of the views from first floor patios are obstructed by vegetation. Thus, if you stay in one of the seven older longhouses, ask for a room on the third floor. The newer buildings offer full balconies on both the second and third floors along with patios on the first floor.

Most of the restaurants and shops, as well as the resort lobby, guest services, and the bus and monorail stations, are located in the Great Ceremonial House. Unfortunately, the longhouses most convenient to the Great Ceremonial House, namely Fiji, Tonga, Rarotonga, Niue, and Samoa offer views of the swimming complex, small marina, or inner gardens. In other words, there are no lagoon views except for oblique views from the upper floors of Fiji and Samoa, and a tunnel view from Tonga. Samoa, however, by virtue of its proximity to the main swimming complex is a good choice for families who plan to spend a lot of time at the pool. If your children are under eight, go for a first-floor room on the Nanea Volcano Pool side of Samoa. If your children are older, rooms 2915 to 2918 and 3015 to 3018 offer good, though slightly oblique, views of the lagoon from full balconies.

For an unobstructed view of the lagoon, go for lagoon side rooms on the second or third floor in Tahiti, the first or third floor in Hawaii, or the third floor in Tuvalu. For the record, the landscaping at the Polynesian is superb, so garden-view rooms are generally a cut above garden view or standard-view rooms at the other resorts. Remember though, in the older buildings, ask for the third floor. Aside from second-floor rooms in the older buildings (with fake balconies), also avoid the monorail side rooms in the Rarotonga and Rapa Nui buildings. Garden-view rooms in Aotearoa are especially nice, but be advised that the monorail, though quiet, runs within spitting distance.

Finally, if you plan to spend a lot of time at Epcot, the Tahiti and Rapa Nui longhouses are within easy walking distance of the Ticket and Transportation Center and the Epcot monorail. Even if you are going to the Magic Kingdom, it's less of a walk to the TTC and the Magic Kingdom monorail than to the monorail station at the Great Ceremonial House. Conversely, Tahiti and Rapa Nui are the most distant accommodations from the Polynesian Resort bus stop.

Disney's Wilderness Lodge and Villas   This deluxe Walt Disney World resort is inspired by turn-of-the-century national park lodges. The Wilderness Lodge and Villas ranks with the Animal Kingdom Lodge as the most impressively themed and meticulously detailed of the Disney resorts. Situated on Bay Lake, the Wilderness Lodge and Villas features an eight-story central building flanked by two seven-story guest-room wings and a new wing of studio and one- and two-bedroom condominiums. The rustic hotel features exposed timber columns, log cabin–style facades, and dormer windows. The Lodge is surrounded by evergreen pine and pampas grass landscaping. An eight-story lobby boasts an 87-foot stone fireplace and two 55-foot Pacific Northwest totem poles. In addition to these centerpieces, details like timber pillars; giant teepee chandeliers; and stone, wood, and marble-inlaid floors maintain the resort's feeling of rustic luxury. Although the Wilderness Lodge and Villas is not situated on vast acreage, it does have a beach and a delightful pool. The pool, with its mountain hot-spring atmosphere, is modeled after a stone quarry and offers a waterfall and a geyser.

The 728 guest rooms at the Wilderness Lodge are suited with darkly stained mission-style furniture, which is accented by the primary colors in the decor. The Native American–patterned bedspreads, animal-motif armoires, and faux-calfskin fixtures create a cozy feeling. At 340 square feet, average rooms at the Lodge are the smallest Walt Disney World "deluxe" rooms. Typical rooms have two queen-size beds, and some have one queen-size bed and bunk beds. All rooms have a table and chairs, and a vanity outside the bathroom. Most rooms have balconies.

Part of the Disney Vacation Club time-share program, the Wilderness Lodge Villas are studio and one- and two-bedroom villas in a free-standing building to the right of the Wilderness lodge. Studios offer kitchenettes, while one- and two- bedroom villas come with full kitchens. The rustic décor of the Wilderness Lodge is extended to the villas, which can be booked by non–Vacation Club members on a space-available basis. The villas share restaurants, pools, and other amenities with the Wilderness Lodge.

Service at the Wilderness Lodge and Villas is rated as excellent. There are two full-service restaurants, with several more a boat ride away. The

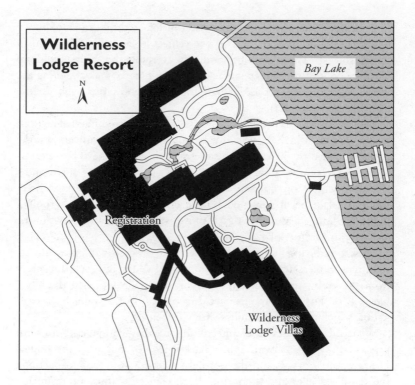

resort is connected to the Magic Kingdom by boat and to other Disney theme parks by bus. Walking time to the bus and boat loading areas from the most remote rooms is about five to eight minutes.

WILDERNESS LODGE & VILLAS

Strengths	Weaknesses
Magnificently rendered theme	Boat service only to Magic Kingdom
Good on-site dining	Lack of direct bus service to many
Great views from guest rooms	destinations
Interesting architecture	
Extensive recreational options	
Romantic setting	
Swimming complex	
Health and fitness center	
Child-care facility on site	

Good Rooms and Not So Good Rooms at the Wilderness Lodge & Villas Resort   Rooms in the V-shaped Lodge building offer either courtyard or external views, presenting guests with a choice between vistas of the lively Silver Creek Pool area or the nearby woods. A few unlucky external-view rooms overlook the parking lot at the bottom of the **V** (which points southwest) or a service vehicle lot and drainage pond to the northeast. Those on the southeast overlook the Villas building. Guests who want the added privacy and quiet of a room overlooking the woods should request one furthest from the lobby, preferably in the northernmost rooms.

The few rooms on the end of the wings offer coveted Bay Lake vistas, which are best at higher levels. If you're planning to rise early and hit the parks, you just might catch the sun rising over the lake. The interior-facing rooms on the ends of the wings allow lake views at an angle, and a few rooms above the courtyard actually face northeast, which is the direction of the lake beyond the pool. However, the balcony dividers, though they offer some measure of privacy, mostly obscure sideways views of the lake from most interior-facing rooms.

Closest to the lobby, a lush garden occupies the courtyard, presenting a calming and pleasant scene to the rooms overlooking it. Proceeding away from the lobby, rooms directly overlook waterfalls and then the Silver Creek Pool. First-floor rooms have direct access to the water from their patios, which is ideal for families with children.

What the villas lack in architectural flare, they compensate for with privacy and quiet. All villa rooms have balconies; not so at the Lodge. However, only a few—on the northern side near the lobby—overlook the resort's smaller Hidden Springs Pool. Generally, those rooms facing the lake, even on the uppermost third story, can scarcely see beyond the pines. The villas are buffered by woods on all sides, but those rooms furthest from the lodge overlook the closest thing to wilderness at Wilderness Lodge and Villas.

Disney's Contemporary Resort   This deluxe resort is the least themed of the Walt Disney World–owned properties. The Contemporary is unique in its A-frame design that permits the Magic Kingdom monorail to pass through the structure's cavernous atrium. The only real source of color in the atrium is a 90-foot mosaic depicting Native American children and nature scenes. The white cement A-frame tower is flanked by two three-story "garden" buildings. The landscaping at the Contemporary is a little bizarre, with trees and shrubs trimmed like overgrown poodles. Situated on Bay Lake, the Contemporary offers a marina and a white-sand beach. Its swimming pool, at 6,500 square feet, is the largest of all Walt Disney World resorts.

The rooms in the Contemporary's tower building enjoy fantastic views of either Bay Lake or the Magic Kingdom. At 436 square feet, the rooms are only slightly smaller than those at the Grand Floridian. All of the rooms are tasteful albeit somewhat dull, with simple lines and neutral colors. The Contemporary is a bit cold in our opinion, and the angular lines of the furnishings make the ambiance somewhat uninviting. Most rooms have two queen-size beds, a daybed, and a table and chair. All tower rooms have balconies.

The Contemporary has a 6,500-square-foot pool with slides and waterfalls. The resort is home to two full-service restaurants (including the well-known California Grill), a buffet restaurant, and a counter-service restaurant. There are six shops at the Contemporary. This resort is within easy walking distance to the Magic Kingdom, and transportation via monorail is available to both the Magic Kingdom and Epcot. Other Walt Disney World destinations can be accessed by bus or boat. Walking time to transportation loading areas from the most remote rooms is six to nine minutes.

CONTEMPORARY RESORT

Strengths	Weaknesses
On Magic Kingdom monorail	Sterility of theme and decor
Ten-minute walk to Magic Kingdom	
Interesting architecture	
Great views from guest rooms	
Good on-site dining	
Best lounge at Walt Disney World	
Restaurant selection via monorail	
Recreational options	
Swimming complex	
Child-care facility on site	
Health and fitness center	

Good Rooms and Not So Good Rooms at the Contemporary Resort
There are three guest room buildings at the Contemporary: the 15-story A-frame tower, and the North and South Garden buildings. Rooms in the a-frame overlook either Bay Lake and the resort marina and swimming complex on one side, or the parking lot with the Seven Seas Lagoon and the Magic Kingdom in the proximate background on the other. All of the guest rooms have a balcony furnished with two chairs and a table. If you stay on the Magic Kingdom side, ask for a room on the 9th floor or higher. The parking lot and connecting roads are less distracting (and noisy) the higher up you are. On the Bay Lake side the view is fine from all floors, though higher floors are preferable here as well.

In the Garden buildings, all ground floor rooms have patios. Only end rooms on the second and third floors of the buildings nearest Bay Lake have full balconies. All other rooms (the vast majority) have balconies only a foot deep: fine for standing at the rail but not enough room to sit

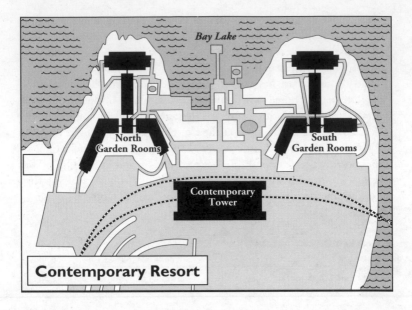

outdoors. Both Garden buildings are a fair walk from the restaurants, shops, front desk, guest services, and monorail station located in the a-frame. This isolation, however, is a plus when it comes to the scenery and peaceful tranquility offered by some of the guest rooms.

In general the North Garden building is more serene and offers better views than the South Garden building. In the North Garden building, rooms 8108 to 8124, 8208 to 8224, and 8308 to 8324 are so close to the lake that you could cast a fishing rod from your patio. The view is of the quietest part of the lake with just a slip of a sand beach graced by stately cypress trees between you and the water. The same view can be enjoyed from rooms 7129 to 7139, 7229 to 7251, and 7329 to 7351, though from a bit farther away across a lawn. These rooms, particularly those on the first floor, represent the best views for the dollar at any Disney resort.

There's a lot of boat traffic in the lake and canal alongside the South Garden building. Closest to the lake and quietest (in this building) are rooms 6116 to 6123, 6216 to 6223, 6316 to 6323. Right at water's edge but noisier are rooms 6107 to 6115, 6207 to 6215, and rooms 6307 to 6315. Flanking the canal that connects Bay Lake to the Seven Seas Lagoon are rooms 5128 to 5143, 5228 to 5251, and 5328 to 5351. All of these rooms have nice views of the canal and lake beyond, but are subjected to a lot of noise from passing watercraft.

Both buildings have a number or rooms that face the marina, pool, and playground—that works well for families with small children. The view isn't comparable to views from the rooms previously listed, but ground-floor rooms 7101 to 7126 in the North Garden building, and 5110 to 5125 in the South Garden Building make for easy coming and going to the pool.

In addition to offering some of the most scenic and tranquil guest rooms in all of Walt Disney World, the North and South Garden buildings likewise contain some of the most undesirable rooms. In the North Garden building, avoid any room with a room number ending in numbers 58 to 88. In the South garden building, avoid room numbers ending in numbers 52 to 70. Almost all of these rooms look directly onto a parking lot.

Shades of Green This deluxe resort is owned and operated by the U.S. Armed Forces and is available only to U.S. military personnel (including the National Guard, reserves, Public Health Service, and Department of Defense). Shades of Green consists of one three-story building nestled among three golf courses. Tastefully nondescript, Shades of Green is at the same time pure peace and quiet. There is no beach or lake at Shades of Green, but there are several pools, including one shaped like Mickey's head. Although Shades of Green is open only to the military, the surrounding golf courses are open to all Walt Disney World guests.

At 455 square feet, the 587 guest rooms at Shades of Green are larger than those at the Grand Floridian. The rooms are luxuriously decorated with an English-countryside theme, with light-oak furniture, dust ruffles, and soft colors. Most rooms have two queen-size beds, a daybed, and a table and four chairs, as well as a television in an armoire. All rooms have either a patio or balcony.

Even though Shades of Green is not operated by Disney, the service here is comparable to the deluxe Walt Disney World properties. The single restaurant at Shades of Green offers both buffet and menu service. Transportation to all theme parks is by bus, with a transfer required to almost all destinations. Walking time to the bus loading area from the most remote rooms is about five minutes. Shades of Green is immensely popular; make reservations five to seven months in advance.

SHADES OF GREEN

Strengths	Weaknesses
Large, beautiful guest rooms	Limited on-site dining
Informality	Limited bus service
Quiet setting	
Views of golf course from guest rooms	
Convenient self-parking	

Shades of Green will be closed until September of 2003 while a major expansion is under way. When completed, the project will add 290 new guest rooms, a multi-level parking structure, an Italian restaurant, and a new family-style restaurant. While Shades of Green is closed, service members can obtain comparable rates at the Contemporary Resort.

The Epcot Resorts

Disney's Yacht and Beach Club Resorts & Villas   These adjoined five-story deluxe resorts are similarly themed. Both resorts have clapboard facades with whitewashed-wood trim. The Yacht Club is painted a subdued gray, while the Beach Club is painted a brighter blue. The Yacht Club has a nautical theme with model ships and antique navigational instruments gracing the public areas. The Beach Club is appointed with beach scenes in foam green and white. Both resorts have themed lobbies, with a giant globe in the Yacht Club and sea-horse fixtures in the Beach Club. The resorts face 25-acre Crescent Lake and share an elaborate swimming complex.

There are 630 guest rooms at the Yacht Club and 583 at the Beach Club and 205 studio, and one- and two-bedroom villas at the new Beach Club Villas (part of the Disney Vacation Club time-sharing program). Most of the hotel rooms are 381 square feet and contain two queen-size beds, a daybed, and a table and two chairs. Like the Grand Floridian, rooms here have a lot of drawer space. Rooms at the Yacht Club are decorated with navy blue and white, while rooms at the Beach Club offer a more muted, soft-green look. Some rooms have balconies.

The new (September 2002) Beach Club Villas are evocative of seaside cottages of the Victorian era. Studio accommodations offer kitchenettes while the one- and two-bedroom villas come with a full kitchen. Subject to availability, the villas are open to the public as well as to Disney Vacation Club (time-share) members. The villas share restaurants, pools, and other amenities with the Yacht and Beach Club Resorts.

As deluxe Walt Disney World resorts, the Yacht and Beach Clubs provide excellent service. The resorts house nine restaurants and lounges and are within walking distance of Epcot and Disney's BoardWalk. Transportation to other destinations is by bus or boat. Walking time to the transportation loading areas from the most remote rooms is seven minutes.

Good Rooms and Not So Good Rooms at the Yacht and Beach Club Resorts & Villas   Although the Yacht and Beach Club Resorts are arrayed along Crescent Lake opposite Disney's Boardwalk, a relatively small percentage of guest rooms actually overlook the lake. Many additional rooms have an oblique view of the lake but actually face a courtyard or garden. To complicate matters, the resorts do not differentiate between a room with a view of the lake and a room that overlooks a swimming pool, pond, or canal. All are considered water views. We receive a number of letters each year from readers complaining that their "water view" was a rather distant, sidelong peek at a swimming pool. Disappointments like

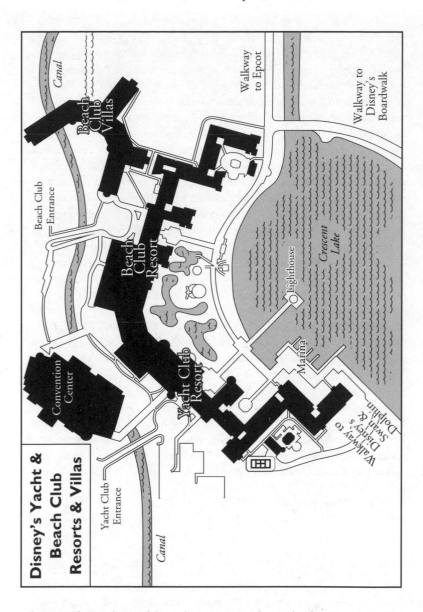

Disney's Yacht & Beach Club Resorts & Villas

Canal

Beach Club Villas

Beach Club Entrance

Beach Club Resort

Convention Center

Yacht Club Resort

Yacht Club Entrance

Canal

Walkway to Epcot

Walkway to Disney's Boardwalk

Crescent Lake

Lighthouse

Marina

Walkway to Disney's Swan & Dolphin

these might explain why readers consistently grade the resorts a very mediocre "C" in value.

The resorts consist of four- and five-story interconnected buildings with private guest-room patios on the ground floor and balconies on the upper floors. All balconies at the Yacht Club are full sized, but balconies at the Beach Club vary. Some balconies are full sized and provide space for sitting with railings that afford good visibility. Rooms on the top floor of the Beach Club have smaller, inset, solidly enclosed balconies that limit visibility when seated. A third type of balcony offers enough room only for standing.

The best rooms at both resorts offer full balconies with frontal views of Crescent Lake. Our favorite views at the Beach Club are from full-balconied, odd-numbered rooms located in the U-configured buildings closest to Epcot. At the Yacht Club the best views are from L-configured buildings that overlook the marina, floors 2 and higher. Go for odd-numbered rooms 2045—2055, 3045—3055, 4057—4065, except 4059 and 4061. In addition to a nice view of the lake, it's possible to watch the Illuminations fireworks at Epcot (about a half mile distant) from the balconies of these rooms. Be forewarned that the rooms recommended, both at the Beach Club and the Yacht Club, are the most distant from the lobbies, main swimming complex, shopping, restaurants, and bus stops. For rooms offering great views, easy access to pools and restaurants, and a tolerable walk to Epcot, try for odd-numbered Beach Club rooms 2641 to 2647, 5641 to 5647, 3683 to 3691, 5683 to 5691.

Avoid standard-view rooms at both resorts, with the exception of even-numbered rooms 2512 to 2596 and 4512 to 4596 at the Beach Club, which overlook a dense pine thicket. In addition to offering a nice view, these standard rooms are the closest rooms of any resorts surrounding Crescent Lake to Epcot.

Although the Beach Club Villas had not opened when the *Unofficial Guide* went to press, we can tell you that the best villas are those which overlook the pine forest between the Villas and Epcot and are farthest away from noisy Epcot Resorts Boulevard. Oddly, for accommodations called Beach Club Villas, the only water visible is that of a diminutive canal. For sure there isn't any beach.

YACHT & BEACH CLUB RESORTS

Strengths	Weaknesses
Attractive guest rooms	No transportation to Epcot main
Good on-site dining	entrance
Selection of nearby off-site dining	Distant guest self-parking within
Ten-minute walk to Epcot	
Ten-minute walk to BoardWalk nightlife	
Swimming complex	
Health and fitness center	
View from waterside guest rooms	
Child-care facility on site	
Nautical/New England theme	

Disney's BoardWalk Inn and BoardWalk Villas   Situated on Crescent Lake across from the Yacht and Beach Club Resorts, the BoardWalk Inn is one of the newer Walt Disney World deluxe resorts. Viewed from Crescent Lake, the complex is a detailed replica of an early-twentieth-century Atlantic coast boardwalk. Varied facades of hotels, diners, and shops create a waterfront skyline that is both inviting and exciting. In reality, the BoardWalk Inn and Villas form a single integrated structure behind the varied facades. Restaurants and shops occupy the boardwalk level, while Inn and Villas accommodations rise up to six stories above. Painted bright red and yellow along with weathered pastel greens and blues, the BoardWalk resorts are the only Disney hotels that use neon signage as architectural detail. The Inn and Villas share a single, old-fashioned amusement park–themed swimming pool.

The 375 deluxe rooms of the BoardWalk Inn measure 422 square feet, and most contain two queen-size brass beds, a child's cherry daybed, a cherry table and two chairs, and ceiling fans. Decorating touches include blue and yellow gingham wallpaper and print curtains with a blue postcard pattern. Rooms at the BoardWalk have more closet space than other deluxe Disney rooms. Most rooms have balconies.

The 517 BoardWalk Villas are decorated with warmer tones and primary colors, with bright tiles in the kitchen and bathrooms. Villas range in size from 359 to 1,071 square feet (studio through three-bedroom), and sleep 4–12 people. Many villas have full kitchens, laundry rooms, and whirlpool bathtubs. The BoardWalk Villas tend to be more expensive than similar accommodations at other Disney resorts—you pay for the address.

As the newest Epcot deluxe resort, the BoardWalk Inn and Villas are very well staffed and offer excellent service. Additionally, some of Disney World's finest restaurants and shops are located at the BoardWalk. The Inn and Villas are within walking distance of Epcot and are connected to other destinations by bus and boat. Walking time to transportation loading areas from the most remote rooms is five to six minutes.

Good Rooms and Not So Good Rooms at the Boardwalk Inn and Villas
The BoardWalk complex is made up of several wings radiating out from the lobby complex, roughly in the shape of a giant H. Crescent Lake and the Promenade are to the north, the entrance is to the south, and the canal that runs to Disney-MGM Studios is to the west. As with other Disney resorts, the water part of "water view" can mean many things—at the BoardWalk, it can mean Crescent Lake, the canal, or a small pool. There are also two levels of concierge floors for those interested in a little extra service.

All rooms at both the Inn and Villas have either a balcony or patio, though the size of the balconies on the standard upper-floor rooms alternates between large and medium. The BoardWalk Inn and Villas each share about half the frontage on the Promenade, which in turn looks out

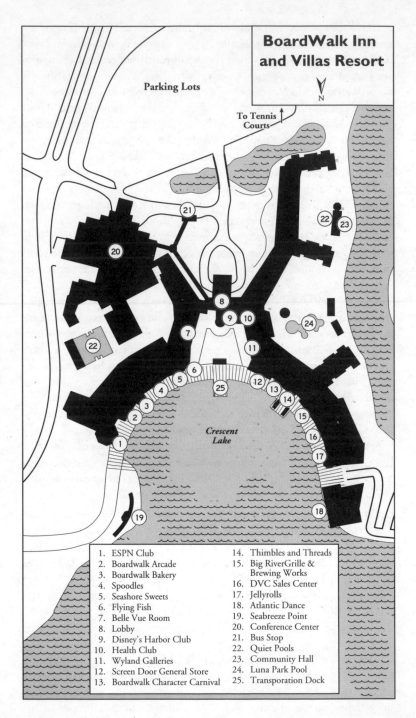

BoardWalk Inn and Villas Resort

Parking Lots

N

To Tennis Courts

Crescent Lake

1. ESPN Club
2. Boardwalk Arcade
3. Boardwalk Bakery
4. Spoodles
5. Seashore Sweets
6. Flying Fish
7. Belle Vue Room
8. Lobby
9. Disney's Harbor Club
10. Health Club
11. Wyland Galleries
12. Screen Door General Store
13. Boardwalk Character Carnival
14. Thimbles and Threads
15. Big RiverGrille & Brewing Works
16. DVC Sales Center
17. Jellyrolls
18. Atlantic Dance
19. Seabreeze Point
20. Conference Center
21. Bus Stop
22. Quiet Pools
23. Community Hall
24. Luna Park Pool
25. Transporation Dock

over Crescent Lake. The Promenade's clubs, stores, and attractions are spread about equally among the two sections, leading to approximately similar levels of noise and commotion. However, the Inn side is closer to Epcot and the nearby access road; this makes for better views of the Epcot fireworks and easier access to that park, but it also increases foot traffic and road noise on the Promenade side of the Inn.

Otherwise, the Inn is actually less noisy than the more expensive Villas; there is one tranquil, enclosed courtyard, and another half-enclosed area with a quiet pool (this is where the BoardWalk's Garden Suites are located). Notwithstanding the noise of the Promenade, the only really bad views in the Inn are from rooms facing the hotel's traffic loop or from those rooms overlooking the unattractive roof of the conference facility.

The majority of the BoardWalk Villas face the canal to the west; beyond and above the natural setting of the canal, the view of most of these rooms is dominated by the hulking Swan resort. Promenade-facing Villa rooms have identical noise issues as their Inn counterparts. The middle section of the canal-facing Villa rooms look out on the Luna Park Pool, a carnival-themed family-pool complex that gets extremely noisy during the day. However, possibly our favorite rooms at the BoardWalk are found immediately to the south, with views of the canal and a partially-enclosed quiet pool. Noise is practically nonexistent around these rooms; the only downside is that they are relatively distant from the Promenade and Epcot. Rooms on the opposite side of this wing are almost as quiet, but they face the BoardWalk's parking lot and are thus less than desirable.

BOARDWALK INN & VILLAS

Strengths	Weaknesses
Attractive guest rooms	No transportation to Epcot main entrance
Ten-minute walk to Epcot	
Swimming complex	No restaurants in hotel
Health and fitness center	Distant guest self-parking
Three-minute walk to BoardWalk nightlife	
Selection of off-site dining within walking distance	
View from waterside guest rooms	
Child-care facility on site	
Nautical/New England theme	

The Walt Disney World Swan and Dolphin Although these resorts are inside Walt Disney World and Disney handles their reservations, they are owned by Sheraton (Dolphin) and Westin (Swan). The resorts face each other and are situated on either side of an inlet of Crescent Lake. The Dolphin is a 27-story triangular turquoise building. On its roof are two

56-foot-tall fish balanced with their tails in the air. The Swan has a 12-story main building flanked by two seven-story towers. Two 47-foot-tall swans adorn its roof, staring incredulously at the fish across the way. The Swan and Dolphin have been described as "bizarre" and stylistically disjointed. At the very least they are eclectic in their theming. Disney, for its part, claims that you will step into a "fantasy world." For our part, however, the experience is more akin to art deco gone haywire. The giant swans look swanlike enough, but the fish on the Dolphin are more like catfish from outer space. The mood at these properties could be described alternately as adventurous or confusing, depending on how much you value the work of a good interior decorator.

The restyled lobby at the Dolphin is the more ornate, featuring a rotunda with corridors branching off like spokes to shops, restaurants, and other public areas. At the other end of the spectrum, the lobby of the Swan is so small as to appear an afterthought. Both resorts feature artwork of wildly different styles and eras (from Matisse to Roy Lichtenstein). The resorts each have their own pool. The Dolphin's "Grotto" pool is shaped like a seashell and has a waterfall, while the Swan's pool is of a conventional rectangular configuration.

The rooms at the two properties are decorated similarly, with fine art prints and bold colors. However, the rooms at the Dolphin are slightly larger, with an extra vanity. The 1,509 guest rooms at the Walt Disney World Dolphin are 360 square feet, and the 758 rooms at the Swan are 340 square feet. Both are decorated in bright turquoise and peach. Most rooms have two queen-size beds, a desk, and a reading chair. The furniture is modern, with wood and metal marine-inspired accents. Some rooms at the Dolphin have balconies.

Since the Walt Disney World Swan and Dolphin are not run by Disney, the service at these resorts is less sugar-coated than service at other Disney resorts. The Swan and Dolphin collectively house more than a dozen restaurants and lounges and are within easy walking distance from Epcot and the BoardWalk. The resorts are connected to other destinations by bus and boat. Walking time from the most remote rooms to the transportation loading areas is seven to nine minutes.

None of the Epcot resorts offer transportation to the main entrance of Epcot. As a Greenville, South Carolina, mom points out, this omission can occasion substantial inconvenience:

I would like to point out one inconvenience of staying in the Epcot area resorts. The only transportation to Epcot is by boat or foot. There is no bus available to take you to the front gates of Epcot. We had to walk through the International Gateway and all the way to the front of Epcot to ride Future World attractions. And if we finished Epcot at the end of the day

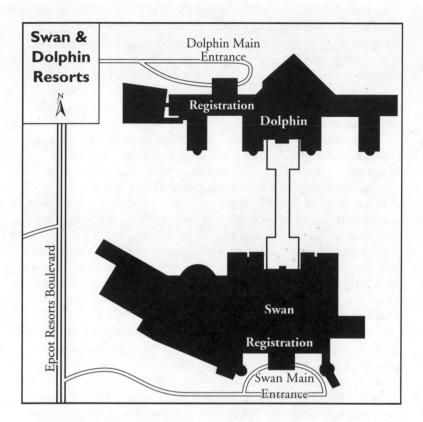

near the front entrance, the only way back home was a long hike through
Future World and the International Gateway.

**Good Rooms and Not So Good Rooms at the Swan and Dolphin
Resorts** These two sprawling hotels are configured very differently, and
their irregular shapes mean that it's mostly easier to discuss groups of
rooms in relation to exterior landmarks and compass directions rather
than by room numbers. When speaking with a Disney reservationist, just
use our tips when asking for a particular view or area.

The Swan The Swan's prime views are from its east-facing rooms, particularly in the upper half of the eight-story wing above Palio. From this vantage point, guests overlook a canal and the BoardWalk, with Epcot in the
distance. The fireworks of IllumiNations enliven the view nightly. However,
the rooms in the wing closest to the hotel's main section have the southern
portion of their view obscured by the easternmost portion of the building,
which juts east beyond the eight-story wing. There are some eastern-facing
rooms on that portion of the main section, sans balconies. Note that lofty
palm trees obscure the view from east-facing rooms below the fourth floor.

North-facing rooms afford views of the Dolphin across Crescent Lake and (generally) of the courtyard. The exceptions are the north-facing rooms on the easternmost portion of the main section, which look across Crescent Terrace to the BoardWalk. These afford angled views of Epcot and are buffered by palms on the lowest three floors. The few north-facing rooms at the end of the Swan's two eight-story wings directly overlook Crescent Lake. However, the bulk of the north-facing rooms are in the main section and directly overlook the courtyard, with greenery, fountains, and an indoor café in its center. Courtyard-facing rooms are subject to more noise from below, though never very much.

Above the eighth floor, north-facing rooms in the main section overlook the roofs of the shorter wings below. In these rooms, height enhances the vista out your window, but only near the center of the hotel is the view not seriously marred by rooftops below.

North-facing main-section rooms have a more direct view of the Dolphin across the lake than the courtyard-facing rooms in either eight-story wing. However, most wing rooms can view the lake at an angle. Those on the northern edge of the western wing are also able to view the Board-Walk at an angle.

Most courtyard-facing rooms have balconies, though not all. Only 224 of the Swan's 758 rooms are so equipped, and these balconies offer panoramic 180° views. Of course, from most rooms at the Swan, part of any 180° view will include another section of the hotel.

The hotel's worst views are from west-facing rooms above the fourth floor, which overlook the unsightly roof of the hotel's western wing, home to the health club, game room, and the Garden Grove restaurants. The northernmost rooms in the wing directly above Kimonos are an exception to this, as their balconies overlook the pool and the beach on Crescent Lake's western shore. Although you'll be nearest the pool in these rooms, you won't have improved access. Since the hotel's bottom floor has no rooms, proximity to the pool won't free you from walking down the hall and taking the elevator.

Above the Swan's main entrance, south-facing rooms overlook the parking lot, with forest and Disney-MGM Studios in the distance. However, the canal is also visible to the east. These rooms lack balconies.

The Dolphin   Comprised of a central **A**-frame with large wings jutting off each side and four additional smaller arms extending from the rear of the building, the Dolphin is semi-attached to a large conference center, which means that the vast majority of guests are ostensibly there on business. Many of the vacation amenities found at true Disney properties are nonexistent (such as extensive playgrounds) or available in limited supply (the Dolphin sports only a single pool). All parks are accessible from either a shttle stop or a boat dock located between the Dolphin and the Swan.

If you want a room with easy access to shopping, dining, and transport to and from the parks, most any room in the Dolphin will do. The shuttle (located outside the main entrance) and the boat dock are equidistant from the main front and rear exits. Restaurants and shopping are located primarily on the first and third floors. If you would also like a view of something other than parking lot asphalt, your choices narrow considerably. The rooms in the Dolphin which provide pleasant views are located in the four arms on the rear of the building. Rooms on all the arms sport balconies from the first through fourth floors, then alternate between balconies or windows on floors five through nine.

One of the best views from the Dolphin overlooks the Grotto Pool on the far right of the building. A man-made beach, complete with a small waterfall, is visible from rooms at the very end of the large right wing. None of these rooms has a balcony, but that might be a blessing, since the pool is between you and the grotto and comes complete with canned tiki music and a bar. A better bet would be to ask for a room on the far right side of the first rear arm. These outer rooms do have balconies and are a bit more removed from the pool. The rooms on the inner part of that arm overlook a bladderwort-encrusted reflecting pool; these are not recommended. Nor are the facing rooms on the next arm.

Between the second and third arms looms the monstrous Dolphin fountain, and the better choices here are on the top two floors. There, from arm two, you can see the BoardWalk (including any nighttime fireworks), and from arm three the Grotto Pool. Otherwise, you may find you have a lovely view of massive, green concrete fish scales. Note that the noise from the water is quite loud, and the fountain geysers away continuously. Depending upon your personality, this is either soothing or maddening.

Arm three and arm four are again situated around a reflecting pool. While your view of the lagoon is certainly better than that of the rooms surrounding the other such pool, these rooms are not recommended due in part to the malodorous state of the these pools. Another concern for rooms in this area is the ferry that toots its horn every time it approaches and departs the boat dock. Its path runs right by these rooms, and the horn blows just as it passes. The first time that happens, it's quaint. By the 17th, your hair will be coming out in clumps.

The lagoon side of arm four, and the small jut of the large Dolphin wing perpendicular to it, offer arguably the best views. You have an unobstructed view of the lagoon and any ensuing fireworks, a fine BoardWalk view for people-watching, and, from the higher floors, the beach of the Beach Club across the lagoon is visible. There is still ferry noise to contend with, but all in all these rooms have the most going for them.

SWAN & DOLPHIN RESORTS

Strengths	Weaknesses
Exotic architecture	No transportation to Epcot main
Good on-site dining	entrance
Health and fitness center	Distant guest self-parking
View from guest rooms	Garish decor
Ten-minute walk to BoardWalk nightlife	Confusing layout
Selection of off-site dining within walking distance	

Disney's Caribbean Beach Resort   The Caribbean Beach Resort is situated on 200 acres surrounding a 45-acre lake called Barefoot Bay. This mid-priced Disney resort, modeled after resorts of the Caribbean islands, is comprised of the registration area, called the "Custom House," and five two-story "villages" named after Caribbean islands. Each village has its own pool, laundry room, and beach. The Caribbean motif is maintained with red-tile roofs, widow's walks, and wooden railed porches. The atmosphere at this resort is cheerful, with buildings painted blue, lime green, and sherbet orange. In addition to the five village pools, the main swimming pool at the Caribbean Beach is themed as an old Spanish fort, complete with slides and water cannons.

Most of the 2,112 guest rooms at the Caribbean Beach are 315 square feet and contain two double beds and a table and two chairs. Some of the rooms are decorated with bright tropical colors, while others are decorated with neutral beachy tones. All of the rooms are suited with the same light-oak furniture. Rooms do not have balconies. Some rooms at the Caribbean are in need of refurbishment. When you make your reservations, request a recently renovated room. Also, be aware that the Caribbean Beach Resort is not known for its check-in efficiency.

Regarding the quality of the guest rooms, a couple from Alexandria, Virginia, offered this:

The Caribbean Beach Resort was easily the biggest disappointment of our trip (we did not read your guide until after we booked our reservations at the CBR). The resort's rather drab rooms were little better than the Howard Johnson rooms where we stayed during our visit to Universal, yet the CBR rate was nearly three times as much as the HoJo rate. Add my voice to the chorus of complaints about this sub-par resort.

One of the most centrally located of the Disney resorts, the Caribbean Beach Resort offers transportation to all Walt Disney World destinations

Caribbean Beach Resort

Trinidad South
Trinidad North
Old Port Royale Centre Town
Promenade
Martinique
Barbados
Jamaica
Promenade
Sea Breeze Dr.
Custom House Registration
Aruba
Victory Way
Buena Vista Drive

🏖 Beach 🧒 Playground
🚌 Bus Stop 🏊 Pool

by bus. Though the Caribbean Beach has one full-service restaurant and a food court, food service is woefully inadequate for the size of the resort. Because food service at the Caribbean is limited and because it is immensely time consuming to commute to other resorts by Disney bus, guests at the Caribbean Beach should seriously consider renting a car. Walking time to the bus loading area from the most remote rooms is seven to ten minutes.

Good Rooms and Not So Good Rooms at the Caribbean Beach Resort
Once you get out of the drab rooms, the grounds of the Caribbean Beach resort are actually quite pleasant. The landscaping is not particularly colorful—lots of ferns and palm trees—but it's quite verdant, especially in the courtyards. Divided into six "islands" or groups of buildings clustered around Barefoot Bay, it's all identical, motel-style, two-story structures, though they are arranged various ways to face courtyards, pools, the bay, and so forth. The whole setup is similar to Disney's Coronado Springs Resort in most every way but theme.

In general, corner rooms at the Caribbean Beach Resort are preferable since they have more windows. Standard-view rooms face either the parking lots or courtyards, and the usual broad interpretation about water views is in play here. Beyond that, your main choices will revolve around your preference for proximity to (or distance from) the Custom House, pools, parking lots, or beaches on Barefoot Bay. Each of the six islands has direct access to at least one beach, playground, bus stop, and parking lot.

The island of Barbados is the closest to the Custom House, but its central location guarantees that it also experiences the most foot traffic and road noise. It also shares its only beach and playground with Martinique, which is probably the best area for families; Martinique has access to two beaches, is adjacent to the main pool and playground at the Old Port Royale Town Center, and yet is removed enough from the Custom House to offer a little serenity for parents. The islands of Aruba and Jamaica are similar in character to Martinique, but they each have only one beach, and you must walk across a footbridge to reach the facilities at Old Port Royale. Trinidad North is only comprised of three buildings, and its thin layout means that noise penetrates its courtyard both from surrounding roads and from rambunctious kids at Old Port Royale next door. The quietest island is Trinidad South, which is also the most remote from resort facilities. It does have its own playground and beach, and the beach in particular has a special bonus: the view across Barefoot Bay is of wild, undeveloped Florida forest, a rarity on a Disney property.

CARIBBEAN BEACH RESORT

Strengths	Weaknesses
Caribbean theme	Guest rooms
Children's play areas	On-site dining
Convenient self-parking	No easily accessible off-site dining
	Extreme distance of many guest rooms from dining and services
	Slow check-in process
	Large, confusing layout
	Bus service

The Bonnet Creek Resorts

Disney's Old Key West Resort   This is the first of the Disney Vacation Club properties. Although the resort is a time-share property, units not being used by owners are rented on a nightly basis. Old Key West is a large aggregation of two- to three-story buildings modeled after Caribbean residences and guest houses of the Florida Keys. Arranged subdivision-style around a golf course and along Bonnet Creek, the buildings are situated in small neighborhoodlike clusters. They feature pastel-colored facades, white trim, and shuttered windows. The registration area is housed in the Conch Flats Community Hall, along with a full-service restaurant, modest fitness center, marina, and sundries shop. There is a quiet pool in each cluster of accommodations and a larger pool at the Conch Flats Community Hall.

With studios at 376 square feet, one-bedroom villas at 942 square feet, and two-bedroom villas at 1,333 square feet, this resort offers some of the

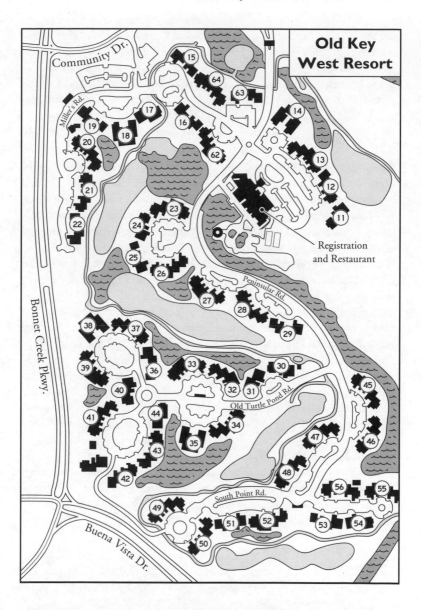

roomiest accommodations at Walt Disney World. Studios contain two queen-size beds, a table and two chairs, and an extra vanity outside the bathroom. One-bedroom villas contain a king-size bed in the master bedroom, a queen-size sleeper sofa in the living room, a laundry room, and a fully equipped kitchen. Two-bedroom villas include an additional bedroom with two queen-size beds. All of the villas have enough closet space to bring your whole wardrobe.

Each villa at the Old Key West has its own private balcony that opens onto a delightfully landscaped private courtyard. Finally, rooms and villas at the Old Key West are tastefully decorated, with wicker and upholstered furniture, and peach and light-green color schemes.

As a Disney Vacation Club resort, Old Key West's service is very personal. Transportation to other Walt Disney World destinations is by bus. Walking time to transportation loading areas from the most remote rooms is about six minutes.

Good Rooms and Not So Good Rooms at the Old Key West Resort
Old Key West is a huge resort with 56 three-story villa buildings. Each building contains a mix of studio and multi-room villas. The views are nice from almost all of the villas. To enhance the view, all multi-room villas and some studios offer a large balcony furnished with a table and chairs. Though nice vistas are easy to come by, quiet is more elusive. Because Old Key West is bordered by busy Bonnet Creek Parkway and even busier Buena Vista Drive, the best villas are those as far away as possible from the highway noise. For quiet isolation and a lovely river view ask for building 55, 46, or 45, in that order. For a lake and golf course view away from road noise but closest to restaurants, recreation, the marina, the main swimming complex, and shopping, ask for building 13. Nearby buildings 12 and 11 are likewise both quiet and convenient choices, but offer views primarily of the golf course. Next best choices are buildings 32 and 34. 32 looks out onto a lake with the golf course in the background while 34 faces the golf course with tennis courts off to the left and a lake to the right. None of the buildings recommended are more than a two- to five-minute walk to the nearest bus stop or pool. Buildings to avoid are 19–22, 38–39, 41–42, and 49–51.

Ground floor villas make lugging in suitcases and groceries less taxing. Though the top floor requires a three-story climb, views from on high are superior. The top floor also insures that you'll have no noisy neighbors clomping around above you.

OLD KEY WEST RESORT

Strengths	Weaknesses
Extremely nice guest rooms and condos	Substandard bus service
Quiet, lushly landscaped setting	Limited on-site dining
Convenient self-parking	No easily accessible off-site dining
Old Key West theme	Large, confusing layout
	Extreme distance of many guest rooms from dining and services

Disney's Port Orleans Resort The Port Orleans and Dixie Landings Resorts were merged in 2001. The combined midpriced resort, called Port Orleans, is divided into two sections. The smaller, southern part that was previously Port Orleans is now called the French Quarter. The larger section encompassing the former Dixie Landings is now labeled the Riverside.

Port Orleans French Quarter The French Quarter section is a sanitized Disney version of the New Orleans French Quarter. Comprised of seven three-story guest-room buildings situated next to Bonnet Creek, the resort gives you an idea of what New Orleans would look like if its buildings were painted every year and the garbage collectors never went on strike. There are very prim pink-and-blue guest buildings, with wrought-iron filigree, shuttered windows, and old-fashioned iron lampposts. In keeping with the Crescent City theme, the French Quarter is landscaped with magnolia trees and overgrown vines. The centrally located "Mint" houses the registration area and restaurants, and is a reproduction of a turn-of-the-century building where Mississippi Delta farmers sold their harvests. The registration desk features a vibrant Mardi Gras mural and old-fashioned bank-teller windows. "Doubloon Lagoon," the pool in the French Quarter section, surrounds a colorful fiberglass creation depicting Neptune riding a sea serpent.

The 1,008 guest rooms in the French Quarter each measure 315 square feet. Most contain two double beds, a table and two chairs, and a vanity outside the bathroom. The gold-and-deep-green rooms feature hardwood furniture and valances over the curtains. None of the rooms have private balconies.

There is a food court but no full-service restaurant. Walking time to bus loading areas from the most remote French Quarter rooms is seven to ten minutes.

Good Rooms and Not So Good Rooms at the Port Orleans French Quarter Resort There are seven guest-room buildings situated to either side of the pool and guest-services building with its food court, shopping, and bus stop. The best views are from the rooms that directly face the river and the natural pine forest on the opposite bank. Wings of buildings 1, 2, 5, 6, and 7 flank the river and provide the best river views in either the French Quarter or Riverside sections of Port Orleans resort. River-view rooms in buildings 1, 6, and 7 are a long walk from French Quarter public areas and common facilities, but are the most tranquil accommodations. Families with children should ask for river-view rooms in buildings 2 and 5, closest to the swimming complex. Make sure the reservationist understands that you are specifically requesting a "river-view," as opposed to a "water-view" room. All river-view rooms are also water-view rooms, but not all water-view rooms overlook the river.

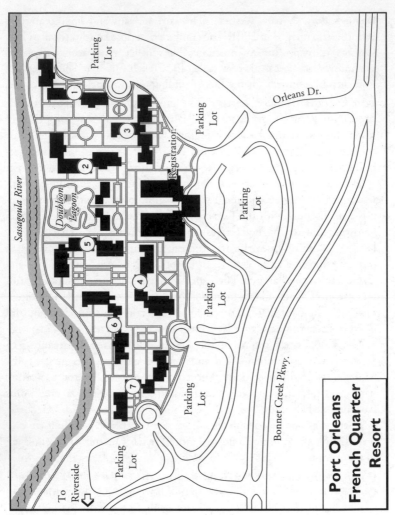

Port Orleans
French Quarter
Resort

Following are the best river-view rooms in each building:

Building 1	Rooms 1127–1132, 1227–1232, 1327–1332
Building 2	Rooms 2127–2132, 2227–2232, 2327–2332
Building 5	Rooms 5117–5122, 5217–5222, 5317–5322
Building 6	Rooms 6123–6126, 6223–6226, 6323–6326, 6133–6140, 6233–6240, 6333–6340, 6141–6148, 6241–6248, 6341–6348
Building 7	Rooms 7141–7148, 7241–7248, 7341–7348

Standard-view rooms in the French Quarter look out onto either a
courtyard or a parking lot. Although there are no private balconies, you

can turn your exterior access walkway into a balcony by bringing along a lawn chair or two. You'll have to make way, of course, for fellow guests coming and going to their rooms, but most of the time you'll be able to sit outdoors undisturbed.

Port Orleans Riverside The Riverside section of Port Orleans draws on the lifestyle and architecture of Mississippi River communities in antebellum Louisiana, though it conveniently ignores any reference to slavery. Spread along Bonnet Creek, which encircles "Old Man Island" (the section's main swimming area), Riverside is divided into yet two more themed areas: the "mansion" area, which features plantation-style architecture, and the "bayou" area, with tin-roofed rustic (imitation) wooden buildings. The mansions are three stories tall, while the bayou guest houses are a story shorter. The theme is augmented by landscaped groves of azalea and juniper. Southern river life is also depicted at Riverside's food court, which houses a working cotton press powered by a 32-foot waterwheel.

The 2,048 rooms at Riverside each measure 315 square feet. Most provide two double beds, a table and two chairs, and two pedestal sinks outside the bathroom. Some rooms also contain a child's trundle bed. All rooms feature brass bathroom fixtures, hickory-branch bedposts, and quilted bedspreads. The rooms are decorated in tasteful neutrals and blues. None of the rooms have private balconies.

Riverside has one full-service restaurant as well as a food court. The resort is served by the Disney bus system, which connects it to all Walt Disney World destinations. Walking time from the most remote rooms to the transportation loading areas is ten minutes.

When the old Port Orleans and Dixie Landings Resorts merged, Disney permanently closed one of two full-service restaurants. This leaves a single remaining full-service restaurant (and two food courts) to handle the dining needs of a 3,056-room resort. Located in the Riverside section, the restaurant is a 15-minute walk from many of the guest buildings. Guests depending on Disney transportation to travel to restaurants in other hotels can expect a commute time of 40–60 minutes *each way*. Also closed was the marina in the French Quarter section.

Good Rooms and Not So Good Rooms at the Port Orleans Riverside Resort Port Orleans Riverside is so large that we use bicycles whenever we work there. All told, there are 20 guest-room buildings (not counting flanking wings on two of the buildings). Divided into two sections, Alligator Bayou and Magnolia Bend, Port Orleans Riverside is arrayed around two pine groves and a watercourse that Disney calls the Sassagoula River. Magnolia Bend consists of four three-story, grand-plantation-style complexes, respectively named Acadian House, Magnolia Terrace, Oak Manor, and Parterre Place. Though situated on the river, only about 15%

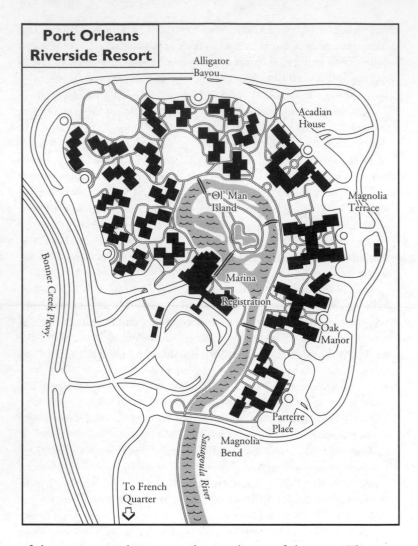

of the guest rooms have an unobstructed view of the water. The vast majority of rooms overlook a courtyard or parking lot. Many of the rooms that actually face the river have trees and other vegetation blocking the view. The best views in Magnolia Bend can be had from the third floor, river side of Acadian House (building 80), which looks down on the river and Ol' Man Island, Riverside's main swimming complex.

To the south are Magnolia Terrace (building 85) and Oak Manor (building 90), both configured in an H shape. In these buildings, only second and third floor rooms on the very top of the H (facing the river) have an unobstructed water view. Rooms to ask for are 9416, 9417,

9039, 9042, and 9239 to 9242. Both H-shaped buildings, however, are closer to the front desk, restaurant, lounge, and shopping complex than is the Acadian House. Continuing south, Panterre Place (building 95) has a number of rooms overlooking the river, but unfortunately they also overlook the parking lot on the far shore. Generally speaking (other than the few exceptions described above), if you really want a nice river view, you're better off opting for Port Orleans French Quarter down river.

The other part of Port Orleans Riverside, Alligator Bayou, forms an arch around the northern half of the resort. In all there are 16 two-story guest-room buildings. These smaller buildings, surrounding two pine groves and graced by abundant gardens, offer a cozy, more tranquil alternative to the more imposing structures of the Magnolia Bend section of Port Orleans Riverside, and of Port Orleans French Quarter. If you want to see the river, ask for a second story water-view room in buildings 27 or 38. Building 14 also offers some river-view rooms and it is quite convenient to shops, front desk, and restaurant, but it's in a noisy, high-traffic area. A good compromise building for families is building 18. It's insulated from traffic and noise by landscaping, yet is next to a satellite swimming pool and is within easy walking distance of the main guest-services building.

We should mention that the Disney Port Orleans Riverside map shows two lakes situated north of the river bend, suggesting additional water views in Alligator Bayou. In fact, these are dried up lakes now forested with pine. This area, however, is richly landscaped to compliment the "pine islands," and though out of site of water, offers the most peaceful and serene accommodations in the entire Port Orleans Resort. Our recommended buildings in this area are numbers 26, 25, and 39, in that order. While quite restful, be aware that these buildings are somewhat distant from the resort's central facilities and that there is no adjacent parking. Buildings to avoid in Alligator Bayou are buildings 15, 16, 17, and 24, all of which are subject to motor traffic noise from nearby Bonnet Creek Parkway.

Finally, understand that all Port Orleans guest buildings have exterior corridors. When you look out your window, therefore, there will be a safety rail in the immediate foreground, and other guests periodically walking past.

PORT ORLEANS RESORT

Strengths	Weaknesses
Swimming areas	Insufficient on-site dining
Nice guest rooms	No easily accessible off-site dining
Food courts	Large, confusing layout
Convenient self-parking	Extreme distance of many guest
Children's play areas	rooms from dining and services

The Villas at the Disney Institute

Following the tourism downturn of 2001–2002, Disney closed all of its lodging accommodations at the Disney Institute. The golf courses remain open, as do spa and health club facilities, and some use is being made of the various meeting and teaching facilities. The rest, however, are not expected to be restored to service until 2004 or later. All this could change in an instant if Walt Disney World attendance suddenly balloons, but for now the Disney Institute is Mickey's upscale ghost town.

The Animal Kingdom Resort Area

Animal Kingdom Lodge   The Animal Kingdom Lodge, situated in the far northwest corner of Walt Disney World and a short distance from the Animal Kingdom theme park, opened in April 2001. Designed by Peter Dominick of Disney's Wilderness Lodge fame, the Animal Kingdom Lodge fuses African tribal architecture with the exotic, rugged style of grand East African national park lodges. Five-story, thatched-roof guest-room wings fan out from a vast central rotunda housing the lobby and featuring a huge mud fireplace. The public areas, as well as approximately half of the guest rooms, offer panoramic views of a private 33-acre plain punctuated with elevated kopje (rock outcroppings) and flowing streams and populated with 200 free-roaming animals and 130 birds. Most guest rooms are 344 square feet in size and boast hand-carved furnishings and richly colored soft goods. Almost all have full balconies.

Billed as a deluxe property, the Animal Kingdom Lodge offers fine dining in a casual setting at Jiko. Twin wood-burning ovens are the focal point of the restaurant, which serves primarily light, simple meals. Boma, the Animal Kingdom's family restaurant, is an African version of the Whispering Canyon eatery at the Wilderness Lodge and Villas. Boma serves a buffet with food prepared in an exhibit kitchen featuring a wood-burning grill and rotisserie. Dining tables are situated under thatched roofs. Mara, a quick-service restaurant with extended hours, and Victoria Falls, a delightful mezzanine lounge overlooking Boma, round out the Animal Kingdom's food and beverage service. Other amenities of the 1,307-room lodge include an elaborate swimming area and a village marketplace retail venue.

The Animal Kingdom Lodge is connected to the theme parks and the rest of Walt Disney World by the Disney bus system, but because of the lodge's remote location, you should seriously consider renting a car if you opt to stay there.

ANIMAL KINGDOM LODGE

Strengths	Weaknesses
Exotic theme	Remote location
Uniquely appointed guest rooms	Distant guest self-parking
Views from guest rooms	
Swimming area	
On-site dining	
Health and fitness center	
Child-care center on site	
Recreational options	

Good Rooms and Not So Good Rooms at the Animal Kingdom Lodge
A quick glance at the Animal Kingdom Lodge resort map will tell you
where the best rooms are. Two wings branching from the rear of the main
lodge, respectively called Kudu Trail and Zebra Trail, curve to make a half-
circle around the center wildlife savanna. On each wing, or trail, there are
seven five-story guest buildings with guest rooms on floors 2 through 5.
Five buildings on each wing form the semicircle, while the remaining two
jut outward away from the center. The best rooms are on floors 3 and 4,

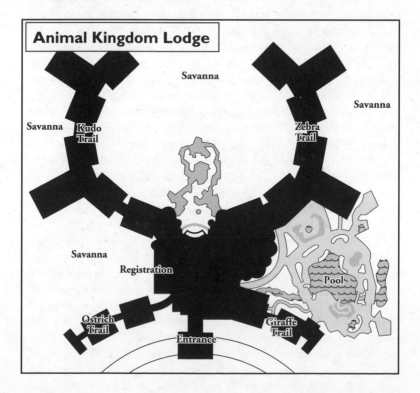

Animal Kingdom Lodge

Savanna

Savanna

Savanna

Kudo Trail

Zebra Trail

Savanna

Registration

Pool

Ostrich Trail

Giraffe Trail

Entrance

facing into the circle. These rooms are high enough to survey the entire savanna, but low enough to let you appreciate the ground-level detail of this amazing natural-habitat wildlife exhibit. Second-floor rooms really can't take in the panoramic vista, and fifth-floor rooms are a little too high for intimate viewing of the animals. For the best wildlife viewing coupled with easy access to the main lodge, book a third or fourth floor, interior-facing room in the third building from the end of either trail.

Most rooms in the outward-jutting buildings, as well as rooms that face away from the interior, also survey a savanna scene, but one not as compelling as that of the inner circle. On the Zebra Trail, the first two buildings plus the first jutting building provide savanna views on one side and look onto the resort swimming complex on the opposite side (water/pool view).

Less attractive still are two smaller wings, the Ostrich Trail and the Giraffe Trail, branching from either side of the lodge near the main entrance. Some rooms in the Ostrich Trail, on the left, overlook a small savanna. Rooms on the opposite side of the same buildings command a view of the front entrance. Least desirable of all is the Giraffe Trail, emanating from the right side of the lobby. Rooms in this wing either survey the pool area (water/pool view) or the resort entrance (standard view).

Disney's Coronado Springs Resort   The Coronado Springs Resort, located near the Animal Kingdom, is Disney's only midpriced convention property. Inspired by northern Mexico and the American Southwest, the resort is divided into three separately-themed areas. The two- and three-story Ranchos call to mind vast Southwestern cattle ranches, while the two- and three-story Cabanas are modeled after Mexican beach resorts. Finally, the multistoried Casitas embody elements of Spanish architecture found in Mexico's great cities. The lobby is part of the Casitas and features a mosaic ceiling and tiled floor. The vast resort surrounds a 15-acre lake, and there are three small pools as well as one large main swimming complex. The main pool is designed to look like ancient ruins and features a reproduction of an Aztec/Mayan steppe pyramid with a waterfall cascading down its side.

There are 1,965 guest rooms at the Coronado Springs. Most of the rooms measure 315 square feet and contain two double beds, a table and chairs, and a vanity outside the bathroom. They are decorated with the colors of the sunset and feature handpainted Mexican wall hangings. All rooms have coffeemakers. None of the rooms have their own balcony.

The Coronado Springs offers one full-service restaurant as well as the most interesting food court at Walt Disney World. Unfortunately, however, there is not nearly enough food service for a resort this large and remote. If you book the Coronado Springs, we suggest that you rent a car to expand your dining options. The resort is connected to other Walt

Disney World destinations by bus only. Walking time from the most remote rooms to the bus stop is eight to ten minutes.

As a convention hotel, the Coronado Springs is somewhat peculiar. Unlike most convention hotels, where everything is centrally located, with the guest rooms in close proximity, guest rooms at the Coronado Springs are arrayed around a huge lake. If you are assigned one of the rooms on the opposite side of the lake from the meeting and convention area (and restaurants!) plan on a 11- to 15-minute hike every time you leave your room. If your organization books the Coronado Springs for a meeting, think about having your meals catered. The hotel's restaurants simply do not have the capacity during a large convention to accommodate the morning breakfast rush or to serve a quick lunch between meeting sessions.

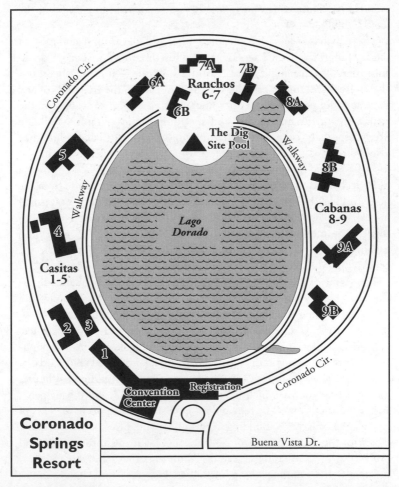

Coronado Springs Resort

Good Rooms and Not So Good Rooms at the Coronado Springs Resort
The Coronado Springs Resort encircles a large, man-made lake called
Lago Dorado. In addition to the main building (El Centro) which holds
the shopping venues, restaurants, and a conference center, there are three
communities of accommodations, each different in appearance and layout. The Cabanas, beach house–style buildings, are nearest El Centro
and the walkway to the main pool; the Ranchos, rustic lodges directly
across Lago Dorado from El Centro, are closest to buses to the parks; and
the Casitas, the four-story "high rises" of the complex, are closest to the
convention center.

A great many guest rooms in Coronado Springs can boast a water view
but, sadly, none of the rooms have private balconies. Here, as at other
resorts, Disney uses the term "water view" loosely, meaning by "water"
everything from a courtyard fountain to a small swimming pool to the
Lago Dorado.

The Cabanas are closest to the main pool and playground, and most of
the buildings overlook Lago Dorado. This proximity to Lago Dorado
and the resort's prime play area is a mixed blessing—it's convenient, but
also noisy. If you prefer to be in the thick of things, the front side of any
Cabana building is going to offer fine water views and easy access to the
attractions of the main lobby and shopping/dining complex. Building
8A is especially so, rooms -40 through -47 in particular since they
directly overlook the pool complex. Our favorites here are rooms -20
though -31 and -40 through -42 on the rear of building 9B. They have a
more secluded water view, one sheltered from the bulk of noise from the
pool complex by virtue of being on the back side overlooking a small
inlet of the Lago. Building 9A has some of the least desirable rooms in
this community, with -20 through -31 and -80 through -83 right off a
parking lot. The same fate is shared by building 8B, with all rooms to the
rear looking directly onto a sea of asphalt.

The Ranchos are conveniently located near the main pool and are the
closest to Disney bus stops. They are also farthest from the shopping and
dining at El Centro. Though they have virtually no true water views,
their proximity to the bus stops and the giant pool-and-play area, where
kids are encouraged to "excavate" at the dig site, makes them very popular. Most of the rooms at the Ranchos overlook landscaped courtyards, or
even nicer, a small "forest" adjacent to the dig site. Building 6B houses
most of these rooms, which include -30 through -37, -50 through -57,
and -60 through -63. The remainder of guest rooms in 6B have views of
landscaped courtyards. Building 7B also has some nice rooms, including
a view of the "quiet pool" from -40 through -45, -50 through -59, and
-80 through -83. Buildings 6A and 7A, on the other hand, are too close
to street traffic and the parking lots to be a first or second choice.

The Casitas are nearest the convention center and close to El Centro. Unfortunately, the high-rise setup lacks the charm of the other areas, and every building backs up to a parking lot except Building 3. The Casitas are dotted with charming inner courtyards, tiled reflecting pools, and fountains, in addition to Lago Dorado and their own "quiet pool." Some of the better water views: Building 1, rooms -70 through -91; Building 2, -40 through -47; Building 3, -80 through -87 and -66 through -74; Building 4, -30 through -32 and -60 through -66; Building 5, -00 through -07, -20 through -27, -30 through -37, and -50 through -55. All these rooms have a view of the lake, or at minimum a pretty pool and fountain--many have all three. We found the best lake views to be from the higher floors (four & five), since there is little in the way of vegetation to block the scene.

CORONADO SPRINGS RESORT

Strengths	Weaknesses
View from waterside guest rooms	Remote location
Swimming area	Insufficient on-site dining
Nice guest rooms	Extreme distance of many guest
Food court	rooms from dining and
Convenient self-parking	services

Disney's All-Star Sports, All-Star Music, and All-Star Movie Resorts
Disney's version of a budget resort features three distinct themes executed in the same hyperbolistic style. Spread over a vast expanse, the resorts are comprised of almost 35 three-story motel-style guest-room buildings. Although the three resorts are neighbors, each has its own lobby, food court, and registration area. The All-Star Sports Resort features huge sports icons: bright football helmets, tennis rackets, and baseball bats, all taller than the buildings they adorn. Similarly, the All-Star Music Resort features 40-foot guitars, maracas, and saxophones, while the All-Star Movie Resort showcases giant popcorn boxes and icons from Disney films. Lobbies of all three resorts are loud (in both decibels and brightness) and cartoonish, with checkerboard walls and photographs of famous athletes, musicians, and film stars. There's even a photo of Mickey Mouse with Alice Cooper. (Does Mickey know that Alice is a man who wears sun-dresses and bites the heads off bats during rock concerts?) The swimming pool at the Music Resort is shaped like a giant guitar, and the pool at the Sports Resort features plastic replicas of the Disney characters shooting water pistols. At the All-Star Movie Resort, the pool is star shaped.

At 260 square feet, the guest rooms at each of the All-Star Resorts are very small. They are so small that a family of four attempting to stay in one room might well redefine family values by the end of the week. Each room has two double beds, a separate vanity area, and a table and chairs. The bed-spreads feature famous athletes, movie stars, and musicians, and the light fixtures are star shaped. None of the rooms at the All-Stars have balconies.

If you are planning to save for years for your grand Disney vacation, save enough money for a bigger room. Also, the prevalence of young children running wild makes the All-Stars the noisiest of the Disney resorts, though the guest rooms are well soundproofed and quiet.

With a low ratio of staff to guests, service is not the greatest. Additionally, there are no full-service restaurants at the resorts. Because the All-Stars are the second most remote of the Walt Disney World resorts, the bus ride to a full-service restaurant at another resort takes about 45 minutes each way. There is, however, a McDonalds about a quarter of a mile away. Bus service to the theme and water parks is pretty efficient. Walking time to the bus stop from the most remote guest rooms is about eight minutes.

We receive a lot of reader mail commenting on the All-Star Resorts. The following are representative:

First, from a family group of 13 from East Greenbush, New York:

The All-Star Resorts are perfectly family-oriented. Some nice touches that were not mentioned in your guide—a small amphitheater set up in the lobby to occupy the kids while you check in, soft sidewalk material surrounding the kiddie pool, which is only about 10 inches deep. And the playground has two separate jungle-gyms—one for older kids and one for younger kids.

Regardless of your personal preference, if you are going to stay at an All-Star Resort, stay at Sports. The sole reason is that the shuttle buses pick up and drop off at the All-Star Resorts in this order: Sports, Music, Movies. That little difference can mean a lot when traveling with kids or with a group.

An Orland Park, Illinois, family had a tough time with their All-Star neighbors, copying us on a letter to Disney:

I am not a person who usually complains, but I had to write and tell you how extremely disappointed I was with the accommodations we had at the All Star Sports. I was expecting that a Disney Resort would be geared toward families. Boy was I mistaken! What we mostly had staying with us were young teenagers who were extremely loud and foul mouthed. We could hardly get any rest. We had groups of people outside our room partying on the football field one night until midnight before someone finally closed them down. Then in the morning (one time as early as 6:30 a.m.) we had cheerleaders practicing right outside our door, shouting their cheers.

A Canadian family had a similar experience:

The guide did not prepare us for the large groups of students that take over the resorts. They are very noisy and very pushy when it comes to getting on buses. Our scariest experience was when we tried getting on a bus and got mobbed by about 100 students. We didn't know if our children would come out alive from the experience. We don't think we would go back to the All Star Resort for this reason (they offer packages to student groups). Also, the motel does not want to hear your complaints at all.

But a Baltimore family had a very positive experience, writing:

We decided early on that we'd rather spend more money on food than lodging. We love to eat, and figured that we wouldn't spend that much time in the room, so we picked the All-Star Movies resort. We were pleasantly surprised. Yes, the rooms are small. But the overall magic there is amazing. The lobby played Disney movies, which is perfect if you get up early and the buses aren't running yet. There are great photo ops everywhere (Donald and Daisy were awesome). It's heaven for fans of Fantasia 2000. Customer service was impeccable. Everyone seems to bust on the food court, which let's face it — is crap... except for the refrigerator cases where you can buy (albeit expensive) fresh-tasting fruit, water, healthy snacks, and great chicken-salad sandwiches. Further, despite forewarnings of loud children, we were in the Love Bug building and found it very quiet. The express checkout service was also a godsend.

From a Massachusetts family of four:

I would never recommend the All-Star for a family. It was like dormitory living. Our room was about one mile from the bus stop, and the food court got old very quickly. Buses were great, but the room was tiny. I'm in the hotel business, and it was one of the smallest I've been in. You needed to step into the bathroom, shut the door, then step around the toilet that blocked half the tub.

And finally, a family from the United Kingdom reports:

We stayed at All-Star Sports. For younger kids the other themed hotels can be a bit too adult—my kids don't know much about Dixie/N'Awlins (yet!), but they loved the theme at All-Star Sports. Perhaps again it is a foreign thing, but we all loved the over-the-top decor. Can you say something nice about it, please?

Good Rooms and Not So Good Rooms at the All Star Resorts The All-Star Resort is divided into three themed sections: movies, music, and sports. Though the layout of each section is unique, the buildings are identical three-story, three-winged structures. The T-shaped buildings are further grouped into pairs, generally facing one another, that share a common sub-theme. For example, there is a Toy Story pair in the movies section. In addition to being named by theme, i.e. Fantasia, buildings are numbered 1–10 in each section. Rooms are accessed via a motel-style outdoor walkway, but, fortunately, each building has an elevator.

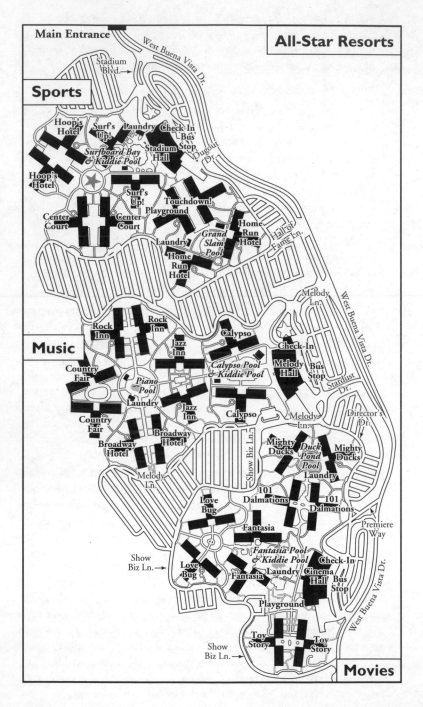

As with a motel, there is plenty of parking at the All-Star, all in sprawling lots buffering the three sections. A room near a parking lot means easier loading and unloading, but also unsightly views of the lot during your stay. (The resort offers a luggage service, but it often takes up to an hour for your bags to arrive.) Disney has taken care to leave wooded parcels, mostly pines, between the lots and buildings. However, this greenery fails to spare everyone. Generally, and unsurprisingly, rooms on the ends of a wing that juts toward a parking lot are most likely to overlook it, while those near the buildings' inner corners—where wings meet—are best insulated by trees.

The sure way to avoid a parking lot vista is to opt for a room facing a courtyard or pool. The trade-off is noise. Cars starting in the parking lot are no match for shrieking children or hooting teenagers cavorting in the pool. Of course, they're also not as entertaining. But don't count on a good view of the pool, even if your room faces it directly. The buildings' themed façade decorations are placed on their widest face—the top of the **T**—which is also the side facing the pool or courtyard. In some cases, as with the surfboards in the sports section, these significantly obstruct the view from nearby rooms. Additionally, there are floodlights trained on these facades. So, if you step out of your room at night to view the action below, looking straight down may result in temporary blindness.

The sort of traveler you are should dictate the sort of room you request at the All-Star Resort. If you choose the resort because you'd rather spend time and money at the parks than at your hotel, then opt to be near the bus stop, your link to the rest of Walt Disney World. Note that buses leave from the central public building of each section, dubbed "halls," which are near the larger, noisier pools. If you're planning to return to your room for an afternoon nap, seek a room further from the pools. Also consider an upper-story room to minimize foot traffic past your door. On the other hand, if you choose the All-Star for its kid-friendly aspects—themes obvious to youngsters, large pools with kiddie pools attached, smaller secondary pools, arcades, and food courts for picky eaters—then consider roosting near the action. A bottom-floor room provides easy pool access, and a room looking out on a courtyard or pool allows you to keep an eye on children playing outside.

For travelers not bringing young children (infants excluded), the best bets for privacy and quiet are the buildings that overlook the forest behind the resort, buildings 2–4 in All-Star Sports and 4–7 in All-Star Music. Interior-facing rooms in these buildings (and their partners) also fit the bill, since they look out on the courtyards furthest from the large pools. The courtyards themselves vary with theme but are generally only mildly amusing. For example, the New Orleans–style garden in the Jazz

Inn courtyard is positively verdant compared to the all-blacktop court-yard of its Broadway Hotel neighbor.

Nevertheless, if you're travelling with children, it makes sense to opt for a section and building with a theme that appeals to your kids. Often, that will be a film—movies are the lifeblood of the Disney empire—but it might well be a sport. If you're staying in Home Run Hotel, don't forget the ball and gloves to maximize the experience. Just keep games of catch away from the pool. Older elementary- and middle-school children will most likely want to spend hotel time in or near the bigger pools or the arcades in the nearby halls. Periodically, cadres of teenagers—too cool for their younger siblings—effectively commandeer the smaller secondary pools. There are playgrounds tucked behind Building 9 in All-Star Music and behind Building 6 in All-Star Sports, so rooms facing these are ideal for families with children too young or timid for the often-chaotic larger pools. In All-Star Movies, the playground is closer to the food court than to any rooms.

ALL-STAR RESORTS

Strengths	Weaknesses
Low (for Disney) rates	No full-service dining
Food courts	Small guest rooms
Convenient self-parking	Remote location
	Large, confusing layout

Disney's Pop Century Resorts   Located across from Disney's Wide World of Sports on Osceola Parkway, the Pop Century is the newest of the Disney-owned resorts. It is to be completed in phases, but the first section, scheduled to open in December 2001, was put on indefinite hold following the events of 9/11 and their devastating impact on travel. The second phase, which would have brought the full compliment of 5,760 guest rooms by 2003, is likewise in limbo.

Pop Century is a Disney economy resort, meaning rooms will average about $80–110 per night. In terms of layout, architecture, and facilities, Pop Century is almost a perfect clone of the All-Star Resorts (i.e., three-story, motel-style buildings built around a central pool, food court, and registration area). Aside from location, the only difference between the All-Star and Pop Century Resorts are the decorative touches. Where the All-Star Resorts are distinguished (if you can call it that) by larger-than-life icons from sports, music, and movies, Pop Century draws its icons from various decades of the twentieth century. Look for such oddities as building-size Big Wheels, hula hoops, and the like, punctuated by sil-houettes of people dancing the in-dance of the decade.

There is no full-service restaurant at Pop Century, and guest rooms are small and whimsically (as opposed to tastefully) decorated. The resort is

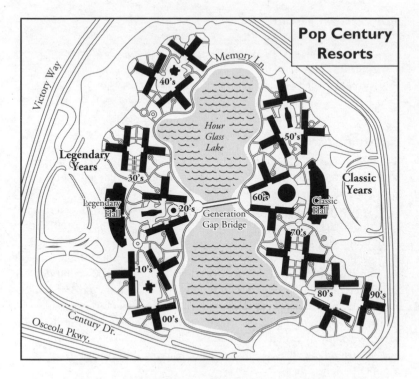

connected to the rest of Walt Disney World by bus, but because of the limited dining options we recommend renting a car.

Good Rooms and Not So Good Rooms at the Pop Century Resort
Because the Pop Century Resort had not opened by press time, our room recommendations will be elaborated in the next edition. For the moment, however, we can tell you that guest rooms do not have private patios or balconies. If you bring along a lawn chair, however, you can sit on the railed walkway that serves as the guest-room access corridor on each floor. The best rooms in terms of both view and convenience are the lake-view rooms in buildings 4 and 5, representing the 1960s decade. The downside for the intermediate term, however, is that these rooms will be subjected to highway noise from Victory Way and Osceola Parkway across the lake. If work resumes on the other half of the Pop Century, these rooms will also have to put up with the sights and noise of construction. A safer short-term bet, though with an admittedly less compelling view, are east-facing rooms in the same building, i.e., rooms facing the registration and food court building. Next best choices are the east-facing rooms of building 3 in the 1950s, and of building 6 in the 1970s. To be avoided are south-facing rooms in 1980s building 7 and 1990s building 8. Both buildings are echo chambers for traffic noise on nearby Osceola Parkway.

POP CENTURY RESORTS

Strengths	Weaknesses
Low (for Disney) rates	No full-service dining
Food courts	Small guest rooms
Convenient self-parking	Remote location
	Large, confusing layout

Camping at Walt Disney World

Fort Wilderness Campground is a spacious resort campground for tent and RV camping. Fully equipped, air-conditioned prefab log cabins are also available for rent.

Sites are priced according to utilities furnished. Sites with water and electric only go for $34–$65 per night, depending on the season. Sites with water, electric, and sewer run $39–$76. If you add cable the price is $47–$80. All sites are arranged on loops accessible from one of three main roads. There are 28 loops altogether, with loops 100–2000 dedicated to tent and RV campers, and loops 2100–2800 offering prefab log cabin accommodations. All sites are level and provide a picnic table, a waste container, and a grill. No fires are permitted except in the grills. RV sites are roomy by eastern US standards, but tent campers will probably feel a little cramped. On any given day, about 90% or more of the campers will be RVers.

Fort Wilderness Campground arguably offers the most recreational facilities and activities of any Disney resort. Among other things, there are two video arcades, nightly campfire programs, Disney movies, a dinner theater, two swimming pools, a beach, the River Country swimming park, walking paths, bike, boat, canoe, golf cart, and water ski rentals, a petting zoo, horseback riding, hay rides, fishing, and tennis, basketball, and volleyball courts. There are two convenience stores, a restaurant, and a tavern. Comfort stations with toilets, showers, pay phones, ice machine, and laundry facilities are within easy walking distance of all campsites.

Access to the Magic Kingdom is by boat from Fort Wilderness Landing and by bus with a transfer at the Ticket and Transportation Center. Transportation to all other Walt Disney World destinations is by bus. Motor traffic within the campground is permitted only when entering or exiting. Options for getting around within the campground include bus, golf cart, or bike, the latter two of which are available for rent.

FORT WILDERNESS CAMPGROUND

Strengths	Weaknesses
Informality	Complicated bus service
Children's play areas	Lack of privacy
Recreational options	Very limited dining options
Special day and evening programs	Confusing campground layout
Campsite amenities	Small baths in cabins and trailers
Number of shower/toilet facilities	Distance to store and restaurant from many campsites

For tent and RV campers there's a fairly stark trade-off between sites convenient to pools, restaurant, trading posts, and other amenities and those that are most scenic, shady, and quiet. RVers who prefer to be where the action is, close to guest services, the marina, the beach, the restaurant and tavern, and the River Country water park, should go for loops 100, 200, 700, and 400 (in that order). Loops close to the campground's secondary facility area with pool, trading post, bike and golf cart rentals, and campfire program, are 1400, 1300, 600, 1000, and 1500 in order of preference. If you're looking for a quiet, tranquil, scenic setting among more mature trees, we recommend loops 1800, 1900, 1700, 1600, in that order, and the backside sites on the 700 loop. The best loop of all, and the only loop to offer both a lovely setting and close proximity to key amenities is loop 300. The best loops for tent and pop-up campers are loops 1500 and 2000, with 1500 being closest to a pool, convenience store, and the campfire program.

With the exception of loops 1800 and 1900, avoid sites within 40 yards of the loop entrance. These sites are almost always flanked by one of the main traffic arteries within Fort Wilderness. Further, sites on the outside of the loop are almost always preferable to those in the center of the loop. RVers should be forewarned that all the sites are back-ins, and that although most RV sites will accommodate large rigs, the loop access roads are pretty tight and narrow.

Rental cabins offer a double bed and two bunk beds in the only bedroom, augmented by a Murphy bed (pulls down from the wall) in the living room. There is one rather small bathroom with shower and tub.

All cabins offer air conditioning, color television with VCR, a fully equipped kitchen, and a dining table. Housekeeping service is provided daily. Most of our readers are crazy about the cabins. Here are a couple of representative comments:

First, from a Lancaster, New York, family of five:

Fort Wilderness Cabins are underrated. It's a great place for our family of 5. If you don't mind cooking breakfast and a few other meals during your stay,

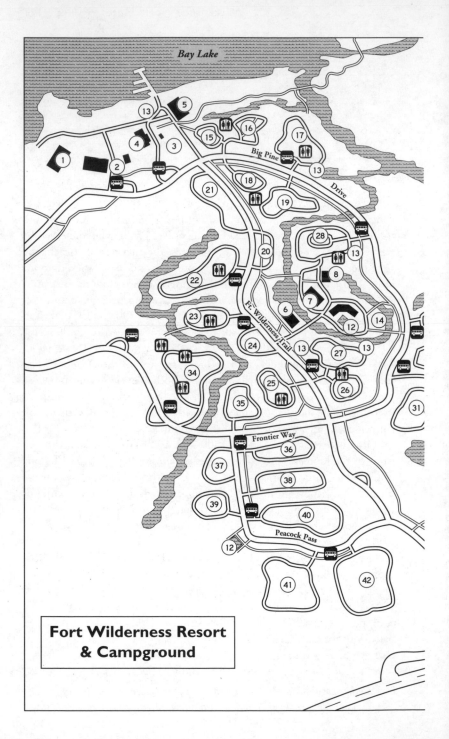

Bay Lake

Big Pine

Drive

Ft. Wilderness Trail

Frontier Way

Peacock Pass

Fort Wilderness Resort & Campground

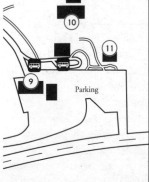

1. Pavillon
   Petting Farm/Ranch
2. Coachmen RV Display
3. Pioneer Hall
      Guest Services
      Trail's End Restaurant
      Crockett's Tavern
      Hoop-Dee-Doo Revue
4. Settlement Trading Post
5. Meadow Trading Post
6. Bike Barn/Golf Cart Rentals
7. Campfire Program
8. Reception Outpost
9. Trail Ride
10. Kennel
11. Arcade
12. Pool
13. Playground
14. Tennis Courts

Campsite Loops
15. Bay Tree Lake
16. Palmetto Path
17. Cypress Knee Circle
18. Whispering Pine Way
19. Buffalo Bend
20. Sunny Sage Way
21. Cinnamon Fern Way
22. Jack Rabbit Run
23. Quail Trail
24. Raccoon Lane
25. Possum Path
26. Dogwood Drive
27. Tumblewood Turn
28. Little Bear Path & Big Bear Path
29. Cottonwood Curl
30. Timber Trail
31. Hickory Hollow
32. Conestoga Trail
33. Wagon Wheel Way
34. Spanish Moss Lane
35. Bobcat Bend
36. Arrowhead Way
37. Shawnee Bend
38. Settler's Bend
39. Cedar Circle
40. Moccasin Trail
41. Heron Hollow
42. Willow Way

Bus Stop
Comfort Station/Laundry Facility

you can actually save on food at restaurants. This makes up for the extra money spent on accommodations. The cabins are more spacious and much more comfortable than a basic hotel room. The bedroom is great for the kids to have an afternoon rest or for getting them to bed early so parents can relax and unwind after a long day.

And from another New York family, this time from Wappingers Falls:

We stayed at Fort Wilderness Campgrounds in a cabin because:
We wanted a separate bedroom area.
We wanted a kitchen.
Our kids are very lively and the cabins were apart from each other so we wouldn't disturb other guests.
We thought the kids might meet other children to play with.
It was close to River Country.

The cabins worked out just right for us. Although the kids did not meet any other children to play with, they had a ball chasing the little lizards and frogs, kicking around pinecones, sitting on the deck to eat ice pops, and sleeping in bunk beds. We went to the campfire twice (we brought our own marshmallows and sticks). Our cabin was a short walk to our bus stop and two "blocks" away from the pool and laundry. I loved the dishwasher, the generous storage space, the extra towels, the air conditioning, and the daily cleaning service. There was no canned music or fake bird calls in the tress, just peace and quiet.

If you rent a cabin or camp in a tent or RV, particularly in the fall or spring, keep abreast of local weather conditions. This is definitely not the place where you want to be if the area is under a tornado warning.

How to Evaluate a Walt Disney World Travel Package

Hundreds of Walt Disney World package vacations are offered each year. Some are created by the Walt Disney Travel Company, others by airline touring companies, independent travel agents, and wholesalers. Almost all include lodging at or near Disney World and theme-park admissions. Packages offered by airlines include air transportation.

Prices vary seasonally; mid-February to the end of April and holiday periods are the most expensive. Off-season, forget packages: there are plenty of empty rooms, and you can negotiate great discounts (especially at non-Disney properties). Similarly, airfares and rental cars are cheaper off-peak.

Almost all package ads are headlined "5 Days at Walt Disney World from $645" (or such). The key word is "from." The rock-bottom price includes the least desirable hotels. If you want better or more convenient digs, you'll have to pay more, often much more.

Packages offer a wide selection of hotels. Some, like the Disney resorts, are very dependable. Others run the gamut of quality. If you consider a non-Disney hotel, check its quality as reported in an independent rating such as those offered by the *Unofficial Guides, AAA Directories, Mobil Guides,* or *Frommer's Guides.* Checking two or three independent sources is best. Also, before you book, ask how old the hotel is and when the guest rooms were last refurbished. Locate the hotel on a map to verify its proximity to Disney World. If you won't have a car, make sure the hotel has an adequate shuttle service.

Packages with non-Disney lodging are much less expensive. But guests at Disney-owned properties get free parking and access to the Disney transportation system. These privileges don't apply to guests at the seven independent hotels of the Disney Village Hotel Plaza (Wyndham Palace, Grosvenor Resort, DoubleTree Guest Suites Resort, The Hilton Resort, Courtyard by Marriott, Hotel Royal Plaza, and Best Western Hotel).

Packages should be a win/win proposition for both buyer and seller. The buyer makes only one phone call and deals with one salesperson to set up the whole vacation (transportation, rental car, admissions, lodging, meals, and even golf and tennis). The seller, likewise, deals with the buyer only one time. Some packagers also buy airfares in bulk on contract, like a broker playing the commodities market. By buying a large number of airfares in advance, the packager saves significantly over posted fares. The practice is also applied to hotel rooms. Because selling packages is efficient and because the packager often can buy package components (airfare, lodging, etc.) in bulk at discount, savings in operating expenses realized by the seller are sometimes passed on to the buyer, making the package both convenient and an exceptional value.

In practice, however, the seller may realize all of the economies and pass on no savings to the buyer. In some instances, packages are loaded with extras that cost the packager almost nothing but run the retail price of the package sky-high. Not surprisingly, the savings passed on to customers are still somewhere in Fantasyland.

Choose a package that includes features you're sure to use. Whether you use all of the features or not, you will pay for them. If price is more important than convenience, call around to see what the package would cost if you booked its components on your own. If the package price is less than the à la carte cost, the package is a good deal. If costs are about equal, the package probably is worth it for the convenience. Most of the time, however, you'll find that there are significant saving to be had buying the components of the package individually.

An Example A popular package offered by the Walt Disney Travel Company is the *Disney Resort Magic* plan, which includes:

1. Three or more nights' accommodation at your choice of any Disney resort. Rates vary with choice of lodging; the Grand Floridian is the most expensive, and the All-Star Resorts are the least expensive.

2. Unlimited use of the Walt Disney World transportation system.

3. Admission and unlimited use of all Walt Disney World theme parks during your stay.

4. Admission and unlimited use of Pleasure Island nighttime entertainment complex; River Country, Typhoon Lagoon, and Blizzard Beach swimming parks; and Disney's Wide World of Sports during your stay. (Admission becomes effective upon check-in and is valid until midnight of your check-out day.)

5. Free parking.

The *Disney Resort Magic* plan also includes a "flex feature," which consists of one of the following per person:

1. One Mickey 'n You photo session.

2. Disney character breakfast.

3. Disney's Magical Moments Pin

4. 30-minute mini powerboat rental

Loaded with benefits and amenities, this is one of Walt Disney World's most popular packages (price varies with hotel and room choice and length of stay). Depending on how you use it, you can come out a winner or a loser.

Our sample analysis is done for a couple from Fairfield, Connecticut, on a six-night package, traveling in August and arriving in Orlando by air. The couple's choice of hotels is Port Orleans Riverside Resort, connected to the theme parks by bus. Because check-in time at Port Orleans is 3 p.m. or later, the couple plans to arrive at Walt Disney World in the late afternoon and begin touring the theme parks the next day. Their itinerary calls for additional touring on their check-out day prior to leaving for the airport. The package in 2002 costs $1,034 for each adult (two to a room), or $2,069 for the couple (tax included). Their round-trip airfare from Hartford and transportation from and to the airport are in addition to the package price.

Six days' use of the transportation system is no big deal. Anyone who buys a regular five- or six-day admission can ride all day on the buses, boats, and monorails.

The package provides six days' admission to the major theme parks as well as River Country, Blizzard Beach, Typhoon Lagoon, and Pleasure Island. Since it takes at least five days to see the major theme parks, little time is left to visit Typhoon Lagoon, Blizzard Beach, River Country, and Pleasure Island.

Another problem with the six days' admission is that whatever you don't use, you lose. Admissions are good only for the days of the package, unlike the non-package Hopper Passes. Unused days on the Hopper and Hopper Plus are good forever. If you come back next month or three years from now, you'll be able to finish using your pass. Not so with the package admission.

The package's "flex features" can all be purchased à la carte. And the private photo session with Mickey may be more of a liability than an asset, as a Texas gentleman notes:

Included in our vacation package was a photograph session with Mickey at You & Me Kid, a shop in the Downtown Disney Marketplace (aka WDW Village). Two caveats emptor here: First, the procedure for the photo session was very poorly arranged and executed with molasses-like speed (much to the ire of a gaggle of bedraggled parents). Second, we suspect that the delay was at least partially intentional: the more hours you were detained at the Disney Village before your appointment with The Mouse, the more steadily your billfold could be emptied on the relentless parade of Disney merchandise. Indeed, since this shopping center was the only location given for this special photo-op, our hunch is that the whole affair is little more than a lure to draw families off the beaten path to a nice but très expensive Disney Marketplace.

In the final analysis, the *Disney Resort Magic Plan* is best suited to vacationers who plan to be on the go from dawn until midnight and visit the theme parks every day. And, you may have concluded, it's set up in a way that makes it almost impossible not to waste many of its benefits.

Getting Down to Dollars and Cents   If you exclude the recreational extras, here's how the package compares with going it your own:

Option A:	*Disney Resort Magic Plan* for two people in August, sharing a water-view room at the Port Orleans Resort:	$1,034 per person × 2 = $2,068
Option B:	Creating your own vacation with the same basic features of the *Disney Resort Magic Plan*. The Port Orleans Resort (same room as package) for six nights with tax included for two adults	$1,026
	Two 6-Day Park-Hopper Plus Passes (unlimited admission to four major parks and three visits to the minor parks) with tax	$587
	A 30-minute mini powerboat rental	$22
	Grand total for two people	$1,635
	Amount saved by arranging things yourself	$433

The Disney Central Reservations Office (CRO) quoted us the room-only rate of $1,026 for the six-night stay. When (because we were merely collecting price quotes for this edition) we did not make a reservation, the CRO fished around and found a special deal that gave us the same room for the same dates at $626 tax inclusive! This additional $400 savings pushed our total do-it-yourself savings to $833, a walloping 40% savings over the package price. Because the travel market was still somewhat soft when we called, deals might have been more readily available than when you book. Even so, we would not have even bumped into the deal had we not been booking our own room through CRO.

Another Example   Most Delta Dream Vacations offer almost the same features as *Disney's Resort Magic Plan,* plus round-trip air transportation. If a couple from Los Angeles buys a six-night Delta package for late August at the Wilderness Lodge and Villas Resort, they'll pay $3,129 for both people. If they book the same components themselves, the cost will be $2,054 *before* buying airline tickets.

If you subtract the à la carte costs of package components from the package price ($3,129 minus $2,054), the remainder ($1,075) is what the couple is being charged for airfare, in this case $537.50 per person ($1,075 divided by two). If they can fly round trip to Orlando from Los Angeles for less than $537.50 a person, the package isn't such a great deal. If airfares from Los Angeles equal or exceed $537.50 per person, the package makes sense.

If you buy a package from Disney, don't expect reservationists to offer suggestions or help you sort out your options. Generally, they won't volunteer information and will respond only to your specific questions, ducking queries that require an opinion. A reader from North Riverside, Illinois, complains:

I have received various pieces of literature from WDW, and it is very confusing to figure out everything. My wife made two telephone calls, and the representatives from WDW were very courteous. However, they only answered the questions posed and were not eager to give advice on what might be most cost effective. [The] WDW reps would not say if we would be better off doing one thing over the other. I feel a person could spend eight hours on the phone with WDW reps and not have any more input than you get from reading the literature.

If you can't get the information you need from Disney, contact a good travel agent. Chances are the agent can help you sort out your options. A dad from Valley Stream, New York, used the Walt Disney Travel Company, travel wholesalers, and travel agents to comparison-shop successfully:

Nothing pays greater dividends than planning in advance. A year before our vacation we joined the Magic Kingdom Club [now the Disney Club]. Some 8–9 months before our vacation I secured a package price from the Magic Kingdom Club, which I was able to use to negotiate a lower package with *my travel agent. Yes, the travel agent packages are negotiable (much to my own surprise). What I now realize is that travel agents get WDW packages from different wholesalers and may not be immediately inclined to give you a package offered through the lowest-priced wholesaler. The first quotes I received were from AAA and Liberty Travel but, unbeknownst to me, both packages were, in fact, purchased through Delta Airlines. It was only after I was able to obtain a lower land package price by booking directly through Disney (as a Magic Kingdom Club member) that I was assured by each agent that they could beat the price I was able to secure—and they did, saving me several hundred dollars. The air package was another reason to book through a travel agent. Our agent reserved seats for us on one airline only to call us three weeks later to tell us of discounts being offered through another airline. We acted quickly and bought the discounted tickets, saving another $200 on our air package.*

Information Needed for Evaluation   If you have web access, pull up disneyworld.com. On the home page look for the brown "Vacations Savings" block on the upper left. Start here. There might be a special for a room-only deal or even for a package that fits your needs. If the block does not appear on the home page, or if there are no deals that work for you, click on "Reservations & Tickets" in the upper right. This will bring up a page where you can click "Book Your Vacation Package" or "Book Your Room Reservation." You can also price admission options on this page by clicking "Buy Tickets and Passes." Once you access the Vacation Package page, you can enter your dates, the number of persons in your party, your preferred resort, and the package you're interested in (they're all described). Without asking you to provide any personal information, the site will compute the total cost for you.

Now that you know the price you have to beat, go to the Room Reservation page, punch in your dates, number of people, and choice of hotel. The page will calculate the tax inclusive room rate for you. Go next to the Tickets and Passes page to determine the cost of your passes. Don't be afraid to click on "Buy Now." It's the only way to get total calculated costs, and you'll get the info you need before you're asked to enter any personal info.

Once you've costed all the individual components of the package, you'll know how much you'll save by buying each component individually. When you're ready to actually book, whether a package or individual components, do it via phone with the Disney Central Reservations Office (CRO) at (407) W-DISNEY. Getting a live sales agent on the phone will allow you to inquire about special deals and extra savings. When we get to this point, we go one step further and give our travel agent the opportunity to better the price.

If you don't have Internet access, obtain a Walt Disney World Travel Company 2003 (or 2002 if applicable) Florida Vacations booklet from any local travel agent. The booklet will contain all the information you'll need to price a package. Remember that all packages are priced on a per-person basis at two to a room (double occupancy), and that there is an 11% combined sales and room tax. Once you've calculated the cost of the package, call the CRO at (407) W-DISNEY for room-only accommodations and ticket prices. Don't forget to ask about specials. Once you've obtained your comparative data, let your travel agent make the reservations. It's all about relationships. One of these days you'll need a loyal travel agent.

Some Tips from Mary Waring

Mary Waring, webmaster at Mousesavers.com (see page 25), knows more about Disney packages than anyone on the planet. Here's what she suggests:

Book "room only"   Disney likes to sell packages, because they are easy and profitable. When you buy a package you are typically paying a premium for convenience, and packages are cunningly designed to include extras you are unlikely to use. You can often save money by putting together your own "package." It's not difficult. Just book a "room only" resort reservation and buy your passes, meals, and extras separately.

Need another reason to consider a "room only" reservation? Packages require full payment well in advance and have far less desirable change and cancellation policies than "room only" reservations. Booking "room only" requires a deposit of just one night's room rate, with the remainder due at check-in, and your reservation can be changed or cancelled for any reason until 5 days before check-in.

Be aware that all reservations using the Disney Club member discount are considered packages. In order to justify this, Disney automatically adds tickets to the Wide World of Sports Complex or mini-golf to a "room only" Disney Club reservation and calls it a "Basic Plan" package. If you don't want a package, don't use Disney Club.

For best results when booking a "room only" reservation, keep these five important points in mind:

The phone number you use may make a difference   All reservations phone calls go to the Disney Reservations Center, but within the center there are two kinds of agents: those primarily focused on selling packages for the Walt Disney Travel Company (WDTC) and those who sell "room only" reservations for the Central Reservations Office (CRO). If you call a number provided on a package brochure, or the number on your Disney Club card, you will be connected to a WDTC agent. If you call the CRO number, (407) W-DISNEY, you will usually get a CRO agent—at busy times your call may roll over to a WDTC agent.

Know how to work with Disney's phone reservations agents   CRO agents deal with "room only" reservations all day long and naturally will be experts at booking such reservations. WDTC agents are able to book "room only" reservations, but they prefer to book packages and occasionally they are not very cooperative about doing anything else. If you find yourself talking to a WDTC agent and you don't want a package, be pleasant but firm. Tell the agent very clearly that you want a "room only" reservation. If the first agent you reach isn't helpful, politely end the call and try again. There are hundreds of agents and you're unlikely to reach the same one twice.

Use discount codes to reduce your "room only" rate by up to 45% Discount codes are used by Disney to push unsold rooms at certain times of year. They are published in newspaper ads, on Disney's website, and in e-mails and postcards sent out by Disney. You can check a website like **mousesavers.com** (see page 25) to learn about any discount codes that may be available for the dates of your vacation. Many of the discount codes are available to anyone (including international visitors), though a few are specific to residents of certain states, Annual Passholders, etc. Code discounts are not always available at every hotel or for every date, and they typically don't appear until 2–6 months in advance. The good news is, you can usually apply a code to an existing "room only" reservation (but not to a package). Simply call CRO and inquire whether there are any rooms available at your preferred hotel for your preferred dates, using the code.

Be flexible   Buying a room with a discount code is a little like shopping for clothes at a discount store. If you wear size XX-Small or XXXX-Large, or you like green when everyone else is wearing pink this year, you're a lot more likely to score a cheap deal. Likewise, discounts at the Disney resorts are only going to happen when Disney has excess rooms. You're more likely to get a discount during less-popular times of year (i.e., Value Season) and at larger or less-popular resorts. Animal Kingdom Lodge and Old Key West often seem to have more discounted room availability than the other resorts, while scoring a discounted room at the very popular All Star Movies is a major coup.

Be persistent   This is the most important tip of all. Disney allots a certain number of rooms to each discount; reportedly this averages 100 rooms per night per code. Once the discounted rooms are gone, you won't be able to get that rate unless someone cancels. Fortunately, people change and cancel reservations all the time. If you can't get your preferred dates or hotel with a certain discount code, try an alternate code (if available) or keep calling back first thing in the morning to check on whether there have been any cancellations. The system resets overnight and any reservations with unpaid deposits are automatically released for resale.

Hotels outside Walt Disney World

Selecting and Booking a Hotel outside Walt Disney World

Lodging costs outside Walt Disney World vary incredibly. If you shop around, you can find a clean motel with a pool within 20 minutes of the World for as low as $35 a night. You also can find luxurious, expensive hotels with all the extras. Because of hot competition, discounts abound, particularly for AAA and AARP members.

There are three primary out-of-the-World areas to consider:

1. International Drive Area   This area, about 15–20 minutes east of Walt Disney World, parallels I-4 on its southern side and offers a wide selection of both hotels and restaurants. Accommodations range from $40 to $320 per night. The chief drawbacks of the International Drive area are its terribly congested roads, countless traffic signals, and inadequate access to westbound I-4. While the biggest bottleneck is the intersection with Sand Lake Road, the mile of International Drive between Kirkman Road and Sand Lake Road stays in near-continuous gridlock. It's common to lose 25–35 minutes trying to navigate this stretch.

Regarding International Drive (known locally as I-Drive) traffic, the following comments are representative.

From a Seattle mom:

After spending half our trip sitting in traffic on International Drive, those Disney hotels didn't sound so expensive, after all.

A convention-goer from Islip, New York, weighed in with this:

When I visited Disney World with my family last summer, we wasted huge chunks of time in traffic on International Drive. Our hotel was in the section between the big McDonald's [at Sand Lake Drive] and Wet 'n' Wild [at Universal Boulevard]. There are practically no left turn lanes in this section, so anyone turning left can hold up traffic for a long time. Recently, I returned to Orlando for a trade show and stayed at a hotel on International Drive near the convention center. This section was much saner and far less congested. It's also closer to Disney World.

If you stay on I-Drive, you can avoid the worst traffic as well as the infamous Sand Lake Road intersection by using Universal Boulevard. Universal Boulevard originates north of I-4, crosses the interstate, and then intersects International Drive. It continues south, crossing Sand Lake Road, and eventually reconnects with I-Drive south of the Orange County Convention Center. Turning left onto I-Drive, it's a short hop (about one-third mile) to the I-Drive/Beeline Expressway interchange.

Get on the Beeline Expressway heading west (no toll), and it will drop you right onto I-4. Proceed south on I-4 to the exits for Walt Disney World.

Traffic aside, a gentleman from Ottawa, Canada, extols his International Drive experience:

International Drive is the place to stay when going to Disney. Your single paragraph description of this location failed to point out that [there are] several discount stores, boutiques, restaurants and mini-putts, and other entertainment facilities, all within walking distance of remarkably inexpensive accommodations and a short drive away from WDW. Many of the chain motels and hotels are located in this area, and the local merchants have created a mini-resort to cater to the tourists. It is the ideal place to unwind after a hard day visiting WDW. I have recommended this location for years and have never heard anything but raves about the wisdom of this advice.

Hotels in the International Drive area are listed in the *Orlando Official Accommodations Guide* published by the Orlando/Orange County Convention and Visitors Bureau. For a copy, call (800) 255-5786 or (407) 363-5872.

2. Lake Buena Vista and the I-4 Corridor A number of hotels are situated along FL 535 and north of I-4 between Walt Disney World and I-4's intersection with the Florida Turnpike. These properties are easily reached from the interstate and are near a large number of restaurants, including those on International Drive. Driving time to Disney World is 5 to 15 minutes. Most hotels in this area are listed in the *Orlando Official Accommodations Guide.*

3. US 192 This is the highway to Kissimmee, southeast of Walt Disney World. In addition to a number of large, full-service hotels are many small, privately owned motels that are often a good value. Several dozen properties on US 192 are closer to the Disney theme parks than are the more expensive hotels in Walt Disney World Village and the Disney Village Hotel Plaza. The number and variety of restaurants on US 192 has increased markedly in the past several years, easing the area's primary shortcoming.

We're happy to report that the construction project on US 192 east and west of the entrance to Walt Disney World has been completed. The highway has been widened and landscaped medians and shoulders, lined with stately palms, have been added. The flow of traffic has improved considerably and the improved appearance of the highway is remarkable. What once looked like an endless strip mall has now assumed the lush appearance of a real resort area.

Although traffic now moves fluidly along US 192, there remain a number of traffic signals. If your hotel on US 192 is east of the Walt Disney

World entrance, you can bypass the lights by using the Osceola Parkway toll road that parallels US 192 to the north. From US 192 take FL 535 or Poinciana Boulevard north to access the parkway.

A senior citizen from Brookfield, Connecticut, was surprised and pleased with lodging in the US 192/Kissimmee area:

We were amazed to find that from our cheaper and superior accommodations in Kissimmee it took only 5 minutes longer to reach the park turnstiles than it did from the Disney accommodations. Kissimmee is the way to go, in our opinion.

Hotels on US 192 and in Kissimmee are listed in the *Kissimmee–St. Cloud Visitor's Guide*, available at (800) 327-9159 or www.floridakiss.com.

Driving Time to the Theme Parks for Visitors Lodging outside Walt Disney World

For those staying outside Walt Disney World, we've calculated the approximate commuting time to the major theme parks' parking lots from several off-World lodging areas. Add a few minutes to our times to pay your parking fee and park. Once parked at the Transportation and Ticket Center (Magic Kingdom parking lot), it takes an average of 20–30 additional minutes to reach the Magic Kingdom. To reach Epcot from its parking lot, add 7–10 minutes. At Disney-MGM Studios and the Animal Kingdom, the lot-to-gate transit is 5–10 minutes. If you haven't purchased your theme-park admission in advance, tack on another 10–20 minutes.

DRIVING TIME TO THE THEME PARKS

Minutes From	To Magic Kingdom Parking Lot	Epcot Parking Lot	Disney–MGM Studios Parking Lot	Animal Kingdom Parking Lot
Downtown Orlando	39	36	38	41
North International Dr. and Universal Studios	24	21	22	26
Central International Dr.– Sand Lake Road	26	23	24	27
South International Dr. SeaWorld	18	15	16	20
FL 535	12	9	10	13
US 192, north of I-4	10–20	10–20	8–15	8–15
US 192, south of I-4	10–25	10–22	8–18	8–17

Getting a Good Deal on a Room outside Walt Disney World

Hotel development at Walt Disney World has sharpened the competition among lodgings throughout the Disney World/Orlando/Kissimmee area.

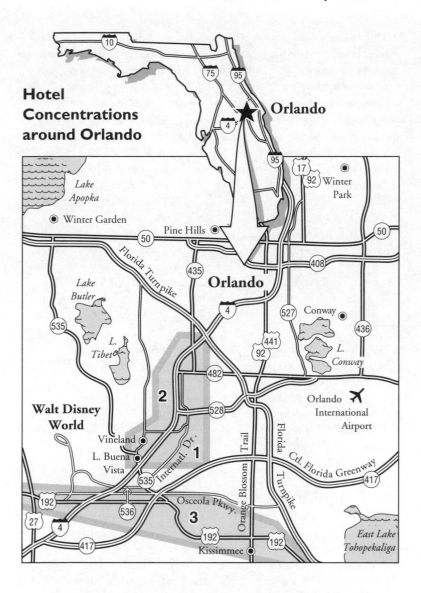

Hotels outside Disney World, in particular, struggle to fill their guest rooms. Unable to compete with Disney resorts for convenience or perks, off-World hotels lure patrons with bargain rates. The extent of the bargain depends on the season, day of the week, and area events. In high-season, during holiday periods, and during large conventions at the Orange County Convention Center, even the most modest lodging properties are sold out. Here are tips and strategies for getting a good deal on a room outside Disney World.

The following list may seem intimidating and may refer to travel-market players unfamiliar to you, but many tips we provide for getting a good deal at Disney World work equally well almost any other place you need a hotel. Once you understand these strategies, you'll routinely be able to obtain rooms at the best hotels for the lowest possible rates.

1. Orlando MagiCard   Orlando MagiCard is a discount program sponsored by the Orlando/Orange County Convention and Visitors Bureau. Cardholders are eligible for discounts of 20–50% at approximately 50 participating hotels. The MagiCard is also good for discounts at area attractions, including SeaWorld, Cypress Gardens, the Universal parks, several dinner theaters, and Disney's Pleasure Island. Valid for up to six persons, the card isn't available for groups or conventions.

To obtain an Orlando MagiCard and a list of participating hotels and attractions, call (800) 255-5786 or (407) 363-5874. Anyone older than 18 years is eligible, and the card is free. If you miss getting a card before you leave home, you can get one at the Convention and Visitors Bureau at 8723 International Drive in Orlando. When you call for a MagiCard, also request the *Orlando Official Accommodations Guide* and the Orlando Vacation Planner.

2. Exit Information Guide   Exit Information Guide publishes a book of discount coupons for bargain rates at hotels statewide. The book is free in many restaurants and motels on main highways leading to Florida. Because most travelers make reservations before leaving home, picking up the coupon book en route doesn't help much. If you call and use a credit card, EIG will send the guide first class for $3 ($5 U.S. for Canadian delivery). Contact:

Exit Information Guide
4205 N.W. 6th Street
Gainesville, FL 32609
(352) 371-3948

3. Hotel Shopping on the Internet   To read the popular press, you'd think hotels were giving away rooms on the Internet. While they're not, of course, it is true that hotels are increasingly using the Internet to fill rooms during slow periods and to advertise time-limited specials. The Internet is one of many communications tools in the hotel's toolbox, and hotels use it along with more traditional practices, such as promoting specials through travel agents. If you enjoy cyber shopping, by all means have at it, but hotel shopping on the Internet is not nearly as quick or convenient as handing the task to your travel agent. And, you'll be hard-pressed to find a deal that is not also available through your agent. When we bump into a great deal on the web, we call our travel agent. Often our agent can beat the deal or improve on it (as in the case of an upgrade). Although a good travel agent working alone can achieve great things, the same agent working with a savvy, helpful client can work wonders.

Websites we've found most dependable for Walt Disney Area hotel discounts are:

Expedia.com	An Internet travel superstore
HotelKingdom.com	Will meet the price you find elsewhere and pay you $5 a night
ValueTrips.com	Specializes in budget accommodations
Travelocity.com	An Internet travel superstore
RoomSaver.com	Specializes in budget accommodations
FloridaKiss.com	Operated by Kissimmee-St. Cloud Visitors Bureau

Potential Best Site for Non-Disney Hotels   As the Guide was going to press, we found a website that seemed to offer fantastic deals on non-Disney hotels in the Orlando area: **www.2000orlando-florida.com/ hotels.htm.** A wholesale company runs the site and uses its bulk-buying power to negotiate discounted rates with local hotels. For example, the site offered a rate of $48 per night at the Holiday Inn Nikki Bird for a six-night stay six weeks in advance. In comparison, the best we could do online or over the phone was a rate of $70 per night. Be advised that the cancellation policy for rooms booked through this site is much stricter than booking through the hotel directly—$15 for cancellations made 48 hours after the reservation is made, and possibly more.

Because we found the site so close to press time, we were unable to book rooms ourselves and verify that we'll actually get the rates advertised. Our due diligence, however, turned up a satisfactory rating by the Better Business Bureau, and no complaints on the web. We would like to hear from readers who book rooms through this site. As always, if you book rooms online, get a printout of the screen showing the room costs and your confirmation number when you make your reservation.

4. Half-Price Programs   Larger discounts on rooms (35–60%), in the Disney World area or anywhere else, are available through half-price hotel programs, often called travel clubs. Program operators contract with hotels to provide rooms at a deep discount, usually 50% off the rack rate, on a space-available basis. Generally, space available means you can reserve a room at the discount whenever the hotel expects occupancy will be less than 80%. To increase your chances for the discount, check the calendar to avoid high-season, big conventions, holidays, and special events.

Most half-price programs charge an annual membership or directory subscription fee of $25–125. Once enrolled, you're mailed a membership card and directory listing participating hotels. There are lots of restrictions and exceptions. Some hotels, for instance, "black out" (exclude) certain times. Others may offer the discount only on certain days of the week or may require you to stay a certain number of nights. Still others may offer a discount much smaller than 50%.

More established programs offer members up to 4,000 hotels in the United States. All of the programs have a heavy concentration of hotels in California and Florida. Offerings elsewhere in the United States vary considerably. The programs with the largest selection of hotels in the Disney World area are Encore, at (800) 638-0930, and Entertainment Publications, at (800) 285-5525. The Disney Club partners with Entertainment Publications. When you join the club, Disney sends you a booklet listing hotels available through Entertainment at a discount. Guess what: no Kissimmee, Orlando, Lake Buena Vista, or Walt Disney World hotels are listed. Disney Club membership provides a smaller discount of Disney hotels extrinsic of Entertainment, but if you want Entertainment's hotel listings in the Orlando/Walt Disney World area, you must sign up directly with them.

One problem with half-price programs is that not all hotels offer a full 50% discount. Another is the base rate against which the discount is applied. Some hotels figure the discount on an exaggerated rack rate that virtually no one pays. A few participating hotels may deduct the discount from the rate for a "superior" or "upgraded" room, though the room assigned is the hotel's standard accommodation. The majority of participants base discounts on rates published in the *Hotel & Travel Index* (a quarterly reference journal used by travel agents) and work within the spirit of their agreement with the program operator. As a rule, if you travel several times a year, your savings will more than pay for your program membership.

A footnote to this information is that rooms through half-price programs aren't commissionable to travel agents. This means you usually must make your own inquiries and reservations. If you work frequently with your agent, however, he or she will probably do your legwork, lack of commission notwithstanding.

5. Wholesalers, Consolidators, and Reservation Services Wholesalers and consolidators buy rooms, or options on rooms (room blocks), from hotels at a low, negotiated rate. They then resell the rooms at a profit through travel agents and tour packagers, or directly to the public. Most wholesalers and consolidators make provisions for returning unsold rooms to participating hotels but are disinclined to do so. The wholesaler's or consolidator's relationship with any hotel is tied to volume. If unsold rooms are returned, the hotel might not make as many rooms available the next time. So wholesalers and consolidators often offer rooms at rates from 15 to 50% off rack rate, occasionally sacrificing profit to avoid returning the rooms unsold.

When wholesalers and consolidators deal directly with the public, they frequently represent themselves as "reservation services." When you call, ask for a rate for your chosen hotel or for the best deal in the area where you'd like to stay. Say if there's a maximum amount you're willing to pay. The service likely will find something for you, even if it has to shave off a dollar or two of profit. You may have to pay by credit card when you reserve a room. Other times, you pay when you check out. Here are three services that frequently offer substantial discounts:

Accommodations Express	(800) 444-7666 or
	www.accommodationsexpress.com
Hotel Reservations Network	(800) 964-6835 or
	www.hoteldiscounts.com
Hotel Discounts	(800) 715-7666 or
	www.hoteldiscounts.com

6. If You Make Your Own Reservation   Always call the hotel in question, not the hotel chain's national 800 number. Often, reservationists at the 800 number are unaware of local specials. Always ask about specials before you inquire about corporate rates. Don't hesitate to bargain, but do it before you check in. If you're buying a hotel's weekend package, for example, and want to extend your stay, you can often obtain at least the corporate rate for the extra days.

7. Condominium Deals   A large number of condo resorts, time-shares, and all-suite properties in the Kissimmee/Orlando area rent to vacationers for a week or less. Look for bargains, especially during off-peak periods. Reservations and information can be obtained from:

Condolink	(800) 733-4445
Holiday Villas	(800) 344-3959
Kissimmee–St. Cloud Reservations	(800) 333-5477
Vistana Resort	(800) 877-8787
Ramada Suites by SeaWorld	(800) 633-1405
Holiday Inn Family Suites	(877) 387-KIDS
Vacation Homes at Disney	(800) 288-6608

We frequently receive letters from readers extolling the virtues of renting a condo or vacation home. This endorsement by a family from Ellington, Connecticut, is typical:

Our choice to stay outside Disney was based on cost and sanity. We found over the last couple of years that our children can't share the same bed. We have also gotten tired of having to turn off the lights at 8 p.m. and lie quietly in the dark waiting for our children to fall asleep. With this in mind, we needed a kind of condo/suite layout. Anything in Disney offering this option (e.g. Boardwalk Villas, [Old Key West, etc.]) was going to cost approximately $400–$500 a night. This was not built into our Disney budget. We decided on the Sheraton Vistana Resort. We had a two-bedroom *villa with full kitchen, living room, 3 TVs and washer/dryer. I packed for half the trip and did laundry almost every night. The facilities offered a daily children's program and several pools, kiddy pools, and "playscapes". Located on FL 535, we had a 5–10 minute drive to most attractions, including SeaWorld, Disney, and Universal.*

A majority of rental condos are listed with travel agents. Condo owners often pay an enhanced commission to agents who rent the units for reduced consumer rates.

The Best Hotels for Families outside Walt Disney World

What makes a super family hotel? Roomy accommodations, in-room fridge, great pool, complimentary breakfast, child-care options, and special programs for kids are but a few of the things the *Unofficial* hotel team checked out to select the top hotels for families from among hundreds of lodging properties in the Walt Disney World area. Some of our picks, of course, are expensive, but others are quite reasonable, and some are even a bargain. Regardless of price, you can be assured that these hotels understand the needs of a family. *Note:* Though all the hotels listed below offer some type of shuttle service to the theme parks, some offer very limited service. Call the hotel before you book to find out what the shuttle schedule will be at the time of your visit. Since families, like individuals, have different wants and needs, we have not ranked the following properties; they are listed by zone and alphabetically.

Zone 1: International Drive

Doubletree Castle Hotel

8629 International Drive, Orlando; (407) 345-1511 or (800) 952-2785;
www.doubletreecastle.com

Rate per Night $100 **Pool** ★★★ **Fridge in Room** Yes **Shuttle to Parks** Yes (Disney, Universal, and SeaWorld) **Maximum Persons per Room** 4

Special Comments Add $10 to room rate and up to four people receive continental breakfast; two signature chocolate-chip cookies come with every room

You can't miss this one—it's the only castle on I-Drive. Inside you'll find royal colors (purple dominates), opulent fixtures, European art, Renaissance music, and, of course, a mystical Castle Creature at the door. The 216 guest rooms also receive the royal treatment when it comes to decor, and some may find them on the gaudy side; however, they are fairly large and well equipped with TV with Sony PlayStation, fridge, three phones, coffee maker, iron and board, hair dryer, and safe. Guests can enjoy full or continental breakfast in the Castle Cafe located off the lobby. A court jester appears at breakfast four days a week to entertain with juggling and balloon sculptures. For lunch or dinner, you might walk next door to either Vito's Chop House or Café Tu Tu Tango (an *Unofficial* favorite). The heated circular pool is five feet deep and features a fountain in the center, a poolside bar, and a whirlpool. *Note:* there is no separate kiddie pool. Other on-site amenities include a fitness center, arcade, gift shop, lounge, valet laundry service and facilities, and guest services desk with park passes for sale and baby-sitting recommendations. A nice security feature: all elevators require an electronic guest card key.

Hard Rock Hotel

5800 Universal Boulevard, Orlando; (407) 503-ROCK; www.universalorlando.com

Rate per Night $185 **Pool** ★★★★ **Fridge in Room** No but available for $10 per day **Shuttle to Parks** Yes (Universal, SeaWorld, and Wet n' Wild) **Maximum Persons per Room** 4

Special Comments Microwaves available for $15 per day

Located on the Universal property, the 650-room Hard Rock Hotel is nirvana for any kid over age eight, especially those interested in music. The hotel's architecture is California mission style, and rock memorabilia is displayed throughout. If you're planning to spend at least a few days at the Universal parks, this is an excellent upscale option. Hotel guests receive special theme-park privileges such as early theme-park admission on select days and all-day access to the Universal Express line-breaking program, plus delivery of packages to their hotel room and priority seating at select Universal restaurants. The music-filled pool area is a big draw with a white sand beach, water slide, underwater audio system, and ultra-hip pool bar. You'll also find two restaurants, including the world-renowned Palm Restaurant, a chic lounge, a fitness center, and a Hard Rock merchandise store (watch your teens closely here). Guest rooms are ultra-hip too, of course, with cutting-edge contemporary decor, a CD sound system, TV with pay-per-view movies and video games, coffee maker, iron and board, robes, hair dryer, and two phones. There's also a supervised children's activity center for kids ages 4–14.

Holiday Inn Family Suites Resort

14500 Continental Gateway, Orlando; (407) 387-5437 or (877) 387-5437; www.hifamilysuites.com/bro

Rate per Night $159–179 **Pools** ★★★★ **Fridge in Room** Yes **Shuttle to Parks** Yes (Disney only) **Maximum Persons per Room** 5

Special Comments Complimentary hot breakfast buffet

Set on 24 sprawling acres, this new resort is about as kid-friendly as they come. Little ones will love the locomotive theme, which is consistently carried throughout the property. Kids are engaged the moment they arrive with a kids' check-in desk designed to look like a caboose. Don't take your eyes off the tikes or they might hop the kiddie train for a ride around the property. The options here will make your head spin. Guests can choose from 800 suites with seven different themes: two-bedroom Classic, two-bedroom Kidsuites, Sweet Heart, Cinema, Residential, Business, and Fitness. All suites are approximately 485 square feet and include microwave, fridge, coffee maker, TV and VCR, iron and board, two hair dryers, and a safe. Kidsuites feature a semiprivate kids' bedroom with bunk beds, pull-out sleeper bed, 20-inch TV and VCR, Nintendo 64, CD/cassette player, and activity table with chairs. All suites offer contemporary and comfortable decor but are a bit chopped up and don't receive much natural light. You can either stay in the more family-oriented East Track Courtyard or the West Track Courtyard, which has a more adult atmosphere. Additional amenities include high-tech game room, casual-dining restaurant (kids age 12 and under eat free with a paying adult), food court, convenience store, lounge, gift shop, fitness center, washer and dryer in each courtyard, and guest activities desk (where you can purchase Disney park passes and get a recommendation on local baby-sitting services). Two pools provide aquatic fun for all: adults will enjoy the Olympic-size lap pool, while kids will like the huge zero-depth entry pool with fountains, water toys, kiddie pool, and a soft tubular playground with slide. Afternoon pool activities for kids are scheduled seasonally. The resort teems with families even in the off-season—it's mondo but can still get crowded.

Portofino Bay Hotel

5601 Universal Boulevard, Orlando; (407) 503-1000; www.universalorlando.com

Rate per Night $240 **Pools** ★★★★ **Fridge in Room** Mini bar; fridge available for $10 per day **Shuttle to Parks** Yes (Universal, SeaWorld, and Wet n' Wild) **Maximum Persons per Room** 4

Special Comments Character dinner on Monday and Friday

Also located in Universal, the 750-room Portofino Bay Hotel is themed like a seaside village on the Italian Riviera. Like at the Hard Rock Hotel, Portofino guests receive special theme-park privileges such as early theme-park admission on select days and all-day access to the Universal Express line-breaking program, plus delivery of packages to their hotel room and priority seating at select Universal restaurants. The guest rooms are ultra luxurious by any standard, with Italian furnishings, opulent baths, and soothing neutral hues. Standard guest room amenities include mini bar, coffee maker, iron and board, hair dryer, safe, umbrella, and TV with pay-per-view movies. Microwaves are available for $15 a day. Camp Portofino offers nightly supervised activities from 5 to 11:30 p.m. for children ages 4–14. Cost is $45 per child and $35 for each additional child in the same family and includes dinner. Activities might include movies, video games, and arts and crafts. Trattoria del Porto, one of the Portofino's casual-dining restaurants, offers a character dinner on Monday and Friday, 6:30–9:30 p.m. Food is served buffet style, and characters such as Scooby Doo and Woody Woodpecker attend. Cost is $19.50 for adults and $12.75 for children ages 12 and under; children under 3 eat free. The Portofino also has four other Italian restaurants (all with children's menus), an Italian bakery (which also serves gelato), and two bars. Three elaborately designed pools, gardens, jogging trails, and a spa and fitness center round out the major Portofino amenities. If you have the bank account to pay for it and plan to spend some time at Universal, you can't go wrong here.

Renaissance Orlando Resort

6677 Sea Harbor Drive, Orlando; (407) 351-5555 or (800) 327-6677; www.renaissancehotels.com

Rate per Night $129 **Pool** ★★★½ **Fridge in Room** Yes **Shuttle to Parks** Yes (Disney, Universal, SeaWorld) **Maximum Persons per Room** 4

Special Comments Babysitting and child care services available, and pets are permitted

The Renaissance Orlando Resort is not the most kid-focused possibility in the area, as it does a lot of convention business. However, its large size and convenience to SeaWorld and Universal make it an acceptable alternative if the more family-friendly options are sold out or not to your liking. Rooms are decorated in light and bright colors, albeit in a largely ho-hum style. In-room amenities for families are limited; though the staff will help by arranging child care or bringing up cribs, you'll have to largely make do with repurposed business amenities (i.e. cramming your own perishables in the mini-bar). Dining options range from casual sandwiches at the poolside bar and grill to a continental restaurant serving dinner only. The sizable pool is the main draw for kids, as it has enough square footage to exhaust even the most determined small fry. The large central atrium of the hotel also has a small tropical bird aviary; local songbirds, perhaps drawn by their imprisoned kin, are often seen flitting about the wide central space and stealing potato chips from abandoned lunches.

Sheraton Studio City

5905 International Drive, Orlando; (407) 351-2100 or (800) 327-1366;
www.sheratonstudiocity.com

Rate per Night $139 **Pool** ★★½ **Fridge in Room** No **Shuttle to Parks** Yes (Universal, SeaWorld, and Wet 'n Wild) **Maximum Persons per Room** 4

Special Comments Across the street from Wet 'n Wild

It's not for little ones, but preteens and teens will love the hip atmosphere at Sheraton Studio City. And movie buffs will appreciate the theme—a tribute to feature films of the 1940s and 1950s. The lobby is reminiscent of a 1950s movie house lobby with a slick black-and-white color scheme, cool art deco furnishings, and photos of classic movie stars. The art deco theme continues in the 302 guest rooms, which also offer subdued teal and silver hues, elegant marble baths, 25-inch TV with Sony PlayStation, two phones, iron and board, coffee maker, hair dryer, and safe. The 21-story hotel is round, which makes guest rooms somewhat pie-shaped but still spacious enough. Request a room on one of the upper floors for an outstanding view. The heated pool is on the smallish side but has a jumping fountain over it, a kiddie pool, and a très cool poolside bar with more movie motif. The Starlight Room serves breakfast, lunch, and dinner, while Oscar's Lounge features a nightly champagne celebration for adults. Other major on-site amenities and services include fitness center, arcade, gift shop, hair salon, Alamo car rental, one-hour photo service, and Universal park passes for sale in the lobby.

Sheraton World Resort

10100 International Drive, Orlando; (407) 352-1100 or (800) 327-0363;
www.sheratonworld.com

Rate per Night $159 **Pools** ★★★½ **Fridge in Room** Yes **Shuttle to Parks** Yes (Disney only) **Maximum Persons per Room** 4

Special Comments A good option if you're visiting SeaWorld

Set on 28 acres, the Sheraton World Resort offers plenty of room for kids to roam. And with three heated pools, two kiddie pools, a small playground, an arcade, and a complimentary mini golf course (very mini, indeed), this resort offers more than enough kid-friendly diversions. The main pool is especially pleasant with fountains, lush landscaping, and a poolside bar. Other on-site amenities and services include fitness center, massage therapy, gift shop, guest services desk, and lounge. A golf club is located one mile away. We recommend booking a room in the new tower if possible even though it's set away from the kiddie pools and playground. The tower rooms are a bit larger and more upscale than the low-rise rooms, some of which could use a renovation. All 1,102 guest rooms include fridge, coffee maker, TV with Nintendo, iron and board, hair dryer, and safe. The Sheraton has one restaurant and a deli with a Pizza Hut. If your family loves SeaWorld, you're in luck here—Shamu and friends are within walking distance.

Zone 2: Lake Buena Vista and I-4 Corridor

Hilton Disney Village

1751 Hotel Plaza Boulevard, Lake Buena Vista; (407) 827-4000 or (800) 782-4414; www.hilton-wdwv.com

Rate per Night $150 **Pools** ★★★½ **Fridge in Room** Mini bar **Shuttle to Parks** Yes (Disney theme and water parks only) **Maximum Persons per Room** 4

Special Comments Sunday character breakfast and Surprise Mornings program available

Located in the Disney Village, the Hilton offers 814 guest rooms and suites set on 23 landscaped acres. Since it's an official Walt Disney World hotel, guests can take advantage of the Surprise Mornings program, which allows hotel guest to enter a selected Disney park one hour before official opening time. At press time, the Hilton was the only hotel in the Disney Village to offer this privilege. Hilton guest rooms are spacious, luxurious, and tasteful. Decorated in earth tones and complete with marble baths, all standard rooms are equipped with iron and board, hair dryer, two phones, desk, mini bar, coffee maker, and cable TV with pay-per-view movies and video games. One big-plus family amenity offered by the Hilton is its character breakfast. Offered on Sunday only from 8:30 to 11 a.m., the food is served buffet style, and four characters attend but only two are present at a time. When we visited the characters were Minnie Mouse, Brer Bear, Donald Duck, and Pluto. Reservations are not accepted for the character breakfast. Other important family amenities include the Hilton Vacation Station, where kids ages 4–12 can take part in supervised activities; baby-sitting services; an arcade and pool table; and two beautifully landscaped heated swimming pools, as well as a kiddie pool. Adults and older children can blow off steam after a long day at the parks in the fitness center. And nine on-site restaurants, including Benihana, add to the hotel's convenience.

Holiday Inn SunSpree Resort

13351 State Road 535, Lake Buena Vista; (407) 239-4500 or (800) 366-6299; www.kidsuites.com

Rate per Night $109 **Pool** ★★★ **Fridge in Room** Yes **Shuttle to Parks** Yes (Disney only) **Maximum Persons per Room** 4–6

Special Comments The first hotel in the world to offer Kidsuites

Put on your sunglasses—you'll know you're there when the hot pink, bright blue, green, and yellow exterior comes into view. Once inside kids get into the action from the very beginning at their own check-in counter, where they'll receive a free goody bag. Max, Maxine, and the Kidsuite Gang, the character mascots here, come out to play with the kids at scheduled times during the day. But the big lure is the Kidsuites, which are 405-square-foot rooms with a separate area for kids. Themes include a tree house, circus tent, jail, space capsule, igloo, fort, and many more. The kids' area sleeps three to four children and has either two sets of bunk beds or one bunk bed and a twin, plus a cable TV and VCR, Nintendo, radio/cassette or CD player, fun phone, and game table and chairs. The separate adult area has its own TV and VCR, safe, hair dryer, and a mini kitchenette with fridge, microwave, sink, and coffee maker. Standard guest rooms are also available and offer the same amenities found in the adult areas of the Kidsuites. Other kid-friendly amenities include free bedtime tuck-in service by a member of the Kidsuite Gang (reservations required); the tiny Castle Movie Theater, which shows continuous movies daily and clown and magic shows nightly; a playground; a state-of-the-art arcade with Sega games and air hickey among many other games; a basketball court; and Camp Holiday, a free supervised activities program for kids ages 3–12. Held every day in Max's Magic Castle, Camp Holiday activities might include movies and cartoons, clown and magic shows, bingo, face painting, karaoke, and computer and arcade games. There's also a large, attractive free-form pool, complete with kiddie pool and two whirlpools, and a fitness center. You won't go hungry with Maxine's Food Emporium on site. Open 7 a.m.–10 p.m., it includes Little Caesars, A&W Restaurant, Otis Spunkmeyer Cookies and Muffins, TCBY, and more. There's also a mini mart. Another perk: kids ages 12 and under eat free from a special menu when dining with one paying adult; there's a maximum of four kids per paying adult.

Hyatt Regency Grand Cypress

One Grand Cypress Boulevard, Lake Buena Vista; (407) 239-1234;
www. hyattgrandcypress.com

Rate per Night $209 **Pool** ★★★★★ **Fridge in Room** Mini bar; fridge available on request **Shuttle to Parks** Yes (Disney only) **Maximum Persons per Room** 4

Special Comments Wow, what a pool!

There are myriad reasons to stay at this 1,500-acre resort, but in our book, the pool ranks as number one. It's a sprawling, 800,000-gallon tropical paradise with a 125-foot water slide, ubiquitous waterfalls, caves and grottos, and a suspension bridge. The only problem is your kids may never want to leave the pool to visit the theme parks. The Hyatt is also a golfer's paradise. With a 45-hole championship Jack Nicklaus–designed course, an 18-hole course, a 9-hole pitch and putt course, and a golf academy, there's something for golfers of all abilities. Other recreational perks include a racquet facility with hard and clay courts, a private lake complete with beach, a fitness center, and miles of nature trails for biking, walking or jogging, and horseback riding. The 750 standard guest rooms are 360 square feet and provide a casual but luxurious Florida ambience, with green and reddish hues, touches of rattan, and private balconies. In-room amenities include mini bar, iron and board, safe, hair dryer, ceiling fan, and cable TV with pay-per-view movies and video games.

Suite and villa accommodations offer even more amenities. Camp Hyatt provides supervised programs for kids, and in-room baby-sitting is also available. Five restaurants provide plenty of dining options, and four lounges offer nighttime entertainment. If outdoor recreation is high on your family's list, the Hyatt is an excellent high-end choice.

Marriott Village at Little Lake Bryan

8623 Vineland Avenue, Lake Buena Vista; (407) 938-9001 or (877) 682-8552; www.marriott-village.com

Rate per Night $79–159 **Pools** ★★★ **Fridge in Room** Yes **Shuttle to Parks** Yes (Disney, Universal, SeaWorld, and Wet n' Wild) **Maximum Persons per Room** 4

Special Comments Complimentary continental breakfast at Fairfield Inn and Spring Hill Suites

This brand new fully gated community includes a 388-room Fairfield Inn, a 400-suite Spring Hill Suites, and 312-room Courtyard. Whatever your travel budget, you'll find a room to fit it here. For a bit more space, book the Spring Hill Suites; if you're looking for a good value, try the Fairfield Inn; and if you need limited business amenities, reserve at the Courtyard. In-room amenities at all three properties include fridge, cable TV with Sony PlayStation, iron and board, and hair dryer. Additionally, the Spring Hill Suites have microwaves in all suites, and all Courtyard rooms feature Web TV. Cribs and rollaway beds are available at no extra charge at all locations. Pools at all three hotels are attractive and medium-sized with children's interactive splash zones and whirlpools, and all properties have their own fitness center. An incredibly convenient feature here is the Village Marketplace food court, which includes Pizza Hut Pizza, TCBY Yogurt, Oscar Mayer Hot Dog Construction Company, Oscar Mayer 1883 Deli, Village Grill, Gourmet Bean Coffee and Pastry Shop, and a 24-hour convenience store. And if you're looking for a full-service restaurant experience, Bahama Breeze, Fish Bones, and Golden Corral restaurants are adjacent and within walking distance of the compound. Each hotel also features its own Kids Club. For kids ages 4–8, Kids Clubs have a theme (backyard, tree house, and library) and feature a big-screen TV, computer stations, and three educational centers (math and science, reading, and creative activities). They operate approximately six hours per day with a staff member on duty at all times. And best of all, there's no extra charge to participate in the Kids Club program. Marriott Village also offers a Kids Night Out program (for ages 4–10), which runs on select nights from 6 to 10 p.m. Cost is $35 per child and includes activities and dinner. The program is supervised by two staff members. A Disney planning station and attraction ticket sales, an arcade, and a Hertz car rental desk complete the Marriott Village services and amenities. And last but not least, shoppers in the family will be pleased to know that Marriott Village is located adjacent to the new Orlando Premium Outlets. You'll get a lot of bang for your buck at Marriott Village.

Sheraton Safari Hotel

12205 Apopka-Vineland Road, Lake Buena Vista; (407) 239-0444 or (800) 423-3297; www.sheraton.com

Rate per Night $115 **Pool** ★★★ **Fridge in Room** In safari suites only **Shuttle to**

Parks Yes (Disney complimentary; other parks for a fee) **Maximum Persons per Room** 4–6

Special Comments Cool python water slide

The Sheraton Safari offers a more low-key theme experience. The safari theme is nicely executed throughout the property—from the lobby dotted with African artifacts and native decor to the 79-foot python water slide dominating the pool. The 393 guest rooms and 90 safari suites also sport the safari theme with tasteful animal print soft goods in brown, beige, and jewel tones and African-inspired art. In-room amenities include cable TV with Sony PlayStation, coffee maker, iron and board, hair dryer, and safe. The safari suites are a good option for families since they provide added space with a separate sitting room and a kitchenette with a fridge, microwave, and sink. The first thing your kids will probably want to do is hit the pool and take a turn on the python water slide. It's pretty impressive, but as one Unofficial researcher pointed out, it's somewhat of a letdown that the python doesn't actually spit you out of its mouth. Instead you're deposited below the snake. Details, details. Other on-site amenities include a restaurant (children's menu available), deli, lounge, arcade, and fitness center. Should you want to escape for a night of strictly adult fun, baby-sitting services are available.

Sheraton Vistana Resort

8800 Vistana Center Drive, Lake Buena Vista; (866) 208-0003; www.starwoodvo.com

Rate per Night $149 **Pools** ★★★½ **Fridge in Room** Mini bar **Shuttle to Parks** Yes (Disney, Universal, SeaWorld) **Maximum Persons per Room** 6

Special Comments Though actually timeshares, the villas are rented nightly as well

The Sheraton Vistana is deceptively large, stretching as it does across either side of Vistana Center Drive. Since Sheraton's sales emphasis is on ownership of the timeshares, the rental angle is a small secret in local lodging. But it's worth considering for visiting families, as the Vistana is one of the best off-Disney properties in Orlando. If you want to have a very serene retreat from your days in the theme parks, this is an excellent home base. You may even have difficulty prying yourself out of here to go to the parks. The spacious "villas" come in one-bedroom, two-bedroom, and two-bedroom-with-lockoff combinations. All are cleanly decorated in simple pastels, but the main emphasis is on the profusion of amenities. Each villa comes with full kitchen (including fridge with freezer, microwave, oven/range, dishwasher, toaster, and coffeemaker, with an option to pre-stock with groceries), clothes washer and dryer, TVs in the living room and each bedroom (one with VCR), stereo with CD player, separate dining area, and private patio or balcony in most. The grounds themselves have resort amenities close at hand, with seven swimming pools (four with poolside bars), four playgrounds, three restaurants, game rooms, fitness centers, a mini-golf course, sport equipment rental (including bikes), and courts for basketball, volleyball, tennis, and shuffleboard. The resort organizes a mind-boggling array of activities for kids (and adults) of all ages, from arts and crafts to a variety of games and sports tournaments. Of special note is the fact that the Vistana is extremely secure, with locked gates bordering all guest areas, so children can have the run of the place without parents worrying about their wandering off.

Wyndham Palace

1900 Buena Vista Drive, Lake Buena Vista; (407) 827-2727 or (800) WYNDHAM; www.wyndham.com

Rate per Night $129 **Pools** ★★★½ **Fridge in Room** Mini bar **Shuttle to Parks** Yes (Disney only) **Maximum Persons per Room** 4

Special Comments Sunday character breakfast available

Located in the Disney Village, the Wyndham Palace is an upscale and convenient choice for your Disney vacation headquarters. Surrounded by a manmade lake and plenty of palms, the attractive and spacious pool area contains three heated pools, the larger of which is partially covered by a pool house (nice for when you're ready for a little shade), a whirlpool, and a sand volleyball court. Plus, there's even a pool concierge who will fetch your favorite magazine or fruity drink. On Sunday, the Wyndham offers a character breakfast at the Watercress Cafe. Cost is $19 for adults and $11 for children. Minnie Mouse, Pluto, and Goofy were in attendance when we visited. The 1,014 guest rooms are posh and spacious, and each comes with a desk, coffee maker, hair dryer, cable TV with pay-per-view movies, iron and board, and mini bar. There are also 112 suites. Children ages 4–12 can participate in supervised programs through the Wyndy Harbour Kids' Klub, and in-room baby-sitting is available through the All about Kids child-care service. Three lighted tennis courts, a European-style spa offering 60 services, a fitness center, an arcade, a playground, and a beauty salon round out the hotel's amenities. You won't have a problem finding a decent meal with three restaurants and a mini market on site. And if you're not wiped out after spending time in the parks, you might consider the Laughing Kookaburra Good Time Bar for live entertainment and dancing. Note: all these amenities and services come at a price—an $8 per night resort fee will be added to your bill.

Zone 3: US 192

Comfort Suites Maingate Resort

7888 West US 192, Kissimmee; (407) 390-9888

Rate per Night $89 **Pool** ★★★ **Fridge in Room** Yes **Shuttle to Parks** Yes (Disney, Universal, SeaWorld, and Wet 'n Wild) **Maximum Persons per Room** 6

Special Comments Complimentary continental breakfast daily

This nice new property has 150 spacious one-room suites with double sofa bed, microwave, fridge, coffee maker, TV, hair dryer, and safe. The suites aren't lavish but are clean and contemporary with a muted deep purple and beige color scheme. Extra counter space in the bathroom is especially convenient for larger families. The heated pool is large and amoeba shaped with plenty of lounge chairs and moderate landscaping. A kiddie pool, whirlpool, and poolside bar complete the courtyard area. Other on-site amenities include an arcade and gift shop. But the big plus for this place is its location—right next door to a shopping center with just about everything a traveling family could possibly need. Here's what you'll find: seven dining options, including Outback Steakhouse, Dairy Queen, Subway, TGI Friday's, and Chinese, Japanese, and Italian eateries; a Goodings supermarket; one-hour film developing; a hair salon; a bank; a dry cleaner; a tourist information center with park passes for sale; and a Centra Care walk-in clinic, among other services. All this just a short walk from your room.

Gaylord Palms Resort

6000 West Osceola Parkway, Kissimmee; (407) 586-0000; www.gaylordpalms.com

Rate per Night $325 **Pool** ★★★★ **Fridge in Room** Yes **Shuttle to Parks** Yes (Disney) **Maximum Persons per Room** 4

Special Comments Probably the closest thing to Disney-level extravagance off Disney grounds

Originally meant to be an Opryland Resort, this place had its name changed before opening due to the owners' loss of confidence in the Opryland name as brand. Regardless of whether "Gaylord Palms" results in better name recognition, this is a decidedly upscale resort. Though it has a colossal convention facility and strongly caters to its business clientele, the Gaylord Palms is still a nice (if pricey) family resort. Since it just opened in 2001, the property is also quite new. The hotel wings are defined by the three themed, glass-roofed atriums they overlook. Key West features design reminiscent of island life in the Florida Keys; the Everglades are an overgrown spectacle of shabby swamp chic, complete with piped-in cricket noise and a robotic alligator; and the immense, central St. Augustine hearkens back to old Spanish Colonial Florida. Lagoons, streams, and waterfalls cut through and connect all three, and little walkways and bridges abound. The rooms themselves reflect the color schemes of their respective areas, though there's no particular connection in decor (the St. Augustine atrium view rooms are the most opulent, but they're not in any way Spanish). The fourth wing of rooms, the Emerald Tower, overlooks the Emerald Bay shopping and dining area of the St. Augustine atrium; these rooms are the nicest and most expensive, and they're mostly used by convention-goers. Though rooms do have fridges and stereos with CD (as well as other high-end perks, like high-speed Internet access), the rooms themselves really work better as retreats for adults than for kids. However, children will enjoy wandering the themed areas, playing in the family pool (complete with giant water-squirting octopus), or participating in the La Petite Academy Kids Station, which organizes a range of games and activities for wee ones.

Holiday Inn Nikki Bird Resort

7300 West US 192, Kissimmee; (407) 396-7300 or (800) 20-OASIS

Rate per Night $100 **Pools** ★★★½ **Fridge in Room** Yes **Shuttle to Parks** Yes (Disney only) **Maximum Persons per Room** 5 (2 adults; 3 small children)

Special Comments Kids 12 and under eat free from special menus with a paying adult; room service includes Pizza Hut pizza

In the Orlando hotel world, you're nobody unless you have a mascot. Here it's the Nikki Bird and Wacky the Wizard, who stroll the resort interacting with kids and posing for photos. This Holiday Inn offers standard guest rooms as well as Kidsuites. All rooms feature microwave, fridge, TV with Sony PlayStation, coffee maker, iron and board, hair dryer, and safe. Additionally, Kidsuites offer a themed kids area within the guest room with kid-size bunk beds and twin bed, TV/VCR, radio/CD player, and Playstation. Kidsuites are most suitable for families with children age nine and under; children over nine will have a hard time fitting into the kids' beds. Parents beware: kid-suites here also come with extremely bright decor. Sunglasses recommended. Standard rooms are spacious, but the Kidsuites are a bit cramped with the children's area. This sprawling resort offers three pools with whirlpools and two kiddie pools with squirt fountains and small playgrounds, so you won't have to walk far to cool off. On-site volleyball and tennis provide more outdoor recreation. Fitness equipment is also available. And a large arcade has air hockey, pool, and Sega games. Guest services include car rental and a tour desk with park passes for sale. The resort can also arrange a baby-sitter for $10 per hour, plus a $10 transportation fee; the minimum is four hours, so you'll drop at least $50. The full-service Angel's Diner has 1950s-style diner decor and a good buffet with American cuisine and some theme nights. After dinner, you'll find nightly family entertainment at "Nikki's Nest" with songs, puppet and magic shows, and games.

Howard Johnson EnchantedLand

4985 West Highway 192, Kissimmee; (407) 396-4343 or (888) 753-4343

Rate per Night $79 **Pool** ★★ **Fridge in Room** Yes **Shuttle to Parks** Yes (Disney, Universal, and SeaWorld) **Maximum Persons per Room** 4

Special Comments Complimentary ice cream party; free video library

Fairies, dragons, and super heroes have invaded the HoJo. If you stay here, be sure you book what they call a Family Value Room: a standard room that has been transformed into a kids suite. Approximately 300 square feet, these rooms feature a themed kids area (choose from a treehouse, fairies, or action heroes) with a twin daybed that converts to two twins or one king, TV and VCR, microwave, fridge, coffee maker, and safe. Note that the kids area is separated from the double bed by a mere half-wall divider, so if you're looking for privacy and space from the kids, this probably isn't the place for you. While you're taking care of the real bill, kids can check in at their own desk in the form of a treehouse. For $5 per child, the Adventure Club, based in a small playroom, offers supervised activities, games, and movies in the evenings Thursday–Saturday. There is a small market on site, and breakfast is served every morning from 7 to 11 a.m. (kids age 12 and under eat free with a paying adult). Other on-site amenities include a small arcade and a whirlpool. It may not offer the myriad amenities found in more deluxe properties, but EnchantedLand is a good value for your theme buck.

Radisson Resort Parkway

2900 Parkway Boulevard, Kissimmee; (407) 396-7000 or (800) 634-4774

Rate per Night $149 **Pool** ★★★★½ **Fridge in Room** Mini bar **Shuttle to Parks** Yes (Disney, Universal, and SeaWorld) **Maximum Persons per Room** 4

Special Comments Kids 10 and under eat free with a paying adult at any hotel restaurant

Although the pool alone is worth a stay here, fortunately the Radisson Resort gets high marks in all areas. But first the pool: it's a huge free-form affair with a waterfall and water slide surrounded by lush palms and flowering plants, plus an additional smaller heated pool, two whirlpools, and a kiddie pool. Other outdoor amenities include two lighted tennis courts, volleyball, a playground, and jogging areas. Kids can also blow off steam at the arcade, while adults might visit the fitness center with a sauna. The recently renovated guest rooms are elegant and feature Italian furnishings with clean lines and marble baths. Rooms are fairly large and include mini bar, coffee maker, color TV, iron and board, hair dryer, and safe. Dining options include The Court for breakfast and dinner buffets and a 1950s-style diner serving burgers, sandwiches, shakes, and Pizza Hut pizza, among other fare. A sports lounge with an 11-by-6-foot TV offers nighttime entertainment. Guest services can help with special tours, park passes, car rental, and baby-sitting. The only downside here is no organized children's programs. The good news is parents don't sacrifice their vacation for the kids—all will be equally happy here.

Hotels and Motels: Rated and Ranked

In this section, we compare hotels in three main areas outside Walt Disney World (pages 182–185) with those inside the World.

In addition to Disney properties and the three lodging areas we rate, there are hotels at the intersection of US 27 and I-4, on US 441 (Orange Blossom Trail), and in downtown Orlando. All of these require more than 20 minutes' commuting time to Walt Disney World. We also haven't rated lodging east of Siesta Lago Road on US 192.

What's in a Room?

Except for cleanliness, state of repair, and decor, travelers pay little attention to hotel rooms. There is, of course, a clear standard of quality and luxury that differentiates Motel 6 from Holiday Inn, Holiday Inn from Marriott, and so on. Many hotel guests, however, fail to appreciate that some rooms are better engineered than others. Making the room usable to its occupants is an art, a planning discipline that combines both form and function.

Decor and taste are important, certainly. No one wants to stay in a room that is dated, garish, or ugly. But beyond decor, how "livable" is the room? In Orlando, for example, we have seen some beautifully appointed rooms that simply aren't well designed for human habitation. The next time you stay in a hotel, note the details and design elements of your room. Even more than decor, these are the things that will make you feel comfortable and at home.

ROOM STAR RATINGS

★★★★★	*Superior Rooms*	Tasteful and luxurious by any standard
★★★★	*Extremely Nice Rooms*	What you would expect at a Hyatt Regency or Marriott
★★★	*Nice Rooms*	Holiday Inn or comparable quality

★★	*Adequate Rooms*	Clean, comfortable, and functional without frills—like a Motel 6
★	*Super Budget*	

Room Ratings

To evaluate properties for their quality, tastefulness, state of repair, cleanliness, and size of their *standard rooms,* we have grouped the hotels and motels into classifications denoted by stars. Star ratings in this guide apply to Orlando-area properties only and don't necessarily correspond to ratings awarded by Frommer, Mobil, AAA, or other travel critics. Because stars have little relevance when awarded in the absence of recognized standards of comparison, we have tied our ratings to expected levels of quality established by specific American hotel corporations.

Star ratings apply *only to room quality* and describe the property's standard accommodations. For most hotels and motels, a standard accommodation is a hotel room with either one king bed or two queen beds. In an all-suite property, the standard accommodation is either a one- or two-room suite. In addition to standard accommodations, many hotels offer luxury rooms and special suites, which aren't rated in this guide. Star ratings for rooms are assigned without regard to whether a property has restaurant(s), recreational facilities, entertainment, or other extras.

In addition to stars (which delineate broad categories), we use a numerical rating system. Our rating scale is 0–100, with 100 as the best possible rating and zero (0) as the worst. Numerical ratings are presented to show the difference we perceive between one property and another. Rooms at both the Disney Port Orleans Resort and Grosvenor Resort are rated as three-and-a-half stars (★★★½). In the supplemental numerical ratings, Port Orleans is an 81, and the Grosvenor Resort a 76. This means that within the three-and-a-half-star category, Port Orleans has slightly nicer rooms than the Grosvenor Resort.

The location column identifies the area around Walt Disney World where you will find a particular property. The designation "WDW" means that the property is inside Walt Disney World. A "1" means that the property is on or near International Drive. Properties on US 192 (a.k.a. Irlo Bronson Memorial Highway, Vine Street, and Space Coast Parkway) are indicated by a "3." All others are marked with "2" and for the most part are along the I-4 corridor, though some are in nearby locations that don't meet any other criteria.

Properties along US 192 also carry location designations with their names, such as the Holiday Inn Maingate East. The consensus in Orlando seems to be that the main entrance to Walt Disney World is the broad interstate-type road that runs off of US 192. This is called Maingate. Properties along US 192 call themselves Maingate East or West to differentiate their positions along the highway. So, driving southeast from Clermont or the Florida Turnpike, the properties before you reach the Maingate turnoff are called Maingate West, while the properties after you pass the Maingate turnoff are called Maingate East.

LODGING AREAS

WDW	Walt Disney World
1	International Drive
2	I-4 Corridor
3	US 192 (Irlo Bronson Memorial Highway)

How the Hotels Compare

Cost estimates are based on the hotel's published rack rates for standard rooms. Each "$" represents $50. Thus a cost symbol of "$$$" means a room (or suite) at that hotel will be about $150 a night.

Here's a hit parade of the nicest rooms in town. We've focused strictly on room quality and excluded consideration of location, services, recreation, or amenities. In some instances, a one- or two-room suite is available for the same price or less than that of a hotel room.

If you have used an earlier edition of this guide, you'll notice that new properties have been added and many ratings and rankings have changed, some because of room renovation or improved maintenance and housekeeping. Failure to maintain guest rooms or lax housekeeping can bring down ratings.

Before you shop for a hotel, consider this letter we received from a man in Hot Springs, Arkansas:

We canceled our room reservations to follow the advice in your book and reserved a hotel highly ranked by the Unofficial Guide. *We wanted inexpensive, but clean and cheerful. We got inexpensive, but [also] dirty, grim, and depressing. I really felt disappointed in your advice and the room. It was the pits. That was the one real piece of information I needed from your book! The room spoiled the holiday for me aside from our touring.*

This letter was as unsettling to us as the bad room was to our reader. Our integrity as travel journalists is based on the quality of the information we provide our readers. Even with the best of intentions and the most conscientious research, we can't inspect every room in every hotel. What we do, in statistical terms, is take a sample: we check several rooms selected at random in each hotel and base our ratings and rankings on those rooms. The inspections are conducted anonymously and without the knowledge of the property's management. Although unusual, it's certainly possible that the rooms we randomly inspect aren't representative of the majority of rooms. Another possibility is that the rooms we inspect in a hotel are representative, but by bad luck a reader is assigned an inferior room. When rechecking the hotel our reader disliked, we discovered our rating was correctly representative, but that he and his wife had unfortunately been assigned one of a small number of threadbare rooms scheduled for renovation.

The key to avoiding disappointment is to snoop in advance. Ask the hotel to send a photo of its standard guest room before you book, or at least get a copy of the hotel's promotional brochure. Be aware that some hotel chains use the same guest-room photo in promotional literature for *all* hotels in the chain and that the guest room in a specific property may not resemble the photo in the brochure. When your travel agent or you call, ask how old the property is and when the guest room you are being assigned was last renovated. If you arrive and are assigned a room inferior to that which you had been led to expect, demand to be moved.

HOW THE HOTELS COMPARE

Hotel	Location	Overall Room Rating	Room Quality Rating	Cost ($=$50)	Phone (area code 407)
Hard Rock Hotel	1	★★★★★	96	$$$$–	503-ROCK
WDW Grand Floridian Resort	WDW	★★★★★	96	$$$$$$+	934-7639
WDW Animal Kingdom Lodge	WDW	★★★★★	95	$$$$$–	934-7639
Portofino Bay Hotel	1	★★★★½	94	$$$$$–	503-1000
WDW Boardwalk Inn	WDW	★★★★½	93	$$$$$$–	934-7639
Embassy Vacation Resort	2	★★★★½	92	$$$–	238-2500
Royal Pacific Resort	1	★★★★½	92	$$$$+	(888) 322-5541
WDW Beach Club Resort	WDW	★★★★½	92	$$$$$$–	934-7639
WDW Yacht Club Resort	WDW	★★★★½	92	$$$$$$–	934-7639
WDW Old Key West Resort	WDW	★★★★½	92	$$$$$$$–	934-7639
WDW Beach Club Villas	WDW	★★★★½	91	$$$$$$–	934-7639
WDW Boardwalk Villas	WDW	★★★★½	91	$$$$$$–	934-7639
WDW Wilderness Villas	WDW	★★★★½	91	$$$$$$–	934-7639

HOW THE HOTELS COMPARE (continued)

Hotel	Location	Overall Room Rating	Room Quality Rating	Cost ($=$50)	Phone (area code 407)
Shades of Green	WDW	★★★★½	91	n/a	824-3400
Radisson Resort Parkway	3	★★★★½	90	$$$–	396-7000
Celebration Hotel	WDW	★★★★½	90	$$$+	566-6000
Hyatt Regency Grand Cypress	2	★★★★½	90	$$$$+	239-1234
Marriott Orlando World Center	2	★★★★½	90	$$$$$–	239-4200
Gaylord Palms Resort	3	★★★★½	90	$$$$$$	586-0000
WDW Polynesian Resort	WDW	★★★★½	90	$$$$$$–	934-7639
Peabody Orlando	1	★★★★½	90	$$$$$$$+	352-4000
Radisson Hotel	1	★★★★	88	$$$– (800)	327-2110
Crowne Plaza Resort	1	★★★★	87	$$$–	239-1222
WDW Contemporary Resort	WDW	★★★★	87	$$$$$$–	934-7639
Wyndham Palace	WDW	★★★★	86	$$$–	827-2727
WDW Wilderness Lodge	WDW	★★★★	86	$$$$+	934-7639
WDW Dolphin Resort	WDW	★★★★	86	$$$$$	934-7639
WDW Swan	WDW	★★★★	86	$$$$$	934-7639
Hilton Disney Village	WDW	★★★★	85	$$$	827-4000
Sheraton Vistana Resort	2	★★★★	85	$$$ (866)	208-0003
Hotel Royal Plaza (tower rooms)	WDW	★★★★	85	$$$+	828-2828
Residence Inn	1	★★★★	84	$$	313-3600
Hyatt Orlando	3	★★★★	84	$$+	396-1234
Doubletree Guest Suites	WDW	★★★★	84	$$$+	934-1000
Embassy Suites Orlando Intl.	1	★★★★	84	$$$$+	352-1400
Radisson Barcelo Inn International (tower rooms)	1	★★★★	83	$$–	345-0505
WDW Coronado Springs Resort	WDW	★★★★	83	$$$–	934-7639
Embassy Suites Plaza Intl.	1	★★★★	83	$$$+	345-8250

HOW THE HOTELS COMPARE (continued)

Hotel	Location	Overall Room Rating	Room Quality Rating	Cost ($=$50)	Phone (area code 407)
Sierra Suites Lake Buena Vista	2	★★★★	83	$$$+	239-4300
Sierra Suites Pointe Orlando	1	★★★★	83	$$$+	903-1500
Summerfield Suites Lake Buena Vista	2	★★★★	83	$$$+	238-0777
Cypress Pointe Resort	2	★★★★	83	$$$+	238-2300
The Castle Hotel (Doubletree)	1	★★★½	82	$$	345-1511
Sheraton Royal Safari	2	★★★½	82	$$+	(800) 423-3297
Sheraton Studio City	1	★★★½	82	$$$−	351-2100
Holiday Inn Family Suites Resort	1	★★★½	82	$$$+	387-5437
Summerfield Suites	1	★★★½	82	$$$+	352-2400
Clarion Suites Resort World (suites)	3	★★★½	82	$$$$−	396-8300
Club Hotel by Doubletree	2	★★★½	81	$$−	239-4646
Wyndham Orlando	1	★★★½	81	$$−	351-2420
Hawthorne Suites Orlando	1	★★★½	81	$$+	351-6600
Buena Vista Suites	3	★★★½	81	$$$−	239-8588
Doubletree Orlando Suites & Villas	3	★★★½	81	$$$−	397-0555
WDW Port Orleans Resort	WDW	★★★½	81	$$$−	934-7639
Amerisuites Orlando Convention Center	1	★★★½	81	$$$+	370-4720
Embassy Suites Resort	2	★★★½	81	$$$+	239-1144
Radisson Inn Lake Buena Vista	2	★★★½	81	$$$+	239-8400
Rosen Plaza Hotel	1	★★★½	81	$$$+	352-9700
Holiday Inn Nikki Bird Resort	3	★★★½	80	$$	396-7300
Renaissance Orlando Resort	1	★★★½	80	$$$−	351-5555
Caribe Royale Resort Suites	3	★★★½	80	$$$$−	238-8000

HOW THE HOTELS COMPARE *(continued)*

Hotel	Location	Overall Room Rating	Room Quality Rating	Cost ($=$50)	Phone (area code 407)
Rosen Centre Hotel	1	★★★½	80	$$$$	354-9840
Homewood Suites International	1	★★★½	79	$$$−	248-2232
Sheraton World Resort (tower rooms)	1	★★★½	79	$$$+	352-1100
Country Inn & Suites (suites)	2	★★★½	78	$$+	239-1115
Courtyard by Marriott	1	★★★½	78	$$$−	351-2244
Renaissance by Marriott Resort	3	★★★½	77	$$−	396-1400
Residence Inn Convention Center	1	★★★½	77	$$−	226-0288
Grosvenor Resort	WDW	★★★½	76	$$−	828-4444
Radisson Barcelo Inn Intl. (garden rooms)	1	★★★½	76	$$−	345-0505
AmeriSuites Universal	1	★★★½	76	$$+	351-0627
Residence Inn Orlando	1	★★★½	76	$$$−	345-0117
WDW Caribbean Beach Resort	WDW	★★★½	76	$$$−	934-7639
Westgate Towers	3	★★★½	76	$$$−	396-2500
WDW Fort Wilderness Resort (cabin)	WDW	★★★½	76	$$$$$+	934-7639
Courtyard Disney Village	WDW	★★★½	75	$$+	828-8888
Holiday Inn Universal Studios	1	★★★	74	$$$+	351-3333
Homewood Suites Maingate	3	★★★	74	$$$+	396-2229
Marriott Village Spring Hill Suites	2	★★★	74	$$$+	938-9001
Quality Suites Intl. Drive	1	★★★	74	$$−	363-0332
RUI Orlando	2	★★★	74	$$−	239-8500
Comfort Suites	3	★★★	73	$$−	390-9888
La Quinta Inn Intl.	1	★★★	73	$$−	351-1660
WDW All-Star Resort	WDW	★★★	73	$$−	934-7639
Quality Suites Maingate East	3	★★★	73	$$$−	396-8040

HOW THE HOTELS COMPARE *(continued)*

Hotel	Location	Overall Room Rating	Room Quality Rating	Cost ($=$50)	Phone (area code 407)
Westgate Lakes	1	★★★	73	$$$$$$–	352-8051
Holiday Inn Intl. Resort	1	★★★	72	$$	351-3500
Country Inn & Suites (rooms)	2	★★★	72	$$+	239-1115
Spring Hill Suites by Marriott	1	★★★	72	$$$–	345-9073
Days Suites Maingate East	3	★★★	72	$$$+	396-7900
Clarion Maingate	3	★★★	71	$$–	396-4000
Holiday Inn Hotel & Suites Maingate East (rooms)	3	★★★	71	$$–	396-4488
Ramada Plaza and Inn Gateway (tower rooms)	3	★★★	71	$$$	396-4400
Marriott Village Courtyard	2	★★★	71	$$$+	938-9001
Best Western Disney Village	WDW	★★★	70	$$+	828-2424
Comfort Suites Orlando	1	★★★	69	$$	351-5050
Holiday Inn Sun Spree Resort	2	★★★	69	$$+	239-4500
Best Western Movieland	1	★★★	68	$$–	351-3900
Hotel Royal Plaza (garden rooms)	WDW	★★★	68	$$$–	828-2828
Sheraton World Resort (garden rooms)	1	★★★	68	$$$+	352-1100
Travelodge Suites Eastgate	3	★★★	67	$+	396-7666
Wellesley Inn	1	★★★	67	$+	370-5100
Best Western Lake Cecile	3	★★★	67	$$–	396-2056
Hampton Inn Universal Studios	1	★★★	67	$$–	351-6716
Sheraton Four Points Hotel by Lakeside	3	★★★	67	$$–	396-2222
Clarion Universal	1	★★★	67	$$+	351-5009
Courtyard by Marriott	2	★★★	67	$$+	239-6900
Delta Orlando Resort	1	★★★	67	$$$–	351-3340

HOW THE HOTELS COMPARE (continued)

Hotel	Location	Overall Room Rating	Room Quality Rating	Cost ($=$50)	Phone (area code 407)
Enclave Suites	1	★★★	67	$$$−	351-1155
Red Roof Inn Kissimmee	3	★★★	66	$−	396-0065
Hampton Inn Maingate	3	★★★	66	$$−	396-8484
Hampton Inn Sandlake	1	★★★	66	$$−	363-7886
Howard Johnson EnchantedLand Resort Hotel	3	★★★	66	$$−	396-4343
Ramada Eastgate Fountain Park	3	★★★	66	$$−	396-1111
Holiday Inn Hotel & Suites Maingate East (suites)	3	★★★	66	$$$−	396-4488
Hampton Inn Convention Center	1	★★★	65	$+	354-4447
Quality Inn Intl.	1	★★★	65	$+	351-1600
Holiday Inn Maingate West	3	★★★	65	$$−	396-1100
Howard Johnson Plaza Resort	1	★★★	65	$$−	351-2000
Days Inn Lake Buena Vista	2	★★★	65	$$$+	239-4441
Days Inn Eastgate	3	★★½	64	$+	396-7700
Howard Johnson Maingate West	3	★★½	64	$+	396-9300
Travelodge Maingate East	3	★★½	64	$+	396-4222
Quality Inn Lake Cecile	3	★★½	64	$+	396-4455
Hampton Inn Kirkman	1	★★½	64	$$−	345-1112
Marriott Village Fairfield Inn	2	★★½	64	$$−	938-9001
Ramada Resort Florida Center	1	★★½	64	$$+	351-4600
MIC Lakefront Inn	1	★★½	63	$+	345-5340
Sleep Inn Maingate	3	★★½	63	$+	396-1600
Howard Johnson South Intl. Drive	1	★★½	63	$$−	351-5100
Holiday Inn Express	1	★★½	63	$$	351-4430
Days Inn	3	★★½	62	$	(800) 544-5713

HOW THE HOTELS COMPARE (continued)

Hotel	Location	Overall Room Rating	Room Quality Rating	Cost ($=$50)	Phone (area code 407)
Ramada Inn Westgate	3	★★½	62	$+	(863) 424-2621
Best Western Plaza Intl.	1	★★½	62	$$–	345-8195
Howard Johnson Express Inn and Suites (suites)	3	★★½	62	$$–	396-4762
Quality Inn Plaza	1	★★½	62	$$–	345-8585
Days Inn Maingate East	3	★★½	61	$+	396-7900
Ramada Inn	1	★★½	61	$+	351-4410
Ramada Resort Maingate	3	★★½	61	$$–	396-4466
Comfort Inn at Lake Buena Vista	2	★★½	60	$+	239-7300
Days Inn Orlando Lakeside	1	★★½	60	$+	351-1900
Days Inn Universal Studios	1	★★½	60	$+	351-3800
Super 8 Maingate	3	★★½	60	$+	396-7500
Travelodge Intl.	1	★★½	60	$+	(800) 327-0750
Clarion Suites Resort World (rooms)	3	★★½	60	$$–	396-8300
Diplomat Resort	3	★★½	60	$$+	396-6000
Days Inn SeaWorld/ Convention Center	1	★★½	60	$$$–	352-8700
Magic Castle	3	★★½	59	$–	396-2212
Travelodge Maingate	3	★★½	59	$–	396-0100
Econo Lodge Maingate Hawaiian	3	★★½	59	$+	396-2000
Fairfield Inn Intl.	1	★★½	59	$+	363-1944
Howard Johnson Inn	1	★★½	59	$+	351-2900
Wynfield Inn Westwood	1	★★½	59	$+	(800) 346-1551
Ramada Plaza and Inn Gateway (garden rooms)	3	★★½	59	$$	396-4400
Red Roof Inn Orlando	1	★★½	58	$–	352-1507
Days Inn Maingate West	3	★★½	58	$+	396-1000
Quality Inn Maingate West	3	★★½	58	$+	396-1828

HOW THE HOTELS COMPARE *(continued)*

Hotel	Location	Overall Room Rating	Room Quality Rating	Cost ($=$50)	Phone (area code 407)
Sleep Inn and Suites Universal	1	★★½	58	$+	363-1333
Days Inn Intl. Drive	1	★★½	58	$$+	351-1200
Best Western Eastgate	3	★★½	57	$−	396-0707
Howard Johnson Express Inn and Suites (rooms)	3	★★½	57	$+	396-4762
Howard Johnson Inn Maingate East	3	★★½	57	$+	396-1748
Super 8 Maingate	3	★★½	57	$+	396-8883
Wynfield Inn Maingate	3	★★½	57	$+	396-2121
Kissimmee Super 8 Motel	3	★★½	56	$	396-1144
Ramada Limited Universal Maingate	1	★★½	56	$+	354-3996
Riande Continental Plaza	1	★★½	56	$+	352-8211
Rodeway Inn Intl.	1	★★½	56	$+	351-4444
Super 8 Universal	1	★★½	56	$+	352-8383
Travelodge Suites Maingate	3	★★½	56	$+	396-1780
Knights Inn Maingate	3	★★	55	$+	396-4200
Masters Inn	3	★★	55	$+	396-4020
Masters Inn Maingate	3	★★	55	$+	396-7743
Larson's Inn Maingate	3	★★	55	$$−	396-6100
Golden Link Motel	3	★★	54	$−	396-0555
Universal Inn	1	★★	54	$−	351-4100
Park Inn Intl.	3	★★	53	$−	396-1376
Sun Motel	3	★★	53	$−	396-2673
Knights Inn Maingate East	3	★★	52	$	396-8186
Motel 6 Maingate East	3	★★	52	$−	396-6333
Motel 6 Maingate West	3	★★	52	$−	396-6427
Traveler's Inn	3	★★	52	$−	396-1668
Central Motel	3	★★	51	$−	396-2333

		Overall Room Rating	Room Quality Rating	Cost ($=$50)	Phone (area code 407)
HOW THE HOTELS COMPARE *(continued)*					
Hotel	Location				
Red Carpet Inn East	3	★★	50	$–	396-1133
Motel 6 Intl. Drive	1	★★	49	$	351-6500
Monte Carlo	3	★★	48	$–	396-4700

The Top 30 Best Deals

Having listed the nicest rooms in town, let's take a look at the best combinations of quality and value in a room. As before, the rankings are made without consideration of location or the availability of restaurant(s), recreational facilities, entertainment, and/or amenities.

A reader recently wrote us to complain that he had booked one of our top-ranked rooms in terms of value and had been very disappointed in the room. We noticed that the room the reader occupied had a quality rating of ★★½. We would remind you that the list of top deals are intended to give you some sense of value received for dollars spent. A ★★½ room at $50 may have the same value as a ★★★★ room at $115, but that does not mean the rooms will be of comparable quality. Regardless of whether it's a good deal or not, a ★★½ room is still a ★★½ room.

Listed below are the top 30 room buys for the money, regardless of location or star classification, based on average rack rates. Note that a suite can sometimes cost less than a hotel room.

Hotel	Location	Overall Room Rating	Room Quality Rating	Cost ($=$50)	Phone (area code 407)
THE TOP 30 BEST DEALS					
Red Roof Inn Kissimmee	3	★★★	66	$–	396-0065
Grosvenor Resort	WDW	★★★½	76	$$–	828-4444
Radisson Barcelo Inn International (tower rooms)	1	★★★★	83	$$–	345-0505
Travelodge Maingate	3	★★½	59	$–	396-0100
Red Roof Inn Orlando	1	★★½	58	$–	352-1507
Days Inn	3	★★½	62	$	(800) 544-5713
Travelodge Suites Eastgate	3	★★★	67	$+	396-7666
Magic Castle	3	★★½	59	$–	396-2212
Residence Inn Convention Center	1	★★★½	77	$$–	226-0288

THE TOP 30 BEST DEALS (continued)

Hotel	Location	Overall Room Rating	Room Quality Rating	Cost ($=$50)	Phone (area code 407)
Wellesley Inn	1	★★★	67	$+	370-5100
Best Western Eastgate	3	★★½	57	$−	396-0707
The Castle Hotel (Doubletree)	1	★★★½	82	$$	345-1511
Wyndham Orlando	1	★★★½	81	$$−	351-2420
Club Hotel by Doubletree	2	★★★½	81	$$−	239-4646
La Quinta Inn Intl.	1	★★★	72	$$−	351-1660
Hampton Inn Convention Center	1	★★★	65	$+	354-4447
Kissimmee Super 8 Motel	3	★★½	56	$	396-1144
Quality Inn Intl.	1	★★★	65	$+	351-1600
Embassy Vacation Resort	2	★★★★½	92	$$$−	238-2500
Days Inn Universal Studios	1	★★½	60	$+	351-3800
Super 8 Maingate	3	★★½	60	$+	396-7500
Radisson Resort Parkway	3	★★★★½	90	$$$−	396-7000
Crowne Plaza Resort	1	★★★★	87	$$$−	239-1222
Golden Link Motel	3	★★	54	$−	396-0555
Radisson Barcelo Inn Intl. (garden rooms)	1	★★★½	76	$$−	345-0505
Wyndham Palace	WDW	★★★★	86	$$$−	827-2727
Clarion Maingate	3	★★★	71	$$−	396-4000
Travelodge Maingate East	3	★★½	63	$+	396-4222
Ramada Inn Westgate	3	★★½	62	$+	(863) 424-2621
Hard Rock Hotel	1	★★★★★	96	$$$$−	503-ROCK

Part Four

The Disney Cruise Line

The Mouse at Sea

In case you've been raising chinchillas on Venus, here's the news: the Walt Disney Company is now in the cruise business with two almost identical ships called *Disney Wonder* and *Disney Magic*. Cruises originate at Port Canaveral (about an hour's drive from the Orlando airport) and visit Nassau in the Bahamas and Castaway Cay, Disney's private island, on three- and four-day itineraries. Seven-day eastern-Caribbean itineraries include port calls at St. Maarten and St. Thomas as well as Castaway Cay. Western Caribbean itineraries are offered on alternate weeks. Ports of call include Key West, Grand Cayman, Cozumel, and Castaway Cay.

Cruises can be purchased separately or as part of weeklong packages that split the seven days between the cruise and three or four days at Walt Disney World. Included in the packages are your Disney World hotel, theme-park admissions, transportation (called transfers) from Walt Disney World or the airport to the ship, and the cruise.

From the outset, Disney assembled a team of highly respected veterans of the cruise industry and dozens of the world's best-known ship designers and put them together with their own unrivaled team of creative talent. Together, they conceptualized and created the Disney ships, recognizing that every detail would be critical to the line's success. Their task was to design a product that makes every adult on board feel the vacation is intended for them, while at the same time, giving every kid the same impression.

The first surprise is the appearance of the Disney ships. They are simultaneously classic and innovative. The exteriors are based on traditional lines, reminiscent of the great oceanliners of the past, but even in that respect, you'll find a Disney twist or two. Inside, they are up-to-the-minute technologically and full of novel ideas for dining, entertainment, cabin design, and entertainment facilities. Even Disney's exclusive cruise terminal at Port Canaveral is an integral part of the overall strategy, aiming to make enjoyable even embarkation and debarkation—shown by Disney's market research to be a cruising negative.

The major innovation is in dining. Each evening on board you dine in a different restaurant with a different motif, but your waiters and dining companions move with you. Overcoming another cruising negative—the hassle of tendering passengers—was also an important consideration for Disney in selecting its private Bahamian island that is included on all cruises; namely, finding one with deep water where facilities could be built for their ships to pull dockside.

Disney's plan has been to create a "seamless vacation package" combining a three- or four-day stay at Walt Disney World with a cruise. Disney Cruise Line passengers are met at the airport by Disney staff and transported to the terminal in easily identifiable Disney Cruise Line buses. During the hour-long ride from the airport to Port Canaveral, they watch a video preview of the cruise. To smooth embarkation, Disney has streamlined check-in. When your cruise is packaged with a stay at a Disney hotel, you check in once. The same key that unlocks your hotel room door opens the door to your cruise ship cabin.

The Disney Cruise Line targets first-time cruisers, counting on Disney's reputation for quality, service, and entertainment to dispel noncruisers' doubts about cruise vacations. At the same time, a great deal of time and effort has been spent to ensure that the ships are designed to appeal to adults—with or without children—as much as to accommodate children and families. Adults are catered to in myriad ways and presented with an extensive menu of adult-oriented activities. For example, the ships have an alternative restaurant, swimming pool, and nightclub for use by adults only, and entertainment choices range from family musicals to adults-only improv comedy. Meanwhile, from virtually sunrise to almost midnight, children are offered an equally varied selection of programs from which to choose. Because the programs for both adults and for children are offered on an à la carte basis, families can choose how much time to spend together or pursuing separate interests.

If you need a breather from the kids, you won't have much trouble escaping, even with hundreds of children on board. The children's programs are excellent—in fact, they are rated as the best in the cruise industry in the current edition of the *Unofficial Guide to Cruises,* by Kay Showker with Bob Sehlinger. Thus, it's no surprise that many parents see their kids only at breakfast and dinner. Much more difficult to escape than children, however, is Disney's syrupy, wholesome, cuter-than-a-billion-Beanie-Babies brand of entertainment, which permeates every cruise. Expressed differently, to enjoy a Disney cruise you'd better love Disney.

DISNEY CRUISE LINE STANDARD FEATURES

Officers   Multinational.

Staffs   Cabin, dining/Multinational; Cruise/American.

Dining Facilities   Three themed family restaurants with "rotation" dining; alternative adults-only restaurant; indoor/outdoor cafe for breakfast, lunch, snacks, and buffet dinner for children; pool bar/grill for burgers, pizza, and sandwiches; ice cream bar.

Special Diets   On request; health-conscious cuisine program.

Room Service   24 hours.

Dress Code   Casual by day; casual and informal in the evenings.

Cabin Amenities   Direct-dial telephone with voicemail; tub and shower; TV; safe; hair dryer; mini-bar stocked for fee.

Electrical Outlets   110 AC.

Wheelchair Access   Yes.

Smoking   Smoking not allowed except in special areas.

Disney Suggested Tipping   Waiter: 3-night cruise, $11; 4-night, $14.75; assistant waiter, $8 and $10.75. Cabin steward: 3-night cruise, $11; 4-night, $14.75; 15% service charge added to bar bills.

Credit Cards   For cruise payment and on-board charges, all major credit cards.

The Ships

Disney Magic and *Disney Wonder* are modern cruise ships with long, sleek lines, twin smokestacks, and nautical styling that recalls a classic ocean-liner but with instantly recognizable Disney signatures. The colors—black, white, red, and yellow—and the famous face-and-ears silhouette on the stacks are clearly those of Mickey Mouse. Look closely and you'll see that *Magic*'s figurehead is a 15-foot Goofy (Donald Duck on *Wonder*) swinging upside down from a boatswain's chair, "painting" the stern.

Interiors combine nautical themes with art deco inspiration, but Disney images are everywhere, from Mickey's profile in the wrought-iron balustrades to the bronze statue of Helmsman Mickey at the center of the three-deck Grand Atrium. Disney art is on every wall, stairwell, and corridor. Some are valuable prints of Disney animated cartoon characters. A grand staircase sweeps from the atrium lobby to shops selling Disney Cruise Line–themed clothing, collectibles, jewelry, sundries, classic Disney toys, T-shirts, and souvenirs. (The shops are always full of eager buyers; some people speculate that the cruise line will derive as much revenue here as other lines do from their casinos, which the Disney ships do not have.)

The ships have two lower decks with cabins, three decks with dining rooms and show rooms, then three decks of cabins, and two sports and sun decks with separate pools and facilities for families and for adults without kids. Signs with arrows point the way to lounges and facilities, and all elevators are clearly marked forward, aft, or amidship.

Our main complaint concerning the design of the ships is that all outdoor public areas focus inward toward the pools as opposed to seaward, as if Disney wanted you to forget you are on a cruise liner. There's no public place on any deck where you can curl up in a shady spot and watch the ocean (at least not without a wall of Plexiglas between you and it). If this quintessential cruise pleasure ranks high on your hit parade, your only option is to spring for a cabin with a private veranda. A second predictable but nonetheless irritating design characteristic is the extent to which the ship is childproofed. There's enough Plexiglas on *Magic* and *Wonder* to build a subdivision of transparent houses. On the pool decks (Deck 9) especially, it feels as if the ships are hermetically sealed.

Cabins

Cabins and suites are spacious with generous wood paneling throughout. About three-fourths are outside, almost half with private verandas. The 12 cabin categories range from standard to deluxe, deluxe with veranda, family suite, one- and two-bedroom suites, and royal suite. Categories are similar to those at Walt Disney World hotels. Passengers who spend three or four days at a Disney resort are matched with a cabin in a comparable category.

Note: If you're staying at a Disney resort before your cruise, be sure to complete and return your cruise forms at the hotel. By showing your shoreside room key card at the cruise terminal, you can bypass lines and board directly. Cruise-only passengers may encounter a wait at check-in.

The design of the cabins, particularly, reveals Disney's finely tuned sense of the needs of families and children and offers a cruise industry first: a split bathroom with bathtub/shower and sink in one room and toilet, sink, and vanity in another. This configuration, found in all but the standard inside cabins, allows any member of the family to use the bathroom without monopolizing it entirely. All bathrooms have both tub and shower.

The decor has unusual features, such as bureaus designed to look like steamer trunks—a nod to tradition. The cabins also have a direct-dial telephone with voicemail messaging; TV; hair dryer; and mini-bar. In some cabins, pull-down Murphy beds allow for additional daytime floor space. Storage space is generous with deep drawers and large closets.

On each ship the cabin inventory includes 252 inside cabins and 625 outside cabins; 276 suites with verandas, 82 family suites, 16 one-bedroom suites, 2 two-bedroom suites, 2 royal suites; 14 wheelchair-accessible accommodations. Most cabins accommodate three people;

inside cabins up to four; deluxe with verandas up to four; family and one-bedroom suites up to five.

Services and Amenities

Passengers lavishly praise Disney cast members. They are among the most accommodating you will ever encounter in travel, and they try hard to smooth your way from boarding to departure. *Unofficial Guide* cruise writer Kay Showker related, "More than once when I stopped to get my bearings, a Disney cast member was there within seconds to help me."

You will be given a Disney Magic Passport, a convenient purse-sized booklet that covers just about everything you need to know for your cruise. Daily in your cabin, you will receive "Your Personal Navigator" listing onboard entertainment and daily activities separated into options for teens, children, adults, and families, as well as information on shore excursions.

Dining

Dining is Disney's most innovative area. Ships have three different family restaurants, plus an alternative restaurant for adults only. Each night passengers move to a different family restaurant, each with a different theme and menu, taking their table companions and wait staff with them. In each restaurant, tableware, linens, menu covers, and waiters' uniforms have been designed specifically to fit the theme.

On *Magic,* Lumière's, named for the candlestick character from *Beauty and the Beast,* is a handsome, art-deco venue serving continental cuisine. A mural depicts *Beauty and the Beast* (the equivalent restaurant on *Wonder* is called Triton, themed after *The Little Mermaid*).

Parrot Cay dishes up Caribbean-accented food in a colorful, fun, tropical setting that reminds most Disney veterans of the Enchanted Tiki Room. Parrot Cay is the most popular of the three for breakfast. Children particularly enjoy the decor and festivity, but the food, although adequate, is not up to the standard of the other restaurants.

But it's Animator's Palate that reflects the creative genius of Disney animation and is the ships' dining pièce de résistance (or for some, the straw that broke the camel's back). Diners are given the impression that they have entered a black-and-white sketchbook. Over the course of the meal, the sketches on the walls are transformed through fiber optics into a full-color extravaganza. Waiters change their costumes from black and white to color. The first course is a montage of appetizers served on a palette-shaped plate, and dessert—a tasteless mousse in the shape of Mickey—comes with a parade by waiters bearing trays of colorful syrups—mango, chocolate, and strawberry—used to decorate it. The food is less than inspired, and hot dishes are likely to arrive cold. But no ones seems to care—they are too absorbed in watching Disney perform its magic. Conversation is often difficult, and the entertainment, though creative, is the ultimate in Disney cute (and totally inescapable). Children predictably love it, but for many adults it's a little overwhelming.

Palo, the casual Italian restaurant named for the pole gondoliers use to navigate Venetian canals, is the intimate, adults-only alternative restaurant. It's the best on board and has its own kitchen. The lovely semicircular room has a sophisticated ambience with soft lighting, Venetian glass, inlaid wood, and a back-lit bar. Northern Italian cuisine is featured. Food and presentation are excellent. More than two dozen wines are available by the glass for $5.50 to $30. There is a $5-per-person cover charge (but no signs in the restaurant, on the menu, or in the ship literature alert you to it). Service is attentive but leisurely, though it may just seem that way in comparison to the staccato dining pace of the other restaurants on board. Reservations are required; make them as soon as you board or risk being shut out. (Disney underestimated demand for this venue.)

There are two seatings, at 6 and 8:30 p.m., for dinner at Lumière's (Triton), Animator's Palate, and Parrot Cay. If your children are 12 or younger and you plan to dine as a family, we recommend the early seating. If your kids are involved in programs where they dine with the other children, go with your own preference. All three restaurants offer special kid's meals if your picky eaters can't find something they like on the regular menu.

On a three-day cruise, your normal rotation will have you dine one night each at Lumière's (Triton), Animator's Palate, and Parrot Cay. If you sign up to dine at Palo (adults only), you will skip the regular restaurant designated for that night on your rotation. Thus, choose your Palo night carefully. Our vote for the most expendable restaurant on the rotation is Parrot Cay. In any event, if you miss Parrot Cay for dinner, you can still try it at lunch or breakfast. On a four-day cruise, one of the regular restaurants will pop up twice on your rotation. If you want to eat at all of the restaurants, including Palo, make your Palo reservation on the night that you are scheduled to repeat one of the basic three.

Shortly after boarding Disney gives you the opportunity to both make Palo reservations (taken in the restaurant) and/or change your restaurant rotation if you desire. In our opinion, one night each at Animator's Palate or Parrot Cay is enough. If your rotation calls for you to repeat a night in either, eliminate the repeat by booking Palo or substituting a second night at Lumière's (Triton).

If you're wondering what to do with your children while you dine at Palo, you have several options: make a late reservation for Palo, then keep your children company (but don't eat) while they dine at the regularly assigned restaurant (this only works if you normally eat at the first seating); place your children in a program where they'll eat dinner with the other enrolled kids; take your children to Pluto's Dog House, poolside on Deck 9, for hot dogs and burgers; or order the kids a room service dinner and arrange for a private sitter.

Buffet & Fast Food Other dining options include Topsiders (Beach Blanket Buffet on *Wonder*), an indoor/outdoor cafe serving breakfast, lunch, snacks, and a buffet dinner for children; a pool bar and grill for hamburgers, hot dogs, and sandwiches; Pinocchio's Pizzeria; an ice cream and frozen yogurt bar; and 24-hour room service. Topsiders is the weak sister of the bunch: It's OK for breakfast, but long on bulk and short on flavor for lunch. The pizza, dogs, burgers, yogurt, and ice cream are good.

Facilities and Entertainment

Nightly entertainment is unlike any other cruise line's and features quality, Disney-produced shows. The 977-seat Walt Disney Theater stages a different musical production each night, with talented actors, singers, and dancers. These family musicals are on the level of Disney theme parks' entertainment rather than Broadway and will probably appeal more to children than adults.

Disney Dreams has about every Disney character and song ever heard and offers a light plot wherein Peter Pan visits a girl who dreams of Disney's famous characters. It's pure schmaltz, but audiences give it a standing ovation. As for kids at the late show, many had dozed off to their own dreamland before the curtain fell.

Another night offers *Hercules, The Muse-ical,* a musical comedy that is the least saccharine of the lot. Substituted as a low-budget replacement for a third musical production is the Disney Trivia Game Show. Do you know Goofy's middle name? On seven-night cruises, a Welcome Aboard Variety Show and Magical Farewell production are added along with a magic show.

In the smaller Buena Vista Theater with full-screen cinema and Dolby sound, passengers watch first-run movies and classic Disney films.

Studio Sea, modeled after a television- or film-production set, is a family-oriented nightclub offering dance music, family-oriented cabaret acts, passenger game shows, and multimedia entertainment. The art deco Promenade Lounge offers a haven for reading and relaxation by day and cocktails and piano music by night. ESPN Skybox, a sports bar in the ship's forward, decorative funnel, has a big screen TV for viewing sporting events and a small viewing area with stadium seating.

Magic features Beat Street, an adult-oriented evening entertainment district with shops and three themed nightclubs—Rockin' Bar D, with live bands playing rock and roll, Top 40, and country music; Off Beat, an improv comedy club; and Sessions, a casual yet sophisticated place to relax and enjoy easy-listening music. On *Wonder,* Beat Street is replaced with the Route 66 three-club complex. Wavebands features live bands playing current pop and oldies. Barrel of Laughs offers dueling pianos and sing-alongs, while Cadillac Lounge is the place for atmosphere and quiet music.

Disney ships have no casinos (research showed its target markets weren't interested in gambling at sea, Disney says) or libraries.

Children's Programs

Playrooms and other kids' facilities occupy more than 15,000 square feet. Programs of age-specific activities are among the most extensive in cruising. They include challenging interactive activities and play areas supervised by trained counselors. There are separate programs for ages 3–5, 6–8, 9–10, 11–12, and teens. Baby-sitting for tots is provided in the Flounders Reef nursery for ages 12 weeks to 3 years old; this service operates 2–4 p.m. and 7 p.m.–midnight daily. Cost is $6 per child per hour; $5 per hour for each additional child.

The Oceaneer's Adventure program encompasses Oceaneer's Club (ages 3–7), themed to resemble Captain Hook's pirate ship, with plenty of places for activity; and Oceaneer's Lab (ages 8–12), with high-tech play including video games, computers, and lab equipment, and a small area for listening to CDs. Kids wear ID bracelets, and parents receive pagers for staying in touch with their playing children. Both parents and children give youth programs high marks. Children in the drop-off program are taken to dinner at Topsiders.

Common Grounds (Deck 9) is a teen area themed after a trendy coffee bar and has a game arcade, a selection of videos, and a CD-listening lounge. There are also organized activities, including nighttime volleyball. The program is a hit, as teens enjoy having a large part of the upper deck to themselves in the evenings. Teen activities are supervised in a way that makes the participants feel unfettered and autonomous. For example, other than counselors, no adults are allowed in the Common Grounds teen club.

Sports, Fitness, and Beauty

Of three top-deck pools, one has a Mickey Mouse motif and water slide and is intended for families. Another is set aside for team sports; the third is exclusively for adults. At night the pool area can be transformed into a stage for deck parties and dancing.

The 8,500-square-foot, ocean-view Vista Spa and Salon above the bridge offers Cybex exercise equipment, an aerobics room, exercise instruction, thermal-bath area, saunas, and steam rooms. It's supervised by a qualified fitness director. The spa, run by the British-based Steiner group, offers pricey beauty treatments along with a sales pitch on Steiner products. Despite high prices, the spa has proved to be very popular; it's generally booked for the entire cruise within hours of embarkation. Passengers in Deck 8 concierge-level suites can have a private massage in their suite or veranda. A 50-minute massage costs $108 (prices vary).

The Sports Deck has a paddle tennis court, Ping-Pong, basketball court, and shuffleboard. A full promenade deck lures walkers and joggers but has no lounge chairs.

Castaway Cay

Each Disney cruise includes a day at Castaway Cay, Disney's 1,000-acre private island. The natural environment and beauty of the island has been preserved. Miles of white sand beaches are surrounded by clear, emerald water. A pier allows access without tendering. A four-car open tram (like those at WDW theme parks) carries you from the ship to Scuttle's Cove family beach. The shuttle runs every five minutes. En route, a recording narrates a mythical version of the island's history. You could walk the quarter-mile to the beach, but it's inadvisable in the blistering heat. (Bring sunblock and wear a hat.) Strollers are available, as are rental floats, bikes, kayaks, and snorkel gear. Lounge chairs under pastel-colored umbrellas are plentiful, and some hammocks swing under the palms, but otherwise there's very little shade.

Disney Imagineers have created shops, rest rooms, and pavilions that give the impression they have been there for years. A supervised children's area includes a "dig" at a half-buried whale skeleton. Water sports are offered in a protected lagoon. One snorkeling course is near shore; the other, farther out, requires more endurance. On the distant course, snorkelers see a variety of fish they identify from a waterproof card provided with rental equipment. Lifeguards watch snorkelers all around the courses. The cruise line has also planted several "shipwrecks." On one in about ten feet of water, snorkelers can see Mickey Mouse riding the bow of the ship. There's also a treasure chest, its contents guarded by large fish. Rental equipment costs $25 for adults and $10 for children (ages 3–9). Nature trails and bike paths are provided. The main beach offers kids' activities, live Bahamian music, and shops. Cookie's Bar-B-Cue serves a buffet lunch of burgers, pork ribs, hot dogs, baked beans, slaw, corn on the cob, fruit, and potato chips.

A second tram connects to Serenity Bay, the adult beach on the island's opposite side. The adult beach is a long sweep of sugary sand. A bar serves drinks, and passengers can enjoy a massage in one of the private cabanas with shuttered doors opening on the sea. Passengers must be back on the ship by 3:15 p.m. Most say they would have liked more time on the island.

Rates

Although Disney bundles its cruises with a stay at Walt Disney World, you can usually beat the package price by buying your vacation components à la carte. Disney cruise-only brochure rates start at $450 per person (based on double occupancy) for a standard inside cabin on a three-day cruise and run to about $1,500 for a cabin with a veranda on a four-day cruise. Suites cost up to $3,500 for a four-day cruise. Seven-day packages that include a stay at Walt Disney World start at $829 and run to about $4,800 per person. Fares for children sharing a cabin with their parents run $99–$799. Port charges are included in the price.

Our advice is to shop the non-Disney cruise discount agencies. Some agencies sell only cruises, but others can sell the entire Disney cruise/land package. So far, however, we haven't seen a package that we couldn't beat by purchasing the components individually ourselves.

CRUISE DISCOUNT AGENCIES

All Cruise Travel	(800) 227-8473	www.allcruise.com
Crown Travel	(800) 869-7447	www.crowncruise.com
Cruise Match	(800) 925-8572	www.cruisematch.com
Cruise Value Center	(800) 231-7407	www.cruisevalue.com
Cruises Only	(800) 895-3771	www.mytravelco.com
Mann Travel & Cruises	(800) 438-3709	www.travelcruises.com

As a courtesy, once you've shopped around and determined the lowest price available, give your regular travel agent the opportunity to match or beat it. In addition to discounts offered by cruise sellers like those listed above, additional savings ("early bird" discounts) can be had by booking well in advance. If for some reason you prefer to book directly with Disney, here's how to get in touch:

Disney Cruise Line
210 Celebration Place, Suite 400
Celebration, FL 34747-4600
(800) 951-6499 or (800) 951-3532
fax: (407) 566-7739; www.disneycruise.com

A Few Tips

1. If you opt for a week that includes the cruise and a stay at Walt Disney World, go to Disney World first. Taking the cruise at the end of your vacation will ensure that you arrive home relaxed and rested.

2. Board the ship as early as possible. Check your dining rotation, and arrange for changes if you desire. Make reservations for Palo as soon as the reservations desk at the restaurant opens, usually 2 p.m.

3. After firming up your dining arrangements, register your children at Oceaneer Club (ages 3–7) and/or Oceaneer Lab (ages 8–12). If you board before 1:30 p.m., register your kids first and then attend to your dining arrangements.

4. If you are interested in a massage or other spa services, sign up between 2 and 4 p.m. at the spa.

5. Disney requests that gentlemen wear jackets (no ties required) in the evening at Palo and Lumière's (Triton).

6. If you are staying at a Disney resort prior to your cruise, be sure to fill out and hand in your cruise forms at the hotel. By flashing your shoreside room key card at the cruise terminal, you can bypass lines and board the ship directly. If you are a "cruise-only" passenger, you might encounter a wait at check-in.

7. Because most cabins have a mini-fridge, we recommend bringing your own snacks and beverages.

8. The Sessions/Cadillac Lounge piano bar is one of the most relaxing and beautiful lounges we have ever seen on a cruise ship. Make a before- or after-dinner drink at The Sessions part of your daily routine. It's on Deck 3, forward.

9. Don't miss the Offbeat comedy club, located on Deck 3, forward.

10. Don't miss the various kids' programs.

11. WARNING: Since September 11, 2001, Disney has tightened security on both ships. Knives of any kind, scissors, corkscrews, and anything else that can be used as a weapon are prohibited. Both carry-on and checked luggage are checked. Contraband items are confiscated and returned at the end of the cruise on disembarkation.

Part Five

Walt Disney World with Kids

The Ecstasy and the Agony

So overwhelming is the Disney media and advertising presence that any child who watches TV or shops with Mom is likely to get revved up about going to Walt Disney World. Parents, if anything, are even more susceptible. Almost every parent has brightened with anticipation at the prospect of guiding their children through the wonders of this special place. But the reality of taking a young child (particularly in summer) is usually closer to the agony than the ecstasy.

A mother from Dayton, Ohio, describes taking her five-year-old to Disney World in July:

> I felt so happy and excited before we went. I guess it was all worth it, but when I look back I think I should have had my head examined. The first day we went to [the Magic Kingdom] and it was packed. By 11 in the morning we had walked so far and stood in so many lines that we were all exhausted. Kristy cried about going on anything that looked or even sounded scary and was frightened by all of the Disney characters (they are so big!) except Minnie and Snow White.
>
> We got hungry about the same time as everyone else, but the lines for food were too long and my husband said we would have to wait. By one in the afternoon we were just plugging along, not seeing anything we were really interested in, but picking rides because the lines were short, or because whatever it was was air-conditioned. We rode Small World three times in a row, and I'll never get that song out of my head (Ha!). At around 2:30 we finally got something to eat, but by then we were so hot and tired that it felt like we had worked in the yard all day. Kristy insisted on being carried, and we had 50 fights about not going on rides where the lines were too long. At the end, we were so P.O.'d and uncomfortable that we weren't having any fun. Mostly by this time we were just trying to get our money's worth.

Before you stiffen in denial, let me assure you that the Ohio family's experience is fairly typical. Most young children are as picky about the rides as they are about what they eat, and more than half of preschoolers are intimidated by the friendly Disney characters. Few humans (of any age) are mentally or physically equipped to march all day in a throng of 50,000 people in the hot Florida sun. And would you be surprised to learn that almost 60% of preschoolers said the thing they liked best about their Disney World vacation was the hotel swimming pool?

Reality Testing—Whose Dream Is It?

Remember when you were little and you got that nifty electric train for Christmas, the one Dad wouldn't let you play with? Did you ever wonder who that train was really for? Ask yourself the same question about your vacation to Walt Disney World. Whose dream are you trying to make come true: yours or your child's?

Young children are adept at reading their parents' emotions. When you ask, "Honey, how would you like to go to Disney World?" your child will respond more to your smile and excitement and the idea of doing something with Mom and Dad than to any notion of what Disney World is all about. The younger the child, the more this is true. For many preschoolers, you could elicit the same enthusiasm by asking, "Honey, how would you like to go to Cambodia on a dogsled?"

So, is your happy fantasy of introducing your child to Disney magic a pipe dream? Not necessarily, but you have to be practical and open to reality testing. For example, would you increase the probability of a happy, successful visit by waiting a couple of years? Is your child adventuresome enough to sample the variety of Disney World? Will your child have sufficient endurance and patience to cope with long lines and large crowds?

Recommendations for Making the Dream Come True

When planning a Disney World vacation with young children, consider:

Age   Although the color and festivity of Disney World excite all children and specific attractions delight toddlers and preschoolers, Disney entertainment is generally oriented to older children and adults. Children should be a fairly mature seven years old to *appreciate* the Magic Kingdom and the Animal Kingdom, and a year or two older to get much out of Epcot or Disney-MGM Studios.

Not unexpectedly, our readers engage in a lively and ongoing debate over how old a child should be, or what the ideal age is, to go to Walt Disney World. A Waldwick, New Jersey, mother reports:

My kids, not in the least shy or clingy, were frightened of many attractions. I thought my six-year-old was the "perfect age" but quickly realized this was not the case. Disney makes even the most simple, child-friendly story into a major theatrical production, to the point where my kids couldn't associate their beloved movies to the attraction in front of them.

A Rockaway, New Jersey, mom provided this feedback:

You were absolutely right about young kids—I found myself re-reading your section "The Ecstasy and the Agony." Unfortunately, our experience was pure agony, with the exception of our hotel pool. It was the one and only thing our kids wanted to do. I planned this trip and saved for over a year and cried all week at the disappointment that our kids just wanted to swim.

A Dallas, Texas, dad had this to say:

I must echo the thoughts of readers about parents who bring infants and toddlers to WDW. Are these people nuts? They should find a better way to waste their hard-earned vacation dollars. These children (and therefore their parents) cannot ride any of the best rides and won't remember the ones they do ride five minutes after they get off. It is tough enough walking these huge parks without pushing around one or more children in a stroller. My advice to these parents is to go to a nice beach, rest, let the kids play in the sand, spend less money, and come back in a few years. Disney World will still be there.

A couple from Lexington, Kentucky, agrees and offers this advice:

To the folks with kids in strollers . . . Six years ago we carried an infant in a Snugli, pushed another child in a stroller, and carried the diaper bag from hell. This year, all were on their own foot power. What a difference. Those of you with preschoolers, please wait until they are older. The kids will have just as much fun and may even remember it when they are older. You will actually enjoy the trip instead of being a Grand Canyon pack mule. Your children will not bad-mouth you to Oprah if they don't get to WDW until they are six or seven instead of two or three.

But a Cleveland, Ohio, mother takes exception:

The best advice for parents with young kids is to remember who you are there for and if possible accommodate the kids' need to do things again and again. I think you underestimate Disney's appeal to young children. Since we've gotten home my four-year-old has said "I don't want to live in Cleveland. I want to live at Disney World" at least five times a day.

A New York mother of two very young children believes mental preparation is the key:

I disagree with what you say about toddlers being too young. My two-year-old had a great time! He loved the Animal Kingdom, the characters, and many of the rides. Even my seven-month-old enjoyed Disney World. He had a *good time just looking at the colors and lights. As long as you understand that going with babies will take a little extra work, you can have a good time. I was not one of those parents with screaming kids! If one of my children was cranky, we just left.*

A mother of two toddlers from Lawrenceville, Georgia, thinks it's better to maintain the childrens' normal schedule than to get to the parks early:

The first day, we tried your suggestion about an early start, so we woke the children (ages four and two) and hurried them to get going. BAD IDEA with toddlers. This put them off schedule for naps and meals the rest of the day. It is best to let young ones stay on their regular schedule and see Disney at their own pace and you'll have much more fun.

Finally, a northern Alabama woman encourages parents to be more open-minded about taking toddlers to Walt Disney World:

Parents of toddlers, don't be afraid to bring your little ones! Ours absolutely loved it, and we have priceless photos and videos of our little ones and their grandparents together with Mickey and the gang. For all those people in your book who complained about our little sweethearts crying, sorry, but we found your character-hogging, cursing, ill-mannered, cutting-in-line, screaming-in-our-ears-on-the-roller-coasters teens and preteens much more obnoxious. Guess it's just what you're used to.

Hmmm . . . don't you hate it when people won't tell you what they *really* think?

Time of Year to Visit　Avoid the hot, crowded summer months, especially if you have preschoolers. Go in October, November (except Thanksgiving), early December, January, February, or May. If you have children of varied ages and they're good students, take the older ones out of school and visit during the cooler, less-congested off-season. Arrange special assignments relating to the educational aspects of Disney World. If your children can't afford to miss school, take your vacation as soon as the school year ends in late May or early June. Alternatively, try late August before school starts. Nothing, repeat, nothing will enhance your Walt Disney World vacation as much as avoiding summer and holiday periods.

Build Naps and Rest into Your Itinerary　The theme parks are huge; don't try to see everything in one day. Tour in early morning and return to your hotel around 11:30 a.m. for lunch, a swim, and a nap. Even during off-season when the crowds are smaller and the temperature more pleasant, the size of the major theme parks will exhaust most children under age eight by lunchtime. Return to the park in late afternoon or early evening and continue touring. A family from Texas underlines the importance of naps and rest:

Despite not following any of your "tours," we did follow the theme of visiting a specific park in the morning, leaving midafternoon for either a nap back at the room or a trip to the [hotel] pool, and then returning to one of the parks in the evening. On the few occasions when we skipped your advice, I was muttering to myself by dinner. I can't tell you what I was muttering....

When it comes to naps, this mom does not mince words:

One last thing for parents of small kids: take the book's advice and get out of the park and take the nap, take the nap, TAKE THE NAP! Never in my life have I seen so many parents screaming at, ridiculing, or slapping their kids. (What a vacation!) WDW is overwhelming for kids and adults. Even though the rental strollers recline for sleeping, we noticed that most of the toddlers and preschoolers didn't give up and sleep until 5 p.m., several hours after the fun had worn off, and right about the time their parents wanted them to be awake and polite in a restaurant.

A mom from Rochester, New York, was equally adamant:

[You] absolutely must rest during the day. Kids went from 8 a.m. to 9 p.m. in the Magic Kingdom. Kids did great that day, but we were all completely worthless the next day. Definitely must pace yourself. Don't ever try to do two full days of park sight-seeing in a row. Rest during the day. Go to a water park or sleep in every other day.

If you plan to return to your hotel in midday and would like your room made up, let housekeeping know.

Where to Stay   The time and hassle involved in commuting to and from the theme parks will be lessened if you can afford to stay in the World. But even if you lodge outside, it's imperative that you take young children out of the parks each day for a few hours of rest. Neglecting to relax is the best way we know to get the whole family in a snit and ruin the day (or the vacation).

If you have young children, you must plan ahead. Make sure your hotel is within 20 minutes of the theme parks. Naps and relief from the frenetic pace of the theme parks, even during off-season, are indispensable. It's true you can revive somewhat by retreating to a Disney hotel for lunch or by finding a quiet restaurant in the theme parks, but there's no substitute for returning to the familiarity and comfort of your own hotel. Regardless of what you have heard, children too large to sleep in a stroller won't relax unless you take them back to your hotel. If it takes renting a car to make returning to your hotel practicable, rent the car.

Thousands of new rooms have been built in and near Disney World, many of them affordable. With sufficient lead time, you should have no difficulty finding accommodations that meet your requirements.

If you are traveling with children age 12 and younger, we recommend the Polynesian, Grand Floridian, or Wilderness Lodge and Villas Resorts (in that order) if they fit your budget. For less expensive rooms, try the Port Orleans Resort. Bargain accommodations are available at the All-Star and Pop Century Resorts. Fully equipped log cabins at Fort Wilderness Campground are also good economy lodging. Outside Walt Disney World, check out our top hotels for families on pages 192–203.

Be in Touch with Your Feelings   When you or your children get tired and irritable, call time out and regroup. Trust your instincts. What would feel best? Another ride, an ice cream break, or going back to the room for a nap?

The way to protect your considerable investment in your Disney vacation is to stay happy and have a good time. You don't have to meet a quota for experiencing attractions. Do what you want.

Least Common Denominators   Somebody is going to run out of steam first, and when they do the whole family will be affected. Sometimes a snack break will revive the flagging member. Sometimes, however, as Marshall Dillon would say: Get out of Dodge. Pushing the tired or discontented beyond their capacity will spoil the day for them—and you. Accept that energy levels vary and be prepared to respond to members of your group who poop out. *Hint:* "We've driven a thousand miles to take you to Walt Disney World and now you're ruining everything!" is not an appropriate response.

Building Endurance   Though most children are active, their normal play usually doesn't condition them for the exertion required to tour a Disney theme park. We recommend starting a program of family walks four to six weeks before your trip to get in shape. A mother from Wesconsville, Pennsylvania, reports:

We had our six-year-old begin walking with us a bit every day one month
  before leaving—when we arrived [at Walt Disney World], her little legs
  could carry her and she had a lot of stamina.

Setting Limits and Making Plans   Avoid arguments and disappointment by establishing guidelines for each day, and get everybody committed. Include:

1. Wake-up time and breakfast plans.
2. When to depart for the park.
3. What to take with you.
4. A policy for splitting the group or for staying together.
5. What to do if the group gets separated or someone is lost.
6. How long you intend to tour in the morning and what you want to see, including plans in the event an attraction is closed or too crowded.

7. A policy on what you can afford for snacks.

8. A time for returning to the hotel to rest.

9. When you will return to the park and how late you will stay.

10. Dinner plans.

11. A policy for buying souvenirs, including who pays: Mom and Dad or the kids.

12. Determination of bedtimes.

Be Flexible   Any day at Walt Disney World includes some surprises; be prepared to adjust your plan. Listen to your intuition.

About the _Unofficial Guide_ Touring Plans   Parents who adopt one of our touring plans are often frustrated by interruptions and delays caused by their young children. Here's what to expect:

1.   Character encounters can wreak havoc with the touring plans. Many young children will stop in their tracks whenever they see a Disney character. Attempting to haul your child away before he has satisfied his curiosity is likely to cause anything from whining to a full-scale revolt. Our advice is to either go with the flow or set aside a certain morning or afternoon for photos and autographs. Be aware, however, that queues for autographs, especially in Toontown at the Magic Kingdom and Camp Minnie-Mickey at the Animal Kingdom, are every bit as long as the queues for major attractions.

2.   Our touring plans call for visiting attractions in a sequence, often skipping attractions along the way. Children don't like skipping anything! If something catches their eye, they want to see it that moment. Some children can be persuaded to skip attractions if parents explain their plans in advance. Other kids flip out at skipping something, particularly in Fantasyland. A mom from Charleston, South Carolina, writes:

We did not have too much trouble following the touring plans at [Disney-]
   MGM and at Epcot. The Magic Kingdom plan, on the other hand, turned
   out to be a train wreck. The main problem with the plan is that it starts in
   Fantasyland. When we were on Dumbo, my five-year-old saw eight dozen
   other things in Fantasyland she wanted to see. The long and the short is
   that after Dumbo, there was no getting her out of there.

A mother of two from Burlington, Vermont, adds:

I found out that my kids were very curious about the castle because we had
   read Cinderella at home. Whenever I wanted to leave Fantasyland, I would
   just say, "Let's go to the castle and see if Cinderella is there." Once we got
   as far as the front door to the castle, it was no problem going out to the
   [central] hub and then to another land.

3.   Children have an instinct for finding rest rooms. We have seen adults with maps search interminably for a rest room. Young children, on the

other hand, including those who can't read, will head for the nearest rest room with the certainty of a homing pigeon. You can be sure your children will ferret out (and want to use) every rest room in the theme park.

4. If you are using a stroller, you won't be able to take it into attractions or onto rides. This applies to rides such as the Walt Disney World Railroad that are included in the touring plans as in-park transportation.

5. You probably won't finish the touring plan. Varying hours of operation, crowd levels, the size of your group, the ages of your children, and your stamina will all affect how much of the plan you will complete. Unless you tailor your expectations to this reality, you're likely to experience the frustration expressed by this mother of two from Nazareth, Pennsylvania:

> We do not understand how anyone could fit everything you have on your plans into the time allotted while attending to small children. We found that long lines, potty stops, diaper changes, stroller searches, and autograph breaks ate huge chunks of time. And we were there during the off-season.

While our touring plans will allow you to make the most of your time at the theme parks, it's impossible to define what "most" will be. It differs from family to family. If you have two young children, you probably won't see as much as will two adults. If you have four children, you probably won't see as much as will a couple with only two children.

Overheating, Sunburn, and Dehydration   These are the most common problems of younger children at Disney World. Carry and use sunscreen. Be sure to put some on children in strollers, even if the stroller has a canopy. Some of the worst cases of sunburn we've seen were on the exposed foreheads and feet of toddlers and infants in strollers. Protect skin from overexposure. To avoid overheating, rest regularly in the shade or in an air-conditioned restaurant or show.

Don't count on keeping young children hydrated with soft drinks and stops at water fountains. Long lines may hamper buying refreshments, and fountains may not be handy. Further, excited children may not realize or tell you that they're thirsty or hot. We recommend renting a stroller for children age six and younger and carrying plastic bottles of water. Plastic squeeze bottles with caps are sold in all major parks for about $3.

Blisters and Sore Feet   Guests of all ages should wear comfortable, well-broken-in shoes and two pairs of thin socks (better than one pair of thick socks). If you or your children are susceptible to blisters, bring pre-cut Moleskin bandages. They offer the best protection, stick great, and won't sweat off. When you feel a hot spot, stop, air out your foot, and place a Moleskin bandage over the area before a blister forms. Moleskin comes in five-by-four-inch sheets, so you'll need a pair of scissors to cut the Moleskin to size. Moleskin is available by name at all drug stores.

Young children may not tell their parents about a developing blister until it's too late, so inspect the feet of preschoolers two or more times a day.

First Aid   Each major theme park has a first-aid center. In the Magic Kingdom, it's behind the refreshment corner to the left after you enter. At Epcot, it's on the World Showcase side of the Odyssey Center. At Disney-MGM, it's in the Guest Relations Building just inside the main entrance. At Animal Kingdom, it's in Discovery Island. If you or your children have a medical problem, go to a first-aid center. Disney first-aid centers are warmer and friendlier than most doctor's offices and are accustomed to treating everything from paper cuts to allergic reactions.

Children on Medication   Some parents of hyperactive children on medication discontinue or decrease the child's normal dosage at the end of the school year. If you have such a child, be aware that Disney World might overly stimulate him/her. Consult your physician before altering your child's medication regimen.

Walkie-Talkies   An increasing number of readers stay in touch while on vacation by using walkie-talkies. Here's what they have to say:

From a Cabot, Arkansas, family:

Borrow or get walkie-talkies! The vacation is expensive enough so get some walkie-talkies! Our youngest was too scared or too short for some rides, plus I was expecting, so we would sit outside or go to a snack area, but we were always in contact. My husband, Joe, could tell me how long the wait was, when he was about to come down Splash Mountain (for me to take a photo!), or where to meet.

A dad from Roanoke is on the same wavelength:

The single best purchase we made was Motorola TalkAbout walkie-talkies. They have a two-mile range and are about the size of a deck of cards. We first started using them at the airport when I was checking the bags and she took the kids off to the gate. At the parks, the kids would invariably have diverse interests. With walkie-talkies, however, we could easily split up and simply communicate with each other when we wanted to meet back up. At least a half dozen times, exasperated parents asked where they could rent/buy the walkie-talkies.

If you go the walkie-talkie route, get a set that operates on multiple channels or opt for cellular phones as a Duluth, Georgia, family did:

I spoke with a woman who invested $100 in walkie-talkies. All day long all she could hear were other people's conversations as so many people are using them. My husband and I used our cellular phones, and they worked beautifully. Even though I pay roaming charges on mine, there's no way I could use $100 worth!

Sunglasses   If you want your younger children to wear sunglasses, put a strap or string on the frames so that the glasses will stay on during rides and can hang from the child's neck while indoors.

Things You Forgot or Things You Ran Out Of   Rain gear, diapers, diaper pins, formula, film, aspirin, topical sunburn treatments, and other sundries are sold at all major theme parks and at Typhoon Lagoon, Blizzard Beach, River Country, and Downtown Disney. Rain gear is a bargain, but most other items are high. A good place to find diapers is at the Baby Centers—two diapers plus ointment are $3.50. Ask for goods you don't see displayed.

Infants and Toddlers at the Theme Parks   The major theme parks have centralized facilities for infant and toddler care. Everything necessary for changing diapers, preparing formulas, and warming bottles and food is available. Baby supplies are for sale, and there are rockers and special chairs for nursing mothers. At the Magic Kingdom, the Baby Center is next to the Crystal Palace at the end of Main Street. At Epcot, Baby Services is near the Odyssey Center, right of the Test Track in Future World. At Disney-MGM Studios, Baby Care is in the Guest Relations Building left of the entrance. At the Animal Kingdom, Baby Changing/Nursing is in Discovery Island in the center of the park. Dads in charge of little ones are welcome at the centers and can use most services offered. In addition, many men's rooms in the major theme parks have changing tables.

Infants and toddlers are allowed to experience any attraction that doesn't have minimum height or age restrictions. But as a Minneapolis mother reports, some attractions are better for babies than others:

Theater and boat rides are easier for babies (ours was almost one year old, not yet walking). Rides where there's a bar that comes down are doable, but harder. Peter Pan was our first encounter with this type, and we had barely gotten situated when I realized he might fall out of my grasp. The standing auditorium films are too intense; the noise level is deafening, and the images unescapable. You don't have a rating system for babies, and I don't expect to see one, but I thought you might want to know what a baby thought (based on his reactions). [At the Magic Kingdom:] Jungle Cruise—Didn't get into it. Pirates—Slept through it. Riverboat—While at Aunt Polly's, the horn made him cry. Aunt Polly's—Ate the chicken while watching the birds in relative quiet. Small World—Wide-eyed, took it all in. Peter Pan—Couldn't really sit on the seat. A bit dangerous. He didn't get into it. Carousel of Progress—Long talks; hard to keep him quiet; danced during song. WDW RR—Liked the motion and scenery. Tiki Birds—Loved it. Danced, clapped, sang along. At Epcot: Honey, I Shrunk the Audience—We skipped due to recommendation of Disney worker that it got too loud and adults screamed throughout. Journey into Imagination—

*Loved it. Tried to catch things with his hands. Bounced up and down, chor-
tled. The Land—Watchful, quiet during presentation. Food Rocks—Loved
it, danced. El Río del Tiempo—Loved it.*

The same mom also advises:

*We used a baby sling on our trip and thought it was great when standing in
lines—much better than a stroller, which you have to park before getting
in line (and navigate through crowds). The food at WDW [includes] almost
nothing a baby can eat. No fruits or vegetables. My baby was still nursing
when we went to WDW. The only really great place I found to nurse in MK
was a hidden bench in the shade in Adventureland in between the freezee
stand (next to Tiki Birds) and the small shops. It is impractical to go to
the baby station every time, so a nursing mom better be comfortable
about nursing in very public situations.*

If you think you might try nursing during a theater attraction, be
advised that most shows run about 17–20 minutes. Exceptions are *The
Hall of Presidents* at the Magic Kingdom and *The American Adventure* at
Epcot that run 23 and 29 minutes respectively.

Strollers The good news is that strollers are available for a modest
rental fee at all four theme parks. The better news is that Disney has
replaced the ancient blue clunkers at Epcot and the Magic Kingdom with
brand new strollers. The parks experimented with several models to
determine which design guests liked best, phasing out the old strollers at
the same time. If you rent a stroller at the Magic Kingdom and decide to
go to Epcot, the Animal Kingdom, or Disney-MGM Studios, turn in
your Magic Kingdom stroller and present your receipt at the next park.
You'll be issued another stroller without additional charge.

Strollers can be obtained to the right of the entrance at the Magic
Kingdom, to the left of the Entrance Plaza at Epcot, and at Oscar's Super
Service just inside the entrance of Disney-MGM Studios. Stroller rentals
at the Animal Kingdom are just inside the entrance and to the right.
Rental at all parks is fast and efficient, and returning the stroller is a
breeze. Even at Epcot, where as many as 900 strollers are turned in after
the evening fireworks, there's almost no wait or hassle. If you don't mind
forfeiting your dollar deposit, you can ditch your rental stroller anywhere
in the park when you're ready to leave.

Readers inform us that there is a lively "gray market" in strollers at the
parks. Families who arrive late look for families who are heading for the
exit and "buy" their stroller at a bargain price. A Chester, New Hampshire, mom, ever vigilant for a bargain, reported: "We 'bought' strollers
for $3 when we saw people returning them. Also, we 'sold' our strollers
when leaving for $3."

When you enter a show or board a ride, you must park your stroller, usually in an open, unprotected area. If it rains before you return, you'll need a cloth, towel, or diaper to dry it.

Strollers are a must for infants and toddlers, but we have observed many sharp parents renting strollers for somewhat older children (up to five or so years old). The stroller prevents parents from having to carry children when they sag and provides a convenient place to carry water and snacks.

If you go to your hotel for a break and intend to return to the park, leave your rental stroller by an attraction near the park entrance, marking it with something personal like a bandanna. When you return after your break, your stroller will be waiting for you.

Be aware that rental strollers are too large for all infants and many toddlers. If you plan to rent a stroller for your infant or toddler, bring along some pillows, cushions, or rolled towels to buttress him in.

It's permissible to bring your own stroller. Remember, however, that only collapsible strollers are permitted on monorails, parking-lot trams, and buses. Your stroller is unlikely to be stolen, but mark it with your name.

Kerri, a Mechanicsville, Virginia, mother of two toddlers, found having her own stroller indespensible, writing:

How I was going to manage to get the kids from the parking lot to the park was a big worry for me before I made the trip. I didn't read anywhere that it was possible to walk to the entrance of the parks instead of taking the tram so I wasn't sure I could do it.

I found that for me personally, since I have two kids aged one and two, that it was easier to walk to the entrance of the park from the parking lot with the kids in [my own] stroller than to take the kids out of the stroller, fold the stroller (while trying to control the two kids and associated gear), load the stroller and the kids onto the tram, etc.... No matter where I was parked I could always just walk to the entrance... it sometimes took awhile but it was easier for me.

A mom from Secaucus, New Jersey weighed all the considerations in exemplary Type-A fashion, writing:

If your child is under age 2, bring your own stroller. Three reasons to bring your own: First, you have all the way from your car to the TTC to the monorail (or ferry) to the stroller rental without a stroller, but with your child, diaper bag, and own self and stuff in tow. Not half as bad as doing it in reverse when leaving, when you're exhausted and have added to your luggage with purchases and the toddler who might have walked in wants to be carried out. Second, the WDW stroller is simply too large for most children under two to be comfortable without significant padding. The seat is so low that the child is forced to keep their legs straight out in front of them. Third, despite being sooo big, there is NO PLACE to store anything.The body of the stroller is so low, there is no underneath storage for the diaper bag.There is a small net bag on the back of the carriage, but it seems designed to hold, at most, a small purse. If you hang a diaper bag by its straps from the handle, the stroller will tip backwards very, very easily.And you can't balance it on the top or the canopy won't stay open. It amazed me that the Disney folks did not provide ample space for all the souvenirs they want you to buy!

Now, if your child is past needing a diaper bag, the WDW strollers seem like a pretty good deal.You won't need the storage space, and they do maneuver very well.They seem especially good for children who no longer need a stroller at home (ages 4 – 6) but who won't make it walking all day.

If your child is between ages 2 and 3, it's a toss up. If you're a type-A mom, like me, who carries extra clothes, snacks, toys, enough diapers for three days, along with a pocketbook, and extra-jackets-for-everyone-just-in-case, you've probably found a stroller that suits your needs, and will be miserable with the WDW kind. If you're a Type B, "we can get everything else we need at the park, I'll just throw a diaper in my back pocket" mom, you'll probably be tickled with the WDW strollers.Also consider your toddler's personality.Will his familiar stroller add a level of comfort to a pretty intense experience? Or will he enjoy the novelty of the new wheels?

Stroller Wars Sometimes strollers disappear while you're enjoying a ride or show. Disney cast members will often rearrange strollers parked outside an attraction. Sometimes this is done to "tidy up." At other times, strollers are moved to clear a walkway. Don't assume your stroller has been stolen because it isn't where you left it. It may be "neatly arranged" a few feet away.

Sometimes, however, strollers are taken by mistake or ripped off by people not wanting to spend time replacing one that's missing. Don't be alarmed if yours disappears. You won't have to buy the missing stroller, and you'll be issued a new one for your continued use. In the Magic Kingdom, replacements are available at Tinker Bell's Treasures in Fantasyland, at Merchant of Venus in Tomorrowland, and at the main rental facility near the park entrance. At Epcot, get replacements at the Entrance Plaza rental headquarters and at the International Gateway (in World Showcase between the United Kingdom and France). Strollers at Disney-MGM can be replaced at Oscar's Super Service and at Endor Vendors near Star Tours. In the Animal Kingdom, stroller replacements are available at Garden Gate Gifts and Mombasa Marketplace.

While replacing a stroller is no big deal, it's inconvenient. A family from Minnesota complained that their stroller had been taken six times in one day at Epcot and five times in a day at Disney-MGM Studios. Even with free replacements, larceny on this scale represents a lot of wasted time. Through our own experiments and readers' suggestions, we have developed techniques for hanging on to a rented stroller: affix something personal (but expendable) to the handle. Evidently, most strollers are pirated by mistake (they all look alike) or because it's easier to swipe someone else's stroller than to replace one when it disappears. Since most stroller "theft" results from confusion or laziness, the average pram pincher will hesitate to haul off a stroller bearing another person's property. After trying several items, we concluded that a bright, inexpensive scarf or bandanna tied to the handle works well. A sock partially stuffed with rags or paper works even better (the weirder and more personal the object, the greater the deterrent). Best of all might be an Ann Arbor, Michigan, mother's strategy:

We used a variation on your stroller identification theme. We tied a clear plastic bag with a diaper in it on the stroller. Jon even poured a little root beer on the diaper for effect. Needless to say, no one took our stroller and it was easy to identify.

Strollers As Lethal Weapons   A father of one from Purcellville, Virginia, wrote complaining about how inconsiderate some parents are:

The biggest problem is surviving the migrating herds of strollers. The drivers of these contraptions appear to believe they have the right-of-way in all situations and use the strollers as battering rams to enforce their perceived right. I know they will not be banned from the parks, but how about putting speed governors on these things?

In fact, you would be amazed at how many people are injured by strollers pushed by parents who are driving aggressively, in a hurry, or in the ozone. Though you may desire to use your stroller as a battering ram or to wedge through crowds like Moses parting the seas, think twice. It's very un-Disney to steamroll other guests.

Lost Children

Although it's amazingly easy to lose a child (or two) in the theme parks, it usually isn't a serious problem. All Disney employees are schooled in handling the situation. If you lose a child in the Magic Kingdom, report it to a Disney employee, then check at the Baby Center and at City Hall, where lost-children "logs" are kept. At Epcot, report the loss, then check at Baby Services near the Odyssey Center. At Disney-MGM Studios, report the loss at the Guest Relations Building at the entrance end of Hollywood Boulevard. At Animal Kingdom, go to the Baby Center in Discovery Island. Paging isn't used, but in an emergency an "all-points bulletin" can be issued throughout the park(s) via internal communications. If a Disney employee encounters a lost child, he or she will take the child immediately to the park's guest relations center or its baby-care center.

We suggest that children younger than eight be color-coded by dressing them in purple T-shirts or equally distinctive clothes. It's also smart to sew a label into each child's shirt that states his name, your name, and the name of your hotel. The same thing can be accomplished by writing the information on a strip of masking tape. Hotel security professionals suggest the information be printed in small letters and the tape be affixed to the outside of the child's shirt, five inches below the armpit. Also, special name tags can be obtained at the major theme parks.

How Kids Get Lost

Children get separated from their parents every day at Disney parks under remarkably similar (and predictable) circumstances:

1. Preoccupied Solo Parent   In this situation, the party's only adult is preoccupied with something like buying refreshments, loading the camera, or using the rest room. Junior is there one second and gone the next.

2. The Hidden Exit   Sometimes parents wait on the sidelines while two or more young children experience a ride together. Parents expect the kids to exit in one place and, lo and behold, the youngsters pop out somewhere else. Exits from some attractions are distant from the entrances. Make sure you know exactly where your children will emerge before letting them ride by themselves.

3. After the Show   At the end of many shows and rides, a Disney staffer will announce, "Check for personal belongings and take small children by the hand." When dozens, if not hundreds, of people leave an attraction simultaneously, it's easy for parents to lose contact with their children unless they have them directly in tow.

4. Rest Room Problems   Mom tells six-year-old Tommy, "I'll be sitting on this bench when you come out of the rest room." Three possibilities: One, Tommy exits through a different door and becomes disoriented (Mom may not know there is another door). Two, Mom decides she also will use the rest room, and Tommy emerges to find her gone. Three, Mom pokes around in a shop while keeping an eye on the bench, but misses Tommy when he comes out.

If you can't be with your child in the rest room, make sure there's only one exit. The rest room on a passageway between Frontierland and Adventureland in the Magic Kingdom is the all-time worst for disorienting visitors. Children and adults alike have walked in from the Adventureland side and walked out on the Frontierland side (and vice versa). Adults realize quickly that something is wrong. Young children, however, sometimes fail to recognize the problem. Designate a distinctive meeting spot and be thorough in your instructions: "I'll meet you by this flagpole. If you get out first, stay right here." Have your child repeat the directions back to you. When children are too young to leave alone, sometimes you have to think outside the box as Kerri from Virginia [quoted above] did:

It was very scary for me at times being alone with children that had just turned one and two. I'm reminded of the time on the trip when I couldn't fit the double stroller into the bathroom. I was at Epcot inside one of the buildings and I had to leave my kids with a WDW employee outside of the restroom because the stroller just wouldn't fit inside with me. Thinking about the incident now makes me laugh. The good news is that I found that most WDW bathrooms can accommodate a front-and-back, double stroller inside the handicapped stall [with you]. When you are alone with two little ones they have to go EVERYWHERE you go!

5. Parades   There are many parades and shows at which the audience stands. Children tend to jockey for a better view. By moving a little this way and that, the child quickly puts distance between you and him before either of you notices.

6. Mass Movements   Be on guard when huge crowds disperse after fireworks or a parade, or at park closing. With 20,000–40,000 people at once in an area, it's very easy to get separated from a child or others in your party. Use extra caution after the evening parade and fireworks in the Magic Kingdom, *Fantasmic!* at the Disney-MGM Studios, and *IllumiNations* at Epcot. Families should have specific plans for where to meet if they get separated.

7. Character Greetings   Activity and confusion are common when the Disney characters appear, and children can slip out of sight. See "Then Some Confusion Happened" (page 262).

8. Getting Lost at the Animal Kingdom   It's especially easy to lose a child at the Animal Kingdom, particularly in the Oasis entryway, on the Maharaja Jungle Trek, and on the Pangani Forest Exploration Trail. Mom and Dad will stop to observe an animal. Junior stays close for a minute or so, and then, losing patience, wanders to the other side of the exhibit or to a different exhibit.

Especially in the multi-path Oasis, locating a lost child can be maddening, as a mother from Safety Harbor, Florida, describes:

Manny wandered off in the paths that lead to the jungle village while we were looking at a bird. It reminded me of losing somebody in the supermarket when you run back and forth looking down each aisle but can't find the person you're looking for because they are running around, too. I was nutso before we even got to the first ride.

A mother from Flint, Michigan, came up with yet another way to lose a kid: abandonment.

From the minute we hit the park it was gripe, whine, pout, cry, beg, scream, pick, pester, and aggravate. When he went to the rest room for the ninth time before 11 a.m., I thought I'M OUTTA HERE ... let the little snothead walk back to Flint. Unfortunately, I was brought up Catholic with lots of guilt so I didn't follow through.

Disney, Kids, and Scary Stuff

Disney rides and shows are adventures, and they focus on themes of all adventures: good and evil, death, beauty and the grotesque, fellowship and enmity. As you sample the attractions at Walt Disney World, you transcend the spinning and bouncing of midway rides to thought-provoking and emotionally powerful entertainment. All of the endings are happy, but the adventures' impacts, given Disney's gift for special effects, often intimidate and occasionally frighten young children.

There are rides with menacing witches, burning towns, and ghouls popping out of their graves, all done with a sense of humor, provided you're old enough to understand the joke. And bones. There are bones everywhere: human bones, cattle bones, dinosaur bones, even whole skeletons. There's a stack of skulls at the headhunter's camp on the Jungle Cruise, a platoon of skeletons sailing ghost ships in Pirates of the Caribbean, and a haunting assemblage of skulls and skeletons in The Haunted Mansion. Skulls, skeletons, and bones punctuate Snow White's Adventures, Peter Pan's Flight, and Big Thunder Mountain Railroad. In the Animal Kingdom, there's an entire children's playground comprised exclusively of giant bones and skeletons.

Monsters and special effects at Disney-MGM Studios are more real and sinister than those in the other parks. If your child has difficulty coping with the witch in Snow White's Adventures, think twice about exposing him to machine-gun battles, earthquakes, and the creature from *Alien* at the Studios.

One reader tells of taking his preschool children on Star Tours:

We took a four-year-old and a five-year-old, and they had the shit scared out of them at Star Tours. We did this first thing, and it took hours of Tom Sawyer Island and Small World to get back to normal. Our kids were the youngest by far in Star Tours. I assume other adults had more sense or were not such avid readers of your book.

Preschoolers should start with Dumbo and work up to the Jungle Cruise in late morning, after being revved up and before getting hungry, thirsty, or tired. Pirates of the Caribbean is out for preschoolers. You get the idea.

SMALL-CHILD FRIGHT-POTENTIAL CHART

Our "Fright-Potential Chart" is a quick reference to identify attractions to be wary of, and why. The chart represents a generalization, and all kids are different. It relates specifically to kids ages three to seven. On average, children at the younger end of the range are more likely to be frightened than children in their sixth or seventh year.

MAGIC KINGDOM

Main Street, U.S.A.

Walt Disney World Railroad   Not frightening in any respect.

Main Street Vehicles   Not frightening in any respect.

Adventureland

Swiss Family Treehouse   Not frightening in any respect.

Jungle Cruise   Moderately intense, some macabre sights. A good test attraction for little ones.

Enchanted Tiki Birds   A thunderstorm, loud volume level, and simulated explosions frighten some preschoolers.

Pirates of the Caribbean   Slightly intimidating queuing area; intense boat ride with gruesome (though humorously presented) sights and a short, unexpected slide down a flume.

Magic Carpets of Aladdin   Much like Dumbo. A favorite of most younger children.

Frontierland

Splash Mountain   Visually intimidating from outside, with moderately intense visual effects. The ride, culminating in a 52-foot plunge down a steep chute, is somewhat hair-raising for all ages. Switching off option provided (pages 254–257).

Big Thunder Mountain Railroad   Visually intimidating from outside, with moderately intense visual effects. The roller coaster is wild enough to frighten many adults, particularly seniors. Switching off provided (pages 254–257).

Tom Sawyer Island   Some very young children are intimidated by dark, walk-through tunnels that can be easily avoided.

Country Bear Jamboree   Not frightening in any respect.

Frontierland Shootin' Arcade   Not frightening in any respect.

Diamond Horseshoe Saloon Revue   Not frightening in any respect.

Liberty Square

The Hall of Presidents   Not frightening, but boring for young ones.

Liberty Belle Riverboat   Not frightening in any respect.

Mike Fink Keelboats   Not frightening in any respect.

The Haunted Mansion   Name raises anxiety, as do sounds and sights of waiting area. Intense attraction with humorously presented macabre sights. The ride itself is gentle.

Fantasyland

Mad Tea Party   Midway-type ride can induce motion sickness in all ages.

The Many Adventures of Winnie the Pooh   Frightens a small percentage of pre-schoolers.

Snow White's Adventures   Moderately intense spook-house-genre attraction with some grim characters. Absolutely terrifies many preschoolers.

Dumbo the Flying Elephant   A tame midway ride; a great favorite of most young children.

Cinderella's Golden Carrousel   Not frightening in any respect.

It's a Small World   Not frightening in any respect.

Peter Pan's Flight   Not frightening in any respect.

Mickey's Toontown Fair

All attractions except roller coaster   Not frightening in any respect.

The Barnstormer at Goofy's Wiseacres Farm (children's roller coaster)   May frighten some preschoolers.

Tomorrowland

Alien Encounter   Extremely intense. Capable of frightening all ages. Not for young children. Switching off provided (pages 254–257).

Buzz Lightyear's Space Ranger Spin   Dark ride with cartoonlike aliens may frighten some preschoolers.

Tomorrowland Transit Authority   Not frightening in any respect.

Space Mountain   Very intense roller coaster in the dark; the Magic Kingdom's wildest ride and a scary roller coaster by any standard. Switching off provided (pages 254–257).

Astro Orbiter   Visually intimidating from the waiting area. The ride is relatively tame. See safety warning on page 261.

Walt Disney's Carousel of Progress (open seasonally)   Not frightening in any respect.

Tomorrowland Speedway   Noise of waiting area slightly intimidates preschoolers; otherwise, not frightening.

Timekeeper (open seasonally)   Both loud and intense, with frightening film scenes. Audience must stand.

EPCOT

Future World

Spaceship Earth   Dark and imposing presentation intimidates a few preschoolers.

Innoventions East and West   Not frightening in any respect.

Universe of Energy   Dinosaur segment frightens some preschoolers; visually intense, with some intimidating effects.

Wonders of Life—Body Wars   Very intense, with frightening visual effects. Ride causes motion sickness in riders of all ages. Switching off provided (pages 254–257).

Wonders of Life—Cranium Command   Not frightening in any respect.

Wonders of Life—The Making of Me   Not frightening in any respect.

Mission Space (opens 2003)   Extremely intense space simulation ride frightens guests of all ages. Switching off provided (pages 254–257).

Test Track   Intense thrill ride may frighten any age. Switching off provided (pages 254–257).

Journey into Imagination—Honey, I Shrunk the Audience   Extremely intense visual effects and loudness frighten many young children.

Journey into Your Imagination Ride   Loud noises and unexpected flashing lights startle younger children.

SMALL-CHILD FRIGHT-POTENTIAL CHART *continued*

EPCOT (continued)

Future World (continued)

The Land—Living with the Land   Not frightening in any respect.

The Land—Circle of Life Theater   Not frightening in any respect.

The Land—Food Rocks   Not frightening in any respect, but loud.

World Showcase

Mexico—El Río del Tiempo   Not frightening in any respect.

Norway—Maelstrom   Visually intense in parts. Ride ends with a plunge down a 20-foot flume. A few preschoolers are frightened.

China—Wonders of China   Not frightening in any respect.

Germany   Not frightening in any respect.

Italy   Not frightening in any respect.

The American Adventure   Not frightening in any respect.

Japan   Not frightening in any respect.

Morocco   Not frightening in any respect.

France—Impressions de France   Not frightening in any respect.

United Kingdom   Not frightening in any respect.

Canada—O Canada!   Not frightening in any respect, but audience must stand.

DISNEY-MGM STUDIOS

The Twilight Zone Tower of Terror   Visually intimidating to young children; contains intense and realistic special effects. The plummeting elevator at the ride's end frightens many adults. Switching off provided (pages 254–257).

The Great Movie Ride   Intense in parts, with very realistic special effects and some visually intimidating sights. Frightens many preschoolers.

Who Wants to Be a Millionaire   Not frightening in any respect.

Sounds Dangerous   Noises in the dark frighten some preschoolers.

Indiana Jones Epic Stunt Spectacular!   An intense show with powerful special effects, including explosions. Presented in an educational context that young children generally handle well.

Rock 'n' Roller Coaster   The wildest coaster at Walt Disney World. May frighten guests of any age. Switching off provided (pages 254–257).

Star Tours   Extremely intense visually for all ages. Not as likely to cause motion sickness as Body Wars at Epcot. Switching off provided (pages 254–257).

Disney-MGM Studios Backlot Tour   Sedate and nonintimidating except for "Catastrophe Canyon," where an earthquake and a flash flood are simulated. Prepare younger children for this part of the tour.

You can reliably predict that Walt Disney World will, at one time or another, send a young child into system overload. Be sensitive, alert, and prepared for almost anything, even behavior that is out of character for your child at home. Most young children take Disney's macabre trappings in stride, and others are easily comforted by an arm around the shoulder or a squeeze of the hand. Parents who know that their children

Backstage Walking Tours   Not frightening in any respect.

Jim Henson's MuppetVision 3D   Intense and loud, but not frightening.

Honey, I Shrunk the Kids Movie Set Adventure Playground   Everything is oversized, but nothing is scary.

Voyage of the Little Mermaid   Not frightening in any respect.

The Magic of Disney Animation   Not frightening in any respect.

Walt Disney: One Man's Dream   Not frightening in any respect.

Playhouse Disney: Live on Stage   Not frightening in any respect.

Fantasmic!   Terrifies some pre-schoolers

ANIMAL KINGDOM

The Boneyard   Not frightening in any respect.

Rafiki's Planet Watch   Not frightening in any respect.

Dinosaur   High-tech thrill ride rattles riders of all ages. Switching off provided (pages 254–257).

TriceraTop Spin   A midway-type ride that will frighten only a small percentage of younger children.

Pimeval Whirl   A beginner roller coaster. Most children age 7 and over will take it in stride.

Festival of the Lion King   A bit loud, but otherwise not frightening in any respect.

Flights of Wonder   Swooping birds alarm a few small children.

Pangani Forest Exploration Trail   Not frightening in any respect.

Pocahontas and Her Forest Friends   Not frightening in any respect.

It's Tough to Be a Bug!   Very intense and loud with special effects that startle viewers of all ages and potentially terrify young children.

Kilimanjaro Safaris   A "collapsing" bridge and the proximity of real animals make a few young children anxious.

Maharaja Jungle Trek   Some children may balk at the bat exhibit.

The Oasis   Not frightening in any respect.

Kali River Rapids   Potentially frightening and certainly wet for guests of all ages. Switching off provided (pages 254–257).

Theater in the Wild   Not frightening in any respect, but loud.

Wildlife Express Train   Not frightening in any respect.

tend to become upset should take it slow and easy, sampling more benign adventures like the Jungle Cruise, gauging reactions, and discussing with the children how they felt about what they saw.

Sometimes young children will rise above their anxiety in an effort to please their parents or siblings. This doesn't necessarily indicate a mastery of fear, much less enjoyment. If children leave a ride in apparently good shape, ask if they would like to go on it again (not necessarily now, but sometime). The response usually will indicate how much they actually enjoyed the experience. There's a big difference between having a good time and mustering the courage to get through something.

Evaluating a child's capacity to handle the visual and tactile effects of Disney World requires patience, understanding, and experimentation. Each of us, after all, has our own demons. If a child balks at or is frightened by a ride, respond constructively. Let your children know that lots of people, adults and children, are scared by what they see and feel. Help them understand that it's okay if they get frightened and that their fear doesn't lessen your love or respect. Take pains not to compound the discomfort by making a child feel inadequate; try not to undermine self-esteem, impugn courage, or ridicule. Most of all, don't induce guilt by suggesting the child's trepidation might be ruining the family's fun. It is also sometimes necessary to restrain older siblings' taunting or teasing.

A visit to Walt Disney World is more than an outing or an adventure for a young child. It's a testing experience, a sort of controlled rite of passage. If you help your little one work through the challenges, the time can be immeasurably rewarding and a bonding experience for you both.

The Fright Factor

While each youngster is different, there are seven attraction elements that alone or combined could punch a child's buttons:

1. Name of the Attraction Young children will naturally be apprehensive about something called "The Haunted Mansion" or "Tower of Terror."

2. Visual Impact of the Attraction from Outside Splash Mountain and Big Thunder Mountain Railroad look scary enough to give adults second thoughts, and they terrify many young children.

3. Visual Impact of the Indoor Queuing Area Pirates of the Caribbean's caves and dungeons and The Haunted Mansion's "stretch rooms" can frighten children even before they board the ride.

4. Intensity of the Attraction Some attractions are overwhelming, inundating the senses with sights, sounds, movement, and even smell. Epcot's *Honey, I Shrunk the Audience,* for example, combines loud sounds, lasers, lights, and 3-D cinematography to create a total sensory experience. For some preschoolers, this is two or three senses too many.

5. Visual Impact of the Attraction Itself Sights in various attractions range from falling boulders to lurking buzzards, from grazing dinosaurs to attacking white blood cells. What one child calmly absorbs may scare the bejabbers out of another the same age.

6. Dark Many Disney World attractions operate indoors in the dark. For some children, this triggers fear. A child who is frightened on one dark ride (Snow White's Adventures, for example) may be unwilling to try other indoor rides.

7. The Tactile Experience of the Ride Itself Some rides are wild enough to cause motion sickness, wrench backs, and discombobulate patrons of any age.

A Bit of Preparation

We receive many tips from parents telling how they prepared their young children for the Disney experience. A common strategy is to acquaint children with the characters and the stories behind the attractions by reading Disney books and watching Disney videos at home. A more direct approach is to rent Walt Disney World travel videos that show the actual attractions. Of the latter, a father from Arlington, Virginia, reports:

My kids both loved The Haunted Mansion, with appropriate preparation. We rented a tape before going so they could see it, and then I told them it was all "Mickey Mouse Magic" and that Mickey was just "joking you," to put it in their terms, and that there weren't any real ghosts, and that Mickey wouldn't let anyone actually get hurt.

A mother from Teaneck, New Jersey, adds:

I rented movies to make my five-year-old more comfortable with rides (Star Wars; Indiana Jones; Honey, I Shrunk the Kids). We thought we might go to Universal, so I rented King Kong, and it is now my kid's favorite. If kids are afraid of rides in dark (like ours), buy a light-up toy and let them take it on the ride.

A Gloucester, Massachusetts, mom solved the fright problem on the spot:

The three-and-a-half-year-old liked It's a Small World, [but] was afraid of The Haunted Mansion. We just pulled his hat over his face and quietly talked to him while we enjoyed [the ride].

Sometimes when children balk it has nothing to do with being frightened. Some children turn up their nose at any attraction that isn't a ride, as a reader from Lenexa, Kansas, reports:

The one thing I would do differently is prepare my kids for the different kinds of entertainment each park offers. Some have more rides, some more shows, some street performers (very fun), and some interesting things about the world. My eight-year-old especially had trouble admitting he liked anything that wasn't a ride (even if he did).

Attractions that Eat Adults

You may spend so much energy worrying about Junior that you forget to take care of yourself. If the motion of a ride is potentially disturbing, persons of any age may be adversely affected. Several attractions are likely to cause motion sickness or other problems for older children and adults.

<u>**Attractions That Eat Adults**</u>

Magic Kingdom	Tomorrowland—Space Mountain
	Tomorrowland—*Alien Encounter*
	Fantasyland—Mad Tea Party
	Frontierland—Big Thunder Mountain Railroad
	Frontierland—Splash Mountain
Epcot:	Future World—Body Wars
	Future World—Test Track
	Future World—Mission: Space (opens 2003)
Disney-MGM Studios	Star Tours
	The Twilight Zone Tower of Terror
	Rock 'n' Roller Coaster
Animal Kingdom	Dinosaur
	Kali River Rapids

A Word about Height Requirements

A number of attractions require children to meet minimum height and age requirements, usually 44 inches tall to ride with an adult or 44 inches and seven years of age to ride alone. If you have children too short or too young to ride, you have several options, including switching off (described later in this chapter). Although the alternatives may resolve some practical and logistic issues, be forewarned that your smaller children may nonetheless be resentful of their older (or taller) siblings who qualify to ride. One link you may visit is the Height Calculator at **www.go2orlando.com/heightcalc**. A mom from Virginia bumped into just such a situation, writing:

> *You mention height requirements for rides but not the intense sibling jealousy this can generate. Frontierland was a real problem in that respect. Our very petite five-year-old, to her outrage, was stuck hanging around while our eight-year-old went on Splash Mountain and [Big] Thunder Mountain with grandma and grandad, and the nearby alternatives weren't helpful [too long a line for rafts to Tom Sawyer Island, etc.]. If we had thought ahead, we would have left the younger kid back in Mickey's Toontown with one of the grown-ups for another roller coaster ride or two and then met up later at a designated point. The best areas had a playground or other quick*

attractions for short people near the rides with height requirements, like the Boneyard near the dinosaur ride at the Animal Kingdom.

The reader makes a valid point, though in practical terms splitting the group and meeting later can be more complicated than she might imagine. If you choose to split up, ask the Disney greeter at the entrance to the attraction(s) with height requirements how long the wait is. If you tack five minutes for riding onto the anticipated wait and add five or so minutes to exit and reach the meeting point, you'll have an approximate sense of how long the younger kids (and their supervising adult) will have to do other stuff. Our guess is that even with a long line for the rafts, the reader would have had more than sufficient time to take her daughter to Tom Sawyer Island while the sibs rode Splash Mountain and Big Thunder Mountain with the grandparents. For sure she had time to tour the Swiss Family Treehouse in adjacent Adventureland.

Waiting-Line Strategies for Adults with Young Children

Children hold up better through the day if you minimize the time they spend in lines. Arriving early and using our touring plans immensely reduce waiting. Here are additional ways to reduce stress for children:

1. Line Games Wise parents anticipate children's getting restless in line and plan activities to reduce the stress and boredom. In the morning, have waiting children discuss what they want to see and do during the day. Later, watch for and count Disney characters or play simple guessing games like "20 Questions." Lines move continuously; games requiring pen and paper are impractical. Waiting in the holding area of a theater attraction, however, is a different story. Here, tic-tac-toe, hangman, drawing, and coloring make the time fly by.

2. Last-Minute Entry If an attraction can accommodate an unusually large number of people at once, it's often unnecessary to stand in line. The Magic Kingdom's *Liberty Belle* Riverboat is a good example. The boat holds about 450 people, usually more than are waiting in line. Instead of standing uncomfortably in a crowd, grab a snack and sit in the shade until the boat arrives and loading is well under way. After the line is almost gone, join it.

At large-capacity theaters like that for Epcot's *The American Adventure,* ask the entrance greeter how long it will be until guests are admitted for the next show. If it's 15 minutes or more, take a rest room break or get a snack, returning a few minutes before the show starts. You aren't allowed to carry food or drink into the attraction, so make sure you have time to finish your snack before entering.

Attractions You Can Usually Enter at the Last Minute

Magic Kingdom

Liberty Square	*The Hall of Presidents*
	Liberty Belle Riverboat

Epcot

Future World	*The Circle of Life* (except during mealtimes)
	Food Rocks (except during mealtimes)
World Showcase	*Wonders of China*
	The American Adventure
	O Canada!

Disney-MGM Studios	*Sounds Dangerous*
	Backlot Tour

Animal Kingdom	*Flights of Wonder*

3. The Hail Mary Pass   Certain lines are configured to allow you and your smaller children to pass under the rail to join your partner just before actual boarding or entry. This technique allows children and one adult to rest, snack, cool off, or go potty while another adult or older sibling stands in line. Other guests are very understanding about this strategy when used for young children. You're likely to meet hostile opposition, however, if you try to pass older children or more than one adult under the rail.

Attractions Where You Can Usually Complete a Hail Mary Pass

Magic Kingdom

Adventureland	Swiss Family Treehouse
Frontierland	*Country Bear Jamboree*
Fantasyland	Mad Tea Party
	Snow White's Adventures
	Dumbo the Flying Elephant
	Cinderella's Golden Carrousel
	Peter Pan's Flight

Epcot

Future World	Spaceship Earth
	Living with the Land

Disney-MGM Studios	*Sounds Dangerous*
	Indiana Jones Epic Stunt Spectacular!

Animal Kingdom	Dinoland USA
	TriceraTop Spin

4. Switching Off (a.k.a. The Baby Swap)   Several attractions have minimum height and/or age requirements, usually 44" tall to ride with an adult, or age 7 *and* 44" tall to ride alone. Some couples with children too small or too young forgo these attractions, while others take turns to ride. Missing some of Disney's best rides is an unnecessary sacrifice, and waiting in line twice for the same ride is a tremendous waste of time.

Instead, take advantage of the "switching off" option, also called "The Baby Swap." To switch off, there must be at least two adults. Everybody waits in line together, adults and children. When you reach an attendant (called a "greeter"), say you want to switch off. The greeter will allow everyone, including the young children, to enter the attraction. When you reach the loading area, one adult rides while the other stays with the kids. Then the riding adult disembarks and takes charge of the children while the other adult rides. A third adult in the party can ride twice, once with each of the switching off adults, so that the switching off adults don't have to experience the attraction alone.

Most rides with age and height minimums load and unload in the same area, facilitating switching off. An exception is Space Mountain, where the first adult at the conclusion of the ride must also inform the unloading attendant that he or she is switching off. The attendant will admit the first adult to an internal stairway that goes back to the loading area.

Attractions at which switching off is practiced are oriented to more mature guests. Sometimes it takes a lot of courage for a child just to move through the queue holding Dad's hand. In the boarding area, many children suddenly fear abandonment as one parent leaves to experience the attraction. Unless your children are prepared for switching off, you might have an emotional crisis on your hands. A mom from Edison, New Jersey, advises:

Once my son came to understand that the switch-off would not leave him abandoned, he did not seem to mind. I would recommend to your readers that they practice the switch-off on some dry runs at home, so that their child is not concerned that he will be left behind. At the very least, the procedure could be explained in advance so that the little ones know what to expect.

Finally, a mother from Ada, Michigan, who discovered the procedure for switching off varies from attraction to attraction, offered this suggestion:

Parents need to tell the very first attendant they come to that they would like to switch off. Each attraction has a different procedure for this. Tell every other attendant too because they forget quickly.

Attractions Where Switching Off Is Common

Magic Kingdom

Tomorrowland	Space Mountain
	Alien Encounter
Frontierland	Splash Mountain
	Big Thunder Mountain Railroad

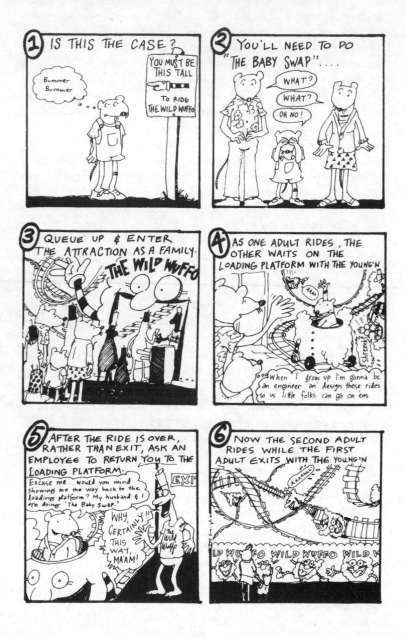

Attractions Where Switching Off Is Common *(continued)*

Epcot	
Future World	Body Wars
	Test Track
	Mission: Space (opens 2003)
Disney-MGM Studios	Star Tours
	The Twilight Zone Tower of Terror
	Rock 'n' Roller Coaster
Animal Kingdom	
DinoLand U.S.A.	Dinosaur
Asia	Kali River Rapids
	Primeval Whirl

---

5. How to Ride Twice in a Row without Waiting   Many young children like to ride a favorite attraction two or more times in succession. Riding the second time often gives them a feeling of mastery and accomplishment. Unfortunately, even in early morning, repeat rides can be time-consuming. If you ride Dumbo as soon as the Magic Kingdom opens, for instance, you will wait only a minute or two for your first ride. When you come back for your second, the wait will be about 12 minutes. If you want to ride a third time, count on 20 minutes or longer.

The best way to get your child on the ride twice (or more) without blowing your morning is to use the "Chuck Bubba Relay" (named in honor of a Kentucky reader):

a. Mom and little Bubba enter the waiting line.

b. Dad lets a specific number of people go in front of him (24 at Dumbo), then gets in line.

c. As soon as the ride stops, Mom exits with Bubba and passes him to Dad to ride the second time.

d. If everybody is really getting into this, Mom can hop in line again, no fewer than 24 people behind Dad.

The Chuck Bubba Relay won't work on every ride, because waiting areas are configured differently (i.e., it's impossible in some cases to exit the ride and make the pass). For those rides where the Bubba Relay works, here are the numbers of people to count off:

Magic Kingdom

> Mad Tea Party 53
>
> Snow White's Adventures 52
>
> Dumbo the Flying Elephant 24
>
> Cinderella's Golden Carrousel 75
>
> Peter Pan's Flight 64
>
> Magic Carpets of Aladdin 48

Animal Kingdom
TriceraTop Spin 56

If you're the second adult in the relay, you'll reach a place in line where it's easiest to make the hand-off. This may be where those exiting the ride pass closest to those waiting to board. In any event, you'll know it when you see it. If you reach it and the first parent hasn't arrived with Bubba, let those behind you pass until Bubba shows up.

6. Last-Minute Cold Feet If your young child gets cold feet just before boarding a ride where there is no age or height requirement, you usually can arrange with the loading attendant for a switch off. This is common at Pirates of the Caribbean, where children lose their courage while winding through the dungeon-like waiting area.

No law says you have to ride. If you reach the boarding area and someone is unhappy, tell an attendant you've changed your mind and you'll be shown the way out.

7. Elevator Shoes for the Short and the Brave If you have a child who is begging to go on the rides with height requirements but who is a little too short, slip heel lifts into his Nikes before he reaches the measuring point. Be sure to leave the heel lifts in, because he may be measured again before boarding.

A Huntsville, Alabama, mom has the heel lift problem under control:

Knowing my wild child three-year-old as I do, I was interested in your comment regarding shoe lifts. I don't know about other places, but in the big city of Huntspatch where we live, one has to have a prescription for lifts. Normal shoe repair places don't make them. I couldn't think of a material with which to fashion a homemade lift that would be comfortable enough to stand on while waiting in line. I ended up purchasing some of those painfully ugly two-inch chunky-heeled sandals at my local mart where they carried these hideous shoes in unbelievably tiny sizes ($12). Since they didn't look too comfortable, we popped them on her right before we entered the ride lines. None of the height checkers ever asked her to remove them and she clip clopped onto Splash Mountain, Big Thunder Railroad (Dat BIG Choo-Choo), Star Wars, and The Tower of Terror—twice! However, the same child became so terrified at the Tiki Bird show that we were forced to leave—go figure! For adventuresome boys, I would suggest purchasing some of those equally hideous giant-heeled cowboy boots.

Along similar lines, a Long Pond, Pennsylvania, mom had this to offer:

Tower of Terror, Star Tours, and Body Wars are 40" requirements. Being persistent with a 39" child, we tried these several times. She got on Tower of Terror two of three times, Body Wars one of one time, and Star Tours one of two tries. She wore elevator shoes and a bun hairstyle to increase height.

8. Throw Yourself on the Grenade, Mildred! For conscientious parents determined to sacrifice themselves on behalf of their children, we provide a Magic Kingdom One-Day Touring Plan called the "Dumbo-or-Die-in-a-Day Touring Plan, for Parents with Small Children." This plan (page 491) will ensure that you run yourself ragged. Designed to help you forfeit everything of your personal interest for the sake of your children's pleasure, the plan guarantees to send you home battered and exhausted, with extraordinary stories of devotion and perseverance. By the way, the plan really works. Anyone under age eight will love it.

9. Catch-22 at Tomorrowland Speedway Though Tomorrowland Speedway is a great treat for young children, they're required to be 4'4" tall in order to drive. Few children age six and younger measure up, so the ride is essentially withheld from the very age group that would most enjoy it. To resolve this Catch-22, go on the ride with your small child. The attendants will assume that you will drive. After getting into the car, shift your child over behind the steering wheel. From your position, you will still be able to control the foot pedals. Your child will feel like she is really driving, and because the car travels on a self-guiding track, there's no way she can make a mistake while steering.

10. Astro Orbiter—A Safety Warning Parents often board the rocket before lifting their child aboard. Because the attendant can't see small children beside the vehicle from his control station, the ride may start before a child is safely in the cockpit. If you take a small child on this ride, put the child in the rocket, then get in.

The Disney Characters

The large and friendly costumed versions of Mickey, Minnie, Donald, Goofy, and others—known as "Disney characters"—provide a link between Disney animated films and the theme parks. To people emotionally invested, the characters in Disney films are as real as next-door neighbors, never mind that they're drawings on plastic. In recent years, theme-park personifications of the characters also have become real to us. It's not just a person in a mouse costume they see; it is Mickey himself. Similarly, meeting Goofy or Snow White in Fantasyland is an encounter with a celebrity, a memory to be treasured.

While there are hundreds of Disney animated film characters, only about 250 have been brought to life in costume. Of these, a relatively small number (less than a fifth) are "greeters" (characters who mix with patrons). The remaining characters perform in shows or parades. Originally confined to the Magic Kingdom, characters are now found in all the major theme parks and Disney hotels.

Character Watching   Character watching has become a pastime. Families once were content to meet a character occasionally. They now pursue them relentlessly, armed with autograph books and cameras. Because some characters are only rarely seen, character watching has become character collecting. (To cash in on character collecting, Disney sells autograph books throughout the World.) Mickey, Minnie, and Goofy are a snap to bag; they seem to be everywhere. But Daisy Duck seldom comes out. Other characters appear regularly, but only in a location consistent with their starring role. Cinderella, predictably, reigns at Cinderella Castle in Fantasyland, while Brer Fox and Brer Bear frolic in Frontierland near Splash Mountain.

A dad from Brooklyn thinks the character autograph–hunting craze has gotten out of hand, complaining:

Whoever started the practice of collecting autographs from the characters should be subjected to Chinese water torture! We went to WDW eleven years ago, with an eight-year-old and an eleven-year-old. We would bump into characters, take pictures, and that was it. After a while, our children noticed that some of the other children were getting autographs. We managed to avoid joining in during our first day at the Magic Kingdom and our first day at Epcot, but by day three our children were collecting autographs. However, it did not get too out of hand, since it was limited to accidental character meeting.

This year when we took our youngest child (who is now eight), he had already seen his siblings' collection, and was determined to outdo them. However, rather than random meetings, the characters are now available practically all day long at different locations, according to a printed schedule, which our son was old enough to read. We spent more time standing in line for autographs than we did for the most popular rides!

A family from Birmingham, Alabama, found some benefit in their children's relentless pursuit of characters, writing:

We had no idea we would be caught up in this madness, but after my daughters grabbed your guidebook to get Pocahontas to sign it (we had no blank paper), we quickly bought a Disney autograph book and gave in. It was actually the highlight of their trip, and my son even got into the act by helping get places in line for his sisters. They LOVED looking for characters (I think it has all been planned by Kodak to sell film). The possibility of seeing a new character revived my seven-year-old's energy on many occasions. It was an amazing, totally unexpected part of our visit.

Preparing Your Children to Meet the Characters   Almost all characters are quite large, and several, like Brer Bear, are huge! Small children don't expect this, and preschoolers especially can be intimidated.

Discuss the characters with your children before you go. On first encounter, don't thrust your child at the character. Allow the little one to deal with this big thing from whatever distance feels safe. If two adults are present, one should stay near the youngster while the other approaches the character and demonstrates that it's safe and friendly. Some kids warm to the characters immediately; some never do. Most take a little time and several encounters.

There are two kinds of characters: those whose costume includes a face-covering headpiece (animal characters and such humanlike characters as Captain Hook) and "face characters," those who resemble the characters so no mask or headpiece is necessary. Face characters include Mary Poppins, Ariel, Jasmine, Aladdin, Cinderella, Belle, Snow White, Esmarelda, and Prince Charming.

Only face characters speak. Headpiece characters don't make noises of any kind. Because cast members couldn't possibly imitate the distinctive cinema voice of the character, Disney has determined it's more effective to keep them silent. Lack of speech notwithstanding, headpiece characters are very warm and responsive, and communicate very effectively with gestures. Tell children in advance that headpiece characters don't talk.

Some character costumes are cumbersome and give cast members very poor visibility. (Eye holes frequently are in the mouth of the costume or even on the neck or chest.) This means characters are somewhat clumsy and have limited sight. Children who approach the character from the back or side may not be noticed, even if the child touches the character. It's possible in this situation for the character to accidently step on the child or knock him down. It's best for a child to approach a character from the front, but occasionally not even this works. Duck characters (Donald, Daisy, Uncle Scrooge), for example, have to peer around their bills. If a character appears to be ignoring your child, pick up your child and hold her in front of the character until the character responds.

It's okay for your child to touch, pat, or hug the character. Understanding the unpredictability of children, the character will keep his feet very still, particularly refraining from moving backward or sideways. Most characters will sign autographs or pose for pictures. If your child collects autographs, it's a good idea to carry a pen the width of a magic marker. Costumes make it exceedingly difficult for characters to wield a pen, so the bigger the better.

The Big Hurt   Many children expect to meet Mickey the minute they enter the park and are disappointed when he isn't around. If your children can't enjoy things until they see Mickey, ask a cast member where to find him. If the cast member doesn't know, he or she can call to learn exactly where the characters are at any time.

"Then Some Confusion Happened"   Young children sometimes become lost at character encounters. Usually, there's a lot of activity around a character, with both adults and children touching it or posing for pictures. Most commonly, Mom and Dad stay in the crowd while Junior approaches to meet the character. In the excitement and with people milling and the character moving around, Junior heads off in the wrong direction to look for Mom and Dad. In the words of a Salt Lake City mom: "Milo was shaking hands with Dopey one minute, then some confusion happened and [Milo] was gone."

Families with several young children and parents who are busy with cameras can lose a youngster in a heartbeat. Our recommendation for parents with preschoolers is to stay with the kids when they meet characters, stepping back only to take a quick picture.

Character Hogs   While we're on the subject of cameras, give other families a chance. Especially if you are shooting video, consider the perspective of this mom from Houston:

One of the worst parts to deal with are the people with movie cameras who take about three minutes filming their child with Mickey, asking everyone else to move. A 35mm camera takes about two seconds.

Meeting Characters for Free

You can *see* Disney characters in live shows at all the theme parks and in parades at the Magic Kingdom and Disney-MGM Studios. Consult your daily entertainment schedule for times. If you want to *meet* the characters, get autographs, and take photos, consult the park map or the handout *Times Guide* sometimes provided to supplement the park map. If there is a particular character you're itching to meet, ask any cast member to call the character hotline for you. The hotline will tell you (via the cast member) if the character is out and about, and if so, where to find it.

At the Magic Kingdom   Characters are encountered more frequently here than anywhere else in Walt Disney World. There almost always will be a character next to City Hall on Main Street and usually one or more in Town Square or near the railroad station. If it's rainy, look for characters on the veranda of Tony's Town Square Restaurant or in the Town Square Exposition Hall next to Tony's. Characters appear in all the lands but are more plentiful in Fantasyland and Mickey's Toontown Fair. At Mickey's Toontown Fair, you can meet Mickey privately in his "Judge's Tent." Characters actually work shifts at the Toontown Hall of Fame next to Mickey's Country House. Here, you can line up to meet three different assortments of characters. Each assortment has its own greeting area and, of course, its own line. One group, variously labeled Mickey's Pals, Toon Pals, Famous Friends, or some such, will include Minnie, Pluto, Goofy, Donald, and sometimes Chip 'n' Dale, Daisy, and Uncle Scrooge. The other two assortments vary and are more ambiguously defined. The 100 Acre Wood Friends are mostly Winnie the Pooh characters, while Fairy Tale Friends include Snow White, assorted dwarfs, Sleeping Beauty, the Beast, Belle, Cinderella, Prince Charming, etc. Sometimes, however, it's Villains (Captain Hook, Cruella DeVil, Jabar, et al.), and Princesses (Sleeping Beauty, Mary Poppins, yadda, yadda, yadda). In Fantasyland, Cinderella regularly greets diners at Cinderella's Royal Table in the castle, and Ariel holds court in her own grotto. Nearby, check out the Fantasyland Character Festival by the lagoon opposite Dumbo. Also look for characters in the central hub and by Splash Mountain in Frontierland.

Characters are featured in afternoon and evening parades and also play a major role in Castle Forecourt shows (at the entrance to the castle on the moat side) and at the Galaxy Palace Theater in Tomorrowland. Find performance times for shows and parades in the park's daily entertainment schedule or *Times Guide*. Sometimes characters stay to greet the audience after shows.

At Epcot   At first Disney didn't think characters would be appropriate for the more serious, educational style of Epcot. Later, in response to criticism that Epcot lacked warmth and humor, characters were imported.

To integrate them thematically, new and often bizarre costumes were created. Goofy roams Future World in a metallic silver cape reminiscent of Buck Rogers. Mickey greets guests at the American Adventure dressed like Ben Franklin.

Although chance encounters with characters are less frequent at Epcot than at other parks, Epcot compensates by periodically bringing in characters by the busload, literally. Several times each day, a platoon of characters piles into a British double-decker bus and sets out for one of the countries in the World Showcase. When the bus stops, the characters hop off and mingle with the crowd, posing for pictures and signing autographs. Mickey, Minnie, Goofy, Chip and Dale, and Pluto are almost always on the bus, and are frequently accompanied by Ballou, Tigger, Eyeore, the Genie from Aladdin, Jasmine, Mushu, Timor, and Snow White. The bus is dispatched about eight to ten times a day. Specific times and stops are listed in the Epcot handout park map. If you position yourself at a scheduled stop a few minutes before the bus arrives, you can score photos and autographs before everyone else arrives. In fact, the bus offers the easiest access to the most characters in one place in all of Walt Disney World. However, once the crowd in the immediate area gets the drift, the characters are mobbed. In addition to the bus, character shows are performed daily at the American Gardens Theater in World Showcase. Check the park's daily entertainment schedule for times.

Characters may be rarer at Epcot, but they're often easier to meet. A father from Effingham, Illinois, writes:

Trying to get autographs and pictures with Disney characters in the Magic Kingdom was a nightmare. Every character we saw was mobbed by kids and adults. Our kids had no chance. But at Epcot and Disney-MGM, things were much better. We got autographs, pictures, and more involvement. Our kids danced with several characters and received a lot of personal attention.

At Disney-MGM Studios   Characters are likely to turn up anywhere at the Studios but are most frequently found in front of the Animation Building, along Mickey Avenue (leading to the soundstages), at Al's Toy Barn, and at the end of New York Street on the backlot. Mickey and his "friends" pose for keepsake photos (about $14 each) on Hollywood Boulevard and Sunset Boulevard. Characters are also prominent in shows, with *Voyage of the Little Mermaid* running almost continuously and an abbreviated version of *Beauty and the Beast* performed several times daily at the Theater of the Stars. Check the daily entertainment schedule for show times.

At the Animal Kingdom   Camp Minnie-Mickey in the Animal Kingdom is a special location designed specifically for meeting characters. There are designated character greeting "trails" where you can meet Mickey, Minnie, and various characters from *The Jungle Book* and *The Lion King*. Also at Camp Minnie-Mickey are two stage shows featuring characters from *The Lion King* and *Pocahontas*.

Disney has taken several initiatives intended to satisfy guests' inexhaustible desire to meet characters. Most important, Disney assigned Mickey and a number of other characters to all-day duty in Mickey's Toontown Fair in the Magic Kingdom and Camp Minnie-Mickey in the Animal Kingdom. While making the characters more available has taken the guesswork out of finding them, it has robbed encounters of much of their spontaneity. Instead of chancing on a character, it's much more common now to wait in line to meet the character. Speaking of which, be aware that lines for face characters move m-u-c-h more slowly than do lines for nonspeaking characters. Because face characters are allowed to talk, they often engage children in lengthy conversations, much to the dismay of families still in the queue.

At the Disney Resorts As a paltry peace offering for terminating the popular theme park early entry program, Disney now sends a bus loaded with characters to the resorts. The idea is that the characters will be at the resort entrance and lobby to see you off as you depart for the theme parks. Problem is, nobody's quite sure where and when the bus will turn up. Consequently, the characters usually descend on a sparsely populated, if not deserted, lobby, and run around frantically looking for a kid to hug. Not exactly something to plan your day around. Maybe by the time you visit they will have sent the characters back to Toontown or at least developed a dependable schedule. By the way, Disney introduced this brain burp as a substitute for early entry, because, according to them, resort guests ask for it. Right.

Character Dining

Fraternizing with characters has become so popular that Disney offers character breakfasts, brunches, and dinners where families can dine in the presence of Mickey, Minnie, Goofy, and other costumed versions of animated celebrities. Besides grabbing customers from Denny's and Hardee's, character meals provide a familiar, controlled setting in which young children can warm gradually to characters. All meals are attended by several characters. Adult prices apply to persons age 12 or older, children's prices to ages 3–11. Little ones under age three eat free. For additional information on character dining, call (407) 939-3463 (WDW-DINE).

Because character dining is very popular, we recommend that you arrange priority seating as far in advance as possible by calling (407) 939-3463. Priority seating is not a reservation, only a commitment to seat you ahead of walk-in patrons at the scheduled date and time. A reserved table

CHARACTER MEAL HIT PARADE

RANK	RESTAURANT	LOCATION	MEALS SERVED	CHARACTERS
1.	Cinderella's Royal Table	Magic Kingdom	Breakfast	Cinderella, Snow White, Belle, Jasmine, Aladdin
2.	Chef Mickey's	Contemporary	Breakfast	Minnie, Mickey, Chip, Pluto, Goofy
			Dinner	Mickey, Pluto, Chip, Dale, Goofy
3.	Crystal Palace	Magic Kingdom	Breakfast	Pooh, Tigger, Eeyore Piglet
			Lunch/ Dinner	Pooh, Tigger, Eeyore
4.	1900 Park Fare	Grand Floridian	Breakfast	Alice, Mad Hatter, Geppeto, Mary Poppins
			Dinner	Cruella de Vil, Gov. Ratcliff, Prince John, Queen of Hearts, Captain Hook
5.	Garden Grill	Epcot	Breakfast/ Lunch/ Dinner	Chip, Dale, Mickey, Pluto
6.	Liberty Tree Tavern	Magic Kingdom	Dinner/ Lunch seasonally	Minnie, Pluto, Goofy, Chip and/or Dale

won't await you, but you will be seated ahead of patrons who failed to call ahead. Even with priority seating, expect to wait at least 10–30 minutes to be seated.

Character Dining: What to Expect

Character meals are bustling affairs, held in hotels' or theme parks' largest full-service restaurants. Character breakfasts offer a fixed menu served individually, family style, or on a buffet. The typical individual or family-style breakfast includes scrambled eggs; bacon, sausage, and ham; hash browns; waffles or French toast; biscuits, rolls, or pastries; and fruit. With family-style service, the meal is served in large skillets or platters at your

SERVED	SETTING	TYPE OF SERVICE	FOOD VARIETY & QUALITY	NOISE LEVEL	CHARACTER TO GUEST RATIO
Daily	★★★★★	Limited Menu	★★★½	Quiet	1 to 26
Daily	★★★	Buffet	★★★	Loud	1 to 56
Daily	★★★	Buffet	★★★½	Loud	1 to 56
Daily	★★★	Buffet	★★½	Very Loud	1 to 67
Daily	★★★	Buffet	★★★	Very Loud	1 to 89
Daily	★★★	Buffet	★★★	Moderate	1 to 54
Daily	★★★	Buffet	★★★½	Moderate	1 to 44
Daily	★★★★½	Family Style	★★★	Very Quiet	1 to 46
Daily	★★★★½	Family Style	★★½	Very Quiet	1 to 46
Daily	★★★★½	Family Style	★★½	Very Quiet	1 to 46
Daily	★★★½	Family Style	★★★	Moderate	1 to 47

table. If you run out of something, you can order seconds (or thirds) at no extra cost. Buffets offer much the same fare, but you have to fetch it yourself.

Character dinners range from a set menu served family-style to buffets or ordering off the menu. The character dinner at the Liberty Tree Tavern in the Magic Kingdom, for example, is served family-style and consists of turkey, ham, marinated flank steak, salad, mashed potatoes, green vegetables, and, for kids, macaroni and cheese. Dessert is extra. Character dinner buffets, such as those at 1900 Park Fare at the Grand Floridian and Chef Mickey's at the Contemporary Resort, offer separate adults' and children's serving lines. Typically, the children's buffet includes hamburgers,

CHARACTER MEAL HIT PARADE *(continued)*

RANK	RESTAURANT	LOCATION	MEALS SERVED	CHARACTERS
7.	Coral Cafe *	Dolphin	Breakfast	Chip, Dale, Goofy, Pluto
8.	Olivia's *	Old Key West	Breakfast	Pooh, Eyeore, Tigger
9.	Donald's Breakfastosaurus	Animal Kingdom	Breakfast	Mickey, Donald Pluto, Goofy
10.	Cape May Cafe	Beach Club	Breakfast	Goofy, Chip, Dale, Pluto
11.	Artist Point *	Wilderness Lodge	Breakfast	Pooh, Eyeore, Tigger
12.	Hollywood & Vine	Disney-MGM Studios	Breakfast	Minnie, Goofy, Pluto, Chip
			Lunch	Minnie, Donald, Goofy, Chip
13.	Ohana	Polynesian Resort	Breakfast	Mickey, Goofy, Chip, Dale
14.	Garden Grove Cafe	Swan	Breakfast	Goofy, Pluto
15.	Gulliver's Grill	Swan	Dinner	Goofy & Pluto or Rafiki & Timon

*These character meals are were suspended in 2002, but they may be reinstated.

hot dogs, pizza, fish sticks, fried chicken nuggets, macaroni and cheese, and peanut butter and jelly sandwiches. Selections at the adult buffet usually include prime rib or other carved meat, baked or broiled Florida seafood, pasta, chicken, an ethnic dish or two, vegetables, potatoes, and salad.

At both breakfasts and dinners, characters circulate around the room while you eat. During your meal, each of the three to five characters present will visit your table, arriving one at a time to cuddle the kids (and sometimes the adults), pose for photos, and sign autographs. Keep autograph books (with pens) and loaded cameras handy. For the best photos, adults should sit across the table from their children. Always seat the children where characters can reach them most easily. If a table is against a wall, for example, adults should sit with their backs to the wall and children on the aisle.

At some of the larger restaurants, including 'Ohana at the Polynesian Resort and Chef Mickey's at the Contemporary, character meals involve

SERVED	SETTING	TYPE OF SERVICE	FOOD VARIETY & QUALITY	NOISE LEVEL	CHARACTER TO GUEST RATIO
Sunday	★★★	Buffet	★★★½	Moderate	1 to 66
S, M, W	★★½	Family Style	★★½	Loud	1 to 32
Daily	★★★	Buffet	★★★	Very Loud	1 to 112
Daily	★★★	Buffet	★★½	Moderate	1 to 67
Daily	★★★★	Family Style	★★½	Moderate	1 to 83
Daily	★★½	Buffet	★★½	Moderate	1 to 71
Daily	★★½	Buffet	★★½	Moderate	1 to 71
Daily	★★½	Family Style	★★½	Moderate	1 to 57
Saturday	★★★	Buffet/Menu	★★★½	Moderate	1 to 216
S–M, W–F	★★★	Buffet/Menu	★★★½	Moderate	1 to 198

impromptu parades of characters and children around the room, group singing, napkin waving, and other organized mayhem.

Disney people don't rush you to leave after you have eaten. You can get seconds on coffee or juice and stay as long as you wish to enjoy the characters. Remember, however, that there are lots of eager children and adults waiting not so patiently to be admitted.

When to Go

Though a number of character breakfasts are offered around Walt Disney World, attending them usually prevents you from arriving at the theme parks in time for opening. Because early morning is best for touring the parks and you don't want to burn daylight lingering over breakfast, we suggest:

1. Substitute a character breakfast for lunch. Have a light breakfast from room service or your cooler first thing in the morning to tide you over. Then tour the

"Casting? This is George at the character breakfast. There's been a mistake. We were supposed to get the Assorted Character Package with one Mickey, one Goofy, one Donald, one Pluto . . ."

theme park for an hour or two before breaking off around 10:15 a.m. to go to the character breakfast of your choice. Make a big brunch of your character breakfast and skip lunch. You should be fueled until dinner.

2. Go on your arrival or departure day. The day you arrive and check in is usually good for a character dinner. Settle in at your hotel, swim, then dine with the characters. This strategy has the added benefit of exposing your children to the characters before chance encounters at the parks. Some children, moreover, won't settle down to enjoy the parks until they have seen Mickey. Departure days also are good for a character meal. Schedule a character breakfast on your check-out day before you head for the airport or begin your drive home.

3. Go on a rest day. If you plan to stay five or more days, you probably will take a day or a half day from touring to rest or do something else. These are perfect days for a character meal.

4. Go for a character dinner or lunch in the afternoon or evening instead of breakfast; it won't conflict with your touring schedule.

How to Choose a Character Meal

We receive a lot of mail asking for advice about character meals. This question from a Waterloo, Iowa, mom is typical:

Are all character breakfasts pretty much the same or are some better than others? How should I go about choosing one?

In fact, some *are* better than others, sometimes much better. Here's what we look for when we evaluate character meals:

1. The Characters The various meals offer a diverse assortment of Disney characters. Selecting a meal that features your children's special favorites is a good first step. Check the Character-Meal Hit Parade chart to see which characters are assigned to each meal. With the exception of 1900 Park Fare at the Grand Floridian, most restaurants stick with the same characters from year to year. Even so, it's wise to check the character line-up when you phone to make your priority seating, as this mom from Austin, Texas, attests:

> We went to two character meals at 1900 Park Fare. We ate dinner there the night we arrived unaware that the characters would all be villains. My four-year-old was a little scared of the witch from Snow White but amazingly kept his cool! Cruella De Vil, Captain Hook, and Prince John (from Robin Hood) were also there. My son asked the next morning if that witch was going to be at the theme parks, too. Needless to say, we did not ride the Snow White ride in MK! (The character breakfast was kinder and gentler.)

Unfortunately, a family from Michigan did not fare as well:

> Our character meal at 1900 Park Fare was a DISASTER!!! Please warn other readers with younger children that if they make a priority seating and the characters are villains, they may want to rethink their options. We went for my daughter's fifth birthday, and she was scared to death. The Queen of Hearts chased her sobbing and screaming down the hallway. Most young children we saw at the dinner were very frightened. Captain Hook and Prince John were laid-back, but Governor Ratcliff (from Pocahontas) and the Queen were amazingly rude and intimidating. I was very disappointed in our meal and the characters.

The villains have abdicated 1900 Park Fare in favor of more benign, cuddly characters, but you never know where they might show up next. Moral? Always call before making priority seatings to determine which characters you'll be dining with.

2. Attention from the Characters In all character meals the characters circulate among the guests hugging children, posing for pictures, and signing autographs. How much time a character spends with you and your children depends primarily on the ratio of characters to guests. The more characters and fewer guests the better. Because many character meals never fill to capacity, the Character-to-Guest Ratios found in our Character-Meal Hit Parade chart below have been adjusted to reflect an average attendance as opposed to a sell-out crowd. Even so, there's quite a range. The best character-to-guest ratio is at Cinderella's Royal Table where there is approximately 1 character to every 26 guests. The worst ratio can be found at the Garden Grove Cafe at the Swan Resort. Here there is only 1 character for every 216 guests. What this means in practical terms is that your family will get eight times more attention from the characters at Cinderella's Royal Table than from those at the Garden Grove Cafe. As an aside, many children particularly enjoy meals with characters such as Snow White, Belle, Jasmine, Cinderella, Aladdin, etc. These so-called "face characters" speak and are thus able to engage children in a way not possible for the mute animal characters.

3. The Setting Some character meals are staged in exotic settings, while for others, moving the venue to an elementary school cafeteria would be an improvement. In our chart we rate the setting of each character meal with the familiar scale of 0–5 stars. Two restaurants, Cinderella's Royal Table in the Magic Kingdom and the Garden Grill in the Land pavilion at Epcot, deserve special mention. Cinderella's Royal Table is situated on the first and second floors of Cinderella Castle in Fantasyland, offering guests a look at the inside of the castle. The Garden Grill is a revolving restaurant that overlooks several scenes from the Living with the Land boat ride attraction. Although Chef Mickey's at the Contemporary Resort is rather sterile and cold in appearance, it affords a great view of the monorail running through the interior of the hotel. The respective themes and settings of the remaining character meal venues, while readily apparent to adults, will be lost on most children.

4. The Food Although some food served at character meals is quite good, most is average—in other words palatable but nothing to get excited about. In terms of variety, consistency, and quality, restaurants generally do a better job with breakfast than with lunch or dinner (if served). Some restaurants offer a buffet, while others opt for "one-skillet," family-style service where all the hot items on the bill of fare are served from the same pot or skillet. A few restaurants offer traditional table service where a waiter serves a preset meal to each guest individually. This last type of service provides for dishes that are fresher than those that languish under buffet heat lamps or dry out in metal skillets and pots. However, like most generalizations, this has its exceptions. To help you sort it out, we rate the food at each character meal in our chart below using the tried-and-true five-star scale.

5. The Program Some larger restaurants stage modest performances where the characters dance, head up a parade, conga line around the room, or lead songs and cheers. For some guests these productions lend a celebratory air to the proceedings; for others they turn what was already mayhem into absolute chaos. In either event the antics consume time that the characters could be spending with families at their table.

6. Noise If you want to eat in peace, character meals are a bad choice.

That having been said, some are much noisier than others. Once again, our chart gives you some idea of what to expect.

7. Which Meal? Although character breakfasts seem to be the most popular, character lunches and dinners are usually more practical because they do not interfere with your early morning touring. During hot weather especially, a character lunch at midday can be heavenly.

8. Cost Dinners cost more than lunches, and lunches are more than breakfasts. Prices for any given meal vary only about $3 from the least expensive to the most expensive restaurant. Breakfasts run $15–$17 for adults and $8–$10 for children ages 3–9. For character lunches, expect to pay $17–$20 for adults and $10–$11 for kids. Dinners are $21–$22 for adults and $10–$12 for children. Little ones ages two and under eat free.

9. Reservations The Disney dining reservations system makes priority seatings for character meals up to 60 days prior to the day you wish to dine. Priority seating for most character meals is easy to obtain even if you forget to call until a couple of weeks before you leave home. Breakfasts at Cinderella's Royal Table are another story. To get a breakfast table at Cinderella's, you'll need our strategy (see pages 274–278), as well as the help of Congress and the Pope.

10. Homeless Characters Because of decreased attendance at Walt Disney World in the fall of 2001 and through much of 2002, several character meals were suspended, including breakfasts at the Coral Cafe in the Dolphin, at Artist Point at the Wilderness Lodge, and at Olivia's at Old Key West. It's possible that these character meals will be reinstated, but it's also possible that additional meals will be eliminated. Our advice is reconfirm all character meal priority seatings a week or so before you leave home by calling (407) WDW-DINE.

11. Friends For some venues, Disney has stopped specifying the characters scheduled for a particular character meal. Instead, they tell you that it's a certain character "and friends." For example, "Pooh and friends," meaning Eeyore, Piglet, and Tigger, or some combination thereof, or "Mickey and friends" with some assortment chosen from among Minnie, Goofy, Pluto, Donald, Daisy, Chip, and Dale. Most are pretty self-evident, but others such as "Mary Poppins and friends" are unclear. Who knows who Mary Poppins hangs out with? Don't expect Dick van Dyke.

12. Oddities Character meals are odd affairs at best, with the name "character meal" rather implying that you eat the characters. Yet, although we have seen characters savagely gnawed, we have not seen one devoured. Semantics aside, the oddities we refer to here are ones that may confuse or disappoint you. In the confusion department, the Garden Grove Cafe at the Swan Resort changes its name to Gulliver's Grill for dinner, and while it does not accept priority seatings for its breakfast character meal, it does accept them for its character dinner. If you ask, Garden Grove Cafe/Gulliver's Grill will tell you that two characters attend each meal. What you need to know, however, is that they work alternating 30-minute shifts, so there is usually only one character in the restaurant at a time.

Many people who fail to obtain a priority seating for the character breakfast at Cinderella's Royal Table reserve a table at the restaurant for lunch or dinner instead. Unfortunately, neither lunch nor dinner is a character meal. Although Cinderella and Snow White have been known to make an impromptu appearance during lunch or dinner, there's no guarantee. Finally, 1900 Park Fare at the Grand Floridian Resort trots out five characters for dinner but only four for breakfast. Conversely, the Crystal Palace features four characters for breakfast but only three for lunch and dinner.

Getting a Priority Seating at Cinderella's Royal Table

The character breakfast at Cinderella's Royal Table is extremely popular, as this frustrated reader from Golden, Colorado, complained:

> *I don't know what you have to do to get a priority seating for Cinderella's [Royal] Table in the castle. I called Disney Dining every morning at 7 [a.m.], which was 5 [a.m.] where I live! It was like calling into one of those radio shows where the first person to call wins a prize. Every time I finally got through all the tables were gone. I am soooo frustrated and mad I could spit. What do you have to do to get a table for Cinderella's breakfast?*

Admittedly, the hardest ticket to obtain at Walt Disney World is a priority seating for the character breakfast at Cinderella's Royal Table, located in the castle at the Magic Kingdom. Why? For starters, Cinderella's Royal Table is Disney's tiniest character meal restaurant, accommodating only about 130 diners at a time. Second, the character breakfast at Cinderella's is included in certain Walt Disney World vacation packages, which means the number of remaining seats available for distribution through Disney's central reservations is small. If you're considering a Disney package vacation anyway, buying one that includes the Cinderella character breakfast is the easiest and least complicated way to get a table. However, don't spring for an expensive Disney package just to get into Cinderella's Royal Table. The character breakfast is good but not *that* good.

If you don't purchase a package that includes the breakfast, the only way to get a table is to obtain a priority seating through Disney's central dining reservations. You must call (407) WDW-DINE at 7 a.m. exactly 60 days before the day you want to eat at Cinderella's. Okay, it's 6:50 a.m. EST and all the Disney dining reservationists are warming up their computers to begin filling available seats at 7 a.m. As the clock strikes seven, Disney dining is blasted with an avalanche of calls, all trying to make priority seatings for the character breakfast at Cinderella's Royal Table. There are over 100 reservationists on duty, and most priority seatings can be assigned in two minutes or less. Thus, the coveted seats go quickly, selling out as early as 7:02 a.m. on many days.

To be among the fortunate few who score a priority seating, try the following. First, be sure to call on the right morning. Use a calendar and count backwards exactly 60 days from (but not including) the day you wish to dine. (The computer doesn't understand months, so you can't, for example, call on February 1st to make a priority seating for April 1st because, count 'em, that's fewer than 60 days.) If you want to eat on May 2nd, for example, begin your 60-day countdown on May 1st. If you count correctly, you will find that the correct morning to call is that of March 3rd. If you don't feel like counting days, call (407) WDW-DINE and the Disney folks will calculate it for you. Call them during the afternoon when they are less busy about 70 days prior to your trip. Let them know when you'd like your priority seating, and they will tell you the exact morning to call.

To get a table you must dial in almost exactly at 7 a.m. EST on the dot. Disney does not calibrate its clock with the correct time as determined in the United States by the U.S. Naval Observatory or the National Institute of Standards and Technology, but by conducting synchronizing tests, we determined that Disney reservation system clocks are accurate within 1–3 seconds. Several Internet sites will give you the exact time. Our favorite is **www.atomictime.net.** This service offers the exact time in counting displays that show hours, minutes, and seconds. Once the Atomic Time home page is up, click on "html multi-zone continuous" and look for the Eastern Time Zone. Using this site or your local "Time of Day" number from the phone directory, synchronize your watch TO THE SECOND. About 18–20 seconds before 7 a.m. dial (407) WDW-DIN, waiting to dial the final "E" in "DINE" until the count of 7 seconds before the hour.

Continue hanging up and redialing until the call is answered. WDW-DINE changed the answering recording in 2002 to offer a menu. When your call is answered, the recorded menu will instruct you to dial 1 for Cinderella or 2 for other priority seatings. Hit 1 as the call is answered, not waiting for the recording to play.

If the above seems too complicated (not to mention anal), start dialing (407) WDW-DINE about 50 seconds before 7 a.m. If the reservation center is not yet open you'll get a recorded message telling you so. When this happens, hang up and call back immediately. If you have a redial button on your phone, use it (it will speed up the dialing process). Continue hanging up and redialing as fast as you can until you get a recording say-ing "all agents are busy helping other customers." This recording verifies that your call has been placed in the service queue in the order in which it was received. If you were among the first to get through, a Disney reservationist will pick up within 3–20 seconds.

What happens next depends on how many others got through ahead of you, but chances are good that you'll be able to get a priority seating. First, speak clearly but quickly with as few words as necessary. "Four per-sons at 8:30 for Cinderella's Royal Table, please," will get the job done. Bear in mind that while you're talking, other agents are confirming prior-ity seatings for other guests, so you don't want to get into a long-winded conversation. Flexibility on your part counts. It's much harder to get a seating for a large group, so give some advance thought to possibly break-ing your group into numbers that can be accommodated at tables for four or even tables for two. Likewise, be flexible concerning the time of your priority seating. If you are willing to accept whatever is available, say so up front, for example, "Cinderella's Table for four persons at 9, or whatever's available, please."

Because requesting a specific seating time wastes valuable seconds, you might want to say, "Party of 4 for X date for first available time." If you ask for a specific time slot and it's already full, you probably won't have time to make a second request before all seating times are filled.

All priority seatings for Cinderella's Royal Table Character Breakfast now require a credit card deposit (not guarantee) of $10 per adult and $5 per child at the time of the booking. No changes may be made to the name on the booking once the priority seating is made. Priority seatings may be cancelled with the deposit refunded in full by calling (407) WDW-DINE at least 24 hours before the seating time.

While many readers have been successful using our strategies, some have not, as this reader reported:

> *[Regarding] reservations for breakfast as Cinderella's castle. I did exactly what you suggested, five days in a row, and was unable to get through to an actual person until after 7:15 each day (although I was connected and put on hold at exactly 7 a.m. each time). Of course, by then, all reservations were gone (this was for the first week in May, not a peak time).*

On most days, a couple hundred calls slam the Disney's automated call queuing system literally within milliseconds seconds of each other. With this call volume, 1/20 of a second or less can make the difference between getting and not getting a table. As it happens there are a number of vari-ables that are beyond your control. When you hit the first digit of a long distance phone number, your phone system leaps into action. As you continue entering digits your phone system is already searching for the best path to the target switch, i.e., the number you're calling. According to federal regulation, a phone system must connect the call to the target number within 20 seconds of you entering the last digit of the number called. In practice, most systems make the connection much faster, but then again, your system could be pokey. How fast your call is connected, therefore, is a function of the connection speed of your local phone system, and even this varies according to traffic volume and available routing paths for individual calls. Distance counts too, although we're talking milliseconds. Thus, it will take just a little bit longer for a call to reach Walt Disney World from Chicago than from Atlanta, and longer yet if you're calling from San Francisco.

So, if you're having trouble getting a priority seating at Cinderella's Royal Table using the strategies outline earlier, here are our suggestions. Make a test call to (407) WDW-DINE at 7 a.m. EST a couple of days before you actually call in earnest. Using a stopwatch or the stopwatch function on your watch, time the interval between entering the last digit of the number and when the phone starts to ring on the other end. This exercise will provide a rough approximation of the call connection speed at that time of day from your area, taking into account both speed of service and distance. For most of you, the connection interval will be very short. Some of you, however, might discover that your problem in getting through is because of slow service. Either way, factor in the connection interval in timing your call to Disney. Phone traffic is heavier on weekdays than weekends, so if you plan to call for reservations on a weekday, conduct your test on a weekday also. Finally, don't use a cell phone to make the call. The connection time will usually be slower and certainly less predictable.

Thought it's one of the most widely used sections in this guidebook, we find it amazing that anyone would go to this much trouble to eat with Cinderella . . . atomic clocks, split-second timing, test calls . . . yikes! Maybe it's time for a nice relaxing week at the beach.

As a postscript, we've found it's often easier to get through to Disney's central reservations if you call on Saturday or Sunday. Presumably, folks don't mind calling in at the break of dawn if they are up getting ready for work but object to interrupting their beauty rest on weekends.

If You Can't Get a Priority Seating   If you insist on breakfast at Cinderella's but can't get a priority seating, go to the restaurant on the morning you wish to dine and try to score a table as a walk-in. This is a long shot, though sometimes possible during the least busy times of year. There's also a fair shot at success on very cold or rainy days when there's an above-average probability of no-shows. If you try to walk in, your chances are best during the last hour that breakfast is served.

If none of the above works, consider this suggestion from a Providence, Rhode Island, mother of three:

> We were not able to get [priority seating] for Cinderella's breakfast at the castle, so we booked a character breakfast at our hotel and then lunch at [Cinderella's Royal Table] for later in the week. This way our kids were able to eat with Mickey one day and see the inside of the castle a few days later. Incidentally, getting the [priority seating] for lunch at the castle was easy.

Neither lunch nor dinner at Cinderella's is a character meal, but Cinderella or Snow White sometimes look in—no guarantees, though. Even without characters, a meal in the castle costs a bundle, as this Snellville, Georgia, mom points out:

> We ate at Cinderella's Castle to fulfill my longtime dream. The menu was very limited and expensive. For three people, no appetizers or dessert, the bill was $100.

In case you're wondering, no alcoholic beverages either. No alcohol is served in the Magic Kingdom.

Campfire Program

A campfire and sing-along are held nightly (times vary depending on the season) near the Meadow Trading Post and Bike Barn at Fort Wilderness Campground. Chip 'n' Dale lead the songs, and two Disney films are shown afterward. The program is free and open to resort guests. For a schedule, call (407) 824-2788.

Baby-Sitting

Childcare Centers   Childcare isn't available within the theme parks, but each Magic Kingdom resort connected by the monorail or boat, each Epcot resort (BoardWalk Inn and Villas, Yacht and Beach Club resorts), and the Animal Kingdom Lodge have a childcare center for potty-trained children older than three. Services vary, but children generally can be left between 4:30 p.m. and midnight. Milk and cookies and blankets and pillows are provided at all childcare centers, and dinner is provided at most. Play is supervised but not organized, and toys, videos, and games are plentiful. Guests at any Disney resort or campground may use the childcare services.

The most elaborate of the childcare centers (variously called "clubs" or "camps") is Neverland Club at the Polynesian Resort. The rates for children ages 4–12 are $8 per hour per child.

All clubs accept advance reservations (some six months in advance!) with a credit card guarantee. Either call the club directly or reserve through Disney central reservations at (407) WDW-DINE. Most clubs require a 24-hour cancellation notice and levy a hefty penalty charge of $16 per child for no-shows. A limited number of walk-ins are usually available on a first-come, first-serve basis.

If you're staying in a Disney resort that doesn't offer a childcare club and you *don't* have a car, you're better off using in-room baby-sitting. Trying to take your child to a club in another hotel via Disney bus requires a 50- to 90-minute trip each way. By the time you have deposited your little one, it will almost be time to pick him up again. Be aware that the childcare clubs shut down at or before midnight. If you intend to make a late night of it, in-room baby-sitting is your best bet.

Kinder-Care Learning Centers also operate childcare facilities at Disney World. Originally developed for use by Disney employees, the centers now also take guests' children on a space-available basis. Kinder-Care provides basically the same services as a hotel club, except that the daytime "Learning While Playing Development Program" is more structured and educational. Employees are certified in CPR and first aid. Kinder-Care is open Monday–Friday, 6 a.m.–9 p.m., and Saturday and Sunday, 6 a.m.–6 p.m. Accepted are children ages 1 (provided they're walking and can eat table food) through 12. $10 per hour, per child. For reservations, call (407) 827-5437 or (407) 824-3290.

CHILDCARE CLUBS*			
Hotel	Name of Program	Ages	Phone
Wyndham Palace	All About Kids	All	(407) 812-9300
BoardWalk Inn & Villas	Harbor Club	4–12	(407) 939-6301
Contemporary Resort	Mouseketeer Clubhouse	4–12	(407) 824-3038 ext. 3700
Grand Floridian Beach Resort	Mouseketeer Club	4–12	(407) 824-2985
The Hilton	All about Kids	4–12	(407) 812-9300
Polynesian Resort	Neverland Club	4–12	(407) 939-3463
Wilderness Lodge & Villas	Cub's Den	4–12	(407) 824-1083
Yacht and Beach Club Resorts	Sandcastle Club	4–12	(407) 934-8000
Animal Kingdom Lodge	Simba's Cubhouse	4–12	(407) 938-4760

*Childcare clubs operate afternoons and evenings. Before 4 p.m., call the hotel rather than the number listed above. All programs require reservations.

In-Room Baby-sitting   For those staying in the World, in-room baby-sitting is offered by Kinder-Care (phone (407) 827-5444) and the Fairy

Godmothers (no kidding) service described below. All services described below will take your kids to the theme parks

Base rates for Kinder-Care are $13.50 an hour for one child, $15.50 an hour for two, and $17.50 an hour for three. If you have four or more kids, call for rates. Kinder-Care sitters are 18 or older, are insured and bonded, and have had previous childcare experience. Additionally, they undergo a complete police background check and reference checks and are certified in CPR and first aid. Disney hotel guests can charge baby-sitting services. Non-Disney hotel guests, including guests at the Swan and Dolphin, must pay cash. Reservations can be made up to 30 days in advance. Though there are no guarantees, Kinder-Care tries to accommodate same-day calls and requests for unusual hours. A four-hour minimum is required.

All About Kids (phone (407) 812-9300) offers in-room service to all Buena Vista–area hotels. Sitters range in age from college students to grandparents and are licensed, bonded, and insured. Base rates are $11 an hour (add $1 an hour for each additional child), with a four-hour minimum and an $8 travel fee. For jobs that start after 9 p.m., add $2 an hour. They will even take your child to the theme parks if you pay the sitter's admission.

Outside of Walt Disney World, childcare services and in-room sitting can be arranged through most larger hotels and motels or by calling the Fairy Godmothers. Godmothers are on-call 24 hours a day (you never get an answering machine) and offer the most flexible and diversified service in town. They will come to any hotel at any hour. No child is too young or too old, and Godmothers also care for the elderly and pets. All sitters are female nonsmokers. Base rates are $12 an hour for up to three children (in the same family), with a four-hour minimum and a $12 travel fee. For additional children in the same family, add $2 per child per hour. Godmothers will also tend a group of four or fewer children from different families for $8 an hour per family. For each additional child in excess of four, add $2 per child per hour to the base rate. Wishing won't get you a Godmother; you have to call (407) 277-3724 or (407) 275-3326.

Special Programs for Children

When the Disney Institute eliminated programs for all but large, organized groups, most of the children's educational programs were terminated as well. Several new programs for children are now available, but they lack the educational focus of the old curriculum.

Let the Kids Play Pirate   This program originates at the Grand Floridian and is open to all Walt Disney World resort guests ages 3–10. Children don bandanas and cruise to other resorts situated on Bay Lake and the

Seven Seas Lagoon following a treasure map and discovering clues along the way. At the final port of call, kids gobble down a snack and locate the buried treasure (dubloons, beads, and rubber bugs!). The two-hour cruise operates Monday–Thursday and costs $24.95 per child. Reservations can be made up to 120 days in advance by calling (407) WDW-DINE.

Wonderland Tea Party   Although the name of this enchanting soiree is enough to make most boys break out in hives, it is nevertheless available at the Grand Floridian on Monday, Wednesday, and Friday afternoons for $24.99 per child for ages 3–10. The program consists of making cupcakes, arranging flower bouquets, and having lunch and tea with characters from *Alice in Wonderland*. Reservations can be made up to 120 days in advance by calling (407) WDW-DINE.

Magic Kingdom Family Magic Tour   This is a two-hour guided tour of the Magic Kingdom for the entire family. Even children in strollers are welcome. The tour combines information about the Magic Kingdom with the gathering of clues that ultimately lead the group to a character greeting at the tour's end. Definitely not for the self-conscious, the tour involves skipping, hopping, and walking sideways as you progress from land to land. There's usually a marginal plot, such as saving Wendy from Captain Hook, in which case the character at the end of tour is Wendy. You get the idea. The tour departs daily at 9:30 and 11:30 a.m. The cost is $25 per person, plus a valid Magic Kingdom admission. The maximum group size is 18 people. Reservations can be made up to one year in advance by calling (407) WDW-TOUR.

Disney's The Magic Behind Our Steam Trains   You must be age 10 or older for this two-hour tour presented every Monday, Thursday, and Saturday. Kicking off at 7:30 a.m., you join the crew of the Walt Disney World Railroad as they prepare their steam locomotives for the day. Cost is $30 per person, plus a valid Magic Kingdom admission. Call (407) WDW-TOUR for additional information and reservations.

Birthdays and Special Occasions

If someone in your family celebrates a birthday while you're at Walt Disney World, don't keep it a secret. A Lombard, Illinois mom put the word out and was glad she did:

Regarding birthday celebrations – my daughter was turning 5 while we were there and I asked about special things that could be done. Our hotel asked me who her favorite character was and did the rest. We came back to our room on her birthday and there were helium balloons, a card, and a Cinderella 5x7 photo autographed in ink!! When we entered the Magic Kingdom, we received an "It's My Birthday Today" pin (FREE!) and at the restaurant she got a huge cupcake with whipped cream, sprinkles, and a candle. IT PAYS TO ASK!!

An Ohio mom celebrate her child's first haircut at the Magic Kingdom barber shop, reporting:

The barber shop at the entrance of MK makes a big deal with baby's first haircut—pixie dust, photos, a certificate and "free" mouse ears hat! ($12 total).

Part Six

Special Tips for Special People

Walt Disney World for Singles

Walt Disney World is great for singles. It is safe, clean, and low-pressure. If you're looking for a place to relax without being hit on, Disney World is perfect. Bars, lounges, and nightclubs are the most laid-back and friendly you're likely to find anywhere. In many, you can hang out and not even be asked to buy a drink (or asked to let someone buy a drink for you). Parking lots are well lighted and constantly patrolled. For women alone, safety and comfort are unsurpassed.

There's also no need to while away the evening hours alone in your hotel room. Between the BoardWalk and Downtown Disney, nightlife options abound. Virtually every type of entertainment performed fully clothed is available at an amazingly reasonable price at a Disney nightspot. If you drink more than you should and are a Disney resort guest, Disney buses will return you safely to your hotel.

You can meet people from all over the world in the World, and you'll often find that people from the farthest away are the most friendly. Foreign tourists especially can be very eager for conversation and any tips you might have (assuming you share a common language). Even so, the majority of park guests you'll encounter will be tourists much like yourself, and your relations, though pleasant, will often be as ultimately transient as the line you're standing in.

If, however, you're looking to meet someone new and exciting, there are better places than Walt Disney World. Most singles at Disney World work there. Even at the Pleasure Island entertainment complex, you need to check your dancing partner's wristband to determine whether he or she is old enough to buy a drink.

Far fewer single men vacation at Disney World than do single women. There are men, both single for real and single for the moment, attending meetings and conventions at the resorts, but their schedules rarely permit development of anything meaningful. Filling the void are local single (and married) men who understand that single women on vacation may be vulnerable. Avoid these guys.

The easiest and safest way to meet anyone at Disney World—either just for friendly companionship or for something more—is at the theme parks, including the water theme parks. (Most local cruisers aren't going to shell out the price of admission and hang around the park all day.) Parks give guests something to talk about, and there's no easier place to strike up a conversation than waiting in line for an attraction. A more organized way to meet people is to take a tour for adults.

Many readers take us to task for our singles coverage. An angry Texas woman wrote, asking, "Do you really think all of us single people are running around Disney World looking for sex?" Of course we don't, but we also know from experience that almost all Walt Disney World visitors let their guard down because they think of the World as a "safe" place, with no room for the steamy or tawdry inclinations of human nature. Our job, like it or not, is to give you a heads-up for potential trouble spots. We know there are predators at Walt Disney World—our female researchers have been hit on by a few. We'd be seriously remiss if we didn't let you know. End of story.

Going Solo

Of course, "single" can mean traveling solo as well as unmarried, and being by yourself doesn't mean you can't have a really great time in the World. **WDWIG.com** webmaster and Walt Disney World guru Deb Wills offers the following advice:

Tips for Going Solo to WDW

Some people may say that visiting Walt Disney World by yourself can't possibly be fun. They couldn't be more wrong, as there are many good reasons for going to WDW on your own.

Whether you're in Orlando on business and you're visiting the parks to kill time, or you came specifically to get away from it all, visiting the parks by yourself needn't be a lonely experience. It affords you the unique opportunity to see and do what you want, when you want, so take advantage of that. For those of you who are hesitating—JUST DO IT! You'll be glad you did. Here are some ways to maximize your experience when alone at WDW.

While the tendency might be to plan your days full of activity, I would suggest just the opposite—don't plan much at all. That's right . . . go with your schedule as wide open as you can. This is one of the best parts about traveling solo—you can be your own boss, and you don't have to answer to anyone. Sleep in, have a leisurely morning coffee on the balcony, relax by the pool . . . or not. If you'd rather get up and go early, who's going to stop you?

One of my favorite things to do when I'm traveling solo is to play photographer. How often do you walk past folks taking photos of each other? Ask if they would like to all be in one photo, then offer to snap the picture. This is a great way to make some quick friends.

Get your favorite Disney snack, find a bench, and people-watch. You'll be amazed at what you see: the young couple on their honeymoon wearing bride and groom mouse ears, the toddlers giving Mickey and the characters their first hugs, the grandparents smiling indulgently as their grandchildren smear ice cream all over their faces. If you're missing the smiles of your own children, buy a couple of balloons and give them away. You'll help make the kids near you very, very happy.

Learn how some of the magic is created. Take one of the behind-the-scenes tours (see our write-ups in each park's chapter) or even one of the deluxe hotel tours.

Visit the Animal Kingdom Lodge and relax at one of the animal viewing areas. While there, find one of the animal keepers—they'll be happy to discuss the care of the wild animals around the resort.

Don't hesitate to strike up conversations with cast members or other guests you may be in line with. The foreign cast members in Epcot's World Showcase are more than happy to share stories about their homelands with you.

With no one pulling to go to Space Mountain, get a snack, or go to the bathroom, you can enjoy a leisurely shop around the World. Some stores (Arribas Brothers in Downtown Disney, and Mitsukoshi Department Store in the Japan section of Epcot's World Showcase) have really neat displays and exhibits you'll be hard pressed to find elsewhere in the States.

This is the time to go to that restaurant you've always wanted to try, but the picky eater you know has always declined. You don't even have to order a full meal—you could try several appetizers or, better yet, just dessert.

You don't want the folks at home to think you've forgotten them, so go to Innoventions in Epcot to e-mail a photo of yourself to your family.

Use common sense when it comes to your own personal security. While I feel very comfortable and safe traveling alone at Walt Disney World (and have done so many times), I still don't do things I wouldn't do at home (like announce to anyone listening that you're traveling solo). If you are not comfortable walking back to your room alone, stop by the front desk and ask for a security escort. Use extra caution in the parking lots at night (again, just like you would at home).

Walt Disney World for Couples

So many couples marry or honeymoon at Walt Disney World that a department has been formed to take care of their needs. Disney's Fairy Tale Weddings & Honeymoons department offers a range of wedding venues and services, plus honeymoon packages.

Weddings

It takes big bucks to marry at Disney World. Disney's Intimate Wedding (six or fewer guests) includes four nights' lodging for the wedding couple, admission to the parks, a wedding officiant, and one dinner at a Disney "fine-dining" establishment—for $4,000! This price includes a musician, flower bouquet, limousine ride, and a wedding coordinator, as well. For even more, you can arrive at your wedding in Cinderella's glass coach, have Goofy as best man and Minnie as maid of honor, and drive away after the ceremony in a limo chauffeured by Mickey. If you don't have many friends, you can rent additional Disney characters by the half hour to attend your wedding. Volume discounts are available; characters cost $550 for one, $850 for two, $1,150 for three, and so on. If character prices sound steep, be comforted that they don't eat or drink. If you invite more than six guests to your wedding, you must purchase Disney's customized wedding package, which starts at $7,500.

Indoor and outdoor sites are available for weddings at theme parks as well as the Grand Floridian, Yacht Club, Beach Club, BoardWalk Inn and Villas, Contemporary, Wilderness Lodge and Villas, Polynesian, and Disney Village Resorts. You can have a nautical wedding aboard the

Kingdom Queen sternwheeler on Bay Lake or the riverboat at the Walt Disney World Village. Wedding sites for the nocturnal are available at Pleasure Island nightclubs. If it's a short ceremony you're looking for, you can actually tie the knot on a plummeting elevator at the Tower of Terror in Disney-MGM Studios (I swear I'm not making this up). Disney operates its Fairy Tale Wedding pavilion on a private island near the Grand Floridian. The glass-enclosed pavilion is nondenominational and accommodates 250 guests as well as smaller, more intimate nuptials.

One of the more improbable services available is bachelor parties (obtain information at (407) 828-3400). What goes on at a Disney bachelor party? Stag cartoons or a private showing of *The Making of Me?* Get down!

If you wish to marry at Walt Disney World, you can get a marriage license ($89) at any Florida county courthouse. Cash, traveler's checks, or money orders are accepted. There's no waiting period; your license is issued when you apply. The ceremony must occur within 60 days. Blood tests aren't required, but you must present ID (driver's license, passport, or birth certificate). If you were divorced within the year, you must produce a copy of your divorce decree. Call the wedding coordinator at (407) 828-3400 or (877) 566-0969 or check out **www.disneywedding.com** for more information.

Honeymoons

Honeymoon packages are adaptations of the regular Walt Disney Travel Company vacations. No special rooms or honeymoon suites are included unless you upgrade. In fact, the only honeymoon features are room service (in one package) and a photo session and keepsake album (in two others). Package rates range from $1,170–$4,100.

If you're interested in a Disney wedding or honeymoon, contact:
Disney's Fairy Tale Weddings & Honeymoons
P.O. Box 10000
Lake Buena Vista, FL 32830-0020
(800) 370-6009
www.disney.go.com

An Easton, Pennsylvania, couple enjoyed the reception they received at Walt Disney World and offer advice on how to make it even warmer:

We found that everyone, guests and cast members, bent over backwards for us when they learned it was our honeymoon. I highly recommend buying the bride and groom mouse ears, and wearing them everywhere. I know most men will be hesitant, as was my husband, but once you see what you get, you'll wear them gladly.

Romantic Getaways

Walt Disney World is a favorite getaway for honeymooners and other couples. You don't have to buy a honeymoon package to enjoy a romantic interlude, but not all Disney hotels are equally romantic. Some are too family oriented; others swarm with convention-goers. We recommend these Disney lodgings for romantics:

- Animal Kingdom Lodge
- Polynesian Resort
- Wilderness Lodge and Villas
- Grand Floridian Beach Resort
- BoardWalk Inn and Villas
- Yacht and Beach Club Resorts

All of these properties are expensive. There are also secluded rooms in Alligator Bayou section of Port Orleans Riverside. In Part Three: Selecting Your Hotel, we provide specific recommendations for the best rooms in each of the Disney resorts taking into consideration view, quiet, and convenience.

Quiet, Romantic Places to Eat

Quiet, romantic restaurants with good food are rare in the theme parks. Only the Coral Reef, the terrace at the Rose & Crown, and the San Angel Inn at Epcot satisfy both requirements. Waterfront dining is available at Portobello Yacht Club and Fulton's Crab House at Pleasure Island, and Narcoossee's at the Grand Floridian.

The California Grill atop the Contemporary Resort has the best view at Walt Disney World. If window tables aren't available, ask to be served in the adjoining lounge. Victoria & Albert's at the Grand Floridian is the World's showcase gourmet restaurant; expect to pay big bucks. Other good choices for couples include Shula's Steakhouse and Kimonos at the Swan and Dolphin Resorts, Jiko at the Anilam Kingdom Lodge, and Spoodles and The Flying Fish Cafe at the BoardWalk.

Eating later in the evening and choosing among the restaurants we've mentioned will improve your chances for quiet, intimate dining, but children—well-behaved or otherwise—are everywhere at Walt Disney World, and you won't escape them. Honeymooners from Slidell, Louisiana, write:

We made dinner reservations at some of the nicer Disney restaurants. When
we made reservations, we made sure they were past the dinner hours and
we tried to stress that we were on our honeymoon. [In] every restaurant we
went to, we were seated next to large families. The kids were usually tired
and cranky. After a whole day in the parks, the kids were not excited about

sitting through a long meal. It's very difficult to enjoy a romantic dinner when there are small children crawling around under your table. We looked around the restaurant and always noticed lots of nonchildren couples. Our suggestion is this: Seat couples without children together and families with kids elsewhere. If Disney is such a popular honeymoon destination, then some attempt should be made to keep romantic restaurants romantic.

A couple from Woodbridge, Virginia, adds:

We found it very difficult to find a quiet restaurant for dinner anywhere. We tried a restaurant which you recommended as quiet and pleasant. We even waited until 8:30 p.m. to eat and we were still surrounded by out-of-control children. The waiters were even singing the Barney the Dinosaur theme song. The food was very good, but after a long day in the park, our nerves were shot.

For complete information about Disney restaurants, as well as recommendations for off-World dining, see Part Nine: Dining in and around Walt Disney World.

Romantic Stuff to Do

Couples, like everyone else, have their own agenda at Disney World. Nonetheless, here are romantic diversions you might not have on your list:

1. Visit a Lounge   Atop the Contemporary Resort is a nice but pricey lounge. It's great for watching a sunset or viewing nighttime fireworks over the nearby Magic Kingdom. If you want to go for the view and not drink, access an outside promenade through a set of glass doors at the end of the lounge. Also wonderful is Mizner's Lounge on the Alcazar level of the Grand Floridian. It overlooks the hotel grounds and pools and the Seven Seas Lagoon. Each evening, a six-piece dance band plays 1920s and 1930s music on the adjacent landing.

2. View the Floating Electrical Pageant   One of Disney's most romantic entertainments, the pageant consists of a train of barges, each with a spectacular light display depicting sea creatures. The show starts after dark to music by Handel played on synthesizers. You see only the lights. The best places to watch are from the piers at the Polynesian, Wilderness Lodge and Villas, the Grand Floridian, or Fort Wilderness.

3. Ride a Boat   Small launches shuttle guests to and from the Grand Floridian, Polynesian, Magic Kingdom, Wilderness Lodge and Villas, and Fort Wilderness Campground well into the night. On a summer night, take a tranquil cruise around Bay Lake and the Seven Seas Lagoon. Boats also cruise the canal connecting Disney-MGM Studios and Epcot, stopping at the Swan and Dolphin, Disney's BoardWalk, and the Yacht and Beach Club Resorts.

During daytime at the Fort Wilderness dock, you can rent boats for exploring Bay Lake and the Seven Seas Lagoon. The adjacent Fort Wilderness Campground is honeycombed with footpaths that are lovely for early-morning or early-evening walks.

4. Head for the Woods   If you enjoy hiking and boating, visit Juniper Springs Recreation Area in the Ocala National Forest. About an hour and a half north of Disney World, the forest is extraordinarily beautiful. Trails are well marked, and canoes are available for rent (shuttle included). Paddling down Juniper Springs is like floating through a natural version of the Jungle Cruise. For Juniper Springs information, call (352) 625-2808.

5. Watch the Animals   Spend an afternoon watching African wildlife from the covered viewing towers overlooking the savanna at the Animal Kingdom Lodge. In the evening there are stories outside around a fire pit. Visitors are not admitted to visit the Animal Kingdom Lodge, however, unless they have a priority seating at either the Jiko or Boma restaurant. Both restaurants serve excellent food and are definitely worth a try. Boma is an African buffet while Jiko offers upscale dining with cuisine that might be classified as African fusion. Though it sounds very exotic, even the pickiest meat and potato lover will find plenty to like. Of the two, Jiko is the more romantic by far.

6. Have a Picnic   During more temperate months, picnic on the beaches of Bay Lake and the Seven Seas Lagoon. Room service at Disney resorts will prepare a carry-along lunch to order. Drinks, including wine and beer, are less expensive at hotel convenience shops. Fort Wilderness Campground also is good for picnics.

7. Dine and Dance on the BoardWalk   Disney's BoardWalk offers several nice restaurants and an upscale dance club featuring music from the 1920s to the 1990s. Even if you don't dine or dance, the BoardWalk is romantic and picturesque for strolling.

8. Go Bicycling   Rent a bike at Wilderness Lodge and Villas and explore the paths and roads of nearby Fort Wilderness Campground. Maps are available at the bike-rental shed.

Things to Bring

Once ensconced in your Disney World hideaway, it can be inconvenient to go out for something you've forgotten. Many couples write us to list things they wish they'd remembered to bring. Here are items most often mentioned:

1. Wine (Wine is sold by the bottle at Disney World, but the selection is pretty dismal. The best nearby selection of beer, wine, and liquor is at the ABC store at

11951 Apopka-Vineland Road about a mile northeast of the Crossroads Shopping Center.)

2. Corkscrew (Wine glasses are available from room service.)

3. Liquor, aperitifs, and cordials

4. Mixers for fancy drinks such as margaritas, olives for martinis, lemons, and limes

5. Portable tape or disc player and your favorite music

6. Bicycles

7. Picnic basket and blanket or tablecloth

8. Candles and holders

9. Cooler

10. Special snacks such as caviar, chocolates, cheeses (with knife), and fruit

Walt Disney World for Expectant Mothers

It is said that a good shepherd will lay down his life for his sheep. Heaven knows we have tried to be good shepherds for you. We have spun around in teacups and been jostled in simulators until we turned green. We have baked in the sun, flapped in the wind, and come close to drowning in the rain, all while researching this guide. But for expectant mothers we have failed. Try as he might, the author has never become pregnant, and as a consequence, the *Unofficial Guide* has never included good, first-hand information for mothers-to-be. Then, in our darkest hour, to the rescue came Debbie Grubbs, a reader from Colorado in her fifth month of pregnancy. Fearless and undaunted, Debbie waddled all over Walt Disney World, compiling observations and tips for expectant moms. The following is what she had to say.

I was very disappointed to find no information specifically directed to pregnant women, particularly concerning which attractions at the theme parks you can and cannot ride. Generally speaking, pregnant women can experience more attractions than not at Walt Disney World. Therefore, I will outline only those rides that are prohibited to pregnant women and the reasons why. There were several rides that I just knew I could ride even though they were restricted, so I sent my husband and friends to ride first and they reported why they thought I could or could not ride.

MAGIC KINGDOM

Splash Mountain *is restricted obviously due to the drop, or so I thought. It turns out that the seat configuration in the "logs" has more to do with it than the drop. The seats are made so that your knees are higher than your rear, causing compression on the abdomen (when it is this large). This is* *potentially harmful to the baby. As always, better safe than sorry. I really hated to miss this one.*

Big Thunder Mountain Railroad *is restricted for obvious reasons as well. It's just not a good idea to ride roller coasters when you are pregnant.*

Mad Tea Party *may be okay if you don't spin the cups. We didn't ride this one because I was advised by my doctor not to ride things with centrifugal [or centripetal] force. Dumbo and the Astro Orbiter (Tomorrowland) are okay, but the Mad Tea Party is too fast if you spin the cups.*

Space Mountain *is restricted. It's one of my favorite rides, but a roller coaster nonetheless.*

Tomorrowland Speedway *is not recommended due to the amount of rear-ending that always occurs due to overzealous younger drivers.*

EPCOT

Body Wars *and* **Test Track** *are restricted, as are all simulator rides. They are too rough and jerky, much like a roller coaster.* **Mission: Space** *(opens 2003) will also be a no-go. [Non-moving seats are available in some simulation attrations—ask a cast member.]*

DISNEY-MGM STUDIOS

Tower of Terror *is restricted for the drop alone, and* **Star Tours** *is restricted because it is a simulator. Although not as rough as Body Wars, Star Tours is still a no-no. The* **Rock 'n' Roller Coaster** *is clearly off limits.*

There might be some question about the **Backlot Tour** *due to Catastrophe Canyon, where there is a simulated earthquake. It is very tame compared to Earthquake! at Universal Studios and posed no hazard to me. I rode with no problems.*

ANIMAL KINGDOM

Dinosaur *is very jerky and should be avoided. Same for* **Primeval Whirl.**
Kali River Rapids *is a toss-up—it's somewhat bouncy and very wet.*

WATER THEME PARKS

All of the slides are off-limits to pregnant women. You can, however, do Shark Reef at Typhoon Lagoon with an extra-large wetsuit vest. The wave pools and floating creeks are great for getting the weight off your feet.

A mother of three from Bethesda, Maryland, adds the following:

First, anyone who is pregnant should go to their local golf shop and buy one of those canes that has a seat attached to it. They are lightweight and easy to carry. Without a seat, I would have been gone. Second, a pregnant woman must come with some type of support or "Belly Bra."

More Tips

In addition to Debbie's tips, here are a few of our own:

1. Go over your Walt Disney World vacation plans with your obstetrician well in advance of your trip.

2. Be prepared for a lot of walking at Walt Disney World. Get in shape by walking at home, building up endurance and distance gradually.

3. While on vacation, get as much rest as you need, even if you have to sacrifice some time at the theme parks. Try to work in an afternoon nap each day.

4. Make sure you eat properly. Drink plenty of water throughout the day, especially if you visit during the warmer seasons.

5. Use in-park transportation whenever available to cut down on walking.

6. Stay in Walt Disney World if possible. This will make it easier to separate from your group and return to your hotel for rest.

Walt Disney World for Seniors

Seniors' problems and concerns are common to Disney visitors of all ages. Seniors do, however, often get into predicaments caused by touring with people younger than they are. Run ragged and pressured by grandchildren to endure a frantic pace, many seniors concentrate on surviving Disney World rather than enjoying it. The parks have as much to offer older visitors as they do children, and seniors must either set the pace or dispatch the young folks to tour on their own.

An older reader in Alabaster, Alabama, writes:

> The main thing I want to say is that being a senior is not for wussies. At Disney World particularly, it requires courage and pluck. Things that used to be easy take a lot of effort, and sometimes your brain has to wait for your body to catch up. Half the time, your grandchildren treat you like a crumbling ruin and then turn around and trick you into getting on a roller coaster in the dark. What you need to tell seniors is that they have to be alert and not trust anyone. Not their children or even the Disney people, and especially not their grandchildren. When your grandchildren want you to go on a ride, don't follow along blindly like a lamb to the slaughter. Make sure you know what the ride is all about. Stand your ground and do not waffle. He who hesitates is launched!

Most seniors we interview enjoy Disney World much more when they tour with folks their own age. If, however, you're considering going to Disney World with your grandchildren, we recommend an orientation visit without them first. If you know first-hand what to expect, it's much easier to establish limits, maintain control, and set a comfortable pace when you visit with the youngsters.

If you're determined to take the grandkids, read carefully those sections of this book that discuss family touring. *(Hint:* The Dumbo-or-Die-in-a-Day Touring Plan has been known to bring grown-ups of any age to their knees.*)*

Because seniors are a varied and willing lot, there aren't any attractions we would suggest they avoid. For seniors, as with other Disney visitors, personal taste is more important than age. We hate to see mature visitors pass an exceptional attraction like Splash Mountain because younger visitors call it a "thrill ride." Splash Mountain is a full-blown adventure that gets its appeal more from music and visual effects than from the thrill of the ride. Because you must choose among those attractions that might interest you, we provide facts to help you make informed decisions.

We know it's easy to get caught up in the spectacle and wonder of Disney World, so much so that you follow a crowd onto something you hadn't fully considered. Here are some of the attractions to know before you enter.

Magic Kingdom

Space Mountain   If you thought the roller coaster at Coney Island was a thrill, this won't be far behind, with dips and pops that pull you through curves and over humps. This ride vibrates a lot. Put your glasses in your fanny pack; we can't guarantee they'll stay in your pocket.

Big Thunder Mountain Railroad   Although sedate compared with Space Mountain, this ride is very jarring. Cars jerk back and forth along the track, though there are few drops. It's the side-to-side shaking that gets to most people.

Splash Mountain   This ride combines the whimsy of Disney with the thrill of a log flume. There's one big drop near the end and some splash (engineered by spray guns and a water cannon, not the drop itself). The enchanting Brer Rabbit story is worth getting wet for.

Swiss Family Treehouse   This isn't a thrill ride, but it does involve lots of stair climbing and a very unsteady pontoon bridge.

Mad Tea Party   An adaptation of a carnival ride, big tea cups spin until riders are nauseated. If you approach this instrument of the devil while it's motionless, your cunning grandchildren may try to pass it off as an al fresco dining patio.

Epcot

Body Wars   This ride jolts more than Star Tours (at Disney-MGM Studios) and is more likely to cause motion sickness than the Mad Hatter's tea cups. It's like a graphic anatomy lesson combined with the trauma of being chauffeured by a teenager driving his first stick shift.

Test Track   This thrill ride in Future World simulates test driving a car. Both fast and bumpy, Test Track whizzes you around hairpin turns, over rough road, down straightaways, and up and down steep inclines.

Mission: Space   (opens 2003) Although this is another fairly wild simulator ride, it will supposedly usher in a new generation of Disney attraction. In other words, we expect it to be pretty special. We also expect it to have some non-moving seats and perhaps a viewing capsule for guests in wheelchairs. Ask a cast member.

Disney-MGM Studios

Star Tours   Using the plot and characters from *Star Wars,* this flight-simulation ride is a Disney masterpiece. If you're extremely prone to motion sickness, this ride will affect you. Otherwise, it might be the highlight of your Walt Disney World vacation.

The Twilight Zone Tower of Terror   Though most of the thrills are visual, the Tower of Terror features a gut-gripping simulation of an elevator in free fall after its cable has broken.

Rock 'n' Roller Coaster   This is Disney's wildest coaster. If you thought Space Mountain was rough, stay away from this one.

Animal Kingdom

Dinosaur   The show consists primarily of startling visual effects, but the ride is pretty jerky.

Kali River Rapids   This ride simulates a whitewater raft trip. It's not all that rough, but it's very wet.

Primeval Whirl   This ride, though quite jerky, is not as bad as it looks, and you can pretty much check out the whole thing from out front.

Getting Around

Many seniors like to walk, but a seven-hour visit to one of the theme parks normally includes four to eight miles on foot. If you aren't up for that much hiking, let a more athletic member of your party push you in a rented wheelchair. The theme parks also offer fun-to-drive electric carts (convenience vehicles). Don't let your pride get in the way of having a good time. Sure you could march ten miles if you had to, but *you don't have to!*

Your wheelchair-rental deposit slip is good for a replacement wheelchair in any park during the same day. You can rent a chair at the Magic Kingdom in the morning, return it, go to Epcot, present your deposit slip, and get another chair at no additional charge.

Timing Your Visit

Retirees should make the most of their flexible schedules and go to Disney World in fall or spring (excluding holiday weeks), when the weather is nicest and the crowds are thinnest. Crowds are also sparse from the end of January through the beginning of February, but the weather is unpredictable. If you visit in winter, bring coats and sweaters, plus warm-weather clothing. Be prepared for anything from near-freezing rain to afternoons in the 80s.

The Price of Admission

Only Florida residents get senior discounts on Disney World admission (page 48). For additional information, see our section on admission options (pages 45–52).

Lodging

If you can afford it, stay in Walt Disney World. If you're concerned about the quality of your accommodations or the availability of transportation, staying inside the Disney complex will ease your mind. The rooms are some of the nicest in the Orlando/Kissimmee area and are always clean and well maintained. Plus, transportation is always available to any destination in Disney World at no additional cost.

Disney hotels reserve rooms closer to restaurants and transportation for guests of any age who can't tolerate much walking. They also provide golf carts to pick up from and deliver guests to their rooms. Cart service can vary dramatically depending on the time of day and the number of guests requesting service. At check-in time (around 3 p.m.), for example, the wait for a ride can be as long as 40 minutes.

Though there are many good-quality hotels in the area, here are five reasons to consider staying in Walt Disney World:

1. The quality of the properties is consistently above average.

2. Transportation companies that operate buses for "outside" hotels run only every hour or so. Disney buses run continuously. Staying in Disney World guarantees you can get transportation whenever you need it.

3. Boarding pets overnight at the kennels is available only to Disney resort guests.

4. You get free parking in the major theme-park lots.

5. You get preferential tee times on resort golf courses.

All Disney hotels are large and spread out. While it's easy to avoid most stairs, it is often a long hike to your room from the parking lot, bus stops, or public areas. Seniors intending to spend more time at Epcot and Disney-MGM Studios than at the Magic Kingdom or the Animal Kingdom should consider the Yacht and Beach Club Resorts, Swan and Dolphin, or BoardWalk Inn.

The Contemporary Resort is a good choice for seniors who want to be on the monorail system. So are the Grand Floridian and Polynesian Resorts, though both sprawl over many acres, necessitating a lot of walking. For a restful, rustic feeling, choose the Wilderness Lodge and Villas. If you want a kitchen and all the comforts of home, book Old Key West Resort, the Beach Club Villas, or BoardWalk Villas. If you enjoy watching birds and animals, try Animal Kingdom Lodge.

RVers will find pleasant surroundings at Disney's Fort Wilderness Campground. There are also several KOA campgrounds within 20 minutes of Walt Disney World. None offer the wilderness setting or amenities that Disney does, but they cost less.

Transportation

Roads in Walt Disney World can be daunting. Armed with a moderate sense of direction and an above-average sense of humor, however, even the most timid driver can learn to get around in the World. If you're easily intimidated, book a hotel on the monorail and stay off the road.

If you drive, parking isn't a problem. Lots are served by trams that link the parking area and the theme park's front gate. For guests with mobility problems, parking spaces for the disabled are available adjacent to each park's entrance. The attendant at the pay booth will give you a special ticket for your dashboard and will direct you to the reserved spaces. Though Disney requires that you be recognized officially as handicapped to use this parking, temporarily disabled or injured persons also are permitted access.

Senior Dining

Eat breakfast at your hotel restaurant or save money by having juice and rolls in your room. Although you aren't allowed to bring food into the parks, fruit, fruit juice, and soft drinks are sold throughout Disney World. Make your lunch priority seating for before noon to avoid the lunch crowds. Follow with an early dinner and be out of the restaurants, rested and ready for evening touring and fireworks, long before the main crowd begins to think about dinner.

We recommend seniors fit dining and rest times into the day. Remember Dad on the Dumbo-or-Die-in-a-Day Touring Plan? He'll be gobbling fast foods as he hauls his toddlers around the park at breakneck speed. Reserve a window table for your early lunch and wave to him as he races by. Plan lunch as your break in the day. Sit back, relax, and enjoy. Then return to your hotel for a nap.

Have a Plan

From planning the time to visit to observing our first rule of touring ("Arrive early! Arrive early! Arrive early!"), seniors generally are the perfect *Unofficial Guide* patrons. Those who can get by on less sleep enjoy the stress-free pleasure of touring the parks in early morning. Late sleepers should visit Disney World during less crowded, off-peak times.

It's imperative to follow our maxim, "Have a plan or get a frontal lobotomy." Select a touring plan. Before you go to the park, read the ride and show descriptions and pick what you want to see or skip so that you'll be able to efficiently follow the plan. Arrive at the park's gates at least a half hour before official opening. Move as fast as you can early in the day so that you'll be able to slow down after an hour or so, knowing the most strenuous part of the plan and potential bottlenecks are behind you.

Seniors who ask us whether the touring plans work for folks who want to take things a little slower should take heart:

My mother (age 77) and myself (age 47) visited Disney for the first time. We followed your "Type A" schedule and really enjoyed the challenge of it. We were standing in line for Star Tours and the friendly attendant was advising us on the popular attractions to see. He suggested Tower of Terror, Indiana Jones, Voyage of the Little Mermaid, and Muppet Vision 3D. We said we had already seen them all. He said, "It's only 10 o'clock in the morning and you have seen all of those already?" We said, "Yes," and held up your guidebook.

Every senior should take at least one behind-the-scenes tour, most of which are at Epcot. They offer an in-depth look at Walt Disney World operations. Especially worthwhile are Hidden Treasures and Gardens of the World. If you don't have time for these lengthy tours, the shorter Greenhouse Tour at Epcot's The Land pavilion is a "must-see." Backstage Magic visits behind-the-scenes locations at several theme parks, while Keys to the Kingdom provides a glimpse of the history and hidden operations of the Magic Kingdom. Ranging in duration from one to seven hours and in price from $5 to $160 per person, all tours require a lot of walking and standing.

Finally, include quiet time in your itinerary. We recommend Disney patrons of all ages return to their hotel during the hot, crowded part of the day for lunch, a nap, and even a swim.

When You Need to Contact the Outside World

Pay telephones are located throughout Walt Disney World. Amplified handsets are available for the hearing-impaired in all four major theme parks. Handset locations are marked on each park's map, provided free when you enter. A Telecommunication Device for the Deaf (TDD) is available at Guest Relations in all theme parks.

Telephones that guests in wheelchairs can reach are scattered throughout all parks except the Magic Kingdom, where they're under the Walt Disney World Railroad Station.

Walt Disney World for Disabled Guests

Walt Disney World is so attuned to guests with disabilities that unscrupulous folks have been known to fake a disability in order to take unfair advantage. If you have a disability, or even a restricted diet (including kosher preparations), Walt Disney World is prepared to meet your needs.

Valuable information for trip planning is available on-line at **www. disneyworld.com.** At Walt Disney World, each of the major theme parks offers a free booklet describing disabled services and facilities at that park. The Disney people are somewhat resistant to mailing you the theme-park booklets in advance, but if you are polite and persistent they can usually be persuaded.

For specific requests, including specialized accommodations at the resort hotels or on the Disney Transportation System, call (407) 939-7807 [voice] or (407) 939-7670 [TTY]. When the recorded menu comes up, touch "1" on your Touch-Tone phone. Calls to this number should be strictly limited to questions and requests regarding disabled services and accommodations. Other questions should be addressed to (407) 824-4321.

The following equipment, services, and facilities are available at Walt Disney World resort hotels, though not all hotels offer all of the items listed:

Wheelchairs	Knock and phone alerts
Bed and bathroom rails	Closed-captioned televisions
Wider bath doors	TTYs
Roll-in showers	Strobe-light smoke detectors
Shower benches	Double peep holes in doors
Hand-held shower heads	Braille on signs and elevators
Accessible vanities	Portable commodes
Rubber bed pads	Lower-level kitchen appliances and
Lower beds	cupboards
Refrigerators	

Much of the Walt Disney World transportation system is accessible to guests with disabilities. Monorails can be accessed by either ramp or elevator, and all bus routes are serviced by buses with wheelchair lifts, though unusually wide or long wheelchairs (or motorized chairs) may not fit the lift. Watercraft accommodations for wheelchairs are iffier. If you plan to stay at the Wilderness Lodge and Villas, Fort Wilderness Campground, or one of the Epcot resorts, call the special requests number provided above for the latest information on watercraft accessibility.

Food and merchandise locations at the theme parks, Downtown Disney, and hotels are generally accessible, but some fast-food queues and shop aisles are too narrow for wheelchairs. At these locations you can ask a cast member or member of your party for assistance.

Disabled guests and their families give Walt Disney World high marks for accessibility and general consideration for the needs of disabled patrons. An Arlington, Virginia, woman writes:

Before the trip, I thought of Disney as a sort of corporate monster that successfully accessed my pocketbook through my innocent and trusting children with its diabolical marketing expertise. I also considered a Disney vacation pretty ersatz compared to, say, a week in Provence. However, I must say that Disney is dynamite in its treatment of handicapped vacationers and this perspective has turned me into a fan. My mom has mobility problems that got a lot worse between the time my Dad made reservations and the time we arrived, and she was worried about getting around. Disney supplied a free wheelchair, and every bus had kneeling steps for wheelchair users. The disabled brochures for each park were incredibly informative about access for each attraction, and the hosts sprang into action when they saw us coming.

Visitors with Special Needs

Wholly or Partially Nonambulatory   Guests may rent wheelchairs. Most rides, shows, attractions, rest rooms, and restaurants in the World accommodate the nonambulatory disabled. If you're in a theme park and need assistance, go to Guest Relations.

A limited number of electric carts (motorized convenience vehicles) are available for rent. Easy and fun to drive, they give nonambulatory guests a tremendous degree of freedom and mobility. For some reason, vehicles at the Magic Kingdom are much faster than those at other parks.

Close-in parking is available for disabled visitors at all Disney lots. Request directions when you pay your parking fee. All monorails and most rides, shows, rest rooms, and restaurants accommodate wheelchairs.

An information booklet for disabled guests is available at wheelchair rental locations in each park. Theme-park maps issued to each guest on admission are symbol-coded to show nonambulatory guests which attractions accommodate wheelchairs.

Even if an attraction doesn't accommodate wheelchairs, nonambulatory guests still may ride if they can transfer from their wheelchair to the ride's vehicle. Disney staff, however, aren't trained or permitted to assist in transfers. Guests must be able to board the ride unassisted or have a member of their party assist them. Either way, members of the nonambulatory guest's party will be permitted to go along on the ride.

Because waiting areas of most attractions won't accommodate wheelchairs, nonambulatory guests and their party should request boarding instructions from a Disney attendant as soon as they arrive at an attraction. Almost always, the entire group will be allowed to board without a lengthy wait.

A woman from New Orleans who traveled with a nonambulatory friend writes:

The most recent trip is what I really wanted to tell you about. I went with a very dear friend of mine who is a paraplegic, confined to a wheelchair. It was his first trip to WDW, and I knew that it was a handicap-friendly place, but we were still a little apprehensive about how much we would be able to do. The official pamphlet distributed by the WDW staff is helpful, but it implies limitations, such as stating that one must be able to navigate (i.e., walk) the catwalks of Space Mountain in case of emergency. After reading this, Brian and I thought that we would end up walking around the MK looking at the rides, not riding them. The reality is, nonambulatory visitors are able to do much more—one only has to ask the cast members what is really allowed. Of course, I'm sure the WDW publication is written to cover liability purposes; also, Brian is a very active person who is able to transfer from his wheelchair without too much difficulty, so we were able to ride almost everything we wanted! We both had a terrific time. The only ride that it seems we should have been able to ride but couldn't was Pirates of the Caribbean, and [this was] only because the railings at the loading site are just a few inches too close together for a wheelchair to pass through. Anyway, my point is that it may be encouraging to disabled readers of the Unofficial Guide *to know that there are options available; of course, with the caveat that it depends on the individual's mobility. I would recommend to anyone to not avoid a ride—ask first.*

Visitors with Dietary Restrictions can be assisted at Guest Relations in the theme parks. For Walt Disney World restaurants outside the theme parks, call the restaurant a day in advance for assistance.

Sight- and/or Hearing-Impaired Guests aren't forgotten. Guest Relations at the theme parks provide complimentary tape cassettes and portable tape players to assist sight-impaired guests ($25 refundable deposit required). At the same locations, TDDs are available for hearing-impaired guests. In addition to TDDs, many pay phones in the major parks are equipped with amplifying headsets. See your Disney map for locations.

In addition, braille guide maps are available from Guest Relations at all theme parks. Some rides provide closed captioning, while many theater attractions provide reflective captioning. Walt Disney World will provide an interpreter for the live theater shows. To reserve an interpreter, call (407) 824-4321 (voice) or (407) 939-8255 (TTY).

Friends of Bill W. A mom from Linthicum, Maryland suggested this inclusion: a great idea and long overdue. Here's what she had to say:

> We went on this vacation with an recovering alcoholic. He was able to attend daily 3–4 p.m. meetings that were held just outside the park in one of the hotels. It would be helpful if you mentioned that there are meetings available for Alcoholics Anonymous. Disney does not sponsor them. This is a very sensitive issue for many that are too afraid to ask for fear of public ridicule. The person in our group took a cab from the resort the first time and never had to after that. There are regulars in the meetings that will pick up anyone from their resorts that need a ride. Thanks for letting me include this. I wouldn't want someone to be afraid to come to Disney because they feared a setback in their recovery.

Visitors from Other Countries

Foreign visitors are warmly welcomed at Walt Disney World and represent a large percentage of its guests. Most Magic Kingdom and Animal Kingdom attractions are straightforward and easily understood by visitors with limited English. Many attractions at Epcot and Disney-MGM Studios, however, depend heavily on narration. A Scandinavian visitor urges us:

> You should write something about how interesting the attractions are to people who don't have English as their mother tongue. We are Norwegians, we all know English fairly well, but we still had problems understanding significant parts of some attractions because the Disney people talk too fast. That goes especially for Body Wars, which we all thought was boring, but also for the Jungle Cruise and the Backstage Tour.

European guests frequently contrast the Magic Kingdom with Disneyland Paris. This comment from an English gentleman is typical:

> The Magic Kingdom was a great disappointment. We all felt it was too crowded, whatever the time of day. For European visitors, we recommend they visit Disneyland Paris instead of the Magic Kingdom. It is much prettier and far better laid out. Their rides are also better.

The size of the portions in restaurants at Walt Disney World astounds many visitors from abroad, including this man from Surrey, England:

Please warn your readers who are not American about the very big helpings at all of the restaurants. We usually found that a starter alone or a main course shared between two was sufficient (even though at home we consider ourselves big eaters). We rarely made it to the dessert menu.

Incidentally, many Walt Disney World restaurants have menus available in French, German, Japanese, and Spanish.

Foreign language assistance is available throughout the World. Call (407) 824-4321 or stop by Guest Relations in the parks. There are also park maps available in German, Spanish, Japanese, Portuguese, and French.

The parks' unabashedly patriotic atmosphere is expressed in flag raisings, attractions that chronicle U.S. history, and entire themed areas inspired by events in America's past (Frontierland and Liberty Square in the Magic Kingdom, for example). While most patriotic fanfare is festive and enjoyable to anyone, *The Hall of Presidents* in the Magic Kingdom and *The American Adventure* at Epcot may be an overdose for some foreign visitors.

Foreign currency of most countries can be exchanged for dollars at the Guest Relations windows of the Ticket and Transportation Center and at the Guest Relations window in the ticketing areas of the theme parks. The amount these locations can exchange is limited. For large transactions, use the American Express office just outside the main entrance to Epcot. Also, Goodings Supermarket on FL 535 (phone (407) 827-1200) operates a foreign currency exchange booth from 7:30 a.m. to 11 p.m.

Part Seven

Arriving and Getting Around

Getting There

Directions

Motorists can reach any Walt Disney World destination via World Drive off US 192, or via Epcot Drive off I-4 (see map, pages 312–313).

Warning! I-4, connecting Daytona and Tampa, generally runs east to west but takes a north/south slant through the Orlando/Kissimmee area. This directional change complicates getting oriented in and around Disney World. Logic suggests that highways branching off I-4 should run north and south, but most run east/west here. Until you're somewhat familiar with the area, have a good map at your side.

From I-10 Take I-10 east across Florida to I-75 southbound. Exit I-75 onto the Florida Turnpike. Exit onto I-4 westbound. Take Exit 67, marked Epcot/Downtown Disney, and follow the signs to your Disney destination.

From I-75 Southbound Follow I-75 south to the Florida Turnpike. Exit onto I-4 westbound. Take Exit 67, marked Epcot/Downtown Disney, and follow the signs to your Disney destination.

From I-95 Southbound Follow I-95 south to I-4. Go west on I-4, passing through Orlando. Take Exit 67, marked Epcot/Downtown Disney, and follow the signs to your Disney destination.

From Daytona or Orlando Go west on I-4 through Orlando. Take Exit 67, marked Epcot/Downtown Disney, and follow the signs.

From the Orlando International Airport Leaving the airport, go southwest on the Central Florida Greenway (FL 417), a toll road. Take Exit 6 onto FL 536. FL 536 will cross over I-4 and become Epcot Drive. From here, follow the signs to your destination. An alternate route is to take FL 528 (Beeline Highway toll road) west for approximately 12 miles to the intersection with I-4. Go west on I-4 to Exit 67, marked Epcot/Downtown Disney, and follow the signs.

From Miami, Fort Lauderdale, and Southeastern Florida   Head north on the Florida Turnpike to I-4 westbound. Take Exit 67, marked as Epcot/Downtown Disney, and follow the signs.

From Tampa and Southwestern Florida   Take I-75 northbound to I-4. Go east on I-4, take Exit 64 onto US 192 westbound, and then follow the signs.

Walt Disney World Exits Off I-4

Going east to west (in the direction of Orlando to Tampa), three I-4 exits serve Walt Disney World. Note that exit numbers changed in 2002.

Exit 68 (old Exit 27) (marked FL 535/Lake Buena Vista) primarily serves the Disney Village Hotel Plaza and Downtown Disney, including the Disney Village Marketplace, Pleasure Island, and Disney's West Side. This exit puts you on roads with lots of traffic signals. Avoid it unless you're headed to one of the above destinations.

Exit 67 (old Exit 26) (marked Epcot/Downtown Disney) delivers you to a four-lane expressway right into the heart of Disney World. It's the fastest and most convenient way for westbound travelers to access almost all Disney World destinations except the new Animal Kingdom and Disney's Wide World of Sports.

Exit 64 (old Exit 25) (marked US 192/Magic Kingdom) is the best route for eastbound travelers to all Disney World destinations. For westbound travelers, it's the best exit for accessing the Animal Kingdom and Disney's Wide World of Sports.

Getting to Walt Disney World from the Airport

If you arrive in Orlando by plane, there are three basic options for getting to Walt Disney World:

1. Taxi   Taxis carry four to eight passengers (depending on the type of vehicle). Rates vary according to distance. If your hotel is in Walt Disney World, your fare will be about $35, not including tip. For the US 192 "Main Gate" area, your fare will be about $45. If you go to International Drive or downtown Orlando, expect to pay about $35.

2. Shuttle Service   Mears Motor Transportation Service (phone (407) 423-5566), operate from Orlando International Airport. Although this is the shuttle services that will provide your transportation if "airport transfers" are included in your vacation package, you do not have to be on a package to avail yourself of their services. In practice, both companies collect passengers until they fill a van, or sometimes in the case of Mears, a bus. Once the vehicle is full or close to full, it's dispatched. Mears charges the same *per-person* rates (children under age four ride free). Both one-way and round-trip service are available.

From the Airport to:	One-Way	Round Trip
International Drive	$16	$28
Downtown Orlando	$16	$28
Walt Disney World/Lake Buena Vista	$16	$28
US 192 "Main Gate" Area	$16	$28

You might have to sit a spell at the airport waiting for a vehicle to fill to capacity and be dispatched. Once underway, your shuttle will probably make several stops to disembark other passengers before it reaches your hotel. We get a lot of reader mail discussing the shuttle services, and it would be fair to say that nobody accuses them of being overly expeditious. Transtar has an edge over Mears because they do not use any buses (but, on the other hand, Transtar doesn't run as often). Obviously, it takes less time to collect enough passengers to fill a van compared to a bus, as well as less time to deliver and unload those passengers at their destination hotels.

Readers debate the relative merits of Transtar and Mears. This dad from Fairfax, Virginia, prefers Mears because of the frequency of their service, writing:

DO NOT recommend Transtar Shuttle like you do in the book. They do not run as often, and we ended up at the airport way too early. Mears runs every hour from the resorts; Transtar every two hours!

Though Mears has more capacity than Transtar, it nevertheless gets maxed out periodically as this Philadelpha reader reports:

Oh yeah—speaking of busses—Mears should pay us to ride them! The confusion at the airport was atrocious! I'm kind of aggressive, so I got my husband and myself on the third bus that left, leaving 100 or more angry travelers behind. [Later] to get to Universal two times and SeaWorld once, we had to pay $12 a day. The bus was invariably late picking us up at either end and made us generally miserable.

For the record, we've used both services. Neither service scores particularly well in regard to managing a large number of people arriving at once. Given that their modest-sized waiting and loading areas constrain operations, they do about as well as you can expect.

On the return trip from your hotel to the airport, you're most likely be transported in a van irrespective of which company you use (r you are part of a large tour group, in which case Mears might send In our experience, because the shuttle services pick folks up at hotels, they ask you to be ready for pick-up much earlier than ordinarily depart if you were taking a cab or returning a ren

3. Town Car Service Similar to taxi service, a town car service will transport you directly from Orlando International Airport to your hotel. Instead of hailing a car outside the airport, however, the town car driver will usually be waiting for you in the baggage claim area of your airline.

Each of the town car services we surveyed offers large, well-appointed late-model sedans, such as the Lincoln Town Car ES series. These cars hold four adults or two adults and three children comfortably. Car seats for small children are available, but you'll have to call ahead to reserve one. Golfers will appreciate the generous luggage space in these cars. We're sure it's just coincidence that every driver we interviewed quantified his car's trunk capacity using dead bodies as the unit of measure.

Tiffany Towncar Service (phone (888) 838-2161 or (407) 251-5431 or check **www.tiffanytowncar.com**) provides a prompt, clean ride. They also received the best reviews from Disney bellhops. A round-trip to a Disney resort will cost $85, while the round-trip fee to a non-Disney resort is $80, not including tip. Figure on about half as much for a one-way trip. What Tiffany offers that other taxi and town car services do not is a free stop at a local Publix supermarket on the way to your hotel. You can save considerable time and money if you stock up on breakfast and snack items here rather than purchase them in the parks. Also, be sure to check Tiffany's website for a coupon worth $5 off a round-trip.

Mears and Transtar also offer town car services. Transtar (phone (800) 543-6681) charges $61 for one-way or $122 for a round-trip for up to three people. Mears town car rates vary based on the number of passengers. For comparison, however, they quoted a price of $61 one-way for three passengers to a Disney resort, or $122 round-trip (i.e. the same as Transtar). Mears can be reached at (407) 423-5566.

4. Rental Cars Rental cars are readily available for both short- and long-term rentals. Most rental car companies allow you to drop a rental car at certain hotels or one of their subsidiary locations in the Walt Disney World general area if you do not want the car for your entire stay. Likewise, you can pick up a car at any time during your stay at the same hotels and locations without trekking back to the airport.

Dollars and Sense Which option is the best deal depends on the number of people in your party and the value you attach to your time. If you're traveling solo or only have two in your party, and you're pretty sure you won't need a rental car, the shuttle service is your least expensive bet. A cab for two people makes sense if you want to get there faster than the shuttle service can arrange. The cab will cost about $36 including tip. Splitting the fare equally, this is $18 for each of you. The same shuttle service will cost $14 each, a savings of $4. It's up to you to decide whether the timeliness and convenience of the cab is worth the extra four bucks. A one-day car rental will cost you anywhere from $34–$70 once all taxes and extras are figured in, plus you'll have to go to the trouble of completing the paperwork, retrieving the vehicle, and presumably filling the tank before you turn it in. If there are more than two of you, a cab becomes a more economical option than the shuttle. Likewise with the rental car, though the cab will still get you there faster. If saving time and hassle is worth the extra bucks, go for a town car.

Renting a Car

Readers planning to stay in the World frequently ask if they will need a car. If your plans don't include restaurants, attractions, or other destinations outside of Disney World, the answer is a very qualified no. You won't require a car, but, after considering the thoughts of this reader from Snohomish, Washington, you might want one:

We rented a car and were glad we did. It gave us more options, though we used the [Disney] bus transportation quite extensively. With a car we could drive to the grocery store to restock our snack supply. It also came in handy for our night out. I shudder at how long it might have taken us to get from the Caribbean Beach to the Polynesian to leave our kids [at the childcare facility], then to Pleasure Island, then back to the Polynesian [to get the kids], and then back to the Caribbean Beach. At $8 an hour [for childcare] you don't want to waste time! It was also nice to drive to Typhoon Lagoon with a car full of clothes, lunches, and other paraphernalia. It was also easier to drive to the other hotels for special meals. And, of course, if you plan to travel out of the World during your stay, a car is a must.

Being openminded regarding renting a car is no longer a problem for this reader:

I read what you said about using our own transportation between the parks but I did not believe you. Duh! That won't happen again. I may be a bit hard-headed, but I am still quite educable. I had not been to "The World" since the early 1980s and did not remember having any problem getting around on the Disney Transportation System. I will never forget all of the waiting we did this trip. There is nothing more frustrating than to get in sight of your bus stop and see your bus driving off because you know it is going to be near twenty minutes before the next one pulls up

A dad from Avon Lake, Ohio, adds:

It was unbelievable how often we used our rental car. Although we stayed at the Grand Floridian, we found the monorail convenient only for the Magic Kingdom. Of the six nights we stayed, we used our car five days.

A family from Lynn Haven, Florida, had this to say:

The transportation system (buses specifically) was a mess. Nothing like the efficient system they had when we visited four years ago. What has happened? It took us an hour and 45 minutes to get from the BoardWalk to Fort Wilderness by bus. Bus transportation was very bad the whole time. Boat transportation was just fine.

A family from Portland, Maine, experienced problems with non-Disney transportation:

We stayed outside WDW and tried to commute on the bus furnished by our hotel. After two days, we gave up and rented a car.

Plan to Rent A Car:

1. If your hotel is outside Walt Disney World.
2. If your hotel is in Walt Disney World and you want to dine someplace other than the theme parks and your own hotel.
3. If you plan to return to your hotel for naps or swimming during the day.
4. If you plan on going to other area theme parks or swimming parks (including Disney's).

Renting a Car at Orlando International Airport

The airport has two terminals—A and B. Each airline serving Orlando is assigned to one of the two. Each terminal has three levels and an adjacent parking garage. Level Three is where you'll find the airline ticket counters. On Level Two you'll find the baggage claim, and Level One is where the car rental counters are located, or, if your rental company is located off-site, where you'll catch a courtesy vehicle to its headquarters.

Orlando is the largest rental car market in the world. At last count, there were 22 rental car companies competing for your business. Five companies—Avis, Budget, Dollar, L&M, and National—have rental counters on Level One of both terminals. Alamo, Enterprise, Hertz, Thrifty, and 13 other companies have locations near the airport and provide courtesy shuttles that pick you up outside both terminals on Level One. Most shuttles run continuously, so you don't have to call to arrange a pick-up. We prefer using one of the five companies located in the airport because (1) you can complete your paperwork while you wait for your checked luggage to arrive at baggage claim and (2) it's a short walk to the adjacent garage to pick up your car (i.e., you don't have to catch a courtesy shuttle).

If you rent from one of the on-site companies, you'll return your car to the garage adjacent to whichever terminal your airline is assigned. If you accidentally return your car to the wrong garage, you'll have to haul all your luggage on foot from one side of the airport to the other in order to reach your airline's terminal for check-in.

Finally, either pre-pay for a tank of gas (so you can return the car empty) or alternatively fill up in the area of your hotel. There are no convenient gas stations near the airport, and most rental car companies will charge you about $4 per gallon if they fill the tank.

How the Orlando Rental-Car Companies Stack Up

Unofficial Guide readers provide us with a lot of information about the quality of the car and service they receive from Orlando car-rental companies. In general, most folks are looking for:

1. Quick, courteous, and efficient processing on pick-up.

2. A nice, well-maintained, late-model automobile.

3. A car that is clean and odor-free.

4. Quick, courteous, and efficient processing on return.

5. If applicable, an efficient shuttle service between the rental agency and the airport.

Most of our readers rent cars from Alamo, Avis, Budget, Dollar, Hertz, or National. On a scale of 0 (worst) to 100 (best), the following table shows how they rate the Orlando operations of each company, based on the five items listed above.

If you would like to participate in our rental car survey, send us your completed *Unofficial Guide* Reader Survey form from the back of this book.

Company	Pick-Up Efficiency	Condition of the Car	Cleanliness of the Car	Return Efficiency	Shuttle Efficiency
Alamo	69	85	85	84	83
Avis	87	93	95	94	na
Budget	74	90	90	94	na
Dollar	87	89	90	90	na
Enterprise	77	93	93	92	95
Hertz	78	88	91	90	88
National	83	90	93	93	na

If you rent a car, a 6–7% sales tax, a $2.35-per-day state surcharge, and a 40-cents-per-day vehicle license recovery fee will be heaped onto your rental fee. If you rent from an agency with airport facilities or shuttles, an additional 10% airport tax will be charged.

Remember that you can wait and rent a car at your hotel on the day you actually need it.

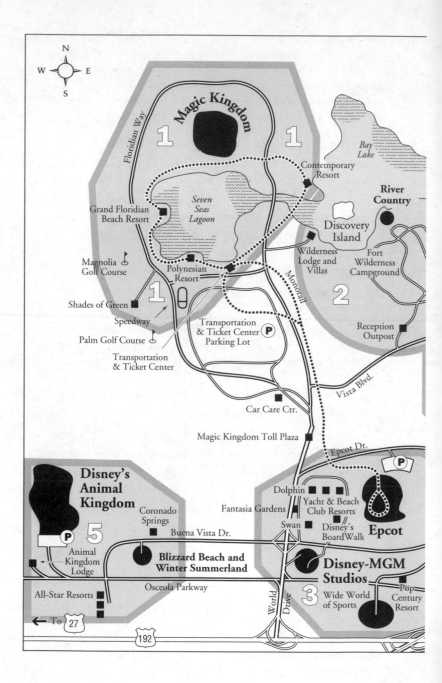

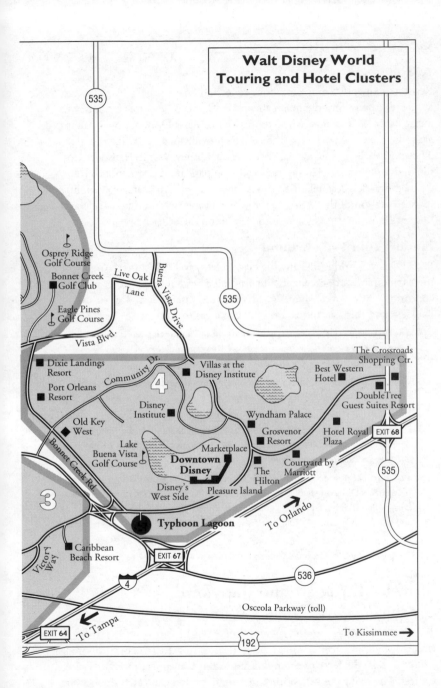

Walt Disney World Touring and Hotel Clusters

535

535

Osprey Ridge
Golf Course

Bonnet Creek
Golf Club

Live Oak
Lane

Buena Vista Drive

Eagle Pines
Golf Course

535

Vista Blvd.

The Crossroads
Shopping Ctr.

Dixie Landings
Resort

Community Dr.

Villas at the
Disney Institute

Best Western
Hotel

Port Orleans
Resort

4

DoubleTree
Guest Suites Resort

Disney
Institute

Wyndham Palace

Old Key
West

Grosvenor
Resort

Hotel Royal
Plaza

EXIT 68

Lake
Buena Vista
Golf Course

Marketplace

**Downtown
Disney**

The
Hilton

Courtyard by
Marriott

535

Bonnet Creek Rd.

Disney's
West Side

Pleasure Island

To Orlando

3

Typhoon Lagoon

Victory Way

Caribbean
Beach Resort

EXIT 67

4

536

Osceola Parkway (toll)

EXIT 64

To Tampa

To Kissimmee →

192

Getting Oriented

A Good Map

Readers frequently complain about signs and maps provided by Disney. While it's easy to find the major theme parks, it can be quite an odyssey to locate other Walt Disney World destinations. Many Disney-supplied maps are stylized and hard to read, while others provide incomplete information. The most easily obtained map is the Walt Disney World Transportation Guide/Map. Available at any resort, theme-park bus information station, or theme-park guest relations office, the Guide/Map features a slightly reduced version of the Walt Disney World Property Map on one side and Disney Transportation System information on the other.

Finding Your Way Around

Walt Disney World is like any big city. It's easy to get lost there. Signs for the theme parks are excellent, but finding a restaurant or hotel is often confusing, even for Disney World veterans. The easiest way to orient yourself is to think in terms of five major areas, or clusters:

1. The first major cluster encompasses all the hotels and theme parks around the Seven Seas Lagoon. This includes the Magic Kingdom, hotels connected by the monorail, the Shades of Green resort, and two golf courses.

2. The second cluster includes developments on and around Bay Lake: Wilderness Lodge and Villas, Fort Wilderness Campground, River Country, and two golf courses.

3. Cluster three contains Epcot, Disney-MGM Studios, Disney's BoardWalk, Disney's Wide World of Sports, the Epcot resort hotels, the Pop Century Resorts, and the Caribbean Beach Resort.

4. The fourth cluster encompasses Walt Disney World Village; the Disney Institute; Downtown Disney (including the Disney Village Marketplace, Pleasure Island, and Disney's West Side); Typhoon Lagoon; a golf course; Disney Village Hotel Plaza; and the Port Orleans and Old Key West Resorts.

5. The fifth and newest cluster contains the Animal Kingdom, Blizzard Beach, and the Disney All-Star, Coronado Springs, and Animal Kingdom Lodge Resorts.

How to Travel around the World (or the *Real* Mr. Toad's Wild Ride)

Trying to commute around Walt Disney World can be frustrating. A Magic Kingdom street vendor, telling me how to get to Epcot, proposed, "You can take the ferry or the monorail to the Transportation and Ticket Center. Then you can get another monorail, or you can catch the bus, or you can take a tram out to your car and drive over there yourself." What he didn't say was that it would be easier to ride a mule than to take any conceivable combination from this transportation smorgasbord.

There's no simple way to travel around the World, but there are ways to make it easier. Just don't wait to get moving until ten minutes before you're due somewhere.

Transportation Trade-Offs for Guests: Lodging outside Walt Disney World

Disney day-guests (those not staying inside Disney World) can use the monorail system, the bus system, and the boat system. If, for example, you go to Disney-MGM Studios in the morning, then decide to go to Epcot for lunch, you can take a bus directly there. The most important advice we can give day-guests is to park your car in the lot of the theme park (or other Disney destination) where you plan to finish your day. This is critical if you stay at a park until closing time.

Moving Your Car from Lot to Lot on the Same Day

Once you have paid to park in any major theme-park lot, hang on to your receipt. If you visit another park later in the same day, you'll be admitted to that park's lot without additional charge when you show your receipt. Disney lodging guests park free in any theme-park lot.

If you move your car from park to park or arrive at a theme park after noon, there will be a number of open parking spaces up close. Instead of following Disney signage or being directed to a far-flung space by a cast member, head for the front and hunt for a space like you would at the mall.

All You Need to Know about Driving to the Theme Parks

1. Positioning of the Parking Lots   The Animal Kingdom, Disney-MGM Studios, and Epcot parking lots are adjacent to the park entrance. The Magic Kingdom parking lot is adjacent to the Transportation and Ticket center (TTC). From the TTC you can take a ferry or monorail to the Magic Kingdom entrance.

2. Paying to Park   Disney resort guests and annual passholders park free. All others pay. If you pay to park, keep your receipt. If you move your car during the day to another theme park you will not have to pay again if you show your receipt.

3. Finding Your Car when It's Time to Depart   The theme park parking lots are huge. Jot down the section and row where you park. If you are driving a rental car, jot down the license number (you wouldn't believe how many white rental cars there are).

4. Getting from Your Car to the Park Entrance   Each parking lot provides trams to transport you to the park entrance, or in the case of the Magic Kingdom, to the TTC. If you arrive early in the morning, you may find that it is faster to walk to the entrance (or to the TTC) than to take the tram.

5. A Tip for Parking at the Disney-MGM Studios   The Disney-MGM Studios has two parking entrances, one off World Drive and one off Buena Vista Drive. If you want to park within walking distance of the park entrance, access the Studios from World Drive (cars from the Buena Vista entrance are parked in the boonies no matter how early they arrive).

6. How Much Time to Allot for Parking and Getting to the Park Entrance   At Epcot and the Animal Kingdom, it will take about 15–20 minutes to pay, park, and walk or ride to the park entrance. At the Disney-MGM Studios, allow 10–15 minutes; at the Magic Kingdom, it's 15 minutes to get to the TTC and another 15–20 to reach the park entrance via the monorail (3 ½ minutes one way) or the ferry (6½ minutes one way).

7. Commuting from Park to Park   You can commute to the other theme parks via Disney bus, or to and from the Magic Kingdom and Epcot by monorail. You can also, of course, commute via your own car. Using Disney transportation or your own car, allow 45–60 minutes entrance to entrance one way. If you plan to park hop, make sure your car is parked in the lot of the theme park where you plan to finish the day.

8. Leaving the Park at the End of the Day   If you stay at a park until closing expect the parking lot trams, the monorails, and the ferries to be mobbed. If the wait for the parking lot tram is unacceptable, you can either walk to your car, or walk to the first tram stop on the route and wait there until a tram arrives. When some people get off, you can get on and continue to your appropriate stop.

9. Dinner and a Quick Exit   One way to beat closing crowds at the Magic Kingdom is to arrange a priority seating for dinner at one of the restaurants at the Contemporary Resort. When you leave the Magic kingdom to go to dinner, move your car from the TTC lot to the Contemporary Resort. After dinner, either walk (eight minutes) or take the monorail back to the Magic Kingdom. When the park closes and everyone else is fighting their way onto the monorail or ferry, you can stroll leisurely back to the Contemporary, pick up your car, and be on your way. You can pull the same trick at Epcot by arranging a priority seating at one of the Epcot resorts. After *IllumiNations* when the park closes, simply exit the park by the International Gateway and walk back to the resort where your car is parked.

10. Car Trouble   All the parking lots have security patrols that circulate through the lots. If you have a dead battery or some other automotive problem, the security patrols will help get you going.

11. Scoring a Great Parking Place   Anytime you arrive at a park after noon, there will some empty spots right up front vacated by early arriving guests who have already departed. Here's an approach that a Coopersburg, Pennsylvania couple used to get one of those spots (in this case their own):

After leaving Epcot on our first day for a lunch break, we returned to find a fullish parking lot. We were unhappy because we had left a third-row parking spot. My husband told the attendant that we had left just an hour ago and that there were lots of spaces up front. Without a word of protest he waved us to the front and we got the same spot we had left!

Taking a Shuttle Bus from Your Out-of-the-World Hotel

Many independent hotels and motels near Walt Disney World provide trams and buses. They're fairly carefree, depositing you near theme-park entrances and saving you parking fees. The rub is that they might not get you there as early as you desire (a critical point if you take our touring advice) or be available when you wish to return to your lodging. Also, some shuttles go directly to Disney World, while others stop at additional area lodgings. Each service is a bit different; check the particulars before you make reservations.

Warning: Most hotel shuttles don't add vehicles at park opening or closing times. In the mornings, you may not get a seat. At closing or during a hard rain, expect a mass exodus from the park. More people will be waiting for the shuttle than the bus will hold, and some will be left behind. Most (not all) shuttles return for stranded guests, but the guests may wait 20 minutes to over an hour for a ride.

If you're depending on shuttles, leave the park at least 45 minutes before closing. If you stay until closing and lack the energy to hassle with the shuttle, take a cab. Cabstands are near the Bus Information buildings at the Animal Kingdom, Epcot, Disney-MGM Studios, and the Transportation and Ticket Center. If no cabs are on-hand, staff at Bus Information will call one for you. If you're leaving the Magic Kingdom at closing, it's easier to take the monorail to a hotel and catch a cab there (rather than the TTC taxi stand).

The Disney Transportation System

The Disney Transportation System is large, diversified, and generally efficient, but it sometimes is overwhelmed during peak periods, particularly at park opening and closing times. If you could be assured of getting on a bus, boat, or monorail at these critical times, we would advise you to leave your car at home. However, the reality is that when huge crowds want to go somewhere at the same time, delays are unavoidable. In addition, some destinations are served directly, while many others require one or more transfers. Finally, it's sometimes difficult to figure how the buses, boats, and monorails interconnect.

In the most basic terms, the Disney Transportation System is a "hub and spoke" system. Hubs include the Transportation and Ticket Center, Downtown Disney, and all four major theme parks (from two hours before official opening time to two to three hours after closing). Although there are some exceptions, there is direct service from Disney resorts to the major theme parks and to Downtown Disney, and from park to park. If you want to go from resort to resort or most anywhere else, you will have to transfer at one of the hubs.

If a hotel offers boat or monorail service, its bus service will be limited, meaning you'll have to transfer at a hub for many Disney World destinations. If you're staying at a Magic Kingdom resort served by monorail (Polynesian, Contemporary, Grand Floridian), you'll be able to commute efficiently to the Magic Kingdom via monorail. If you want to visit Epcot, you must take the monorail to the TTC and transfer to the Epcot monorail. (Guests at the Polynesian can eliminate the transfer by walking five to ten minutes to the TTC and catching the direct monorail to Epcot.)

If you're staying at an Epcot resort (Swan, Dolphin, Yacht and Beach Club Resorts, BoardWalk Inn and Villas) you can walk or commute via boat to the International Gateway (back door) entrance of Epcot. Although direct buses link Epcot resorts to the Magic Kingdom and the Animal Kingdom, there's no direct bus to Epcot's main entrance or to Disney-MGM Studios. To reach the Studios from Epcot resorts, you must take a boat.

The Caribbean Beach, Pop Century, Port Orleans, Coronado Springs, Old Key West, Animal Kingdom Lodge, and All-Star Resorts offer direct buses to all the theme parks. The rub is that guests sometimes must walk a long way to bus stops or endure more than a half-dozen additional pick-ups before actually heading for the park(s). Commuting in the morning from these resorts is generally no sweat, though you may have to ride standing up. Returning in the evening, however, can be a different story. Shades of Green runs continuous shuttles from the resort to the TTC, where guests can transfer to their final destination.

The hotels of the Disney Village Hotel Plaza terminated their guest-transportation contract with Disney Transportation Operations, so they provide service with another carrier. The substitute, which we feel doesn't measure up, constitutes a real problem for guests at these hotels. Before booking a hotel in the Plaza, check the nature and frequency of shuttles. Fort Wilderness guests must use the campground's own buses to reach boat landings or the Pioneer Hall bus stop. From these points, respectively, guests can travel directly by boat to the Magic Kingdom or by bus to Disney-MGM Studios, or to other destinations via transfer at the TTC. With the exception of commuting to the Magic Kingdom, the best way for Fort Wilderness guests to commute in Disney World is to drive their own car.

The Walt Disney World Transportation System vs. Driving Your Own Car

To enable you to assess your transportation options, we have developed a chart comparing the approximate commuting times from Disney resorts to various Walt Disney World destinations, using Disney transportation or your own car.

Disney Transportation   Times on the chart in the Disney Transportation System (DTS) columns represent a best case/worst case range. For example, if you want to go from the Caribbean Beach Resort to Epcot, the chart indicates a range of 12–45 minutes. The first number (12) is how long your commute will take if everything goes perfectly (your bus is at the stop when you walk up, departs for your destination as soon as you board, and isn't delayed by traffic jams or other problems en route). If you're staying at a resort where the bus makes numerous stops within the complex, the first number assumes that you board at the last embarkation point before the bus heads for its final destination. The second number (45) represents a worst-case scenario. (The bus is pulling away as you arrive at the stop, and you must wait 20 minutes for the next one. When you finally board, the bus makes six more stops in the Caribbean complex before heading for Epcot. Once en route, the bus hits every red light.)

On busier days, buses run every 20 minutes all day. On slower days, some buses (at Old Key West, among others) run only once every 45 minutes between noon and 6 p.m. Our worst-case scenario assumes that buses run every 20 minutes. If they're running only every 45 minutes, you must add the difference (25 minutes) to the second number to calculate the worst-case commute. If buses run from the Caribbean Beach complex to Epcot every 45 minutes, for example, it could take as long as 1 hour and 10 minutes (45 minutes + 25 minutes) to complete the commute. Be sure to ask at your hotel how frequently buses will run during your stay. If your bus makes intermediate stops after leaving your resort, the time spent making the stops is figured into both the best and worst times, because the stops are unavoidable in either case.

DOOR-TO-DOOR COMMUTING TIMES
In Your Car versus the Disney Transportation System†

Time (in minutes) From	To Magic Kingdom		To Epcot		To MGM Studios	
	Your Car	Disney System	Your Car	Disney System	Your Car	Disney System
All-Star Resorts	26–47	11–31	13–23	8–28	11–20	7–27
Animal Kingdom	25–48	30–61	14–17	16–36	14–17	10–34
Animal Kingdom Lodge	27–50	25–49	16–19	18–38	16–19	12–36
Beach Club	25–46	14–34	11–21	5–28*	9–18	16–36
Blizzard Beach	25–46	17–37	13–23	29–62	13–22	30–50
BoardWalk Inn and Villas	25–46	11–31	11–21	5–28*	9–18	16–36
Caribbean Beach	26–47	13–40	13–23	12–45	10–19	6–33
Contemporary	NA	12–23	16–26	13–29	18–27	22–42
Coronado Springs	26–47	11–31	13–23	8–28	11–20	7–27
Disney-MGM Studios	25–46	14–34	14–24	10–34		
Disney Institute	27–48	15–45	13–23	10–37	15–24	8–35
Dixie Landings	27–48	11–36	15–25	9–33	15–24	9–34
Dolphin	24–45	18–38	10–20	10–35*	10–19	12–32
Downtown Disney	27–49	24–58	14–25	21–57	12–22	30–69
Epcot	25–46	16–35			14–23	8–30
Fort Wilderness	26–47	13–33	13–23	14–60	14–23	17–50
Grand Floridian	NA	4–7	13–23	20–42	15–24	9–29
Magic Kingdom			12–39	13–42	13–29	14–34
Old Key West	25–46	12–40	13–23	7–35	13–22	9–36
Polynesian	NA	7–13	12–22	23–48	14–23	12–32
Pop Century Resorts	29–51	18–50	18–28	19–51	15–24	14–40
Port Orleans	26–47	19–39	14–24	15–35	14–23	17–37
Shades of Green	20–36	22–45	13–23	20–42	15–24	10–29
Swan	24–45	21–41	10–20	10–35*	10–19	12–32
Typhoon Lagoon	26–47	18–51	13–23	29–62	10–19	38–75
Village Hotel Plaza	30–51	20–74	16–26	12–50	15–24	9–49
Wilderness Lodge	NA	11–41	15–25	12–42	17–26	18–48
Yacht Club	25–46	11–31	11–21	5–28*	9–18	16–36

† Driving time vs. time on DTS. Driving times include time in your car, stops to pay tolls, time to park, and transfers to Disney trams and monorails where applicable.

TO AND FROM THE DISNEY RESORTS AND PARKS

To Animal Kingdom		To Typhoon Lagoon		To Downtown Disney		To Blizzard Beach	
Your Car	Disney System	Your Car	Disney System	Your Car	Disney System	Your Car	Disney System
9–12	8–25	10–13	9–29	11–14	15–40	4–7	17–38
		15–19	43–57	17–21	33–53	7–13	7–30
7–10	6–23	17–21	45–59	20–24	35–55	8–14	15–40
15–18	14–33	7–10	22–42	8–11	13–35	10–13	21–41
7–13	8–40	11–14	33–76	12–15	44–77		
15–18	12–30	7–10	24–44	8–11	15–37	10–13	21–41
15–18	15–46	4–7	7–39	5–8	9–43	10–13	23–54
18–21	28–48	15–18	17–40	15–17	28–51	13–16	36–56
9–12	8–31	10–13	9–29	11–14	15–40	4–7	17–37
14–17	10–34	6–9	30–73	7–10	41–74	9–12	30–50
19–22	23–45	7–10	13–37	4–7	5–30	14–17	21–48
18–21	14–43	8–11	9–35	9–12	15–40	13–16	22–49
14–17	20–35	8–11	27–47	9–12	18–40	9–12	8–31
17–21	33–53	4–7	5–28			12–16	30–50
14–17	26–48	10–13	22–43	11–14	30–54	9–12	23–45
22–25	23–56	8–11	18–51	9–12	27–60	17–20	31–56
16–19	16–36	13–16	24–53	14–17	37–64	11–14	24–44
15–18	30–61	15–31	17–53	17–36	30–64	10–13	22–55
17–20	18–43	6–9	9–35	7–10	9–36	12–15	23–49
15–18	18–38	12–15	27–59	13–16	40–70	10–13	27–46
12–16	18–38	9–14	26–50	13–16	18–40	8–12	20–51
17–20	25–43	7–10	16–36	8–11	24–44	12–15	37–57
16–19	16–36	13–16	24–53	15–20	37–64	11–14	24–44
14–17	23–38	8–11	30–50	9–12	20–42	9–12	10–32
15–19	43–57			4–7	5–28	11–14	40–57
19–22	30–53	7–10	5–7	4–7	NA	14–17	30–50
18–21	23–51	15–18	23–46	16–19	27–67	13–16	31–54
15–18	16–36	7–10	24–44	8–11	15–37	10–13	21–41

*This hotel is within walking distance of Epcot Center; time given includes boat ride from International Gateway, if necessary.

Driving Your Own Car The "Your Car" column on the chart indicates the best-case/worst-case situation for driving. To make these times directly comparable to Disney system times, we have added the time it takes to get from your parked car to the park's entrance. While Disney buses and monorails deposit guests at the front door, those who drive must sometimes take a tram from their car to the gate, or walk. At the Magic Kingdom, you must take a tram from the parking lot to the TTC, then catch a monorail or ferry to the park's entrance.

Walt Disney World Transportation System for Teenagers

If you're staying at Walt Disney World and have teens in your party, familiarize yourself with the Disney bus system. Safe, clean, and operating until 1 a.m. on most nights, buses are a great way for teens to get around the World.

Walt Disney World Bus Service

Buses in Disney World have an illuminated panel above the front windshield that flashes the bus's destination. Also, theme parks have designated waiting areas for each Disney World destination. To catch the bus to the Caribbean Beach Resort from Disney-MGM Studios, for example, go to the bus stop and wait in the area marked "To the Caribbean Beach Resort." At the resorts, go to any bus stop and wait for the bus with your destination displayed on the illuminated panel. Directions to Disney World destinations are available when you check in or at your hotel's guest relations desk. The clerk at guest relations can also answer your questions about the Disney Transportation System.

Service from the resorts to the major theme parks is fairly direct. You may have to endure intermediate stops, but you won't have to transfer. More problematic, and sometimes requiring transfers, is service to the swimming theme parks and other Disney World hotels.

The fastest way to commute from resort to resort by bus is to take a bus from your resort to one of the major theme parks and from there transfer to your resort destination. This only works, of course, when the major theme parks are open (actually from two hours before opening until two to three hours after closing). If you are attempting to commute to another resort for a late dinner during the off-season when the major parks close early, you will have to transfer at Downtown Disney or at the Transportation and Ticket Center.

Buses begin service to the theme parks at about 7 a.m. on days when the parks' official opening time is 9 a.m. Generally, buses run every 20 minutes. Buses to Disney-MGM Studios, Epcot, or the Animal Kingdom deliver you to the park entrance. Until one hour before the park opens (before 8 a.m. in this example), buses to the Magic Kingdom deliver you to the TTC, where you transfer to the monorail or ferry to complete your commute. Buses take you directly to the Magic Kingdom starting one hour before the park's stated opening.

To be on-hand for the real opening time (when official opening is 9 a.m.), catch direct buses to Epcot, the Animal Kingdom, and Disney-MGM Studios between 7:30 and 8 a.m. Catch direct buses to the Magic Kingdom between 8 and 8:15 a.m. If you must transfer to reach your park, leave 15–20 minutes earlier. On days when official opening is 7 or 8 a.m., move up your departure time accordingly.

For your return bus trip in the evening, leave the park 40 minutes to an hour before closing to avoid the rush. If you're caught in the mass exodus, you may be inconvenienced, but you won't be stranded. Buses, boats, and monorails continue to operate for two hours after the parks close.

Not All Hubs Are Created Equal

As mentioned earlier, all major theme parks, Downtown Disney, and the Transportation and Ticket Center (TTC) serve as hubs on the Disney bus system. If your route requires you to transfer at a hub, make your transfer at the closest theme park or the TTC, *except at theme-park closing time.* Avoid using Downtown Disney as a transfer point. Because each bus makes multiple stops within the Downtown Disney complex, it takes 16–25 minutes just to get out of Downtown Disney!

Bus Transportation to the Water Parks

Evidently Disney assumes you will spend the entire day at the water park because direct service from and to the resorts is scheduled only in the early morning and late afternoon. At other times during the day, you must transfer at the TTC.

Disney Village Hotel Plaza Bus Service

Although located in Walt Disney World, the hotels of the Disney Village Hotel Plaza provide their own bus service—one that many, including a family from Prospect, Connecticut, find inferior:

> We were disappointed in the shuttle bus for the Village hotels. They do not run often enough, and there is no schedule. [The b]us at the parks picks up in [the] middle of busy parking lots. Treats you as second class [compared] to Disney resort guests. Take a cab instead of waiting late at night to get back to [your] hotel. Costs only $9.

Walt Disney World Monorail Service

Picture the monorail system as three loops. Loop A is an express route that runs counterclockwise connecting the Magic Kingdom with the

Transportation and Ticket Center (TTC). Loop B runs clockwise alongside Loop A, making all stops, with service to (in this order) the TTC, Polynesian Resort, Grand Floridian Beach Resort, Magic Kingdom, Contemporary Resort, and back to the TTC. The long Loop C dips southeast like a tail, connecting the TTC with Epcot. The hub for all three loops is the TTC (where you usually park to visit the Magic Kingdom).

The monorail system serving Magic Kingdom resorts usually starts an hour and a half before official opening on other days. If you're staying at a Magic Kingdom resort and wish to be among the first in the Magic Kingdom when official opening is 9 a.m., board the monorail at the times indicated below.

From the Contemporary Resort	7:45–8 a.m.
From the Polynesian Resort	7:50–8:05 a.m.
From the Grand Floridian Beach Resort	8–8:10 a.m.

What's that? You don't have the circadian rhythms of a farmer? Get with the program, Bubba! This is a *Disney* vacation. Haul your buns out of bed and go have fun!

If you're a day-guest you'll be allowed on the monorail at the TTC between 8:15 and 8:30 a.m. on a day when official opening is 9 a.m. If you want to board earlier, walk from the TTC to the Polynesian Resort and board there.

The monorail loop connecting Epcot and the TTC begins operating at 7:30 a.m. on days when Epcot's official opening is 9 a.m. To be at Epcot when the park opens, catch the Epcot monorail at the TTC by 8:05 a.m.

While your multiday pass suggests you can flit at will among parks, actually getting there is more complex. For example, you can't go directly from the Magic Kingdom to Epcot. You must catch the express monorail (Loop A) to the TTC and transfer to the Loop C monorail to Epcot. If lines to board either monorail are short, you can usually reach Epcot in 30–40 minutes. But should you want to go to Epcot for dinner (as many do) and you're departing the Magic Kingdom in late afternoon, you may have to wait 30 minutes or more to board the Loop A monorail. Adding this delay bumps up your commute to 50–60 minutes.

Monorails usually run for two hours after closing to ensure that everyone is served. If a train is too crowded or you need transportation after the monorails have stopped running, catch a bus.

It's great fun to ride in the front cab of the monorail with the conductor. All you have to do is ask, according to a mom from Richmond, Virginia:

Speaking of the monorail—don't hesitate to ask about sitting up front—even if you aren't the first ones there. People are somewhat timid about asking, and the monorail attendants won't ever suggest it, so ask! We got to ride up front three times during our stay.

Some Canadian friends wrote sharing their strategy for riding up front:

I highly recommend that parents ask the monorail staff if their family can sit up front with the driver. It's a real thrill for the kids and gives even adults a very different perspective. Since you'll find a lot of people making this request at the TTC in the a.m. and Magic Kingdom in the p.m., a good trick is to make the request at the TTC in the p.m. or at the Magic Kingdom in the a.m. (i.e. reverse of where it's busiest) or at a hotel station where there are less people getting on. You may have to wait for a few trains to go by before you get a turn, but it's worth it. The monorail staff was very accommodating. The driver explained things to the kids like they were the first kids he'd ever had up front!

Part Eight

Bare Necessities

Credit Cards and Money

Credit Cards

- MasterCard, VISA, American Express, Discover, Diners Club, JCB, and the Disney Credit Card, as well as traveler's checks, are accepted throughout Walt Disney World.

Financial Matters

Cash Bank service at the theme parks is limited to ATMs. Branches of Sun Bank are across the street from Downtown Disney Marketplace and at 1675 Buena Vista Drive. Both branches will:

- *Provide cash advances* on MasterCard and VISA (no minimum; maximum equals the patron's credit limit).

- *Cash personal checks* of $200 or less drawn on Sun Bank upon presentation of a driver's license and major credit card.

- *Cash and sell traveler's checks.* The bank cashes the first check up to $100 without charge but levies a $2 service fee for each additional check.

- *Facilitate wiring of money* from the visitor's bank to Sun Bank.

- *Exchange foreign currency* for dollars.

Most VISA and MasterCard cards are accepted at ATMs at Walt Disney World. To use an American Express card, however, you must sign an agreement with American Express before your trip. If your credit card doesn't work in the ATMs, a teller will be able to process your transaction at any Sun Bank full-service location.

A License to Print Money

One of Disney's more sublime ploys for separating you from your money is the printing and issuing of Disney Dollars. Available throughout Disney World in denominations of $5 (Goofy Greenbacks), $10 (Minnie Money or Simba Sawbucks), and $20 (Mickey Moolah), the colorful cash can be used for purchases at Walt Disney World, Disneyland, and Disney Stores nationwide. Disney Dollars can also be exchanged one for one with U.S. currency. Disney money is sometimes included as a perk (for which you're charged dollar for dollar) in Walt Disney Travel Company packages.

While the idea of Disney Dollars seems fun and innocent, it's one of Disney's better moneymakers. Some guests take the money home as souvenirs. Others forget to spend or exchange it before they leave the World, then fail to go to a Disney Store or to exchange the money by mail. Usually the funny money ends up forgotten in a drawer—exactly as Disney hoped.

A Michigan family, however, found a way to make their Disney Dollars useful:

Your criticism of Disney Dollars is valid if people are dumb enough not to cash them in or use them in their local Disney store. We used them. Since we had planned on going to Disney a year ahead of time, we asked people giving our children money for birthdays, Christmas, Tooth Fairy, etc., to give Disney Dollars instead. This forced both of our children (ages five and seven) to save the money for the trip instead of spending it beforehand.

The P. T. Barnum Memorial Walkway

Oh my stars and garters, Mildred, you won't believe what they're doing now! For only $110, you can buy a 10-inch hexagonal brick with your name on it. If you want to go all out, you can purchase a granite brick for $225. Of course, you aren't allowed to take your brick home. Disney is going to use it to build a walkway around a big lake down at Walt Disney World. (They need that walkway really bad in case the monorails and the ferry boats all break down at the same time.) Here's the really good news: it will cost us and our friends who buy bricks only about $9.6 million to build the whole dadgum thing, and we can visit our brick anytime we want . . . if we can find it. Maybe when they get our little sidewalk finished, they'll build another one from Walt Disney World out to Disneyland in California. Those interstate highways are about worn out, you know.

Problems and Unusual Situations

Attractions Closed for Repairs

Check in advance with Disney World to see what rides and attractions may be closed for maintenance or repair during your visit. If you're interested in a specific attraction, the call could save you a lot of disappointment. A mother from Dover, Massachusetts, laments:

We were disappointed to find Space Mountain, Swiss Family Treehouse, and the Liberty Belle Riverboat closed for repairs. We felt that a large chunk of the Magic Kingdom was not working, yet the tickets were still full price and expensive!

A woman from Pasadena, California, adds:

Rides can close without warning. I had called in advance and knew that River Country [and] Horizons would be closed. Our hotel even gave us a list of closed attractions. So, imagine our surprise when we get to the Magic Kingdom and find that Space Mountain is closed with no prior warning. Needless to say, we were disappointed.

Car Trouble

Security or tow truck patrols will help you if you lock the keys in your parked car or return to find the battery dead. For more serious problems, the closest repair center is Maingate Exxon, US 192 west of I-4, (407) 396-2721. Disney security will help you contact the service station. Arrangements can be made to take you to your Disney World destination or the nearest phone.

Lost and Found

If you lose (or find) something in the Magic Kingdom, go to City Hall. At Epcot, Lost and Found is in the Entrance Plaza. At Disney-MGM Studios, it's at Hollywood Boulevard Guest Relations, and at the Animal Kingdom, it's at Guest Relations at the main entrance. If you discover your loss after you have left the park(s), call (407) 824-4245 (for all parks). See page 28 for the number to call in each park if you're still at the park(s) and discover something is missing.

Medical Matters

Relief for a Headache   Aspirin and other sundries are sold at the Emporium on Main Street in the Magic Kingdom (they're kept behind the counter; you must ask), at most retail shops in Epcot's Future World and World Showcase, and in Disney-MGM Studios and the Animal Kingdom.

If You Need a Doctor   Main Street Physicians provides 24-hour service. Doctors are available for house calls to all area hotels and campgrounds (Disney and non-Disney). House calls are $165–$170 per visit. If your problem doesn't require a house call, visit the clinic on a walk-in basis (no appointments taken) at 2901 Parkway Boulevard, Suite 3-A, in Kissimmee. Minimum charge for a physician consultation at the clinic is $80. The clinic is open daily from 8 a.m. to 8 p.m., and its main phone is (407) 396-1195.

Centra Care walk-in clinic operates two locations that are across the street from one another. The first is at 12500 S. Apopka-Vineland Road and is open on weekdays from 8 a.m. to midnight and on weekends from 8 a.m. to 8 p.m. The second location is at 12139 S. Apopka-Vineland Road and is open every day from 9 a.m. to 9 p.m. They operate a total of four locations in the Disney area. Call (407) 239-7777 for fees and information. Centra Care also operates an "in-room," 24-hour physician (house call) service and runs a shuttle that will pick you up free of charge. Phone (407) 238-2000.

Prescription Medicine   The closest pharmacy is Walgreen's Lake Buena Vista (phone (407) 238-0600). Turner Drugs (phone (407) 828-8125) charges $5 to deliver a filled prescription to your hotel's front desk. The service is available to Disney resort guests and guests at non-Disney hotels in the Turner Drugs area, and the fee is charged to your hotel account.

Sergeant Blisterblaster's Guide to Happy Feet at Walt Disney World

1. On Your Feet!   Get up, Easy-Boy rider: when you go to Walt Disney World, you'll have to walk a lot farther than to the refrigerator. You can log 5–12 miles a day no problem at the Disney parks, so now's the time

"No, no, really, it's okay. It's just not what I expected."

to get them dogs in shape. Start with some short walks around the neighborhood and increase your distance gradually until you can do six miles on weekends without CPR.

2. A-TEN-SHUN! During your pre-Disney training program, pay attention when those puppies growl. They will give you a lot of information about your feet and the appropriateness and fit of your shoes. Listen up! No walking in flip-flops, loafers, or sandals. Wear well-constructed, broken-in running or hiking shoes. If you feel a "hot spot," that means a blister is developing. The most common sites for blisters are the heels, the toes, and the balls of your feet. If you note a tendency to develop a hot spot in the same place every time you walk, cover it prophylactically with Moleskin (available in drugstores without prescription) before you set out. No, Sofa Bunny, I did not tell you to wear condoms on your feet! *Prophylactically* means to anticipate the problem and treat it in advance. One more thing: keep your toenails cut short and straight across.

3. Sock It Up, Trainee! Good socks are as important as good shoes. When you walk, your feet sweat like a mule in a peat bog, and moisture increases friction. To minimize friction, wear two pairs of socks. The pair next to your feet should ideally be polypropylene thin socks or sock liners. The outer sock can be either a natural fiber like cotton or wool, or a synthetic fiber. To further combat moisture, dust your dogs with some antifungal talcum powder.

4. Who Do You Think You Are, John Wayne? Don't be a hero. The time to take care of a foot problem is the minute you notice it. Carry a small foot emergency kit for your platoon. The kit should contain gauze, Betadyne antibiotic ointment, Moleskin or Spenco second skin, scissors, a sewing needle or some such to drain blisters, as well as matches to sterilize the needle. An extra pair of dry socks and some talc is optional.

5. Bite the Bullet! If you develop a hot spot, cover it ASAP with Moleskin or Spenco second skin. Cut the covering large enough to cover the skin surrounding the hot spot. If you develop a blister, air out and dry your foot. Next, drain the fluid, but do not remove the top skin. Clean the area with your Betadyne, place a gauze square over the blister, and cover the whole shooting match with Moleskin. If you do not have Moleskin or Spenco second skin, do not try to cover the hot spot or blister with Band-Aids. Band-Aids slip and wad up.

6. Take Care of Your Platoon. If you have a couple of young green troops in your outfit, they might not sound off when a hot spot comes on. Stop several times a day and check their feet. If you forgot your emergency foot kit and a problem arises, don't be reluctant to call the Disney medics. They have all the stuff you need to keep your command in action.

Okay troops, prepare to move out. Hit the dusty trail and *move* those feet: left, right, left. When you get back old Sarge will teach you how to avoid VD at Walt Disney World.

Rain

Weather bad? Go to the parks anyway. Crowds are lighter, and most attractions and waiting areas are under cover. Showers, especially during warmer months, are short.

Rain gear is one of the few bargains at the parks. It isn't always displayed in shops; you have to ask for it. Ponchos are available for about $7; umbrellas go for about $13. Ponchos sold at Walt Disney World are all yellow. Picking out somebody in your party on a rainy day is like trying to identify a certain, individual bumblebee in a swarm. Sometimes this can be disconcerting, as a Bethesda, Maryland, mom reported:

Bring your own rain ponchos, especially for your children. When everyone races to the gift shops to buy the ponchos and then puts them on, everyone looks alike. I got so scared I was going to lose my kids I almost left for the day. I ended up using a black marker and making my own design on the ponchos so I could tell my children apart.

Some unusually heavy rain precipitated (no pun intended) dozens of reader suggestions for dealing with soggy days. Nobody, however, had their act together as well as this mom from Memphis, Tennessee. Here are her tips:

1. Rain gear should include poncho and umbrella. Umbrellas make the rain much more bearable. When rain isn't beating down on your ponchoed head, it's easier to ignore.

2. Buy blue ponchos at Walgreens. We could keep track of each other much easier because we had blue ponchos instead of yellow ones.

Sun, Heat, and Humidity

Florida's sun, heat, and humidity can be brutal from late April through mid-October. A woman from Durham, North Carolina, advises:

Be prepared for the heat. I am a 24-year-old former aerobics instructor and felt dizzy after a long day in the Magic Kingdom. Carry clear water bottles, as they are the only beverages allowed on rides.

A lady from Ardsley, New York, writes:

I would advise that people carry umbrellas for shelter against the sun. I was the only one with an umbrella, and every time I used it, I would hear people around me say, "She's smart. She brought an umbrella." This came in handy during the wait for the live show [at Disney-MGM Studios]. The show is absolutely the best event in all three parks (and I should know, because I'm a singer and musician), but the wait is absolutely the worst. They line you up on this open piece of pavement for at least 30 minutes. There is absolutely no shade or breeze, and the cement has been baking in the sun all day. If you bring umbrellas and lots of water to throw on the kids, you might make it until show time.

The latest fad is wearing your own air conditioner. A shopping savvy reader offers this advice:

When we were there, the craze seemed to be water spray bottles fitted with a fan to spray water and cool you down. These were priced at $18 [at the theme parks] and of course a huge hit with the children. We found them priced at $7 outside the park, exactly the same.

St. Louis Encephalitis

Although contraction occurs very rarely, St. Louis Encephalitis is an ongoing concern for Florida's health officials. The disease is transmitted to humans by mosquito bites, and is often more severe in children and the elderly. In spite of regular warnings by state and county agencies, many people (including Disney cast members) are still unsure how much of a threat the mosquito-borne infection poses. A reader from New York City wrote:

Something very important to keep in mind: our resort's pools were closed by 6 p.m. every night. Why? Mosquitoes. We heard from a cast member that there was an encephalitis scare, so pools were closed early to protect guests from possible exposure. Alternately, we heard it was encephalitis season—implying that this wasn't an isolated scare, but an annual event. We couldn't substantiate this, but either way, you should inform your readers, even if it's not annual. People should know to bring bug spray, and they should plan on possibly not having any late night swims.

Since mosquitoes flourish during periods of summer rain, it can be said that Florida undergoes an annual "encephalitis season." However, encephalitis is not a common disease in Florida, and most summers see no cases reported. Rather, health officials advise taking precautions during periods of warmth and moisture. Precautions include:

- Avoid outdoor activities between dusk and dawn, when mosquitoes are most active.

- If you must be outside at night, wear long pants and long-sleeved shirts, as well as insect repellent on exposed skin.

- Avoid water, and especially standing water, at night.

There is no vaccine for St. Louis Encephalitis since it occurs in humans so rarely. The good news is that, due to conscientious preventive measures on the part of Florida locals as well as tourists, only a handful of cases were reported last year.

How to Lodge a Complaint with Disney

Lodging a complaint about a leaky faucet or not having enough clean towels is pretty straightforward, and you will usually find the Disney folks extremely responsive. However, a gripe that is larger, more global, or beyond an on-site manager's ability to resolve is likely to founder in the labyrinth of Disney bureaucracy.

One of the foremost gripes voiced by readers related to Disney's lack of responsiveness in fielding complaints. The remarks of this Providence, Rhode Island, dad are typical:

It's all warm fuzzies and big smiles until you have a problem. Then everybody plays [hide and seek]. The only thing you know for sure is that it's never the responsibility of the Disney person you are talking to.

A Mobile, Alabama, mother echoes the Providence dad's comment:

I made call after call, with one [Disney] person passing me on to the next, until finally I ran out of steam. Basically, I had to choose between getting my problem addressed, which was pretty much a full-time job, or going ahead with my vacation.

A Portland, Maine, reader summed it up in quintessential New England style:

Lodging a complaint with Disney is like shouting at a brick.

Like most companies, Disney would rather hear from you when the message is good. Concerning complaints, they prefer to receive the complaint in writing, but by the time you get home and draft a letter, it's often too late to correct the problem. And though Disney would have you believe that it's a touchy-feely outfit, it's not generally the kind of company that will "make things right for you" after the fact. You may get a letter thanking you for writing and expressing generalized regret without acknowledging responsibility (as in "We're sorry you *felt* inconvenienced," as if the perception arose from your imagination), but it's not likely they will offer or commit to do anything remedial. That having been said, if you want to lodge a complaint once you've returned home, write:

Walt Disney World Guest Communications
P.O. Box 10000
Lake Buena Vista, Florida 32830-1000

If you're really hot, try writing:

Michael Eisner	Al Weiss
Chairman and CEO	President
The Walt Disney Company	The Walt Disney World Resort
500 South Buena Vista Street	P.O. Box 10040
Burbank, CA 91521-4873	Lake Buena Vista, FL 32830

Paul Pressler
Chairman and President
Walt Disney Parks & Resorts
500 South Buena Vista Street
Burbank, CA 91521-4873

If Disney doesn't respond, you can always go public by writing:

Letters to the Editor	*Consumer Reports Travel*
The Orlando Sentinel	*Newsletter*
633 North Orange Avenue	101 Truman Avenue
Orlando, FL 32801-1349	Yonkers, NY 10703-1057
	talkback@travel.consumer.org

If you're at Walt Disney World and really need to get an issue settled, keep your resort general manager in the middle of the fray and hold his feet to the fire until he hooks you up with the right person.

Visiting More than One Park in a Single Day

If you have a pass that allows you to visit the Magic Kingdom, the Animal Kingdom, Epcot, and Disney-MGM Studios in the same day, it will be validated with the date when you enter your first park. If you decide to go later to another park, you must have your hand stamped for re-entry before you leave. If you start the day at the Magic Kingdom, for example, then go to Epcot for dinner, you must get a re-entry stamp when you leave the Magic Kingdom. At Epcot, you'll have to present your pass and show your hand stamp. The stamp is visible only under ultraviolet light and usually won't come off if you wash your hands or swim.

Services

Messages

Messages left at City Hall in the Magic Kingdom, Guest Relations at Epcot, Hollywood Boulevard Guest Relations at Disney-MGM Studios, or Guest Relations at the Animal Kingdom can be retrieved at any of the four.

Pet Care

Pets aren't allowed in the major or minor theme parks. But never leave an animal in a hot car while you tour; the pet will die. Kennels and holding facilities are provided for temporary care of your pets. They're located adjacent to the Transportation and Ticket Center, left of the Epcot entrance plaza, left of the Disney-MGM Studios entrance plaza, at the outer entrance of the Animal Kingdom, and at Fort Wilderness Campground. If you insist, kennel staff will accept about any type of animal (except natural wildlife pets), though owners of exotic and/or potentially vicious pets must place their charge in its assigned cage. Small pets (mice, hamsters, birds, snakes, turtles, alligators, etc.) must stay in their own escape-proof carrier.

Here are several additional details you may need to know:

- When traveling with your pet in Florida, bring proof of vaccination and immunization, including bordatella for dogs.

- It is against the law in Florida to leave a pet in a closed vehicle.

- Advance reservations for animals aren't accepted.

- Kennels open one hour before the park opens and close 30 minutes to one hour after the park closes. The kennels, however, are staffed 24 hours a day.

- Disney resort guests may board a pet overnight for $9 per pet, per night. Other patrons are charged $11 per pet, per night. Day care of pets for all guests costs $6 per day. The kennels aren't really set up for multiday boarding. You must exercise your own pet.

- Guests leaving exotic pets should supply their food.

- Pets are allowed at a limited number of sites at Fort Wilderness Campground. $5 per day, per pet.

For more information on pet care, call (407) 824-6568.

Religious Services

On Sundays at the Polynesian Resort, mass for Catholics is celebrated at 8 and 10:15 a.m., and nondenominational Protestant services are held at 9 a.m. For a schedule of services at churches and temples in the Walt Disney World area, inquire at your hotel's front desk.

Interestingly, we've been receiving mail from Roman Catholic readers about the Mary, Queen of the Universe Shrine, located across I-4 from Walt Disney World. Here's what a Roselle Park, New Jersey gentleman confided after going to the Shrine for a regularly scheduled mass:

This "church" held about 2,000 people, and we were encouraged to squeeze toward the end of the row like in the amusement parks to fit more people in. After the entrance hymn, a priest greeted the crowd, then proceeded to give a history of the "little church." Next, he began suggesting how donations would sure help keep the church going for vacationers, saying two collections would follow, the first of which donors usually put a check in the basket! Well, after 15 minutes of this not-so-Catholic mass, I got up and left. As I made my way [out], I met a priest who greeted me warmly. I told him my opinion of the commercial I just sat through and he had no comment at all. He just looked down and walked away.

Several of our *Unofficial Guide* research team are Catholic, so we sent them to Mary Queen of the Universe to determine first hand if the reports we've been receiving from readers are representative. Here's their report:

You've got to be suspicious of any church that features its gift shop on its website, and the Shrine is no exception. If overt fundraising makes you uncomfortable, this is not the place for you. Upon entering the church, guests are handed a small pamphlet best described as a "rate card." Mine said I could get a roof tile with my name on it for only $50. For $900 I could get an entire pew seat. If you thought indulgences were a thing of the past, the rate card notes that donors will receive "... remembrance in daily Mass; and all the spiritual benefits accorded the family of Mary, Queen of the Universe Shrine." Donation envelopes are stored like napkins in the pews. The Shrine purports to be a Catholic church, but is not affiliated with any diocese or parish. That whirring sound you hear is Martin Luther spinning in his grave.

Excuse Me, but Where Can I Find ...

Someplace to Put All These Packages?   Lockers are available on the ground floor of the Main Street railroad station in the Magic Kingdom, to the right of Spaceship Earth in Epcot, and on the east and west ends of the TTC. At Disney-MGM Studios, lockers are to the right of the entrance on Hollywood Boulevard at Oscar's Super Service. At the Animal Kingdom, lockers are inside the main entrance to the left. Lockers are $4 a day plus a $2 deposit.

Package Pick-up is available at each major theme park. Ask the salesperson to send your purchases to Package Pick-up. When you leave the park, they'll be waiting for you. Epcot has two exits, thus two Package Pick-ups, so specify whether you want your purchases sent to the main entrance or to the International Gateway.

A Mixed Drink or a Beer?   Alcoholic beverages aren't sold in the Magic Kingdom; you must leave and go to a resort hotel to get one. Everywhere else in Disney World, wine, beer, and mixed drinks are readily available.

Cameras and Film?   Camera Centers at the major theme parks sell disposable cameras for about $10 ($19 with flash). Film is sold throughout the World. Developing is available at most Disney hotel gift shops and at Camera Centers. For two-hour developing, look for the Photo Express sign in the theme parks. Drop your film in the container and pick up your pictures at the Camera Center as you leave the park. If you use the express service and intend to stay in the park until closing, pick up your pictures earlier in the evening to avoid the end-of-day rush. The Magic Kingdom Camera Center almost always develops film within the advertised two hours. Camera Centers at the other parks frequently run late.

Photo tips and recommendations for settings and exposures are detailed in the respective maps provided free when you enter the theme parks.

Suntan Lotion?   Suntan lotion and other sundries are sold at the Emporium on Main Street in the Magic Kingdom (they're kept behind the counter; you must ask) and in Epcot at many Future World and World Showcase shops. At Disney-MGM Studios and the Animal Kingdom, suntan lotion is sold at almost all shops.

Chewing Gum?   Sorry, it isn't sold in any theme park. B.Y.O.

A Grocery Store?   Goodings Supermarket in the Crossroads Shopping Center (across FL 535 from the entrance to Walt Disney World) is a large, designer grocery with everything from sushi to fresh-baked doughnuts. If you're looking for gourmet foods, a good wine selection, or something exotic, it's your best bet. If you just want to stock up on staples, however, you'll find the prices higher than the Tower of Terror, and just about as frightening. For more down-to-earth prices, try Publix Supermarket on the corner of FL 535 and US 192. There are also supermarkets on US 192, north of Walt Disney World's main gate. At readers' request, we've added the Marketplace store located on US 192 near the entrance to Splendid China. Though large, this store lacks the breadth of goods available at Goodings and Publix.

As a test, we compiled a list of common vacation grocery items and went shopping. None of the items purchased were offered at a special sale or promotional price. Here's how prices at the Marketplace, Publix, and Goodings compared:

Item	Goodings	Publix	Market-place
Dozen donuts	4.89	3.99	3.99
Maxwell House coffee	4.69	2.29	3.49
Mr. Coffee coffee filters, 100	1.98	1.19	1.49
One gallon of milk	3.89	2.99	3.99
Tropicana orange juice, 64 oz.	3.99	2.99	3.99
Cheerios, 10 oz.	3.99	3.29	3.99
Coca Cola, 12-pack of cans	4.29	3.29	4.99
Lay's Potato Chips, 12¼ oz.	2.99	2.99	2.99
Sugar, 2 lbs.	1.69	1.19	1.99
Chips Ahoy cookies, 12 oz.	3.29	2.69	3.59
Budweiser, 6-pack of cans	4.99	4.69	5.79
Bananas, 4 lbs.	2.76	1.96	3.16
Merita white bread, 20 oz.	1.99	1.59	1.89
Jif Creamy Peanut Butter, 12 oz.	2.69	1.69	2.49
Welch's Grape Jelly, 18 oz.	2.39	1.59	2.39
Oral B Advantage toothbrush	4.19	3.29	3.19
Hawaiian Tropic SPF 15 sunscreen, 8 oz.	10.99	8.49	7.99
Kodak Gold 200 film, 24 exposures	6.69	3.91	6.69
Total	$72.38	$55.01	$68.09

Part Nine

Dining in and around Walt Disney World

Dining outside Walt Disney World

Unofficial Guide researchers love good food and invest a fair amount of time scouting new places to eat. And, because food at Walt Disney World is so expensive, we (like you) have an economic incentive for finding palatable meals outside the World. Unfortunately, the area surrounding Disney World is not exactly a culinary nirvana. If you thrive on fast food and the fare at chain restaurants (Denny's, T.G.I. Fridays, Olive Garden, etc.), you'll be as happy as an alligator on a chicken farm. If, however, you'd like a superlative dining experience, you'll find the pickings outside the World about the same as those inside, only less expensive.

Some ethnic cuisines aren't represented in Walt Disney World restaurants. If you want Indian, Thai, Greek, or Caribbean, you'll have to forage in surrounding communities. Among specialty restaurants in and out of the World, location and price will determine your choice. There are, for example, decent Italian restaurants in Walt Disney World and adjoining tourist areas. Which one you select depends on how much you want to spend and how convenient the place is. Our recommendations on specialty and ethnic fare served in and out of Dinsey World are summarized in the table below.

Better restaurants outside Walt Disney World cater primarily to adults and aren't as well equipped to deal with children. If, however, you're looking to escape children or want to eat in peace and quiet, you're more likely to find such an environment outside the World.

IN OR OUT OF THE WORLD FOR ETHNIC CUISINE?

American Good selections both in and out of the World.

Barbecue Better out of the World.

Buffets This is a toss-up. Disney buffets are expensive but offer excellent quality and extensive selections. Off-World buffets aren't as upscale, but they are inexpensive.

Chinese Eat out of the World.

French   Toss-up. Reasonably good but expensive both in and out of the World.

German   Passable, but not great, in or out of the World.

Italian   Tie on quality; better value out of the World.

Japanese   Teppanyaki Dining Room at Epcot is tops for teppan (table grill) dining. For sushi and sashimi, go off-World, or try Kimonos at the Swan Resort.

Mexican   San Angel Inn at Epcot is good but expensive. For good food and value, try Jalapeños Grill on US 192.

Middle Eastern   More choice and better value out of the World.

Seafood   Toss-up.

Steak/Prime Rib   Try Shula's Steak House at the WDW Swan or Charlie's off US 192 out of the World.

Take Out Express

If you're staying in a hotel *outside* Disney World, **Take Out Express** (phone (407) 352-1170) will deliver a meal from your choice among 20 restaurants, including T.G.I. Fridays, Ming Court, Passage to India, Siam Orchid, Bella Roma, Chili's, Ocean Grille, Houlihans, Italianni's, and Sizzler. The delivery charge is $5–$10 per restaurant (depending on your distance from the restaurant), with a minimum $15 order. Tips aren't included. Cash, traveler's checks, MasterCard, Visa, and American Express are accepted. Hours are 4:30–11 p.m.

Dining at Universal's CityWalk

Universal rolled out its answer to Downtown Disney with a vengeance in 1999. Like Downtown Disney, CityWalk is a combination of entertainment and dining with a focus on adults. Restaurant tastes run the gamut, from the elegant (Emeril's Orlando) to the base (NASCAR Cafe), or, if you prefer, from the sublime to the ridiculous. All the restaurants share one common trait: they are loud. But there is good food to be found inside some of them. Most of the restaurants are partners with Universal's culinary team.

Emeril's Orlando   Chief among these offerings, Emeril's Orlando is Emeril Lagasse's Florida version of his New Orleans restaurant. Lagasse is on hand from time to time, though he tends to stay in the kitchen. But even when he's not there, you're in for some good eating. The food is Louisiana style with a creative flair.

Pastamoré   This is the requisite Italian restaurant. The decor is modern and stylish, and the food—with portions big enough to share—is better than average.

NBA City   NBA City opened as a partnership with Hard Rock Cafe, which is next door (and the largest HRC in the world), but the two have since split. NBA City serves good theme-restaurant eats, with quality that's a little higher than you'd expect. The dining area looks like a miniature basketball arena, and televisions throughout play videos of famous basketball players and key moments in roundball history.

Jimmy Buffett's Margaritaville A large and noisy tribute to the head Parrothead. None of the food, including the cheeseburger, will make you think you're in paradise, but fans don't seem to care. The focal point is a volcano that erupts from time to time, spewing margarita mix instead of lava.

Latin Quarter A large and noisy tribute to all Latin American nations. The restaurant features a cuisine it calls nuevo latino, which means it can do whatever it wants with the food. Still, the quality is mostly good. In the late evening (after 10 p.m.), the focus of the establishment shifts from being a restaurant to being a nightclub, and you'll be discouraged from ordering more than nibbles.

Motown Cafe This is the rhythm-and-blues version of Hard Rock Cafe. The food here is about as satisfying as trying to listen to an old 45-rpm record on a player without an adapter for the hole, but there is a good floor show with singers performing classic Motown hits.

NASCAR Cafe A large and noisy tribute to all things motorized. You may find yourself sitting under a full-sized race car that from time to time starts up and roars at a too-realistic sound level. The food? See all the logos for oil companies on the walls?

Bob Marley—A Tribute to Freedom The Bob Marley place (a medium-sized and moderately loud tribute), **Pat O'Brien's**, and **City-Jazz** are mostly music venues that serve some food. Pat O'Brien's, behind a facade that looks remarkably like the New Orleans original, has the best bites (try the jambalaya).

One Man's Treasure

A man from Richland, Washington, urges:

I think that you should in future editions promote the Crossroads of Buena Vista [Shopping Center] a little stronger. There are plenty of non-WDW restaurants at non-WDW prices. The Crossroads is nothing less than a small city that can service all of your needs.

Crossroads Shopping Center is on FL 535 directly across from the entrance to Walt Disney World Village and Disney Village Hotel Plaza. As the reader suggests, it offers about everything you need. Fast food is sold at McDonald's, Burger King, and Taco Bell. Up a notch are T.G.I. Fridays, Perkins, Jungle Jim's, Pizzeria Uno, and Red Lobster. For a really nice meal, pick Pebbles, featuring fresh Florida seafood. When you finish eating, shop for sportswear, swimwear, and athletic shoes.

Buffets and Meal Deals outside Walt Disney World

Buffets, restaurant specials, and discount dining abound in the area surrounding Walt Disney World, especially on US 192 (locally known as the Irlo Bronson Highway) and along International Drive. The local visitor

WHERE TO EAT OUTSDE WALT DISNEY WORLD

American

Cafe Tu Tu Tango 8625 International Drive, Orlando; inexpensive to moderate; (407) 248-2222 Mediterranean-style tapas in an artist's garret setting.

Chatham's Place 7575 Dr. Phillips Boulevard, Orlando; moderate to expensive; (407) 345-2992 New American cuisine: the dining room is small and unappealing, but the food and service are some of the best in Orlando.

Manuel's on the 28th 390 North Orange Avenue, Orlando; expensive; (407) 246-6580 Creative American overlooking downtown Orlando from the 28th floor of the Barnett Bank building.

Pebbles 12551 FL 535, Crossroads Shopping Center, Lake Buena Vista; moderate to expensive; (407) 827-1111 A casual homegrown chain featuring a Florida version of California cuisine.

Sam Snead's Tavern 2461 South Hiawassee Road, Orlando; inexpensive to moderate; (407) 295-9999 A golfer's version of the Hard Rock Cafe.

Wild Jack's 7364 International Drive, Orlando; moderate; (407) 352-4407 Cowboy cuisine in a Rodeo Drive setting.

Barbecue

Bubbalou's Bodacious B-B-Q 5818 Conroy Road, Orlando (near Universal Studios Florida); inexpensive; (407) 295-1212 Tender smoky barbecue with a tomato-based "killer" sauce.

Beef

Butcher Shop Steakhouse 8445 International Drive, Mercado Mediterranean Village, Orlando; moderate; (407) 363-9727 High-quality beef you can cook at the open pit.

Charlie's Steak House 6107 South Orange Blossom Trail, Orlando; moderate; (407) 851-7130 There are other locations for this small chain, including one just south of the I-4 interchange on US 192.

Del Frisco's 729 Lee Road, Orlando (quarter-mile west of I-4); expensive; (407) 645-4443 A little pricey, but if you're in the mood for a great steak, it's worth it.

Vito's Chop House 8633 International Drive, Orlando; (407) 354-2467 Surprisingly upscale meat house with a taste of Tuscany.

Caribbean

Bahama Breeze 8849 International Drive, Orlando; moderate; (407) 248-2499 A creative—and tasty—version of Caribbean cuisine from the owners of the Olive Garden and Red Lobster chains.

Chinese

Ming Court 9188 International Drive, Orlando; expensive; (407) 351-9988 Ask to see the dim sum menu.

Cuban

Numero Uno 2499 South Orange Avenue, Orlando; inexpensive; (407) 841-3840 No trip to Florida is complete without a sampling of Cuban food.

Rolando's 870 Semoran Boulevard, Casselberry; inexpensive; (407) 767-9677 Some of the best Cuban around, served by some of the friendliest people.

French

Le Coq au Vin 4800 South Orange Avenue, Orlando; moderate; (407) 851-6980 A perennial local favorite featuring country French in a not-too-stuffy atmosphere. Reservations are required.

German/Eastern European

Chef Henry's Cafe 3716 Howell Branch Road, Winter Park; moderate; (407) 657-2230   A small family-run cafe with authentic and delicious Eastern European dishes. Don't leave without having a slice (or five) of the apple streudel.

Old Munich 5731 South Orange Blossom Trail, Orlando; moderate; (407) 438-8997 Nothing special, but if you've just got to have some sauerbraten . . .

Indian

Kohinoor Ethan Allen Plaza, 249 W. State Road 436, Altamonte Springs; moderate; (407) 788-6004   Try the lamb korma.

Memories of India 7625 Turkey Lake Road, Orlando; moderate; (407) 370-3277 A quiet atmosphere with some of the best Indian cuisine in the area. A bit more reasonable than some other I-Drive–area Indian restaurants.

Passage to India 5532 International Drive, Orlando; moderate; (407) 351-3456 A lot of locals brave International Drive just to dine here.

Shamiana 7040 International Drive, Orlando; inexpensive; (407) 354-1160 Also serves Pakistani cuisine.

Italian

Capriccio Peabody Orlando, 9801 International Drive, Orlando; moderate to expensive; (407) 345-4450   This upscale Italian restaurant serves a good Sunday brunch.

Antonio's 7559 W. Sand Lake Road, Orlando; moderate to expensive; (407) 363-9191   Upscale Italian that's a popular choce among locals.

Japanese/Sushi

Hanamizuki 8255 International Drive, Orlando; moderate to expensive; (407) 363-7200   Usually filled with Japanese visitors; expensive, but very authentic.

Ichiban 19 South Orange Avenue, Orlando (near Church Street Station); moderate; (407) 423-2688   Sit on the floor or at a table; good sushi and tempura.

Mexican

Don Pablo's 8717 International Drive, Orlando; inexpensive; (407) 354-1345 A pretty good chain that uses fresh ingredients. Can be a bit noisy.

Middle Eastern

Aladdin's Cafe 1015 East Semoran Boulevard, Casselberry; moderate; (407) 331-0488   Call for belly dancer's schedule.

Seafood

Chinatown 1103 North Mills Avenue, Orlando; moderate to expensive; (407) 896-9383   Yes, it's a Chinese restaurant, but it also has a fresh seafood market attached. How fresh? It's still swimming when you order it.

Sunset Sam's Fish Camp Gaylord Palms Hotel, 6000 Osceola Parkway, Kissimmee; (407) 586-1101   The setting is half the fun: a three-mast ship floating in an indoor lagoon with a Key West theme. The seafood is fresh and well prepared.

Thai

Royal Thai 1202 North Semoran Boulevard, Orlando; inexpensive to moderate; (407) 275-0776   If you like hot Thai food, you'll love this place; have the lemon fish.

Siam Orchid 7575 Universal Boulevard, Orlando; moderate to expensive; (407) 351-0821   Fancier than most Thai places and a bit pricier, but the best Thai in the tourist areas.

magazines, distributed free at non-Disney hotels among other places, are packed with advertisements and discount coupons for seafood feasts, Chinese buffets, Indian buffets, breakfast buffets, and a host of combination specials for everything from lobster to barbecue. For a family trying to economize on meals, some of the come-ons are mighty appealing. But are these places any good? Is the food fresh, tasty, and appealing? Are the restaurants clean and inviting? Armed with little more than a roll of Tums, the *Unofficial* research team tried all the eateries that advertise heavily in the free tourist magazines. Here's what we discovered.

Chinese Super Buffets   Whoa! Talk about an oxymoron. If you've ever tried preparing Chinese food, especially a stir-fry, you know that split-second timing is required to avoid overcooking. So it should come as no big surprise that Chinese dishes languishing on a buffet lose their freshness, texture, and flavor in hurry. As a rule, Chinese dishes simply do not work on a buffet. The exception might be a busy local Chinese lunch spot where buffet items are replenished every five or so minutes. Even then, however, the food doesn't measure up to dishes that are cooked to order and served fresh out of the wok. At the so-called Chinese super buffets, the food often sits a long time. We tried all the buffets advertised in the visitor magazines (and a few that were not), and while a number of them had great eye appeal, the food was inevitably lackluster. **China Jade Buffet** (7308 International Drive) is no exception in regard to food on the serving line, but it offers a Mongolian Grill where they'll whip up a custom-made stir-fry for you. Even with this exotic-sounding extra, however, the meal remains bland overall.

Indian Buffets   Indian food works much better on a buffet than Chinese food. The mainstay of Indian buffets is curries. Curry, you may be surprised to know, is essentially the Indian word for stew. Curry powder, as sold in the United States, is nothing more than a blend of spices prepackaged to flavor a stew. In India, each curry is prepared with a different combination of spices, and no self-respecting cook would dream of using an off-the-shelf mix. The salient point about Indian buffets is that stews, unlike stir-frys, actually improve with a little aging. If you've ever heated a leftover stew at home and commented that it tasted better than when originally served, it's because the flavors and ingredients continued to marry during the storage period, making it richer and more tasty.

In the Walt Disney World area, most Indian restaurants offer a buffet at lunch only—not too convenient if you plan on spending your day at the theme parks. If you're out shopping or taking a day off, here are some Indian buffets worth trying:

Passage to India	5532 International Drive	(407) 351-3456
Shalimar	7342 International Drive	(407) 226-9797

Punjab	7451 International Drive	(407) 352-7887
India Palace at Vista Shoppes	8530 Palm Parkway	(407) 238-2322

General Buffets There are two buffets, the **Las Vegas Buffet** on US 192 and **Bill Wong's** on International Drive, that offer fair value for the dollar. The Las Vegas Buffet (5269 West US 192; (407) 397-1288), the better of the two, features a carving station with prime rib, ham, turkey, and sometimes lamb. Bill Wong's represents itself as a Chinese buffet but shores up its Chinese selections with peel-and-eat shrimp, prime rib, and a nice selection of hot and cold vegetables. Discount coupons for both buffets are readily available.

Seafood and Lobster Buffets These affairs do not exactly fall under the category of inexpensive dining. Prices range from $20 to $24 for early birds (4–6 p.m.) and $25 to $29 after 6 p.m. The main draw (no pun intended) is all the lobster you can eat. The problem is lobsters, like Chinese food, don't wear well on a steam table. After a few minutes on the buffet line, they make better tennis balls than dinner. If, however, you have someone in the kitchen who knows how to steam a lobster, and if you grab your lobster immediately after a fresh batch has been brought out, it will probably be fine. There are two lobster buffets on US 192 and another two on International Drive. Although all four do a reasonable job, we prefer **Angel's** on US 192 (7300 Irlo Bronson Highway; (407) 397-1960) and the **International Lobster Feast** on I-Drive (8735 International Drive; (407) 248-8606). In both cases, there's enough other good stuff on the buffet, including prime rib, to have a good meal even if the lobsters are sub-par. If you put our two favorites head-to-head, the International Lobster Feast offers greater variety, especially in terms of shellfish, but is also about $4 more expensive. Both places are cavernous noisy joints. Finally, be aware that the other International Drive lobster buffet is called the International *Lighthouse* Lobster Feast. A lot of folks get the names and the restaurants confused. Discount coupons are available in local visitor magazines.

Breakfast Buffets and Entree Buffets Entree buffets are offered by most of the area chain steakhouses such as **Ponderosa, Sizzler, Western Sizzlin, Western Steer,** and **Golden Corral.** Between the five, there are 18 locations in the Walt Disney World area. All serve breakfast, lunch, and dinner. At lunch and dinner you get the buffet when you buy an entree, usually a steak. Generally speaking, the buffets are less elaborate than a stand-alone buffet and considerably more varied than a salad bar. Breakfast service is a straightforward buffet (i.e., no obligation to buy an entree). Concerning the food, it's chain restaurant quality but pretty decent all the same. Prices are a bargain, and you can get in and out at lightning speed, important at breakfast when you're trying to get to the theme park early. Some locations offer lunch and dinner buffets at a set price without buying an entree. In addition to the steakhouses, area **Shoney's** also offer breakfast, lunch, and dinner buffets. Local freebie visitor magazines are full of discount coupons for all of the above.

Meal Deals Discount coupons are available for a wide range of restaurants, including some wonderful upscale ethnic places like **Siam Orchid** (Thai) and **Ming's** (Chinese). For those who crave both beef and a bargain, try **JT's Prime Time Restaurant and Bar** (8553 West Irlo Bronson; (407) 239-6555). JT's serves all-you-can-eat prime rib for $15. They slice it a little thin but are very attentive in regard to bringing you additional helpings. Other prime rib specials can be found at **Cattleman's Steakhouse** with locations on I-Drive a quarter of a mile north of the convention center (407) 354-9888 and on US 192 at FL 535 (407) 397-1888. Our favorite prime rib option is **Wild Jack's** at 7364 International Drive (407) 352-4407. The decor is strictly cowboy modern, but the beef is some of the best in town and the price is right. Another meat-eater's delight is the Feast for Four at **Sonny's Real Pit Bar-B Q,** a Florida chain that turns out good barbecue. For $26–$30 per family of four you get sliced pork or beef, plus chicken, ribs, beans, slaw, fries, garlic bread, and soft drinks or tea, all served family style. Locations include: 4220 Vine Street, Kissimmee, (407) 847-8888 and on US 192 at 4475 13th Street, (407) 892-2285. No coupons are needed or available for JT's or Sonny's but are available for the other meateries.

Dining in Walt Disney World

This section aims to help you find good food without going broke or tripping over one of Disney World's many culinary landmines. More than 100 restaurants operate in Walt Disney World, including about 70 full-service restaurants, 23 of which are inside the theme parks. Collectively, Disney restaurants offer exceptional variety, serving everything from Cajun to French, from Moroccan to Texas barbecue. Most restaurants are expensive, and many serve less than distinguished fare, but the culinary scene at Disney World gets better every year. You can find good deals if you know where to look, and there are ethnic delights rarely found outside of America's largest cities.

Getting It Right

Although we work hard to be fair, objective, and accurate, many readers, like this one from Couderport, Pennsylvania, think we are too critical of Disney restaurants. He writes:

You are tough on all Disney dining... Everyone has to eat while there, so it benefits no one to be this critical. Lighten up a little bit and make your dining recommendations in the same spirit as the rest of the book.

In a similar vein, a Charleston, West Virginia, woman came out swinging:

Get a life! It's crazy and unrealistic to be so snobbish about restaurants at a theme park. Considering the number of people Disney feeds each day, I think they do a darn good job. Also, you act so surprised that the food is expensive. Have you ever eaten at an airport? HELLO, IN THERE?... Surprise, you're a captive! It's a theme park!

And a mom from Erie, Pennsylvania, struck a practical note, writing:

Most of the food [at Walt Disney World] is OK. Certainly in our experience, more of it is good than bad. If you pay attention to what other visitors say and what's in the guidebooks, you can avoid the yucky places. It's true that you pay more than you should, but it's more convenient [to eat in Walt Disney World] than to run around trying to find cheaper restaurants somewhere else. When it comes to Walt Disney World, who needs more running around.

As you might infer from the reader comments above, getting our dining coverage right is a bit of a challenge. While researching and reviewing restaurants may appear to be a straightforward endeavor, we can assure you that it is fraught with peril. We have read dining reviews by writers who turn up their noses at anything except four-star French restaurants (of which there are a whole lot fewer than people think). Likewise, we have seen reviewers who totally avoid Thai and Indian restaurants–– among others—because they do not understand those cuisines. We have read reviews absolutely devoid of criticism, written by "experts" unwilling to risk offending the source of their free meals. Finally, we've seen reviews in dining guides that are wholly based on surveys submitted by diners whose credentials for evaluating fine dining are mysterious at best and questionable at least.

How, then, do you go about presenting the best possible dining coverage? What is the best way to get it right? At the *Unofficial Guide,* we have elected to begin with highly qualified culinary experts and then balance their opinions with those of our readers. It's necessary, we believe, to present both an expert and a popular opinion of each restaurant.

The expert opinion is essential because it's important to be able to differentiate what the restaurant really serves from what it purports to serve. Many years ago in Lexington, Kentucky, by way of example, there was only one Chinese restaurant. It was wildly successful in spite of the fact that it was Chinese in name only. Even so, its specialty dishes, essentially American vegetable casseroles smothered in cornstarch, were happily gobbled up by loyal patrons who had never been exposed to real Chinese cooking. The food was not bad, mind you, but it was not Chinese either.

Visitors from out of town, inquiring about a good local Chinese restaurant, were invariably directed to this place. As you would expect, they were routinely horrified by the fare.

In this guide, we think you deserve to know whether or not you're getting the real thing. If we recommend the bastilla (a Moroccan pastry) at the Restaurant Marrakesh, it's pretty essential that our dining critics know what bastilla is, how it's properly prepared, how it should be served, and how it should taste. Likewise with the Bernaise sauce served at the Yachtsman Steakhouse, or the Jagerschnitzel at the Biergarten. In our opinion, it's almost impossible to publish a creditable restaurant review without the help of a knowledgeable, professional dining critic.

The ultimate test of success for a restaurant, however, is not the authenticity of its dishes, but the level of satisfaction of its patrons. If diners have a bad experience and don't come back, the restaurant will fail. Thus, in this guide, we regard our expert's opinion and our readers' opinions as two halves of a whole. Both are necessary to give you the information you need to make your dining decisions.

Our experts are knowledgeable, seasoned professionals who have studied culinary arts around the world and who have written cookbooks or columns. They are well versed in ethnic dishes and have studied many of the cuisines of the world in their native lands. As at home in a Tupelo, Mississippi, catfish shack as in an exclusive French restaurant on New York's Upper East Side, they have no prejudice about high or low cuisine. Equally important, our experts conduct their reviews anonymously, and always pay full menu prices for their meals.

To be as fair and thorough as possible, we display our readers' opinion of each restaurant right alongside that of our dining critics and encourage you to take both into consideration when selecting a restaurant. Likewise, we encourage you to send us the dining-survey form in the back of this guide so we can include your opinions in our tabulations. If you want to share your dining experience in great depth write us at the address listed on page 12 or e-mail us at unofficialguides@menasharidge.com.

Disney Dining 101

Priority Seating

Disney ceaselessly tinkers with its restaurant reservations policy. Since 1997, reservations have been replaced with "Priority Seating." When you call, your name and essential information are taken as if you were making a reservation. The Disney representative then says you have priority seating for the restaurant on the date and time you requested and usually explains that priority seating means you will be seated ahead of walk-ins, i.e., those without priority seating.

THE COST OF COUNTER-SERVICE FOOD

To help you develop your dining budget, here are prices of common counter-service items. Sales tax isn't included.

Food

Bagel/Muffin	$1.70–$2.50
Barbecue Platter	$8.00
Brownie	$1.50–$2.00
Cake or Pie	$2.20–$2.65
Cereal with Milk	$3.50
Cheeseburger with Fries	$5.20–$6.00
Chicken Breast Sandwich (grilled)	$4.55–$6.95
Children's Meals	$3.50–$3.90
Chips	$1.30–$2.40
Cookies	$1.50–$1.90
Sub/Deli Sandwich	$4.95–6.50
Fish Basket (fried) with Fries	$6.30
French Fries	$1.80–$3.05 (loaded)
Fried Chicken Nuggets with Fries	$5.60
Fruit (whole piece)	$0.80–$1.50
Fruit Cup/Fruit Salad	$2.20–$2.80
Hot Dogs	$3.70–$4.80
Ice Cream Bars	$2.35–$2.95
Nachos with Cheese	$4.25
Pasta Salad	$1.35–$5.85
Pizza (per slice)	$3.50–$5.35
Pizza (individual)	$5.30–$6.00
Popcorn	$2.35–$3.30
Salad (entree)	$4.10–$6.40
Salad (side)	$2.00
Smoked Turkey Leg	$4.50
Soup/Chili	$2.00–$4.95
Taco	$4.75 for two tacos
Taco Salad	$5.75

Drinks	**Small**	**Large**
Beer (not available in the Magic Kingdom)	$3.75	$5.00
Bottled Water	$2.00	$2.50
Cappuccino/Espresso	$2.95	
Coffee	$1.60	$1.80
Fruit Juice	$1.50	NA
Milk	$1.00	NA
Soft Drinks, Iced Tea, and Lemonade	$2.00	$2.30
Hot Tea and Cocoa	$1.60	NA

Behind the Scenes at Priority Seating
Central Reservations

Disney restaurants operate on what they call a "template system." Instead of scheduling priority seatings for actual tables, reservationists fill time slots. The number of time slots available is based on the average observed length of time that guests occupy a table at a particular restaurant, adjusted for seasonality. Here's a rough example of how it works. Let's say the Coral Reef Restaurant at Epcot has 40 tables for four and 8 tables for six and that the average length of time for a family to be seated, order, eat, pay, and depart is 40 minutes. Add 5 minutes to bus the table and set it up for the next guests, and they are turning the table every 45 minutes. The restaurant provides central reservations (aka WDW-DINE) with a computer template of its capacity along with the average time the table is occupied. Thus, when WDW-DINE makes a priority seating for four people at 6:15 p.m., the system removes one table for four from overall capacity for 45 minutes. The template on the reservationist's computer indicates that the table will not be available for reassignment until 7 p.m. (45 minutes later). So it goes for all the tables in the restaurant, each being subtracted from overall capacity for 45 minutes, then listed as available again, and then assigned to other guests and subtracted again, and so on, throughout the meal period. WDW-DINE tries to fill every time slot for every seat in the restaurant or come as close to filling every slot as possible. No seats, repeat none, are reserved for walk-ins.

Templates are filled differently depending on the season of the year. During slower times of year when priority seatings are easier to get, WDW-DINE will overbook the restaurant for each time slot on the assumption that there will be a lot of no-shows. During busy times of year when priority seatings are harder to come by, there are very few no-shows, so the restaurant is booked according to its actual capacity. The no-show rate in January, a slow month, is about 33%, while in July it's less than 10%.

Even though, as discussed above, no seats are reserved for walk-ins, it's easy to get a walk-in seat during slower times of the year (with the exception of Cinderella's Royal Table). During high season it's tougher to get seated as a walk-in, but by no means impossible. As we've seen, you can score a seat in the event of no-shows, but you can also sometimes get in if the tables turn over more rapidly than usual. Hosts in each restaurant are responsible for keeping every table full. If additional guests can be accommodated, you can bet the host will jump to fill those slots.

With priority seating, your wait almost always will be less than 20 minutes during peak hours, and often less than 10 minutes. If you just walk in, especially during busier seasons, expect to wait 40–75 minutes.

Getting Your Act Together

If you want to patronize any of the Walt Disney World Resort full-service restaurants, buffets, character meals, or dinner shows, you should make priority seatings in advance. Following is a listing of how far in advance you can make priority seating:

730 Days (two years) in Advance
Hoop-Dee-Doo Revue
Polynesian Luau

365 Days (one year) in Advance
All American Backyard BBQ

180 Days in Advance
Victoria & Albert's

120 Days in Advance
All Walt Disney World Resort hotel restaurants
Epcot full-service restaurants except Bistro de Paris
Animal Kingdom Breakfastosaurus character breakfast
Animal Kingdom Rainforest Cafe
Grand Floridian 1900 Park Fare character meals
Grand Floridian Traditional Afternoon Tea
Grand Floridian Wonderland Tea Party
Contemporary Resort Chef Mickey character meals
Polynesian Resort Ohana character breakfast
Beach Club Cape May character breakfast

60 Days in Advance

Disney-MGM Studios full service restaurants and character meals

Magic Kingdom full-service restaurants and character meals

Wolfgang Puck Cafe (Downtown Disney)

Cinderella's Royal Table character breakfast

30 Days in Advance

Bistro de Paris at Epcot

Fulton's Crab House (Downtown Disney)

For most full-service restaurants, buffets, and character meals, you can make priority seatings 120 days in advance. Exceptions include the character breakfast at Cinderella's Royal Table where priority seating arrangement can be made 60 days in advance, and Disney dinner shows such as the *Polynesian Luau* and the *Hoop-Dee-Doo Revue* where priority seatings can be scheduled two years in advance.

If you fail to make priority seating before you leave home, or if you want to make your dining decisions spontaneously while at Walt Disney World, your chances of getting a table at the restaurant of your choice is pretty good, but not a slam dunk. The *Hoop-Dee-Doo Revue* and Cinderella's Royal Table breakfast will most certainly be sold out, as will several of the other more popular character meals. as will Boma, a buffet at the Animal Kingdom Lodge. Other restaurants will still have priority seatings available if you call at least a day in advance. Whether you reserve early or make arrangements once you're there, the number to call is (407) WDW-DINE.

Once in the theme parks, you can make priority seatings in person at the door of the restaurant, at Guest Services at Epcot,, or at the kiosk at the intersection of Hollywood and Sunset Boulevards at the Disney-MGM Studios. With a few exceptions, you'll have no problem getting your priority seating at the park. If you fail to make priority seatings, most full-service theme park restaurants will take you as a walk-in between 2:30 and 4:30 p.m.

Getting your act together in regard to counter-service restaurants in the parks is more a matter of courtesy than necessity. Rude guests ranked fifth among reader complaints, while a mother from Fort Wayne, Indiana, points out that indecision can be as maddening as outright discourtesy, especially when you're hungry:

Every fast-food restaurant has menu signs the size of billboards, but do you think anybody reads them? People waiting in line spend enough time in front of these sings to memorize them, and still don't have a clue what they want when they finally get to the order taker. If by some miracle they've managed to choose between the hot dog and the hamburger, they

*then fiddle around another ten minutes deciding what size coke to order.
Tell your readers PULEEEZ get their order together ahead of time!*

Dress

Dress is informal at all theme-park restaurants. While theme-park attire
(shorts, T-shirts, sneakers, etc.) is tolerated at hotel restaurants, you probably would feel more comfortable if you dressed up a bit. The only
restaurant requiring jackets for men and dressy clothes for women is Victoria & Albert's at the Grand Floridian.

A Few Caveats

Before you commence eating your way through the World, you need to
know:

1. However creative and enticing the menu descriptions, avoid fancy food,
    especially at full-service restaurants in the Magic Kingdom and Disney-
    MGM Studios. Order dishes the kitchen is unlikely to botch. An excep-
    tion to this caveat is the Brown Derby Restaurant at the Studios.

2. Don't order baked, broiled, poached, or grilled seafood unless the
    restaurant specializes in seafood or rates at least ★★★★ on our restau-
    rant profile.

3. Theme-park restaurants rush their customers in order to make room
    for the next group of diners. Dining at high speed may appeal to a

family with young, restless children, but for people wanting to relax, it's more like Beat the Clock than fine dining.

If you want to linger over your expensive meal, do not order your entire dinner at once. Order drinks. Study the menu while you sip, then order appetizers. Tell the waiter you need more time to decide among entrees. Order your main course only after appetizers have been served. Dawdle over coffee and dessert.

4. If you're dining in a theme park and cost is an issue, make lunch your main meal. Entrees are similar to those on the dinner menu, but prices are significantly lower.

Walt Disney World Restaurant Categories

In general, food and beverage offerings at Walt Disney World are defined by service, price, and convenience:

Full-Service Restaurants   Full-service restaurants are in all Disney resorts except the All-Star and Pop Century, and in all major theme parks, Downtown Disney Marketplace, Pleasure Island, and Disney's West Side. Disney operates the restaurants in the theme parks and its hotels. Contractors or franchisees operate the restaurants in hotels of the Disney Village Hotel Plaza, the Swan and Dolphin Resorts, Pleasure Island, Disney's West Side, and some in the Marketplace. Priority seating (explained above), arranged in advance, is recommended for all full-service restaurants except those in Disney Village Hotel Plaza. The restaurants accept VISA, MasterCard, American Express, Discover, Diners Club, and the Disney Credit Card.

Buffets   There has been an explosion of buffets at Disney World during recent years. Many have Disney characters in attendance, and most have a separate children's menu featuring hot dogs, burgers, chicken nuggets, pizza, macaroni and cheese, and spaghetti and meatballs. In addition to the buffets, several restaurants serve a family-style, all-you-can-eat, fixed-price meal. Priority seating arrangements are required for character buffets and recommended for all other buffets and family-style restaurants. Most major credit cards are accepted.

The table below lists buffets (where you can belly up for bulk loading) at Walt Disney World.

WALT DISNEY WORLD BUFFETS

Location	Restaurant	Cuisine	Meals Served	Disney Characters Present
Magic Kingdom	Crystal Palace	American	B, L, D	Yes
Epcot	Biergarten	German	L, D	No
Epcot	Restaurant Akershus	Scandinavian	L, D	No
Disney-MGM Studios	Hollywood and Vine	American	L	Yes
Animal Kingdom	Restaurantosaurus	American	B	Yes
Contemporary Resort	Chef Mickey's	American	B, D	Yes
Beach Club Resort	Cape May Cafe	Clambake	B, D	No
Grand Floridian	1900 Park Fare	American	B, D	Yes
Fort Wilderness Campground	Trail's End	American	B, L, D	No
Dolphin	Tubbi's Buffeteria	American	B, L, D	No
Animal Kingdom Lodge	Boma	African	B, D	No
Boardwalk	Spoodles	American/ Mediterranean	B, Sunday Brunch	No
Dolphin	Coral Cafe	American/ Japanese	B	No
Swan	Garden Grove Cafe	American	B	No

If you want to eat a lot but don't feel like standing in yet another line, consider one of the all-you-can-eat "family-style" restaurants. These feature platters of food brought to your table in courses by a server. You can sample everything on the menu and eat as much as you like. You can even go back to a favorite appetizer after you finish the main course. Food tends to be a little better than you'll find on a buffet line.

Family-style all-you-can-eat service is available at the Liberty Tree Tavern in the Magic Kingdom and The Garden Grill Restaurant in the Land pavilion in Epcot (both with character dining); or at 'Ohana in the Polynesian Resort and Whispering Canyon Cafe in the Wilderness Lodge.

Cafeterias and Food Courts   Cafeterias, in all the major theme parks, offer a middle ground between full-service and counter-service dining. Food courts, featuring a collection of counter-service eateries under one roof, are found at the theme parks as well as at the moderate (Coronado Springs, Caribbean Beach, Port Orleans) and budget (All-Star and Pop Century) Disney resorts. No priority seating is required or available at cafeterias or food courts.

Counter Service   Counter-service fast food is available in all theme parks and at Downtown Disney Marketplace, Pleasure Island, Disney's BoardWalk, and Disney's West Side. The food compares in quality with McDonald's, Captain D's, or Taco Bell, but is more expensive, though often served in larger portions.

Vendor Food Vendors abound at the theme parks, Downtown Disney Marketplace, Pleasure Island, Disney's West Side, and Disney's Board-Walk. Offerings include popcorn, ice cream bars, churros (Mexican pastry), soft drinks, bottled water, and (in theme parks) fresh fruit. Prices include tax, and payment must be in cash.

Hard Choices

Dining choices will definitely impact your Walt Disney World experience. If you're short on time and you want to see the theme parks, avoid full-service restaurants. Ditto if you're short on funds. If you want to try a Disney full-service restaurant, arrange priority seating in advance. That won't reserve you a table, but it will minimize your wait.

Integrating Meals into the Unofficial Guide *Touring Plans*

Arrive before the park of your choice opens. Tour expeditiously, using your chosen plan (taking as few breaks as possible), until about 11–11:30 a.m. Once the park becomes crowded around midday, meals and other breaks won't affect the plan's efficiency. If you intend to stay in the park for evening parades, fireworks, or other events, eat dinner early enough to be finished in time for the festivities.

Character Dining

A number of restaurants, primarily those serving all-you-can-eat buffets and family-style meals, offer character dining. At character meals, you pay a fixed price and dine in the presence of one to five Disney characters that circulate throughout the restaurant, hugging children (and sometimes adults), posing for photos, and signing autographs. Character breakfasts, lunches, and dinners are served at restaurants in and out of the theme parks. For an extensive discussion of character dining, see Part Five: Walt Disney World with Kids.

Full-Service Dining for Families with Young Children

Disney restaurants offer an excellent (though expensive) opportunity to introduce young children to the variety and excitement of ethnic food. No matter how formal a restaurant appears, the staff is accustomed to wiggling, impatient, and often boisterous children. Chefs de France at Epcot, for example, may be the nation's only French restaurant where most patrons wear shorts and T-shirts and at least two dozen young diners are attired in basic black . . . mouse ears. Bottom line: Young children are the rule, not the exception, at Disney restaurants.

Almost all Disney restaurants offer children's menus, and all have booster seats and highchairs. They understand how tough it may be for children to sit for an extended period, and waiters will supply little ones with crackers and rolls and serve your dinner much faster than in comparable restaurants elsewhere. Letters from readers suggest that being served too quickly (not having enough time to relax) is much more common than having a long wait.

Good Walt Disney World Theme-Park Restaurants for Children

In Epcot, preschoolers most enjoy the Biergarten in Germany, San Angel Inn Restaurante in Mexico, and Coral Reef in The Living Seas pavilion in Future World. The Biergarten combines a rollicking and noisy atmosphere with good basic food, including roast chicken. A German oompah band entertains. Children often have the opportunity to participate in Bavarian dancing. San Angel Inn is in the Mexican village marketplace. From the table, children can watch boats on El Río del Tiempo drift beneath a smoking volcano. With a choice of chips, tacos, and other familiar items, picky children usually have no difficulty finding something to eat. The Coral Reef, with tables beside windows looking into The Living Seas aquarium, offers a satisfying mealtime diversion for all ages. If your kids don't eat fish, Coral Reef also serves chicken.

The Biergarten offers reasonable value, plus good food. The Coral Reef and San Angel Inn are overpriced, though the food is palatable.

Cinderella's Royal Table in Cinderella Castle is the big draw in the Magic Kingdom. Interestingly, other Magic Kingdom full-service restaurants hold little appeal for children. For the best combination of food and entertainment, book a character meal at the Liberty Tree Tavern or The Crystal Palace.

At Disney-MGM Studios, all ages enjoy the atmosphere and entertainment at the Sci-Fi Dine-In Theater Restaurant and the 50's Prime Time Cafe. Unfortunately, the Sci-Fi's food is close to dismal and the Prime Time's is uneven. Eat only dessert at these restaurants.

The only full-service restaurant at the Animal Kingdom is the Rainforest Cafe, which is a great favorite of children.

Fast Food in the Theme Parks

Because most meals during a Disney World vacation are consumed on the run while touring, we'll tackle counter-service and vendor foods first. Plentiful in all theme parks are hot dogs, hamburgers, chicken breast sandwiches, green salads, and pizza. They're augmented by special items that relate to the park's theme or the part of the park you're touring. In Epcot's Germany, for example, counter-service bratwurst and beer are sold. In Frontierland in the Magic Kingdom, vendors sell smoked turkey legs. Counter-service prices are fairly consistent from park to park. Expect to pay the same for your coffee and hot dog at the Animal Kingdom as at Disney-MGM Studios.

Healthful Food in Walt Disney World

One of the most commendable developments in food service at Walt Disney World has been the introduction of more healthful foods and snacks. Diabetics, vegetarians, weight-watchers, those requiring kosher meals, and guests on restricted diets should have no trouble finding *something* to eat. Ditto for anyone seeking wholesome, nutritious food. Healthful food is available at most fast-food counters and even from vendors. All major theme parks, for example, have fruit stands.

A Nashville, Tennessee, mom was delighted to see the changes, writing:

I was very happy to see vegetarian items on almost every menu. What a difference from a couple of years ago.

Cutting Your Dining Time at the Theme Parks

Even if you confine your meals to vendor and counter-service fast food, you lose a lot of time getting food in the theme parks. At Walt Disney World, everything begins with a line and ends with a cash register. When it comes to fast food, "fast" may apply to the time you spend eating it, not the time invested in obtaining it.

A New York reader agrees, writing:

In terms of lunch, we found the lines, staff, and general service incredibly slow, unappetizing, and annoying. How is it that ski resorts throughout the country feed hordes of people at precisely the same time and offer an extensive array of quality food with a broad selection, prompt service, and quick check out? Perhaps WDW should visit Vail or Steamboat and learn a thing or two.

Here are suggestions for minimizing the time you spend hunting and gathering food:

1. Eat breakfast before arriving. Don't waste touring time eating breakfast at the parks. Besides, restaurants outside the World offer some outstanding breakfast specials. Some hotels furnish small refrigerators in their guest rooms or rent them. If you can get by on cold cereal, rolls, fruit, and juice, having a fridge in your room will save a ton of time. If you can't get a fridge, bring a cooler.

2. After a good breakfast, buy snacks from vendors in the parks as you tour, or stuff some snacks in a fanny pack. This is very important if you're on a tight schedule and can't spend a lot of time waiting in line for food.

3. All theme-park restaurants are busiest between 11:30 a.m. and 2:15 p.m. for lunch and 6 and 9 p.m. for dinner. For shorter lines and faster service, avoid eating during these hours.

4. Many counter-service restaurants sell cold sandwiches. Buy a cold lunch (except for drinks) before 11 a.m. and carry it until you're ready to eat. Ditto for dinner. Bring small plastic bags in which to pack the food. Purchase drinks at the appropriate time from any convenient vendor.

5. Most fast-food eateries have more than one service window. Regardless of time of day, check the lines at all windows before queuing. Sometimes a window that's manned but out of the way will have a much shorter line or none at all. Note, however, that some windows may offer only certain items. For example, some windows may serve only soup and salad, while others serve sandwiches.

6. If you're short on time and the park closes early, stay until closing and eat dinner outside Disney World before returning to your hotel. If the park stays open late, eat dinner about 4 or 4:30 p.m. at the restaurant of your choice. You should miss the last wave of lunchers and sneak in just ahead of the dinner crowd.

Beyond Counter Service:
Tips for Saving Money on Food

Though buying food from counter-service restaurants and vendors will save time and money (compared to full-service dining), additional strategies can bolster your budget and maintain your waistline. Here are some suggestions our readers have made over the years:

1. Go to Disney World during a period of fasting and abstinence. You can save a fortune and save your soul at the same time!

2. Wear clothes that are slightly too small and make you feel like dieting (no spandex allowed!).

3. Whenever you're feeling hungry, ride the Mad Tea Party, Body Wars, or other attractions that induce motion sickness.

4. Leave your cash and credit cards at your hotel. Buy food only with money your children fish out of fountains and wishing wells.

Cost-conscious readers also have volunteered ideas for stretching food dollars. A family from Lee's Summit, Missouri, tells us:

Last year we requested a small refrigerator for our room and were given one for no charge. This year we were charged $5 a day [now it's $10 a day!] for use of the fridge, but it was definitely worth it for us to be able to eat breakfast in the room to save time and money.

A Missouri mom writes:

I have shared our very successful meal plan with many families. We stayed six nights and arrived at WDW after some days on the beach south of Sarasota.

We shopped there and arrived with our steel Coleman cooler well stocked with milk and sandwich fixings. I froze a block of ice in a milk bottle, and we replenished it daily with ice from the resort ice machine. I also froze small packages of deli-type meats for later in the week. We ate cereal, milk, and fruit each morning, with boxed juices. I also had a hot pot to boil water for instant coffee, oatmeal, and soup.

Each child had a belt bag of his own, which he filled from a special box of "goodies" each day. I made a great mystery of filling that box in the weeks before the trip. Some things were actual food, like packages of crackers and cheese, packets of peanuts and raisins. Some were worthless junk, like candy and gum. They grazed from their belt bags at will throughout the day, with no interference from Mom and Dad. Each also had a small, rectangular plastic water bottle that could hang in the belt. We filled these at water fountains before getting into lines and were the envy of many.

We left the park before noon, ate sandwiches, chips, and soda in the room, and napped. We purchased our evening meal in the park, at a counter-service eatery. We budgeted for both morning and evening snacks from a vendor but often did not need them. It made the occasional treat all the more special. Our cooler had been pretty much emptied by the end of the week, but the block of ice was still there.

We interviewed one woman who brought a huge picnic for her family of five packed in a large diaper/baby paraphernalia bag. She stowed the bag in a locker under the Main Street Station and retrieved it when the family was hungry. A Pennsylvania family adds:

Despite the warning against bringing food into the park, we packed a double picnic lunch in a backpack and a small shoulder bag. Even with a small discount, it cost $195 for the seven of us to tour the park for a day, and I felt that spending another $150 or so on two meals was not in the cards. We froze juice boxes to keep the meat sandwiches cool (it worked fine) and had an extra round of juice boxes and peanut butter sandwiches for a late-afternoon snack. We took raisins and a pack of fig bars for sweets, but didn't carry any other cookies or candy to avoid a "sugar-low" during the day. Fruit would have been nice, but it would have been squashed.

Note: Disney has a rule against bringing your own food and drink into the park. Although after 9/11 all packs, purses, diaper bags, etc., are being searched, security usually does not enforce this ban.

Suggestions for Eating at the Theme Parks

Below are suggestions for dining at each of the major theme parks. If you are interested in trying a theme-park full-service restaurant, be aware that the restaurants continue to serve after the park's official closing time. For example, we showed up at The Hollywood Brown Derby just as Disney-MGM Studios closed at 8 p.m. We were seated almost immediately and enjoyed a leisurely dinner while the crowds cleared out. Incidentally, don't worry if you are depending on Disney transportation: buses, boats, and monorails run two to three hours after the parks close.

At the Magic Kingdom

Food at the Magic Kingdom has improved noticeably over the past several years. The Crystal Palace at the end of Main Street offers a good, albeit pricey, buffet, chaperoned by Disney characters, while the Liberty Tree Tavern in Liberty Square features hearty family-style dining, also with Disney characters in attendance. Cinderella's Royal Table, a full-service restaurant on the second floor of the castle, delivers palatable meals in one of the World's most unique settings.

THE MAGIC KINGDOM

Author's Favorite Counter-Service Restaurants

Cosmic Ray's—Tomorrowland
The Plaza Pavilion—Tomorrowland
Aunt Polly's Dockside Inn—Frontierland
Pecos Bill's Tall Tale Inn & Cafe—Frontierland
The Diamond Horseshoe Saloon Revue—Liberty Square

Fast food at the Magic Kingdom is, well, fast food. It's more expensive, of course, than what you would pay at McDonald's, but what do you expect? It's like dining at an airport—you're a captive audience. On the positive side, portions are large, sometimes large enough for children to share. Overall, the variety of fast food offerings provides a lot of choice, though the number of selections at any specific eatery remains quite limited. Check our mini-profiles of the park's counter-service restaurants before you queue up.

Here are dining recommendations for your day at the Magic Kingdom:

1. Take the monorail to one of the hotels for lunch. The trip over and back takes very little time, and because most guests have left the hotels for the parks, the resorts' restaurants are often uncrowded. The food is better than in the Magic Kingdom; the service is faster; the atmosphere is more relaxed; and beer, wine, and mixed drinks are available. Decent dinner buffets are served at Chef Mickey's at the Contemporary and at 1900 Park Fare at the Grand Floridian. Both feature characters; don't expect quiet dining. Commuting to the buffets is a snap by monorail. A more adult option is the family-style skillet dinner served at Whispering Canyon Cafe in the Wilderness

Lodge and Villas. Lunch is also available. To reach the Wilderness Lodge and Villas, take the boat from the Magic Kingdom docks.

2. If you choose to eat in the Magic Kingdom during the midday rush (11:30 a.m.–2:15 p.m.) or the evening rush (5–8 p.m.), try Aunt Polly's Dockside Inn (closes at dusk) on Tom Sawyer Island. Another option is The Diamond Horseshoe Saloon Revue, which serves sandwiches between shows. All theme-park counter-service restaurants are profiled later in this section.

3. Full-service restaurants that accept priority seating for lunch and/or dinner fill quickly. To obtain priority seating in advance, call (407) 939-3463 or hotfoot to your chosen restaurant as soon as you enter the park. Priority seating is explained and all Magic Kingdom full-service restaurants are profiled later in this section.

4. Of the park's four full-service restaurants, Liberty Tree Tavern in Liberty Square is the best. Tony's Town Square Restaurant on Main Street and Cinderella's Royal Table in the castle also serve decent food. Because children love Cinderella and everyone's curious about the inside of the castle, you need to make a priority seating before you leave home if you want to eat breakfast at Cinderella's Royal Table (see pages 274–278). Priority seatings for lunch or dinner are easier to arrange.

6. A good rule at any full-service restaurant in the park is to keep it simple. Order sandwiches or basic dishes (roast turkey and mashed potatoes, for example).

At Epcot

From the beginning, dining has been an integral component of Epcot's basic entertainment product. The importance of dining is reflected both in the number of restaurants and their ability to serve consistently interesting and well-prepared meals. This is in stark contrast, say, to the Magic Kingdom, where, until recently, food service was seemingly a perfunctory afterthought, with quality and selection a distant runner-up to logistical efficiency.

For the most part, Epcot's restaurants have always served decent food, though the World Showcase restaurants have occasionally been timid about delivering an honest representation of the host nation's cuisine. While these eateries have struggled with authenticity and have sometimes shied away from challenging the meat-and-potatoes palate of the average tourist, they are bolder now, encouraged by America's exponentially expanding appreciation of ethnic dining. True, the less adventuresome can still find sanitized and homogenized meals, but the same kitchens will serve up the real thing for anyone with a spark of curiosity and daring.

FULL-SERVICE RESTAURANTS IN EPCOT

Future World

Coral Reef	The Living Seas
The Garden Grill Restaurant	The Land

World Showcase

Biergarten	Germany
Le Cellier Steakhouse	Canada
Bistro de Paris	France
Chefs de France	France
L'Originale Alfredo di Roma Ristorante	Italy
Restaurant Akershus	Norway
Restaurant Marrakesh	Morocco
Tempura Kiku	Japan
Teppanyaki Dining Room	Japan
Nine Dragons Restaurant	China
Rose & Crown Dining Room	United Kingdom
San Angel Inn Restaurante	Mexico

EPCOT

Author's Favorite Counter-Service Restaurants

Pure and Simple	Rose and Crown Pub
Kringla Bakeri og Kafé	Sommerfest
Yakitori House	

Many Epcot restaurants are overpriced, most conspicuously Nine Dragons Restaurant (China) and the Coral Reef (The Living Seas). Representing relatively good value through the combination of ambiance and well-prepared food are Chefs de France (France), Restaurant Akershus (Norway), Biergarten (Germany), and Restaurant Marrakesh (Morocco). The Biergarten and the Marrakesh also have entertainment.

If cost is an issue, make lunch your main meal. Entrees are similar to those on the dinner menu, but prices are significantly lower.

Epcot has 13 full-service restaurants: 2 in Future World and 11 in World Showcase. With a couple of exceptions, these are among the best restaurants at Disney World, in or out of the theme parks. Profiles of Epcot full-service restaurants are presented at the end of this section.

While eating at Epcot can be a consummate hassle, an afternoon without priority seating for dinner in World Showcase is like not having a date on the day of the prom. Each pavilion has a beautifully seductive ethnic restaurant, offering the gastronomic delights of the world. To tour these exotic settings and not partake is almost beyond the limits of willpower. And although the fare in some World Showcase restaurants isn't always compelling, the overall experience is exhilarating. If you fail to dine in World Showcase, you'll miss one of Epcot's more delightful features.

If you want to sample the ethnic foods of World Showcase without eating in restaurants requiring priority seating, we recommend these counter-service specialties:

Norway	Kringla Bakeri og Kafé, for pastries, open-face sandwiches, and Ringnes beer (our favorite)
Germany	Sommerfest, for bratwurst and Beck's beer
Japan	Matsu No Ma Lounge, for sushi and sashimi
Japan	Yakitori House, for yakitori (meat or vegetables on skewers)
France	Boulangerie Pâtisserie, for French pastries
United Kingdom	Rose & Crown Pub, for Guinness, Harp, and Bass beers and ales

Epcot counter-service restaurants are profiled at the end of this section.

At Disney-MGM Studios

Dining at Disney-MGM Studios is more interesting than in the Magic Kingdom and less ethnic than at Epcot. Disney-MGM has five restaurants where priority seating is recommended: The Hollywood Brown Derby, 50's Prime Time Cafe, Sci-Fi Dine-In Theater Restaurant, Mama Melrose's Ristorante Italiano, and the Hollywood and Vine Cafeteria. The upscale Brown Derby is by far the best restaurant at the Studios. For simple Italian food, including pizza, Mama Melrose's is fine. Just don't expect anything fancy (except the prices). At the Sci-Fi Dine-In, you eat in little cars at a simulated drive-in movie of the '50s. Though you won't find a more entertaining restaurant in Walt Disney World, the food is quite disappointing. Ditto for the 50's Prime Time Cafe, where you sit in Mom's kitchen of the '50s and scarf down meat loaf while watching clips of vintage TV sitcoms. Like the Sci-Fi, the 50's Prime Time Cafe is fun, but the food is expensive and lackluster. The best way to experience either restaurant is to stop in for dessert or a drink between 2:30 and 4:30 p.m.

DISNEY-MGM STUDIOS

Author's Favorite Counter-Service Restaurants

Toy Story Pizza Planet	Backlot Express
ABC Commissary	Toluca Legs Turkey Co.
Studio Catering	

We receive considerable mail from readers recounting their Disney-MGM dining experiences. A man from Sumter, South Carolina, writes:

We had lunch at the Sci-Fi Dine-In. In the guide you gave it a terrible review, but I have always felt you guys are too hard on the Disney restaurants, so we went ahead and ate there. Well, on this one you were right on target! While the atmosphere was fun, and the clips were a hoot, the food was lousy . . . and expensive!

A Mechanicsville, Virginia, family agreed:

You tried to warn us about the Sci-Fi Dine-In, but my four-year old was dying to eat there. The food was even worse than you said—and the cost! $9.50 for a hot dog and fries.

From a Maryland reader:

Prime Time Cafe was a fun experience, but again, the food quality was, at best, mediocre. If my mom really did cook that way, I would have many times run away from home. Our poor reaction to the food quality pushed us quickly into the car and out of WDW. I never thought I would get down on my knees and kiss the sidewalk outside of a Perkins Pancake House.

But a West Newton, Massachusetts, family loved the Prime Time:

50's Prime Time Cafe: We know you guys didn't rate it very well, but we decided to go against your recommendation and give it a shot. We're so glad we did! For the five of us (ages 16–20), this dining experience was a blast. Our waiter (and big brother for the meal), "Leroy," came and sat at our table and helped us set our places so we wouldn't get in trouble with "Mom." When one member of our party cursed, "Mom" arrived to punish him, making him clear the table onto her tray, which he did shamefully. Overall, the experience was a total kick, which we talked about for the rest of the trip.

Disney-MGM Studios' full-service restaurants are profiled at the end of this section. If you arrive at Disney-MGM Studios without previously arranging priority seating for meals, do so at the the priority seating kiosk at the corner of Hollywood and Sunset boulevards or at the restaurants.

If you have no priority seating and become hungry during meal times, try the deli sandwiches at the Studio Catering Company. On the park's opposite side, try Toy Story Pizza Planet. Both are sometimes overlooked by the teeming hordes.

Disney-MGM Studios counter-service restaurants are profiled at the end of this section.

At the Animal Kingdom

Because touring the Animal Kingdom takes less than a day, crowds are heaviest from 9:30 a.m. until about 3:30 p.m. Expect a mob at lunch and thinner crowds at dinner. We recommend you tour early after a good breakfast, then eat a very late lunch or graze on vendor food. If you tour later in the day, eat lunch before you arrive, then enjoy dinner in or out of the theme park.

The Animal Kingdom mostly offers counter-service fast food. Although grilled meats are available, don't expect a broad choice of exotic dishes. Most Animal Kingdom eateries serve up traditional Disney theme-park fare: hot dogs, hamburgers, deli sandwiches, and the like. Even so, we found Animal Kingdom fast food to be a cut above the average Disney fare. Flame Tree Barbeque in Safari Village is our pick of the litter, both in terms of food quality and atmosphere. For a quiet refuge away from the crowds, you can't beat Flame Tree Barbeque's waterfront dining pavilions.

THE ANIMAL KINGDOM
Author's Favorite Counter-Service Restaurant

Flame Tree Barbecue

The only full-service restaurant is the Rainforest Cafe, with entrances both inside and outside the theme park (you don't have to purchase theme-park admission, in other words, to eat at the restaurant). Unlike the Rainforest Cafe at the Downtown Disney Marketplace, the Animal Kingdom branch accepts priority seatings.

Readers' Comments about Walt Disney World Dining

Eating is a popular topic among *Unofficial Guide* readers. In addition to participating in our annual restaurant survey, many readers share their thoughts. The following comments are representative.

A reader from Carbondale, Illinois, exhorts other readers to be adventuresome in their choice of restaurants:

Please advise your readers to try "different" restaurants at EPCOT! We had a blast dining at Akershus and Marrakesh! The service was great, food was different, but not weird. My husband is a picky eater, but even he was able to say that he tried Norwegian and Moroccan food at the end of our vacation! I feel like Marrakesh is not popular because people think the food is too ethnic. Well it was ethnic enough, but not too hot or spicy, and the atmosphere was great. To me, it was the most themed restaurant—the inside SCREAMED Mediterranean and the belly dancer was GREAT! I think it would be a fun restaurant for anyone, with kids as well.

Another Illinois reader, this one from Glendale, had a positive experience with Disney food, writing:

On the food: In general, we were pleasantly surprised. I expected it to be over-priced, generally bad, and certainly unhealthy. There were a lot of options—and almost all restaurants (including counter service) had generally good food, and some healthy options. It is not the place to expect fine cuisine—and is certainly overpriced, but if you understand the parameters—you can eat quite well. One thing I appreciated was having a children's menu that did not consist only of hot dogs and french fries. My children ate well and we were able to get them a good variety of food—with plenty of fruits and vegetables.

The Sci-Fi Diner at the Disney-MGM Studios is always a lightning rod for reader comments. Here are couple from this year's batch. First, from a Pennsylvania reader:

The Sci-Fi Dine-In Theater Restaurant was even worse than I remembered. However, the behavior of the would-be/never-will-be actors of serving staff was unforgivable. At particular points of the movie trailers playing, the entire serving staff is supposed to pretend (pretend?) they are bored and yell the movie dialogue at the top of their lungs with the film. Do you know what that is like when carrying on a conversation? Do you know what that is like while asking the server questions or ordering? We picked up and left with the server chasing us to come back. I do not care if the servers want to be actors. Paying more attention to the film than customers and screaming instead of concentrating on business is unforgivable!

A Houston, Texas family thought the food at the Sci-Fi was vastly improved, writing:

We thought the food at the Sci-Fi Theater was wonderful! I could picture the meeting of top brass reading your book, and some guy at the head of the table pounding his fist on the table and demanding that they improve the food or else everyone was fired—because the food was remarkably good!

Four adults from Lake Charles, Louisiana loved Alfredo's at Epcot:

We really enjoyed L'Originale Alfredo Restauranto. It was the best meal we had in WDW, and that's high praise since we had a Tuscan and a Sicilian in the group! Am glad we went against your recommendation.

Another big thumbs up from Terre Haute, Indiana for the California Grill:

I had what might be the most memorable meal of my life at the California Grill. We left the kids with a sitter, (Vivian from Fairy Godmother's: "You'll like her—she's been with me twenty years."), and went out for a romantic evening. You mentioned being seated at the counter overlooking the show kitchen, which I'm sure would be great, but for a romantic dinner, you can't beat the smaller dining room. We didn't know it existed, but we were led through the end of the main dining room through large glass doors to a table in the corner of a smaller dining room with only seven other tables. Away from the cacophony of the main dining room, this was a quiet haven with a spectacular view. We watched as a thunderstorm with all its lightning glory rolled toward, then over us. Afterward, we were awed by a stunning full rainbow. It was a nice treat for our 10th anniversary. The food was out of this world, and the service (by Judy) was impeccable.

A family of five loved Whispering Canyon at the Wilderness Lodge:

Our best experience for dining was at the Whispering Canyon. My girls (6, 10, 11) thought the servers were great. They joked with each other, shouted and laughed with the kids. They had wooden pony races around the restaurant for the kids. Our waiter even sat down with our kids and helped my oldest "finish" her salad and showed my youngest how to eat whipped cream off her nose. Out of all the places we ate, this was my kids (and Mom and Dad's) favorite. Oh, and the food was pretty good too.

We've received consistent raves for Boma:

Boma (the African Buffet at the Animal Kingdom Lodge) is terrific!!

A Lombard, Illinois, mom underscores the need to make priority seatings in advance:

Please stress that if you want a "normal" dining hour at a specific restaurant, call them 60 or 45 days in advance—IT IS WORTH IT! One reservation I wanted to change about two weeks before our arrival date and I had a choice of dinner times of either 7:45 or 9 p.m. (not feasible with little ones).

A Baltimore, Maryland, reader thinks we failed to give Wolfgang Puck his due:

Bob, you greatly underestimated the Wolfgang Puck Express in Marketplace. It's not five-star, but it is a great fast-food alternative. We got yummy gourmet pizzas, and rotisserie chicken ... but the best part were the beer barrels. We ended up eating there on two occasions.

I was apprehensive about the food, [but] our experiences were very good overall at both the full-service and counter-service restaurants. Face it, you don't go to Disney for the dinner bargains.

A Greenwood, Indiana, family agrees:

The food was certainly expensive, but contrary to many of the views expressed in the Unofficial Guide, we all thought the quality was excellent. Everything we had, from chicken strips and hot dogs in the parks to dinner at the Coral Reef, tasted great and seemed very fresh.

A family from Youngsville, Louisiana, got a leg up on other guests:

The best thing we ate were the smoked turkey legs.

A mom from Aberdeen, South Dakota, writes:

When we want great food we'll be on a different vacation. Who wants to waste fun time with the kids at a sit-down restaurant when you know the food will be mediocre anyway.

A woman from Verona, Wisconsin, offers this:

We think the character meals are under-rated in all guidebooks. These meals are in pleasant settings and provide an easy, efficient way for little kids to interact with characters while providing adults with an opportunity to relax. For value and good food, we especially like the breakfasts. Yes, they're a little pricey, but you get more than food. Probably our favorite is at The Garden Grill at The Land at Epcot. This year they even gave us souvenir hats.

A mother of three from Jamaica, New York, waited two hours and 40 minutes for a table at the Rainforest Cafe and still had a good time:

The Rainforest Cafe was an absolute delight. Our six-year-old sat right next to a gorilla that ranted every few minutes; our ten-month-old loved the huge fish tanks; and they loved the food. Our wait for a table was two hours, so we went back to the hotel and returned two hours later. We still had to wait 40 minutes, but it was worth it. The gorilla room had more of a jungle feel than the elephant room.

On the topic of saving money, a Seattle woman offered the following:

For those wanting to save a few bucks (or in some cases several bucks) we definitely suggest eating outside WDW for as many meals as possible. To keep down our costs, we ate a large breakfast before leaving the hotel, had a fast-food lunch in the park, a snack later to hold us over, and then ate a good dinner outside the park. Several good restaurants in the area have excellent food at reasonable prices, notably Cafe Tu Tu Tango and Ming [Court], both on International Drive. We also obtained the "Entertainment Book" for Orlando, which offers 50% off meals all over town.

Cap'n Jack's Oyster Bar at Downtown Disney has taken the place of Cinderella's Royal Table as the punching bag for dissatisfied diners. These remarks from a Winston Salem, North Carolina, reader are typical:

Also, we ate at Cap'n Jack's Friday night. Not very good. We were hard-pressed to remember a more disappointing meal in WDW. Dinner for five with two shared appetizers and no alcohol was around $130, excluding gratuity. We couldn't identify the origin of most of the seafood bits in the seafood pasta—you couldn't point to anything and say "That's a clam," for *example. My brother's vegetables included part of the cardboard box they came in. The sesame-coated tuna steak, while correctly cooked, was almost flavorless.*

Counter-Service Restaurant Mini-Profiles

To help you find palatable fast-service food that suits your taste, we have developed mini-profiles of Walt Disney World theme-park counter-service restaurants. The restaurants are listed alphabetically by theme park.

For convenience, we've repeated our lists of favorite counter-service restaurants here. The restaurants profiled below are rated for quality and portion size (self-explanatory), as well as for value. The value rating ranges from A to F as follows:

A = Exceptional value, a real bargain
B = Good value
C = Fair value, you get exactly what you pay for
D = Somewhat overpriced
F = Extremely overpriced

THE MAGIC KINGDOM

Author's Favorite Counter-Service Restaurants

Cosmic Ray's—Tomorrowland
The Plaza Pavilion—Tomorrowland
Aunt Polly's Dockside Inn—Frontierland
Pecos Bill's Tall Tale Inn & Cafe—Frontierland
The Diamond Horseshoe Saloon Revue—Liberty Square

Aunt Polly's Dockside Inn

Frontierland, on Tom Sawyer Island

QUALITY Good | VALUE B | PORTION Medium

Selection Turkey- and ham-and-swiss sandwiches; child's plate with peanut-butter-and-jelly sandwich (includes cookie and a child's beverage); ice-cream cones, floats, chocolate brownies, and apple pie.

Comments Scenic and off the beaten path. One of our great favorites for lunch with seats in the shade. A decent amount of food for the money. Closes at dusk.

Casey's Corner

Main Street, U.S.A.

QUALITY Good | VALUE B | PORTION Medium

Selection Quarter-pound hot dogs and fries; and brownies.
Comments A little pricey on the dogs and very crowded—keep walking.

Columbia Harbour House
Liberty Square

QUALITY Fair | VALUE C | PORTION Medium

Selection Fried fish and chicken strips; ham-and-cheese, veggie, and tuna-salad sand-wiches; child's plate with bologna-and-cheese sandwich or macaroni and cheese, cookie, and child's beverage; New England clam chowder (in bread bowl) and vegetable chili; cole slaw; chips; fries; garden salad with chicken; and apple pie and cookies.

Comments Fried items aren't appetizing, but the soups and sandwiches and their unusual sides (hummus, broccoli slaw) are a nice change from the usual pizza/burger fare. Tables usually available upstairs. Quickest service within spitting distance of Fantasyland.

Cosmic Ray's Starlight Cafe
Tomorrowland

QUALITY Good | VALUE B | PORTION Large

Selection Rotisserie chicken meal; deli sandwiches; cheesesteak subs; fried and grilled chicken sandwiches; burgers (including vegetarian); chicken strips; hot dogs; child's plate with corn dog–nuggets; vegetable and cream of chicken soups; chicken Caesar salads; fries, mashed potatoes, veggie pasta salad; and ice-cream bars.

Comments Big place. Tables inside usually available. Out-of-this-world entertainment on stage. This is the place if everybody in your party is picky—you'll have plenty of options. Nice burger-fixin' bar.

The Diamond Horseshoe Saloon Revue
Liberty Square

QUALITY Good | VALUE B | PORTION Medium

Selection Ham-and-cheese, smoked-turkey, and roast-beef sandwiches; garden and chicken Caesar salads; veggie wraps; child's plates with peanut-butter-and-jelly sandwich, chips, and child's beverage; chips; ice-cream cones and floats; brownies; and hot-fudge sundaes.

Comments Combine lunch with a show. First come, first served. They also serve a small selection of continental breakfast items (cereal, muffins, etc.) during pre-lunch hours.

El Pirata y el Perico
Adventureland

QUALITY Fair | VALUE B | PORTION Medium to large

Selection Nachos; taco salad; tacos; beef empanada with black beans and rice; chili with cheese; churros; and ice cream.

Comments Large, shaded eating area. Open seasonally and often overlooked.

The Lunching Pad
Tomorrowland

QUALITY Good | VALUE C | PORTION Medium

Selection Smoked turkey legs; Disney-character cookies; and frozen sodas.
Comments Smack in the middle of Tomorrowland, The Lunching Pad is good for a quick snack or for waiting for people on nearby rides.

Pecos Bill's Tall Tale Inn & Cafe
Frontierland

QUALITY Good | VALUE B | PORTION Medium to large

Selection Cheeseburgers; hot dogs; chicken wraps; chicken salad; chili; child's plate with hot dog, cookie, and child's beverage; fries and chili cheese fries; root-beer floats; brownies.
Comments Use the great fixin's station to garnish your burger or dog.

The Pinocchio Village Haus
Fantasyland

QUALITY Fair to good | VALUE B | PORTION Medium

Selection Quarter-pound cheeseburger; double cheeseburger; quarter-pound hot dog; turkey sandwich; garden salad (with or without chicken); child's plate with peanut-butter-and-jelly sandwich or hot dog, chips, and a child's beverage; fries; fresh fruit; and brownies.
Comments Almost always crowded. Try Columbia Harbour House on the border with Liberty Square. And for the same burger/dog fare, Pecos Bill's gets higher marks.

The Plaza Pavilion
Tomorrowland

QUALITY Good | VALUE B | PORTION Medium to large

Selection Six-inch pizzas; pizza combo meal with small salad; bread sticks; salads; deli sandwiches; chicken strips; child's plate with peanut-butter-and-jelly sandwiches, chips, and a child's beverage; fries; and ice-cream bars.
Comments Usually not too crowded. Along with Cosmic Ray's, our pick for best menu selection in the Magic Kingdom.

Plaza Restaurant
Main Street USA

QUALITY Excellent | VALUE B | PORTION Large

Selection Club, Reuben, cheesesteak, turkey, grilled chicken, and veggie sandwiches as well as burgers. Also big ice cream sundaes.
Comments This restaurant serves mostly sandwiches, but very good ones. Most days you can get a table pretty easily. Off hours, the Plaza Restaurant is a great place for hearty desserts.

EPCOT

Author's Favorite Counter-Service Restaurants

Pure and Simple

Kringla Bakeri og Kafé

Yakitori House

Rose and Crown Pub

Sommerfest

Boulangerie Pâtisserie

World Showcase, France

QUALITY Good | VALUE B | PORTION Small to medium

Selection Coffee, croissants, and pastries; cheese plate; ham-and-cheese croissant; quiche Lorraine; and French wine and beer.

Comments Okay for a light meal, better for a snack. A few outside tables.

Cantina de San Angel

World Showcase, Mexico

QUALITY Fair | VALUE C | PORTION Medium

Selection Chicken hard and soft tacos; burritos; ensalada Mexicana; child's plate with burrito, chips , and child's beverage; nachos, churros; XX Lager and frozen margaritas.

Comments Most meals are served with refried beans and salsa. Tables are outdoors.

Electric Umbrella Restaurant

Future World, Innoventions, Plaza East

QUALITY Good | VALUE B | PORTION Medium

Selection Breakfast pizza and breakfast burrito, French toast, cereal; burgers, veggie burgers, and chicken tenders with fries; chicken sandwiches; child's plates with hot dogs or cheese and pepperoni pizza; chicken tenders; hot dogs; chicken Caesar salad; fruit cup; chocolate-chip cookies, chocolate cream pie, and apple pie; Budweiser and Bud Light; breakfast menu also available.

Comments All items are served with french fries.

Kringla Bakeri og Kafé

World Showcase, Norway

QUALITY Good to Excellent | VALUE B | PORTION Small to medium

Selection Pastries; open-faced sandwiches (smoked ham, smoked turkey, and smoked salmon); green salad, fruit cup; sweet pretzels with raisins and almonds; cinnamon rolls; waffles; and Ringnes beer on tap.

Comments Good but pricey.

Liberty Inn

World Showcase, The American Adventure

QUALITY Fair | VALUE C | PORTION Medium

Selection Burgers and french fries; hot dogs; portobello mushroom sandwich; chicken strips; turkey club and grilled-chicken sandwiches; chicken Caesar and garden vegetable salads; child's hot dog and child's chicken-nugget plate; apple pie, chocolate-chip cookies, chocolate-mousse cake, frozen yogurt, and root-beer floats; and Samuel Adams, Budweiser, and Bud Light.

Comments The only place in World Showcase for American fast food. Ample seating.

Lotus Blossom Cafe
World Showcase, China
QUALITY Fair | VALUE D | PORTION Medium

Selection Stir-fried beef, chicken, and vegetable dishes; sweet-and-sour chicken; egg rolls; fried rice; veggie and sesame noodle plates; salad; hot and sour soup; ginger ice cream, fruit cup with lychee, and fortune cookies; child's plate with sweet-and-sour chicken or eggroll and pork fried rice (includes beverage); and Chinese beer and wine.

Comments Marginal Chinese at fancy prices.

Pure and Simple
Future World, Wonders of Life
QUALITY Good to excellent | VALUE B | PORTION Medium

Selection Turkey wrap and fruit or chips; hot dogs; chili; fruit cups; smoothies (natural fruit-blend drinks and papaya juice); yogurt sundaes, low-fat mousse, sugar-free brownies, and root-beer floats; waffles, bagel sandwiches, muffins, cereal, and breakfast platters.

Comments A good spot for those seeking low-fat, heart-healthy meals. This is also a good option for breakfast until 11 a.m.

Refreshment Port
Between the World Showcase and Future World
QUALITY Good | VALUE B | PORTION Medium

Selection Chicken nuggets; fries; McFlurry dessert.
Comments Though now a thinly disguised McDonald's, it's still a convenient place for a snack.

Rose & Crown Pub
World Showcase, United Kingdom
QUALITY Good | VALUE C | PORTION Medium

Selection Cornish pasties; fish and chips, sausage rolls; shortbread; fruit and cheese; and Guinness, Harp, and Bass beers and ales, as well as other spirits.
Comments The attraction here is the pub atmosphere and the draft beer. Note that the restaurant requires priority seating while the pub does not.

Sommerfest
World Showcase, Germany

QUALITY Good | VALUE B | PORTION Medium

Selection Bratwurst and frankfurter sandwiches with kraut; chicken schnitzel; soft pretzels; soup; apple strudel and Black Forest cake; and German wine and beer (Beck's).
Comments Tucked in the entrance to the Biergarten restaurant, Sommerfest is hard to find from the street. Very limited seating.

Sunshine Season Food Fair
Future World, The Land

QUALITY Fair to good | VALUE C | PORTION Medium

Selection Potatoes with cheese and bacon, and chicken and vegetables; soups and salads; barbecued chicken and ribs and smoked sandwiches with corn on the cob and fries; deli sandwiches; chicken Parmesan; pastas; veggie wrap; fruit-and-yogurt cups; brownies and cookies; ice cream and freshly baked goods; and beer.
Comments This is a food court with eight different counters. Most of the counters offer adult and child combo meals, and several feature heart-healthy options. Most counters serve beverages, so you don't have to queue up twice. Very crowded at mealtimes, making empty tables difficult to find.

Tangierine Cafe
World Showcase, Morocco

QUALITY Good | VALUE B | PORTION Medium

Selection Chicken and lamb shawarma; hummus; tabbouleh; braised-lamb plate; lentil salad; chicken with couscous; roast leg of lamb; seafood, chicken, or tabouleh wraps; olives; child's meal of Mediterranean pizza or hamburger with fries and small beverage; Casablanca beer; baklava.
Comments You won't get the belly dancers that entertain inside the pavilion at Restaurant Marrakesh, but the food here is good with an authentic flavor. The best seating is at the outdoor tables.

Yakitori House
World Showcase, Japan

QUALITY Excellent | VALUE B | PORTION Small to medium

Selection Shogun combo meal with beef and chicken teriyaki and rice (adult and child versions); shrimp, chicken, and beef skewers with rice; beef curry; shrimp tempura and beef udon; side salad; fruit cup; sushi; seafood salad; pickled radishes; edamamei; miso soup; child's fried chicken with vegetables and rice; ginger, green tea, and red-bean ice cream; and Kirin beer, sake, and plum wine.
Comments A great place for a light meal. Limited seating.

DISNEY-MGM STUDIOS

Author's Favorite Counter-Service Restaurants

Toy Story Pizza Planet
ABC Commissary
Studio Catering

Backlot Express
Toluca Legs Turkey Co.

ABC Commissary

Backlot

QUALITY Good | VALUE B | PORTION Medium to large

Selection Tabouleh wrap; chicken yakitori; vegetable noodle stir-fry; fish and chips; tomato salad; child's chicken-nugget or fish 'n' chips plate; fries; Asian slaw; ice-cream bars; and pie.
Comments Indoors, centrally located, air-conditioned, and usually not too crowded. Also offers a great traditional breakfast.

Backlot Express

Backlot

QUALITY Good | VALUE B | PORTION Medium to large

Selection Burgers and fries or fruit; chicken strips; hot dogs; chicken Caesar salad; tuna subs; and carrot cake or chocolate cake.
Comments Often overlooked. Great burger-fixin' bar. Indoor and outdoor seating.

Catalina Eddie's

Sunset Boulevard

QUALITY Fair | VALUE B | PORTION Medium

Selection Cheese, pepperoni, and vegetable pizzas; side salads; and pie and cake.
Comments Seldom crowded.

Min and Bill's Dockside Diner

Echo Lake

QUALITY Fair | VALUE C– | PORTION Small to medium

Selection Shakes and beverages; chips; and cookies and brownies.
Comments Limited outdoor seating.

Rosie's All American Cafe

Sunset Boulevard

QUALITY Good | VALUE B | PORTION Medium to large

Selection Cheeseburgers, bacon cheeseburgers, and veggie burgers; chicken strips' soup; side salads; apple pie; and chocolate cake.
Comments Was better as a hot dog stand. Sandwiches are premade. Backlot Express is a better option for the same fare.

Starring Rolls Bakery
Sunset Boulevard

QUALITY Fair to good | VALUE C | PORTION Small to medium

Selection Pastries, pies, cookies, cake, bagels, and rolls.

Comments Open for breakfast on some mornings. Slowest service of any counter-service eatery. Pastries look better than they taste.

Studio Catering Co.
Backlot

QUALITY Good | VALUE B | PORTION Large

Selection Stacked sandwiches (roast beef with Swiss, Italian, club, and turkey with cheddar), child's sandwich; pretzels; popcorn; chips; fruit cups; ice-cream cones, sundaes, and brownies.

Comments Ice cream has separate service lines. Good place for a break while your kids enjoy the *Honey, I Shrunk the Kids* playground. Shady outside seating.

Toluca Legs Turkey Co.
Sunset Boulevard

QUALITY Good | VALUE B | PORTION Medium to large

Selection Smoked turkey legs, hot dogs, Polish sausage, baked potatoes, pretzels, beer, and bottled soda.

Comments This vendor stall serves up some of the tastiest fast food in the park. Often overlooked. Covered outside seating.

Toy Story Pizza Planet
Backlot

QUALITY Excellent | VALUE B+ | PORTION Large

Selection Cheese, pepperoni, and veggie pizzas; salads; and chips.

Comments The place for pizza at the Studios. Fresh ingredients. Gets good marks from readers. Combo meals are great values.

THE ANIMAL KINGDOM

Author's Favorite Counter-Service Restaurant

Flame Tree Barbecue

Chakranadi Chicken Shop
Asia

QUALITY Good | VALUE C– | PORTION Small

Selection Chicken satay; Oriental noodle bowl; rotisserie chicken; chicken fried rice; roasted corn.

Comments Tasty food, tiny portions.

Flame Tree Barbecue
Safari Village
QUALITY Good | VALUE B– | PORTION Large

Selection Pork shoulder and chicken sandwiches; barbecue ribs; combination barbecue platters; crisp greens salad with chicken; child's plate of peanut-butter-and-jelly sandwich and chips, or franks-and-beans with cookie; steak fries; and Key lime pie and frozen lemonade.

Comments Queues very long at lunch time, but seating is ample and well shaded. One of our favorites for lunch.

Pizzafari
Safari Village
QUALITY Fair | VALUE B | PORTION Medium

Selection Personal pizzas: cheese; pepperoni; spinach, ham, tomato, pesto, pepperoni; or spinach, tomato, pesto, portabello mushrooms. Mesquite chicken Caesar salad; Italian deli sandwiches; penne pasta with meat sauce; cheese bread with sauce; child's cheese pretzel; chocolate-mousse cake, carrot cake, frozen lemonade; and draft beer.

Comments A favorite with children. Hectic at peak mealtimes. The pizza is pretty unimpressive—toppings resemble those on a cheap frozen pizza.

Restaurantosaurus
Dinoland U.S.A.
QUALITY Good | VALUE B+ | PORTION Medium to large

Selection Cheeseburgers and hot dogs; McDonald's Chicken McNuggets and Happy Meals; turkey wraps; mesquite-grilled chicken salad and vegetarian platter; fries, brownies, lemon bars, and cookies; and beer.

Comments Picky children might enjoy Restaurantosaurus. Others will do better at another eatery.

Tamu Tamu
Africa
QUALITY Good | VALUE C | PORTION Large

Selection Various flavors of yogurt or ice cream, available in cones or as sundaes; ice-cream floats; and smoothies.

Comments Seating is behind building and could easily be overlooked.

Tusker House Restaurant
Africa
QUALITY Good | VALUE C | PORTION Medium to large

Selection Half rotisserie chicken; fried chicken dinner; turkey and veggie wraps; smoked turkey on focaccia; grilled-chicken sandwich; roasted vegetable sandwich with

tabouli; hot ham and Swiss sandwich; child's plate with macaroni and cheese; cinnamon rolls, cake, and cookies.
Comments Excellent selections for health-conscious diners. Salads are refreshing. Separate line for bakery items. Also serves a nice sit-down breakfast.

Walt Disney World Restaurants: Rated and Ranked

To help you in your dining choices, we have developed profiles of full-service restaurants at Disney World. Each profile allows you to quickly check the restaurant's cuisine, location, star rating, cost range, quality rating, and value rating. *Profiles are listed alphabetically by restaurant.*

Star Rating The star rating represents the entire dining experience: style, service, and ambiance, in addition to taste, presentation, and quality of food. Five stars is the highest rating and indicates that the restaurant offers the best of everything. Four-star restaurants are above average, and three-star restaurants offer good, though not necessarily memorable meals. Two-star restaurants serve mediocre fare, and one-star restaurants are below average. Our star ratings don't correspond to ratings awarded by AAA, Mobil, Zagat, or other restaurant reviewers.

Cost The next rating tells how much a complete meal will cost. We include a main dish with vegetable or side dish, and a choice of soup or salad. Appetizers, desserts, drinks, and tips aren't included. We've rated the cost as inexpensive, moderate, or expensive.

Inexpensive	$12 or less per person
Moderate	$13–$23 per person
Expensive	More than $23 per person

Quality Rating The food quality is rated on a scale of one to five stars, five being the best rating attainable. The quality rating is based expressly on the taste, freshness of ingredients, preparation, presentation, and creativity of food served. There is no consideration of price. If you are a person who wants the best food available and cost is not an issue, you need look no further than the quality ratings.

Value Rating If, on the other hand, you are looking for both quality and value, then you should check the value rating, expressed as stars.

★★★★★	Exceptional value, a real bargain
★★★★	Good value
★★★	Fair value, you get exactly what you pay for
★★	Somewhat overpriced
★	Significantly overpriced

Payment   We've listed the types of payment accepted at each restaurant using the following codes:

VISA	VISA
AMEX	American Express
MC	MasterCard
D	Discover
CB	Carte Blanche
DC	Diners Club
JCB	Japanese Credit Bureau
DCC	Disney Credit Card

Readers' Restaurant Survey Responses

For each Disney World restaurant profiled, we include the results of last year's readers' survey responses. Results are expressed as a percentage of responding readers who liked the restaurant well enough to eat there again (Thumbs Up), as opposed to the percentage of responding readers who had a bad experience and wouldn't go back (Thumbs Down). (Readers tend to be less critical than our *Unofficial Guide* restaurant reviewers.) If you would like to participate in the survey, complete and return the restaurant form on the last page of this book.

WALT DISNEY WORLD RESTAURANTS BY CUISINE

(Full restaurant reviews arranged alphabetically follow this listing.)

Type of Restaurant	Location	Overall Rating	Price	Quality Rating	Value Rating
African					
Boma	Animal Kingdom Lodge	★★★½	Moderate	★★★★	★★★★★
Jiko	Animal Kingdom Lodge	★★★	Expensive	★★★	★★★
American					
California Grill	Contemporary	★★★★½	Expensive	★★★★★	★★★
Artist Point	Wilderness Lodge	★★★½	Moderate	★★★★	★★★
Planet Hollywood	Pleasure Island	★★★½	Moderate	★★★★	★★★
The Hollywood Brown Derby	Disney-MGM	★★★	Expensive	★★★★	★★★
Kona Cafe	Polynesian	★★★	Moderate	★★★★	★★★★
House of Blues	West Side	★★★	Moderate	★★★½	★★★
Olivia's Cafe	Old Key West	★★★	Moderate	★★★½	★★★
Yacht Club Galley	Yacht Club	★★★	Moderate	★★★½	★★★
Wolfgang Puck Cafe	West Side	★★★	Expensive	★★★½	★★★

WALT DISNEY WORLD RESTAURANTS BY CUISINE (continued)

Type of Restaurant	Location	Overall Rating	Price	Quality Rating	Value Rating
American (continued)					
Whispering Canyon Cafe	Wilderness Lodge	★★½	Moderate	★★★½	★★★★
Hollywood & Vine	Disney-MGM	★★½	Inexpensive	★★★	★★★
Liberty Tree Tavern	Magic Kingdom	★★½	Moderate	★★★	★★★
Boatwright's Dining Hall	Dixie Landings	★★½	Moderate	★★★	★★
Cinderella's Royal Table	Magic Kingdom	★★½	Moderate	★★★	★★
Rainforest Cafe	Downtown Disney/Animal Kingdom	★★½	Moderate	★★★	★★
Baskervilles	Grosvenor Resort	★★	Moderate	★★★	★★★
ESPN Club	BoardWalk	★★	Moderate	★★★	★★★
The Garden Grill Restaurant	Epcot	★★	Moderate	★★★	★★★
Pleasure Island Jazz Company	Pleasure Island	★★	Moderate	★★★	★★★
Big River Grille & Brewing Works	Boardwalk	★★	Moderate	★★★	★★
Coral Cafe	Dolphin	★★	Moderate	★★★	★★
50's Prime Time Cafe	Disney-MGM	★★	Moderate	★★★	★★
Grand Floridian Cafe	Grand Floridian	★★	Moderate	★★★	★★
Sci-Fi Dine-In Theater Restaurant	Disney-MGM	★★	Moderate	★★★	★★
Gulliver's Grill at Garden Grove	Swan	★★	Expensive	★★★	★★
Buffet					
Boma	Animal Kingdom Lodge	★★★½	Moderate	★★★★	★★★★★
Cape May Cafe	Beach Club	★★★½	Moderate	★★★★	★★★★
Restaurant Akershus	Epcot	★★★½	Moderate	★★★★	★★★★
The Crystal Palace	Magic Kingdom	★★½	Moderate	★★★½	★★★
1900 Park Fare	Grand Floridian	★★½	Moderate	★★★½	★★★
Hollywood & Vine	Disney-MGM	★★½	Inexpensive	★★★	★★★
Biergarten	Epcot	★★½	Moderate	★★★	★★★
Chef Mickey's	Contemporary	★★	Moderate	★★★	★★★
Trail's End	Fort Wilderness	★★	Moderate	★★★	★★★

WALT DISNEY WORLD RESTAURANTS BY CUISINE *(continued)*

Type of Restaurant	Location	Overall Rating	Price	Quality Rating	Value Rating
Chinese					
Nine Dragons Restaurant	Epcot	★★½	Expensive	★★★	★
Cuban					
Bongos Cuban Cafe	West Side	★★	Moderate	★★★	★★
English					
Rose & Crown Dining Room	Epcot	★★★	Moderate	★★★★	★★
French					
Chefs de France	Epcot	★★★★	Moderate	★★★★	★★★
Bistro de Paris	Epcot	★★★	Expensive	★★★	★★
German					
Biergarten	Epcot	★★½	Moderate	★★★	★★★
Gourmet					
Victoria & Albert's	Grand Floridian	★★★★½	Expensive	★★★★★★	★★
Arthur's 27	Wyndham Palace	★★★★	Expensive	★★★★	★★★
Italian					
Portobello Yacht Club	Pleasure Island	★★★½	Expensive	★★★★	★★
Palio	Swan	★★★	Expensive	★★★½	★★★
Tony's Town Square Restaurant	Magic Kingdom	★★½	Moderate	★★★½	★★
Mama Melrose's Ristorante Italiano	Disney-MGM	★★½	Moderate	★★★	★★
L'Originale Alfredo di Roma Ristorante	Epcot	★★½	Expensive	★★★	★★
Japanese					
Kimonos	Swan	★★★★	Moderate	★★★★	★★★
Teppanyaki Dining Room	Epcot	★★★½	Expensive	★★★★	★★★
Tempura Kiku	Epcot	★★★	Moderate	★★★★	★★★
Benihana— The Japanese Steakhouse	Hilton	★★½	Moderate	★★★	★★★
Mediterranean					
Citricos	Grand Floridian	★★★★	Expensive	★★★★	★★★
Spoodles	BoardWalk	★★★½	Moderate	★★★★	★★★

WALT DISNEY WORLD RESTAURANTS BY CUISINE *(continued)*

Type of Restaurant	Location	Overall Rating	Price	Quality Rating	Value Rating
Mediterranean *(continued)*					
San Angel Inn Restaurante	Epcot	★★★	Expensive	★★★★	★★
Maya Grill	Coronado	★★	Expensive	★★★	★★
Moroccan					
Restaurant Marrakesh	Epcot	★★★	Moderate	★★★★	★★★
Norwegian					
Restaurant Akershus	Epcot	★★★½	Moderate	★★★★	★★★★
Polynesian					
'Ohana	Polynesian	★★★	Moderate	★★★	★★★
Seafood					
Flying Fish Cafe	BoardWalk	★★★★	Expensive	★★★★★	★★★
Artist Point	Wilderness Lodge	★★★½	Moderate	★★★★	★★★
Narcoossee's	Grand Floridian	★★★½	Expensive	★★★★	★★
Cap'n Jack's Oyster Bar	Downtown Disney Marketplace	★★½	Moderate	★★★	★★
Coral Reef	Epcot	★★½	Expensive	★★★	★★
Fulton's Crab House	Pleasure Island	★★½	Expensive	★★★	★★
Captain's Tavern	Caribbean Beach	★★	Moderate	★★★	★★★
Finn's Grill	Hilton	★	Moderate	★★	★★
Steak					
Shula's Steak House	Dolphin	★★★½	Expensive	★★★★	★★★
Yachtsman Steakhouse	Yacht Club	★★★	Expensive	★★★½	★★
Concourse Steakhouse	Contemporary	★★½	Moderate	★★★	★★
Le Cellier Steakhouse	Epcot	★★	Moderate	★★★	★★★
The Outback	Wyndham Palace	★★	Expensive	★★★	★★

Restaurant Profiles

ALL STAR CAFE   ★★½

AMERICAN | MODERATE | QUALITY ★★★ | VALUE ★★★

READER'S SURVEY RESPONSES 84% 👍 16% 👎

Disney's Wide World of Sports; (407) 827-8326

Customers People attending sporting events **Reservations** Recommended **When to go** Anytime **Entree range** $9.50–$17.95 **Payment:** AMEX, MC, VISA **Service** ★★ **Friendliness** ★½ **Parking** Wide World of Sports' lot **Bar** Full service **Wine selection** Minimal **Dress** Jerseys if you've got 'em **Disabled access:** Yes

Lunch & dinner Daily, 11:30 a.m.–9 p.m.

Setting & atmosphere Think Hard Rock Cafe but with sports memorabilia instead of music instruments. Dozens of television screens in varying sizes play whatever game happens to be on at the time.

House specialties Burgers, sandwiches, and steaks.

Entertainment & amenities Televised sporting events.

Summary & comments This was originally the Official All Star Cafe, part of the Planet Hollywood company backed by such sports stars as Shaquille O'Neal and Wayne Gretzky. Planet Hollywood is having enough trouble keeping its own doors open lately, so it sold off the All Star Cafes. This one seems to exist only because Disney wants a restaurant next to its sports venue, but you're more likely to find better food from the hot-dog vendor inside the stadium.

ARTHUR'S 27   ★★★★

GOURMET | EXPENSIVE | QUALITY ★★★★ | VALUE ★★★

READER'S SURVEY RESPONSES 76% 👍 24% 👎

Wyndham Palace, Disney Village Hotel Plaza; (407) 827-3450

Customers Hotel guests and locals **Reservations** Necessary **When to go** Sunset or during fireworks at any of the three parks **Entree range** $20–$36 **Payment** VISA, MC, AMEX, DC **Service** ★★ **Friendliness** ★★ **Parking** Complimentary valet **Bar** Full service **Wine selection** Excellent **Dress** Jackets preferred, tie optional **Disabled access** Yes

Dinner Daily, 6–10 p.m.

Setting & atmosphere From its perch on the 27th floor of the Wyndham Palace, Arthur's gives a breathtaking view of the glittering lights of the Downtown Disney Marketplace and the twirling searchlights of Pleasure Island. Diners sit at large booths, all set apart from each other with their own windows.

House specialties A la carte menu; Florida Gulf shrimp; herb-crusted tuna; medallions of veal; breast of duckling.

Other recommendations Loin of lamb; salmon in strudel leaves; chilled breast of chicken Alexandra.

Entertainment & amenities Live entertainment in lounge.

Summary & comments The best values at this overpriced restaurant are the four- and five--course table d'hôte offerings for $62, $68. If you're not looking for a lot of food, you'll pay too much for what you get. Still, it is one of the most impressive views in the area, although only if you are facing the Disney side. Otherwise, you'll be looking at the taillights on Interstate 4 and you'll know what all the locals know: Florida is flat.

Honors & awards DiRoNa winner.

ARTIST POINT ★★★½

SEAFOOD | MODERATE | QUALITY ★★★★ | VALUE ★★★

READER'S SURVEY RESPONSES 88% 👍 12% 🗨

Disney's Wilderness Lodge and Villas; (407) 824-3200

Customers Hotel guests, some locals **Priority seatings** Recommended for dinner and character breakfasts **When to go** Anytime **Entree range** $20–$35 **Payment** VISA, MC, AMEX **Service** ★★★★ **Friendliness** ★★★★★ **Parking** Hotel lot **Bar** Full service **Wine selection** Selections from wineries in America's Northwest **Dress** Casual **Disabled access** Yes

Dinner Daily, 5:30–10 p.m.

Setting & atmosphere Two-story-high paintings depicting the landscapes of the Pacific Northwest dominate the interior walls of this casually appointed restaurant. Tall windows offer guests a view of the lake or a waterfall that flows off high rocks and past wildflowers. Huge cast-iron chandeliers hold 12 lanterns with milk-glass panes. Tables are uncovered, and each has a bust of an animal native to the Northwest engraved in it.

House specialties Pan-roasted sea scallops; savory rabbit sausage with frisée; grilled lamp chops with smokey red lentils.

Other recommendations Roasted cedar plank salmon; grilled buffalo top sirloin; omelets; duck hash with egg.

Summary & comments Unlike other large hotels, the Wilderness Lodge's top-of-the-line restaurant is not an elegant gourmet room. Still, the beauty of the artwork and the room itself make dining here a pleasure. Breakfast is especially nice, as the landscaping can be fully appreciated in the sunlight.

BASKERVILLES ★★

AMERICAN | MODERATE | QUALITY ★★★ | VALUE ★★★

READER'S SURVEY RESPONSES 77% 👍 23% 🗨

Grosvenor Resort, Disney Village Hotel Plaza; (407) 828-4444

Customers Hotel guests **Reservations** Accepted **When to go** Anytime **Entree range** $10–$30 **Payment** VISA, MC, AMEX, DC, D **Service** ★★★ **Friendliness** ★★ **Parking** Hotel lot **Bar** Full service **Wine selection** Good **Dress** Casual **Disabled access** Yes

Breakfast Daily, 7–11:30 a.m.
Lunch Monday–Friday, 11:30 a.m.–1 p.m.
Dinner Daily, 5–10 p.m.

Setting & atmosphere This is a half-hearted attempt to create an English drawing-room atmosphere. Unfortunately, it looks way too much like a cafeteria in a college dormitory.

House specialties Prime rib; specialty buffets.

Other recommendations Grilled grouper; stir-fried vegetables; Sherlock's breakfast combo.

Entertainment & amenities Murder-mystery Saturdays where guests solve the crime (priority seatings required).

Summary & comments Elementary fare. If you're having trouble being entertained, try the murder-mystery dinner—it might make the food a little more exciting. Otherwise, the only reason to dine here is if you're just too tired to leave the hotel or you can't get a priority seating anywhere else. Or if you really have your heart set on an average piece of prime rib.

BENIHANA—THE JAPANESE STEAKHOUSE   ★★½

JAPANESE | MODERATE | QUALITY ★★★½ | VALUE ★★★

READER'S SURVEY RESPONSES 58% 👍 42% 🗨

The Hilton, Disney Village Hotel Plaza; (407) 827-4865

Customers Hotel guests and some locals **Reservations** Recommended **When to go** Anytime **Entree range** $16–$43 **Payment** VISA, MC, AMEX, DC, JCB, D, CB **Service** ★★★★ **Friendliness** ★★★★ **Parking** Hotel lot **Bar** Full service **Wine selection** Good **Dress** Casual **Disabled access** Yes

Dinner Daily, 5:30–10:30 p.m.

Setting & atmosphere Large tables with built-in grills are crammed into small rooms decorated with rice-paper panels and Japanese lanterns. Lighting is low and focused on the stage—the chef's grill.

House specialties Teppanyaki service at large tables (where the chef cooks dinner in front of you). Specialties include New York steak; lobster tail; hibachi vegetables.

Other recommendations Japanese onion soup.

Entertainment & amenities Dinner is the show at this teppanyaki-service restaurant where the chef does a lot of noisy chopping and grilling.

Summary & comments If you're looking for a nice, quiet dinner, be aware that diners sit at tables of eight and private conversation is almost impossible.

BIERGARTEN ★★½

GERMAN | MODERATE | QUALITY ★★★½ | VALUE ★★★

READER'S SURVEY RESPONSES 77% 👍 23% 💬

Germany, World Showcase, Epcot; (407) 939-3463

Customers Theme-park guests **Priority seatings** Recommended **When to go** After 6 p.m. **Entree range** $14, lunch; $20, dinner **Payment** VISA, MC, AMEX, D, DC **Service** ★★★ **Friendliness** ★★★ **Parking** Epcot lot **Bar** Full service **Wine selection** German **Dress** Casual **Disabled access** Yes

Lunch Daily, noon–3:45 p.m.

Dinner Daily, 4–8:30 p.m.

Setting & atmosphere Biergarten serves a fairly extensive German buffet that has improved substantially. Choices include schnitzel, various wursts, spaetzle, rot kraut and sour kraut, roast chicken, sauerbraten (dinner only), and a variety of salads, breads, and desserts. Not light fare to be sure, but satisfying. Additionally, you'll have no problem finding items the kids will eat. Guests sit at long tables in a tiered dining area that surrounds a sort of town square of a German village, with the exteriors of shops and houses as the backdrop for the bandstand and dance floor. An oompah band plays on the stage and encourages diners to join them in sing-alongs and dancing. You may even find yourself swept up in a German version of a conga line.

House specialties German potato salad; lentil salad; various sausages and wieners; spaetzle with gravy; and hot dogs in sauerkraut. There is also rotisserie chicken, which looks and tastes like the rotisserie chicken you would get at any other country in World Showcase—or in the world, for that matter. The buffet is set up on wooden barrels, and the food is served from vats.

Other recommendations Bratwurst; beer.

Entertainment & amenities Oompah band and German dancers perform after 12:30 p.m.

Summary & comments Possibly the best of the World Showcase restaurants for picky children, with enough variety and ethnic specialties to satisfy adults. Be aware that you may find yourself seated with other guests.

BIG RIVER GRILLE & BREWING WORKS ★★

AMERICAN | MODERATE | QUALITY ★★★ | VALUE ★★

READER'S SURVEY RESPONSES 64% 👍 36% 💬

Disney's BoardWalk; (407) 560-0253

Customers Tourists **Priority seatings** Not accepted **When to go** Anytime **Entree range** $10–$25 **Payment** VISA, MC, AMEX **Service** ★★ **Friendliness** ★★★ **Parking** BoardWalk lot; valet parking is free before 5 p.m., $5 after (for nonresort guests only) **Bar** Full service **Wine selection** Minimal **Dress** Casual **Disabled access** Good

Lunch & dinner Daily, 11:30 a.m.–midnight

Setting & atmosphere Industrial cubist murals of factories, machinist-metal and wood chairs and tables, and a midnight-blue neon river that flows along the ceiling of the restaurant set a working-class atmosphere. The place is small—it seems like the huge copper brewing tanks take up more room than what is allotted to the diners.

House specialties Hazelnut crusted chicken, sautéed and served in sundried cherry sauce; flame-grilled meatloaf, topped with rich brown gravy; drunken rib-eye marinated in Rocket Red Ale and topped with sundried tomato and oregano.

Summary & comments Big River is out-sourced to a Tennessee company and is the first brewpub at Walt Disney World. The Brewing Works brews four regular beers and one or two specialty ales. If you're a beer drinker and like trying something new, you should like this. If you're a beer drinker and have a craving for your favorite brew, you're out of luck—the hand-crafted beers are the only beers sold here. The food is okay, though nothing special. It's another good late-night choice. There is outside seating and service, weather permitting.

BISTRO DE PARIS   ★★★

FRENCH | EXPENSIVE | QUALITY ★★★½ | VALUE ★★

READER'S SURVEY RESPONSES 74% 👍 26% 👎

France, World Showcase, Epcot; (407) 939-3463

Customers Theme park guests **Priority seatings** Recommended **When to go** Late dinner **Entree range** $27–$35 **Payment** AMEX, MC, VISA **Service** ★★★ **Friendliness** ★★★★ **Parking** Epcot lot or BoardWalk lot and enter through back gate **Bar** Full service **Wine selection** Good but pricey; several by the glass **Dress** Casual **Disabled access** Elevator to second level

Dinner Daily, 6–8:45 p.m.

Setting & atmosphere The paint is yellow and it is a bright contrast against the oxblood color of the leather banquettes. The bistro is on the second level of the France pavilion. A few windows look out over the World Showcase lagoon (good for watching *IllumiNations* if you can snag one of those tables), but otherwise there isn't a whole lot to look at here.

House specialties Lobster fricassee and zucchini stuffed crab cake; roasted duck breast with cherry brandy sauce; double-cut veal chop with roasted garlic cloves; honey roasted rack of lamb with thyme flower.

Summary & comments The food can be good, but it has been spotty lately. The real focus of the staff here seems to be the restaurant downstairs. The Bistro is used more as an overflow space when Chefs de France is full, which hasn't been too often in recent months.

BOATWRIGHT'S DINING HALL   ★★½

AMERICAN/CAJUN | MODERATE | QUALITY ★★★ | VALUE ★★ ·

READER'S SURVEY RESPONSES 87% 👍 13% 👎

Disney's Port Orleans Resort; (407) 934-5000

Customers Hotel guests **Priority seatings** Recommended for dinner **When to go** Early evening **Entree range** $16–$23 **Payment** VISA, MC, AMEX **Service** ★★ **Friendliness** ★★★★ **Parking** Hotel lot **Bar** Full service **Wine selection** Fair; the beer selection is better. **Dress** Casual **Disabled access** Good

Breakfast Daily, 7–11:30 a.m.
Dinner Daily, 5–10 p.m.

Setting & atmosphere Diners sit in a large, noisy room under the skeleton of a riverboat under construction that looks sort of like the carcass of a mastodon. Tables are set with a boatwright's tool kit that contains condiments instead of tools. The real tools—the two-handed saws, hatchets, chisels, and a few that are too foreign to identify—hang along the walls.

House specialties Bayou salmon with crawfish dill cream, jambalaya with andouille sausage.

Other recommendations Pirogue of pasta and seafood *(pirogue* means boat*)*; crescent city ribs; boat builder chicken.

Summary & comments Servers can get a little caught up in the theme, a working riverboat-building operation, and forget the basics of good service. Long waits gain no apologies. Fans of true Cajun food may be disappointed with this version, which has been toned down to please the masses. There is, however, a fine selection of regional beers, including Dixie, Blackened Voodoo, and Abita. You'll have a chance to decide which is your favorite while you're waiting for your table.

BOMA—THE FLAVORS OF AFRICA   ★★★½

AFRICAN | MODERATE | QUALITY ★★★½ | VALUE ★★★★★

READER'S SURVEY RESPONSES 91% 👍 9% 👎

Animal Kingdom Lodge; (407) 938-3000

Customers Hotel guests **Reservations** Mandatory **Priority seatings** Required **When to go** Anytime **Entree range** $22; $9 ages 3–11 **Payment** AMEX, MC, VISA **Service** ★★★ **Friendliness** ★★★ **Parking** Complimentary valet or self park in hotel's lot **Bar** Full service **Wine selection** All South African **Dress** Casual **Disabled access** Good

Breakfast Daily, 7–10:45 a.m.
Dinner Daily, 5:30–10 p.m.

Setting & atmosphere An open area with a number of food stations that encourage diners to roam about and graze, just like the animals that wander about the lodge.

House specialties Watermelon rind salad; couscous salad; Moroccan seafood salad; chicken salad with cilantro.

Other recommendations Prime rib; zebra dome; crusted salmon; soups.

Summary & comments The quality of the food, the surroundings, and the selection of dishes make this a terrific deal. Disney doesn't use the word buffet, and indeed this is very different from the typical buffet (there are no steam tables for starters), but for those who like a major bang for their buck, this is the place to go.

BONGOS CUBAN CAFE   ★★

CUBAN | MODERATE | QUALITY ★★★ | VALUE ★★

READER'S SURVEY RESPONSES 81% 👍 19% 🗨

Downtown Disney West Side; (407) 828-0999

Customers Gloria Estefan fans; Disney guests **Reservations** Accepted **When to go** Anytime **Entree range** $12.95–$30 **Payment** VISA, MC, AMEX, DC, D **Service** ★★★ **Friendliness** ★★★ **Parking** Downtown Disney lot **Bar** Full service **Wine selection** Moderate **Dress** Casual **Disabled access** Elevator to second level

Lunch & dinner Monday–Friday, 10:30 a.m.–11 p.m.; Saturday and Sunday, 11 a.m.–11 p.m.

Setting & atmosphere This multilevel restaurant features an airy environment with a tropical theme built around a three-story pineapple. Other touches include a banana-leaf roof, banana-leaf ceiling fans, and palm tree–shaped columns. You'll expect Carmen Miranda to dance through the door any minute. Hand-painted murals and mosaics lend an artistic air. An open wrap-around porch provides a pleasant atmosphere for outdoor dining.

House specialties Arroz con pollo (chicken with rice); camerones al ajillo (shrimp in garlic sauce); ropa vieja (shredded beef in tomato sauce); churrasco (grilled skirt steak).

Entertainment & amenities Latin music.

Summary & comments Miami resident and Latin singer Gloria Estefan and her husband-producer, Emilio, created this large restaurant that marries salsa music with Cuban cuisine. There are any number of mom-and-pop Cuban restaurants in the area (not that the Estefans aren't mom-and-pop) that do a better and more consistent job with this wonderful cuisine. If you've never had Cuban food, try it somewhere else. Come here to have a drink with an umbrella in it and listen to music. It's upbeat but noisy.

CALIFORNIA GRILL   ★★★★½

AMERICAN | EXPENSIVE | QUALITY ★★★★★ | VALUE ★★★

READER'S SURVEY RESPONSES 93% 👍 7% 🗨

Disney's Contemporary Resort; (407) 939-3463

Customers Locals and hotel guests **Priority seatings** Recommended **When to go** During evening fireworks **Entree range** $10–$30 **Payment** AMEX, MC, VISA **Service** ★★★★ **Friendliness** ★★★★ **Parking** Valet on request **Bar** Full service **Wine selection** California wines **Dress** Casual; no tank tops **Disabled access** Yes

Dinner Daily, 5:30–10 p.m.
Lounge Daily, 5:30 p.m.–midnight

Setting & atmosphere From the 15th floor of the Contemporary Resort, California Grill commands one of the most impressive panoramas in central Florida. The dining room is inspired by Wolfgang Puck's Spago restaurant and the Rainbow Room in

New York. A show kitchen where the chefs prepare all the food is the centerpiece of the dining room.

House specialties The catchphrase for the menu is "market inspired," which means the menu changes regularly to take advantage of the freshest produce and available meats and fish. The menu is creative, with Pacific Rim accents. The pork tenderloin is quickly becoming a house favorite and is likely to be kept on most menu rotations.

Other recommendations Sizzled salmon; Tamarind barbecue beef filet; pan-roasted scallops.

Entertainment & amenities The lights are dimmed during the Magic Kingdom fireworks, and the accompanying music is piped in. You can also step outside onto the 15th floor deck for a closer look. Other entertainment includes watching the chefs; instead of begging for a window seat, sit at the counter. The chefs love to slip samples to the people sitting there.

Summary & comments This has been a favorite of central Florida locals for several years—even those who normally wouldn't deign to set foot on Disney property. But at press time the restaurant was under transition: the original chef and manager left, and the chef from Flying Fish Cafe had just taken over the helm. John State had done well with Flying Fish and he's said he won't mess with success, so this should continute to be a good bet.

CAPE MAY CAFE ★★★½

BUFFET | MODERATE | QUALITY ★★★½ | VALUE ★★★★

READER'S SURVEY RESPONSES 84% 👍 16% 👎

Disney's Beach Club Resort; (407) 934-3358

Customers Theme park and hotel guests **Priority seatings** Accepted and recommended **When to go** Anytime **Entree range** Breakfast: $15.99 adults, $8.99 children; dinner: $22.95 adults, $10.50 children **Payment** VISA, MC, AMEX **Service** ★★★★ **Friendliness** ★★★★ **Parking** Hotel lot **Bar** Full service **Wine selection** Limited **Dress** Casual **Disabled access** Yes

Breakfast Daily, 7:30–11 a.m.
Dinner Daily, 5:30–9:30 p.m.

Setting & atmosphere The natural-finish wood furniture and padded booths are in a clean, nautical New England style—bright, airy, and informal.

House specialties The buffet features peel-and-eat shrimp, tasty (albeit chewy) clams; mussels; baked fish; barbecued ribs; corn on the cob; Caesar salad; and a good dessert bar.

Other recommendations Lobster can be ordered as a supplement to the buffet, as can crab legs.

Entertainment & amenities Character breakfast.

Summary & comments This buffet consistently serves some of the best food available at Walt Disney World. While the restaurant is large and tables turn over rapidly, priority seatings are recommended. Because the Cape May is within easy walking distance of the World Showcase entrance to Epcot, it is a perfect and affordable place to dine before *IllumiNations*.

CAP'N JACK'S OYSTER BAR   ★★★½

SEAFOOD | MODERATE | QUALITY ★★★½ | VALUE ★★

READER'S SURVEY RESPONSES 58% 👍 42% 👎

Downtown Disney Marketplace; (407) 828-3971

Customers Tourists **Priority seatings** Not accepted **When to go** Anytime **Entree range** $10–$30 **Payment** VISA, MC, AMEX **Service** ★★★★ **Friendliness** ★★★★ **Parking** Marketplace lot **Bar** Full service **Wine selection** Not a specialty **Dress** Casual **Disabled access** Yes

Lunch & dinner Daily, 11:30 a.m.–10:30 p.m.

Setting & atmosphere An upscale pierhouse on the edge of the Buena Vista Lagoon.

House specialties Cap'n Jack's has a limited menu, but what it does it does well. Choices include New England clam chowder; spicy conch chowder with tomatoes, carrots, and onions; crab cakes made with lump crabmeat and onions; peel-and-eat shrimp; and steamed and baked oysters and clams. You can also get a fresh-fish dinner—usually mahimahi, tuna, or grouper—at a fair price, as well as a stuffed Maine lobster that is more than twice the cost of anything else on the menu. However, you'll be better off sticking with the oyster-bar items.

Entertainment & amenities The lagoonside setting offers views of amateur boaters, and sunsets are pretty here.

Summary & comments Most entrees for dinner are under $25—only the king crab legs climbs higher. But this is really a place for some shrimp or steamed clams and cold beer.

CAPTAIN'S TAVERN   ★★

SEAFOOD | MODERATE | QUALITY ★★★ | VALUE ★★★

READER'S SURVEY RESPONSES 48% 👍 52% 👎

Disney's Caribbean Beach Resort; (407) 939-3463

Customers Resort guests **Priority seatings** Recommended **When to go** Anytime **Entree range** $13.95–$22.95 **Payment** VISA, AMEX, DC **Service** ★★★ **Friendliness** ★★★ **Parking** Resort lot **Bar** Full service **Wine selection** Fair **Dress** Casual **Disabled access** Yes

Dinner Daily, 5–10 p.m.

Setting & atmosphere A dark area across from the resort's food court outlets. It is nautical to the nth degree, with lots of dark woods, slatted blinds, and ship's wheel chandeliers. This is a restaurant that was never supposed to be, and to prove it there is no kitchen. The food court was supposed to meet all the resort's culinary needs, but management discovered that people wanted to be waited on after a long day in the parks. So the food court's eating area was converted to a restaurant, and servers schlep the trays across the hall from the food court's kitchens.

House specialties Ahi tuna, grilled with soy ginger cream sauce; jack-roasted chicken with Parmesan mashed potatoes; Captain Morgan's rib-eye, flavored with brown sugar; tropical pork chop; fresh catch of the day prepared with island spices and lime zest.

Summary & comments The restaurant that wasn't supposed to be should probably cease to be. The limitations of the kitchen—or lack of a proper kitchen—show in the quality of the food. Guests who are too tired to wait in line at the food court should take a nap and then drive to another area restaurant. Guests not staying at the Caribbean Beach Resort may be hassled by the guards at the front gate (they don't believe anyone not staying at the resort would want to come in just to eat).

LE CELLIER STEAKHOUSE ★★

STEAK | MODERATE | QUALITY ★★★ | VALUE ★★★

READER'S SURVEY RESPONSES 78% 👍 22% 🗨

Canada, World Showcase, Epcot; (407) 939-3463

Customers Theme park guests **Priority seatings** Recommended **When to go** Before 6 p.m. **Entree range** $14–$26 **Payment** VISA, MC, AMEX **Service** ★★★ **Friendliness** ★★★★ **Parking** Epcot lot **Bar** Beer and wine only **Wine selection** Canadian wines are featured **Dress** Casual **Disabled access** Yes

Lunch Daily, 11:30 a.m.–3 p.m.

Dinner Daily, from 4:30 p.m. until park closes

Setting & atmosphere Long chided as the worst dining room on Walt Disney World property, this dank space was given a makeover and has risen to palatable mediocrity (actually a big improvement). And it's not quite as depressing as it used to be. The space is more like a wine cellar now than the dungeon it was previously. Wine racks are easily visible with the bright chandeliers and wall sconces with fat candle lamps. There are no windows to the World here, but many guests say they like the sensory deprivation Le Cellier provides.

House specialties Meat. Standouts include filet mignon with mushroom risotto and grilled veal chop.

Other recommendations Roast turkey breast; Canadian cheddar-cheese soup (a lot like Wisconsin cheese soup); smoked beef brisket; chicken and meatball stew.

Summary & comments A steakhouse had been absent from the theme parks until the folks from Canada decided to try their hand. Previously a cafeteria-style restaurant, Le Cellier is now full service with a modest menu of steaks and prime rib.

CHEF MICKEY'S ★★

AMERICAN/BUFFET | MODERATE | QUALITY ★★★ | VALUE ★★★

READER'S SURVEY RESPONSES 89% 👍 11% 🗨

Disney's Contemporary Resort; (407) 939-3463

Customers Theme park guests **Priority seatings** Recommended **When to go** Early evening **Entree range** Breakfast: $15.95 adults, $8.95 children; dinner: $21.95 adults, $9.95 children **Payment** VISA, MC, AMEX **Service** ★★★ **Friendliness** ★★★★ **Parking** Resort valet or lot **Bar** None **Wine selection** Good **Dress** Casual **Disabled access** Yes

Breakfast Daily, 7–11:30 a.m.
Dinner Daily, 5–9:30 p.m.

Setting & atmosphere A futuristic buffet that resembles Disney's idea of how the Jetsons would dine—colorful seatbacks and padded booths, geometric grids, flowing curves, and a buffet line that circles the center of the room. It is a noisy and bustling place, especially when Goofy, Minnie, and Mickey step out of the kitchen to say hello and dance with the diners.

House specialties Breakfast: cooked-to-order pancakes; French toast; biscuits and gravy. Dinner: peel-and-eat shrimp; oven-roasted prime rib.

Other recommendations Fresh greens and mixed salads; pasta selections; mashed potatoes and gravy.

Entertainment & amenities Character visits.

Summary & comments Mickey moved his pots and pans from his Village location to make room for the new Rainforest Cafe. In the process he changed the concept from a full-service restaurant to an all-you-can-eat buffet—something Disney is emphasizing currently. The "state-of-the-art" buffet does not use chafing dishes but places the food in casseroles and platters on special heated countertops. However, that doesn't make much difference in the quality. You've still got buffet food, chafing dishes or not, and it just isn't the same as something cooked fresh.

CHEFS DE FRANCE ★★★

FRENCH | MODERATE | QUALITY ★★★ | VALUE ★★★

READER'S SURVEY RESPONSES 82% 👍 18% 🗨

France, World Showcase, Epcot; (407) 939-3463

Customers Theme park guests **Priority seatings** Recommended **When to go** Anytime **Entree range** $9.25–$17.95, lunch; $9.25–$26.25, dinner **Payment** VISA, MC, AMEX **Service** ★★★★ **Friendliness** ★★★★ **Parking** Epcot lot **Bar** None **Wine selection** Very good **Dress** Casual **Disabled access** Yes

Lunch Daily, noon–3 p.m.
Dinner Daily, 5–9 p.m.

Setting & atmosphere The smell of buttery croissants is as much a part of the decor here as the carefully placed copies of *Le Monde* and the huge mottled mirrors. White tablecloths and padded banquettes accentuate the classic bistro decor of the main dining room. Another room sits off to the side, this one a more casual sunroom with a better view of what's going on outside, but you're there for the illusion—insist on a seat in the main room. A renovation has enclosed the former sidewalk cafe and included that space in the main room. It is brighter than before to reflect a more authentic bistro atmosphere. The second level (the Bistro de Paris) remains unchanged. Downstairs is a better place to sit.

House specialties Chefs de France features some of the dishes served at the real restaurants of the three chefs for whom this restaurant is named: Paul Bocuse, Roger Verge, and Gaston LeNotre. You may sample Verge's brochette of prawns from Moulin de Mougins, LeNotre's fillet of orange roughy in a hazlenut butter from Pre Catelan, or Bocuse's beef braised in burgundy wine from his Lyon restaurant.

Other recommendations Grilled snapper on artichoke and fennel, estouffade de boeuf, pot-au-feu.

Summary & comments Here is your chance to eat in a restaurant supervised by three of France's best chefs. Paul Bocuse and Roger Verge take turns visiting from France and supervising the staff in the preparation of their creations (Gaston LeNotre doesn't make the trip too often anymore), so you just might get a chance to meet a culinary legend. But don't expect them to actually prepare your meal. And don't think what you're served here is even close to what you'd get at one of their hometown restaurants. In the past, most of the food coming out of the kitchen was cooked elsewhere in Disney's commissary and warmed here. The recent renovation installed an impressive kitchen (perhaps the best cooking facility of any Disney restaurant) that allows more à la minute preparations from executive chef Bruno Vrignon. Many of the same entrees are available at lunchtime for a reduced price (and smaller portion). Still, consistency has been a problem here of late.

CINDERELLA'S ROYAL TABLE ★★½

AMERICAN | MODERATE | QUALITY ★★★ | VALUE ★★

READER'S SURVEY RESPONSES 88% 👍 12% 🗨

Cinderella Castle, Fantasyland, Magic Kingdom; (407) 939-3463

Customers Theme park guests **Priority seatings** Required **When to go** Early **Entree range** Lunch $11.95–$15.95 adults, $4.99 children; dinner: $18.95–$25.50 adults, $4.99 children **Payment** VISA, MC, AMEX **Service** ★★★ **Friendliness** ★★★ **Parking** Magic Kingdom lot **Bar** None **Wine selection** None **Dress** Casual **Disabled access** Limited

Lunch Daily, 11:30 a.m.–2:45 p.m.
Dinner Daily, 4 p.m. until park closes

Setting & atmosphere A medieval banquet hall, appointed with the requisite banners and Round Table–like regalia, located on the second floor of Cinderella Castle. Windows look out over the park.

House specialties Prime rib; steak; seafood.

Other recommendations Caesar salad; beef barley soup; grilled swordfish with smoked pepper butter and sautéed beans; sea scallops, shrimp, fish, and vegetables sautéed in white wine and tossed with pasta.

Entertainment & amenities Cinderella makes appearances.

Summary & comments Formerly known as King Stefan's Banquet Hall and long the butt of jokes and unkind remarks from Disney workers and locals, Cinderella's has come a long way in improving the quality of the food. Preparations are more exact, and presentation is pleasing. The grilled swordfish is as good as any you'll find at other Disney seafood restaurants. This is the fanciest full-service restaurant found in the Magic Kingdom—and the priciest. With the name change, Disney officials no longer have to try to explain why Sleeping Beauty's father King Stefan had a restaurant in Cinderella's castle.

CITRICOS   ★★★★

MEDITERRANEAN | EXPENSIVE | QUALITY ★★★★½ | VALUE ★★★

READER'S SURVEY RESPONSES 83% 👍 17% 👎

Disney's Grand Floridian Resort; (407) 824-2496

Customers Hotel guests and locals **Priority seatings** Required **When to go** Anytime **Entree range** $26–$48 **Payment** VISA, MC, AMEX **Service** ★★★★ **Friendliness** ★★★★ **Parking** Valet; self-parking is deceptively far away. **Bar** Full service **Wine selection** Very good **Dress** Casually dressy **Disabled access** Good

Dinner Daily, 5:30–10 p.m.

Setting & atmosphere This is another interior design by Martin Dorf, who also did the stylish California Grill and Flying Fish Cafe. Like those upscale restaurants, Citricos features a show kitchen. Autumnal colors in the carpeting are complemented by lemon, lime, and orange wall tiles (the restaurant name is Spanish for citrus). White tablecloths and napkins embroidered with the restaurant's name add an elegant touch.

House specialties Sautéed shrimp with tomato, lemon, and cheese; sautéed sea scallops with jumbo lump crabmeat; braised veal shank; basil-crusted lamb chops.

Other recommendations Citrus crème brûlée.

Summary & comments Under the direction of chef Gray Byrum, the showcase restaurant has finally found its footing and is sure to be mentioned in the same breath as California Grill and Flying Fish Cafe. The food is inventive without being "overdone" or contrived. Save this one for a special evening.

CONCOURSE STEAKHOUSE   ★★½

STEAK | MODERATE | QUALITY ★★★ | VALUE ★★

READER'S SURVEY RESPONSES 91% 👍 9% 👎

Disney's Contemporary Resort; (407) 939-3463

Customers Hotel guests **Priority seatings** Recommended **When to go** Anytime **Entree range** $14–$24.95 **Payment** VISA, MC, AMEX **Service** ★★★ **Friendliness** ★★★ **Parking** Hotel lot **Bar** Full service **Wine selection** Limited **Dress** Casual **Disabled access** Yes

Breakfast Daily, 7:30–11 a.m.
Lunch Daily, noon–2:30 p.m.
Dinner Daily, 5:30–10 p.m.

Setting & atmosphere The decor is a cross between art deco and *2001: A Space Odyssey*. Large booths sit in the "open air" of the Contemporary's Concourse, with the monorails gliding by overhead on either side.

House specialties Although the name says steaks, sandwiches, burgers, pizzas, and pasta dishes are also available. The burgers are the best at Walt Disney World.

Other recommendations Besides red meat: roasted double breast of chicken; grilled chicken kebabs; grilled shrimp tossed with pasta, garlic, and fresh herbs; roasted salmon coated with maple syrup and black peppercorns; and Caesar salad.

Summary & comments After a poor start over a year ago, the Concourse Steakhouse has done some fine tuning in service and food preparation. There is still a big gap between quality and value and better restaurants are a short monorail ride away, but this steakhouse is acceptable in a pinch. If there is a wait, you will be given a beeper, which reaches as far as the gift shop but not much farther.

CORAL CAFE (SCHEDULED FOR A NAME CHANGE) ★★

AMERICAN | MODERATE | QUALITY ★★★ | VALUE ★★

READER'S SURVEY RESPONSES 71% 👍 29% 🗨

Walt Disney World Dolphin; (407) 934-4000

Customers Hotel guests who can't get into any other restaurants **Priority seatings** Not accepted **When to go** Anytime **Entree range** $12.95–$20.95 **Payment** VISA, MC, AMEX, D **Service** ★★ **Friendliness** ★★ **Parking** Hotel lot **Bar** Full service **Wine selection** Modest **Dress** Casual **Disabled access** Good

Lunch Daily, 11 a.m.–3 p.m.
Dinner Daily, 5–10:30 p.m.

Setting & atmosphere The public relations people would like you to think you're dining in an atmosphere akin to a coral reef, but you're actually in a spot that looks like it never should have been a restaurant. It almost looks like someone said, "Hey, we could put some tables in here and sell food," which would be fine if the food were better.

House specialties Either an all-you-can-stand buffet or an à la carte menu that changes seasonally. The fare looks interesting enough, with such things as duck in plum sauce or chicken with rigatoni. The kitchen just can't seem to pull it off.

Summary & comments This restaurant would be a lot better as an open space for people to sit and plan where they can go for a real meal. If you're determined to eat at the Dolphin, Shula's Steak House is a far better, albeit pricier, option.

CORAL REEF ★★½

SEAFOOD | EXPENSIVE | QUALITY ★★★½ | VALUE ★★

READER'S SURVEY RESPONSES 57% 👍 43% 🗨

The Living Seas, Future World, Epcot; (407) 939-3463

Customers Theme park guests **Priority seatings** Recommended **When to go** Lunch **Entree range** $16–$21 lunch; $18–$32 dinner **Payment** AMEX, MC, VISA

Service ★★★ **Friendliness** ★★★ **Parking** Epcot lot **Bar** None **Wine selection** Good **Dress** Casual **Disabled access** Good

Lunch Daily, 11:30 a.m.–3 p.m.

Dinner Daily, 4:30 p.m. until park closes

Setting & atmosphere Coral Reef has always offered one of the best views anywhere—below the water level of the humongous saltwater tank in The Living Seas pavilion. Sharks, rays, and even humans swim by, and every table has a great view. Even with the main focus of the room outside the room, Disney renovated the place in 1998. Seating still features tiers that afford perfect views, but now special lighting fixtures throw ripple patterns on the ceiling that make diners feel as though they're underwater.

House specialties Seared Atlantic salmon with potato and green-bean salad; whole roasted snapper with roasted vegetables; bacon-wrapped bass; sautéed jumbo shrimp.

Summary & comments There was great hope that a new chef would help raise the quality of the food here (no raising of the prices is necessary), but alas the food is still sub-par and ridiculously overpriced. Why don't they just require a cover charge for the fish-tank view and drop 10 bucks off the prices of the entrees? Piranha was recently added to the menu—you'd think there would be a professional courtesy.

THE CRYSTAL PALACE   ★★½

AMERICAN/BUFFET | MODERATE | QUALITY ★★★½ | VALUE ★★

READER'S SURVEY RESPONSES 92% 👍 8% 🗨

Main Street, U.S.A., Magic Kingdom; (407) 939-3463

Customers Magic Kingdom guests **Priority seatings** Recommended **When to go** Anytime **Entree range** Adults: $15.95 breakfast, $16.95 lunch, $19.95 dinner; children: $8.95 breakfast, $9.25 lunch, $9.95 dinner **Payment** VISA, MC, AMEX **Service** ★★ **Friendliness** ★★★ **Parking** Magic Kingdom lot **Bar** None **Wine selection** None **Dress** Casual **Disabled access** Yes

Breakfast Daily, 7:30–10:30 a.m.

Lunch Daily, 11:30 a.m.–2:45 p.m.

Dinner Daily, 4 p.m. until park closes

Setting & atmosphere A turn-of-the-century glass pavilion awash with sunlight and decorated with plenty of summer greenery. Seating is comfortable (a pleasant respite), and buffet lines are open and accessible. There is a low buffet area for kids to help themselves.

House specialties Waffles and pancakes layered with fresh fruit; muesli; jambalaya; fried chicken with hoisin sauce; grilled vegetable platter; penne pasta tossed with romaine lettuce, grilled chicken, and Parmesan cheese; paella; leg of lamb carving station; grilled mahimahi, salmon, catfish, or marlin, served with caramelized onion relish.

Entertainment & amenities Winnie the Pooh characters dance about and pose with the kids.

Summary & comments Disney continues its latest emphasis on "new-age buffets" with this latest conversion. The Crystal Palace was a counter-service restaurant but now offers an all-you-can-eat buffet similar to the one found at Chef Mickey's in the Contemporary Resort. This state-of-the-art buffet boasts no steam tables. All the foods are presented in casserole dishes and pans that sit on special heated countertops. The steam may be missing, but this is still mass feeding and the quality is reflected. Still, with such limited dining in the Magic Kingdom, one more restaurant—and one less counter-service eatery—is a step in the right direction.

ESPN CLUB ★★

AMERICAN/SANDWICHES | MODERATE | QUALITY ★★★ | VALUE ★★★

READER'S SURVEY RESPONSES 81% 👍 19% 🗨

Disney's BoardWalk; (407) 939-5100

Customers Tourists **Priority seatings** Not accepted **When to go** Anytime **Entree range** $7–$15.95 **Payment** VISA, MC, AMEX, Disney Card **Service** ★★ **Friendliness** ★★★ **Parking** BoardWalk lot; valet parking is free before 5 p.m., $6 after **Bar** Full service **Wine selection** Minimal **Dress** Casual—helmets not required **Disabled access** Good

Open Sunday–Thursday, 11:30 a.m.–1 a.m.; Friday and Saturday, 11:30 a.m.–2 a.m.

Setting & atmosphere This is a sports bar to the nth degree, with basketball court flooring, sports memorabilia, and more television monitors than a network affiliate. The bar area has satellite sports-trivia video games. A large octagonal room with a wall of TV monitors serves as the main dining room and is nonsmoking. Smoking is permitted in the bar.

House specialties Red wings (Buffalo-style wings); half-pound burger with cheddar or Swiss cheese; fresh fin tuna-salad sandwich; penne pasta with grilled vegetables; marinated grilled chicken breast on a roll.

Entertainment & amenities Live sports-trivia contests and televised sports.

Summary & comments Disney is new to the sports bar concept, and it shows here. The first year was a little slow, but things have started to pick up. Service is a little more brusque than at other property restaurants. Portions are large, and the quality is in line with the price. This is a good choice for late-night dining or when you have to choose between going out for a bite and staying in the room to catch "the big game."

50'S PRIME TIME CAFE ★★

AMERICAN | MODERATE | QUALITY ★★★ | VALUE ★★

READER'S SURVEY RESPONSES 73% 👍 27% 🗨

Disney-MGM Studios; (407) 939-3463

Customers Theme park guests **Priority seatings** Suggested **When to go** Anytime **Entree range** $10.95–$15.95 **Payment** VISA, MC, AMEX **Service** ★★★★ **Friendliness** ★★★★ **Parking** Disney-MGM lot **Bar** Full service **Wine selection** Limited **Dress** Casual **Disabled access** Yes

Lunch Daily, 11 a.m.–3:55 p.m.; opens at 10:30 a.m. on Sunday and Wednesday

Dinner Daily, 4 p.m. until park closes

Setting & atmosphere A meal at the 50's Prime Time Cafe is like eating a meal in your own kitchen, 1950s style. Pastel formica, gooseneck lamps, and black-and-white televisions that run vintage sitcoms are the rule.

House specialties Meatloaf, pot roast, chicken, and other homey fare are featured. We get a lot of mail from readers who like the 50's Prime Time Cafe. Most say the food is good, the portions large, and that it is easy to find something the kids like. We, unfortunately, cannot concur in that opinion. By our evaluation the food is bland, more resembling the meals served in an elementary school cafeteria than in someone's home.

Entertainment & amenities 1950s sitcom clips on television.

Summary & comments While we enjoy the ambiance of the 50's Prime Time Cafe and particularly like watching the old sitcoms, we cannot recommend having a meal there. Our suggestion for making the scene is to get late-afternoon or evening priority seatings and order only dessert.

FINN'S GRILL   ★

SEAFOOD | MODERATE | QUALITY ★★ | VALUE ★★

READER'S SURVEY RESPONSES 33% 👍 67% 👎

The Hilton, Disney Village Hotel Plaza; (407) 827-4000

Customers Unsuspecting hotel guests **Reservations** Not necessary **When to go** Anytime **Entree range** $17.95–$26.95 **Payment** VISA, MC, AMEX, DC, D **Service** ★ **Friendliness** ★★ **Parking** Valet or hotel lot **Bar** Full service **Wine selection** Fair **Dress** Casual **Disabled access** Yes

Dinner Daily, 5:30–10:30 p.m.

Setting & atmosphere Walls are painted with the bright colors of the sea and are decorated with stylized fish fins, sort of abstract abalone. The oyster bar area is decorated with crab and lobster traps. Staff members wear silly fish hats that seem to denote some staffing hierarchy. The menu is fraught with puns on the word Finn, such as finn-omenal, finn-icky, and finn-tastic.

House specialties Fresh fish, including snapper, salmon, and swordfish depending on availability, prepared blackened or grilled. Other items include shrimp scampi served with herb butter over yellow rice; Finn's gumbo, with shrimp, crabmeat, chicken, and sausage; and a number of pasta dishes.

Other recommendations Alaskan king crab legs; steamed Maine lobster; fresh oysters; stone crab claws; shrimp.

Summary & comments Someone spent an awful lot of time coming up with pleasing decor and a nice collection of dishes that accompany some of Florida's finest seafood. Unfortunately the rest of the time was spent on clever puns, leaving no time to train the staff on even the most rudimentary service skills. Most of the food is acceptable, but service this poor at a hotel this large is not. It might not be bad for a bucket of steamers and a few cold beers.

FLYING FISH CAFE ★★★★

SEAFOOD | EXPENSIVE | QUALITY ★★★★½ | VALUE ★★★

READER'S SURVEY RESPONSES 90% 👍 10% 🗨

Disney's BoardWalk; (407) 939-3463

Customers Tourists and locals **Priority seatings** Recommended **When to go** Anytime **Entree range** $18–$32 **Payment** VISA, MC, AMEX **Service** ★★★★ **Friendliness** ★★★★ **Parking** BoardWalk lot; valet parking is free before 5 p.m., $6 after **Bar** Full service **Wine selection** Excellent but pricey **Dress** Casual dressy **Disabled access** Good

Dinner Sunday–Thursday, 5:30–10 p.m.; Friday and Saturday, 5:30–10:30 p.m.

Setting & atmosphere A whimsical remembrance of a circa-1920 Coney Island roller coaster served as the inspiration for the decor and the name. Actually the coaster was called The Flying Turns, and one of the cars on the ride was dubbed The Flying Fish. Booth backs resemble the climbs and swoops of a coaster. On the far wall is a Ferris wheel, and overhead fish fly on a parachute ride. Diners may choose to sit at the fishscale-covered counter that overlooks the open kitchen. Children are given a list of "flaws" in the decor to spot, such as the one fish flying backward on the parachute ride. If the decor is reminiscent of California Grill it's because they were both designed by Martin Dorf.

House specialties The creative menu changes weekly. Some samplings of dishes include seared yellowfin tuna with spiced coriander crust and roasted eggplant; grilled Atlantic salmon with sun-dried tomatoes, baby-artichoke risotto, and calamata; and potato-wrapped yellowtail snapper with leek fondue and a cabernet sauvignon reduction (this one is something of a signature dish and is usually available). For dessert, the warm chocolate lava cake with a liquid chocolate center and citrus ice cream is incredibly indulgent—a must.

Summary & comments The design, style, cuisine, and quality are all reminiscent of California Grill at the Contemporary Resort. However, you're more likely to find children here than at C.G. because of the BoardWalk location. Still, the fine food will be more appreciated by adults—and the high cost more respected. If you can't get a table, check on seating availablity at the counter. The service is just as good there, and the show in the kitchen is entertaining. *Note:* At press time a new chef—Robert Curry from Domaine Chandon—had just been hired to replace longtime chef John State, who moved over to the California Grill. The menu is likely to change, but fish will still be the focus.

FULTON'S CRAB HOUSE ★★½

SEAFOOD | EXPENSIVE | QUALITY ★★★½ | VALUE ★★

READER'S SURVEY RESPONSES 81% 👍 19% 🗨

Empress Lilly, Pleasure Island; (407) 934-2627

Customers Locals, Disney guests **Priority seatings** Accepted **When to go** Early evening **Entree range** $21–$43.95 **Payment** VISA, MC, AMEX **Service** ★★★ **Friendliness** ★★★ **Parking** Pleasure Island lot **Bar** Full service **Wine selection** Good; mostly American wines **Dress** Casual **Disabled access** Yes

Lunch Daily, 11:30 a.m.–4 p.m.
Dinner Daily, 5–11 p.m.

Setting & atmosphere Fulton's has taken over the entire three decks of the *Empress Lilly*, which underwent extensive remodeling that removed the rear paddle wheel and the smokestacks (they didn't really work anyway). The third deck is used mainly for banquets. There is a large lounge on the first deck, where you will spend a good deal of time waiting for your table. Separate dining areas include the Market Room, which is a tribute to New York's Fulton Fish Market (for which the restaurant is named); the Constellation Room, a semicircular room with a starlit night sky; and the Industry Room, which is a tribute to the commercial fishing industry.

House specialties Stone crab; fresh fish flown in daily (the airbills are on display inside the front door); blue-crab fingers; fresh-oyster selection; Fulton's seafood chowder; cioppino with crab, shrimp, scallops, and fish in a tomato broth; Alaskan king crab; Alaskan Dungeness crab; calamari steak.

Other recommendations Tuna filet mignon; crab cake and oyster combination; Crab House clam bake; mixed grill of fresh fish.

Summary & comments Fulton's once had some of the best seafood in central Florida, but it has changed its focus from the cutting edge of seafood cuisine to a get-'em-in/get-'em-out volume feeding philosophy. Now selections are mundane, but prices are still high. Waits can be long—over an hour even on weeknights. Have an appetizer in the lounge or on the outside deck while you wait for a table.

THE GARDEN GRILL RESTAURANT ★★

AMERICAN | MODERATE | QUALITY ★★★ | VALUE ★★★

READER'S SURVEY RESPONSES 92% 👍 8% 🗨

The Land, Future World, Epcot; (407) 939-3463

Customers Theme park guests **Priority seatings** Recommended **When to go** Anytime **Entree range** $15.95–$19.95 adults; $9.25–$9.95 children **Payment** VISA, MC, AMEX **Service** ★★★ **Friendliness** ★★★★ **Parking** Epcot lot **Bar** Beer and wine **Wine selection** Fair **Dress** Casual **Disabled access** Yes

Breakfast Sunday, Monday, Wednesday, Thursday, and Saturday, 9:05–11:10 a.m.; Tuesday and Friday, 7:30–11:10 a.m.
Lunch & dinner Daily, 11:30 a.m. until park closing

Setting & atmosphere The Garden Grill is a revolving restaurant, but unlike the ones found at the top of high-rise hotels in large cities, this one is found at ground level and it doesn't even have windows. Instead the booths rotate past the various scenes of the Living with the Land boat ride. Although diners can't see the boats, they can see a rain forest and a prairie, among other things. When you're not looking at the scenes of the rain forest, you'll see brightly painted murals of sunflower fields.

House specialties The restaurant operates via an all-you-can-eat concept of rotisserie chicken and farm-raised fish, which are brought to the table on large platters and served family-style. Accompaniments include salad, bread, grilled vegetables, and potatoes.

Entertainment & amenities The view.

Summary & comments You can bet the vegetables are fresh—many of them are grown in the Epcot experimental farms seen on the pavilion's boat ride. And the lettuce is hydroponically grown.

GRAND FLORIDIAN CAFE   ★★

AMERICAN | MODERATE | QUALITY ★★★ | VALUE ★★

READER'S SURVEY RESPONSES 67% 👍 33% 🗨

Disney's Grand Floridian Beach Resort; (407) 824-2496

Customers Hotel guests **Priority seatings** Required **When to go** Breakfast or late evening **Entree range** $8.95–$24.95 **Payment** VISA, MC, AMEX, D **Service** ★★ **Friendliness** ★★★ **Parking** Valet; self-parking is deceptively far away **Bar** Full service **Wine selection** Very good **Dress** Casual **Disabled access** Yes

Breakfast Daily, 7–11 a.m.
Lunch & dinner Daily, 11:30 a.m.–10 p.m.

Setting & atmosphere The large dining room, with high ceilings and decorative windows, looks out on the hotel's pool and center courtyard.

House specialties Breakfast includes eggs prepared just about every way known to mankind, including omelets, frittatas, and huevos rancheros. Dinnertime appetizers are fairly pedestrian, including fried mozzarella cheese and chicken wings. Entrees have a Southern accent with items such as fried chicken (battered and deep-fried) served with mashed potatoes and gravy (of course); roast prime rib of beef with garlic and pan drippings; deep-fried cornmeal-battered catfish; and seafood "waterzooi" stew with fresh fish, scallops, shrimp, and rice.

Other recommendations If fried Southern cooking and beef with pan drippings aren't on your diet this decade, G.F.C. offers a good selection of nutritional, lighter meals, including a fruit plate; vegetable lasagna; turkey burgers; and a smoked fish platter.

Summary & comments The impersonal service detracts from the overall quality. Try it for breakfast or for a burger after the parks close.

GULLIVER'S GRILL AT GARDEN GROVE   ★★

AMERICAN | EXPENSIVE | QUALITY ★★★ | VALUE ★★

READER'S SURVEY RESPONSES 71% 👍 29% 🗨

Walt Disney World Swan; (407) 934-3000

Customers Hotel guests **Reservations** Required for dinner **When to go** Lunch **Entree range** $10–$30 **Payment** VISA, MC, AMEX, DC **Service** ★★ **Friendliness** ★★ **Parking** Hotel lot **Bar** Full service **Wine selection** Good **Dress** Casual **Disabled access** Yes

Breakfast & lunch Daily, 6:30 a.m.–2 p.m.
Dinner Daily, 5:30–10 p.m.

Setting & atmosphere A large greenhouse-like rotunda with tall palm trees and parrot figures attached to street lamps. Faux-stone tabletops are set with peach placemats and napkins.

House specialties Lunch sandwiches include an Italian sub, chicken salad, French dip, and grilled salmon BLT. Evening appetizers are uninspired. Entrees include steaks, such as New York strip, filet mignon with béarnaise sauce, and 18-ounce porterhouse. Prime rib, swordfish, salmon, and snapper are also available. Dinners include Caesar salad tossed tableside, Italian bread with herb butter and rice, steak fries, or baked potato. Vegetables are extra.

Entertainment & amenities Character breakfasts are held on Wednesdays and Saturdays.

Summary & comments The name has changed because the folks at the hotel believe you can't have a successful restaurant without a gimmick—food apparently doesn't matter. The menu includes a legend of the Gulliver in question (not Jonathan Swift's fictional character, but an even more fictionalized "direct descendant" named Peter Miles Gulliver). The names of the dishes are listed in the language of Brobdingnag, the Land of the Giants. The only item on the dinner menu under $21 is the marinated chicken breast with mushrooms, or kluknkro de sokin & sromes. Oh, please.

HOLLYWOOD & VINE ★★½

AMERICAN | INEXPENSIVE | QUALITY ★★★ | VALUE ★★★

READER'S SURVEY RESPONSES 76% 👍 24% 👎

Disney-MGM Studios; (407) 939-3463

Customers Theme park guests **Priority seatings** Recommended **When to go** Lunch **Entree range** $8.95–$16.95 **Payment** AMEX, MC, VISA **Service** ★★★ **Friendliness** ★★★★ **Parking** Disney-MGM lot **Bar** Full service **Wine selection** Limited **Dress** Casual **Disabled access** Yes

Breakfast Monday–Tuesday and Thursday–Saturday, 8:10–11:30 a.m.; Sunday and Wednesday, 7:30–11:30 a.m.
Lunch & dinner Daily, 11:30 a.m.–park closing

Setting & atmosphere Large art deco–style cafeteria with tile floors and lots of chrome. Walls are decorated with huge murals that resemble old postcards with vintage scenes of old Hollywood and other California landmarks.

House specialties Breakfast: eggs; frittatas; oven-roasted potatoes; smoked salmon; fresh fruit; specialty breads. Lunch and dinner: roasted pork loin; smoked seafood; fried rice; mashed potatoes; salads and fresh fruit.

Summary & comments If you feel the need to stuff yourself, try this all-you-can-eat buffet. Be prepared for lots of noise—with all the glass, tile, and chrome, the noise echoes for days.

THE HOLLYWOOD BROWN DERBY   ★★★

AMERICAN | EXPENSIVE | QUALITY ★★★★ | VALUE ★★★

READER'S SURVEY RESPONSES 83% 👍 17% 👎

Disney-MGM Studios; (407) 939-3463

Customers Theme park guests **Priority seatings** Recommended **When to go** Early evening **Entree range** $12.95–$17.25, lunch; $17.50–$25.95, dinner **Payment** VISA, MC, AMEX **Service** ★★★★ **Friendliness** ★★★★ **Parking** Disney-MGM lot **Bar** Full service **Wine selection** Very good **Dress** Casual **Disabled access** Yes

Lunch Daily, 11:30 a.m.–2:45 p.m.
Dinner Daily, 4:30 p.m. until park closes

Setting & atmosphere A replica of the original Brown Derby restaurant (not the one shaped like a derby) in California, including duplicates of the celebrity caricatures that cover the paneled walls. The elegant sunken dining room has curved booths, tables draped with yards of white linen, and romantic shaded candles. Tall palm trees in huge pots stand in the center of the room and reach for the high ceiling. Waiters wear white jackets and are better dressed than most of the park guests.

House specialties Cobb salad (a Brown Derby creation named for Bob Cobb, not Lee J.); baked grouper (battered and topped with meunière butter and served over pasta).

Other recommendations Udon noodles with tamari-seared tofu; grilled steaks; mixed grill.

Summary & comments The decor is so perfect you'll feel as though you're in 1930s Hollywood. It is so elegant that it is a shame it is located in a theme park full of T-shirted guests. Everyone should really dress in white ties and long chiffon gowns and do their best Fred Astaire and Ginger Rogers impersonations. Don't expect to see any real stars dining in the next booth, however. There is outdoor dining available, but it is much better to sit inside here.

HOUSE OF BLUES   ★★★

REGIONAL AMERICAN | MODERATE | QUALITY ★★★½ | VALUE ★★★

READER'S SURVEY RESPONSES 87% 👍 13% 👎

Downtown Disney West Side; (407) 934-2623

Customers Blues lovers **Priority seatings** Accepted **When to go** Early evening; Sunday gospel brunch **Entree range** $10–$25; brunch, $28 **Payment** VISA, MC, AMEX **Service** ★★★ **Friendliness** ★★ **Parking** Downtown Disney lot; valet $6 **Bar** Full service **Wine selection** Modest **Dress** Casual **Disabled access** Good

Brunch 2 seatings on Sunday, 10:30 a.m. and 1 p.m.
Lunch & dinner Daily, 11 a.m.–1:30 a.m.

Setting & atmosphere You'd think it was a ramshackle hut in the bayous of Louisiana if the place weren't bigger than all of Louisiana. Nearly every available inch of wall space displays some type of folk art, which has a voodoo sort of feel to it. The restaurant area is separate from the performance hall, where blues and rock groups perform. There is often a live band in the restaurant as well. Outdoor dining is available overlooking the lagoon. When recorded music is featured, monitors throughout the restaurant give a detailed description of the artist and the selection.

House specialties The menu features a selection of New Orleans favorites, including étouffée, jambalaya, and po'boy sandwiches with shrimp or catfish.

Other recommendations Cajun meatloaf; fried chicken.

Summary & comments What Hard Rock Cafe is to rock music House of Blues is to rhythm and blues. For a themed restaurant, House of Blues does an impressively good job with the food. If you're planning on taking in one of the acts at the performance space next door, you're better off going there first so you can assure yourself of a good seat and then eating afterwards.

JIKO—THE COOKING PLACE   ★★★½

AFRICAN/EUROPEAN | EXPENSIVE | QUALITY ★★★½ | VALUE ★★★

READER'S SURVEY RESPONSES 89% 👍 11% 👎

Disney's Animal Kingdom Lodge; (407) 938-3000

Customers Hotel guests, locals **Reservations** Mandatory **When to go** Anytime **Entree range** $16.50–$27.50 **Payment** VISA, MC, AMEX **Service** ★★★ **Friendliness** ★★★ **Parking** Complimentary valet or self park in hotel's lot **Bar** Full bar **Wine selection** All South African **Dress** Dressy casual **Disabled access** Good

Dinner Daily, 5–10:30 p.m.

Setting & atmosphere The dining room was conceived by renowned designer Jeffery Beers. The large room features sweeping vistas and a flock of birds (chandeliers) that fly through the room and get smaller as they go (it's supposed to resemble the opening sequence from *The Lion King*). Two large wood-burning ovens dominate the center of the room; this is the cooking place that the restaurant is named for.

House specialties Brick-oven flatbread; maize tamales; banana-leaf steamed sea bass; pan-roasted monkfish; horseradish-crusted salmon; roasted whole papaya.

Other recommendations Duck firecracker; lentil pastilla; Jiko's dumpling; duck two ways.

Summary & comments The decor may bring to mind such Disney restaurants as Citricos or Flying Fish Cafe. Jiko doesn't quite come up to that level, but a new chef, Anette Grecchi-Gray, has been tweaking the menu and is making improvements over the original and ultimately disappointing offering. The food is very good, and the decor makes it a pleasant dining experience. Only South African wines are available, and Disney claims to have the largest collection of such wines in North America.

KIMONOS ★★★★

JAPANESE | MODERATE | QUALITY ★★★★½ | VALUE ★★★

READER'S SURVEY RESPONSES 88% 👍 12% 👎

Walt Disney World Swan; (407) 934-3000

Customers Hotel guests, locals **Reservations** Accepted for parties over 10 **When to go** Anytime **Entree range** Sushi and rolls à la carte, $3.75–$9.95 **Payment** VISA, MC, AMEX, DC, JCB, D **Service** ★★★★ **Friendliness** ★★★★ **Parking** Hotel lot; valet, $10 **Bar** Full service **Wine selection** Very good **Dress** Casual **Disabled access** Yes

Dinner Daily, 5:30 p.m.–1 a.m.; bar opens at 5 p.m.

Setting & atmosphere The decor consists of black lacquered tabletops and counters, tall pillars rising to bamboo rafters with rice-paper lanterns, and elegant kimonos that hang outstretched on the walls and between the dining sections. The chefs will greet you with a friendly welcome, and you'll be offered a hot towel to clean your hands. Even if you're not in the mood for sushi, this is a delightful place to just sit and sip sake.

House specialties Although sushi and sashimi are the focus, Kimonos also serves a number of hot appetizers, including tempura-battered shrimp, fish, and vegetables; skewered chicken yakitori; beef teriyaki and gyoza; and steamed dumplings stuffed with a pork mixture. The crispy soft-shell crab is wonderful.

Summary & comments The skill of the sushi artists is as much a joy to watch as is eating the wonderfully fresh creations. There are no full entrees here, just good sushi and appetizers. The Walt Disney World Swan is host to many Japanese tourists, and you'll find many of them here on any given night. Enough said.

KONA CAFE ★★★

NEW AMERICAN/CARRIBEAN | MODERATE | QUALITY ★★★★ | VALUE ★★★★

READER'S SURVEY RESPONSES 84% 👍 16% 👎

Polynesian Resort; (407) 939-3463

Customers Mostly hotel guests; some locals **Priority seatings** Accepted **When to go** Anytime **Entree range** $6.50–$18.99 **Payment** AMEX, MC, VISA **Service** ★★★ **Friendliness** ★★★★ **Parking** Polynesian lot; valet available **Bar** Full service **Wine selection** Moderate **Dress** Casual **Disabled access** Good

Breakfast Daily, 7–11:45 a.m.
Lunch Monday–Saturday, noon–2:45 p.m.; Sunday, 12:30–2:45 p.m.
Dinner Monday–Saturday, 5–9:45 p.m.

Setting & atmosphere The postmodern decor might remind some regular Disney guests of the dining rooms at California Grill. Arched railings and grillwork cover the ceiling. Instead of a regular "on stage" kitchen, the staff here put the pastry chef out front so you can watch all those lovely calories being loaded onto your plate.

House specialties Ginger-carrot soup; Asian noodle soup; Kona crab cakes; chargrilled seafood served with pan-fried noodles and baby bok choy; Ko ko puffs (miniature cream puffs) and Kilauea torte.

Other recommendations Estate-grown Kona coffee served in a French press pot.

Summary & comments Kona Cafe replaced the Coral Isle Cafe in the Polynesian Resort. But the results of the renovation, both in the design of the restaurant and in the execution of the creative menu, are on a higher plane than your average java joint. It hardly seems necessary to mention chef John Guillemette and pastry chef Isaac Tamada because they will certainly be moved to higher profile positions in fancier restaurants very soon. But they've laid the groundwork for a pleasant dining surprise.

LIBERTY TREE TAVERN ★★½

AMERICAN | MODERATE | QUALITY ★★★ | VALUE ★★★

READER'S SURVEY RESPONSES 88% 👍 12% 👎

Liberty Square, Magic Kingdom; (407) 939-3463

Customers Theme park guests **Priority seatings** Suggested **When to go** Anytime **Entree range Lunch** $9.95–$14.25 adults, $4.75–$5.50 children; dinner: $19.95 adults, $9.95 children **Payment** VISA, MC, AMEX, D **Service** ★★★★ **Friendliness** ★★★★ **Parking** Magic Kingdom lot **Bar** None **Wine selection** None **Dress** Casual **Disabled access** Yes

Lunch Daily, 11:30 a.m.–3 p.m.
Dinner Daily, 4 p.m. until park closes

Setting & atmosphere Low, exposed-beam ceilings in rooms framed by pastel gray chair rails. Colonial-period wall art, much with a nautical theme, accents simple dark wood tables and chairs with woven seats.

House specialties Prime rib; roast turkey; chicken breast with Virginia ham. Family-style character dining.

Other recommendations Sandwiches and salads are good here.

Summary & comments Though the Liberty Tree is the best of the Magic Kingdom's full-service restaurants, it is often overlooked at lunch. A good plan is to make a priority seating here for about an hour or so before parade time. After you eat, you can walk right out and watch the parade.

MAMA MELROSE'S RISTORANTE ITALIANO ★★½

ITALIAN | MODERATE | QUALITY ★★★ | VALUE ★★

READER'S SURVEY RESPONSES 76% 👍 24% 👎

Disney-MGM Studios; (407) 939-3463

Customers Theme park guests **Priority seatings** Suggested **When to go** Anytime **Entree range** $10.95–$22.95 **Payment** VISA, MC, AMEX **Service** ★★★★ **Friendliness** ★★★★ **Parking** Disney-MGM lot **Bar** Full service **Wine selection** Limited **Dress** Casual **Disabled access** Yes

Lunch Daily, 11:30 a.m.–3:30 p.m.
Dinner Daily, 3:30 p.m. until park closes

Setting & atmosphere Mama Melrose's looks like a big-city neighborhood restaurant of the 1930s, with bare wooden floors, red-and-white checkered tablecloths, red vinyl booths, and grapevines hanging from the rafters. By far the most relaxing restaurant at Disney-MGM Studios, Mama Melrose's sports a worn, ethnic look that is as comfortable as an old sweatshirt.

House specialties Pasta and seafood combos are excellent, as are salads and some of the designer pizzas. Bread is served in the traditional style with olive oil.

Other recommendations Veal Parmesan served with pasta; vegetable lasagna; chicken marsala.

Summary & comments Because of its out-of-the-way location, you can sometimes just walk into Mama Melrose's, especially in the evening.

MAYA GRILL ★★

MEXICAN | EXPENSIVE | QUALITY ★★★ | VALUE ★★

READER'S SURVEY RESPONSES 49% 👍 51% 👎

Coronado Springs Resort; (407) 939-3463

Customers Hotel guests **Priority seatings** Recommended **When to go** Anytime **Entree range** $18–$30; breakfast buffet: adult $11.95, child $7.95 **Payment** VISA, MC, AMEX **Service** ★★★ **Friendliness** ★★★ **Parking** Hotel lot; no valet **Bar** Full service **Wine selection** Fair **Dress** Casual **Disabled access** Good

Breakfast Daily, 7–11 a.m.
Dinner Daily, 5–10 p.m.

Setting & atmosphere The dining room is meant to evoke the ancient world of the Maya with, according to the menu, "a harmony of fire, sun and water." The fire is fake and in the form of "flames" made of fabric that is fan-blown at the top of two large columns. Diners sit around the base of a Mayan pyramid. The kitchen is open to view, but so is the barren and starkly lit walkway outside, which detracts a bit from the atmosphere.

House specialties Another attempt to create a new cuisine, this time it's nuevo Latino, for a fusion of New and Old World flavors. This is meant to take Latino foods and marry them with the flavors of the Caribbean, Mexico, and South America. Huachinango features snapper in a pumpkin seed crust. Ropa vieja, braised flank steak, is served on a fresh corn tamale.

Summary & comments Coronado Springs Resort was meant to be for those on a budget, but this restaurant certainly doesn't follow that credo. The prices are way too high here for the quality of the food, which, by the way, is offered by the same company that operates San Angel Inn at the Mexico pavilion in Epcot (the same people run the food court at Coronado Springs as well). The fusion cuisine sometimes works and sometimes falls flatter than a tortilla. Overall the quality doesn't come close to matching the prices, so you're better off eating somewhere else.

NARCOOSSEE'S ★★★½

SEAFOOD | EXPENSIVE | QUALITY ★★★★ | VALUE ★★

READER'S SURVEY RESPONSES 75% 👍 25% 🗨

Disney's Grand Floridian Beach Resort; (407) 939-3463

Customers Hotel guests, locals **Priority seatings** Recommended **When to go** Early evening **Entree range** $20–$52 **Payment** VISA, MC, AMEX **Service** ★★★★ **Friendliness** ★★★★ **Parking** Valet; self-parking is deceptively far away. **Bar** Full service **Wine selection** Good **Dress** Casual **Disabled access** Yes

Dinner Daily, 5–10 p.m.; lounge open, 3–11 p.m.

Setting & atmosphere Part of the Grand Floridian Beach Resort complex, Narcoossee's is a free-standing octagonal building at the edge of Seven Seas Lagoon. It offers a great view of the Magic Kingdom and the boats that dock nearby to pick up guests and drop them off after a day at the park. The lack of carpet and tablecloths, and the high noise level, belie the fine-dining aspect.

House specialties Appetizers include duo of mushroom soup, shredded duck confit salad, and brick-baked focaccia with duck pastrami. Entrees include pan-seared fillet of black grouper with spelt pilaf; crab with potato cakes; and grilled shrimp with saffron couscous.

Other recommendations Grilled filet mignon with mashed red skin potatoes; charred chicken breast with Dijon mustard mayonnaise.

Summary & comments Narcoossee's is back on track in offering some of the best food on the property. Still, prices are extremely high for this atmosphere, which often features children running about delighting in the reverberating acoustics. A good choice for a lunchtime escape from the Magic Kingdom. Prices are more reasonable at lunch.

NINE DRAGONS RESTAURANT ★★½

CHINESE | EXPENSIVE | QUALITY ★★★ | VALUE ★

READER'S SURVEY RESPONSES 62% 👍 38% 🗨

China, World Showcase, Epcot; (407) 939-3463

Customers Theme park guests **Priority seatings** Suggested **When to go** Anytime **Entree range** $9.50–$35, lunch; $12.50–$29.95, dinner **Payment** VISA, MC, AMEX **Service** ★★★ **Friendliness** ★★★★ **Parking** Epcot lot **Bar** Full service **Wine selection** Limited **Dress** Casual **Disabled access** Yes

Lunch Daily, noon–4:30 p.m.
Dinner Daily, 4:45 p.m. until park closes

Setting & atmosphere The Nine Dragons is a stunning restaurant—formal, elegant, and bright. Its decor reflects Asian artistry and sophistication, with combinations of bright lacquered colors and natural wood hues—what every Chinese eatery across America seeks to emulate. There are inlaid ceilings, large and elaborate wood sculptures, and a lush, red, floral-patterned carpet.

House specialties The Nine Dragons' fare, unfortunately, does not live up to its decor. The limited menu features the same tired sweet-and-sour pork, beef with broccoli, and moo goo gai pan that you can buy for one-third the price at your own neighborhood Chinese restaurant.

Summary & comments This should be one of the best Chinese restaurants in the United States, but it's not. The lack of a creative menu, along with assembly-line preparation and service, makes Nine Dragons a lost opportunity at best, and an overpriced tourist trap at worst.

1900 PARK FARE   ★★½

BUFFET | MODERATE | QUALITY ★★★ | VALUE ★★★

READER'S SURVEY RESPONSES 88% 👍 12% 🗨

Disney's Grand Floridian Resort; (407) 824-3000

Customers Hotel and resort guests **Priority seating:** Necessary **When to go** Breakfast or dinner **Buffet cost** Breakfast $17 adults, $10 children; dinner: $22 adults, $13 children **Payment** VISA, MC, AMEX, DC **Service** ★★★ **Friendliness** ★★★ **Parking** Complimentary valet **Bar** Full service **Wine selection** Limited **Dress** Theme park casual **Disabled access** Yes

Breakfast Daily, 7:30–11:30 a.m.
Dinner Daily, 5:15–9:30 p.m.

Setting & atmosphere The cavernous, high-ceilinged, bright room is warmly appointed in pastels. Tables are set with linen. There are no windows. A calliope erupts periodically to provide musical accompaniment to dining (or add to the din, depending on your opinion of calliopes).

House specialties Buffet includes prime rib and nice pasta dishes.

Other recommendations Separate buffet for kids includes burgers, hot dogs, chicken nuggets, and macaroni and cheese.

Entertainment & amenities All meals feature character dining and the calliope.

Summary & comments A good choice for character dining but too bright and loud for adults without children. The dinner buffet is on par with Chef Mickey's (Contemporary Resort) but not as good as the Cape May at the Beach Club. The prime rib is 1900 Park Fare's major draw at dinner, but go someplace else if you prefer your beef on the rare side of medium.

'OHANA   ★★★

POLYNESIAN | MODERATE | QUALITY ★★★½ | VALUE ★★★

READER'S SURVEY RESPONSES 88% 👍 12% 🗨

Disney's Polynesian Resort; (407) 939-3463

Customers Resort guests **Priority seatings** Recommended **When to go** Anytime **Entree range** $21.95 adults; $10.95 children **Payment** VISA, MC, AMEX **Service** ★★★ **Friendliness** ★★★★ **Parking** Hotel lot **Bar** Full service **Wine selection** Limited **Dress** Casual **Disabled access** Yes

Dinner Daily, 5–10 p.m.

Setting & atmosphere This restaurant replaced the Papeete Bay Verandah. A large open pit is the centerpiece of the room. Here the grilled foods are prepared with a flare—literally. From time to time the chef will pour some liquid on the fire, causing huge flames to shoot up. This is usually in response to something one of the strolling entertainers has said, evoking a sign from the fire gods. At any given moment there may be a hula-hoop contest or a coconut race where the children are invited to push coconuts around the dining room with broomsticks.

House specialties Skewer service is the specialty here. There is no menu. As soon as you are seated, your server will begin to deliver food. First a couple of sausages, which are portioned off from long skewers right onto the diner's plate. These are followed by smoked turkey, beef, and chicken. These are accompanied by assorted salads, placed on a lazy Susan in the center of the table, along with pot sticker dumplings and teriyaki noodles.

Entertainment & amenities Strolling singers; games.

Summary & comments 'Ohana, which means family, is a fun place. The food is good but not superior. The method of service and the fact that it just keeps coming make it all taste a little better. Insist on being seated in the main dining room, where the fire pit is located. There are tables around the back, but you can't see what's going on from back there.

OLIVIA'S CAFE ★★★

AMERICAN | MODERATE | QUALITY ★★★★½ | VALUE ★★★

READER'S SURVEY RESPONSES 82% 👍 18% 👎

Old Key West Resort; (407) 939-3463

Customers Resort guests **Priority seatings** Recommended **When to go** Lunch **Entree range** $7.95–$22.95 **Payment** VISA, MC, AMEX **Service** ★★★★ **Friendliness** ★★★★ **Parking** Hotel lot **Bar** Full service **Wine selection** Limited **Dress** Casual **Disabled access** Yes

Breakfast Daily, 7:30–10:15 a.m.
Lunch Daily, 11:30 a.m.–5 p.m.
Dinner Daily, 5–10 p.m.

Setting & atmosphere This is Disney's idea of Key West, with lots of pastels and rough wood siding on the walls, mosaic tile floors, potted palms and tropical trees in the center of the room, and plenty of nautical gewgaws, including vintage photos of Key West and its inhabitants of long ago. (Key West is nothing like this today.) There is some outside seating, which looks out over the waterway. Tile, wood siding, and no tablecloths add up to a very noisy dining room.

House specialties Appetizers include conch chowder; blue lump crab cakes; and guacamole and chips. Entrees feature prime rib; breaded and deep-fried Gulf shrimp; fresh fish grilled with spices; and fried chicken with mashed potatoes and gravy. Many of the dishes are accompanied by what is referred to as real Cuban-style black beans and rice, but these beans would look pretty Americanized to anyone from Havana.

Other recommendations Fried chicken; country-fried steak.

Summary & comments Though perhaps not Key West, the charming atmosphere and low-key pace make the food taste even better than it already is. Not wonderful, just nice. The servers are upbeat and move with alarming speed, though food tends to come out of the kitchen at a more Key Westerly pace (slowly).

L'ORIGINALE ALFREDO DI ROMA RISTORANTE ★★½

ITALIAN | EXPENSIVE | QUALITY ★★★ | VALUE ★★

READER'S SURVEY RESPONSES 84% 👍 16% 👎

Italy, World Showcase, Epcot; (407) 939-3463

Customers Theme park guests **Priority seatings** Recommended **When to go** Midafternoon **Entree range** Lunch, $12.50–$22.50; dinner, $16.50–$32.95 **Payment** VISA, MC, AMEX **Service** ★★★★ **Friendliness** ★★★★ **Parking** Epcot lot **Bar** Beer and wine only **Wine selection** All Italian **Dress** Casual **Disabled access** Yes

Lunch Daily, noon–4:15 p.m.
Dinner Daily, 4:30 p.m. until park closes

Setting & atmosphere The elegant—some would say garish—Roman decor features huge murals of an Italian piazza along the wall behind the upholstered banquettes. Dark woods and latticework on the high ceilings add to a sumptuous atmosphere. It is, however, a noisy dining room, one that is nearly always filled. This is yet another location for the so-called famous restaurant of the inventor of fettucine Alfredo, the favorite dining spot of Mary Pickford and Douglas Fairbanks.

House specialties Fettucine Alfredo (what else?); pasta e fagioli; linguine al pesto; vitello alla Milanese.

Other recommendations Pollo alla Milanese; pollo alla Parmigiana; roasted lamb chop.

Entertainment & amenities Strolling opera singers at dinner.

Summary & comments Although the word "original" appears in the name, the food is a little worn and old. (So what did Mary Pickford and Douglas Fairbanks know about restaurants?) Most of the entrees are heavy and will have you plodding the rest of the way through the park.

THE OUTBACK ★★

STEAK | EXPENSIVE | QUALITY ★★★ | VALUE ★★

READER'S SURVEY RESPONSES 46% 👍 54% 👎

Wyndham Palace, Disney Village Hotel Plaza; (407) 827-2727

Customers Tourists, locals **Reservations** Recommended **When to go** Very early dinner **Entree range** $12.95–$35 **Payment** VISA, MC, AMEX; DC, D **Service** ★ **Friendliness** ★ **Parking** Complimentary valet parking at the rear of the hotel **Bar** Full service **Wine selection** Excellent **Dress** Casual **Disabled access** Yes

Dinner Daily, 5:30–10:45 p.m.

Setting & atmosphere A large, open room with a two-story ceiling and a cascading waterfall. Servers are in Australian bush outfits. That and the menu printed on a boomerang are supposed to make it an Australian restaurant, though the bulk of the menu is what you'd find in just about any American restaurant.

House specialties There aren't many places where you can get kangaroo steak and rattlesnake salad, but you can here if you really want it. Otherwise, there is filet mignon with béarnaise sauce; rack of spring lamb; grilled tuna; and prime rib.

Other recommendations Six-pound live Maine lobster.

Summary & comments For some reason that no one bothers to explain, dinner rolls are delivered to the table at the end of long poles. Staff members tend to treat guests as though they'll never be back. The food isn't good enough to put up with rude service. *Note:* This is not part of the Outback Steakhouse national chain.

PALIO   ★★★

ITALIAN | EXPENSIVE | QUALITY ★★★½ | VALUE ★★★

READER'S SURVEY RESPONSES 89% 👍 11% 🗨

Walt Disney World Swan; (407) 934-3000

Customers Hotel guests **Reservations** Recommended **When to go** Anytime **Entree range** $17–$32 **Payment** VISA, MC, AMEX, DC, JCB, D **Service** ★★★ **Friendliness** ★★★ **Parking** Hotel lot **Bar** Full service **Wine selection** Very good **Dress** Casual **Disabled access** Yes

Dinner Daily, 6–11 p.m.

Setting & atmosphere The name means banner, and they're hanging all over this upscale Italian trattoria and are even draped over the tables. It is a pretty place and bustles with excitement and the sounds of happy diners. Like just about everything else in the hotel, designer Michael Graves had a hand in the decor and design of the restaurant, and it shows. It is a beautiful place.

House specialties Veal alla limone, a scallopine served with lemon butter and linguine; saltimbocca alla Romana, veal medallions topped with prosciutto and sage, served with risotto; osso buco alla Milanese, veal shank braised in white wine and vegetable stock, served with saffron risotto.

Other recommendations Veal picante alla marsala; sautéed chicken breast with tomato; red snapper with sautéed fennel.

Summary & comments The food isn't bad, and the experience is satisfying overall, but there are more exciting dining options available. The roasted-garlic spread served with the hot bread is nice. Fill up on that and then order one of the reasonably priced pizzas.

PLANET HOLLYWOOD   ★★★½

AMERICAN | MODERATE | QUALITY ★★★★ | VALUE ★★★

READER'S SURVEY RESPONSES 64% 👍 36% 🗨

Pleasure Island; (407) 827-7827

Customers Tourists, locals **Priority seatings** Accepted lunch and late-night only **When to go** Late lunch **Entree range** $8.95–$20 **Payment** VISA, MC, AMEX, DC, D **Service** ★★★★ **Friendliness** ★★ **Parking** Pleasure Island lot **Bar** Full service **Wine selection** Limited **Dress** Casual **Disabled access** Yes

Lunch & dinner Daily, 11 a.m.–1 a.m.

Setting & atmosphere A large planet-shaped structure "floating" in the lagoon next to Pleasure Island. Planet Hollywood's decor is something of a movie museum, with memorabilia from famous movies. Orlando is world headquarters for the chain, and the hometown restaurant is really a special structure. Still, the artifacts leave something to be desired. New York's Planet has Judy Garland's ruby slippers; Orlando's has the gilded potty seat from *The Last Emperor*.

House specialties The menu is all over the place: pasta dishes, fajitas, burgers, dinner salads, and pizzas. Burgers are huge (the bleu cheese burger is wonderful). Desserts are incredible, especially the white-chocolate bread pudding.

Other recommendations Chicken fajitas; linguini and sausage; grilled swordfish.

Summary & comments Because of its star power, Planet Hollywood attracts a lot of people. But even with the never-ending stream of guests, the kitchen doesn't slack off. The food is good and well thought out. And while $7.50 may seem like a lot of money for a burger, you'll get a thick, juicy patty, cooked the way you want it, with fries. And to give you an idea of the restaurant's attention to details, the potatoes for the fries are stored on the premises until the proper amount of sweetness from aging is achieved.

PLEASURE ISLAND JAZZ COMPANY ★★

REGIONAL AMERICAN | MODERATE | QUALITY ★★★ | VALUE ★★★

READER'S SURVEY RESPONSES 72% 👍 28% 👎

Pleasure Island; (407) 934-7781

Customers Tourists, locals **Priority seatings** Not accepted **When to go** Early evening to get a good seat for the entertainment **Entree range** $4.50–$9.75 **Payment** VISA, MC, AMEX **Service** ★★ **Friendliness** ★★ **Parking** Pleasure Island lot **Bar** Full service **Wine selection** Moderate **Dress** Casual **Disabled access** Good

Dinner Daily, 8 p.m.–2 a.m.

Setting & atmosphere A large nightclub with tables set up in front of a performance space where jazz musicians play nightly. This is the sort of place where you don't go just to have the food and not stay for the show. However, you'll find plenty of people who come for the music with no intention of having anything to eat.

House specialties Red beans and rice; spicy Cajun chicken stack; Oriental grilled salmon.

Summary & comments Although the jazz club has been serving full dinners for a couple of years, it has remained something of a secret, which is surprising since this is one of the few Downtown Disney eating spots that is not operated by an outside concern. The food is simple, and the service tends to be a bit brusque. But the jazz experience is definitely enhanced when you have a bowl of red beans and rice in front of you.

PORTOBELLO YACHT CLUB   ★★★

ITALIAN | EXPENSIVE | QUALITY ★★★★ | VALUE ★★

READER'S SURVEY RESPONSES 69% 👍 31% 👎

Pleasure Island; (407) 934-8888

Customers Tourists, locals **Priority seatings** Recommended **When to go** Anytime **Entree range** $15–$35 **Payment** VISA, MC, AMEX **Service** ★★★★ **Friendliness** ★★★★ **Parking** Pleasure Island lot **Bar** Full service **Wine selection** Very good; heavy on Italian selections **Dress** Casual **Disabled access** Yes

Lunch Daily, 11:30 a.m.–4 p.m.
Dinner Daily, 4 p.m.–midnight

Setting & atmosphere This restaurant sports an upscale nautical theme with lots of polished brass, dark woods, and canvas window coverings. There is a patio overlooking the lagoon for those days with low humidity.

House specialties Northern Italian cuisine; breaded veal ribeye; charcoal-grilled shrimp on a rosemary skewer; boneless half chicken marinated in olive oil, garlic, and fresh rosemary.

Other recommendations Crispy thin-crust pizza appetizers, including a vegetarian pizza with eggplant, zucchini, and mushrooms and a four-cheese pizza with sun-dried tomatoes. The butterfly pasta with fresh asparagus and snow peas is a good inexpensive selection.

Summary & comments This place, along with Fulton's Crab House (both are Levi Restaurants operations), has been slipping in quality lately. Once a place where visiting celebrities would be wined, it's now left only to unsuspecting walk-ins. Sad. Ask for the patio if it's a cool evening.

RAINFOREST CAFE   ★★½

AMERICAN | MODERATE | QUALITY ★★★ | VALUE ★★

READER'S SURVEY RESPONSES 80% 👍 20% 👎

Downtown Disney Marketplace; (407) 933-2800;
Animal Kingdom; (407) 938-9100

Customers Tourists and locals **Priority seatings** Accepted at Animal Kingdom location only **When to go** Late afternoon, after lunch crunch, and before dinner hour **Entree range** $10–$25 **Payment** VISA, MC, AMEX, DC, D **Service** ★★ **Friendliness** ★★★ **Parking** Marketplace lot **Bar** Full bar **Wine selection** Limited **Dress** Dressy casual **Disabled access** Good

Open *Downtown Disney Marketplace:* Sunday–Thursday, 10:30 a.m.–11 p.m.; Friday and Saturday, 10:30 a.m.–midnight; *Animal Kingdom:* Daily, 8 a.m.–park closes

Setting & atmosphere The Downtown Disney version of the national chain sits beneath a giant volcano that can be seen (and heard) erupting all over the Marketplace. The smoke coming from the volcano is nonpolluting, in accordance with the restaurant's conservation theme. Inside is a huge dining room designed to look like a jungle (imagine all the silk plants in the world tacked to the ceiling), complete with audio-animatronic elephants, bats, and monkeys (not the most realistic animatronics you've seen). There is occasional thunder and even some rainfall. Large aquariums connected with glass "swimways" serve as one of several waiting areas. Next to the dining room is a 5,000-square-foot retail shop. The Animal Kingdom version, featuring a huge waterfall, is easier on the eye externally. Once inside, however, you'll find the same food, decor, and retail space as at the Marketplace.

House specialties "Pieces of ate" eggroll with chicken, red peppers, corn, and black beans wrapped inside wonton skins; seafood Galapagos with fish, zucchini, and shrimp (but no tortoise) served over pasta; Rainforest pita quesadilla with chicken.

Entertainment & amenities After the wait you endure, a chair and some sustenance is all the entertainment you'll need. If you're willing to pay to avoid the long wait, stop by the day before and purchase a Safari Club membership for $10. By presenting your card the on the day you want to dine, you will be seated immediately. Safari Club members can also call ahead for reservations.

Summary & comments Let us say up front that while we are not impressed by the Rainforest Cafes, a lot of our readers rave about them. The slogan for Rainforest Cafe is "a wild place to shop and eat." The shopping experience must be the attraction, because it certainly isn't the food. Preparations are spotty; spicing is uneven; and the quality is not as high as at other area theme restaurants such as Planet Hollywood and Hard Rock Cafe. Waits can be horrendous. Of course, you are expected to shop in the retail space during your wait time. By all means visit the gift shop, but dine somewhere else.

RESTAURANT AKERSHUS ★★★½

NORWEGIAN/BUFFET | MODERATE | QUALITY ★★★★ | VALUE ★★★★

READER'S SURVEY RESPONSES 90% 👍 10% 👎

Norway, World Showcase, Epcot; (407) 939-3463

Customers Theme park guests **Priority seatings** Required **When to go** Anytime **Entree range Lunch** $12.95 adults, $6.25 kids; dinner: $18.50 adults, $7.95 kids **Payment** VISA, MC, AMEX, D **Service** ★★★ **Friendliness** ★★★★ **Parking** Epcot lot **Bar** Full service **Wine selection** Good **Dress** Casual **Disabled access** Yes

Lunch Daily, 11:30 a.m.–4 p.m.
Dinner Daily, 4:15 p.m. until park closes

Setting & atmosphere Modeled on a 14th-century fortress, Akershus entertains its guests in a great banquet hall under high A-framed ceilings and massive iron chandeliers. Stone arches divide the dining rooms. A red carpet alternates with patterned hardwood floors.

House specialties A bountiful hot and cold buffet features salmon; herring; various Norwegian salads and cheeses; hearty stews; and a variety of hot fish and meats. Be sure to try the mashed rutabagas.

Other recommendations Cold Ringnes beer on tap.

Summary & comments Akershus offers a unique introduction to delightful Scandinavian cuisines. The dishes may not be familiar, but the quality is superb, and the overall experience is a real adventure in dining. Akershus's popularity grows every year as word of its quality spreads. We think it's one of the better restaurants at Walt Disney World.

RESTAURANT MARRAKESH ★★★

MOROCCAN | MODERATE | QUALITY ★★★½ | VALUE ★★★

READER'S SURVEY RESPONSES 85% 👍 15% 👎

Morocco, World Showcase, Epcot; (407) 939-3463

Customers Theme park guests **Priority seatings** Required **When to go** Anytime **Entree range** $11.95–$18.50, lunch; $16.95–$25.95, dinner **Payment** VISA, MC, AMEX **Service** ★★★ **Friendliness** ★★★★ **Parking** Epcot lot **Bar** Full service **Wine selection** Limited **Dress** Casual **Disabled access** Yes

Lunch Daily, 11:30 a.m.–3:30 p.m.
Dinner Daily, 4 p.m. until park closes

Setting & atmosphere One of the more exotic World Showcase restaurants, Marrakesh re-creates a Moroccan palace with gleaming tile mosaics, high inlaid-wood ceilings with open beams and brass chandeliers, and red Bukhara carpets.

House specialties Start with bastila (a minced chicken pie sprinkled with confectionary sugar), followed by cornish hen, tangine chicken, or roast lamb. Split an order of couscous. Beef and lamb kebabs are also available.

Other recommendations If you are hungry, curious, or both, go for one of the combination platters for two persons.

Entertainment & amenities Moroccan band and belly dancing.

Summary & comments Interesting fare that is almost impossible to find except in the largest U.S. cities. Unlike diners at most Moroccan restaurants, those at Marrakesh sit at tables (instead of on the floor) and eat with utensils rather than with their hands. Because Moroccan food is unfamiliar to most visitors, Marrakesh sometimes has tables available for walk-ins.

ROSE & CROWN DINING ROOM ★★★

ENGLISH | MODERATE | QUALITY ★★★½ | VALUE ★★

READER'S SURVEY RESPONSES 91% 👍 9% 👎

United Kingdom, World Showcase, Epcot; (407) 939-3463

Customers Theme park guests **Priority seatings** Recommended **When to go** Anytime **Entree range** $9.95–$14.95, lunch; $13.75–$19.95, dinner **Payment** VISA, MC, AMEX **Service** ★★★★ **Friendliness** ★★★★ **Parking** Epcot lot **Wine selection** Limited **Bar** Full bar with Bass ale and Guinness and Harp beers on tap **Dress** Casual **Disabled access** Yes

Lunch Daily, 11:30 a.m.–4 p.m.
Dinner Daily, 4:30 p.m. until park closes

Setting & atmosphere The Rose & Crown is both a pub and dining establishment.

The traditional English pub has a large cozy bar with rich wood appointments and trim, beamed ceilings, and a hardwood floor. The adjoining English country dining room is rustic and simple. Meals are served outdoors overlooking the World Showcase Lagoon when the weather is nice.

House specialties Hearty but simple food; try fish and chips or the Welsh chicken and leek pie, washed down with Bass ale.

Other recommendations Steak and kidney pie; cottage pie; bangers and mash (sausage and mashed potatoes); prime rib.

Summary & comments You do not need priority seatings to stop and refresh yourself on a hot (or cold) afternoon at the friendly bar. The waitresses and barmaids are saucy in the best English tradition and add immeasurably to the experience. Unfortunately, the number of selections on the menu has been cut significantly since our last visit. The Rose & Crown is usually more popular at lunch than at dinner. It is about the fifth Epcot restaurant to book its seatings, owing more to its small size than its popularity.

SAN ANGEL INN RESTAURANTE ★★★

MEXICAN | EXPENSIVE | QUALITY ★★★★ | VALUE ★★

READER'S SURVEY RESPONSES 77% 👍 23% 👎

Mexico, World Showcase, Epcot; (407) 939-3463

Customers Theme park guests **Priority seatings** Recommended **When to go** Anytime **Entree range** $8.95–$16.25, lunch; $17.75–$21.95, dinner **Payment** VISA, MC, AMEX **Service** ★★★★ **Friendliness** ★★★★ **Parking** Epcot lot **Bar** Full service **Wine selection** Limited **Dress** Casual **Disabled access** Yes

Lunch Daily, 11:30 a.m.–4 p.m.
Dinner Daily, 4:30 p.m. until park closes

Setting & atmosphere The San Angel Inn is inside the great Aztec pyramid of the Mexican pavilion. A romantically crafted open-air cantina, the restaurant overlooks both El Río del Tiempo (The River of Time) and the bustling plaza of a small Mexican village.

House specialties In addition to enchiladas, tacos, and other routine Mexican fare, San Angel features (at dinner only) mole poblano (chicken with an exotic sauce made from several kinds of peppers and unsweetened Mexican chocolate) and some interesting regional fish preparations.

Other recommendations Blackened mahimahi or poached red snapper.

Entertainment & amenities Mariachi or marimba bands in the adjacent courtyard.

Summary & comments The San Angel Inn serves good, sometimes excellent, Mexican food at prices much higher than you would find at most Mexican restaurants. The shrimp grilled with pepper sauce, for example, is five medium-sized shrimp for the outrageous sum of $22 ($4.50 per shrimp!). The menu goes beyond normal Mexican selections, offering special and regional dishes that are difficult to find in the United States. If you go, we recommend you skip the tacos and try one of these more unique dishes.

SCI-FI DINE-IN THEATER RESTAURANT ★★

AMERICAN | MODERATE | QUALITY ★★★ | VALUE ★★

READER'S SURVEY RESPONSES 61% 👍 39% 💬

Disney-MGM Studios; (407) 939-3463

Customers Theme park guests **Priority seatings** Required **When to go** Anytime
Entree range $11.95–$16.95, lunch; $14.95–$18.50, dinner **Payment** VISA, MC,
AMEX **Service** ★★★★★ **Friendliness** ★★★★★ **Parking** Disney-MGM lot **Bar**
Full service **Wine selection** Limited **Dress** Casual **Disabled access** Yes

Lunch Sunday and Wednesday, 10:30 a.m.–4 p.m.; Monday–Tuesday and Thursday–
Saturday, 11 a.m.–4 p.m.
Dinner Daily, 4 p.m. until park closes

Setting & atmosphere You sit in little cars in a large building where it is always night
and watch vintage film clips on a drive-in movie screen as you eat.

House specialties The fare consists of sandwiches; burgers; salads; and shakes, as
well as fancier stuff. While we think the food quality is way out of line with the cost, you
can have an adequate meal at the Sci-Fi if you stick with simple fare.

Entertainment & amenities Cartoons and clips of vintage horror and sci-fi movies
are shown, such as *The Attack of the Fifty-foot Woman*, *Robot Monster*, and *Son of the
Blob*. Also shown are lurid previews, proclaiming, "See a sultry beauty in the clutches of
a half-crazed monster!"

Summary & comments We recommend making a late-afternoon or late-evening
priority seating and ordering only dessert. In other words, think of the Sci-Fi as an
attraction (which it is) as opposed to a good dining opportunity (which it is not). If you
want to try the Sci-Fi Dine-In and do not have priority seatings, try walking in at 11 a.m.
or around 3 p.m.

SHULA'S STEAK HOUSE ★★★½

STEAK | EXPENSIVE | QUALITY ★★★★ | VALUE ★★★

READER'S SURVEY RESPONSES 89% 👍 11% 💬

Walt Disney World Dolphin; (407) 934-4000

Customers Hotel guests and locals **Priority seatings** Recommended **When to go**
Anytime **Entree range** $20.95–$65.95 **Payment** VISA, MC, AMEX, D, DC **Service**
★★★ **Friendliness** ★★★ **Parking** Hotel lot; complimentary valet **Bar** Full service
Wine selection Very good; expensive **Dress** Dressy casual **Disabled access** Yes

Dinner Daily, 5–11 p.m.

Setting & atmosphere Clubby and masculine with dark woods and darker lighting.
Large black-and-white photographs of football players in action framed in gold gilt offer
the only decorations. White tablecloths adorn tables.

House specialties Meat—really expensive but very high-quality meat. Only certified
Angus beef is served, with filet mignon, porterhouse (including a 42-ounce version),
lamb chops, and prime rib.

Other recommendations The steak tartare appetizer is special; split lobster cocktail appetizer.

Summary & comments This is the growing chain owned by former Miami Dolphins football coach Don Shula. It's classier than it is kitschy, though printing the menu on the side of a football and placing it on a kickoff tee in the center of the table is a bit over the top. They could also do without the rehearsed spiel from the waiters who present raw examples of the beef selections (not to mention a live lobster) at each table. Once you get past that, however, you're in for some wonderful steaks.

SPOODLES   ★★★½

MEDITERRANEAN | MODERATE | QUALITY ★★★★ | VALUE ★★★

READER'S SURVEY RESPONSES 92% 👍 8% 🗨

Disney's BoardWalk; (407) 939-3463

Customers Tourists and locals **Priority seatings** Recommended **When to go** Anytime **Entree range** $14–$32, dinner; $6.95–$12.50, buffet **Payment** VISA, MC, AMEX **Service** ★★★★ **Friendliness** ★★★★ **Parking** BoardWalk lot; valet parking is free before 5 p.m., $6 after **Bar** Full service **Wine selection** Good selection of Mediterranean countries **Dress** Casual **Disabled access** Good

Breakfast Daily, 7:30–11 a.m.
Lunch Daily, noon–2 p.m.
Dinner Daily, 5–9:30 p.m.

Setting & atmosphere The dining room is designed like a farmhouse you might find in the Mediterranean countryside—a really big farmhouse. Light fixtures of various sizes and styles (no two are alike), Fietsaware plates and cups stacked on wooden tables, and posters of Mediterranean countries reinforce the family-style atmosphere. The open kitchen adds to the noise, which is already extensive because of the size of the room and the sound of people enjoying themselves and passing around plates.

House specialties Less daring than when it first opened (it had to be the only place in the Southeastern United States with zhoug on the menu), Spoodles' menu features pizzas and pastas and a few specialties from non-Italian Mediterranean countries.

Summary & comments It's too bad the menu has been toned down so much because the food here used to be a lot of fun. The food is still good, but it's no more adventurous than you'll find at any other Italian restaurant with Mediterranean touches.

TEMPURA KIKU   ★★★

JAPANESE | MODERATE | QUALITY ★★★★ | VALUE ★★★

READER'S SURVEY RESPONSES 90% 👍 10% 🗨

Japan, World Showcase, Epcot; (407) 939-3463

Customers Theme park guests **Priority seatings** Not accepted **When to go** Lunch **Entree range** $8.95–$12.25, lunch; $12.95–$23.75, dinner **Payment** VISA, MC, AMEX **Service** ★★★★ **Friendliness** ★★★ **Parking** Epcot lot **Bar** Full service **Wine selection** Limited **Dress** Casual **Disabled access** Yes

Lunch Daily, noon–3:45 p.m.

Dinner Daily, 4:30 p.m. until park closes

Setting & atmosphere Tempura Kiku is a small (25-person) tempura bar where most patrons sit around the outside of a square counter. The setting is intimate, almost cramped, and very communal.

House specialties Tempura-battered deep-fried foods featuring chicken, shrimp, and vegetables. The menu tells the story of tempura, which apparently came about when some Portuguese sailors were shipwrecked on a Japanese shore. The Catholic Portuguese did not eat meat on the holy days, which came four times a year and were called quattuor tempora. On these days the sailors ate fried shrimp. The Japanese adapted the word tempura to mean fried shrimp, and the rest of the world adapted it to mean all kinds of fried food.

Other recommendations Kabuki beef; sushi; sashimi.

Summary & comments Not the most appealing restaurant at Epcot, but the tempura is arguably the best in the Japan pavilion. The sushi and sashimi are not heavily marketed, but you can bet the sanitation—important in any restaurant but crucial where sushi is served—is impeccable.

TEPPANYAKI DINING ROOM ★★★½

JAPANESE | EXPENSIVE | QUALITY ★★★★ | VALUE ★★★

READER'S SURVEY RESPONSES 86% 👍 14% 👎

Japan, World Showcase, Epcot; (407) 939-3463

Customers Theme park guests **Priority seatings** Required **When to go** Anytime **Entree range** $8.95–$19.95, lunch; $14.95–$30.25, dinner **Payment** VISA, MC, AMEX **Service** ★★★★ **Friendliness** ★★★★ **Parking** Epcot lot **Bar** Full service **Wine selection** Limited **Dress** Casual **Disabled access** Yes, via elevator

Lunch Daily, noon–3:45 p.m.

Dinner Daily, 4:30 p.m. until park closes

Setting & atmosphere The decor is upscale Japanese, only roomier, with light wood-beam ceilings, grass-cloth walls, and lacquered-finish oak chairs. Overall very clean and spare.

House specialties Chicken, shrimp, beef, scallops, and Oriental vegetables stir-fried on a teppan grill by a knife-juggling chef. Teppanyaki is a fancy version of the Benihana restaurant chain.

Entertainment & amenities Watching the teppan chefs.

Summary & comments While this restaurant offers some of the best teppan dining you will find in the United States, it has missed a wonderful opportunity to introduce the diversity and beauty of authentic Japanese cuisine to the American public. Be aware that diners at the teppan tables (large tables with a grill in the middle) are seated with other parties. Finally, if you would like to try more traditional Japanese fare, consider Tempura Kiku, a small restaurant in the same building.

TONY'S TOWN SQUARE RESTAURANT ★★½

ITALIAN | MODERATE | QUALITY ★★★½ | VALUE ★★

READER'S SURVEY RESPONSES 78% 👍 22% 🗨

Main Street, U.S.A., Magic Kingdom; (407) 939-3463

Customers Theme park guests **Priority seatings** Recommended **When to go** Late lunch or early dinner **Entree range** $9.95–$14.25, lunch; $17.25–$21.95, dinner **Payment** VISA, MC, AMEX **Service** ★★★ **Friendliness** ★★★★ **Parking** Magic Kingdom lot **Bar** None **Wine selection** None **Dress** Casual **Disabled access** Yes

Breakfast Daily, 8:30–10:45 a.m.

Lunch Daily, noon–2:45 p.m.

Dinner Daily, 4 p.m. until park closes

Setting & atmosphere Decorated like a New York Italian eatery, with tile floors, tablecloths, dark woods, and lots of plants. The walls are filled with memorabilia from *Lady and the Tramp*. It is a bright and open place, but it somehow always has a trampled and unkempt appearance.

House specialties Designer pizza; penne with Italian sausage; turkey with wild mushrooms and fettuccini.

Other recommendations Fettuccini with prosciutto (lunch only).

Summary & comments It's perhaps the most pleasant place to dine in the Magic Kingdom and now offers a more interesting menu. The pace can be hectic, but the atmosphere is light and airy and the pictures and other knickknacks from *Lady and the Tramp* are a lot of fun. Go ahead, share a plate of overpriced spaghetti with someone you love.

VICTORIA & ALBERT'S ★★★★½

GOURMET | EXPENSIVE | QUALITY ★★★★★ | VALUE ★★

READER'S SURVEY RESPONSES 74% 👍 26% 🗨

Disney's Grand Floridian Beach Resort; (407) 939-7707

Customers Hotel guests, locals **Priority seatings** Mandatory; must confirm by noon the day of your seating; call at least 120 days in advance to ensure a table **When to go** Anytime **Entree range** Fixed price: $85 per person or up to $120 with wine pairings **Payment** VISA, MC, AMEX, D **Service** ★★★★ **Friendliness** ★★★ **Parking** Valet, $5; self-parking is deceptively far away **Wine selection** Excellent **Dress** Jacket required for men; proper evening attire for women **Disabled access** Yes

Dinner Two seatings nightly at 5:45–6:30 p.m. and 9–9:45 p.m.

Setting & atmosphere Victoria & Albert's is a small, intimate room under a domed ceiling. It is elegantly appointed, with large floral displays, fine china, crystal, and silver.

House specialties The menu changes daily but always features selections of fresh game, poultry, fish, and beef.

Entertainment & amenities A harpist or violinist entertains from the foyer. Guests receive souvenir menus personalized with gold lettering.

Summary & comments Except for one bit of kitsch—instead of waiters, each table is attended by a maid and butler named Victoria and Albert—this is Disney's most elegant restaurant. It also features some of the finest culinary talent in the southeastern United States. Victoria & Albert's dining room is entirely nonsmoking. For a special treat, book the chef's table in the kitchen, where the executive chef will prepare a special meal for you and your guests. There is only one seating each evening, and dinner may take as long as four hours. The cost is at least $115 per person ($160 with wine), but for those who truly love fine food, it's a bargain.

Honors & awards AAA 4-Diamond Award.

WHISPERING CANYON CAFE   ★★½

AMERICAN | MODERATE | QUALITY ★★★½ | VALUE ★★★★

READER'S SURVEY RESPONSES 73% 👍 27% 👎

Disney's Wilderness Lodge and Villas; (407) 939-3463

Customers Hotel guests **Priority seatings** Accepted **When to go** Anytime **Entree range Breakfast** $9.29 adult, $4.99 children; **Lunch** $13.99 adult, $6.95 children; dinner: $21 adult, $8.95 children **Payment** VISA, MC, AMEX, D **Service** ★★ **Friendliness** ★★★ **Parking** Hotel lot **Bar** Full service **Wine selection** Limited **Dress** Casual **Disabled access** Yes

Breakfast Daily, 7:30–11 a.m.
Lunch Daily, noon–3 p.m.
Dinner Daily, 5–10 p.m.

Setting & atmosphere Located just off the hotel's atrium lobby, the restaurant looks out on the lobby on one side and a mountain prairie, created by the Disney landscapers, on the other. Tables have a barrel-top lazy. Susan where the food is placed.

House specialties Barbecue-and-apple-glazed rotisserie chicken; maple-garlic pork spareribs.

Other recommendations Smoked barbecue beef brisket; smoked barbecue veal ribs; porterhouse steak; New York strip steak.

Summary & comments The real value here is in the "family style" service, with all-you-can eat servings brought to you on platters and in crocks to pass around (just your family—you don't have to share with others). There is also an a la carte option for those who don't care to share even with family members, but expect to pay more for your stinginess.

WOLFGANG PUCK CAFE   ★★★

CREATIVE CALIFORNIAN | EXPENSIVE | QUALITY ★★★½ | VALUE ★★★

READER'S SURVEY RESPONSES 81% 👍 19% 👎

Downtown Disney West Side; (407) 938-9653

Customers Tourists and locals **Priority seatings** Upstairs only **When to go** Early evening **Entree range** Cafe, $20–$30; upstairs, $60–$90 **Payment** VISA, MC, AMEX

Service ★★★★ Friendliness ★★★★ Parking Downtown Disney lot; valet evenings, $6 Bar Full service Wine selection Very good Dress Casual in the cafe; collared shirt for men and no jeans upstairs Disabled access Good

Open Cafe: Daily, 11:30 a.m.–11 p.m. Upstairs: 6 p.m.–until last reservation; bar open until midnight

Setting & atmosphere These are actually two restaurants in one—four if you count the attached Wolfgang Puck Express (and there's no reason to count it for anything) and the sushi bar that does a freeform flow into the restaurant's lounge area. The downstairs is the actual cafe, with several open kitchen areas, colorful tile (one designer has called it a tile factory outlet store), and plenty of pictures of Wolfgang Puck hanging around the place. The upstairs is a more formal dining room, but in name only. Both spaces are inordinately loud and conversation is difficult. Throughout the restaurant are TV monitors trained on various culinary stations. One supposes this is so diners can watch their food being prepared (they certainly can't talk to one another), but unless you have excellent vision—and we're talking something along the lines of Superman— you probably won't be able to see anything. The images are like the surveillance cameras in convenience stores.

House specialties Wolfgang Puck became famous with his Spago restaurant in California and is the father of the gourmet pizza. His "signature pizza" features smoked salmon, red onion, dill cream, and chives (none of his pizzas has traditional red sauce). You'll also find smoked sturgeon, roasted lamb chops, Maine lobster with linguine, and blackened catfish. The sushi is quite good. The upstairs dining room has fresh pastas, fish soup, free-range chicken, and Sonoma lamb chops. The Wiener schnitzel, however, is one of the best items on the menu.

Summary & comments Puck, one of the original celebrity chefs, is a master at self-promotion. His cafe, which is really just a chain restaurant, is very much a shrine to his image. But many of the items on the menu are very good, and W.P.C. is one of the better dining options in Downtown Disney. To get out without sticker shock at the end of the meal, go with one of the pizzas and Puck's popular Chinois salad. If you're looking for a quiet, relaxing meal, however, this isn't the place for you. At press time, plans were afoot to convert the upstairs Dining Room to a Spago, Puck's famous California concept. But don't look for the food to change all that much—the Dining Room was already Spago-like.

YACHT CLUB GALLEY ★★★

AMERICAN | MODERATE | QUALITY ★★★½ | VALUE ★★★

READER'S SURVEY RESPONSES 89% 👍 11% 👎

Disney's Yacht Club Resort; (407) 939-3463

Customers Hotel guests **Priority seatings** Not necessary **When to go** Breakfast or lunch **Entree range** $14.95–$26.95 **Payment** VISA, MC, AMEX **Service** ★★★★ **Friendliness** ★★★★ **Parking** Hotel lot **Bar** Full service **Wine selection** Good **Dress** Casual **Disabled access** Yes

Breakfast Daily, 7–11 a.m.

Lunch Daily, 11:30 a.m.–2:30 p.m.
Dinner Daily, 5–10 p.m.

Setting & atmosphere This large and somewhat noisy dining room features a bright nautical theme with colorful pastels, blue-striped wallpaper, and tablecloths. A moving seascape mural is the focal point here.

House specialties Daily fresh-fish specials; barbecued pork ribs; seafood stir-fry with shrimp, scallops, and fish. Breakfast features a buffet or an à la carte menu, with such selections as eggs with grilled sirloin steak.

Other recommendations Roast prime rib with burgundy horseradish sauce; breaded clam strips.

Entertainment & amenities Strolling band in the evening.

Summary & comments Stop here for breakfast or lunch; it's a short walk from Epcot and a good escape if you need to get out of the park and relax.

YACHTSMAN STEAKHOUSE   ★★★

STEAK | EXPENSIVE | QUALITY ★★★½ | VALUE ★★

READER'S SURVEY RESPONSES 79% 👍 21% 👎

Disney's Yacht Club Resort; (407) 939-3463

Customers Hotel guests, locals **Priority seatings** Required **When to go** Anytime **Entree range** $17–$59 **Payment** VISA, MC, AMEX **Service** ★★★ **Friendliness** ★★★★ **Parking** Hotel lot **Bar** Full service **Wine selection** Very good **Dress** Casual **Disabled access** Yes

Dinner Daily, 5:30–10 p.m.

Setting & atmosphere This restaurant is decorated in a country style—lots of knotty pine and chintz tablecloths. A refrigerated display case with big slabs of beef in various stages of the aging process allows you to get acquainted with your steak before you're seated. You can watch it being cooked at the show kitchen, if you wish, and the staff encourages you to ask questions about your meal's preparation. (How about "Is it ready yet?")

House specialties All steaks are cut and trimmed on the premises daily. The Yacht Club porterhouse, Kansas City strip, and prime rib of beef au jus are just some of the cuts. The mixed grill includes filet, lamb chops, and chicken breast served with three sauces. All entrees include baked potato and bread-board assortment. Béarnaise and bordelaise sauces are available to complement your meat selection.

Other recommendations Australian lobster stuffed with crabmeat; full rack of lamb; grilled pork chops.

Entertainment & amenities Strolling musicians (the same ones who stroll through the Yacht Club Galley).

Summary & comments For die-hard meat lovers who don't mind paying a lot for a good steak. The chintz tablecloths keep it from being a male domain, but women should be offended by the "yachtress" cut of meat. Besides a good wine list, the Yachtsman also has an impressive beer list.

Part Ten

The Magic Kingdom

Arriving

If you drive, the Magic Kingdom/TTC parking lot opens about two hours before the park's official opening. After paying a fee, you are directed to a parking space, then transported by tram to the TTC, where you catch either a monorail or ferry to the park's entrance.

If you're staying at the Contemporary, Polynesian, or Grand Floridian Resorts, you can commute directly to the Magic Kingdom by monorail (guests at the Contemporary can walk there more quickly). If you stay at Wilderness Lodge and Villas or Fort Wilderness Campground, you will take a boat. Guests at other Disney resorts can reach the park by bus. All Disney lodging guests, whether they arrive by bus, monorail, or boat, are deposited at the park's entrance, bypassing the TTC.

Getting Oriented

At the Magic Kingdom, stroller and wheelchair rentals are to the right of the train station and lockers are on the station's ground floor. On your left as you enter Main Street is City Hall, the center for information, lost and found, guided tours, and entertainment schedules.

If you don't already have a handout guidemap of the park, get one at City Hall. The guidemap lists all attractions, shops, and eating places; provides helpful information about first aid, baby care, and assistance for the disabled; and gives tips for good photos. It lists times for the day's special events, live entertainment, Disney character parades, and concerts, and it also tells when and where to find Disney characters.

Main Street ends at a central hub from which branch the entrances to five other sections of the Magic Kingdom: Adventureland, Frontierland, Liberty Square, Fantasyland, and Tomorrowland. Mickey's Toontown Fair is wedged like a dimple between the cheeks of Fantasyland and Tomorrowland and doesn't connect to the central hub.

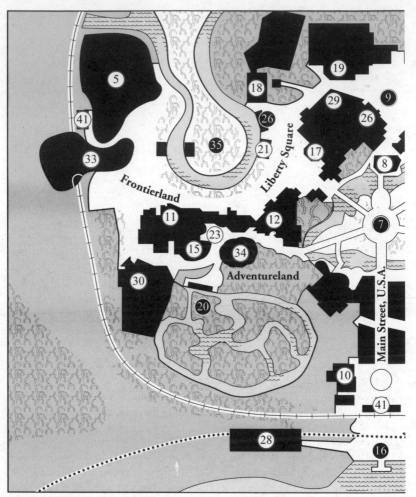

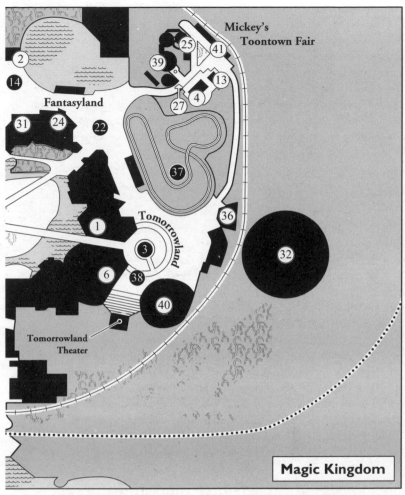

Magic Kingdom

Cinderella Castle is the entrance to Fantasyland and is the Magic Kingdom's visual center. If you start in Adventureland and go clockwise around the Magic Kingdom, the castle spires will always be roughly on your right; if you start in Tomorrowland and go counterclockwise through the park, the spires will always be roughly on your left. Cinderella Castle is an excellent meeting place if your group decides to split up during the day or is separated accidentally. Because the castle is large, designate a very specific meeting spot, like the entrance to Cinderella's Royal Table restaurant at the rear of the castle.

Starting the Tour

Everyone soon finds their favorite and not-so-favorite attractions in the Magic Kingdom. Be open-minded and adventuresome. Our personal experience and research indicate that each visitor differs on which attraction is most enjoyable. Don't dismiss a ride or show until *after* you have tried it.

Take advantage of what Disney does best: the fantasy adventures of Splash Mountain and The Haunted Mansion and the audio-animatronic (talking robots) attractions, including *The Hall of Presidents* and Pirates of the Caribbean. Don't burn daylight browsing the shops unless you plan to spend a minimum of two and a half days at the Magic Kingdom, and even then wait until midday or later. Minimize the time you spend on midway-type rides; you probably have something similar near your hometown. (Don't, however, mistake Space Mountain and Big Thunder Mountain Railroad as amusement park rides. They may be roller coasters, but they're pure Disney genius.) Eat a good breakfast early, and avoid lines at eateries by snacking during the day on food from vendors. Fare at most Magic Kingdom eateries is on a par with Hardee's or McDonald's (nothing special).

FASTPASS at the Magic Kingdom

The Magic Kingdom offers eight FASTPASS attractions, the most in any Disney park. Strategies for using FASTPASS at the Magic Kingdom have been integrated into our touring plans.

MAGIC KINGDOM FASTPASS ATTRACTIONS

Tomorrowland	Space Mountain
	Buzz Lightyear's Space Ranger Spin
Adventureland	Jungle Cruise
Frontierland	Splash Mountain
	Big Thunder Mountain
Liberty Square	The Haunted Mansion

NOT TO BE MISSED AT THE MAGIC KINGDOM

Fantasyland	The Many Adventures of Winnie the Pooh
	Peter Pan's Flight
Adventureland	Pirates of the Caribbean
Frontierland	Big Thunder Mountain Railroad
	Splash Mountain
Liberty Square	The Haunted Mansion
Tomorrowland	Space Mountain
	The Timekeeper (open seasonally)
Special Events	Evening Parade

Main Street, U.S.A.

You begin and end your Magic Kingdom visit on Main Street, which opens a half hour before, and closes a half hour to an hour after, the rest of the park. The Walt Disney World Railroad stops at the Main Street Station; board here for a grand tour of the park or a ride to Frontierland or Mickey's Toontown Fair.

Main Street is a sanitized Disney re-creation of a turn-of-the-century, small-town American street. Its buildings are real, not elaborate props. Attention to detail is exceptional: all interiors, furnishings, and fixtures are true to period. Along the street are shops and eating places, City Hall, and a fire station. Horse-drawn trolleys, double-decker buses, fire engines, and horseless carriages transport visitors along Main Street to the central hub.

MAIN STREET SERVICES

Most park services are centered on Main Street, including:

Wheelchair & Stroller Rental	Right of the main entrance before passing under the railroad station
Banking Services	Automated tellers (ATMs) are underneath the Main Street railroad station
Storage Lockers	Ground floor of the railroad station at the end of Main Street; all lockers are cleaned out each night
Lost & Found	City Hall at the railroad station end of Main Street
Live Entertainment & Parade Info	City Hall at the railroad station end of Main Street
Lost Persons	City Hall
Walt Disney World & Local Attraction Information	City Hall
First Aid	Next to The Crystal Palace, left around the central hub (toward Adventureland)
Baby Center/ Baby-Care Needs	Next to The Crystal Palace, left around the central hub (toward Adventureland)

Walt Disney World Railroad

What It Is Scenic railroad ride around perimeter of the Magic Kingdom, and transportation to Frontierland and Mickey's Toontown Fair

Scope & Scale Minor attraction

When to Go Anytime

Special Comments Main Street is usually the least congested station.

Author's Rating Plenty to see; ★★½

Appeal by Age Group

Pre-school ★★★★	Grade School ★★★	Teens ★★
Young Adults ★★½	Over 30 ★★★	Senior Citizens ★★★

Duration of Ride About 19 minutes for a complete circuit

Average Wait in Line per 100 People ahead of You 8 minutes

Assumes 2 or more trains operating

Loading Speed Fast

Description and Comments A transportation ride blending an unusual variety of sights and experiences with an energy-saving way to get around the park. The train provides a glimpse of all lands except Adventureland.

A Princeton, New Jersey, dad disputes our comment that there's "plenty to see" on the Walt Disney World Railroad:

> I'm not sure why you say there is "plenty to see." We got a great view of lots of trees, a brief glimpse of the queue for Splash Mountain and a scene inside it, an even briefer glimpse of Fantasyland, and a view of Toontown Fair, and that's about it. Yeah, it's kind of fun to ride an old steam engine, and our two-year-old sure likes trains, but I found the sights kind of boring.

Touring Tips Save the train ride until after you have seen the featured attractions, or use it when you need transportation. On busy days, lines form at the Frontierland Station, but rarely at the Main Street and Mickey's Toontown Fair Stations. Strollers aren't allowed on the train. Wheelchair access is available only at the Frontierland and Mickey's Toontown Fair stations.

You cannot take your rental stroller on the train, but you can obtain a replacement stroller at your destination. Just take your personal belongings, your stroller name card, and your rental receipt with you on the train.

Transportation Rides

Description and Comments Trolleys, buses, etc., which add color to Main Street.

Touring Tips Will save you a walk to the central hub. Not worth a wait.

Adventureland

Adventureland is the first land to the left of Main Street. It combines an African safari theme with an old New Orleans/Caribbean atmosphere.

Swiss Family Treehouse

What It Is Outdoor walk-through treehouse
Scope & Scale Minor attraction
When to Go Before 11:30 a.m. and after 5 p.m.
Special Comments Requires climbing a lot of stairs
Author's Rating A visual delight; ★★★
Appeal by Age Group
Pre-school ★★★   Grade School ★★★½   Teens ★★★
Young Adults ★★★   Over 30 ★★★   Senior Citizens ★★★
Duration of Tour 10–15 minutes
Average Wait in Line per 100 People ahead of You 7 minutes
Loading Speed Doesn't apply

Description and Comments An immense replica of the shipwrecked family's treehouse home will turn your children into arboreal architects. It's the king of all treehouses, with its multiple stories, clever jerry-rigging, and mechanical wizardry.

Touring Tips A self-guided walk-through tour involves a lot of stairs up and down, but no ropes, ladders, or anything fancy. People who stop for extra-long looks or to rest sometimes create bottlenecks that slow crowd flow. Visit in late afternoon or early evening if you're on a one-day tour, or in the morning of your second day.

Jungle Cruise (FASTPASS)

What It Is Outdoor safari-themed boat ride adventure
Scope & Scale Major attraction
When to Go Before 10 a.m. or two hours before closing
Author's Rating A long-enduring Disney masterpiece; ★★★
Appeal by Age Group
Pre-school ★★★½   Grade School ★★★½   Teens ★★½
Young Adults ★★★   Over 30 ★★★   Senior Citizens ★★★
Duration of Ride 8–9 minutes
Average Wait in Line per 100 People ahead of You 3½ minutes
Assumes 10 boats operating
Loading Speed Moderate

Description and Comments An outdoor cruise through jungle waterways. Passengers encounter animatronic elephants, lions, hostile natives, and a menacing hippo. Boatman's spiel adds to the fun. Once one of the most grand and elaborate attractions at the Magic Kingdom, the Jungle Cruise's technology now seems dated and worn. Since the advent of the Animal Kingdom, the attraction's appeal has diminished, but in its defense, you can always depend on the Jungle Cruise's robotic critters being present as you motor past.

An Albany, New York, woman agrees that the Jungle Cruise is past its prime:

Jungle Cruise needs updating! My husband gave it a five on the "cheese factor" scale.

Touring Tips   Among the park's oldest attractions and one that occupies a good third of Adventureland. A convoluted queuing area makes it very difficult to estimate the length of the wait for the Jungle Cruise. A mother from the Bronx, New York, complains:

> *The line for this ride is extremely deceiving. We got in line toward early evening; it was long but we really wanted to take this ride. Every time the winding line brought us near the loading dock and we thought we were going to get on, we'd discover a whole new section of winding lanes to go through. It was extremely frustrating. We must have waited 20–30 minutes before we finally gave up and got out.*

Fortunately, the Jungle Cruise is a FASTPASS attraction. Pick up your FASTPASS *before* enjoying other Adventureland and Frontierland attractions. By the time you've toured the Swiss Family Treehouse and experienced Pirates of the Caribbean and perhaps an attraction or two in adjacent Frontierland, it will be time to return and use your FASTPASS for the Jungle Cruise.

Magic Carpets of Aladdin

What It Is   Elaborate midway ride
Scope & Scale   Minor attraction
When to Go   Before 10 a.m. and in the hour before park closing
Author's Rating   An eye-appealing children's ride; ★★★
Appeal by Age Group

Pre-school ★★★★½	Grade School ★★★★	Teens ★½
Young Adults ★½	Over 30 ★½	Senior Citizens ★½

Duration of Ride   1½ minutes
Average Wait in Line per 100 People ahead of You   16 minutes
Loading Speed   Slow

Description and Comments   The first new ride in Adventureland in decades, Magic Carpets of Aladdin is a midway ride like Dumbo, except with magic carpets instead of elephants. Copying the water innovation of the One Fish, Two Fish attraction at Universal's Islands of Adventure, Disney's Aladdin ride has a spitting camel positioned to spray jets of water on carpet riders. Riders can maneuver their carpets up and down and side to side to avoid getting wet.

Touring Tips   Like Dumbo, this ride has great eye appeal but extremely limited capacity (i.e., it's slow-loading). If your younger children see it, they'll probably want to ride. Try to get them on during the first 30 minutes the park is open or try just before park closing.

Pirates of the Caribbean

What It Is   Indoor pirate-themed adventure boat ride
Scope & Scale   Headliner
When to Go   Before noon or after 5 p.m.
Special Comments   Frightens some young children
Author's Rating   Disney Audio-Animatronics at its best; not to be missed; ★★★★★

Appeal by Age Group
Pre-school ★★★   Grade School ★★★★★   Teens ★★★★
Young Adults ★★★★   Over 30 ★★★★½   Senior Citizens ★★★★½
Duration of Ride About 7½ minutes
Average Wait in Line per 100 People ahead of You 1½ minutes
Assumes Both waiting lines operating
Loading Speed Fast

Description and Comments   An indoor cruise through a series of sets depicting a pirate raid on an island settlement, from bombardment of the fortress to debauchery after the victory. Regarding debauchery, Pirates of the Caribbean is one of several Disney attractions that has been administered a strong dose of political correctness. See if you can spot the changes.

Touring Tips   Undoubtedly one of the park's most elaborate and imaginative attractions. Engineered to move large crowds in a hurry, Pirates is a good attraction to see during later afternoon. It has two covered waiting lines.

Enchanted Tiki Birds

What It Is Audio-animatronic Pacific island musical theater show
Scope & Scale Minor attraction
When to Go Before 11 a.m. and after 3:30 p.m.
Special Comments Frightens some preschoolers
Author's Rating Very, very unusual; ★★★½
Appeal by Age Group
Pre-school ★★★★   Grade School ★★★½   Teens ★★★
Young Adults ★★★   Over 30 ★★★   Senior Citizens ★★★
Duration of Presentation 15½ minutes
Preshow Entertainment Talking birds
Probable Waiting Time 15 minutes

Description and Comments   Upgraded in 1998, this theater presentation now features two of Disney's most beloved bird characters: Iago from *Aladdin* and Zazu from *The Lion King*. A new song, "Friend Like Me," and a revamped plotline add some much needed zip, but the production remains (pardon the pun) a featherweight in the Disney galaxy of attractions. Even so, the *Tiki Birds* are a great favorite of the eight-and-under set. Although readers like the *Enchanted Tiki Birds* show, they caution that the new version is more frightening to younger children than was the old. The remarks of this Provo, Utah, mom are typical:

> I want to address the new Tiki Bird show. It was a refreshing change from the other show and is definitely more interesting. Although there is a new element with the Tiki gods that may frighten small children because of loud noises.

Concerning the scary parts, a mother of three from Coleman, Michigan, was somewhat more outspoken:

> The Tiki Bird show was very scary, with a thunder and lightning storm and a loud volcano goddess with glowing red eyes. Can't Disney do anything without scaring young children? It's a bird show!

A New Jersey dad concurred, commenting:

Enchanted Tiki Birds *are now REALLY intense—far more intense than I remember fondly from previous visits. Tiki Gods storming and smoking, the whole room plunged into utter darkness, and thunder and lightning that quite literally shakes the benches you're sitting on—our child (two and a half) was terrified. Definitely not recommended for very young children; it seems the attraction is aimed at older children now.*

Touring Tips One of the more bizarre Magic Kingdom entertainments. Usually not too crowded. We go in the late afternoon when we especially appreciate sitting briefly in an air-conditioned theater.

Frontierland

Frontierland adjoins Adventureland as you move clockwise around the Magic Kingdom. The focus is on the Old West, with stockade-type structures and pioneer trappings.

Splash Mountain (FASTPASS)

What It Is Indoor/outdoor water-flume adventure ride

Scope & Scale Super headliner

When to Go As soon as the park opens, during afternoon or evening parades, just before closing, or use FASTPASS

Special Comments Must be 40" tall to ride; children younger than 7 must ride with an adult. Switching off option provided (pages 254–257).

Author's Rating A wet winner; not to be missed; ★★★★★

Appeal by Age Group

Pre-school †   Grade School ★★★★★   Teens ★★★★★
Young Adults ★★★★★   Over 30 ★★★★★   Senior Citizens ★★★★★

† Many preschoolers are too short to meet the height requirement, and others are visually intimidated when they see the ride from the waiting line. Among preschoolers who actually ride, most give the attraction high marks (3–5 stars).

Duration of Ride About 10 minutes

Average Wait in Line per 100 People ahead of You 3½ minutes

Assumes Operating at full capacity

Loading Speed Moderate

Description and Comments Amusement park flume ride, Disney-style. Bigger than life and more imaginative than anyone thought possible, Splash Mountain combines steep chutes with excellent special effects. The ride covers over half a mile, splashing through swamps, caves, and backwood bayous before climaxing in a five-story plunge and Brer Rabbit's triumphant return home. More than 100 audio-animatronic characters, including Brer Rabbit, Brer Bear, and Brer Fox, regale riders with songs including "Zip-a-Dee-Doo-Dah."

Touring Tips This happy, exciting, adventuresome ride vies with Space Mountain in Tomorrowland as the park's most popular attraction. Crowds build fast in the morn-

ing, and waits of more than two hours can be expected once the park fills. Get in line first thing, certainly no later than 45 minutes after the park opens. Long lines will persist all day.

If you only have one day to see the Magic Kingdom, ride Space Mountain first, then Buzz Lightyear (also in Tomorrowland), then hot-foot it over to Splash Mountain. If the line isn't too long, go ahead and ride. Otherwise, obtain a FASTPASS and return later to enjoy Splash Mountain. FASTPASS strategies have been incorporated into the Magic Kingdom One-Day Touring Plans (see pages 484–493). If you have two mornings to devote to the Magic Kingdom, experience Space Mountain and *Alien Encounter* one morning and Splash Mountain and Big Thunder Mountain the next. Spreading your visit over two mornings will eliminate much crisscrossing of the park as well as the backtracking that is inevitable when you use FASTPASS.

As occurs with Space Mountain, when the park opens, hundreds are poised to dash to Splash Mountain. The best strategy is to go to the end of Main Street and turn left to The Crystal Palace restaurant. In front of the restaurant is a bridge that provides a shortcut to Adventureland. Stake out a position at the barrier rope. When the park opens and the rope drops, move as fast as you comfortably can and cross the bridge to Adventureland.

Here's another shortcut: Just past the first group of buildings on your right, roughly across from the Swiss Family Treehouse, is a small passageway containing rest rooms and phones. Easy to overlook, it connects Adventureland to Frontierland. Go through the passageway into Frontierland and take a hard left. As you emerge along the waterfront, Splash Mountain is straight ahead. If you miss the passageway, don't fool around looking for it. Continue straight through Adventureland to Splash Mountain.

Less exhausting in the morning is to reach Splash Mountain via the Walt Disney World Railroad. Board at Main Street Station and wait for the park to open. The train will pull out of the station at the same time the rope drops at the central hub end of Main Street. Ride to Frontierland Station (the first stop) and disembark. As you come down the stairs at the station, the entrance to Splash Mountain will be on your right. Because of the time required to unload at the station, train passengers will arrive at Splash Mountain about the same time as the lead element from the central hub.

A Suffolk, Virginia, mom contends that there are more important considerations than beating the crowds:

> The only recommendation I do have for the Magic Kingdom plan is to definitely wait to do Splash Mountain at the end of the day. We were seated in the front of the ride and needless to say we were soaked to the bone. If we had ridden the ride [first thing in the morning] according to your plan, I

personally would have been miserable for the rest of the day. Parents, beware! It says you will get wet, not drowned.

At Splash Mountain, if you ride in the front seat, you almost certainly will get wet. Riders elsewhere get splashed, but usually not doused. Since you don't know which seat you'll be assigned, go prepared. On a cool day, carry a plastic garbage bag. Tear holes in the bottom and sides to make a water-resistant (not waterproof) sack dress. Be sure to tuck the bag under your bottom. Leave your camera with a nonriding member of your group or wrap it in plastic.

The scariest part of this adventure ride is the steep chute you see when standing in line, but the drop looks worse than it is. Despite reassurances, however, many children wig out after watching it. A mom from Grand Rapids, Michigan, recalls her kids' rather unique reaction:

> We discovered after the fact that our children thought they would go underwater after the five-story drop and tried to hold their breath throughout the ride in preparation. They were really too preoccupied to enjoy the clever Brer Rabbit story.

Another reader thought he was in the clear after his kids took *Alien Encounter* in stride, writing:

> I'm sure you're going to think our sense of humor is really warped and a sign of the imminent collapse of our civilization, but my ten-year-old son and I found Alien Encounter more funny than scary, and very well done overall. Just to show, though, that it's often hard to predict what will push somebody's buttons the wrong way, at Splash Mountain the drop in the dark and the big final drop terrified both my kids (ages 10 and 13!). And they handled flume rides at other parks without a problem. It will probably be years before they get on a flume ride anywhere again.

Big Thunder Mountain Railroad (FASTPASS)

What It Is Tame, western-mining-themed roller coaster
Scope & Scale Headliner
When to Go Before 10 a.m., in the hour before closing, or use FASTPASS
Special Comments Must be 40" tall to ride; children younger than age 7 must ride with an adult. Switching off option provided (pages 254–257).
Author's Rating Great effects; relatively tame ride; not to be missed; ★★★★
Appeal by Age Group

Pre-school ★★★	Grade School ★★★★	Teens ★★★★
Young Adults ★★★★	Over 30 ★★★★	Senior Citizens ★★★

Duration of Ride Almost 3½ minutes
Average Wait in Line per 100 People ahead of You 2½ minutes
Assumes 5 trains operating
Loading Speed Moderate to fast

Description and Comments Roller coaster through and around a Disney "mountain." The idea is that you're on a runaway mine train during the Gold Rush. This roller coaster is about 5 on a "scary scale" of 10. First-rate examples of Disney

creativity are showcased: realistic mining town, falling rocks, and an earthquake, all humorously animated.

Touring Tips   A superb Disney experience, but not too wild a roller coaster. Emphasis is much more on the sights than on the thrill of the ride.

Nearby Splash Mountain affects the traffic flow to Big Thunder Mountain Railroad. Adventuresome guests ride Splash Mountain first, then go next door to ride Big Thunder. This means large crowds in Frontierland all day and long waits for Big Thunder Mountain. The best way to experience the Magic Kingdom's "mountains" is to ride Space Mountain when the park opens, Splash Mountain immediately afterward, then Big Thunder Mountain. If the wait exceeds 30 minutes when you arrive, use FASTPASS.

Guests experience Disney attractions differently. Consider this letter from a lady in Brookline, Massachusetts:

Being in the senior citizens' category and having limited time, my friend and I confined our activities to those attractions rated as four or five stars for seniors. Because of your recommendation and because you listed it as "not to be missed," we waited for one hour to board the Big Thunder Mountain Railroad, [which you] rated a "5" on a scary scale of "10." After living through three-and-a-half minutes of pure terror, I will rate that attraction a "15" on a scary scale of "10." We were so busy holding on and screaming and even praying for our safety that we did not see any falling rocks, a mining town, or an earthquake. In our opinion, the Big Thunder Mountain Railroad should not be recommended for seniors or preschool children.

Another woman from New England writes:

My husband, who is 41, found Big Thunder Mountain too intense for his enjoyment, and feels that anyone who does not like roller coasters would not enjoy this ride.

A woman from Vermont discovered that there's more to consider about Big Thunder than being scared:

Big Thunder Mountain Railroad was rated a five on the scary scale. I won't say it warranted a higher scare rating, but it was much higher on the lose-your-lunch meter. One more sharp turn and the kids in front of me would have needed a dip in Splash Mountain!

However, a reader from West Newton, Massachusetts, dubbed Big Thunder Mountain "a roller coaster for people who don't like roller coasters."

Country Bear Jamboree

What It Is Audio-animatronic country hoedown theater show
Scope & Scale Major attraction
When to Go Before 11:30 a.m., before a parade, or during the two hours before closing
Special Comments Shows change at Christmas and during summer
Author's Rating A Disney classic; ★★★
Appeal by Age Group

Pre-school ★★★½	Grade School ★★★	Teens ★★½
Young Adults ★★★	Over 30 ★★★	Senior Citizens ★★★

Duration of Presentation 15 minutes
Preshow Entertainment None
Probable Waiting Time This attraction is very popular but has a comparatively small capacity. Waiting time between noon and 5:30 p.m. on a busy day will average 30–50 minutes.

Description and Comments A charming cast of audio-animatronic bears sing and stomp in a western-style hoedown. Although one of the Magic Kingdom's most humorous and upbeat shows, *Country Bear Jamboree* hasn't been revised for many moons, disappointing some repeat visitors.

Readers continue to debate the merits of *Country Bear Jamboree*. The following comments are representative.

First, from a woman who thinks the *Jamboree* is way past its prime:

Country Bear Jamboree—*"A Disney classic ★★★"—You cannot be serious!! Although I must admit my ten-year-old daughter enjoyed it and got very angry about all the jokes we made about it for the remainder of the holiday!*

A Sandy Hook, Connecticut, mom agrees, commenting:

I know they consider it a classic, and kids always seem to love it, but could they PLEASE update it after half a century?

And from a New York woman:

Country Bear Jamboree *should be retired. We walked in from the hot sun with a crowd and were sitting in the cool air-conditioning, which was nice. But then some cutesy voice said "The bears want you to stand up." The crowd shouted in unison, "NO WAY!" I was shocked to laughter by that reaction and was further amused by the complete disdain the audience held for the show.*

A New Jersey family with a terrified child didn't have time to be bored:

We must disagree with your statement that Country Bear Jamboree *has no fear factor whatsoever. When he was two years old, our son was so terrified by the talking heads on the wall that we had to remove him from the show.*

But, a dad from Cape Coral defends the show:

Don't sell the Country Bear Jamboree *short. It may be boring to repeat visitors, but the look on our three-year-old son's face as he saw the show was priceless. In addition, he was astounded when he left the theater and found the mounted heads on the wall of the restaurant still singing away. It was the best thing we saw for him that day.*

Touring Tips The *Jamboree* is extremely popular and draws large crowds, even early in the day.

Tom Sawyer Island and Fort Sam Clemens

What It Is Outdoor walk-through exhibit/rustic playground
Scope & Scale Minor attraction
When to Go Midmorning through late afternoon
Special Comments Closes at dusk
Author's Rating The place for rambunctious kids; ★★★
Appeal by Age Group

Pre-school ★★★★★   Grade School ★★★★★   Teens ★★
Young Adults ★★   Over 30 ★★   Senior Citizens ★★

Description and Comments Tom Sawyer Island is a getaway within the park. It has hills to climb, a cave and windmill to explore, a tipsy barrel bridge to cross, and paths to follow. It's a delight for adults and a godsend for children who have been in tow and closely supervised all day. They love the freedom to explore and the excitement of firing air guns from the walls of Fort Sam Clemens. There is even a "secret" escape tunnel.

Touring Tips Tom Sawyer Island isn't one of the Magic Kingdom's more celebrated attractions, but it's one of the park's better conceived ones. Attention to detail is excellent, and kids revel in its frontier atmosphere. It's a must for families with children ages 5–15. If your group is made up of adults, visit on your second day or stop by on your first day after you've seen the attractions you most wanted to see.

Although children could spend a whole day on the island, plan on at least 20 minutes. Access is by raft from Frontierland; two operate simultaneously and the trip is pretty efficient, though you may have to stand in line to board both coming and going. Despite its limited menu, Aunt Polly's Dockside Inn on Tom Sawyer Island is our favorite place for lunch in the Magic Kingdom.

For a mother from Duncan, South Carolina, Tom Sawyer Island is as much a refuge as an attraction:

I do have one tip for parents. In the afternoon when the crowds were at their peak, the weather [at] its hottest, and the kids started lagging behind, our organization began to suffer. We then retreated over to Tom Sawyer Island, which proved to be a true haven. My husband and I found a secluded bench and regrouped while sipping iced tea and eating delicious soft ice cream. Meanwhile, the kids were able to run freely in the shade. Afterward, we were ready to tackle the park again, refreshed and with direction once more. (Admittedly, I got this tip from another guidebook.)

According to a dad from Hampton, Connecticut, Tom Sawyer Island was a hit with three generations of his family:

Tom Sawyer Island was Grandfather's favorite [attraction]—he fell asleep in the rocking chair on Aunt Polly's Landing while the kids explored the islands and Mom and Dad rested with cool drinks.

And a Chesterfield, Missouri, dad liked the low-tech simplicity:

Tom Sawyer Island was a huge hit with our kids (seven and five). Despite the lack of robots, lasers, or soundtracks, it was pure and simple Disney magic.

The Diamond Horseshoe Saloon Revue

What It Is Live western song and dance show

Scope & Scale Minor attraction

When to Go Check the daily entertainment schedule

Special Comments No Disney characters appear in this show

Author's Rating Fast-paced and funny; ★★★

Appeal by Age Group

Pre-school ★★	Grade School ★★★	Teens ★★
Young Adults ★★★½	Over 30 ★★★½	Senior Citizens ★★★½

Duration of Presentation About 40 minutes

Average Wait in Line per 100 People ahead of You No wait

Description and Comments *The Diamond Horseshoe Saloon Revue* is a PG-rated version of a cattle-town saloon show, with comedy, song, and sometimes dancing. Audience members are conscripted to join the cast.

Touring Tips The *Revue* was reservations-only until 1995, when it was reworked. Now, just walk in, have a seat, and wait for the show to begin. Times are listed in the entertainment column of the official guidemap. Sit in the balcony if you want to avoid being part of the show. Sandwiches, chips, cookies, and soft drinks are available at the bar. *The Diamond Horseshoe* is often overlooked by lunch crowds, especially between shows. We like to catch the *Revue* over lunch or after the afternoon parade.

Frontierland Shootin' Arcade

What It Is Electronic shooting gallery

Scope & Scale Diversion

When to Go Whenever convenient

Special Comments Costs 25¢ per play

Author's Rating Very nifty shooting gallery; ★½

Appeal by Age Group

Pre-school ★★★	Grade School ★★★	Teens ★★★
Young Adults ★★	Over 30 ★★	Senior Citizens ★★

Description and Comments Very elaborate. One of few attractions not included in Magic Kingdom admission.

Touring Tips Not a place to blow your time if you're on a tight schedule. If time allows, go on your second day. The fun is entirely in the target practice—no prizes can be won.

Walt Disney World Railroad

Description and Comments Stops in Frontierland on its circle tour of the park. See the description under Main Street for additional details.

Touring Tips Pleasant, feet-saving link to Main Street and Mickey's Toontown Fair, but the Frontierland Station is usually more congested than those stations. You cannot take your rental stroller on the train. If you don't want to make a round trip to pick up your stroller, take your personal belongings, your stroller name card, and your rental receipt with you on the train. You'll be issued a replacement stroller at your Walt Disney World Railroad destination.

Liberty Square

Liberty Square re-creates Colonial America at the time of the American Revolution. The architecture is Federal or Colonial. A real, 130-year-old live oak (dubbed the "Liberty Tree") lends dignity and grace to the setting.

The Hall of Presidents

What It Is Audio-animatronic historical theater presentation
Scope & Scale Major attraction
When to Go Anytime
Author's Rating Impressive and moving; ★★★
Appeal by Age Group

Pre-school ★	Grade School ★★½	Teens ★★★
Young Adults ★★★½	Over 30 ★★★★	Senior Citizens ★★★★

Duration of Presentation Almost 23 minutes
Preshow Entertainment None
Probable Waiting Time Lines for this attraction look awesome but are usually swallowed up as the theater exchanges audiences. Your wait will probably be the remaining time of the show that's in progress when you arrive. Even during the busiest times, waits rarely exceed 40 minutes.

Description and Comments   President Bush was added in 2001, but the content of the presentation remains largely the same. A 23-minute, strongly inspirational and patriotic program highlights milestones in American history. The performance climaxes with a roll call of presidents from Washington through the present, with a few words of encouragement from President Lincoln. A very moving show, coupled with one of Disney's best and most ambitious audio-animatronic efforts.

Our high opinion notwithstanding, we receive a lot of mail from readers who get more than entertainment from *The Hall of Presidents*. A lady in St. Louis writes:

We always go to *The Hall of Presidents when my husband gets cranky so he can take a nice nap.*

A young mother in Marion, Ohio, adds:

The Hall of Presidents *is a great place to breast-feed.*

Touring Tips   Detail and costumes are masterful. If your children fidget during the show, notice the presidents do, too. This attraction is one of the park's most popular, particularly among older visitors, and draws large crowds from 11 a.m. through about 5 p.m. Don't be put off by long lines. The theater holds more than 700 people, thus swallowing large lines at a single gulp when visitors are admitted. One show is always in progress while the lobby is being filled for the next show. At less busy times, you probably will be admitted directly to the lobby without waiting in line. When the lobby fills, those remaining in line are held outside until those in the lobby move into the theater for the next show, at which time another 700 people are admitted into the lobby.

Liberty Belle *Riverboat*

What It Is Outdoor scenic boat ride
Scope & Scale Major attraction
When to Go Anytime
Author's Rating Slow, relaxing, and scenic; ★★½
Appeal by Age Group

Pre-school ★★★½	Grade School ★★★	Teens ★★½
Young Adults ★★★	Over 30 ★★★	Senior Citizens ★★★

Duration of Ride About 16 minutes
Average Wait to Board 10–14 minutes

Description and Comments Large-capacity paddle-wheel riverboat navigates the waters around Tom Sawyer Island and Fort Sam Clemens. A beautiful craft, the riverboat provides a lofty perspective of Frontierland and Liberty Square.

Touring Tips One of two boat rides that survey the same real estate. Since the Mike Fink Keelboats are slower loading, we prefer the riverboat. If you don't want to ride, see the same sights by hiking around Tom Sawyer Island.

The Haunted Mansion (FASTPASS)

What It Is Haunted-house dark ride
Scope & Scale Major attraction
When to Go Before 11:30 a.m. or after 8 p.m.
Special Comments Frightens some very young children
Author's Rating Some of Walt Disney World's best special effects; not to be missed; ★★★★
Appeal by Age Group

Pre-school [varies]   Grade School ★★★★★ Teens ★★★★
Young Adults ★★★★   Over 30 ★★★★   Senior Citizens ★★★★

Duration of Ride 7-minute ride plus a 1½-minute preshow
Average Wait in Line per 100 People ahead of You 2½ minutes
Assumes Both "stretch rooms" operating
Loading Speed Fast

Description and Comments More fun than scary, with some of the Magic Kingdom's best special effects, the Haunted Mansion is a masterpiece of detail. "Doom Buggies" on a conveyor belt transport you throughout the house from parlor to attic, and then through a graveyard. Disney claims there's a story line, but it's so thin and unemphasized you won't notice.

Although the story line is not obvious to the casual observer, an Australian reader suggests that knowing it in advance really enhances the attraction:

> During our behind-the-scenes tour, we were told the story line for [The Haunted Mansion]. It actually made it much more enjoyable. From my recollection, a lady was about to be married when her groom discovered her with the tailor's arms around her (probably just getting a dress fitting, but we'll never know!). The groom killed the tailor in a rage, and she jumped out the window in distress. This is very cleverly shown throughout the attraction: The carriages rise to the attic to see her in her wedding dress, and while descending the broken window can be seen. At this point, the "guests" assume the role of her ghost, and the gravedigger and faithful dog shiver as the "ghost" passes. The story line really added another dimension to the attraction.

Some children become overly anxious about what they think they'll see. Almost nobody is scared by the actual sights.

The Haunted Mansion is one of veteran *Unofficial Guide* writer Eve Zibart's favorite attractions. She warns:

Don't let the childishness of the old-fashioned Haunted Mansion put you off: This is one of the best attractions in the Magic Kingdom. It's jam-packed with visual puns, special effects, hidden Mickeys, and really lovely Victorian-spooky sets. It's not scary, except in the sweetest of ways, but it will remind you of the days before ghost stories gave way to slasher flicks.

Touring Tips This attraction would be more at home in Fantasyland, but no matter. It's Disney at its best. Lines here ebb and flow more than those at most other Magic Kingdom hot spots because the mansion is near *The Hall of Presidents* and the *Liberty Belle* Riverboat. These two attractions disgorge 700 and 450 people respectively when each show or ride ends, and many of these folks head straight for the mansion. If you can't go before 11:30 a.m. or after 8 p.m., try to slip in between crowds or use FAST-PASS. However note that the Haunted Mansion is such a fast-loading attraction that FASTPASS really isn't warranted, so we advise against using FASTPASS. In the end it will cost you more time than it will save.

Mike Fink Keelboats (open seasonally)

What It Is Outdoor scenic boat ride

Scope & Scale Minor attraction

When to Go Before 11:30 a.m. or after 5 p.m.

Special Comments Open seasonally

Author's Rating ★★

Appeal by Age Group

Pre-school ★★★	Grade School ★★★	Teens ★★½
Young Adults ★★½	Over 30 ★★½	Senior Citizens ★★½

Duration of Ride 9½ minutes

Average Wait in Line per 100 People ahead of You 15 minutes

Assumes 2 boats operating

Loading Speed Slow

Description and Comments Small river keelboats circle Tom Sawyer Island and Fort Sam Clemens. The keelboat's top deck is exposed to the elements.

Touring Tips The boats cruise the same circle traveled by the *Liberty Belle* Riverboat. Because keelboats load slowly, we prefer the riverboat. If you don't want to ride, see the same sights by hiking around Tom Sawyer Island.

Fantasyland

Fantasyland is the heart of the Magic Kingdom, a truly enchanting place spread gracefully like a miniature Alpine village beneath the steepled towers of Cinderella Castle.

It's a Small World

What It Is World brotherhood–themed indoor boat ride

Scope & Scale Major attraction

When to Go Anytime

Author's Rating Exponentially "cute"; ★★★
Appeal by Age Group

Pre-school ★★★½	Grade School ★★★	Teens ★★½
Young Adults ★★½	Over 30 ★★½	Senior Citizens ★★★

Duration of Ride Approximately 11 minutes
Average Wait in Line per 100 People ahead of You 1¾ minutes
Assumes Busy conditions with 30 or more boats operating
Loading Speed Fast

Description and Comments Happy, upbeat, indoor attraction with a catchy tune that will replay in your head for weeks. Small boats carry visitors on a tour around the world, with singing and dancing dolls showcasing the dress and culture of each nation. One of Disney's oldest entertainment offerings, It's a Small World first unleashed its brain-flogging song and adorable ethnic dolls on the real world at the 1964 New York World's Fair. Though it bludgeons you with sappy redundancy, almost everyone enjoys It's a Small World (at least the first time). It stands, however, along with *Enchanted Tiki Birds*, in the "What Kind of Drugs Were They on When They Thought This Up?" category.

A woman from Holbrook, New York, apparently underwhelmed, suggests that "Small World" would be much better "if each person got three to four softballs on the way in!" (We continue to hear from "the Softball Lady." She's still pitching.)

And a mother from Castleton, Vermont, added this:

It's a Small World at Fantasyland was like a pit stop in the Twilight Zone. They were very slow in unloading the boats, and we were stuck in a line of about six boats waiting to get out while the endless chanting of that song grated on my nerves. I told my husband I was going to swim for it just to escape one more chorus.

Touring Tips Cool off here during the heat of the day. It's a Small World loads fast with two waiting lines and usually is a good bet between 11 a.m. and 5 p.m. If you wear a hearing aid, turn it off.

Peter Pan's Flight (FASTPASS)

What It Is Indoor track ride
Scope & Scale Minor attraction
When to Go Before 10 a.m. or after 6 p.m.
Author's Rating Happy, mellow, and well done; ★★★★
Appeal by Age Group

Pre-school ★★★½	Grade School ★★★½	Teens ★★★½
Young Adults ★★★½	Over 30 ★★★½	Senior Citizens ★★★½

Duration of Ride A little over 3 minutes
Average Wait in Line per 100 People ahead of You 5½ minutes
Loading Speed Moderate to slow

Description and Comments Though not considered a major attraction, Peter Pan's Flight is superbly designed and absolutely delightful, with a happy theme uniting some favorite Disney characters, beautiful effects, and charming music. An indoor attraction, Peter Pan's Flight offers a relaxing ride in a "flying pirate ship" over old

London and thence to Never-Never Land. Unlike Snow White's Adventures, there's nothing here that will jump out at you or frighten young children.

Touring Tips Because Peter Pan's Flight is very popular, count on long lines all day. Ride before 10 a.m., during a parade, just before the park closes, or use FASTPASS. If you use FASTPASS, pick up your pass as early in the day as possible. Sometimes Peter Pan exhausts its whole day's supply of FASTPASSes by 2 p.m.

Mickey's PhilharMagic

What It Is 3-D movie
Scope & Scale Major attraction
When to Go Before 11 a.m. and during parades
Author's Rating Not open at press time
Appeal by Age Group Not open at press time
Duration of Presentation About 20 minutes
Probable Waiting Time 12–20 minutes

Description and Comments With the opening of *Mickey's PhilharMagic* in the fall of 2002, there is a 3-D movie attraction at each of the four Disney theme parks. The show features an odd collection of Disney characters, mixing Mickey and Donald with Simba, Arial (the Little Mermaid), as well as Jasmine and Aladdin. *Mickey's PhilharMagic* replaces *Legend of the Lion King* in a theater large enough to accommodate a 150-foot-wide screen, huge by 3-D movie standards. Like the other Walt Disney World 3-D attractionss, the *Mickey's PhilharMagic* movie will be augmented by an arsenal of special effects built into the theater.

Touring Tips All the other 3-D movies are intense, loud, in-your-face productions. *Mickey's PhilharMagic* looks to be a little softer and cuddlier, but what good is 3-D without things coming out of the screen to startle you. Expressed differently, proceed cautiously if you have kids under 7 in your group. Because it's new, the show will be very popular, perhaps popular enough to join the FASTPASS line-up eventually. Try to go before 11 a.m. or during a parade.

Cinderella's Golden Carrousel

What It Is Merry-go-round
Scope & Scale Minor attraction
When to Go Before 11 a.m. or after 8 p.m.
Special Comments Adults enjoy the beauty and nostalgia of this ride
Author's Rating A beautiful children's ride; ★★★
Appeal by Age Group
Pre-school ★★★★   Grade School ★★½   Teens —
Young Adults —   Over 30 —   Senior Citizens —
Duration of Ride About 2 minutes
Average Wait in Line per 100 People ahead of You 5 minutes
Loading Speed Slow

Description and Comments One of the most elaborate and beautiful merry-go-rounds you'll ever see, especially when the lights are on.

A shy and retiring nine-year-old girl from Rockaway, New Jersey, thinks our rating of the carousel for grade schoolers should be higher:

I am nine years old and I want to complain. I went on Cinderella's Golden Carrousel four times and I loved it! Raise those stars right now!! Also kids who don't like things jumping out at them should not go to Honey, I Shrunk the Audience [at Epcot].

Touring Tips Unless young children in your party insist on riding, appreciate this attraction from the sidelines. While lovely to look at, the carousel loads and unloads very slowly. (And yes, there's an extra old-style "r" in Cinderella's Carrousel, but not in the modern-themed *Walt Disney's Carousel of Progress.* Go figure.)

The Many Adventures of Winnie the Pooh (FASTPASS)

What It Is Indoor track ride
Scope & Scale Minor attraction
When to Go Before 10 a.m. or in the 2 hours before closing
Author's Rating Fantasyland's newest attraction: ★★★½
Appeal by Age Group

Pre-school ★★★★½	Grade School ★★★★	Teens ★★★
Young Adults ★★★	Over 30 ★★★	Senior Citizens ★★★

Duration of Ride About 4 minutes
Average Wait in Line per 100 People ahead of You 4 minutes
Loading Speed Moderate

Description and Comments Opened in the summer of 1999, this addition to Fantasyland replaced the alternately praised and maligned Mr. Toad's Wild Ride. Pooh is sunny, upbeat, and fun—more in the image of Peter Pan's Flight or Splash Mountain. You ride a "Hunny Pot" through the pages of a huge picture book into the Hundred Acre Wood, where you encounter Pooh, Piglet, Eeyore, Owl, Rabbit, Tigger, Kanga, and Roo as they contend with a blustery day. There's even a dream sequence with Heffalumps and Woozles, a favorite of this 30-something couple from Lexington, Massachusetts who think Pooh has plenty to offer adults:

The attention to detail and special effects on this ride make it worth seeing, even if you don't have children in your party. The Pooh dream sequence was great!

Touring Tips We're happy to welcome Pooh into the Fantasyland attraction mix. Disney guests, especially younger ones, love Pooh and his friends and have lobbied for a Winnie the Pooh attraction for many years. Because it's new, you can expect larger-than-average crowds for a while. Try to ride before 10 a.m., during a parade, in the hours prior to closing, or use FASTPASS.

Because of its relatively small capacity, the daily allocation of FASTPASSes for Winnie the Pooh is often distributed by noon or 1 p.m. For this same reason, your scheduled return time to enjoy the ride might be hours away. It's not unusual to pick up a FAST-PASS for Winnie the Pooh at 12:30 p.m. with a scheduled return time of 5 p.m. or later.

Snow White's Adventures

What It Is Indoor track ride
Scope & Scale Minor attraction
When to Go Before 11 a.m. and after 6 p.m.
Special Comments Terrifying to many young children
Author's Rating Worth seeing if the wait isn't long; ★★½
Appeal by Age Group

Pre-school ★	Grade School ★★½	Teens ★★
Young Adults ★★½	Over 30 ★★½	Senior Citizens ★★½

Duration of Ride Almost 2½ minutes
Average Wait in Line per 100 People ahead of You 6¼ minutes
Loading Speed Moderate to slow

Description and Comments Mine cars travel through a spook house showing Snow White as she narrowly escapes harm at the hands of the wicked witch. Action and effects are not as good as Peter Pan's Flight or Winnie the Pooh.

Touring Tips We get more mail about this ride than any other Disney attraction. It terrifies many children age 6 and younger. Though a 1995 upgrade gave Snow White a larger role, the witch (who is relentless and ubiquitous) continues to be the focal character. Many readers tell us their children have refused to ride any attraction that operates in the dark after having experienced Snow White's Adventures.

A mother from Knoxville, Tennessee, writes:

The outside looks cute and fluffy, but inside, the evil witch just keeps coming at you. My five-year-old, who rode Space Mountain three times and took The Great Movie Ride's monster from Alien right in stride, was near panic when our car stopped unexpectedly twice during Snow White. [After Snow White] my six-year-old niece spent a lot of time asking "if a witch will jump out at you" before other rides. So I suggest that you explain a little more what this ride is about. It's tough on preschoolers who are expecting forest animals and dwarfs.

A mom from Long Island, New York, adds:

My daughter screamed the whole time and was shot for the day. Grampa kept asking, "Where in the hell is Snow White?"

Ride Snow White if lines aren't too long or on a second day at the park.

Ariel's Grotto

What It Is Interactive fountain and character greeting area
Scope & Scale Minor attraction
When to Go Before 10 a.m. and after 9 p.m.
Author's Rating One of the most elaborate of the character-greeting venues; ★★★
Appeal by Age Group

Pre-school ★★★★★	Grade School ★★★★	Teens ★★
Young Adults ★	Over 30 ★	Senior Citizens ★

Average Wait in Line per 100 People ahead of You 30 minutes

Description and Comments   On the lagoon side of Dumbo, Ariel's Grotto consists of a small children's play area with an interactive fountain and a rock grotto where Ariel, the Little Mermaid, poses for photos and signs autographs. If "interactive fountain" is new to you, it means an opportunity for your children to get ten times wetter than a trout. Can you say "hy-po-ther-mi-a"?

Touring Tips   The Grotto is small, and the wait to meet Ariel is usually long. Because kids in line are fresh from the fountain, it's very difficult for adults to remain dry. A mother from Hagerstown, Maryland, said the experience was "like being packed in a pen with wet cocker spaniels."

If your children spot the Grotto before you do, there's no turning back. Except before 10 a.m., count on a long queue and a 20–40-minute wait to see Ariel. Then there's the fountain. Allow your children to disrobe to the legal limit. (Don't bother with umbrellas or ponchos, because water squirts up from below.) When you're finished meeting Ariel, you will have to navigate an armada of variously aged males plowing upstream through the exit to admire the Little Mermaid's cleavage.

Dumbo the Flying Elephant

What It Is   Disneyfied midway ride

Scope & Scale   Minor attraction

When to Go   Before 10 a.m. and after 9 p.m.

Author's Rating   An attractive children's ride; ★★★

Appeal by Age Group

Pre-school ★★★★★	Grade School ★★★★	Teens ★½
Young Adults ★½	Over 30 ★½	Senior Citizens ★½

Duration of Ride   1½ minutes

Average Wait in Line per 100 People ahead of You   20 minutes

Loading Speed   Slow

Description and Comments   A tame, happy children's ride based on the lovable flying elephant, Dumbo. Despite being little different from rides at state fairs and amusement parks, Dumbo is the favorite Magic Kingdom attraction of many younger children.

A lot of readers take us to task for lumping Dumbo with carnival rides. A reader from Armdale, Nova Scotia, writes:

I think you have acquired a jaded attitude. I know [Dumbo] is not for everybody, but when we took our oldest child (then just four), the sign at the end of the line said there would be a 90-minute wait. He knew and he didn't care, and he and I stood in the hot afternoon sun for 90 blissful minutes waiting for his 90-second flight. Anything that a four-year-old would wait for that long and that patiently must be pretty special.

Touring Tips   If Dumbo is critical to your child's happiness, make it your first stop, preferably within 15 minutes of park opening. Also, consider this advice from an Arlington, Virginia, mom:

Grown-ups, beware! Dumbo is really a tight fit with one adult and two kids. My kids threw me out of their Dumbo and I had to sit in a Dumbo all by myself! Pretty embarrassing, and my husband got lots of pictures.

Mad Tea Party

What It Is Midway-type spinning ride
Scope & Scale Minor attraction
When to Go Before 11 a.m. and after 5 p.m.
Special Comments You can make the tea cups spin faster by turning the wheel in the center of the cup
Author's Rating Fun, but not worth the wait; ★★
Appeal by Age Group

Pre-school ★★★★	Grade School ★★★★	Teens ★★★★
Young Adults ★★★	Over 30 ★★	Senior Citizens ★★

Duration of Ride 1½ minutes
Average Wait in Line per 100 People ahead of You 7½ minutes
Loading Speed Slow

Motion Sickness WARNING!

Description and Comments Riders whirl feverishly in big tea cups. Alice in Wonderland's Mad Hatter provides the theme. A version of this ride, without Disney characters, can be found at every local carnival. Teenagers like to lure adults onto the tea cups, then turn the wheel in the middle, making the cup spin faster, until the adults are plastered against the side of the cup and on the verge of throwing up. Unless your life's ambition is to be the test subject in a human centrifuge, don't even consider getting on this ride with anyone younger than 21.

Touring Tips This ride, well done but not unique, is notoriously slow loading. Skip it on a busy schedule—if the kids will let you. Ride the morning of your second day if your schedule is more relaxed.

Mickey's Toontown Fair

Mickey's Toontown Fair is the first new "land" to be added to the Magic Kingdom since its opening and the only land that doesn't connect to the central hub. Attractions include an opportunity to meet Mickey Mouse, tour Mickey's and Minnie's houses, and ride a child-sized roller coaster.

Mickey's Toontown Fair is sandwiched between Fantasyland and Tomorrowland, like an afterthought, on about three acres formerly part of the Tomorrowland Speedway. It's the smallest of the lands and more like an attraction than a section of the park. Though you can wander in on a somewhat obscure path from Fantasyland or on a totally obscure path from Tomorrowland, Mickey's Toontown Fair generally receives guests arriving by the Walt Disney World Railroad.

Opened in 1988 and reworked in 1996 with a county fair theme, Mickey's Toontown Fair now serves as the Magic Kingdom's character-greeting headquarters. The Fair provides a place where Disney characters are available to guests on a continuing and reliable schedule. Mickey, in the role of the Fair's chief judge, meets guests for photos and autographs in the Judge's Tent. Other characters appear in the Toontown Hall of Fame. Characters are available throughout the day except during parades.

In general, Mickey's Toontown Fair doesn't handle crowds very well. If your children are into collecting character autographs and want to enjoy the various Toontown attractions without extraordinary waits, we recommend touring first thing in the morning. If you only have one day to visit the Magic Kingdom and hitting the children-oriented attractions is a priority, head first to Fantasyland and ride Dumbo, Pooh, and Peter Pan, then split for Toontown. In Toontown, ride Goofy's Barnstormer first and then tour Mickey's and Minnie's houses. Go next to the Toontown Hall of Fame for character pics and autographs. If you plan to remain in the park until closing, follow the example of this family of four from Lewiston, Maine:

A great time to visit [Toontown] is the final hour the Magic Kingdom is open. We rode the small roller coaster several times in a row without ever leaving our seats (a great thrill for a toddler who spent much of his day in lines). Also, no queues for a visit with Mickey. A great, fun, relaxing end to a busy day.

For adults without children, Toontown is visually interesting but otherwise expendable.

Mickey's Country House & Judge's Tent

What It Is Walk-through tour of Mickey's house and meeting with Mickey

Scope & Scale Minor attraction

When to Go Before 11:30 a.m. and after 4:30 p.m.

Author's Rating Well done; ★★★

Appeal by Age Group

Pre-school ★★★½	Grade School ★★★	Teens ★★½
Young Adults ★★½	Over 30 ★★½	Senior Citizens ★★½

Duration of Tour 15–30 minutes (depending on the crowd)

Average Wait in Line per 100 People ahead of You 20 minutes

Touring Speed Slow

Description and Comments Mickey's Country House is the starting point of a self-guided tour through the famous mouse's house, into his backyard, and past Pluto's doghouse. If you want to tour Mickey's house, but skip meeting Mickey, you'll find an exit just before entering his tent.

Touring Tips Discerning observers will see immediately that Mickey's Country House is a cleverly devised queuing area for delivering guests to Mickey's Judge's Tent for the Mouse Encounter. It also heightens anticipation by revealing the corporate symbol on a more personal level. Mickey's Country House is well conceived and contains a lot of Disney memorabilia. Children touch *everything* as they proceed through the house, hoping to find some artifact not welded into the set. (An especially tenacious child actually ripped a couple of books from a bookcase.)

Meeting Mickey and touring his house are best done during the first two hours the park is open, or in the evening. If meeting Mickey is your child's priority, take the railroad from Main Street to Mickey's Toontown Fair as soon as you enter the park. Some children are so obsessed with seeing Mickey that they can't enjoy anything else until they have him in the rearview mirror.

Minnie's Country House

What It Is Walk-through exhibit
Scope & Scale Minor attraction
When to Go Before 11:30 a.m. and after 4:30 p.m.
Author's Rating Great detail; ★★
Appeal by Age Group

Pre-school ★★★	Grade School ★★★	Teens ★★½
Young Adults ★★½	Over 30 ★★½	Senior Citizens ★★½

Duration of Tour About 10 minutes
Average Wait in Line per 100 People ahead of You 12 minutes
Touring Speed Slow

Description and Comments Minnie's Country House offers a self-guided tour through the rooms and backyard of Mickey's main squeeze. Similar to Mickey's Country House, only predictably more feminine, Minnie's also showcases fun Disney memorabilia. Among highlights of the short tour are the fanciful appliances in Minnie's kitchen.

Touring Tips The main difference between Mickey's and Minnie's houses is that Mickey is home to receive guests. Minnie was never home during our visits. We did, however, bump into her on the street and in the Toontown Hall of Fame. Minnie's Country House is one of the more accessible attractions in the Fair, but we nonetheless recommend touring early or late in the day.

Toontown Hall of Fame

What It Is Character-greeting venue
Scope & Scale Minor attraction
When to Go Before 10:30 a.m. and after 5:30 p.m.
Author's Rating You want characters? We got 'em! ★★
Appeal by Age Group

Pre-school ★★★★	Grade School ★★★★	Teens ★★
Young Adults ★★	Over 30 ★★	Senior Citizens ★★

Duration of Greeting About 7–10 minutes
Average Wait in Line per 100 People ahead of You 35 minutes
Touring Speed Slow

Description and Comments The Toontown Hall of Fame is at the end of a small plaza between Mickey's and Minnie's houses. Just inside to the right are entrances to three queuing areas. Signs over each suggest, somewhat ambiguously, which characters you will meet. Character assortments in each greeting area change, as do the names of the assortments themselves. Thus, on a given day you will find two or three groupings available: Famous Friends (also called Toon Pals and sometimes Minnie's Famous Pals) include Minnie, Goofy, Donald, Pluto, and sometimes Uncle Scrooge, Chip 'n' Dale, Roger Rabbit, and Daisy. The 100 Acre Wood Pals are mostly Winnie the Pooh characters but may include any character that fits the forest theme. Fairy Tale Friends are

Snow White, various dwarfs, Belle, the Beast, Sleeping Beauty, Prince Charming, etc. Other categories include Mickey's Pals, Disney Princesses, Disney Villains, and so on.

Each category of characters occupies a greeting room where 15–20 guests are admitted at a time. They're allowed to stay 7–10 minutes, long enough for a photo, autograph, and hug with each character.

Touring Tips   If your children want to visit each category, you'll have to queue up three times. Each line is long and slow-moving, and during busier hours you can lose a lot of time here. While Famous Friends (aka Toon Pals and Minnie's Famous Pals) are slightly more popular than other categories, the longest wait is for groupings that include "face characters." "Face characters" are actors who strongly resemble the character they portray and don't wear any head-covering costume. They are allowed to speak and thus engage children in conversation, prolonging the visit. All characters work in 25-minute shifts, with breaks on the hour and half hour. Because characters in each category change frequently during the day, it's possible to see quite an assortment if you keep recirculating.

If the cast member can't tell you, walk over to the exit and ask departing guests which characters are on duty. Remember that there is some switching of characters on the hour and half hour.

A mother from Winchester, Virginia, reported her solution to seeing characters without waiting in lines:

Some of the things that surprised us, both good and bad, were the crowding and lines to see the characters. We stopped to visit a few, especially when we got lucky with a shorter line, but mostly we couldn't justify stopping at many because we would have missed so many attractions. The best thing we did with regard to the characters was to have the Winnie the Pooh character dinner at The Crystal Palace. Tigger and Pooh are my kids' favorites, and the characters were VERY attentive; my just-turned three-year-old was in heaven and did not have to fight crowds.

A 30-something mother of two comments:

For parents with smaller children at the Magic Kingdom, take the train to Toontown as soon as the park opens—my six-year-old and eight-year-old rode Goofy's Barnstormer roller coaster seven times without getting off. After others wanted on, they moved on to the Toontown Hall of Fame for autographs—No lines!!

A Concord, Massachussets, mom suggests:

Mickey's Toontown was our longest line—should be done RIGHT AT OPENING!

On many days, during the first half hour the park is open, characters are available for pics and autographs outside on the street in Mickey's Toontown Fair. It's just like the old days: spontaneous contact and no lines. After about 30 minutes, they retreat inside.

The Toontown Hall of Fame offers one of the largest and most dependably available collection of characters in Walt Disney World. If your children (or you) are character hounds, visit the Hall of Fame before 10 a.m. In early morning, you can meet all three categories in less than an hour.

The Barnstormer at Goofy's Wiseacres Farm

What It Is Small roller coaster

Scope & Scale Minor attraction

When to Go Before 10:30 a.m., during parades and in the evening, and just before the park closes

Author's Rating Great for little ones, but not worth the wait for adults; ★★

Appeal by Age Group

Pre-school ★★★★	Grade School ★★★	Teens ★★½
Young Adults ★★½	Over 30 ★★½	Senior Citizens ★★

Duration of Ride About 53 seconds

Average Wait in Line per 100 People ahead of You 7 minutes

Loading Speed Slow

Description and Comments The Barnstormer is a very small roller coaster. The ride is zippy but super short. In fact, of the 53 seconds the ride is in motion, 32 seconds are consumed in leaving the loading area, being racheted up the first hill, and braking into the off-loading area. The actual time you spend careering around the track is 21 seconds.

A 42-year-old woman from Westport, Connecticut, warns adults that the Barnstormer may not be as tame as it looks:

Goofy's Barnstormer was a nightmare that should have gone in your "Eats Adults" section. It looked so innocent—nothing hidden in the dark, over quickly. . . . It took hours to stop feeling nauseated and my eight-year-old son and I were terrified.

Though the reader's point is well taken, the Barnstormer is a fairly benign introduction to the roller-coaster genre and a predictably positive way to help your children step up to more adventuresome rides. Simply put, a few circuits on the Barnstormer will increase your little one's confidence and improve his chances for enjoying Disney's more adult attractions. As always, be sensitive and encouraging but respect your child's decision whether or not to ride.

Touring Tips   The cars of this dinky coaster are too small for most adults and whiplash taller people. This plus the limited capacity equal an engineering marvel along the lines of Dumbo. Parties without children should skip the Barnstormer. If you're touring with children, you have a problem. Like Dumbo, the ride is visually appealing. All kids want to ride, subjecting the whole family to slow-moving lines. If the Barnstormer is high on your children's hit parade, try to ride before 9:30 a.m.

Donald's Boat

What It Is Interactive fountain and playground
Scope & Scale Diversion
When to Go Anytime
Special Comments Children can get wet
Author's Rating Spontaneous—yeah! ★★½
Appeal by Age Group

| Pre-school ★★★★ | Grade School ★★½ | Teens ★ |
| Young Adults ★½ | Over 30 ★½ | Senior Citizens ★½ |

Description and Comments   Water spurts randomly from tiny holes in the side of Donald's Boat. The idea is that the boat is springing leaks. Children walk around plugging holes with their hands and trying to guess where the water will squirt next.

Touring Tips   Young children love this attraction and will jump around in the spurting water until they're drenched. Our advice: "GET NAKED!" Even on cooler days, bare skin dries faster than wet clothes. Strip your munchkins to the legal limit and toss them into the fray. If you really want to plan ahead, bring extra underwear and a towel.

A Western Springs, Illinois, woman traveling with small children relates her experience at Donald's Boat:

> I took your advice and insisted we visit Donald's boat (my niece thought we could skip it). We stripped the twins down to their diapers, and I brought extra clothes for Melanie, and a towel, per your suggestion. They must have spent 45 minutes splashing, jumping, and laughing. Your author's rating was only two stars. I think you've underrated it. Mine would be five stars. The kids had so much fun, and it wore them out so they could go back to the hotel and take a good nap.

Tomorrowland

Tomorrowland is a mix of rides and experiences relating to the technological development of man and what life will be like in the future. If this sounds like Epcot's theme, it's because Tomorrowland was a breeding ground for ideas that spawned Epcot. Yet, Tomorrowland and Epcot are very different in more than scale. Epcot is mostly educational. Tomorrow-land is more for fun, depicting the future as envisioned in science fiction. Exhaustive renovation of Tomorrowland was completed in 1995. Before refurbishing, Tomorrowland's 24-year-old buildings resembled 1970s motels more than anyone's vision of the future. The new design is ageless, revealing the future as imagined by dreamers and scientists in the 1920s and 1930s. Today's Tomorrowland conjures visions of Buck Rogers, fanciful mechanical rockets, and metallic cities spread beneath towering obelisks. Disney calls the renovated Tomorrowland the "Future That Never Was," while *Newsweek* dubbed it "retro-future."

Space Mountain (FASTPASS)

Motion Sickness

WARNING!

What It Is Roller coaster in the dark

Scope & Scale Super headliner

When to Go When the park opens, between 6 and 7 p.m., during the hour before closing, or use FASTPASS

Special Comments Great fun and action; much wilder than Big Thunder Mountain Railroad. Must be 44" tall to ride; children younger than age 7 must be accompanied by an adult. Switching off option provided (pages 254–257).

Author's Rating A great roller coaster with excellent special effects; not to be missed; ★★★★

Appeal by Age Group

Pre-school †	Grade School ★★★★★	Teens ★★★★★
Young Adults ★★★★½	Over 30 ★★★★	Senior Citizens †

† Some preschoolers loved Space Mountain; others were frightened. The sample size of senior citizens who experienced this ride was too small to develop an accurate rating.

Duration of Ride Almost 3 minutes

Average Wait in Line per 100 People ahead of You 3 minutes

Assumes Two tracks dispatching at 21-second intervals

Loading Speed Moderate to fast

A teen from Colchester, Connecticut, wrote us about her bad hair day:

> WARN Space Mountain riders to take off hair scrunchies. I lost my best one on it and couldn't get it back. This ride was fast, curvy, and very hairdo messing.

Description and Comments Totally enclosed in a mammoth futuristic structure, Space Mountain has always been the Magic Kingdom's most popular attraction. The theme is a space flight through dark recesses of the galaxy. Effects are superb, and the ride is the fastest and wildest in the Magic Kingdom. As a roller coaster, Space Mountain is much zippier than Big Thunder Mountain Railroad, but much tamer than the Rock 'n' Roller Coaster at the Studios.

Roller coaster aficionados will tell you (correctly) that Space Mountain is a designer version of The Wild Mouse, a carnival and state fair midway ride that's been around for at least 40 years. There are no long drops or swooping hills like on a traditional roller

coaster, only quick, unexpected turns and small drops. Disney's contribution essentially was to add a space theme to The Wild Mouse and put it in the dark. And indeed, this does make the mouse seem wilder.

Touring Tips   People who can handle a fairly wild roller coaster ride will take Space Mountain in stride. What sets Space Mountain apart is that cars plummet through darkness, with only occasional lighting. Half the fun of Space Mountain is not knowing where the car will go next.

Space Mountain is the favorite attraction of many Magic Kingdom visitors ages 7–50. Each morning before opening, particularly during summer and holiday periods, several hundred S.M. "junkies" crowd the rope barriers at the central hub, awaiting the signal to head to the ride's entrance. To get ahead of the competition, be one of the first in the park. Proceed to the end of Main Street and wait at the entrance to Tomorrowland.

Couples touring with children too small to ride Space Mountain can both ride without waiting in line twice by taking advantage of "switching off." Here's how it works: When you enter the Space Mountain line, tell the first Disney attendant (Greeter One) that you want to switch off. The attendant will allow you, your spouse, and your small child (or children) to continue together, phoning ahead to tell Greeter Two to expect you. When you reach Greeter Two (at the turnstile near the boarding area), you'll be given specific directions. One of you will proceed to ride, while the other stays with the kids. Whoever rides will be admitted by the unloading attendant to stairs leading back up to the boarding area. Here you switch off. The second parent rides, and the first parent takes the kids down the stairs to the unloading area where everybody is reunited and exits together. Switching off is also available at Big Thunder Mountain Railroad, Splash Mountain, and *Alien Encounter*.

Seats are one behind another as opposed to side-by-side. Parents whose children meet the height and age requirements for Space Mountain can't sit next to their kids.

If you don't catch Space Mountain early in the morning, use FASTPASS or try again during the hour before closing. Often, would-be riders are held in line outside the entrance until all those previously in line have ridden, thus emptying the attraction. The appearance from the outside is that the line is enormous when, in fact, the only people waiting are those visible. This crowd-control technique, known as "stacking," discourages visitors from getting in line. Stacking is used in several Disney rides and attractions during the hour before closing to ensure that the ride will be able to close on schedule. It is also used to keep the number of people waiting inside from overwhelming the air conditioning. Despite the apparently long line, the wait is usually no longer than if you had been allowed to queue inside.

Splash Mountain siphons off some guests who would have made Space Mountain their first stop. Even so, a mob rushes to Space Mountain as soon as the park opens. If you especially like the thrill attractions and have only one day, see Space Mountain first in the morning, followed by Splash Mountain and Big Thunder Mountain.

Tomorrowland Indy Speedway

What It Is Drive-'em yourself miniature cars

Scope & Scale Major attraction

When to Go Before 11 a.m. and after 5 p.m.

Special Comments Must be 52" tall to drive

Author's Rating Boring for adults (★); great for preschoolers

Appeal by Age Group

Pre-school ★★★★	Grade School ★★★	Teens ★
Young Adults ½	Over 30 ½	Senior Citizens ½

Duration of Ride About 4¼ minutes

Average Wait in Line per 100 People ahead of You 4½ minutes

Assumes 285-car turnover every 20 minutes

Loading Speed Slow

Description and Comments An elaborate miniature raceway with gasoline-powered cars that travel up to seven miles per hour. The raceway, with sleek cars and racing noises, is quite alluring. Unfortunately, the cars poke along on a track, leaving the driver little to do. Pretty ho-hum for most adults and teenagers. The height requirement excludes small children who would enjoy the ride.

Touring Tips This ride is visually appealing but definitely one adults can skip. Preschoolers, however, love it. If your child is too short to drive, ride along and allow the child to steer the car on its guide rail while you work the foot pedal.

A mom from North Billerica, Massachusetts, writes:

I was truly amazed by the number of adults in line. Please emphasize to your readers that these cars travel on a guided path and are not a whole lot of fun. The only reason I could think of for adults to be in the line would be an insane desire to go on absolutely every ride at Disney World. The other feature about the cars is that they tend to pile up at the end, so it takes almost as long to get off as it did to get on. Parents riding with their preschoolers should keep the car going as slow as [possible] without stalling. This prolongs the preschooler's joy and decreases the time you will have to wait at the end.

The line for the Tomorrowland Indy Speedway snakes across a pedestrian bridge to the loading areas. For a shorter wait, turn right off the bridge to the first loading area (rather than continuing to the second).

Astro Orbiter

Motion Sickness

WARNING!

What It Is Buck Rogers–style rockets revolving around a central axis

Scope & Scale Minor attraction

When to Go Before 11 a.m. or after 5 p.m.

Special Comments This attraction, formerly StarJets, is not as innocuous as it appears

Author's Rating Not worth the wait; ★★

Appeal by Age Group

Pre-school ★★★★   Grade School ★★★   Teens ★★½

Young Adults ★★½   Over 30 ★★   Senior Citizens ★

Duration of Ride 1½ minutes

Average Wait in Line per 100 People ahead of You 13½ minutes

Loading Speed Slow

Description and Comments Though recently upgraded and visually appealing, the Astro Orbiter is still a slow-loading carnival ride. The fat little rocketships simply fly in circles. The best thing about the Astro Orbiter is the nice view when you're aloft.

Touring Tips Expendable on any schedule. If you ride with preschoolers, seat them first, then board. The Astro Orbiter flies higher and faster than Dumbo and frightens some young children. It also apparently messes with some adults. A mother from Lev Hashomnon, Israel, attests:

> I think your assessment of [Astro Orbiter] as "very mild" is way off. I was able to sit through all the "Mountains," the "Tours," and the "Wars" without my stomach reacting even a little, but after [Astro Orbiter] I thought I would be finished for the rest of the day. Very quickly I realized that my only chance for survival was to pick a point on the toe of my shoe and stare at it (and certainly not lift my eyes out of the "jet") until the ride was over. My four-year-old was my co-pilot, and she loved the ride (go figure), and she had us up high the whole time. It was a nightmare—people should be forewarned.

Tomorrowland Transit Authority

What It Is Scenic tour of Tomorrowland

Scope & Scale Minor attraction

When to Go During hot, crowded times of day (11:30 a.m.–4:30 p.m.)

Special Comments A good way to check out the crowd at Space Mountain

Author's Rating Scenic, relaxing, informative; ★★★

Appeal by Age Group

Pre-school ★★★½   Grade School ★★★   Teens ★★½

Young Adults ★★½   Over 30 ★★½   Senior Citizens ★★★

Duration of Ride 10 minutes

Average Wait in Line per 100 People ahead of You 1½ minutes

Assumes 39 trains operating

Loading Speed Fast

Description and Comments A once unique prototype of a linear induction–powered mass-transit system, the Authority's tramlike cars carry riders on a leisurely tour of Tomorrowland, including a peek inside Space Mountain. The attraction was formerly called the WEDway PeopleMover.

Touring Tips A relaxing ride, where lines move quickly and you seldom have to wait. It's good to take during busier times of day, and it can double as a nursery.

A Texas mom writes:

The [Transit Authority] is an excellent ride for getting a tired infant to fall asleep. You can stay on for several times around. It is also a moderately private and comfortable place for nursing an infant.

A woman from upstate New York also found it relaxing:

Tomorrowland Transit Authority was a surprising treat; we rode it three times to see everything and to take a break from walking; it's especially nice when it goes through Space Mountain.

Walt Disney's Carousel of Progress (open seasonally)

What It Is Audio-animatronic theater production

Scope & Scale Major attraction

When to Go Anytime

Author's Rating Nostalgic, warm, and happy; ★★★

Appeal by Age Group

Pre-school ★★	Grade School ★★½	Teens ★★½
Young Adults ★★★	Over 30 ★★★	Senior Citizens ★★★½

Duration of Presentation 18 minutes

Preshow Entertainment Documentary on the attraction's long history

Probable Waiting Time Less than 10 minutes

Description and Comments Updated and improved during the Tomorrowland renovation, *Walt Disney's Carousel of Progress* offers a delightful look at how technology and electricity have changed the lives of an audio-animatronic family over several generations. The family is easy to identify with, and a cheerful, sentimental tune bridges the generations.

Touring Tips This attraction is a great favorite among repeat visitors and is included on all of our one-day touring plans. The *Carousel* handles big crowds effectively and is a good choice during busier times of day.

The Timekeeper (open seasonally)

What It Is Time-travel movie adventure

Scope & Scale Major attraction

When to Go Anytime

Special Comments Audience must stand throughout entire presentation

Author's Rating Outstanding; not to be missed; ★★★★

Appeal by Age Group

Pre-school ★★	Grade School ★★★½	Teens ★★★★
Young Adults ★★★★	Over 30 ★★★★	Senior Citizens ★★★★

Duration of Presentation About 20 minutes

Preshow Entertainment Robots, lasers, and movies

Probable Waiting Time 8–15 minutes

Description and Comments Developed as *Le Visionarium* for Disneyland Paris, *The Timekeeper* adds audio-animatronic characters and a story line to the long-successful Circle-Vision 360 technology. The preshow introduces Timekeeper (a humanoid) and 9-Eye (a time-traveling robot so-named because she has nine cameras that serve as eyes). Afterward, the audience enters the main theater, where Timekeeper places 9-Eye into a time machine and dispatches her on a crazed journey into the past and future. What 9-Eye sees on her odyssey is projected onto huge screens that surround the audience with action. The robot travels to prehistoric Europe and then forward to meet French author Jules Verne, who hitches a ride into the future. Circle-Vision 360 technology, audio-animatronics, and high-tech special effects combine to make *The Timekeeper* one of Tomorrowland's premier attractions.

The Timekeeper may be the most underrated attraction in the Magic Kingdom, but as this Westport, Connecticut family attests, it's a "must-see."

We thought The Timekeeper *was the best [audio-animatronics] in the whole of Disney World. Robin Williams was brilliant. We saw it twice— 5 stars!*

A New England family of eight agrees, writing:

The Timekeeper *is an example if how far audio-animatronics has come and when done right, how convincing it can be. A must-see show.*

Touring Tips *The Timekeeper* draws crowds from midmorning on. Because the theater accommodates more than 1,000 guests per show, there never is mcuh wait. Go during early afternoon when the park is hot and crowded.

Buzz Lightyear's Space Ranger Spin (FASTPASS)

What It Is Whimsical space travel–themed indoor ride

Scope & Scale Minor attraction

When to Go Before 10:30 a.m. or after 6 p.m.

Author's Rating A real winner! ★★★★

Appeal by Age Group

Pre-school ★★★★	Grade School ★★★★★	Teens ★★★★½
Young Adults ★★★★	Over 30 ★★★★	Senior Citizens ★★★★

Duration of Ride About 4½ minutes

Average Wait in Line per 100 People ahead of You 3 minutes

Loading Speed Fast

Description and Comments This attraction, based on the space-commando character of Buzz Lightyear from the film *Toy Story*, replaced the Take Flight attraction as the final installment of Tomorrowland's four-year makeover. The marginal story line has you and Buzz Lightyear trying to save the universe from the evil Emperor Zurg. The indoor ride is interactive to the extent that you can spin your car and shoot simulated "laser cannons" at Zurg and his minions.

Touring Tips   Each car is equipped with two laser cannons and a scorekeeping display. Each scorekeeping display is independent, so you can compete with your riding partner. A joy stick allows you to spin the car to line up the various targets. Each time you pull the trigger you'll release a red laser beam that you can see hitting or missing the target. Most folks' first ride is occupied with learning how to use the equipment (fire off individual shots as opposed to keeping the trigger depressed) and figuring out how the targets work. The next ride (like certain potato chips, one is not enough) you'll surprise yourself by how much better you do. *Unofficial* readers are unanimous in their praise of Buzz Lightyear. Some, in fact, spend several hours on it, riding again and again. The following comments are representative:

From a Yorktown, Virginia, mom:

I am a 44-year-old woman who has never been fond of shoot-'em-up arcade games, but I decided I'd better check out Buzz Lightyear's Space Ranger Spin after the monorail driver told us that it, along with Space Mountain, were her favorite rides at the Magic Kingdom. What a blast! My husband and I enjoyed it every bit as much as our ten-year-old daughter. After riding it the first time, we couldn't wait to ride it again (and again) in an effort to improve our scores. Alas, I was never able to advance beyond Ranger 1st Class although my husband made it all the way to Space Ace. Warning— Buzz Lightyear is addictive!

From a father of three from Cleveland, Ohio:

Without question, the favorite ride of my 11-year-old son was the Buzz Lightyear Ride. Come to think about it, it was my favorite too!

From a Snow Hill, Maryland, dad:

Buzz Lightyear was so much fun it can't be legal! We hit it first on early-entry day and rode it ten times without stopping. The kids had fun, but it was Dad who spun himself silly trying to shoot the Zs. This is the most unique, creative ride ever devised.

And finally, from a Massachusetts couple:

Buzz Lightyear was the surprise hit of our trip! My husband and I enjoyed competing for the best score so much that we went on this ride several times during our stay. Definitely a must, especially when there's no wait!

See Buzz Lightyear after riding Space Mountain first thing in the morning or use FASTPASS.

Alien Encounter

What It Is   Theater-in-the-round sci-fi horror show

Scope & Scale   Headliner

When to Go   Before 10 a.m. or after 6 p.m.; try during parades

Special Comments   Frightens children of all ages. Must be 44" tall to ride.

Author's Rating   ★★★

Appeal by Age Group

Pre-school —   Grade School ★★★½   Teens ★★★★

Young Adults ★★★★   Over 30 ★★★★   Senior Citizens ★★★
Duration of Presentation About 12 minutes
Preshow Entertainment About 6 minutes
Probable Waiting Time 12–40 minutes

Description and Comments   Heralded as the showpiece of the "new" Tomorrow-land, *Alien Encounter* is staged in the building that previously housed *Mission to Mars*. Guests witness a demonstration of "interplanetary teleportation," a technique that converts travelers into electrons for transmission to distant locations. In this case, the demonstration goes awry (of course), and an unsavory alien arrives in the theater. Mayhem ensues.

Alien Encounter is the antithesis of most Disney attractions: there is no uplifting message and no happy ending. There is death in this attraction, and its tone is dark and foreboding. While The *Twilight Zone* Tower of Terror at Disney-MGM Studios is suspenseful and subtle, *Alien Encounter* is uncomfortable and gross. The discomfort begins at the preshow when, in a teleportation experiment, a cuddly audio-animatronic character is hideously fried, then vomited, screaming into outer space. Is this someone's idea of entertainment?

Alien Encounter has its advocates, but we consider it mean and twisted. The *coup de grâce*, however, is the hawking of T-shirts (in the adjacent gift shop) decorated with the image of the tortured and maimed audio-animatronic creature. Enough already.

Because *Alien Encounter* is such a departure from typical Disney theme-park entertainment, we consider it prudent to share the observations of readers.

A mother of two from Botswana really let us have it:

> We almost missed *Alien Encounter* due to your report and found it to be the best overall attraction, better than *Terminator 2 3-D [at Universal Studios]* as the audience is smaller and closer to the action. It helped to know it was scary, but we felt your warnings were over the top. The adults laughed throughout.

A Cape May, New Jersey, family agreed:

> We also have to register in on the *Alien Encounter* saga. My ten-year-old and I liked it a lot. We would have gone again except I convinced him that since we already knew the surprises it wouldn't be nearly as scary the second time. When I later let my son read your comments (and others) about the ride, here's his logical reply. "Mom, how could anyone really think a monster was going to get them? It's a ride that millions of people have been on and lived. It's not real after all." How's that for logic? Nonetheless, he screamed with everyone else. Oh, and I looked. I didn't see anyone crying or fainting. Nor was anyone upset at the pre-game show when the little serpent got fried by Tim Curry. It was cartoon violence of a kind reminiscent of the Road Runner and Wiley Coyote, for goodness sakes. Did it really upset you?

A Rochester, New York, woman also comes spiritedly to the defense of *Alien Encounter*, writing:

> I do disagree with you about *Alien Encounter*. Just because Disney is known for cute animals and happy endings, does that condemn them to a future of nothing but singing flowers and dancing hippos? I love A.E. and so did my whole family.... It's not really that bad. But people should know their

own limits and the limits of their children. You say it is too dark and foreboding, but don't analyze it so much.

But a Patterson, Louisiana, mom disagrees:

We took my son (nine) into Alien Encounter on his first night [at WDW],
and I thought I would need a paramedic to resuscitate him after the experience! He clutched onto me the entire time, and his heart was pounding
so hard in his chest I thought it would explode! He was terrified!! We had
discussed the attraction before we left home, and he assured me he knew
the difference between real and make-believe and he would not be scared.
A totally different story in reality!! It just goes to show you never know
what reaction a child will have to any given ride or attraction. (He rode
Rock 'n' Roller Coaster at MGM and loved it.)

A woman from Milford, Michigan, has this to say:

Warning!!! And I can't stress this enough! Alien Encounter is the most
intense attraction in any theme park. It is one of those rides I can say I've
seen and that I have no intention of ever doing again. In fact, parents who
take children under the age of six should be brought up on child abuse.

A parent from Laurel, Maryland, shares her experience:

The preshow is very deceiving. It kind of lulls you into thinking "this isn't so
bad." When the main part came up, I admit the experience gave me the
absolute heebie-jeebies. It is INTENSE! I am grateful nothing touched me
when we were plunged into the dark (my friend and I sat in the middle
row of seats), because I swear I would have either passed out or screamed
bloody murder. If someone is the least bit scared of the dark or is the least
bit fearful, I do not recommend this attraction. (I am never doing that presentation again—it was way too intense for me, and I'm now 27 years of
age!) All sorts of things go running through your mind when it happens. If
you don't keep reminding yourself that it's just a theater, you really can get
the stuffing scared out of you.

In the middle are a group of readers, including this mom from Providence, Rhode
Island, who advocate *Alien Encounter* for adults but warn about taking children:

Alien Encounter was scary in a different way than the other rides. The "theatre of the mind" element really worked. It wasn't just a jarring physical
thing. Disney ought to develop more attractions like this one. Although parents of six- to nine-year-olds should be forewarned that most of the kids
that age were carried out at the end screaming and clinging to their parents. I was in the baby swap holding area (the exit lobby) and was glad I'd
ridden before my husband. If I had seen all those kids shrieking before I'd
queued, I would have chickened out.

Joining the chorus "in favor" is an Amarillo, Texas, mother who regrets subjecting
her child to the attraction:

My personal favorite was Alien Encounter, but it literally scared our daughter
to pieces. She screamed and cried when ol' Mr. Alien busted loose. We
didn't feel like parents of the year, needless to say. I will add that every
other little girl I saw under age eight was crying also. I think they should
have a warning like Terminator 2 3-D does at Universal Studios—PG-13.

A normally fearless New England teenager decided she was not quite "big enough" for *Alien Encounter,* writing:

Alien Encounter was very graphic, loud, and frightening. I am going to be 15 and to me it was too much. I love space and alien movies but that went too far. This place is supposed to be for kids and kids at heart. My feelings toward [Disney's] warnings are very negative. They say it may frighten small children but they don't tell you that it may frighten big "children."

A dad from Greensboro, North Carolina, notes that there is no way possible to comfort your children while the show is in progress, writing:

Alien Encounter should not be seen by pre-adolescents. You are trapped, alone, isolated, with no way to comfort or explain. Our children could not (or would not) speak for an hour afterward.

A mother of four from Winchester, Virginia, tells her family's story:

We mistakenly rode Alien Encounter first. Fortunately the four-year-old and I stayed out. My daughters came out petrified and in tears. Luckily, they recovered quickly. Warn any parents of children seven or younger to ride it first themselves before they subject their kids to it. It's great for adults, though. My vote for best new attraction in the Magic Kingdom.

A mom from Glenview, Illinois, didn't enjoy it:

Alien Encounter was horrible! The seats were uncomfortable and we were strapped in with an overhead harness. This was done, no doubt, to keep all the truly terrified children from trying to escape during the show. An eight- or nine-year-old boy next to me was sobbing after the alien escaped. This attraction is pointless, incomprehensible, intense, and no fun at all. It lacked any Disney creativity and whimsy.

A couple from Laupac, California, was caught off guard by *Alien Encounter:*

Please inform all visitors to read ride descriptions. I avoided the Magic Kingdom section since I felt it was the same as Disneyland. However, we went to Alien Encounter by accident. My 45-year-old wife was terrified. Very un-Disney-like ride. Most children screamed and cried.

Finally, from an Abbott Park, Illinois, dad:

After all the hype, I was a little disappointed. I thought it was a little mean-spirited in a very un-Disneylike way. And though the effects were good, I left with sort of a bad taste in my mouth.

Touring Tips   Disney's most disturbing and frightening attraction, *Alien Encounter* initially was rejected by Walt Disney Company chairman Michael Eisner for not being scary enough. Though reader reaction to *Alien Encounter* is mixed, almost everyone agrees this isn't an attraction for young children. *Alien Encounter* stays busy throughout the day. See it first thing in the morning.

Live Entertainment in the Magic Kingdom

Bands, Disney character appearances, parades, ceremonies, and singing and dancing further enliven the Magic Kingdom. For specific events the day you visit, check the live entertainment schedule in your Disney guidemap (free as you enter the park or at City Hall). Be aware: If you're short on time, it's impossible to see Magic Kingdom feature attractions *and* the live performances. Our one-day touring plans exclude live performances in favor of seeing as much of the park as time permits. This tactical decision is based on the fact that some parades and performances siphon crowds away from the more popular rides, thus shortening lines.

Nonetheless, the color and pageantry of live events are integral to the Magic Kingdom and a persuasive argument for a second day of touring. Here's a list and description of some performances and events presented with regularity that don't require reservations.

Fantasyland Pavilion   Site of various concerts in Fantasyland.

Steel Drum Bands and Luau Dancers   Perform daily at Caribbean Plaza in Adventureland.

Frontierland Stuntmen   Stuntmen stage shootouts in Frontierland; check the daily entertainment schedule.

Castle Forecourt Stage   In 2002, Disney rolled out a new forecourt show call Cinderella's Surprise Celebration featuring a plot, elaborate props (including the castle itself), and a veritable roll call of Disney characters. Like *Fantasmic!,* it's another good vs. evil spectacular, though in distinct contrast to *Fantasmic!,* not at all frightening to pre-schoolers. Because characters pop out of turrets and parapets high up on the castle as well as along the balustrades and on the stage, it's pretty hard to find a viewing perspective where you can see everything. Fortunately, the plot is so simplistic that missing a few things won't compromise your understanding or your enjoyment. The show is performed one to three times each day according to the season with showtimes listed the daily entertainment schedule. During our last visit, we stood on the concrete benches in front of the statue of Mickey and Walt in the central hub.

Storytime with Belle at the Fairytale Garden   Belle and several helpers select children from the small amphitheater audience and dress them up as characters from *Beauty and the Beast.* As Belle tells the story, the children act out the roles. There is a 3–5-minute meet-and-greet with photo and autograph opportunities afterward. Storytime is staged six to eight times each day according to the daily entertainment schedule. To find the Fairytale Garden, follow the path on the Fantasyland side of the castle moat toward Tomorrowland. A reader from Tyler, Texas, enjoyed the short production:

This was actually kind of cute, as the chosen children were hams and very familiar with the story already. The location is sort of set back and down into the ground, thus allowing for a lot of shade and a cooler breeze. It's definitely worth dropping in to sit down and rest in the middle of the afternoon.

Flag Retreat At 5 p.m. daily at Town Square (railroad station end of Main Street). Sometimes performed with great fanfare and college marching bands, sometimes with a smaller Disney band.

Sword in the Stone Ceremony A ceremony based on the Disney animated feature of the same name. Merlin the Magician selects youngsters from the audience to test their courage and strength by removing the sword, Excalibur, from the stone. Staged several times each day behind Cinderella Castle; check the daily entertainment schedule.

Bay Lake and Seven Seas Lagoon Floating Electrical Pageant This is one of our favorites among the Disney extras, but it's necessary to leave the Magic Kingdom to view it. The pageant is a stunning electric light show afloat on small barges and set to nifty electronic music. It's performed at nightfall (about 9 p.m. most of the year) on Seven Seas Lagoon and Bay Lake. Leave the Magic Kingdom and take the monorail to the Polynesian Resort. Get yourself a drink and walk to the end of the pier to watch the show.

Fantasy in the Sky A stellar fireworks display unleashed after dark on nights the park is open late. For an uncluttered view and lighter crowds, watch from the terrace of The Plaza Pavilion restaurant in Tomorrowland. Another good fireworks viewing area is between Dumbo and the carousel.

Fantasy in the Sky Cruise For a different view, you can watch the fireworks from the Seven Seas Lagoon aboard a chartered pontoon boat. The charter costs $120 and accommodates up to 12 persons. Your Disney cast member captain will take you for a little cruise and then position the boat in a perfect place to watch the fireworks. For an additional $80 per each four persons, the captain will provide deli sandwiches, snacks, and beverages. A major indirect benefit of the charter is that you can enjoy the fireworks without fighting the mob afterwards. Because this is a private charter rather than a tour, only your group will be aboard. Life jackets are provided, but you can wear them at your discretion. Because there are few boats, charters sell out fast. To reserve, call (407) WDW-PLAY at exactly 7 a.m. 90 days before the day you want to charter. Because the Disney reservations system counts days in a somewhat atypical manner, we recommend phoning at about 95 days out to have a Disney agent specify the exact morning to call for reservations. Similar charters are available to watch *IllumiNations* at Epcot.

Cosmic Ray's Galaxy Palace Theater and Tomorrowland Stage These stages in Tomorrowland feature Top-40 rock music, rap, and jazz, as well as Disney characters and the Kids of the Kingdom.

Disney Character Shows and Appearances Most days, a character is on duty for photos and autographs from 9 a.m. to 10 p.m. next to City

Hall. Mickey and two or three assortments of other characters are available most of the day at Mickey's Toontown Fair. Shows at the Castle Forecourt Stage and Tomorrowland's Galaxy Palace Theater feature Disney characters several times daily (check the entertainment schedule). In Fantasyland, Ariel can be found in her Grotto daily, while a host of others can be seen at the Character Festival next to Dumbo. Characters also roam the park. For information on character whereabouts on the day you visit, check the *Character Greeting Guide* printed on the inside of the handout park map.

Magic Kingdom Bands   Banjo, Dixieland, steel drum, marching, and fife-and-drum bands roam the park daily.

Tinker Bell's Flight   This nice special effect in the sky above Cinderella Castle heralds the beginning of Fantasy in the Sky fireworks (when the park is open late).

Parades

Parades at the Magic Kingdom are full-fledged spectaculars with dozens of Disney characters and amazing special effects. We rate the afternoon parade as outstanding and the evening parade as "not to be missed."

In addition to providing great entertainment, parades lure guests away from the attractions. If getting on rides appeals to you more than watching a parade, you'll find substantially shorter lines just before and during parades. Because the parade route doesn't pass through Adventureland, Tomorrowland, or Fantasyland, attractions in these lands are particularly good bets. Be forewarned: Parades disrupt traffic in the Magic Kingdom. It's nearly impossible, for example, to get to Adventureland from Tomorrowland, or vice versa, during one.

Afternoon Parade

Usually staged at 3 p.m., the parade features bands, floats, and marching Disney characters. A new afternoon parade is introduced every year or two. While some elements, such as Disney characters, remain constant, the theme, music, and float design change. Seasonal parades during major holidays round out the mix.

Evening Parade(s)

The evening parade is a high-tech affair employing electroluminescent and fiber-optic technologies, light-spreading thermoplastics (do not try this at home!), and clouds of underlit liquid-nitrogen smoke. Don't worry, you won't need a gas mask or lead underwear to watch. For those who flunked chemistry and physics, the parade also offers music, Mickey Mouse, twinkling lights, and snapshots of classic animated features inside giant snow

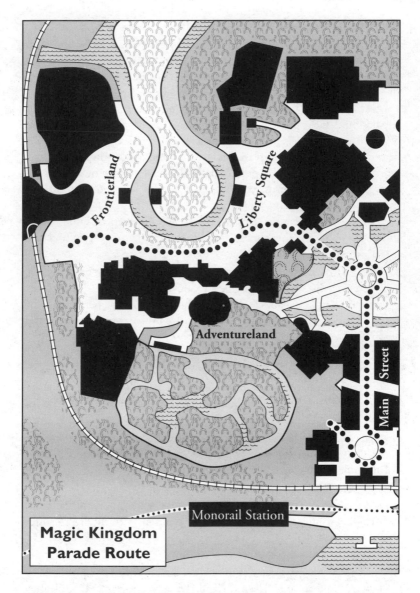

Magic Kingdom Parade Route

Frontierland

Liberty Square

Adventureland

Main Street

Monorail Station

globes. Disney says the snow globes are just part of the show, but we think maybe the characters are worried about anthrax. The evening parade is staged once or twice each evening, depending on the time of year.

During less busy times of year, the evening parade is held only on weekends, and sometimes not even then. Call (407) 824-4321 before you go to be sure the parade is on.

Parade Route and Vantage Points

Magic Kingdom parades circle Town Square, head down Main Street, go around the central hub, and cross the bridge to Liberty Square. In Liberty Square, they follow the waterfront and end in Frontierland. Sometimes they begin in Frontierland and run the route in the opposite direction.

Most guests watch from the central hub, or from Main Street. One of the best and most popular vantage points is the upper platform of the Walt Disney World Railroad station at the Town Square end of Main Street. This is also a good place for watching the Fantasy in the Sky fireworks, as well as for ducking out of the park ahead of the crowd when the fireworks end. Problem is, you have to stake out your position 30–45 minutes before the events.

Because most spectators pack Main Street and the central hub, we recommend watching the parade from Liberty Square or Frontierland. Great vantage points, frequently overlooked, are:

1. Sleepy Hollow snack and beverage shop, immediately to your right as you cross the bridge into Liberty Square. If you arrive early, buy refreshments and claim a table by the rail. You'll have a perfect view of the parade as it crosses the Liberty Square bridge, but only when the parade begins on Main Street.

2. The pathway on the Liberty Square side of the moat from Sleepy Hollow snack and beverage shop to Cinderella Castle. Any point along this path offers a clear and unobstructed view as the parade crosses the Liberty Square bridge. Once again, this spot works only for parades coming from Main Street.

3. The covered walkway between Liberty Tree Tavern and *The Diamond Horseshoe Saloon Revue.* This elevated vantage point is perfect (particularly on rainy days) and usually goes unnoticed until just before the parade starts.

4. Elevated wooden platforms in front of the Frontierland Shootin' Arcade, Frontier Trading Post, and the building with the sign reading FRONTIER MERCHANDISE. These spots usually get picked off 10–12 minutes before parade time.

5. Benches on the perimeter of the central hub, between the entrances to Liberty Square and Adventureland. Usually unoccupied until after the parade begins, they offer a comfortable resting place and unobstructed (though somewhat distant) view of the parade as it crosses Liberty Square bridge. What you lose in proximity, you gain in comfort.

6. Liberty Square and Frontierland dockside areas. These spots usually go early.

7. The elevated porch of Tony's Town Square Restaurant on Main Street provides an elevated viewing platform and an easy path to the park exit when the fireworks are over.

Assuming it starts on Main Street (evening parades normally do), the parade takes 16–20 minutes to reach Liberty Square or Frontierland. On evenings when the parade runs twice, the first parade draws a huge crowd, siphoning guests from attractions. Many folks leave the park after the early parade, with many more departing after the fireworks (scheduled on the hour between the two parades). For optimum touring and less congestion, enjoy attractions during the early parade, then break to watch the fireworks. Continue to tour after the fireworks. This is a particularly good time to see *Alien Encounter*, ride Space Mountain, and enjoy attractions in Adventureland. If you're touring Adventureland and the parade begins on Main Street, you won't have to assume your viewing position in Frontierland until 15 minutes after the parade starts (the time it takes the parade to reach Frontierland). If you watch from the Splash Mountain side of the street and head for the attraction as the last float passes, you'll be able to ride with only a couple of minutes' wait. You might even have time to work in a last-minute ride on Big Thunder Mountain Railroad.

Vantage Points for Fireworks

Anywhere along Main Street is fine for the fireworks. If you plan to leave the park immediately afterwards, watch from the train station end to facilitate a quick departure. Our favorite spot if we intend to remain in the park is the roofless patio of the Plaza Pavilion located in Tomorrowland on the border with Main Street USA.

Leaving the Park after Evening Parades and Fireworks

Armies of guests leave the Magic Kingdom after evening parades and fireworks. The Disney Transportation System (buses, ferries, and monorail) is overwhelmed, causing long waits in boarding areas.

A mother from Kresgeville, Pennsylvania, pleads:

Please stress how terrifying these crowds can be. Our family of five made the mistake of going to the MK the Saturday night before Columbus Day to watch the parade and fireworks. Afterwards, we lingered at The Crystal Palace to wait for the crowds to lessen, but it was no use. We started walking toward the gates and soon became trapped by the throng, not able to go forward or back. There was no way to cross the hordes to get to the dock for our hotel's launch. Our group became separated, and it became a living nightmare. We left the park at 10:30 p.m. and didn't get back to the Polynesian (less than a mile away) until after midnight. How dare they expose children to that nightmare! Even if they were to raise Walt Disney

*himself from cryogenic sleep and parade him down Main Street, I would
never go to the MK on a Saturday night again!*

An Oklahoma City dad offers this advice:

*Never, never leave the Magic Kingdom just after the 10 p.m. fireworks. I have
never seen so many people in one spot before. Go for another ride—no
lines because everyone else is trying to get out!*

Congestion persists from the end of the early evening parade until closing time. Most folks watch the early parade and then the fireworks a few minutes later. If you're parked at the Transportation and Ticket Center and are intent on beating the crowd, view the early parade from the Town Square end of Main Street, leaving the park as soon as the parade ends. Walk (about 12 minutes) or ride the monorail to the Contemporary Resort. Note that the monorail loading platform for the hotels is different from the platform serving the TTC. At the Contemporary Resort, take the elevator to the top floor and go through the lounge (no problem for kids) to the outdoor promenade atop the hotel. There, watch the Magic Kingdom fireworks in a relaxed, uncrowded setting with a perfect, unobstructed view. After the fireworks, return to the TTC on the monorail.

If you're staying at a Disney hotel not served by the monorail and must depend on Disney transportation, watch the early parade and fireworks at the park and then enjoy the attractions until about 20–25 minutes before the late parade is scheduled to begin. At this time, leave the park and catch the Disney bus or boat back to your hotel. Don't cut it too close: Main Street will be so congested that you won't be able to reach the exit.

Here's what happened to a family from Cape Coral, Florida:

*We tried to leave the park before the parade began. However, Main Street
was already packed and we didn't see any way to get out of the park, so
we were stuck. In addition, it was impossible to move across the street, and
even the shops were so crowded that it was virtually impossible to maneuver a stroller through them to get close to the entrance.*

If you don't have a stroller (or are willing to forgo the $1 return refund for rental strollers), catch the Walt Disney World Railroad in Frontierland or Mickey's Toontown Fair and ride to the park exit at Main Street. Be aware that the railroad shuts down during parades because the floats must cross the tracks when entering or exiting the parade route in Frontierland. If you plan to escape by train, don't cut it too close.

If you're on the Tomorrowland side of the park, it's actually possible for you to exit during a parade. Leaving Tomorrowland, cut through The Plaza Pavilion Restaurant to Main Street. Before you reach Main Street, bear left into the side door of the corner shop. Once inside, you'll see that Main Street shops have interior doors allowing you to pass from one shop to the next without having to get on Main Street. Work your way from shop to shop until you reach Town Square (easy, because people will be outside watching the parade). At Town Square, bear left and move to the train station and the park exit.

This strategy won't work if you're on the Adventureland side of the park. You can make your way through Casey's Corner restaurant to Main Street, then work your way through the interior of the Main Street shops, but when you pop out of the Emporium at Town Square, you'll be trapped by the parade. As soon as the last float passes, however, you can bolt for the exit.

Another strategy for beating the masses out of the park (if your car is at the TTC lot) is to watch the early parade and then leave before the fireworks begin. Line up for the ferry. One will depart about every eight to ten minutes. Try to catch the ferry that will be crossing Seven Seas Lagoon while the fireworks are in progress. The best vantage point is on the top deck to the right of the pilot house as you face the Magic Kingdom, and the sight of fireworks silhouetting the castle and reflecting off Seven Seas Lagoon is unforgettable. While there's no guarantee that a ferry will load and depart within three or four minutes of the fireworks, your chances are about 50/50 of catching it just right. If you're in the front of the line for the ferry and don't want to board the boat that's loading, stop at the gate and let people pass you. You'll be the first to board the next boat.

Behind the Scenes in the Magic Kingdom

Keys to the Kingdom takes guests behind the scenes at the Magic Kingdom. This fascinating guided tour provides an informative and detailed look at the park's logistical, technical, and operational sides. Included are the parade assembly area, the waste treatment plant, and tunnels under the theme park. For additional information, call (407) 939-8687. The program ($49 per person) runs about four to five hours. Advance reservations and payment by credit card are required. Park admission is not included. Discounts are usually available; ask when you call to book.

For those interested in the tour, a reader from Ludington, Michigan, offers the following advice:

People thinking of taking the Keys to the Kingdom tour should know that it is not for the faint of heart. This is a four-hour walking tour with only one 15-minute break plus a few minutes to sit while on Pirates of the Caribbean, the Haunted Mansion, and the Tommorowland Transit Authority. It wore me out, and I am on my feet most of any given working day. If you do this, make it the last day of your visit—it took me three days to recover. Oh, by the way, it is worth every penny!

Backstage Magic, a seven-hour, $199 tour, goes behind the scenes at all of parks except the Animal Kingdom. Finally, **Disney's Magic**

behind Our Steam Trains, a two-hour tour for ages ten and up, takes a backstage look at the steam locomotives of the Walt Disney World Railroad. Cost is $30 per person. For reservations and information on all of the tours described, call (407) WDW-TOUR.

Traffic Patterns in the Magic Kingdom

When we research the Magic Kingdom, we study its traffic patterns, asking:

1. Which sections of the park and what attractions do guests visit first? When visitors are admitted to the lands during summer and holiday periods, traffic to Tomorrowland and Frontierland is heaviest, followed by Fantasyland, Adventureland, Liberty Square, and Mickey's Toontown Fair.

During the school year, when fewer young people are in the park, early-morning traffic is more evenly distributed but remains heaviest in Tomorrowland, Frontierland, and Fantasyland. Our researchers tested the frequent claim that most people turn right into Tomorrowland and tour the Magic Kingdom in a counterclockwise sequence. We found it to be baseless. As the park fills, visitors head for the top attractions before lines get long. This, more than any other factor, determines morning traffic patterns.

2. How long does it take for the park to fill up? How are the visitors dispersed in the park? A surge of "early birds" arrives before or around opening time but is quickly dispersed throughout the empty park. After the initial wave is absorbed, there's a lull lasting about an hour after opening. Then the park is inundated for about two hours, peaking between 10 a.m. and noon. Arrivals continue in a steady but diminishing stream until around 2 p.m. The lines we sampled were longest between 1 and 2 p.m., indicating more arrivals than departures into the early afternoon. For touring purposes, most attractions develop long lines between 10 and 11:30 a.m.

Attractions that Are Crowded Early

Tomorrowland	Space Mountain
	Alien Encounter
Frontierland	Splash Mountain
	Big Thunder Mountain Railroad
Fantasyland	Dumbo the Flying Elephant
	The Many Adventures of Winnie the Pooh
	Mickey's PhilharMagic
	Peter Pan's Flight
Adventureland	Jungle Cruise

From late morning through early afternoon, guests are equally distributed through all of the lands. We found, however, that guests concentrate in Fantasyland, Liberty Square, and Frontierland in late afternoon, with a decrease of visitors in Adventureland and Tomorrowland. Adventureland's Jungle Cruise and Tomorrowland's Buzz Lightyear and Space Mountain continue to be crowded, but most other attractions in those lands are readily accessible.

3. How do most visitors tour the park? Do first-time visitors tour differently from repeat guests?   Many first-time visitors are accompanied by friends or relatives familiar with the Magic Kingdom, who guide their tour. These tours may or may not follow an orderly sequence. First-time visitors without personal guides tend to be more orderly in their touring. Many first-time visitors, however, are drawn to Cinderella Castle upon entering the park and thus begin their rotation from Fantasyland. Repeat visitors usually go directly to their favorite attractions.

4. How does FASTPASS affect crowd distributions? The effect is subtle and depends somewhat on the time interval between when the FASTPASS is obtained and the FASTPASS return period. For example, guests who receive a FASTPASS for Splash Mountain at 10 a.m. with an 11:05 a.m.–12:05 p.m. return window tend to tour near Splash Mountain during the interim to minimize the inconvenience of backtracking when it's time to use the pass. However, when the return period is several hours distant, guests don't feel compelled to stay in the immediate area. In general, you won't notice much difference in crowd concentrations because of FASTPASS, but empirically speaking, it increases crowds within proximity of the two anchor attractions, Space Mountain and Splash Mountain, throughout the day.

5. How do special events, such as parades and live shows, affect traffic patterns? Parades pull huge numbers of guests away from attractions and provide a window of opportunity for experiencing the more popular attractions with less of a wait. Castle Forecourt Stage shows also attract crowds but only slightly affect lines.

6. What are the traffic patterns near to and at closing time? On our sample days, in busy times and off-season at the park, departures outnumbered arrivals beginning in midafternoon. Many visitors left in late afternoon as the dinner hour approached. When the park closed early, guests departed steadily during the two hours before closing, with a huge exodus at closing time. When the park closed late, a huge exodus began immediately after the early-evening parade and fireworks, with a second mass departure after the late parade, continuing until closing. Because Main Street and the transportation services remain open after the other six lands close, crowds leaving at closing mainly affect conditions on

Main Street and at the monorail, ferry, and bus boarding areas. In the hour before closing, the other six lands normally are uncrowded.

7. When there are two or more lines, is the shortest wait always in the left line? We don't recommend the "left-line strategy" because, with the occasional exception of food lines, it doesn't hold up. Disney has techniques for both internal and external crowd control that distribute traffic nearly equally. Placing researchers at the same time in each available line, we could discern no consistent pattern of who was served first. Further, researchers entering the same attraction by different lines almost always would exit the attraction within 30 to 90 seconds of each other.

Occasionally guests ignore a second line that has just opened and stay in the established line. As a rule, if you encounter a waiting area with two lines and no barrier to entry for either, and one line is empty or conspicuously shorter than the other, get in the short line.

Magic Kingdom Touring Plans

Our step-by-step touring plans are field-tested for seeing *as much as possible* in one day with a minimum of time wasted in lines. They're designed to help you avoid crowds and bottlenecks on days of moderate to heavy attendance. Understand, however, that there's more to see in the Magic Kingdom than can be experienced in one day. Since we began covering the Magic Kingdom, four headliner attractions and a new land have been added. Today, even if you could experience every attraction without any wait, you still wouldn't be able to see all of the park in a single day.

On days of lighter attendance (see "Selecting the Time of Year for Your Visit," pages 29–34), our plans will save you time but won't be as critical to successful touring as on busier days. Don't worry that other people will be following the plans and render them useless. Fewer than 1 in every 350 people in the park will have been exposed to this information.

Choosing the Appropriate Touring Plan

We present five Magic Kingdom touring plans:

- Magic Kingdom One-Day Touring Plan for Adults
- Author's Selective Magic Kingdom One-Day Touring Plan for Adults
- Magic Kingdom One-Day Touring Plan for Parents with Young Children
- Magic Kingdom Dumbo-or-Die-in-a-Day Touring Plan for Parents with Young Children
- Magic Kingdom Two-Day Touring Plan

If you have two days (or two mornings) at the Magic Kingdom, the Two-Day Touring Plan is *by far* the most relaxed and efficient. The two-day plan takes advantage of early morning, when lines are short and the park hasn't filled with guests. This plan works well year-round and eliminates much of the extra walking required by the one-day plans. No matter when the park closes, our two-day plan guarantees the most efficient touring and the least time in lines. The plan is perfect for guests who wish to sample both the attractions and the atmosphere of the Magic Kingdom.

If you only have one day but wish to see as much as possible, use the One-Day Touring Plan for Adults. It's exhausting, but it packs in the maximum. If you prefer a more relaxed visit, use the Author's Selective One-Day Touring Plan. It includes the best the park has to offer (in the author's opinion), eliminating some less impressive attractions.

If you have children younger than age eight, adopt the One-Day Touring Plan for Parents with Young Children. It's a compromise, blending the preferences of younger children with those of older siblings and adults. The plan includes many children's rides in Fantasyland but omits roller coaster rides and other attractions that frighten young children or are off-limits because of height requirements. Or, use the One-Day Touring Plan for Adults or the Author's Selective One-Day Touring Plan and take advantage of switching off, a technique where children accompany adults to the loading area of a ride with age and height requirements but don't board (pages 254–257). Switching off allows adults to enjoy the more adventuresome attractions while keeping the group together.

The Dumbo-or-Die-in-a-Day Touring Plan for Parents with Young Children is designed for parents who will withhold no sacrifice for the children. On the Dumbo-or-Die plan, adults generally stand around, sweat, wipe noses, pay for stuff, and watch the children enjoy themselves. It's great.

Two-Day Touring Plan for Families with Young Children

If you have young children and are looking for a two-day itinerary, combine the Magic Kingdom One-Day Touring Plan for Parents with Young Children with the second day of the Magic Kingdom Two-Day Touring Plan.

Two-Day Touring Plan for Early Morning Touring on Day One and Afternoon-Evening Touring on Day Two

Many of you enjoy an early start at the Magic Kingdom on one day, followed by a second day with a lazy, sleep-in morning, resuming your touring in the afternoon and/or evening. If this appeals to you, use the Magic Kingdom One-Day Touring Plan for Adults or the Magic Kingdom One-Day Touring Plan for Parents with Young Children on your early day. Adhere to the touring plan for as long as feels comfortable (many folks leave after the afternoon parade). On the second day, pick up where you left off. If you intend to use FASTPASS on your second day, try to arrive at the park by 1 p.m. or the FASTPASSes may be gone. Customize the remaining part of the touring plan to incorporate parades, fireworks, and other live performances according to your preferences.

About Touring Plan Clip-Out Pocket Outlines

Pocket versions of all touring plans presented in this guide begin on page 763. The outlines present the same itineraries as the detailed plans but with vastly abbreviated directions. Select the touring plan appropriate for your party and familiarize yourself with its detailed version. When you understand how the plan works, clip its pocket outline from the back of this guide and carry it as a quick reference when you visit the theme park.

The Single-Day Touring Conundrum

Touring the Magic Kingdom in a day is complicated by the fact that the premier attractions are at almost opposite ends of the park: Splash Mountain and Big Thunder Mountain Railroad in Frontierland and Space Mountain and Buzz Lightyear in Tomorrowland. It's virtually impossible to ride all four without encountering lines at one or another. If you ride Space Mountain and see Buzz Lightyear immediately after the park opens, you won't have much wait, if any. By the time you leave Tomorrowland and hurry to Frontierland, however, the line for Splash Mountain will be substantial. The same situation prevails if you ride the Frontierland duo first: Splash Mountain and Big Thunder Mountain Railroad, no problem; Space Mountain and Buzz Lightyear, fair-sized lines. From ten minutes after opening until just before closing, lines are long at these headliners.

The best way to ride all four without long waits is to tour the Magic Kingdom over two mornings: Ride Space Mountain and Buzz Lightyear first thing one morning, then ride Splash Mountain and Big Thunder Mountain first thing on the other. If you only have one day, be present at opening time. Speed immediately to Space Mountain, then take in Buzz Lightyear. After Buzz Lightyear, rush to Frontierland and scope out the situation at Splash Mountain. If the posted wait time is 30 minutes or less, go ahead and hop in line. If the wait exceeds 30 minutes, get a FASTPASS for Splash Mountain, then ride Big Thunder Mountain..

E-Ride Night

In 2002, Disney offered a program called E-Ride Night. Only Disney resort guests with multiday passports (and annual and seasonal pass holders) are eligible. For $10, you can purchase a pass that allows you to remain in the Magic Kingdom for three hours after the official closing time and enjoy the following attractions:

Space Mountain	Splash Mountain	Big Thunder Mountain
Alien Encounter	Astro Orbiter	Country Bear Jamboree
Buzz Lightyear	The Haunted Mansion	

Disney limits the number of E-Ride Night passes sold to four to five thousand per night, ensuring short-to-nonexistent waits for most attractions. If you have fantasized about riding Space Mountain ten times in a row with practically no waiting, E-Ride Night makes it possible. E-Ride Night, however, is not good for admission to the park by itself. It must be used with a multiday admission used at any of the major theme parks on the day in question. In other words, you can spend the day at the Animal Kingdom (have your hand stamped upon exiting) and then head to the Magic Kingdom for after-hours fun. On arriving at the Magic Kingdom, enter the park before official closing time using your multiday pass. Once inside, take your E-Ride Night voucher to either City Hall, the Tomorrowland Arcade, or Splashdown Photo and exchange it for a wristband that identifies you as eligible to stay in the park. After scheduled park closing, only guests with wristbands are allowed to remain in the park.

Now the bad news. Thus far, Disney has operated this program only during the slower times of year when the Magic Kingdom closes relatively early (7 or 8 p.m.), and even then on just one day each week. It is unlikely that E-Ride Night will ever be operational during summer or holiday periods when the park closes at 10 p.m. or later. As with all things Disney, this program is subject to change or cancellation at any time.

Preliminary Instructions for All Magic Kingdom Touring Plans

On days of moderate to heavy attendance, follow your chosen touring plan exactly, deviating only:

1. When you aren't interested in an attraction it lists. For example, the plan may tell you to go to Tomorrowland and ride Space Mountain, a roller coaster. If you don't enjoy roller coasters, skip this step and proceed to the next.

2. When you encounter a very long line at an attraction the touring plan calls for. Crowds ebb and flow at the park, and an unusually long line may have gathered at an attraction to which you're directed. For example, you arrive at The Haunted Mansion and find extremely long lines. It's possible that this is a temporary situation caused by several hundred people arriving en masse from a recently concluded performance of *The Hall of Presidents* nearby. If this is the case, skip The Haunted Mansion and go to the next step, returning later to retry The Haunted Mansion.

What to Do if You Get Off Track

If an unexpected interruption or problem throws the touring plan off, consult "Magic Kingdom: Recommended Attraction Visitation Times" (page 761) for preferred times of day to visit attractions.

Park Opening Procedures

Your success during your first hour of touring will be affected somewhat by the opening procedure Disney uses that day:

A. All guests are held at the turnstiles until the entire park opens (which may or may not be at the official opening time). If this happens on the day you visit, blow past Main Street and head for the first attraction on the touring plan you're following.

B. Guests are admitted to Main Street a half hour to an hour before the remaining lands open. Access to other lands will be blocked by a rope barrier at the central hub end of Main Street. Once admitted, stake out a position at the rope barrier as follows:

If you're going to Frontierland first (Splash Mountain and Big Thunder Mountain Railroad), stand in front of The Crystal Palace restaurant, on the left at the central hub end of Main Street. Wait next to the rope barrier blocking the walkway to Adventureland. When the rope is dropped, move quickly to Frontierland by way of Adventureland. This is also the place to line up if your first stop is Adventureland.

If you're going to Buzz Lightyear and Space Mountain first, wait at the entrance of the bridge to Tomorrowland. When the rope drops, dash across into Tomorrowland.

If you're going to Fantasyland or Liberty Square first, go to the end of Main Street and line up left of center at the rope.

If you're going to Mickey's Toontown Fair first, go to the Main Street Station of the Walt Disney World Railroad and board the first train of the day. Disembark at the second stop. The train pulls out of the Main Street Station at the same time the rope is dropped at the central hub end of Main Street.

Before You Go

1. Call (407) 824-4321 the day before you go to check the official opening time.
2. Purchase admission before you arrive.
3. Familiarize yourself with park opening procedures (above) and reread the touring plan you've chosen so that you know what you're likely to encounter.

Magic Kingdom One-Day Touring Plan for Adults

For Adults without young children.
Assumes Willingness to experience all major rides (including roller coasters) and shows.

This plan requires considerable walking and some backtracking; this is necessary to avoid long lines. Extra walking plus some morning hustle will spare you two to three hours of standing in line. You might not complete the tour. How far you get depends on how quickly you move from ride to ride, how many times you rest or eat, how quickly the park fills, and what time the park closes.

1. If you're a Disney hotel guest, use Disney transportation to commute to the park, arriving 40 minutes before official opening time.

   If you're a day guest, arrive at the Magic Kingdom's parking lot 50 minutes before official opening time. Arrive 90 minutes before official opening time if it's a holiday period. Add 15 minutes to the above if you have to buy your admission. These arrivals give you time to park and catch the tram to the Transportation and Ticket Center. At the TTC, transfer to the monorail or ferry to reach the park's entrance. If the line for the monorail is short, take the monorail; otherwise, catch the ferry.

2. At the park, proceed through the turnstiles and have one person go to City Hall for guidemaps and the daily entertainment schedule.

3. Regroup and move quickly down Main Street to the central hub. Because the Magic Kingdom has two opening procedures, you probably will encounter one of the following:
   a. The entire park will be open. In this case, proceed quickly to Space Mountain in Tomorrowland.
   b. Only Main Street will be open. In this case, go to the central hub and position yourself at the entrance to Tomorrowland. When the rope barrier is dropped at opening time, walk as fast as possible to Space Mountain. Ride.

4. Backtrack toward the entrance to Tomorrowland, bearing left to Buzz Lightyear's Space Ranger Spin. Ride.

5. After Buzz, proceed to Fantasyland via Tommorowland passing the Tomorrowland Speedway en route. In Fantasyland, experience The Many Adventures of Winnie the Pooh.

6. Exit left from Winnie the Pooh and ride Snow White's Adventure next door.

7. Cross Fantasyland Plaza in the direction of Liberty Square and ride Peter Pan's Flight.

8. Across from Peter Pan, ride It's a Small World.

9. Exit Small World and bear right to Liberty Square. Experience the Haunted Mansion.

10. Proceed right after departing the Haunted Mansion and follow the Liberty Square waterfront into Frontierland and on to Splash Mountain. At Splash Mountain, obtain a FASTPASS.

11. Next door to Splash Mountain, ride Big Thunder Mountain Railroad.

12. Proceed to Adventureland via the bridge in front of Splash Mountain. In Adventureland, experience Pirates of the Caribbean.

13. By now it should be time to return and ride Splash Mountain using your FASTPASS. If you still have some time to kill, try the Swiss Family Treehouse in Adventureland.

14. At this point you will have most of the Magic Kingdom bottlenecks in the rearview mirror. Feel free to stop for lunch, a break, or scheduled live entertainment.

15. Catch the Walt Disney Railroad at the Frontierland station next to Splash Mountain. Ride the train to Mickey's Toontown Fair.

16. Tour Mickey's Toontown Fair.

17. Reboard the train at Mickey's Toontown Fair and complete your round trip, disembarking at the Frontierland Station.

18. Return to Adventureland. Obtain a FASTPASS for the Jungle Cruise.

19. In Adventureland, drop in on the *Enchanted Tiki Birds*.

20. Cross the plaza passing the Aladdin ride and cut through the passage into Frontierland. Bear left (yuk, yuk) and see the *Country Bear Jamboree*.

21. Return to Adventureland through the same passage. Ride the Jungle Cruise using your FASTPASS. Skip to Step 22 if you still have some time to kill before your FASTPASS return window starts.

22. Explore the Swiss Family Treehouse if you didn't see it earlier.

23. Return to Liberty Square via the passage opposite Aladdin. Experience the *Liberty Belle* Riverboat and *The Hall of Presidents* in whichever order is most convenient.

24. Return to Tomorrowland via the central hub and experience *Alien Encounter*.

25. Also in Tomorrowland, ride the Tomorrowland Transit Authority.

26. Also in Tomorowland, see *The Timekeeper* and the *Carousel of Progress* if they are operating (both open only occasionally according to attendance levels).

27. Experience any attractions you might have missed. View any parades, fireworks, or live performances that interest you. Grab a bite. Save Main Street for last because it remains open after the rest of the park closes.

28. Browse Main Street.

Author's Selective Magic Kingdom One-Day Touring Plan for Adults

For Adults touring without young children.
Assumes Willingness to experience all major rides (including roller coasters) and shows.

This plan includes only those attractions the author believes are the best in the Magic Kingdom. It requires a lot of walking and some backtracking to avoid long lines. Extra walking and morning hustle will spare you three or more hours of standing in line. You might not complete the tour. How far you get depends on how quickly you move from ride to ride, how many times you rest or eat, how quickly the park fills, and what time the park closes.

1. If you're a Disney hotel guest, use Disney transportation to commute to the park, arriving 40 minutes before official opening time.

   If you're a day guest, arrive at the parking lot 50 minutes before the Magic Kingdom's official opening time. Arrive 90 minutes earlier than official opening if it's a holiday period. Add 15 minutes to the above if you must buy your admission. These arrivals will give you time to park and catch the tram to the Transportation and Ticket Center. At the TTC, transfer to the monorail or ferry to reach the park's entrance. If the line for the monorail is short, take the monorail; otherwise, catch the ferry.

2. At the park, proceed through the turnstiles and have one person go to City Hall for guidemaps and the daily entertainment schedule.

3. Regroup and move quickly down Main Street to the central hub. Because the Magic Kingdom has two opening procedures, you probably will encounter one of the following:

   a. The entire park will be open. In this case, proceed quickly to Space Mountain in Tomorrowland.

   b. Only Main Street will be open. In this case, proceed to the central hub and position yourself at the entrance to Tomorrowland. When the rope drops, head to Space Mountain.

4. Backtrack toward the entrance to Tomorrowland, bearing left to Buzz Lightyear's Space Ranger Spin. Ride.

5. After Buzz, proceed to Fantasyland via Tommorowland, passing the Tomorrowland Speedway en route. In Fantasyland, experience The Many Adventures of Winnie the Pooh.

6. Exit left from Winnie the Pooh, cross Fantasyland Plaza in the direction of Liberty Square, and ride Peter Pan's Flight.

7. Across from Peter Pan, ride It's a Small World.

8. Exit Small World and bear right to Liberty Square. Experience the Haunted Mansion.

9. Proceed right after departing the Haunted Mansion and follow the Liberty Square waterfront into Frontierland and on to Splash Mountain. At Splash Mountain, obtain a FASTPASS.

10. Next door to Splash Mountain, ride Big Thunder Mountain Railroad.

11. Proceed to Adventureland via the bridge in front of Splash Mountain. In Adventureland, experience Pirates of the Caribbean.

12. By now it should be time to return and ride Splash Mountain using your FASTPASS. If you still have some time to kill, try the Swiss Family Treehouse in Adventureland.

13. At this point, you will have most of the Magic Kingdom bottlenecks in the rearview mirror. Feel free to stop for lunch, a break, or scheduled live entertainment.

14. Catch the Walt Disney Railroad at the Frontierland station next to Splash Mountain. Ride the train to Mickey's Toontown Fair. Toontown doesn't hold much appeal for adults. If you think you can live without it, stay on the train for a round trip all the way back to Frontierland and skip to Step 17.

15. Tour Mickey's Toontown Fair.

16. Reboard the train at Mickey's Toontown Fair and complete your round trip, disembarking at the Frontierland Station.

17. Return to Adventureland. Obtain a FASTPASS for the Jungle Cruise.

18. In Adventureland, drop in on the *Enchanted Tiki Birds*.

19. Cross the plaza passing the Aladdin ride and cut through the passage into Frontierland. Bear left and see the *Country Bear Jamboree*.

20. Return to Adventureland through the same passage. Ride the Jungle Cruise using your FASTPASS. Skip to Step 21 if you still have some time to kill before your FASTPASS return window starts.

21. Explore the Swiss Family Treehouse if you didn't see it earlier.

22. Return to Liberty Square via the passage opposite Aladdin. Experience the *Liberty Belle* Riverboat and *The Hall of Presidents* in whichever order is most convenient.

23. Return to Tomorrowland via the central hub and experience *Alien Encounter*.

24. Also in Tomorrowland, see *The Timekeeper* and the *Carousel of Progress* if they are operating (both open only occasionally according to attendance levels).

25. Experience any attractions you might have missed. View any parades, fireworks, or live performances that interest you. Grab a bite. Save Main Street for last because it remains open after the rest of the park closes.

26. Browse Main Street.

Magic Kingdom One-Day Touring Plan for Parents with Young Children

For Parents with children younger than age eight.

Assumes Periodic stops for rest, rest rooms, and refreshments.

This plan represents a compromise between the observed tastes of adults and those of younger children. Included are many amusement park rides that children may have the opportunity to experience at fairs and amusement parks back home. Although these rides are included in the plan, omit them if possible. These cycle-loading rides often have long lines, consuming valuable touring time:

Mad Tea Party	Dumbo the Flying Elephant
Cinderella's Golden Carrousel	Magic Carpets of Aladdin

This time could be better spent experiencing the many attractions that better demonstrate the Disney creative genius and are found only in the Magic Kingdom. Instead of this plan, try either of the one-day plans for adults and take advantage of "switching off." This allows parents and young children to enter the ride together. At the boarding area, one parent watches the children while the other rides.

Before entering the park, decide whether you will return to your hotel for a midday rest. We strongly recommend that you break from touring and return to your hotel for a swim and a nap (even if you aren't lodging in Walt Disney World). You won't see as much, but everyone will be more relaxed and happy.

This touring plan requires a lot of walking and some backtracking to avoid long lines. A little extra walking and some morning hustle will spare you two to three hours of standing in line. You probably won't complete the tour. How far you get depends on how quickly you move from ride to ride, how many times you rest or eat, how quickly the park fills, and what time the park closes.

1. If you're a Disney hotel guest, use Disney transportation to commute to the park, arriving 40 minutes before official opening time.

   If you're a day guest, arrive at the parking lot 50 minutes before the Magic Kingdom's official opening time. Arrive 90 minutes earlier than official opening if it's a holiday period. Add 15 minutes to the above if you must purchase your admission. These arrivals will give you time to park and catch the tram to the Transportation and Ticket Center. At the TTC, transfer to the monorail or ferry to reach the park's entrance. If the line for the monorail is short, take the monorail; otherwise, catch the ferry.

2. At the Magic Kingdom, proceed through the turnstiles and have one person go to City Hall for guidemaps and the daily entertainment schedule.

3. Rent strollers (if necessary).

4. Move briskly to the end of Main Street. If the entire park is open, go quickly to Fantasyland. Otherwise, position your group by the rope barrier at the central hub. When the park opens and the barrier drops, go through the main door of the castle and ride Dumbo the Flying Elephant in Fantasyland.

5. Enjoy The Many Adventures of Winnie the Pooh. Use the standby line—*not* FASTPASS.

6. Ride Peter Pan's Flight. Use the standby line—*not* FASTPASS.

7. Across the walkway, ride It's a Small World.

8. Head toward the castle. See *Mickey's PhilharMagic* on your right.

9. Exit *Mickey's PhilharMagic* and bear left, passing Peter Pan, and cross into Liberty Square. In Liberty Square, experience the Haunted Mansion, directly on your right.

10. On exiting the Haunted Mansion, head towards Frontierland, keeping the waterfront on your right. To the left of the Frontierland Shootin' Arcade is a passageway the leads directly to Adventureland. Continue to Adventureland and ride the Jungle Cruise. If the wait exceeds 30 minutes, use FASTPASS.

11. Turn left on exiting the Jungle Cruise and head for Frontierland. In Frontierland, take the rafts to Tom Sawyer Island. Allocate at least 30 minutes for your kids to explore the island.

12. Return via raft to the mainland. If you have a FASTPASS for the Jungle Cruise, go ahead and ride. If you need to kill some time before your FAST-PASS time slot, explore the Swiss Family Treehouse, next door to the Jungle Cruise. If you've already experienced the Jungle Cruise, skip ahead to Step 13.

13. Proceed to the Frontierland railroad station, situated on the far right side of Splash Mountain. Take the Walt Disney World Railroad from Frontierland to Main Street USA. Depart the Magic Kingdom for lunch and a nap. If you insist on forgoing the nap, skip the train ride and proceed to Step 15.

14. After your afternoon break, return refreshed to the Magic Kingdom and head for Splash Mountain in Frontierland on foot or via the railroad from the Main Street Station. Be advised that the train is suggested solely to save some walking. There's virtually nothing to see between Main Street and the Frontierland station.

15. In Frontierland, obtain FASTPASSes for Splash Mountain.

16. In Frontierland, see the *Country Bear Jamboree*.

17. Return to Adventureland and ride Pirates of the Caribbean.

18. In Adventureland, explore the Swiss Family Treehouse if you didn't see it earlier.

19. Return to Splash Mountain and ride using your FASTPASSes. If your kids aren't up for Splash Mountain, take advantage of switching off. If you still have some time remaining before your FASTPASS window, ride the *Liberty Belle* Riverboat.

20. After Splash Mountain, cross the park to Tomorrowland via the central hub. On entering Tomorrowland, obtain FASTPASSes for Buzz Lightyear if the return time is acceptable to you. Be aware that on exceedingly busy days, all of the FASTPASSes may have been distributed.

21. In Tomorrowland, ride the Tomorrowland Transit Authority.

22. Keeping the Tomorrowland Indy Speedway on your right, proceed to Mickey's Toontown Fair and explore.

23. If you have FASTPASSes for Buzz Lightyear, return to Tomorrowland and ride. If not, this ends the touring plan. If you have any energy left, check the daily entertainment schedule for live shows, fireworks, and parades.

To Convert This One-Day Touring Plan into a Two-Day Touring Plan

Skip steps 14–23 on the first day. On the second day, arrive 30 minutes prior to opening, take the Walt Disney World Railroad from Main Street to Frontierland, and pick up the plan with step 15, but do not use FAST-PASS unless the wait exceeds 35 minutes.

Magic Kingdom Dumbo-or-Die-in-a-Day Touring Plan for Parents with Young Children

For Adults compelled to devote every waking moment to the pleasure and entertainment of their young children, or rich people who are paying someone else to take their children to the theme park.

Prerequisite This plan is designed for days when the Magic Kingdom doesn't close until 9 p.m. or later.

Assumes Frequent stops for rest, rest rooms, and refreshment.

Note: Name aside, this touring plan is not a joke. Regardless of whether you're loving, guilty, masochistic, selfless, insane, or saintly, this itinerary will provide a young child with about as perfect a day as is possible at the Magic Kingdom.

This plan is a concession to adults determined to give their young children the ultimate Magic Kingdom experience. It addresses the preferences, needs, and desires of young children to the virtual exclusion of those of adults or older siblings. If you left the kids with a sitter yesterday or wouldn't let little Marvin eat barbecue for breakfast, this plan will expiate your guilt. It is also a wonderful itinerary if you're paying a sitter, nanny, or chauffeur to take your children to the Magic Kingdom.

1. If you're a Disney hotel guest, use Disney transportation to commute to the park, arriving 40 minutes before official opening time.

    If you're a day guest, arrive at the parking lot 50 minutes before the Magic Kingdom's official opening time. Arrive 90 minutes earlier than official opening if it's a holiday period. Add 15 minutes to the above if you must purchase your admission. These arrivals will give you time to park and catch the tram to the Transportation and Ticket Center. At the TTC, transfer to the monorail or ferry to reach the park's entrance. If the line for the monorail is short, take the monorail; otherwise, catch the ferry.

2. At the Magic Kingdom, proceed through the turnstiles and have one person go to City Hall for guidemaps and the daily entertainment schedule.

3. Rent a stroller (if needed).

4. Move briskly to the end of Main Street. If the entire park is open, go quickly to Fantasyland. Otherwise, position your group by the rope barrier at the central hub. When the park opens and the barrier is dropped, go through the main door of the castle to Cinderella's Royal Table, on your right as you enter Cinderella Castle.

5. Make a dinner priority seating at the Royal Table for 7 p.m. Eating there will let your kids see the inside of the castle and possibly meet Cinderella. To make your priority seating before you leave home, call (407) 939-3463.

6. Enter Fantasyland. Ride Dumbo the Flying Elephant.

7. Hey, you're on vacation! Ride again, using the Chuck Bubba Relay if there are two adults in your party (page 257–258).

8. Experience The Many Adventures of Winnie the Pooh, near Dumbo. Use the standby line *not* FASTPASS.

9. Ride Peter Pan's Flight. Use the standby line—*not* FASTPASS.

10. Ride Cinderella's Golden Carrousel.

11. In Tomorrowland, ride the Tomorrowland Speedway. Let your child steer (cars run on a guide rail) while you work the foot pedal.

12. Ride the Astro Orbiter. *Safety note:* Seat your children in the vehicle before you get in. Also, the Astro Orbiter goes higher and faster than Dumbo and may frighten some children.

13. Ride Buzz Lightyear's Space Ranger Spin (near Astro Orbiter). Do not use FASTPASS.

14. Return to Main Street via the central hub and leave the park for your hotel. Eat lunch and rest. (Have your hand stamped for re-entry when you leave the park. Keep your parking receipt to show upon return so you won't have to pay again for parking.) If you elect not to take a break out of the park, skip to Step 17.

15. Return to the Magic Kingdom refreshed about 4 or 4:30 p.m. Take the Walt Disney World Railroad to Frontierland.

16. Take the raft to Tom Sawyer Island. Stay as long as the kids want. If you're hungry, Aunt Polly's Dockside Inn on Tom Sawyer Island is a winner for both kids and adults.

17. After you return from the island, see the *Country Bear Jamboree*.

18. Return to the Frontierland Station. Ride the train to Mickey's Toontown Fair.

19. Walk through Mickey's Country House and Minnie's Country House and play on Donald's Boat (tips for the latter are on page 459). Meet Disney characters at the Toontown Hall of Fame and pose for photos.

20. You should be within an hour of your dinner priority seating at Cinderella's Royal Table. Take the direct path from Mickey's Toontown Fair to

Fantasyland. In Fantasyland, if you have 20 minutes or more before your priority seating, ride It's a Small World. Don't forget to sing.

21. After dinner, see *Mickey's PhilharMagic,* also in Fantasyland.

22. Leave Fantasyland and go to Liberty Square. If your children are up to it, see The Haunted Mansion. If not, skip to Step 23.

23. Evening parades are quite worthwhile. If you're interested, adjust the remainder of the touring plan to allow you to take a viewing position about 10 minutes before the early parade starts (usually 8 or 9 p.m.). See our recommendations for good vantage points (pages 474–475). If you aren't interested in the parade, enjoy attractions in Adventureland while the parade is in progress. Lines will be vastly diminished.

24. Go to Adventureland by way of Liberty Square, Frontierland, or the central hub. Take the Jungle Cruise if the lines aren't long. If they're prohibitive, obtain FASTPASSes and experience *Enchanted Tiki Birds,* Magic Carpets of Aladdin, and Swiss Family Treehouse. If your children can stand a few skeletons, also see Pirates of the Caribbean.

25. After the birds, carpets, treehouse, and pirates, return with your FAST-PASSes to ride the Jungle Cruise.

26. If you have time or energy left, repeat any attractions the kids especially liked, or try ones on the plan you might have bypassed because of long lines. Buy Goofy hats if that cranks your tractor.

27. If you're parked at the Transportation and Ticket Center, catch the ferry or express monorail. If the express monorail line is long, catch the resort monorail and disembark at the TTC.

To Convert This One-Day Touring Plan into a Two-Day Touring Plan

Skip steps 19 and 20 on the first day. On the second day, arrive 30 minutes prior to opening and take the Walt Disney World Railroad from Main Street to Mickey's Toontown Fair. See Mickey's Toontown Fair in its entirety.

Magic Kingdom Two-Day Touring Plan

For Parties wishing to spread their Magic Kingdom visit over two days.

Assumes Willingness to experience all major rides (including roller coasters) and shows.

Timing: This two-day touring plan takes advantage of early-morning touring. Each day, you should complete the structured part of the plan by about 4 p.m. This leaves plenty of time for live entertainment. If the park is open late (after 8 p.m.), consider returning to your hotel at midday for a swim and a nap. Eat an early dinner outside Walt Disney World and return refreshed to enjoy the park's nighttime festivities.

Day One

1. If you're a Disney hotel guest, use Disney transportation to commute to the park, arriving 40 minutes before official opening time.

    If you're a day guest, arrive at the parking lot 50 minutes before the Magic Kingdom's official opening time. Arrive 90 minutes earlier than official opening if it's a holiday period. Add 15 minutes to the above if you must purchase your admission. These arrivals will give you time to park and catch the tram to the Transportation and Ticket Center. At the TTC, transfer to the monorail or ferry to reach the park's entrance. If the line for the monorail is short, take the monorail; otherwise, catch the ferry.

2. At the park, proceed through the turnstiles and have one person go to City Hall for guidemaps and the daily entertainment schedule.

3. Move as fast as you can down Main Street to the central hub. Because the Magic Kingdom uses two procedures for opening, you probably will encounter one of the following:
    a. The entire park will be open. In this case, proceed quickly to Space Mountain in Tomorrowland.
    b. Only Main Street will be open. In this case, position yourself in the central hub at the entrance to Tomorrowland. When the park opens and the rope barrier drops, walk as fast as possible to Space Mountain.

4. After exiting Space Mountain, proceed to Fantasyland via the central hub. Bear left after passing through the castle. Experience the Many Adventures of Winnie the Pooh.

5. Exit Pooh and bear left past the carousel to Peter Pan's Flight. Ride.

6. Exit Peter Pan to the right and see *Mickey's PhilharMagic*.

7. Also in Fantasyland, ride It's a Small World.

8. Exit Small World to the right and proceed to Liberty Square. Immediately on entering, turn right to the Haunted Mansion. Enjoy.

9. Also in Liberty Square, ride the riverboat.

10. Feel free to stop for lunch from this point on. Fast food eateries that are generally less crowded include the Columbia Harbour House in Liberty Square and Aunt Polly's Dockside Inn on Tom Sawyer Island. As a lunchtime alternative, check the daily entertainment schedule for the next performance of *The Diamond Horseshoe Saloon Revue*. If the timing is right, grab a sandwich there to eat while enjoying the show.

11. Also in Liberty Square, see *The Hall of Presidents*.

12. Continue along the waterfront into Frontierland. See the *Country Bear Jamboree*. At this point, check the daily entertainment schedule for parades and other live performances that might interest you. Because you already have seen all the attractions that cause bottlenecks and have long lines, interrupting the touring plan here won't cause any problems. Simply pick up where you left off before the parade or show.

13. At the Frontierland waterfront, take a raft to Tom Sawyer Island. Explore.

14. After returning from Tom Sawyer Island, head for Tomorrowland via the central hub.

15. In Tomorrowland, see *Alien Encounter.*

16. Also in Tomorrowland, ride the Tomorrowland Transit Authority.

17. This concludes the touring plan for the day. Enjoy the shops, see some of the live entertainment, or revisit favorite attractions until you're ready to leave.

Day Two

1. If you're a Disney hotel guest, use Disney transportation to commute to the park, arriving 40 minutes before official opening time.

   If you're a day guest, arrive at the parking lot 50 minutes before the Magic Kingdom's official opening time. Arrive 90 minutes earlier than official opening if it's a holiday period. Add 15 minutes to the above if you must purchase your admission. These arrivals will give you time to park and catch the tram to the Transportation and Ticket Center. At the TTC, transfer to the monorail or ferry to reach the park's entrance. If the line for the monorail is short, take the monorail; otherwise, catch the ferry.

2. At the park, proceed through the turnstiles. Stop at City Hall for guidemaps containing the day's entertainment schedule.

3. Proceed to the end of Main Street. If the entire park is open, go immediately to Buzz Lightyear in Tomorrowland and ride. Otherwise, position yourself along the rope at the netrance to Tomorrowland and wait to be admitted. When the rope drops, go directly to Buzz Lightyear.

4. After Buzz Lightyear, head for Frontierland via the central hub. In Frontierland, ride Splash Mountain. Do not use FASTPASS.

5. Ride Big Thunder Mountain Railroad, next to Splash Mountain.

6. Proceed to Adventureland. Ride the Jungle Cruise. If the wait seems prohibitive, use FASTPASS.

7. Across the street, see *Enchanted Tiki Birds.*

8. Walk through the Swiss Family Treehouse.

9. Exit the Treehouse to the left. Enjoy Pirates of the Caribbean. *Note:* At this point, check the daily entertainment schedule to see if any parades or live performances interest you. Note the times, and alter the touring plan accordingly. Since you already have seen all the attractions that cause bottlenecks and have big lines, interrupting the touring plan here won't cause any problems. Simply pick up where you left off before the parade or show.

10. If you're hungry, eat. Fast-food eateries that are generally are less crowded include the Columbia Harbour House in Liberty Square, Aunt Polly's Dockside Inn on Tom Sawyer Island in Frontierland, and The Crystal Palace at the central hub end of Main Street.

11. Exit Adventureland and go to the Frontierland train station between Splash and Big Thunder Mountains. Catch the Walt Disney World Railroad. Disembark at Mickey's Toontown Fair (first stop).

12. Tour the Fair and meet the Disney characters.

13. Exit the Fair via the path to Tomorrowland.

14. In Tomorrowland, if you haven't eaten, try Cosmic Ray's Starlight Cafe or The Plaza Pavilion.

15. See *Walt Disney's Carousel of Progress* (open seasonally).

16. See *The Timekeeper* (open seasonally).

17. This concludes the touring plan. Enjoy the shops, see live entertainment, or revisit your favorite attractions until you are ready to leave.

Part Eleven

Epcot

Overview

Education, inspiration, and corporate imagery are the focus at Epcot, the most adult of the Disney theme parks. What it gains in taking a futuristic, visionary, and technological look at the world, it loses, just a bit, in warmth, happiness, and charm.

Some people find the attempts at education to be superficial; others want more entertainment and less education. Most visitors, however, are in between, finding plenty of entertainment *and* education.

Epcot is more than twice as big as the Magic Kingdom or Disney-MGM Studios and, though smaller than the Animal Kingdom, has more territory to be covered on foot. Epcot rarely sees the congestion so common to the Magic Kingdom, but it has lines every bit as long as those at the Jungle Cruise or Space Mountain. Visitors must come prepared to do considerable walking among attractions and a comparable amount of standing in line.

Epcot's size means you can't see it all in one day without skipping an attraction or two and giving others a cursory glance. A major difference between Epcot and the other parks, however, is that some Epcot attractions can be savored slowly or skimmed, depending on personal interests. For example, the first section of General Motors' Test Track is a thrill ride, the second a collection of walk-through exhibits. Nearly all visitors take the ride, but many people, lacking time or interest, bypass the exhibits.

We have identified several Epcot attractions as "not to be missed." But part of the enjoyment of the park is that there's something for everyone. Ask your group. They're sure to have a variety of opinions as to which attraction is "best."

Operating Hours

Epcot has two theme areas: Future World and World Showcase. Each has its own operating hours. Though schedules change throughout the year,

Future World always opens before World Showcase in the morning and usually closes before World Showcase in the evening. Most of the year, World Showcase opens two hours later than Future World. For exact hours during your visit, call (407) 824-4321.

Arriving

Plan to arrive at the turnstiles 30–40 minutes prior to official opening time. Give yourself an extra 10 minutes or so to park and make your way to the entrance. If you are a guest at one of the Epcot resorts, it will take you about 20–30 minutes to walk from your hotel to the Future World section of Epcot.

Arriving at the park by private automobile is easy and direct. Epcot has its own parking lot and, unlike at the Magic Kingdom, there's no need to take a monorail or ferry to reach the entrance. Trams serve the parking lot, or you can walk to the front gate. Monorail service connects Epcot with the Transportation and Ticket Center, the Magic Kingdom (transfer required), and Magic Kingdom resorts (transfer required).

NOT TO BE MISSED AT EPCOT

World Showcase	The American Adventure
	IllumiNations
Future World	Spaceship Earth
	Living with the Land
	Honey, I Shrunk the Audience
	Test Track
	Body Wars
	Cranium Command
	Mission Space (opens 2003)

Getting Oriented

Epcot's theme areas are distinctly different. Future World combines Disney creativity and major corporations' technological resources to examine where mankind has come from and where it's going. World Showcase features landmarks, cuisine, and culture of almost a dozen nations and is meant to be a sort of permanent World's Fair.

Navigating Epcot is unlike getting around at the Magic Kingdom. The Magic Kingdom is designed so that nearly every location is part of a specific environment—Liberty Square or Main Street, U.S.A., for example. All environments are visually separated to preserve the atmosphere. It wouldn't do for the Jungle Cruise to pass beneath the futuristic spires of Space Mountain, for instance.

Epcot, by contrast, is visually open. And while it seems strange to see a Japanese pagoda and the Eiffel Tower on the same horizon, getting around is fairly simple. An exception is in Future World, where the enormous east and west Innoventions buildings hide everything on their opposite sides.

Cinderella Castle is the central landmark at the Magic Kingdom. At Epcot, the architectural symbol is Spaceship Earth. This shiny, 180-foot geosphere is visible from almost everywhere in the park. Like Cinderella Castle at the Magic Kingdom, Spaceship Earth can help you keep track of where you are in Epcot. But it's in a high-traffic area and isn't centrally located, so it isn't a good meeting place.

Any of the distinctive national pavilions in World Showcase makes a good meeting place, but be specific. "Hey, let's meet in Japan!" sounds fun, but each pavilion is a mini-town with buildings, monuments, gardens, and plazas. You could wander quite awhile "in Japan" without finding your group. Pick a specific place in Japan—the sidewalk side of the pagoda, for example.

The EPCOT Acronym

"Epcot" originally was "EPCOT." When envisioned by Walt Disney as a utopian working city of the future, EPCOT was the acronym for Experimental Prototype Community Of Tomorrow. Corporate Disney ultimately altered Walt's vision and the city became a theme park, but the name remained. Because EPCOT, however, was clearly nothing of the sort, the acronym "EPCOT" became the name "Epcot."

Future World Attractions

Gleaming, futuristic structures of immense proportions define the first theme area you encounter at Epcot. Broad thoroughfares are punctuated with billowing fountains—all reflected in shining, space-age facades. Everything, including landscaping, is sparkling clean and seems bigger than life. Pavilions dedicated to mankind's past, present, and future technological accomplishments form the perimeter of Future World. Front and center is Spaceship Earth, flanked by Innoventions East and West.

Most Epcot services are concentrated in Future World's Entrance Plaza, near the main gate.

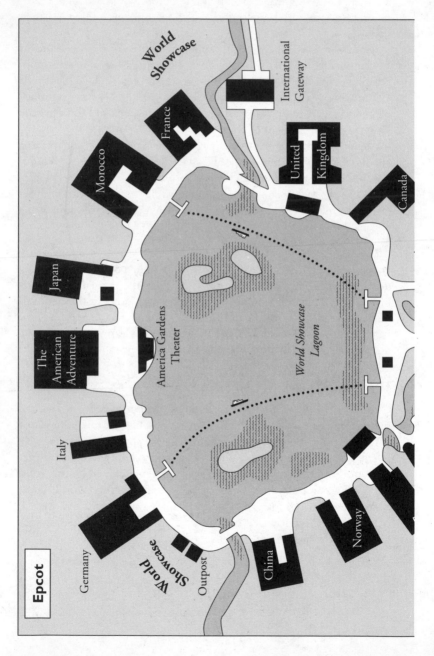

Epcot

World Showcase

International Gateway

France

Morocco

United Kingdom

Canada

Japan

World Showcase Lagoon

The American Adventure

America Gardens Theater

Italy

Germany

World Showcase

Outpost

China

Norway

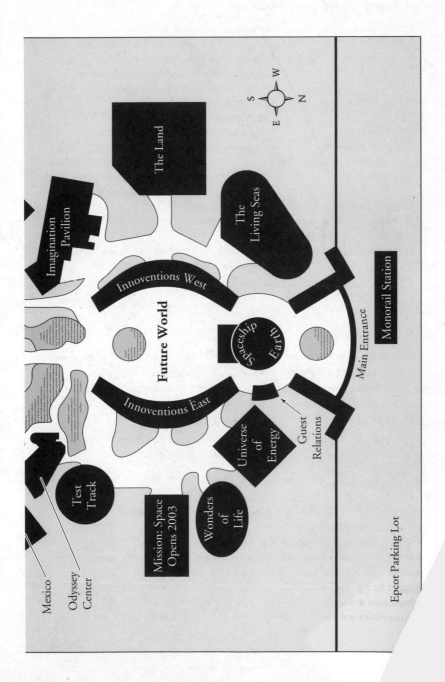

FUTURE WORLD SERVICES

Epcot's service facilities in Future World include:

Wheelchair & Stroller Rental	Inside the main entrance and to the left, toward the rear of the Entrance Plaza
Banking Services	ATMs are outside the main entrance near the kennels, on the Future World bridge, and in World Showcase at the Germany pavilion.
Storage Lockers	Turn right at Spaceship Earth (lockers are cleaned out nightly).
Lost & Found	At the main entrance at the gift shop
Live Entertainment & Parade Information	At Guest Relations, left of Spaceship Earth
Lost Persons	At Guest Relations and the Baby Center on the World Showcase side of the Odyssey Center
Dining Priority Seating	At Guest Relations
Walt Disney World & Local Attraction Information	At Guest Relations
First Aid	Next to the Baby Center on the World Showcase side of the Odyssey Center
Baby Center/ Baby-Care Needs	On the World Showcase side of the Odyssey Center

Guest Relations

Description and Comments   Guest Relations, left of the geodesic sphere, is Epcot's equivalent of the Magic Kingdom's City Hall. It serves as park headquarters and as Epcot's primary information center. Attendants staff information booths and take same-day priority seating for Epcot restaurants.

Touring Tips   If you wish to eat in one of Epcot's sit-down restaurants, you can make your priority seating at Guest Relations.

Spaceship Earth

What It Is Educational dark ride through past, present, and future
Scope & Scale Headliner
When to Go Before 10 a.m. or after 4 p.m.
~ial Comments If lines are long when you arrive, try again after 4 p.m.
's Rating One of Epcot's best; not to be missed; ★★★★
~ge Group

★	Grade School ★★★★	Teens ★★★½
½	Over 30 ★★★★	Senior Citizens ★★★★

Duration of Ride About 16 minutes
Average Wait in Line per 100 People ahead of You 3 minutes
Loading Speed Fast

Description and Comments This AT&T ride spirals through the 18-story interior of Epcot's premier landmark, taking visitors past audio-animatronic scenes depicting mankind's developments in communications, from cave painting to printing to television to space communications and computer networks. The ride is well done and an amazing use of the geosphere's interior.

Touring Tips Because it's near Epcot's main entrance, Spaceship Earth is inundated with arriving guests throughout the morning. If you're interested in riding Test Track, postpone Spaceship Earth until, say, after 4 p.m. Spaceship Earth loads continuously and quickly. If the line runs only along the right side of the sphere, you'll board in less than 15 minutes.

Global Neighborhood

What It Is Interactive communications playground
Scope & Scale Diversion
When to Go After riding Spaceship Earth
Special Comments Spaceship Earth disembarks passengers directly into the Global Neighborhood
Author's Rating AT&T infomercial; ★★
Appeal by Age Group

Pre-school ★½	Grade School ★★	Teens ★★
Young Adults ★★	Over 30 ★★	Senior Citizens ★★

Duration of Attraction Not limited
Average Wait in Line per 100 People ahead of You No wait

Description and Comments Global Neighborhood is at the base of the geosphere. Presented by AT&T, it's a walk-through playground of futuristic, interactive communications devices.

Touring Tips If Spaceship Earth is busy, the Global Neighborhood will be, too. If you want to spend some time there, go during late afternoon or evening. You don't have to ride Spaceship Earth to enter the Global Neighborhood. Walk directly in from the plaza on the far side of the geosphere.

Innoventions

What It Is Static and "hands-on" exhibits relating to products and technologies of the near future
Scope & Scale Major diversion
When to Go On your second day at Epcot or after you have seen all major attractions
Special Comments Most exhibits demand time and participation to be rewarding; not much gained here by a quick walk-through
Author's Rating Vastly improved; ★★★½

Appeal by Age Group

Pre-school ★½   Grade School ★★★½   Teens ★★★★

Young Adults ★★★½   Over 30 ★★★   Senior Citizens ★★★

Description and Comments   Innoventions consists of two huge, crescent-shaped, glass-walled structures separated by a central plaza. Formerly known as CommuniCore, the complex was designed to be the communications and community hub of Epcot, but something was lost in execution. During Epcot's first 12 years, CommuniCore was, at best, a staid museum of science and industry and, at worst, a huge obstacle to circumnavigate when you wanted to cross from one side of Future World to the other.

In 1994, Disney set out to return it to the original concept, this time with a marketplace rather than communications orientation. The result is a huge, busy collection of industry-sponsored, walk-through, hands-on exhibits. Dynamic, interactive, and forward-looking, Innoventions resembles a high-tech trade show. Products preview consumer and industrial goods of the near future. Electronics, communications, and entertainment technology play a prominent role. Exhibits, many of which are changed each year, demonstrate such products as virtual reality games, high-definition TV, voice-activated appliances, future cars, medical diagnostic equipment, and Internet applications. A cool addition in 2002 was the Segway Human Transporter, the much-publicized two-wheeled vehicle where riders look like they're standing on top of a push lawn mower. Each of the major exhibit areas is sponsored by a different manufacturer or research lab, emphasizing the effect of the products or technology on daily living. The most popular Innoventions attraction is an arcade of video and simulator games.

A welcome development at Innoventions is the floor plan introduced recently. For the first time since Innoventions debuted almost a decade ago, there's some logic to the layout. Where previously exhibits were jumbled together in truly bewildering juxtapositions with absolutely no regard to traffic flow, there is now a wide aisle, designed to look like a highway, that runs a nice, orderly route through the exhibits. There is even a printed roadmap available to help you find and identify exhibits.

Exhibits change periodically, and there is a definite trend toward larger, more elaborate exhibits, almost mini-attractions. The newer exhibits are certainly more compelling, but they require waiting in line to be admitted. Because the theater at each exhibit is quite small, you often wait as long for an Innoventions infomercial as for a real attraction elsewhere in the park.

Unofficial Guide reader response to Innoventions is mixed. A family from Port Chester, New York, writes:

> The more unstructured "interactive" parts were incredibly noisy and confusing—rather like a crowded video arcade with games that didn't work very well. Crowd control was poor. The setup leads to pushing and shoving to get to control boards. My kids, being small girls, didn't stand a chance of getting near anything. The display portions of the attraction "Home of the Future," etc., most clearly resembled a trade show at the Javits Center or the fixture displays at Home Depot. This whole pavilion seemed far more commercial than magical.

We receive a lot of complaints about how difficult it is for children (and even adults) to get a turn on Innoventions' more high-tech gadgets. This comment from a Michigan dad is typical:

A warning about Innoventions. All those wonderful Sega games are there, if you can fight off all the pubescent Sega-geeks. And they're free . . . some of them. The ones that your kids will want to play are not free. They are, however, right next to the free games, close enough to tempt your children and result in temper tantrums.

A father of three from Tulsa, Oklahoma, however, liked Innoventions:

The best things at Epcot for my kids were the hands-on exhibits at Innoventions. We bumped into the computer games there as we were passing through en route to something else (I don't remember what, because we never got there).

A mom from Bartlesville, Oklahoma, adds:

My 14-year-old son's favorite attraction was Innoventions. He spent hours there and would have spent more if we'd let him. All those free Sega games were a teenage boy's idea of heaven.

Touring Tips   Innoventions East and West provide visitors an opportunity to preview products of tomorrow in a fun, hands-on manner. Some exhibits are intriguing, while others are less compelling. We observed a wide range of reactions by visitors to the exhibits and can suggest only that you form your own opinion. Regarding touring strategy, spend time at Innoventions on your second day at Epcot. If you have only one day, visit during the evening if you have the time and endurance. Many exhibits, however, are technical and may not be compatible with your mood or energy toward the end of a long day. Also, you can't get much out of a walk-through; you have to invest time to understand what's going on.

The Igloo

Attached to (or growing from) the fountain side of Innoventions West is a tacky, besmirched, white igloo called Ice Station Cool. It doesn't look like much, but inside, this Coca Cola–sponsored exhibit provides free unlimited samples of soft drinks from around the world. Some of the selections will taste like medicine to an American, but others will please. Because it's centrally located in Future World, it makes a good meeting or break place, and you can slake your thirst while you wait for the rest of your party to arrive.

The Living Seas

What It Is   Ride beneath a huge saltwater aquarium, plus exhibits on oceanography, ocean ecology, and sea life
Scope & Scale   Major attraction
When to Go   Before 10 a.m. or after 3 p.m.
Special Comments   The ride is only a small component of this attraction
Author's Rating   An excellent marine exhibit; ★★★½
Appeal by Age Group

| Pre-school ★★★ | Grade School ★★★ | Teens ★★★ |
| Young Adults ★★★★ | Over 30 ★★★★ | Senior Citizens ★★★★ |

Duration of Ride 3 minutes
Average Wait in Line per 100 People ahead of You 3½ minutes
Loading Speed Fast

Description and Comments   The Living Seas is among Future World's most ambitious offerings. Scientists and divers conduct actual marine experiments in a 200-foot-diameter, 27-foot-deep main tank containing fish, mammals, and crustaceans in a simulation of an ocean ecosystem. Visitors can watch the activity through eight-inch-thick windows below the surface (including some in the Coral Reef restaurant) and aboard a three-part adventure ride consisting of a movie dramatizing the link between the ocean and man's survival, a simulated elevator descent to the bottom of the tank, and a three-minute gondola voyage through an underwater viewing tunnel.

The Living Seas' fish population is substantial, but the underwater ride is over almost before you're comfortably settled in the gondola. No matter, the strength of this attraction lies in the dozen or so exhibits offered afterward. Visitors can view fish-breeding experiments, watch short films about sea life, and more. The main aquarium, which the ride transits, can also be viewed through huge windows. Stay as long as you wish in the exhibit areas.

The Living Seas is a high-quality marine/aquarium exhibit, but it's no substitute for visiting SeaWorld, an outstanding marine theme park in Orlando. SeaWorld is on a par with the Disney theme parks in quality, appeal, educational value, and entertainment.

Touring Tips   Exhibits at the end of the ride are the best part of The Living Seas. In the morning, they're often bypassed by guests rushing to stay ahead of the crowd. The Living Seas needs to be lingered over when you aren't in a hurry. Go in late afternoon or evening, or on your second day at Epcot.

The Land Pavilion

Description and Comments   The Land is a huge pavilion containing three attractions and several restaurants. The original emphasis was on farming, but it now focuses on environmental concerns.

Touring Tips   This is a good place for a fast-food lunch. If you're there to see the attractions, however, don't go during mealtimes.

Living with the Land (FASTPASS)

What It Is   Indoor boat-ride adventure through the past, present, and future of U.S. farming and agriculture
Scope & Scale   Major attraction
When to Go   Before 10:30 a.m., after 7:30 p.m., or use FASTPASS
Special Comments   Take the ride early in the morning, but save other Land attractions for later in the day. It's located on the pavilion's lower level.
Author's Rating   Interesting and fun; not to be missed; ★★★★
Appeal by Age Group

Pre-school ★★½	Grade School ★★★	Teens ★★★½
Young Adults ★★★★	Over 30 ★★★★	Senior Citizens ★★★★

Duration of Ride   About 12 minutes

Average Wait in Line per 100 People ahead of You 3 minutes
Assumes 15 boats operating
Loading Speed Moderate

Description and Comments Boat ride takes visitors through swamps, past inhospitable farm environments, and through a futuristic, innovative greenhouse where real crops are grown using the latest agricultural technologies. Inspiring and educational, with excellent effects and good narrative.

Many Epcot guests who read about Living with the Land in guidebooks decide it sounds too dry and educational for their tastes. A woman from Houston, Texas, writes:

I had a bad attitude about Living with the Land, as I heard it was an agricultural exhibit. I just didn't think I was up for a movie about wheat farming. Wow, was I surprised. I really wished I had not had a preconceived idea about an exhibit. Living with the Land was truly wonderful.

Touring Tips See this attraction before the lunch crowd hits The Land restaurants or after 7:30 p.m.

If you really enjoy this ride or have a special interest in the agricultural techniques demonstrated, take the Behind the Seeds Greenhouse Tour. It's a one-hour guided walk behind the scenes for an in-depth examination of advanced and experimental growing methods. It costs $6 for adults and $4 for children ages three to nine. Reservations are made on a space-available basis at the guided tour waiting area (far right of the restaurants on the lower level).

Food Rocks

What It Is Audio-animatronic theater show about food and nutrition
Scope & Scale Minor attraction
When to Go Before 11 a.m. or after 2 p.m.
Special Comments On the lower level of The Land pavilion
Author's Rating Sugar-coated nutrition lesson; ★★½
Appeal by Age Group

Pre-school ★★★	Grade School ★★★	Teens ★★½
Young Adults ★★★	Over 30 ★★★	Senior Citizens ★★★

Duration of Presentation About 13 minutes
Preshow Entertainment None
Probable Waiting Time Less than 10 minutes

Description and Comments Audio-animatronic foods and cooking utensils perform in a marginally educational rock concert. Featured artists include the Peach Boys, Chubby Cheddar, Neil Moussaka, and Pita Gabriel. Little Richard provides the voice of a pineapple singing "Tutti Frutti." Fast-paced and imaginative, *Food Rocks* is better entertainment than its predecessor, *Kitchen Kabaret,* and delivers the proper-diet-and-balanced-nutrition message about as well.

Touring Tips One of the few light-entertainment offerings at Epcot. Slightly reminiscent of the *Country Bear Jamboree* in the Magic Kingdom (but not as humorous or endearing). The theater isn't large, but we have never encountered long waits, even during mealtimes.

Circle of Life Theater

What It Is Film exploring man's relationship with his environment
Scope & Scale Minor attraction
When to Go Before 11 a.m. and after 2 p.m.
Author's Rating Highly interesting and enlightening; ★★★½
Appeal by Age Group
  Pre-school ★★½   Grade School ★★★   Teens ★★½
  Young Adults ★★★   Over 30 ★★★   Senior Citizens ★★★
Duration of Presentation About 12½ minutes
Preshow Entertainment None
Probable Waiting Time 10–15 minutes

Description and Comments The featured attraction is *The Circle of Life,* starring Simba, Timon, and Pumbaa from Disney's animated feature *The Lion King.* This superb film spotlights the environmental interdependency of all creatures on earth, demonstrating how easily the ecological balance can be upset. It's sobering, but not too heavy-handed.

Touring Tips Every visitor should see this film. To stay ahead of the crowd, see it in late afternoon. Long lines usually occur at mealtimes.

Imagination Pavilion

Description and Comments Multi-attraction pavilion on the west side of Innoventions West and down the walk from The Land. Outside is an "upside-down water-fall" and one of our favorite Future World landmarks, the "jumping water," a fountain that hops over the heads of unsuspecting passersby.

Touring Tips We recommend early-morning or late-evening touring. See the individual attractions for specifics.

Journey into Your Imagination with Figment

What It Is Dark fantasy-adventure ride
Scope & Scale Major attraction
When to Go Before 10:30 a.m. or after 6 p.m.
Author's Rating ★★½
Appeal by Age Group
  Pre-school ★★   Grade School ★★   Teens ★★
  Young Adults ★★★   Over 30 ★★★   Senior Citizens ★★★
Duration of Ride About 6 minutes
Average Wait in Line per 100 People ahead of You 2 minutes
Loading Speed Fast

Description and Comments This attraction replaced its dull and vacuous predecessor in the fall of 1999 and was retooled again in 2002 to add the ever-popular purple dragon, Figment. Drawing on the Imagination Institute theme from *Honey, I Shrunk the Audience* in the same pavilion, the new attraction takes you on a tour of the zany Institute. Sometimes you're a passive observer and sometimes you're a test subject as the ride provides a glimpse of the fictitious lab's inner workings. Stimulating all of your senses and then some, you are hit with optical illusions, an experiment where noise generates colors, a room that defies gravity, and other brain teasers. All along the way, Figment makes surprise appearances. After the ride, you can adjourn to an interactive exhibit area offering the latest in unique, hands-on imagery technology.

Although Journey into Your Imagination with Figment is certainlly better than the ride it replaced, it pales in comparison to *Honey, I Shrunk the Audience,* the hilarious 3-D film that occupies the other half of the Imagination Pavilion. Pleasant rather than stimulating, the ride falls short of the promise suggested by its name, though each reincarnation has added a little zip. Will you go to sleep? No. Will you find it amusing? Probably. Will you remember it tomorrow? Only Figment.

Touring Tips Try to ride before 11 a.m. You can enjoy the interactive exhibit without taking the ride, so save it for later in the day.

One of the of the coolest interactive exhibits is a photo-morphing computer. First the machine takes your picture, then you select an image from several categories into which your photo is integrated. The final result can be e-mailed on the spot to family and friends. Best of all, there's no charge. We sent a number of photos where our faces were morphed into pandas, lions, lizards, and birds. I was a great owl!

Honey, I Shrunk the Audience (FASTPASS)

What It Is 3-D film with special effects
Scope & Scale Headliner
When to Go Before 10 a.m. or just before Future World closes
Special Comments Adults should not be put off by the sci-fi theme. The loud, intense show with tactile effects frightens some young children.
Author's Rating An absolute hoot! Not to be missed; ★★★★½
Appeal by Age Group
  Pre-school ★★★½   Grade School ★★★★½ Teens ★★★★½
  Young Adults ★★★★½ Over 30 ★★★★½   Senior Citizens ★★★★
Duration of Presentation About 17 minutes
Preshow Entertainment 8 minutes
Probable Waiting Time 12 minutes (at suggested times)

Description and Comments *Honey, I Shrunk the Audience* is a 3-D offshoot of Disney's feature film, *Honey, I Shrunk the Kids. Honey, I Shrunk the Audience* features an array of special effects, including simulated explosions, smoke, fiber optics, lights, water spray, and moving seats. This attraction is played strictly for laughs, a commodity in short supply in Epcot entertainment.

Touring Tips The sound level is earsplitting, frightening some young children. Many adults report that the loud soundtrack is distracting, even uncomfortable. While *Honey, I Shrunk the Audience* is a huge hit, it overwhelms some preschoolers. A dad from Lexington, South Carolina, writes:

Honey, I Shrunk the Audience *is too intense for kids. Our four-year-old took off his [3-D] glasses five minutes into the movie. Because of this experience, he would not wear glasses in the Muppet movie at MGM.*

A Tucson, Arizona, mom tells of a similar reaction:

Our three- and four-year-olds loved all the rides. They giggled through Thunder Mountain three times, squealed with delight on Splash Mountain, thought Space Mountain was the coolest, and begged to ride Star Tours over and over. They even "fought ghosts" at the Haunted Mansion. But Honey, I Shrunk the Audience dissolved them into sobbing, sniveling, shaking, terrified preschoolers.

Though launched with little fanfare, *Honey, I Shrunk the Audience* has become one of Epcot's most popular attractions. Try to work it into your touring before 10:30 a.m. The show is located to the left of the Journey into Your Imagination ride; it isn't necessary to ride in order to enter the theater. If the wait is prohibitive (very rare), use FASTPASS. Avoid seats in the first several rows: if you're too close to the screen, the 3-D images don't focus properly.

Test Track

Description and Comments   Test Track, presented by General Motors, contains the Test Track ride and TransCenter, a collection of transportation-themed stationary exhibits and mini theater productions. The pavilion is left of Spaceship Earth when you enter, down toward World Showcase from the Universe of Energy pavilion.

Many readers tell us that Test Track "is one big commercial" for General Motors. We agree that promotional hype is more heavy-handed here than in most other business-sponsored attractions. But Test Track is one of the most creatively conceived and executed attractions in Walt Disney World.

Test Track Ride (FASTPASS)

What It Is   Automobile test-track simulator ride
Scope & Scale   Super headliner
When to Go   Before 9:15 a.m. and just before closing
Special Comments   40" height minimum
Author's Rating   Not to be missed; ★★★½
Appeal by Age Group

| Pre-school ★★★★ | Grade School ★★★★ | Teens ★★★★ |
| Young Adults ★★★★ | Over 30 ★★★★ | Senior Citizens ★★★★ |

Duration of Ride   About 4 minutes
Average Wait in Line per 100 People ahead of You   4½ minutes
Loading Speed   Moderate to fast

Description and Comments   Visitors test a future-model car at high speeds through hairpin turns, up and down steep hills, and over rough terrain. The six-guest vehicle is a motion simulator that rocks and pitches. Unlike simulators at Star Tours, Body Wars, and Back to the Future (at Universal Studios), however, the Test Track model is affixed to a track and actually travels.

Though reader comments on Test Track have been mixed, most like it. A Shippensburg, Pennsylvania, couple, for example, gave Test Track two thumbs up:

We did wait about 30 minutes for Test Track and it was worth it! At first we
thought it was a bit of a bust, as the beginning of the ride is not very exciting (though it was interesting), but the last minute or so made up for it! It
was wonderful!

A Westford, Massachusetts, family agrees:

Test Track was the favorite ride at WDW of all five members of our party.
Even my mom (56), who has always refused to go on roller coasters, was
coaxed onto Test Track and loved it. Five stars from one preschooler, three
over-thirties, and a senior citizen!

But a Monona, Wisconsin, couple were somewhat underwhelmed:

In regard to Test Track, while it was a good ride, it was overrated; or perhaps it
just wasn't what I expected. Based on the loud whoosh coming from the
ride, the build-up in the preshow area, and your comments, I expected a
much more intense experience. As it turned out, it just wasn't all that scary.
Compared to the Tower of Terror, Test Track is a Sunday drive in the park.

Touring Tips   Some great technology is at work here. The attraction is so complex,
in fact, that Disney is still trying to work out the kinks. When it's running, it's one of the
park's better attractions. As a Waban, Massachusetts, mother reports, however, it's not
always running:

Test Track was the toughest ride to ride. Either it was broken or the lines were
one and a half to two hours long.

A Bluemont, Virginia, man put it succinctly:

GM's and Disney's inability to keep this ride running consistently is no great
advertisement for GM products.

The opening of super-headliner Mission: Space in spring 2003 will take some of the
pressure off of Test Track. After it opens, you'll want to see Mission: Space first thing
when the park opens and then head directly to Test Track. Until then, get thee to Test
Track ever so fast as your feet will fly, or use FASTPASS.

If you use FASTPASS, be aware that the daily allocation of passes is often distributed
by 12:30 or 1 p.m. If all the FASTPASSes are gone, another time-saving technique is to
join the singles line. A singles line, thus far only available at Test Track, is a separate line
for individuals who are alone or who do not object to riding alone. The objective of the
singles line is to fill the odd spaces left by groups that don't fill up the ride vehicle.
Because there are not many singles, and because most groups are unwilling to split up,
singles lines are usually much shorter than the regular line and can save you a bunch of
time if you don't mind riding by yourself.

Wonders of Life Pavilion

Description and Comments   This multifaceted pavilion deals with the human
body, health, and medicine. Housed in a 100,000-square-foot, gold-domed structure,
Wonders of Life focuses on the capabilities of the human body and the importance of
keeping fit.

Body Wars

Motion Sickness

WARNING!

What It Is Flight-simulator ride through the human body
Scope & Scale Headliner
When to Go Before 10 a.m. or after 6 p.m.
Special Comments Not recommended for pregnant women or people prone to motion sickness; 40" height minimum
Author's Rating Anatomy made fun; not to be missed; ★★★★
Appeal by Age Group

Pre-school ★★★ Grade School ★★★★ Teens ★★★★
Young Adults ★★★★ Over 30 ★★★½ Senior Citizens ★★½

Duration of Ride 5 minutes
Average Wait in Line per 100 People ahead of You 4 minutes
Assumes All simulators operating
Loading Speed Moderate to fast

Description and Comments This thrill ride through the human body was developed along the lines of Disney-MGM Studios' Star Tours space-simulation ride. The story is that you're a passenger in a miniature capsule injected into a human body to pick up a scientist who has been inspecting a splinter in the patient's finger. The scientist, however, is sucked into the circulatory system, and you rush throughout the body to rescue her. The simulator creates a visually graphic experience as it seems to hurtle at fantastic speeds through human organs. The story is more than a little silly, but we nevertheless rate Body Wars as "not to be missed."

Touring Tips Epcot's first thrill ride, Body Wars remains popular with all ages. Ride early in the morning after Test Track and the attractions at the Imagination Institute, or during the hour before closing. Be aware that Body Wars makes a lot of people motion sick; it isn't unusual for a simulator to be taken off-line for attendants to clean up a previous rider's mess. If you're at all susceptible to motion sickness, reconsider riding. If you're on Body Wars and become nauseated, fix your gaze on something other than the screen and as far away as possible (the ceiling or side and back walls). Without the visual effects, the ride isn't rough enough to disturb most guests. If you get queasy, rest rooms are nearby as you get off the ride. Star Tours is just as wild but makes very few people sick. Successfully riding Star Tours doesn't necessarily mean you'll tolerate Body Wars. Conversely, if Body Wars makes you ill, you can't assume that Star Tours will, too.

Reader comments on Body Wars cover the spectrum. These are representative:

The only thing we won't do on this next trip is go on Body Wars in Epcot. The line is so deceptive. We waited almost two hours and then it was only to get motion sickness and feel awful!

and:

Body Wars did not measure up to all the hype and warnings. We expected Space Mountain with visual effects, and it wasn't even close. You weenies!

and:

The ride felt more like the involuntary movements of a hammock.

and finally:

Body Wars at Epcot was great fun. We rode it twice and loved it. A little scary, but exciting. Some of the other things seemed kind of boring after our ride here.

Motion sickness aside, Body Wars is intense—too intense for some, especially preschoolers and seniors. One elderly gentleman confided, "Feeling sick to my stomach took my mind off being terrified."

Cranium Command

What It Is Audio-animatronic theater show about the brain
Scope & Scale Major attraction
When to Go Before 11 a.m. or after 3 p.m.
Author's Rating Funny, outrageous, and educational; not to be missed; ★★★★½
Appeal by Age Group

Pre-school ★★	Grade School ★★★★	Teens ★★★★
Young Adults ★★★★½	Over 30 ★★★★½	Senior Citizens ★★★★½

Duration of Presentation About 20 minutes
Preshow Entertainment Explanatory lead-in to feature presentation
Probable Waiting Time Less than 10 minutes at times suggested

Description and Comments *Cranium Command* is Epcot's great sleeper attraction. Stuck on the backside of the Wonders of Life pavilion and far less promoted than Body Wars, this most humorous Epcot offering is bypassed by many guests. Characters called "Brain Pilots" are trained to operate human brains. The show consists of a day in the life of one of these Cranium Commanders as he tries to pilot the brain of an adolescent boy. Epcot and Walt Disney World could use a lot more of this type of humor.

Touring Tips To understand the program, you need to see the preshow cartoon. If you arrive in the waiting area while it's in progress, be sure you see enough to get a sense of the story before you enter the theater. While most preschoolers enjoy *Cranium Command,* many don't really understand it.

The Making of Me

What It Is Humorous movie about human conception and birth
Scope & Scale Minor attraction
When to Go Early in the morning or after 4:30 p.m.
Author's Rating Sanitized sex education; ★★★
Appeal by Age Group

Pre-school ★½	Grade School ★★★½	Teens ★★½
Young Adults ★★★	Over 30 ★★★	Senior Citizens ★★★

Duration of Presentation 14 minutes
Preshow Entertainment None
Probable Waiting Time 25 minutes or more, unless you go at suggested times

Description and Comments This lighthearted and very sensitive movie about human conception, gestation, and birth was considered a controversial addition to Wonders of Life, but most viewers agree it's tasteful and creative. The plot's main character goes back in time to watch his parents date, fall in love, marry, and, yes, conceive and give birth to him. Look for the biological error in the film. If you spot it, write us.

Sexual material is well handled, with emphasis on loving relationships, not plumbing. Parents of children younger than age seven tell us the sexual information went over their children's heads for the most part. In older children, however, the film precipitates questions. You be the judge.

A father of two from Connecticut weighed in with this opinion:

> [The Making of Me *is*] *very well done . . . but I find it an odd juxtaposition. How many people decide a vacation at Disney World is the time to explain this stuff? Show this in Health Class.*

A gentleman from Cheshire, England, who believes (correctly, in our view) that Americans are sexually repressed, writes:

> *By the standards of sex education programmes shown to English children of ages eight to nine,* The Making of Me *seemed almost Mary Poppinsish in tone. Certainly other Brits found your warnings over content quite puzzling.*

This reader would have a great time in our hometown (Birmingham, Alabama), where some of the local clergy harangued the city council for months to have Bermuda shorts welded onto the bare buttocks of a large statue depicting Vulcan at his forge.

Touring Tips *The Making of Me* is excellent and should be moved from its tiny space to a larger theater. Until (and if) it is, expect long lines unless you go at recommended times.

Fitness Fairgrounds

Description and Comments Participatory exhibits allow guests to test their senses in a fun house, get computer-generated health analyses of their lifestyles, work out on electronically sophisticated exercise equipment, and watch a video called *Goofy about Health* (starring, who else?).

Touring Tips Save the Fitness Fair exhibits for your second day, or the end of your first day at Epcot.

Mission: Space (FASTPASS; opens spring 2003)

Motion Sickness

WARNING!

What It Is Space flight simulation ride
Scope & Scale Super headliner
When to Go As soon as park opens or use FASTPASS
Special Comments Not recommended for pregnant women or people prone to motion sickness.
Author's Rating Not open at press time
Appeal by Age Group Not open at press time
Duration of Ride About 5 minutes plus pre-show
Average Wait in Line per 100 People ahead of You 3 minutes

Description and Comments Mission: Space, among other things, is Disney's reply to all the cutting-edge attractions introduced over the past several years by cross-town rival Universal. The first truly groundbreaking Disney attraction since the Tower of Terror, Mission: Space is certain to become the hottest ticket at Walt Disney World.

Guests enter the NASA Mission: Space Training Center where they are first introduced to the Mission Space deep-space exploration program and then divided into groups for introductory space flight training. After flight orientation, they are strapped into a space capsule for a simulated flight, where, of course, the unexpected happens. Interactive computer controls aboard the capsule allow guests to respond to the emergency and affect the outcome of their mission. The capsules are small and the ride amazingly realistic with convincing simulations of take-off, landing, and even momentary weightlessness.

Touring Tips Experience Mission: Space first thing in the morning or use FASTPASS. If you use FASTPASS, be forewarned that the popularity of this attraction all but insures that all FASTPASSes will be distributed by noon.

Universe of Energy: Ellen's Energy Adventure

What It Is Combination ride/theater presentation about energy
Scope & Scale Major attraction
When to Go Before 11:15 a.m. or after 4:30 p.m.
Special Comments Don't be dismayed by long lines; 580 people enter the pavilion each time the theater changes audiences
Author's Rating The most improved attraction at Walt Disney World; ★★★★
Appeal by Age Group

Pre-school ★★★	Grade School ★★★★	Teens ★★★½
Young Adults ★★★★	Over 30 ★★★★	Senior Citizens ★★★★

Duration of Presentation About 26½ minutes
Preshow Entertainment 8 minutes
Probable Waiting Time 20–40 minutes

Description and Comments Audio-animatronic dinosaurs and the unique traveling theater make this Exxon pavilion one of Future World's most popular. Because this is a theater with a ride component, the line doesn't move while the show is in progress. When the theater empties, however, a large chunk of the line will disappear as people are admitted for the next show. Visitors are seated in what appears to be an ordinary theater while they watch a film about energy sources. Then the theater seats divide into six 97-passenger traveling cars that glide among the swamps and reptiles of a prehistoric forest. Special effects include the feel of warm, moist air from the swamp, the smell of sulphur from an erupting volcano, and the sight of lava hissing and bubbling toward the passengers.

The original film on energy sources (which many guests characterized as boring) was scrapped in 1996 and replaced with a humorous and upbeat flick starring Ellen DeGeneres and Bill Nye. The current film represents a huge improvement for adults, turning a major snoozer into a highly entertaining presentation. For kids, however, Universe of Energy remains a toss-up. The dinosaurs frighten some preschoolers, and kids of all ages lose the thread during the educational segments.

Concerning the education segments, this Columbus, Ohio, dad thought the lesson had been doctored to suit the needs of the attraction sponsor:

I was horrified to see Bill Nye sell out in Exxon's show about energy. The word "conservation" does not appear in the entire script, and Bill blithely tells us global warming is "controversial." It might be controversial in the board-room at Exxon, but in the scientific community, it's an accepted fact.

Touring Tips   This attraction draws large crowds beginning early in the morning. Because Universe of Energy can operate more than one show at a time, lines are generally tolerable. If you decide to skip the show, at least see the great dinosaur topiaries outside the pavilion.

The "Mom, I Can't Believe It's Disney!" Fountain

What It Is   Combination fountain and shower
When to Go   When it's hot
Scope & Scale   Diversion
Special Comments   Secretly installed by Martians during *IllumiNations*
Author's Rating   Yes!! ★★★★
Appeal by Age Group

| Pre-school ★★★★★ | Grade School ★★★★★ | Teens ★★★★ |
| Young Adults ★★★★ | Over 30 ★★★★ | Senior Citizens ★★★★★ |

Duration of Experience   Indefinite
Probable Waiting Time   None

Description and Comments   This simple fountain on the walkway linking Future World to World Showcase isn't much to look at, but it offers a truly spontaneous experience—rare in Walt Disney World, where everything is controlled, from the snow peas in your stir fry to how frequently the crocodile yawns in the Jungle Cruise.

Spouts of water erupt randomly from the sidewalk. You can frolic in the water or let it cascade down on you or blow up your britches. On a broiling Florida day, when you think you might suddenly combust, fling yourself into the fountain and do decidedly un-Disney things. Dance, skip, sing, jump, splash, cavort, roll around, stick your toes down the spouts, or catch the water in your mouth as it descends. You can do all of this with your clothes on or, depending on your age, with your clothes off. It's hard to imagine so much personal freedom at Disney World and almost unthinkable to contemplate soggy people slogging and squishing around the park, but there you have it. Hurrah!

Touring Tips   We don't know how long the fountain will last before its creator is hauled before the Disney Tribunal of People-Who-Sit-on-Sticks, but we hope it's around for a long time. We do know your kids will be right in the middle of this thing before your brain sounds the alert. Our advice: Pack a pair of dry shorts and turn the kids loose. You might even want to bring a spare pair for yourself. Or, maybe not . . . so much advance planning would stifle the spontaneity.

World Showcase Attractions

World Showcase, Epcot's second theme area, is an ongoing World's Fair encircling a picturesque 40-acre lagoon. The cuisine, culture, history, and architecture of almost a dozen countries are permanently displayed in individual national pavilions spaced along a 1.2-mile promenade. Pavilions replicate familiar landmarks and present representative street scenes from the host countries.

World Showcase features some of the most lovely gardens in the United States. Located in Germany, France, England, Canada, and to a lesser extent, China, they are sometimes tucked away and out of sight of pedestrian traffic on the World Showcase promenade. They are best appreciated during daylight hours, as a Clio, Michigan, woman explains:

Make sure to visit the World Showcase in the daylight in order to view the beautiful gardens. We were sorry that we did not do this because we were following the guide and riding the rides that we could have done later in the dark.

Most adults enjoy World Showcase, but many children find it boring. To make it more interesting to children, most Epcot retail shops sell Passport Kits for about $10. Each kit contains a blank passport and stamps for every World Showcase country. As kids accompany their folks to each country, they tear out the appropriate stamp and stick it in the passport. The kit also contains basic information on the nations and a Mickey Mouse button. Disney has built a lot of profit into this little product, but I guess that isn't the issue. More important, parents, including this dad from Birmingham, Alabama, tell us the Passport Kit helps get the kids through World Showcase with a minimum of impatience, whining, and tantrums.

Adding stamps from the Epcot countries was the only way I was able to see all the displays with cheerful children.

Incidentally, if you do not want to spring for the Passport Kit, the Disney folks will be happy to stamp an autograph book or just about anything else (we saw one four-year-old with a stamp from France right in the middle of his forehead).

Children also enjoy "Kidcot Fun Stops," a program Disney designed to make World Showcase more interesting for the 5–12 crowd. So simple and uncomplicated that you can't believe Disney people thought it up, the Fun Stops usually are nothing more than a large table on the sidewalk at each pavilion. Each table is staffed by a Disney cast member who stamps passports and supervises children in modest craft projects relating to the host country. Reports from parents about the Fun Stops have been uniformly positive.

Boats ferry the foot-sore and the weary across the lagoon, although it's almost always quicker to walk.

Moving clockwise around the promenade, here are the nations represented and their attractions.

Mexico Pavilion

Description and Comments   Pre-Columbian pyramids dominate the architecture of this exhibit. One forms the pavilion's facade, and the other overlooks the restaurant and plaza alongside the boat ride, El Río del Tiempo, inside the pavilion.

Touring Tips   Romantic and exciting testimony to Mexico's charms, this installation contains a large number of authentic and valuable artifacts. Many people zip past these treasures without stopping to look. The village scene inside the pavilion is beautiful and exquisitely detailed. We recommend visiting this pavilion before 11 a.m. or after 6 p.m.

El Río del Tiempo

What It Is   Indoor scenic boat ride

Scope & Scale   Minor attraction

When to Go   Before 11 a.m. or after 3 p.m.

Author's Rating   Light and relaxing; ★★

Appeal by Age Group

Pre-school ★★	Grade School ★★	Teens ★½
Young Adults ★★	Over 30 ★★	Senior Citizens ★★½

Duration of Ride   About 7 minutes (plus 1½-minute wait to disembark)

Average Wait in Line per 100 People ahead of You   4½ minutes

Assumes   16 boats in operation

Loading Speed   Moderate

Description and Comments   El Río del Tiempo (The River of Time) cruises among audio-animatronic and cinematic scenes depicting the history of Mexico from the ancient cultures of the Maya, Toltec, and Aztec civilizations to modern times. Special effects include fiber-optic projections that simulate fireworks near the ride's end.

The volcano at the entrance suggests great things to come, but the ride disappoints many. A Troy, New York, woman lambasts El Río del Tiempo:

> My worst nightmare would be to get stuck in It's a Small World or El Río del Tiempo. They were both dreadful, boring, and need updating. I thought El Río was an insult to the Mexico Pavilion—it's a cheap tourist's version of Mexico and hardly a reflection on the culture, history, or people.

We agree. Though tranquil and relaxing, El Río del Tiempo is neither particularly interesting nor compelling, and definitely is not worth a long wait.

Touring Tips   The ride tends to get crowded during early afternoon.

Norway Pavilion

Description and Comments   The Norway pavilion is complex, beautiful, and archi-tecturally diverse. Surrounding a courtyard is an assortment of traditional Scandinavian buildings, including a replica of the 14th-century Akershus Castle, a wooden stave church, red-tiled cottages, and replicas of historic buildings representing the traditional designs of Bergen, Alesund, and Oslo. Attractions include an adventure boat ride in the mold of Pirates of the Caribbean, a movie about Norway, and a gallery of art and artifacts in the stave church. A Viking-ship play area was added in 1999. The pavilion houses Restaurant Akershus, a sit-down eatery (priority seating required) that serves koldtboard (cold buffet), plus a variety of hot Norwegian dishes. An open-air cafe and a bakery cater to those on the run. Shoppers find abundant native handicrafts.

Maelstrom (FASTPASS)

What It Is Indoor adventure boat ride
Scope & Scale Major attraction
When to Go Before noon, after 4:30 p.m., or use FASTPASS
Author's Rating Too short, but has its moments; ★★★
Appeal by Age Group

Pre-school ★★★½	Grade School ★★★½	Teens ★★★
Young Adults ★★★	Over 30 ★★★	Senior Citizens ★★★

Duration of Ride 4½ minutes, followed by a 5-minute film with a short wait in between; about 14 minutes for the whole show
Average Wait in Line per 100 People ahead of You 4 minutes
Assumes 12 or 13 boats operating
Loading Speed Fast

Description and Comments In one of Disney World's shorter water rides, guests board dragon-headed ships for a voyage through the fabled rivers and seas of Viking history and legend. They brave trolls, rocky gorges, waterfalls, and a storm at sea. A new-generation Disney water ride, the Viking voyage assembles an impressive array of special effects, combining visual, tactile, and auditory stimuli in a fast-paced and often humorous odyssey. Afterward, guests see a five-minute film on Norway. We don't have any major problems with Maelstrom, but a vocal minority of our readers consider the ride too brief and resent having to sit through what they characterize as a travelogue.

Touring Tips Sometimes, several hundred guests from a recently concluded screening of *Wonders of China* arrive at Maelstrom en masse. Should you encounter this horde, postpone Maelstrom. If you don't want to see the Norway film, try to be one of the first to enter the theater. You can follow the preceding audience right through the exit doors on the far side.

China Pavilion

Description and Comments A half-sized replica of the Temple of Heaven in Beijing identifies this pavilion. Gardens and reflecting ponds simulate those found in Suzhou, and an art gallery features a lotus blossom gate and formal saddle roof line.

Pass through the Hall of Prayer for Good Harvest to view the Circle-Vision 360 film *Wonders of China*. Warm and appealing, it's a brilliant, albeit politically sanitized, introduction to the people and natural beauty of China. The China pavilion offers two restaurants: a fast-food eatery and a lovely, full-service establishment (priority seating required).

Touring Tips The pavilion is truly beautiful, serene yet exciting. *Wonders of China* plays in a theater where guests must stand, but the film can usually be enjoyed anytime without much waiting. If you're touring World Showcase in a counterclockwise rotation and plan next to go to Norway and ride Maelstrom, position yourself on the far left of the theater (as you face the attendant's podium). After the show, be one of the first to exit. Hurry to Maelstrom as fast as you can to arrive ahead of the several hundred other *Wonders of China* patrons who will be right behind you.

Wonders of China

What It Is Film about the Chinese people and country
Scope & Scale Major attraction
When to Go Anytime
Special Comments Audience stands throughout performance
Author's Rating Well produced, though film glosses over political unrest and events in Tibet; ★★★
Appeal by Age Group

Pre-school ★★	Grade School ★★½	Teens ★★★
Young Adults ★★★½	Over 30 ★★★★	Senior Citizens ★★★★

Duration of Presentation About 19 minutes
Preshow Entertainment None
Probable Waiting Time 10 minutes

Germany Pavilion

Description and Comments   A clock tower, adorned with boy and girl figures, rises above the platz (plaza) marking the Germany pavilion. Dominated by a fountain depicting St. George's victory over the dragon, the platz is encircled by buildings done in traditional German architecture. The main attraction is the Biergarten, a buffet (priority seating required) restaurant serving German food and beer. Yodeling, folk dancing, and oompah band music are included during mealtimes.

Also at Germany, be sure to check out the large and elaborate model railroad located just beyond the rest rooms as you walk from Germany toward Italy.

Touring Tips   The pavilion is pleasant and festive. Tour anytime.

Italy Pavilion

Description and Comments   The entrance to Italy is marked by a 105-foot-tall campanile (bell tower) said to mirror the tower in St. Mark's Square in Venice. Left of the campanile is a replica of the 14th-century Doge's Palace, also in the famous square. Other buildings are composites of Italian architecture. For example, L'Originale Alfredo di Roma Ristorante is Florentine. Visitors can watch pasta being made in this popular restaurant, which specializes in fettucine Alfredo. The pavilion has a waterfront on the lagoon where gondolas are tied to striped moorings.

Touring Tips   Streets and courtyards in the Italy pavilion are among the most realistic in World Showcase. You really feel as if you're in Italy. Because there's no film or ride, tour at any hour.

United States Pavilion

The American Adventure

What It Is Patriotic mixed-media and audio-animatronic theater presentation on U.S. history

Scope & Scale Headliner

When to Go Anytime

Author's Rating Disney's best historic/patriotic attraction; not to be missed; ★★★★

Appeal by Age Group

Pre-school ★★	Grade School ★★★	Teens ★★★
Young Adults ★★★★	Over 30 ★★★★½	Senior Citizens ★★★★★

Duration of Presentation About 29 minutes

Preshow Entertainment Voices of Liberty chorale singing

Probable Waiting Time 16 minutes

Description and Comments The United States pavilion, generally referred to as The American Adventure for the historical production performed there, consists (not surprisingly) of a fast-food restaurant and a patriotic show.

The American Adventure is a composite of everything Disney does best. Located in an imposing brick structure reminiscent of colonial Philadelphia, the production is a stirring, 29-minute sanitized rendition of American history narrated by an audio-animatronic Mark Twain (who carries a smoking cigar) and Ben Franklin (who climbs a set of stairs to visit Thomas Jefferson). Behind a stage almost half the size of a football field is a 28 × 55–foot rear-projection screen (the largest ever used) on which motion picture images are interwoven with action on stage.

Though the production stimulates patriotic emotion in some viewers, others find it overstated and boring. A man from Fort Lauderdale, Florida, writes:

> I've always disagreed with you about The American Adventure. I saw it about ten years ago and snoozed through it. We tried it again since you said it was updated. It was still ponderous. Casey used the time for a nap, and I was checking my watch, waiting for it to be over. I'll try it again in ten years.

An Erie, Pennsylvania, couple resented Disney's squeaky-clean version of American history:

> Our biggest gripe was with The American Adventure. What was that supposed to be? My husband and I were actually embarrassed by that show. They glossed over the dark points of American history and neatly cut out the audio about who bombed Pearl Harbor (after all, Japan is right next door and everyone is happy at WDW). Why do they not focus on the natural beauty of America, the ethnic diversity, immigration, contributions to the world society? No, it's a condensed and Disney-fied history lesson that made us want to pretend to be Canadians after seeing it.

Touring Tips Architecturally, The American Adventure isn't as interesting as most other pavilions. But the presentation, our researchers believe, is the very best patriotic attraction in the Disney repertoire. It usually plays to capacity audiences from around noon to 3:30 p.m., but it isn't hard to get into. Because of the theater's large capacity, the wait during busy times of day seldom approaches an hour, and averages 25–40 minutes. Because of its theme, the presentation is decidedly less compelling to non-Americans. The adjacent Liberty Inn serves a quick, nonethnic, fast-food meal.

Japan Pavilion

Description and Comments   The five-story, blue-roofed pagoda, inspired by a seventh-century shrine in Nara, sets this pavilion apart. A hill garden behind it encompasses waterfalls, rocks, flowers, lanterns, paths, and rustic bridges. The building on the right (as one faces the entrance) was inspired by the ceremonial and coronation hall at the Imperial Palace at Kyoto. It contains restaurants and a large retail store.

Through the center entrance and to the left is the Bijutsu-kan Gallery, exhibiting some exquisite Japanese artifacts. A second gallery, Karakuri, showcases an unusual collection of mechanical dolls.

Touring Tips   Tasteful and elaborate, the pavilion creatively blends simplicity, architectural grandeur, and natural beauty. Tour anytime.

Morocco Pavilion

Description and Comments   The bustling market, winding streets, lofty minarets, and stuccoed archways re-create the romance and intrigue of Marrakesh and Casablanca. Attention to detail makes Morocco one of the most exciting World Showcase pavilions. It also has a museum of Moorish art and the Restaurant Marrakesh, which serves some unusual and difficult-to-find North African specialties.

Touring Tips   Morocco has neither a ride nor theater; tour anytime.

France Pavilion

Description and Comments   Naturally, a replica of the Eiffel Tower (a big one) is this pavilion's centerpiece. In the foreground, streets recall La Belle Epoque, France's "beautiful time" between 1870 and 1910. The sidewalk cafe and restaurant are very popular, as is the pastry shop. You won't be the first visitor to buy a croissant to tide you over until your next real meal.

A group from Chicago found the pavilion's realism exceeds what was intended:

> There were no public rest rooms in the France part of Epcot—just like Paris. We had to go to Morocco to find facilities.

Impressions de France is an 18-minute movie projected over 200° onto five screens. Unlike at China and Canada, the audience sits to view this well-made film introducing France's people, cities, and natural wonders.

Touring Tips   Detail and the evocation of a bygone era enrich the atmosphere of this pavilion. Streets are small and become quite congested when visitors queue for the film.

Impressions de France

What It Is Film essay on the French people and country
Scope & Scale Major attraction
When to Go Before noon and after 4 p.m.
Author's Rating Exceedingly beautiful film; not to be missed; ★★★½
Appeal by Age Group

    Pre-school ★½   Grade School ★★½   Teens ★★★
    Young Adults ★★★★   Over 30 ★★★★   Senior Citizens ★★★★

Duration of Presentation About 18 minutes
Preshow Entertainment None
Probable Waiting Time 12 minutes (at suggested times)

United Kingdom Pavilion

Description and Comments A variety of period architecture attempts to capture Britain's city, town, and rural atmospheres. One street alone has a thatched-roof cottage, a four-story timber-and-plaster building, a pre-Georgian plaster building, a formal Palladian exterior of dressed stone, and a city square with a Hyde Park bandstand (whew!).

The pavilion is mostly shops. The Rose & Crown Pub and Dining Room is the only World Showcase full-service restaurant with dining on the water side of the promenade.

Touring Tips No attractions here create congestion; tour anytime. Priority seating isn't required to enjoy the pub section of the Rose & Crown, making it a nice place to stop for a midafternoon beer. Speaking of which, if you can't make up your mind, a beer sampler is available for $10. Included are 6 ounce servings of Bass Ale, Harp Irish Lager, Tennent Scottish Lager, Guiness Stout, and Boddington Crème Ale. In the category of dubious distinctions, the Rose & Crown Pub is the only place at Epcot where smoking is allowed indoors.

Canada Pavilion

Description and Comments Canada's cultural, natural, and architectural diversity are reflected in this large and impressive pavilion. Thirty-foot-tall totem poles embellish a Native American village at the foot of a magnificent château-style hotel. Nearby is a rugged stone building said to be modeled after a famous landmark near Niagara Falls and reflecting Britain's influence on Canada. The pavilion also has a fine film extolling the nation's many virtues. *O Canada!* is very enlightening and demonstrates the immense pride Canadians have in their beautiful country. Visitors leave the theater through Victoria Gardens, inspired by the famed Butchart Gardens of British Columbia.

Touring Tips *O Canada!*, a large-capacity theater attraction (guests must stand), gets fairly heavy late-morning attendance because Canada is the first pavilion encountered as one travels counterclockwise around World Showcase Lagoon. Le Cellier, a steakhouse on the pavilion's lower level, accepts priority seating but also welcomes walk-ins.

O Canada!

What It Is Film essay on the Canadian people and their country
Scope & Scale Major attraction
When to Go Anytime
Special Comments Audience stands during performance
Author's Rating Makes you want to catch the first plane to Canada! ★★★½
Appeal by Age Group

Pre-school ★★   Grade School ★★½   Teens ★★★
Young Adults ★★★½   Over 30 ★★★★   Senior Citizens ★★★★

Duration of Presentation About 18 minutes
Preshow Entertainment None
Probable Waiting Time 10 minutes

Live Entertainment in Epcot

Live entertainment in Epcot is more diverse than it is in the Magic Kingdom. In World Showcase, it reflects the nations represented. Future World provides a perfect setting for new and experimental offerings. Information about live entertainment on the day you visit is contained in the Epcot guidemap you obtain upon entry or at Guest Relations.

Here are some performers and performances you're apt to encounter:

In Future World A roving brass band, a musical crew of drumming janitors, socializing robots (EpBOTS), and gymnasts in *Alien* attire striking statuesque poses work near the front entrance and at Innoventions Plaza (between the two Innoventions buildings and by the fountain) according to the daily entertainment schedule.

Innoventions Fountain Show Numerous times each day, the fountain situated between the two Innoventions buildings comes alive with pulsating, arching plumes of water synchronized to a musical score. Because there is no posted schedule of performances, the fountain show comes as a surprise to many readers, such as this man from Berwickshire, England:

You don't mention one of the newer joys of Epcot, so the musical fountain came as a real surprise and treat. I sat down and listened to it from start to finish on two different occasions. The music is catchy, and played through the stereo speakers, the soaring effects of both music and water are really beautiful.

A Frankenmuth, Michigan, man was likewise caught off guard:

And, finally, to show that things don't always work out as planned, our children were mesmerized and entertained by something that isn't in any tour plan. At Epcot, there is a fountain between the two Innoventions buildings. During the holidays, the fountain was wonderfully synchronized to Christmas carols. While we [adults] checked our watches to make sure we were on time, our children just wanted to sit and watch the dancing water. Eventually, Mom and Dad sat and watched too. It was better than many of the shows and rides that we encountered during our stay at Disney.

Disney Characters Once believed to be inconsistent with Epcot's educational image, Disney characters have now been imported in significant numbers. In a new program called Disney Characters on Holiday, a dozen or so characters roll around the World Showcase in a British double-decker bus, stopping at times and places listed in the park map entertainment schedule. At each stop, the characters sing a song or two and then wallow into the crowd for autographs and photos.

Characters also appear in live shows at the American Gardens Theatre and at the Showcase Plaza between Mexico and Canada. Times are listed in the daily entertainment schedule in the Epcot guidemap available upon entry and at Guest Relations. Finally, The Garden Grill Restaurant in the Land pavilion offers character meals.

American Gardens Theatre The site of Epcot's premier live performances is in a large amphitheater near The American Adventure, facing World Showcase Lagoon. International talent plays limited engagements there. Many shows spotlight the music, dance, and costumes of the performer's home country. Other programs feature Disney characters.

Tapestry of Nations Parade This parade features 120 20-foot tall "puppets" and 32 drummers accompanied by a recorded musical score. The puppets are evocative of culture and costume around the world. Performed twice nightly according to the daily entertainment schedule, the parade route winds around the World Showcase Lagoon. The second performance is followed by *IllumiNations*. If you watch the second parade, don't count on having much time after the parade to find a viewing spot for *IllumiNations*.

IllumiNations An after-dark program of music, fireworks, erupting fountains, special lighting, and laser technology is performed on World Showcase Lagoon (see page 527–533).

Around World Showcase Impromptu performances take place in and around the World Showcase pavilions. They include a strolling mariachi group in Mexico; street actors in Italy; a fife-and-drum corps or singing group (The Voices of Liberty) at *The American Adventure;* traditional songs, drums, and dances in Japan; street comedy and a Beatles impersonation band in the United Kingdom; white-faced mimes in France; and bagpipes in Canada, among others. Street entertainment occurs about every half hour (though not necessarily on the hour or half hour).

Live entertainment in World Showcase exceeded the expectations of a mother from Rhode Island and led her son to develop a new talent:

You should stress in the new edition that Epcot's World Showcase is really quite lively now. Street performances are scheduled throughout the day in the different pavilions. The schedules were printed on the daily map we picked up at the ticket booth.

My two-year-old was taken with the Chinese acrobats and the Chinese variety performers. We must have watched their shows four times each! As I write this, he's balancing an empty trash can on his feet.

And an Ayden, North Carolina, woman offers this:

I don't feel that you emphasize the street shows at Epcot enough. My husband and I loved the Japanese drumming, the Chinese and Moroccan acrobats, and the street theatre players in Great Britain. These activities were much more indicative of foreign cultures than the rides.

We think the reader's right on target. The quality of street entertainment throughout Epcot has improved exponentially over the last couple of years. Our personal favorite is the Living Statues at France—absolutely brilliant.

Kidcot Fun Zones   In the World Showcase there are Kidcot Fun Zones, where younger children can hear a story or make some small craft representative of the host nation. The Fun Zones are quite informal, usually set up right on the walkway. During busy times of year, you'll find Fun Zones at each country. At slower times, only a couple of zones operate. Parents from Nanticoke, Pennsylvania, who thought Epcot would be a drag for their kids, were quite surprised by their experience:

Unfortunately we saved Epcot for the last day, thinking the children (ages five and six) would be bored. This was a mistake. They wanted to sit for every storyteller. The Tapestry of Nations Parade was special too because so many of the puppets stooped to touch the children's heads or shoulders or even to shake their hands. They loved it! And the best part was the Kidcot Fun Zones in each pavilion. Imagine, something free at Disney World. It's only a stick, but it has a little something from each country added by the child at his whim. They had a ball.

Dinner & Lunch Shows   Restaurants in World Showcase serve healthy portions of live entertainment to accompany the victuals. Find folk dancing and an oompah band in Germany, singing waiters in Italy and Germany, and belly dancers in Morocco. Shows are performed only at dinner in Italy, but at both lunch and dinner in Germany and Morocco. Priority seating is required.

The Best Ways to See *IllumiNations*

IllumiNations is Epcot's great outdoor spectacle, integrating fireworks, laser lights, neon, and music in a stirring tribute to the nations of the world. It's the climax of every Epcot day when the park is open late. Don't miss it.

Unlike earlier *IllumiNations* renditions, this one has a plot as well as a theme and is loaded with symbolism. We'll provide the *Cliffs Notes* version here because it all sort of runs together in the show itself. The show kicks off with colliding stars suggesting the big bang, following which "chaos reigns in the universe." This is soon replaced by twittering songbirds and various other manifestations signaling the nativity of the Earth. Next comes a brief history of time from the dinosaurs to ancient Rome, all projected in images on a huge, floating globe. Man's art and inspiration then flash across the globe "in a collage of creativity." All of this stimulates the globe to unfold "like a massive flower," bringing on the fireworks crescendo heralding the dawn of a new age. Although only the artistically sensitive will be able to differentiate all of this from, say, the

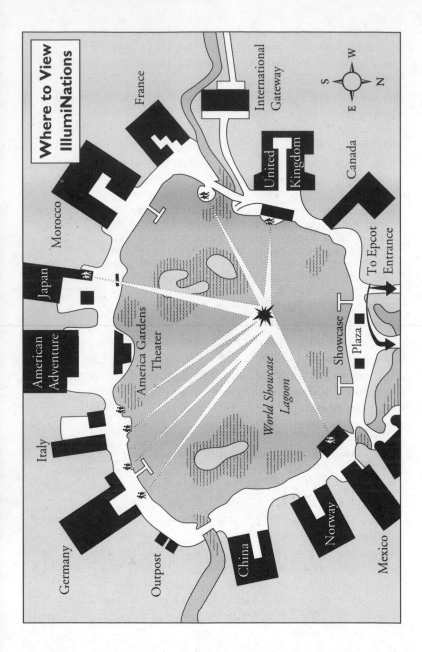

Where to View
IllumiNations

France

International
Gateway

United
Kingdom

Canada

To Epcot
Entrance

Showcase

Plaza

World Showcase
Lagoon

Japan

Morocco

American
Adventure

America Gardens
Theater

Italy

Mexico

Norway

China

Germany

Outpost

S   N
E   W

last five minutes of any Bruce Willis movie, we thought you'd like to know what Disney says is happening.

One practical change affecting *IllumiNations* is that the Tapestry of Nations Parade directly precedes it. Thus, prior to *IllumiNations* you are facing away from the lagoon to watch the parade. Following the parade you must turn around to view *IllumiNations*. In practical terms, it's almost impossible to have a front-of-the-crowd viewing spot for both (an exception is to watch both events from the open veranda of the restaurant in Japan). We recommend, therefore, placing your priority on scoring a good *IllumiNations* viewing spot. The puppets in the parade are 20 feet tall, so you'll be able to see fairly well even if you're not in the front row. A second consideration is that the parade, as well as preparations for it, severely limit your mobility in the hour before *IllumiNations*. Expressed differently, you might be stuck for *IllumiNations* in exactly the same spot where you are when the parade ends.

Getting out of Epcot after IllumiNations (Read This before Selecting a Viewing Spot)

Decide how quickly you want to leave the park after the show, then pick your vantage point. *IllumiNations* ends the day at Epcot. When it's over, only a couple of gift shops remain open. Because there's nothing to do, everyone leaves at once. This creates a great snarl at Package Pick-up, the Epcot monorail station, and the Disney bus stop. It also pushes to the limit the tram system hauling guests to their cars in the parking lot. Stroller return, however, is extraordinarily efficient and doesn't cause any delay.

If you're staying at an Epcot resort (Swan, Dolphin, and Yacht and Beach Club Resorts, and BoardWalk Inn and Villas), watch *IllumiNations* from somewhere on the southern *(The American Adventure)* half of World Showcase Lagoon and then leave through the International Gateway between France and the United Kingdom. You can walk or take a boat back to your hotel from the International Gateway. If you have a car and are visiting Epcot in the evening for dinner and *IllumiNations,* park at the Yacht or Beach Club. After the show, duck out the International Gateway and be on the road to your hotel in 15 minutes. We should warn you that there is a manned security gate at the entrances to most of the Epcot resorts, including the Yacht and Beach Club. You will, of course, be admitted if you have legitimate business, such as dining at one of the hotel restaurants, or, if you park at the BoardWalk Hotel and Villas (requiring a slightly longer walk to Epcot), going to the clubs and restaurants at Disney's BoardWalk. If you're staying at any other Disney hotel and don't have a car, the fastest way home is to join the mass exodus through the main gate after *IllumiNations* and catch a bus or the monorail.

Those who have a car in the Epcot lot have a more problematic situation. If you want to beat the crowd, find a viewing spot at the end of World Showcase Lagoon nearest Future World (and the exits). Leave as soon as *IllumiNations* concludes, trying to exit ahead of the crowd. Be forewarned that thousands of people will be doing exactly the same thing. To get a good vantage point anywhere between Mexico and Canada on the northern end of the lagoon, you'll have to stake out your spot 45–90 minutes before the show. Conceivably, you may squander more time holding your spot before IllumiNations than you would if you watched from the less congested southern end of the lagoon and took your chances with the crowd upon departure.

More groups get separated, and more children lost, after *IllumiNations* than at any other time. In summer, you will be walking in a throng of up to 30,000 people. If you're heading for the parking lot, anticipate this congestion and preselect a point in the Epcot entrance area where you can meet in the event that someone gets separated from the group. We recommend the fountain just inside the main entrance. Everyone in your party should be told not to exit through the turnstiles until all noses have been counted. It can be a nightmare if the group gets split up and you don't know whether the others are inside or outside the park.

For those with a car, the main problem is reaching it. Once there, traffic leaves the parking lot pretty well. If you paid close attention to where

The Smith family from East Wimple stakes out their viewing spot for *IllumiNations*.

you parked, consider skipping the tram and walking. If you walk, watch your children closely and hang on to them for all you're worth. The parking lot is pretty wild at this time of night, with hundreds of moving cars.

Good Locations for Viewing IllumiNations and Other World Showcase Lagoon Performances

The best place to be for any presentation on World Showcase Lagoon is in a seat on the lakeside veranda of the Cantina de San Angel in Mexico. Come early *(at least* 90 minutes before *IllumiNations)* and relax with a cold drink or snack while you wait for the show.

A woman from Pasadena, California, nailed down the seat but missed the relaxation. She writes:

Stake out a prime site for IllumiNations at least two hours ahead, and be prepared to defend it. We got a lakeside table at the Cantina de San Angel at 6:30 p.m. and had a great view of IllumiNations. Unfortunately, we had to put up with troops of people asking us to share our table and trying to wedge themselves between our table and the fence.

The Rose & Crown Pub in the United Kingdom also has lagoonside seating. Because of a small wall, however, the view isn't quite as good as from the Cantina. If you want to combine dinner on the Rose & Crown's veranda with *IllumiNations,* make a dinner priority seating for about 1 hour and 15 minutes before show time. Report a few minutes early for your seating and tell the Rose & Crown host that you want a table outside where you can view *IllumiNations* during or after dinner. Our experience is that the Rose & Crown staff will bend over backward to accommodate you. If you aren't able to obtain a table outside, eat inside, then hang out until show time. When the lights dim, indicating the start of *IllumiNations,* you will be allowed to join the diners on the terrace to watch the show.

Because most guests run for the exits after a presentation, and because islands in the southern *(The American Adventure)* half of the lagoon block the view from some places, the most popular spectator positions are along the northern waterfront from Norway and Mexico on around to Canada and the United Kingdom. Although the northern end of the lagoon unquestionably offers excellent viewing, it's usually necessary to claim a spot 35–60 minutes before *IllumiNations* begins. For those who are late finishing dinner or don't want to spend 45 minutes standing by a rail, here are some good viewing spots along the southern perimeter (moving counterclockwise from the United Kingdom to Germany) that often go unnoticed until 10–20 minutes before show time:

1. **International Gateway Island** The pedestrian bridge across the canal near International Gateway spans an island that offers great

viewing. This island is much more obvious to passersby than the secret park and normally fills 30 minutes or more before show time.

2. **Second-Floor (Restaurant-Level) Deck of the Mitsukoshi Building in Japan**   An Asian arch slightly blocks your sightline, but this covered deck offers a great vantage point, especially if the weather is iffy. Only the Cantina de San Angel in Mexico is more protected. Finally, the deck is the only vantage point that works equally well for *IllumiNations* and the Tapestry of Nations parade.

3. **Gondola Landing at Italy**   An elaborate waterfront promenade offers excellent viewing positions. Claim your spot at least 30 minutes before show time.

4. **The Boat Dock Opposite Germany**   Another good vantage point, the dock generally fills 30 minutes before *IllumiNations*.

5. **Waterfront Promenade by Germany**   Views are good from the 90-foot-long lagoonside walkway between Germany and China.

Do these suggestions work every time? No. A dad from San Ramon, California, writes:

Your recommendations for IllumiNations didn't work out in the time frame you mentioned. People had the area staked out two hours ahead of time.

None of the above viewing locations are reserved for *Unofficial Guide* readers, and on busier nights, good spots go early. But we still won't hold down a slab of concrete for two hours before *IllumiNations* as some people do. Most nights, you can find an acceptable vantage point 15–30 minutes before the show. Because most of the action is significantly above ground level, you don't need to be right on the rail or have an unobstructed view of the water. It's important, however, not to position yourself under a tree, awning, or anything else that blocks your overhead view. If *IllumiNations* is a top priority for you and you want to be absolutely certain of getting a good viewing position, claim your place an hour or more before show time.

A New Yorker who staked out his turf well in advance made this suggestion for staying comfortable until show time:

Your excellent guidebook also served as [a] seat cushion while waiting seated on the ground. Make future editions thicker for greater comfort.

IllumiNations *Cruise*

For a really good view, you can charter a pontoon boat for $120. Captained by a Disney cast member, the boat holds up to 12 guests. Your captain will take you for a little cruise and then position the boat in a perfect place to watch *IllumiNations*. For an additional $80 per each 4 persons, the captain will provide deli sandwiches, snacks, and beverages. Cruises depart from the BoardWalk and Yacht and Beach Club docks. A major indirect benefit of the charter is that you can enjoy *IllumiNations* without fighting the mob afterwards. Because this is a private charter rather than a tour, only your group will be aboard. Life jackets are provided, but you can wear them at your discretion. Because there are few boats, charters sell out fast. To reserve call (407) WDW-PLAY at exactly 7 a.m. 90 days before the day you want to charter. Because the Disney reservations system counts days in a somewhat atypical manner, we recommend phoning about 95 days out to have a Disney agent specify the exact morning to call for reservations. Similar charters are available on the Seven Seas Lagoon to watch the Magic Kingdom fireworks.

Behind-the-Scenes Tours in Epcot

Epcot's **Gardens of the World** offers adults (ages 16 and over) a glimpse of Disney World's gardens, horticulture, and landscaping. The three-hour tour costs $59 plus Epcot admission. Also available is **Hidden Treasures,** a tour exploring the architecture of the international pavilions. The three-and-a-half-hour tour costs $49 plus Epcot admission.

Readers rave about guided walking tours at Epcot. A couple from Los Angeles writes:

The best-kept secret is the adult tour, Hidden Treasures of World Showcase in Epcot. The description is misleading and sounds like a real bore, but we got a behind-the-scenes tour with lots of information on everything we ever wanted to know or were curious about. Definitely the best part of our trip. (This is a walking tour and is mostly outside in the heat.)

A gentleman in Houston, Texas, tells us:

Keep telling people about the Hidden Treasures of World Showcase tour; we finally got to take it, and it was a real highlight. The cast member who took us on the tour (there were only four of us) told us about a tour of the Magic Kingdom, called Keys to the Kingdom, which we took the very next day. It was similar, with backstage touring and a look at the utilidor system, although it also included going on several rides. Tell people about this one, too.

Discounts for these tours are available if you charge them on an American Express card. For reservations, call (407) 939-8687.

The **Behind the Seeds Tour** is shorter and takes guests behind the scenes to vegetable gardens in The Land pavilion. It requires same-day reservations; make them on the lower level of The Land (far right of the fast-food windows). The cost of the hour-long tour is $6 for adults and $4 for children ages three to nine.

Dive Quest

The soggiest behind-the-scenes experience available anywhere is Epcot's Dive Quest, where open-water scuba-certified divers (ages 15 and over) can swim around with the fish at The Living Seas. Offered twice daily, each tour lasts about three and a half hours, including a 30–40-minute dive. The cost is about $140 per diver and includes all gear, a souvenir T-shirt, a dive log stamp, and refreshments. They will make a video recording of your dive, which you can buy for $30. Reservations are required and can be made with a credit card by calling (407) WDW-TOUR. For recorded information, call (407) 560-5590. The experience is for adults only: no junior certifications are accepted.

Dolphins in Depth

This tour (for guests ages 16 and older) visits the dolphin research facility at the Living Seas. There you'll witness a training session and then wade into the water (but not swim) with the two dolphins. Cost for the three-hour experience is $140. Wet suits are provided. Only eight guests per day can participate, so make reservations 90 days in advance by calling (407) WDW-TOUR.

If you really dig dolphins, keep in mind that for $199 (only $59 more), you can visit Discovery Cove, SeaWorld's new park, and actually swim with the dolphins. Though the dolphin swim experience is only about an hour long, the ticket entitles visitors to an entire day at Discovery Cove (where you can snorkel in a manmade coral reef among other activities), plus a decent lunch and a seven-day pass to SeaWorld. For more information on Discovery Cove, see page 655.

Traffic Patterns in Epcot

After long admiring traffic flow in the Magic Kingdom, we were amazed at Epcot's layout. In the Magic Kingdom, Main Street, U.S.A., with its shops and eateries, serves as a huge gathering place when the park opens and funnels visitors to the central hub, where entrances branch off to the lands. Thus, crowds are first welcomed and entertained (on Main Street), then distributed almost equally to the lands.

At Epcot, by contrast, Spaceship Earth, the park's premier landmark and one of its headliner attractions, is just inside the main entrance. When visitors enter the park, they almost irresistibly head for it. Hence, a bottleneck forms less than 75 yards from the turnstiles as soon as the park opens. Visitors aware of the congestion at Spaceship Earth can take advantage of the excellent opportunities it provides for escaping waits at other Future World attractions.

Early-morning crowds form in Future World because most of the park's rides and shows are there. Except at Mission: Space (opens 2003), Test Track, Body Wars (Wonders of Life pavilion), and *Honey, I Shrunk the Audience*, visitors are fairly equally distributed among Future World attractions.

When Mission: Space opens in the spring of 2003, it will edge out Test Track at the top of the pop chart and split the crowd. Most will (correctly) intuit that Mission: Space should be number one on their "to see" list, followed immediately by Test Track, but some will tackle the two attractions in the opposite order. The two together will draw so many guests that the other attractions in Future World will not develop long waits until 11 a.m. or later.

Between 9 and 11 a.m., crowds build in Future World. Even when World Showcase opens (usually 11 a.m.), more people are entering Future World than are leaving for the Showcase. Attendance continues building in Future World between noon and 2 p.m. World Showcase attendance builds rapidly as lunch approaches. Exhibits at the far end of World Showcase Lagoon report capacity audiences from about noon through 6:30 or 7:30 p.m.

The Magic Kingdom's premier attractions are situated on the far perimeters of its lands to distribute crowds evenly. Epcot's cluster of attractions in Future World holds the greater part of the throng in the smaller part of the park. World Showcase has only two major draws (Maelstrom in Norway and *The American Adventure*). There is no compelling reason to rush to see them. The bottom line: Crowds build all morning and into early afternoon in Future World. Not until the evening meal approaches do crowds equalize in Future World and World Showcase. Evening crowds in World Showcase, however, don't compare in size to morning and midday crowds in Future World. Attendance throughout Epcot is normally lighter in the evening.

At the Magic Kingdom, repeat visitors make a mad dash for their favorite ride, and preferences are strong and well defined. At Epcot, by contrast, many returning guests say that with the possible exceptions of Test Track and *Honey, I Shrunk the Audience*, they enjoy the major attractions "about the same." The conclusion suggested is that touring at Epcot is more systematic and predictable (by the numbers, clockwise, or counterclockwise) than at the Magic Kingdom.

Some guests leave Epcot in the early evening, but the vast majority exit en masse after *IllumiNations*. Upwards of 30,000 people head for the parking lot and monorail station at once.

Closing time at Epcot doesn't precipitate congestion as it does at the Magic Kingdom. One primary reason for the easier departure from Epcot is that its parking lot is adjacent to the park, not separated from it by a lake as at the Magic Kingdom. At the Magic Kingdom, departing visitors form bottlenecks at the monorail to the Transportation and Ticket Center and main parking lot. At Epcot, they proceed directly to their cars.

Epcot Touring Plans

Our Epcot touring plans are field-tested, step-by-step itineraries for seeing all major attractions at Epcot with a minimum of waiting in line. They're designed to keep you ahead of the crowds while the park is filling in the morning, and to place you at the less crowded attractions during Epcot's busier hours. They assume you would be happier doing a little extra walking rather than a lot of extra standing in line.

Touring Epcot is much more strenuous and demanding than touring the other theme parks. Epcot requires about twice as much walking. And, unlike the Magic Kingdom, Epcot has no effective in-park transportation; wherever you want to go, it's always quicker to walk. Our plans will help you avoid crowds and bottlenecks on days of moderate to heavy attendance, but they can't shorten the distance you have to walk. (Wear comfortable shoes.) On days of lighter attendance, when crowd conditions aren't a critical factor, the plans will help you organize your tour. We offer four touring plans:

Epcot One-Day Touring Plan   This plan packs as much as possible into one long day and requires a lot of hustle and stamina.

Author's Selective Epcot One-Day Touring Plan   This plan eliminates some lesser attractions (in the author's opinion) and offers a somewhat more relaxed tour if you have only one day.

Epcot Two-Day Sunrise/Starlight Touring Plan   This plan combines the easy touring of early morning on one day with Epcot's festivity and live pageantry at night on the second day. The first day requires some backtracking and hustle but is much more laid-back than either one-day plan.

Epcot Two-Day Early Riser Touring Plan   This is the most efficient Epcot touring plan, eliminating 90% of the backtracking and extra walking required by the others while still providing a comprehensive tour.

Epcot One-Day Touring Plan

For Adults and children eight or older.

Assumes Willingness to experience all major rides and shows.

This plan requires a lot of walking and some backtracking in order to avoid long waits in line. A little extra walking and some early-morning hustle will spare you two to three hours of standing in line. You might not complete the tour. How far you get depends on how quickly you move from attraction to attraction, how many times you rest and eat, how quickly the park fills, and what time it closes.

This plan is not recommended for families with very young children. If you're touring with young children and have only one day, use the

Author's Selective Epcot One-Day Touring Plan. Break after lunch and relax at your hotel, returning to the park in late afternoon. If you can allocate two days to Epcot, use one of the Epcot two-day touring plans.

1. Arrive at the parking lot 40 minutes before official opening time. Mission: Space, Disney's most ambitious and cutting-edge attraction in a decade, is scheduled to open in the spring of 2003, but might open earlier. If you plan to visit during Christmas of 2002 or early 2003, we suggest you call Disney information and inquire about the status of Mission: Space. Inquire again for an up-to-the-minute report as you pass through the turnstiles. If Mission: Space is open, or as the say, "in rehearsal" (not officially open but you can still ride), it should be your first stop, followed immediately by Test Track.

2. When admitted, move quickly (jog if you can, but don't run) around the left side of Spaceship Earth. If so inclined, stop briefly at Guest Relations (to the left of Spaceship Earth) to make priority seatings for Epcot restaurants. Continue through the plaza with the crescent-shaped Innoventions East building on your left until you see an open passage through the building. Turn left through this passage. After emerging on the far side of Innoventions East, proceed straight ahead to Mission: Space if it is operating. Enjoy. If Mission: Space is not open, turn right on the far side of Innoventions East and head directly to Test Track. If you are held up by a rope barrier anywhere along the route from the park entrance to Innoventions East, don't worry. Just stay put and proceed when permitted.

3. Go next to Test Track. If the wait at Test Track when you arrive exceeds 30 minutes, obtain FASTPASSes and return later to ride.

4. After Test Track, bear right and head for the Wonders of Life pavilion located on the same side of Future World as Test Track but back toward the entrance. At the Wonders of Life pavilion, ride Body Wars. Be sure to read our motion sickness warning concerning Body Wars. If you don't want to ride, skip ahead to Step 4.

5. After Body Wars, skip the other attractions in the Wonders of Life pavilion for the time being. Heading back in the direction of Test Track, retrace your path through the Innoventions East passage back into the central plaza. Crossing the plaza, pass through the Innoventions West building on the opposite side. On the far side of Innoventions West, proceed straight to the Land Pavilion.

6. At the Land pavilion, experience the Living With the Land boat ride. Forego the other two attractions for the moment.

7. Exit the Land pavilion and bear right to the Imagination pavilion. Take the Journey Into Your Imagination ride first, and then see the 3-D movie, *Honey, I Shrunk the Audience*.

8. Backtrack to the Land and see *The Circle of Life* and *Food Rocks*, both theater presentations. If you're hungry, scope out the Land's food court or the character meal at the Garden Grill.

9. Exiting The Land, turn left to The Living Seas. Experience The Living Seas.

10. After The Living Seas, bear left and pass back through the Innoventions West building. Ride Spaceship Earth, the attraction in the giant golf ball. Don't be too concerned if the line is long. Spaceship Earth is one of the fastest-loading attractions in the Disney repertoire. At the exit of the ride is a communications electronics exhibit. Our advice is to bypass it for the time being.

11. Following Spaceship Earth, return to the Test Track/Wonders of Life side of Future World, passing once again through Innoventions East. Bear left to the Universe of Energy and see the show. Once again, the line might appear daunting, but because of the immense capacity of the attraction, your wait should be tolerable.

12. Exiting the Universe of Energy, turn left and return to the Wonders of Life Pavilion. See *Cranium Command*.

13. Departing the Wonders of Life pavilion, turn left. Depart Future World and go to the World Showcase, initiating a counterclockwise circuit. If you are primarily interested in the attractions, try to limit your perusal of the dozens of shops.

14. At Canada, see the movie.

15. Next, tour the United Kingdom.

16. Proceed across the bridge to France. See the movie.

17. After France, visit Morocco next door. *Note:* Check your watch. Is your dinner priority seating soon? Suspend touring and go to the restaurant when it's time. Check the daily entertainment schedule for the time of the Tapestry of Nations parade and *IllumiNations,* both worthwhile. Give yourself at least 30 minutes after dinner to locate a good viewing spot.

18. Continue counterclockwise to Japan.

19. After Japan, see *The American Adventure.*

20. Continue to Italy.

21. Go next to Germany.

22. Proceed to China. See the movie.

23. After China, continue on to Norway. Ride Maelstrom if the wait is not prohibitive.

24. Next, tour Mexico and ride El Río del Tiempo.

25. This concludes the touring plan. Unless an unusual holiday schedule is in effect, everything at Epcot closes after *IllumiNations* except for a few shops. Thirty or forty thousand people bolt for the exits at once. Suggestions for coping with this exodus are on pages 529–531.

Author's Selective Epcot One-Day Touring Plan

For All parties.
Assumes Willingness to experience major rides and shows.

This touring plan includes only what the author believes is the best Epcot has to offer. However, exclusion of an attraction doesn't mean it isn't worthwhile.

Families with children younger than eight using this touring plan should review Epcot attractions in the Small-Child Fright-Potential Chart (pages 246–249). Rent a stroller for any child small enough to fit in one, and take your young children back to the hotel for a nap after lunch. If you can allocate two days to see Epcot, try one of the Epcot two-day touring plans.

1. Arrive 40 minutes before official opening time

2. When admitted, move quickly (jog if you can, but don't run) around the left side of Spaceship Earth. If so inclined, stop briefly at Guest Relations (to the left of Spaceship Earth) to make priority seatings for Epcot restaurants. Continue through the plaza with the crescent-shaped Innoventions East building on your left until you see an open passage through the building. Turn left through this passage. After emerging on the far side of Innoventions East, proceed straight ahead to Mission: Space if it is operating. Enjoy. If Mission: Space is not open, turn right on the far side of Innoventions East and head directly to Test Track. If you are held up by a rope barrier anywhere along the route from the park entrance to Innoventions East, don't worry. Just stay put and proceed when permitted.

3. Ride Test Track. If the wait at Test Track when you arrive exceeds 30 minutes, obtain FASTPASSes and return later to ride.

4. After Test Track, bear right and head for the Wonders of Life pavilion located on the same side of Future World as Test Track, but back toward the entrance. At the Wonders of Life pavilion, ride Body Wars. Be sure to read our motion sickness warning concerning Body Wars. If you don't want to ride, skip ahead to Step 5.

5. After Body Wars, skip the other attractions in the Wonders of Life pavilion for the time being. Heading back in the direction of Test Track, retrace your path through the Innoventions East passage back into the central plaza. Crossing the plaza, pass through the Innoventions West building on the opposite side. On the far side of Innoventions West, proceed straight ahead to The Land pavilion. At The Land pavilion ride Living with the Land, a boat ride. Skip the two other attractions in this pavilion.

6. Exit the Land pavilion and bear right to the Imagination pavilion. Take the Journey Into Your Imagination ride first, and then see the 3-D movie, *Honey, I Shrunk the Audience*.

7. Exiting the Imagination pavilion, backtrack past the Land pavilion to see the Living Seas.

8. After The Living Seas, bear left and pass back through the Innoventions West building. Ride Spaceship Earth, the attraction in the giant golf ball. Don't be too concerned if the line is long. Spaceship Earth is one of the fastest loading attractions in the Disney repertoire. At the exit of the ride is a communications electronics exhibit. Our advice is to bypass it for the time being.

9. Following Spaceship Earth, return to the Test Track/Wonders of Life side of Future World, passing once again through Inno-ventions East. Bear left to the Universe of Energy and see the show. Once again, the line might appear daunting, but because of the immense capacity of the attraction, your wait should be tolerable.

10. Exiting the Universe of Energy, turn left and return to the Wonders of Life Pavilion. See *Cranium Command*.

11. Departing the Wonders of Life pavilion, turn left. Depart Future World and go to the World Showcase, initiating a counterclockwise tour. If you are primarily interested in the attractions, try to limit your perusal of the dozens of shops. The street scenes at each World Showcase nation, however, are what make this section of Epcot special. Even when there is not a ride or a show, we recommend you spend some time enjoying the architecture, gardens, and street entertainment. The World Showcase is definitely a smell-the-roses kind of place, so try to relax and not hurry through.

12. There are three movies, two boat rides, and an audio-animatronic attraction *(The American Adventure)* in the World Showcase. As you complete your circuit we recommend experiencing *The American Adventure,* seeing the films at France and China, and taking the boat ride at Norway (if the wait is manageable). The film at Canada is very good, but not as interesting as the other two, in our opinion. The boat ride at Mexico is totally expendable.

13. Check your watch. Is your dinner priority seating soon? Suspend touring and go to the restaurant when it's time. Check the daily entertainment schedule for the time of the Tapestry of Nations parade and *IllumiNations,* both worthwhile. Give yourself at least 30 minutes after dinner to locate a good viewing spot.

14. This concludes the touring plan. Unless an unusual holiday schedule is in effect, everything at Epcot closes after *IllumiNations* except for a few shops. Thirty or forty thousand people bolt for the exits at once. Suggestions for coping with this exodus are on pages 529–531.

Epcot Two-Day Sunrise/Starlight Touring Plan

For All parties.

This touring plan is for visitors who want to tour Epcot comprehensively over two days. Day One takes advantage of early-morning touring opportunities. Day Two begins in late afternoon and continues until the park closes.

Many readers spend part of their Disney World arrival day traveling, checking into their hotel, and unpacking. They aren't free to go to the theme parks until the afternoon. The second day of the Epcot Two-Day Sunrise/Starlight Touring Plan is ideal for people who want to commence their Epcot visit later in the day.

Families with children younger than eight using this plan should review Epcot attractions in the Small-Child Fright-Potential Chart (pages 246–249). Rent a stroller for any child small enough to fit into one. Break off Day One no later than 2:30 p.m. and return to your hotel for rest. If you missed attractions called for in Day One, add them to your itinerary on Day Two.

Day One

1. Arrive at the parking lot 40 minutes before Epcot's official opening time.

2. When admitted, move quickly (jog if you can, but don't run) around the left side of Spaceship Earth. If so inclined, stop briefly at Guest Relations (to the left of Spaceship Earth) to make priority seatings for Epcot restaurants. Continue through the plaza with the crescent-shaped Innoventions East building on your left until you see an open passage through the building. Turn left through this passage. After emerging on the far side of Innoventions East, proceed straight ahead to Mission: Space if it is operating. Enjoy. If Mission: Space is not open, turn right on the far side of Innoventions East and head directly to Test Track. If you are held up by a rope barrier anywhere along the route from the park entrance to Innoventions East, don't worry. Just stay put and proceed when permitted.

3. Ride Test Track. If the wait exceeds 30 minutes, obtain FASTPASSes.

4. After Test Track, backtrack past Mission: Space to the Wonders of Life pavilion. Ride Body Wars.

5. Postponing other Wonders of Life attractions, cross to the opposite side of Future World passing through Innoventions East and Innoventions West enroute. Proceed to The Land pavilion and enjoy the boat ride.

6. Leaving the other Land attractions for later, exit the pavilion, turning right to the Imagination pavilion. Take the Journey Into Your Imagination ride first, and then see the 3-D movie, *Honey, I Shrunk the Audience.*

7. Departing the Imagination pavilion, turn right and proceed to the World Showcase section of Epcot.

8. Turn left and proceed clockwise around the World Showcase Lagoon. Experience El Río del Tiempo boat ride in Mexico. The ride is in the far-left corner of the interior courtyard and isn't very well marked. Consign any purchases to Package Pick-up for collection when you leave the park.

9. Continue left to Norway. Ride Maelstrom. Use FASTPASS if the wait exceeds 20 minutes. *Note:* Check your watch. Is your lunch priority seating soon? Suspend touring and go to the restaurant when it's time. After lunch, resume the touring plan where you left off.

10. Continue left to China. See *Wonders of China.*

11. Visit Germany and Italy. Enjoy the settings; there are no rides or films. If you don't have a restaurant priority seating, Sommerfest (fast food) at Germany serves tasty bratwurst, soft pretzels, desserts, and Beck's beer on draft.

12. Continue clockwise to *The American Adventure.* See the show. If you don't have a restaurant priority seating, the Liberty Inn (left side of *The American Adventure*) serves hamburgers, hot dogs, and chicken breast sandwiches.

13. Visit Japan and Morocco. Consign any purchases to Package Pick-up for collection when you leave the park.

14. This concludes the touring plan for Day One. Attractions and pavilions not included today will be experienced tomorrow. If you're full of energy and wish to continue touring, follow the Epcot One-Day Touring Plan for steps 11–13. If you've had enough, exit through the International Gateway or leave through the main entrance. To reach the main entrance without walking around the lagoon, catch a boat at the dock near Morocco.

Day Two

1. Enter Epcot about 1 p.m. Get a park guidemap and the daily entertainment schedule at Guest Relations.

2. While at Guest Relations, make a dinner priority seating, if you haven't done so already. You can eat your evening meal in any Epcot restaurant without interrupting the sequence and efficiency of the touring plan. We recommend a 7 p.m. priority seating. The timing of the seating is important if you want to see *IllumiNations*, held over the lagoon at 9 p.m.

    If your preferred restaurants and seatings are filled, try for a priority seating at Morocco or Norway. Because these nations' delightful ethnic dishes are little known to most Americans, priority seatings may be available.

3. Ride Spaceship Earth.

4. Cut left through Innoventions East and return to the Wonders of Life pavilion. See *Cranium Command*.

5. Exiting the Wonders of Life pavilion, turn right to the Universe of Energy and see the show.

6. Pass through Innoventions East and West and proceed to The Living Seas. For maximum efficiency, be one of the last people to enter the theater (where you sit) from the preshow area (where you stand). Sit as close to the end of a middle row as possible. This will position you to be first on the ride that follows the theater presentation. Afterward, enjoy the exhibits of Sea Base Alpha.

7. Exit right from The Living Seas to The Land. See *Food Rocks* and The Circle of Life, featuring characters from *The Lion King. Note:* Check your watch. Is your dinner priority seating soon? Suspend touring and go to the restaurant when it's time. After dinner, check the daily entertainment schedule for the time of *IllumiNations*. Don't miss it. Give yourself at least a half hour after dinner to find a good viewing spot along the perimeter of World Showcase Lagoon. For details on the best spots, see pages 527–533.

8. Leave Future World and walk counterclockwise around World Showcase Lagoon to Canada. See *O Canada!*

9. Turn right and visit the United Kingdom.

10. Turn right and proceed to France. See the film.

11. This concludes the touring plan. Enjoy your dinner and *IllumiNations*. If you have time, shop or revisit your favorite attractions.

12. Unless a holiday schedule is in effect, everything at Epcot closes after *Illumi-Nations* except for a few shops. Thirty thousand or more people bolt for the exits at once. Suggestions for coping with this exodus are on pages 529–531.

Epcot Two-Day Early Riser Touring Plan

For All parties.

The Two-Day Early Riser Touring Plan is the most efficient Epcot touring plan, eliminating much of the backtracking and crisscrossing required by the other plans. It takes advantage of easy touring made possible by morning's light crowds. Most folks will complete each day of the plan by midafternoon. While the plan doesn't include *IllumiNations* or other evening festivities, these activities plus dinner at an Epcot restaurant can be added to the itinerary at your discretion.

Families with children younger than eight using this plan should review Epcot attractions in the Small-Child Fright-Potential Chart (pages 246–249). Rent a stroller for any child small enough to fit.

Day One

1. Arrive 45 minutes before official opening time on a day when early entry isn't scheduled.

2. When admitted, move quickly (jog if you can but don't run) around the left side of Spaceship Earth. Continue through the plaza until you see an open passage through Innoventions East on your left. If you are prohibited from proceeding by a rope barrier, position yourself at the barrier to hasten through the passage when the rope is removed. When the rope is dropped, or if you do not encounter a rope, hasten through and proceed directly to Mission: Space (opens 2003) if it is operating. If you really enjoyed Mission: Space, you might consider picking up a FASTPASS as you exit for a later repeat ride. If you obtain a FASTPASS, simply interrupt the touring plan when it is time to return and ride. If Mission: Space is not open, skip ahead to Step 3.

3. After passing through the passage in Innoventions East (and after experiencing Mission: Space if it is operating), head for the Wonders of Life pavilion situated to the immediate left of Mission: Space. Ride Body wars.

4. Also in the Wonders of Life pavilion, see *Cranium Command*. Leave other Wonders of Life exhibits for later and proceed to Step 5.

5. Exit the Wonders of Life pavilion and turn right to the Universe of Energy. Experience the Universe of Energy.

6. After the Universe of Energy, cut back through Innoventions East to the central plaza. Turns right and proceed to Guest Services on your right

across from Spaceship Earth. Make priority seatings for full-service meals later in the day at the Epcot restaurant(s) of your choice.

7. Next, ride Spaceship Earth. Don't worry if the line looks daunting. Your wait will not be long.

8. Following Spaceship Earth, return to the plaza, and from there proceed through Innoventions West to the other side of Future World. Bear right to the Living Seas. Enjoy.

9. After experiencing the Living Seas, proceed next door to the Land pavilion. If the wait for the Living with the Land boat ride is 20 minutes or less, go ahead and ride. If the wait exceeds 20 minutes but the FASTPASS return time is 30-70 minutes away, obtain FASTPASSes for Living with the Land.

10. See *The Circle of Life* and *Food Rocks* in The Land pavilion. Start with whichever one begins first. If you obtained FASTPASSes under the conditions outlined in Step 9, it should be almost time to return and take the boat ride. If the standby wait exceeded 20 minutes and you didn't obtain FASTPASSes, bypass the boats for today. Don't worry, the boat ride will be rescheduled on Day Two of the touring plan.

11. Depart Future World for the World Showcase. Turn right to Canada. See the film.

12. Turning right from Canada visit the United Kingdom. If you are a beer drinker, cap your afternoon with the Rose & Crown Pub's beer sampler.

13. Returning to Future World, check out the exhibits and Innoventions East and West.

14. This concludes Day One of the touring plan. If you linger over exhibits at The Living Seas and Innoventions East and West, it may be late in the day when you finish, and you might consider staying for dinner and *IllumiNations*. If you toured more briskly, you probably will complete the plan by about 2:30 p.m., even with a full-service lunch.

Day Two

1. Arrive 45 minutes before official opening time.

2. When admitted, move quickly (jog if you can, but don't run) around the left side of Spaceship Earth to Guest Relations (across the walkway from the geosphere) and make lunch and dinner priority seatings. If you don't wish to do so or have already made them by phone, skip to Step 3.

3. After making priority seatings for Epcot restaurants, continue as fast as possible through the plaza with the crescent-shaped Innoventions East building on your left until you see an open passage through the building. Turn left through this passage. After emerging on the far side of Innoventions East, turn right and head to Test Track. If you are held up by a rope barrier anywhere along the route from the park entrance to Test Track, don't worry. Just stay put and proceed to Test Track when permitted. Similarly, if you get to Test Track and it's not operating yet, remain in place and be patient. If you do not want to experience Test Track, skip ahead to Step 5.

4. Ride Test Track. If the wait at Test Track when you arrive exceeds 30 minutes, obtain FASTPASSes and return later to ride.

5. After Test Track, cross to the opposite side of Future World, passing through Innoventions East and Innoventions West en route. Proceed to The Land pavilion and enjoy the boat ride. If you experienced the boat ride on Day One of the touring plan, skip ahead to Step 6.

6. Proceed to the Imagination pavilion. Take the Journey Into Your Imagination ride first, and then see the 3-D movie, *Honey, I Shrunk the Audience*. After the movie, check out the exhibits at the Image Works, also in the Imagination pavilion.

7. Departing the Imagination pavilion, turn right and proceed to the World Showcase section of Epcot.

8. Turn left and proceed clockwise around World Showcase Lagoon. Experience the El Río del Tiempo boat ride at Mexico. The ride is in the far-left corner of the interior courtyard and isn't very well marked. Consign any purchases to Package Pick-up for collection when you leave the park.

9. Go left to Norway. Ride Maelstrom. Use FASTPASS if wait exceeds 20 minutes.

10. Go left to China. See *Wonders of China.*

11. Visit Germany and Italy. Enjoy the settings; there are no rides or films. If you don't have a restaurant priority seating, Sommerfest (fast food) at Germany serves tasty bratwurst, soft pretzels, desserts, and Beck's beer on draft.

12. Continue clockwise to *The American Adventure*. See the show. If you don't have a restaurant priority seating, the Liberty Inn (left side of *The American Adventure*) serves hamburgers, hot dogs, and chicken breast sandwiches.

13. Visit Japan and Morocco. Consign any purchases to Package Pick-up for collection when you leave the park.

14. Continue left to France. See *Impressions de France.*

15. Visit the United Kingdom.

16. Go left to Canada. See *O Canada!*

17. This concludes Day Two of the touring plan. If you futzed around in World Showcase shops and it's late in the day, consider staying for dinner and *IllumiNations*. If you caught *IllumiNations* after Day One, consider exiting Epcot through the International Gateway (between the United Kingdom and France) and exploring the restaurants, shops, and clubs of Disney's Board-Walk. The BoardWalk is an easy five-minute walk from the International Gateway.

Part Twelve

Disney's
Animal Kingdom

With its lush flora, winding streams, meandering paths, and exotic setting, the Animal Kingdom is a stunningly beautiful theme park. The landscaping alone conjures images of rain forest, veldt, and even formal gardens. Soothing, mysterious, and exciting all at once, every vista is a feast for the eye. Add to this loveliness a population of more than 1,000 animals, replicas of Africa's and Asia's most intriguing architecture, and a diverse array of singularly original attractions, and you have the most unique of all Disney theme parks. In the Animal Kingdom, Disney has created an environment to savor. And though you will encounter the typical long lines, pricey food, and shops full of Disney merchandise, you will also (with a little effort) experience a day of stimulating private discoveries.

Disney's Animal Kingdom opened in April 1998 amid a storm of controversy. Animal rights activists lambasted Disney, blaming Animal Kingdom zoologists and caretakers for the death of some three dozen various animals. What went largely unreported, however, was that many of these same detractors had for months castigated Disney for pirating away the best zoological talent in the country from America's zoos and research centers. The fact that investigations turned up no evidence of negligence, mistreatment, or neglect did little to satisfy the critics. The Animal Kingdom, for ill or good, is probably destined to be the lightning rod for the ongoing debate concerning the role of zoos and the moral rectitude of confining wild animals in cages (however elaborate) for the pleasure of humans.

At 500 acres, Disney's Animal Kingdom is five times the size of the Magic Kingdom and more than twice the size of Epcot. But like Disney-MGM Studios, most of the Animal Kingdom's vast geography is only accessible on guided tours or as part of attractions. When complete, the Animal Kingdom will feature seven sections or "lands": The Oasis, Discovery Island, DinoLand U.S.A., Camp Minnie-Mickey, Africa, Asia, and an as-yet unnamed land inspired by mythical beasts. Built in phases,

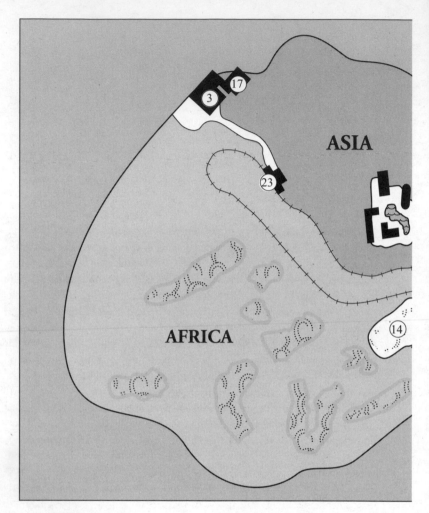

ASIA

AFRICA

1. The Boneyard
2. Character Greeting Area
3. Conservation Station
4. Dinosaur
5. *Festival of the Lion King*
6. *Flights of Wonder*
7. Gibbon Pool
8. Guest Relations
9. Harambe Village
10. Kali River Rapids
11. Kilimanjaro Safaris
12. Maharaja Jungle Trek
13. Main Entrance
14. Pangani Forest Exploration Trail

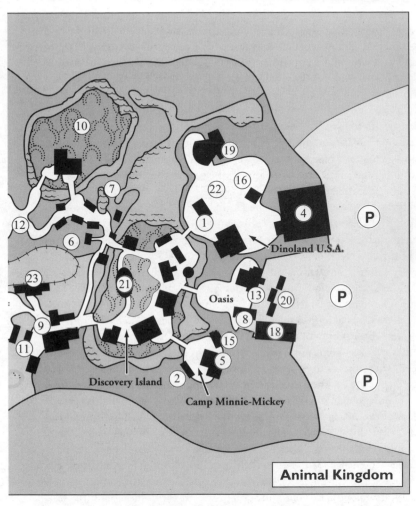

Animal Kingdom

The Oasis, Discovery Island, Camp Minnie-Mickey, Africa, and DinoLand U.S.A. were all operational for the park's opening in 1998, and Asia opened in early 1999. "Beastie Land" (our suggestion) may or may not ever be developed. In any event, it's certainly not on the front burner. Its size notwithstanding, the Animal Kingdom features a limited number of attractions. To be exact, there are six rides, several walk-through exhibits, an indoor theater, four amphitheaters, a conservation exhibit, and a children's playground. However, two of the attractions—Dinosaur and Kilimanjaro Safaris—are among the best in the Disney repertoire.

The evolution of the Animal Kingdom has been interesting in several respects. First, with regard to the Florida theme-park market, it is seen to be taking dead aim at the recently resurgent Busch Gardens in Tampa, a theme park known for its exceptional zoological exhibits and numerous thrill rides. Disney always preferred the neatly controlled movements of audio-animatronic animals to the unpredictable behaviors of real critters. Disney's only previous foray into zoological exhibits landed the Walt Disney Company in court for exterminating a bunch of indigenous birds that tried to take up residence on Disney property. When it comes to "rides," Disney won't even dignify the term. In Disney parks there are no rides, you see—only adventures. Attractions such as modern roller coasters, where the thrill of motion dominates visual, audio, and story-line elements, are antithetical to the Imagineering notion of attraction design.

Unfortunately for Disney, however, the creative, natural-habitat zoological exhibits and state-of-the-art thrill rides developed by Busch Gardens are immensely popular, and as any student of the Walt Disney Company can attest, there is nothing like a successful competitor to make the Disney folks change their tune. So, all the smoke, mirrors, and press releases aside, here's what you get at the Animal Kingdom: natural-habitat zoological exhibits and state-of-the-art thrill rides. Big surprise!

Even if the recipe is tried and true, the Disney version serves up more than its share of innovations, particularly when it comes to the wildlife habitats. In fact, zoologists worldwide are practically salivating at the thought of the Disney Imagineers applying their talent to zoo design. Living up to expectations, the wildlife exhibits at the Animal Kingdom do break some new ground. For starters, there's lots of space, thus allowing for the sweeping vistas that Discovery Channel viewers would expect in, say, an African veldt setting. Then there are the enclosures, natural in appearance, with little or no apparent barriers between you and the animals. The operative word, of course, is "apparent." That flimsy stand of bamboo separating you from a gorilla is actually a neatly disguised set of steel rods imbedded in concrete. The Imagineers even take a crack at certain animals' stubborn unwillingness to be on display. A lion that would rather sleep out of sight under a bush, for example, is lured to center stage with nice, cool, climate-controlled artificial rocks.

A second anomaly in the development of the Animal Kingdom has been its erratic course from design to completion. Far from creating a master plan and sticking to it, the Animal Kingdom has been a continuously evolving project with more midstream about-faces than a kindergarten fire drill. Names of lands and attractions have changed (the land relating to mythical beasts has had no fewer than five names), as have the number of lands and their premier attractions. Some attraction concepts were half executed and then scrapped. The first attraction designed for the park's architectural icon, the Tree of Life, was discarded as the park entered its final stage of construction. Attractions and lands scheduled for Phase I of development were moved back to Phase II, and so on.

All of this, of course, is in the rearview mirror now—yet another example of Disney's penchant for doing things the hard way. What remains is a new star in Disney's growing galaxy of theme parks.

The Animal Kingdom has received mixed reviews in its first several years. Guests have complained loudly about the park layout and the necessity of backtracking through Discovery Island in order to access the various theme areas. Congested walkways, lack of shade, and insufficient air conditioning also rank high on the gripe list. However, most of the attractions (with one or two notable exceptions) have been well received. Also praised are the natural habitat animal exhibits as well as the park architecture and landscaping. At the *Unofficial Guide,* we marvel at how demographically similar readers come away with such vastly differing opinions. A 36-year-old mother of three, for example, exclaims that:

The Animal Kingdom is a monstrous disappointment! Disney should be ashamed to have their name on it!

While a 34-year-old mom with two children reports:

The Animal Kingdom was our favorite theme park at Disney World. We spent four evenings out of our seven-day vacation there.

In truth, the Animal Kingdom is a park to linger over and savor, two things Disney, with its crowds, lines, and regimentation, has conditioned us not to do. But many people intuit that the Animal Kingdom must be approached in a different way, including this mother of three (ages five, seven, and nine) from Hampton Bays, New York.

Despite the crowds, we really enjoyed Animal Kingdom. In order to enjoy it, you really must have the right attitude. It is an educational experience, not a thrill park. Talk to the employees and you won't regret it. We spoke to an employee who played games with the kids—my daughter found a drawer full of butterflies, and the boys located a hidden ostrich egg and lion skull.

If we had not stopped to talk to this guide, we would have joined the hordes running down the trail in search of "something exciting to do."

Arriving

The Animal Kingdom is situated off Osceola Parkway in the southwest corner of Walt Disney World, and is not too far from Blizzard Beach, the Coronado Springs Resort, and the All-Star Resorts. The Animal Kingdom Lodge is about a mile away from the park on its northwest side. From I-4, take Exit 64B, US 192, to the so-called Walt Disney World main entrance (World Drive) and follow the signs to the Animal Kingdom. The Animal Kingdom has its own 6,000-car pay parking lot with close-in parking for the disabled. Once parked, you can walk to the entrance or catch a ride on one of Disney's trademark trams. Be sure to mark the location of your car on your parking receipt and tuck it in a safe place (preferably on your person as opposed to in your car).

"They don't have much experience with real animals,
but I'm sure everything will be fine."

Though there was some discussion about a monorail loop linking the Animal Kingdom with the Transportation and Ticket Center and Disney-MGM Studios, the new park will remain connected to other Walt Disney World destinations only by the Disney bus system for the foreseeable future.

A Word about Admission

Be forewarned that unused days on multiday "hopper" passports issued prior to the opening of the Animal Kingdom are good only for admission to the Magic Kingdom, Epcot, and Disney-MGM Studios. Thus, holders of these older passes must purchase a separate admission for the Animal Kingdom.

Operating Hours

The Animal Kingdom, not unexpectedly, hosted tremendous crowds during its early years. Consequently, Disney management has done a fair amount of fiddling and experimenting with operating hours and opening procedures. In 2002, Disney changed Animal Kingdom opening time to correspond to that of the other parks. Thus, you can expect a 9 a.m. opening during less busy times of the year and an 8 a.m. opening during holidays and high season. The Animal Kingdom usually closes well before the other parks—as early as 5 p.m., in fact, during off-season. More common is a 6 or 7 p.m. closing.

Park opening procedures at the Animal Kingdom vary. Sometimes guests arriving prior to the official opening time are admitted to The Oasis and Discovery Island. The remainder of the park is roped off until official opening time. The rest of the time, those arriving early are held at the entrance turnstiles.

In 2001, Disney laid off a number of cast members and trotted out several cost-cutting initiatives. One of these is to delay the opening of the Asia section of the park, as well as the Boneyard playground, the Wildlife Express train, Rafiki's Planet Watch, and Conservation Station until an hour after the rest of the Animal Kingdom opens. It's not clear whether these delayed openings will be temporary or permanent, or seasonal or year-round.

On holidays and other days of projected heavy attendance, Disney will open the park 30 or 60 minutes early. Our advice is to arrive, admission in hand, an hour before official opening during the summer and holiday periods, and 40 minutes before official opening the rest of the year.

When to Go

For the time being, expect to encounter large crowds at the Animal Kingdom. The best days of the week to go are Monday, Tuesday, and Sunday year-round.

Many guests wrap up their tour and leave by 3:30 or 4 p.m. Lines for the major rides and the 3-D movie in the Tree of Life will usually thin appreciably between 4 p.m. and closing time. If you arrive at 3 p.m. and take in a couple of stage shows (described later), waits should be tolerable by the time you hit the Tree of Life and the rides. As an added bonus for late-afternoon touring, the animals tend to be more active.

ANIMAL KINGDOM SERVICES

Most of the park's service facilities are located inside the main entrance and on Discovery Island as follows:

Wheelchair & Stroller Rentals	Inside the main entrance to the right
Banking Services	ATMs are located at the main entrance and on Discovery Island.
Storage Lockers	Inside the main entrance to the left
Lost & Found	Inside the main entrance to the left
Guest Relations/Information	Inside the main entrance to the left
Live Entertainment/ Parade Information	Included in the park guidemap available free at Guest Relations
Lost Persons	Lost persons can be reported at Guest Relations and at Baby Services on Discovery Island.
First Aid	On Discovery Island, next to the Creature Comforts Shop
Baby Center/ Baby-Care Needs	On Discovery Island, next to the Creature Comforts Shop
Film & Cameras	Just inside the main entrance at Garden Gate Gifts, on Discovery Island at Wonders of the Wild, and in Africa at Duka La Filimu

Getting Oriented

At the entrance plaza are ticket kiosks fronting the main entrance. To your right before the turnstiles are the kennel and an ATM. Passing through the turnstiles, wheelchair and stroller rentals are to your right. Guest Relations, the park headquarters for information, handout park maps, entertainment schedules, missing persons, and lost and found, is to the left. Nearby are rest rooms, public phones, and rental lockers. Beyond the entrance plaza you enter The Oasis, a lushly vegetated network of converging pathways winding through a landscape punctuated with streams, waterfalls, and misty glades, and inhabited by what Disney calls "colorful and unusual animals."

The park is arranged somewhat like the Magic Kingdom, in a hub-and-spoke configuration. The lush, tropical Oasis serves as Main Street, funneling visitors to Discovery Island at the center of the park. Dominated by the park's central icon, the 14-story handcarved Tree of Life, Discovery Island is the park's retail and dining center. From Discovery Island, guests can access the respective theme areas, known as Africa, Camp Minnie-Mickey, Asia, and DinoLand U.S.A. Discovery Island additionally hosts two attractions, a boat ride, a theater in the Tree of Life, and a number of short nature trails.

To help you plan your day, we have profiled all of the Animal Kingdom's major attractions. We suggest, however, that you be open-minded and try everything. Disney rides and shows are rarely what you would anticipate. For the time being, even if you dawdle in the shops and linger over the wildlife exhibits, you should easily be able to take in the Animal Kingdom in one day.

The Oasis

Though the functional purpose of The Oasis is the same as that of Main Street in the Magic Kingdom (i.e., to funnel guests to the center of the park), it also serves as what Disney calls a "transitional experience." In plain English, this means that it sets the stage and gets you into the right mood to enjoy the Animal Kingdom. You will know the minute you pass through the turnstiles that this is not just another Main Street. Where Main Street, Hollywood Boulevard, and the Epcot entrance plaza direct you like an arrow straight into the heart of the respective parks, The Oasis immediately envelops you in an environment that is replete with choices. There is not one broad thoroughfare, but rather multiple paths. Each will deliver you to Discovery Island at the center of the park, but which path you choose and what you see along the way is up to you. There is nothing obvious about where you are going, no Cinderella Castle or giant golf ball to beckon you. There is instead a lush, green, canopied landscape with streams, grottos, and waterfalls, an environment that promises adventure without revealing its nature.

The natural-habitat zoological exhibits in The Oasis are representative of those throughout the park. Although extraordinarily lush and beautiful, the exhibits are primarily designed for the comfort and well-being of the animals. This means in essence that you must be patient and look closely if you want to see the animals. A sign will identify the animal(s) in each exhibit, but there's no guarantee the animals will be immediately visible. Because most habitats are large and provide ample terrain for the occupants to hide, you must linger and concentrate, looking for small movements in the vegetation. When you do spot the animal, you may only make out a shadowy figure, or perhaps only a leg or a tail will be visible. In any event, don't expect the animals to stand out like a lump of coal in the snow. Animal-watching Disney-style requires a sharp eye and a bit of effort.

Touring Tips   The Oasis is a place to linger and appreciate, and although this is exactly what the designers intended, it will be largely lost on Disney-conditioned guests who blitz through at warp speed to queue up for the big attractions. If you are a blitzer in the morning, plan to spend some time in The Oasis on your way out of the park. The Oasis usually opens 30 minutes before and closes 30–60 minutes after the rest of the park.

NOT TO BE MISSED AT THE ANIMAL KINGDOM

Discovery Island	*It's Tough to Be a Bug!*
Camp Minnie-Mickey	*Festival of the Lion King*
Africa	Kilimanjaro Safaris
DinoLand U.S.A.	Dinosaur

Discovery Island

Discovery Island is an island of tropical greenery and whimsical equatorial African architecture, executed in vibrant hues of teal, yellow, red, and blue. Connected to the other lands by bridges, the island is the hub from which guests can access the park's various theme areas. A village is arrayed in a crescent around the base of the Animal Kingdom's signature landmark, the Tree of Life. Towering 14 stories above the village, the Tree of Life is this park's version of Cinderella Castle or Spaceship Earth. Flanked by pools, meadows, and exotic gardens populated by a diversity of birds and animals, the Tree of Life houses a theater attraction inspired by the Disney/Pixar film, *A Bug's Life*.

As you enter Discovery Island via the bridge from The Oasis and the main entrance, you will see the Tree of Life directly ahead at the 12 o'clock position, with the village at its base in a rough semicircle. The bridge to Asia is to the left of the tree at the 2 o'clock position, with the bridge to DinoLand U.S.A. at roughly 4 o'clock. The bridge connecting The Oasis to Discovery Island is at the 6 o'clock position; the bridge to Camp Minnie-Mickey is at 8 o'clock; and the bridge to Africa is at 11 o'clock.

Discovery Island is the park's central shopping, dining, and services headquarters. It is here that you will find the First Aid and Baby-Care Centers. For the best selection of Disney trademark merchandise, try the Island Mercantile or Wonders of the Wild shops. Counter-service food and snacks are available, but there are no full-service restaurants on Discovery Island (the only full-service restaurant in the park is the Rainforest Cafe located to the left of the main entrance).

The Tree of Life/It's Tough to Be a Bug! (FASTPASS)

What It Is 3-D theater show
Scope & Scale Major attraction
When to Go Before 10 a.m. and after 4 p.m.
Special Comments The theater is inside the tree
Author's Rating Zany and frenetic; ★★★★
Appeal by Age Group

Pre-school ★★★½	Grade School ★★★½	Teens ★★½
Young Adults ★★★	Over 30 ★★★	Senior Citizens ★★★

Duration of Presentation Approximately 7½ minutes
Probable Waiting Time 12–30 minutes

Description and Comments   The Tree of Life, apart from its size, is quite a work of art. Although from afar it is certainly magnificent and imposing, it is not until you examine the tree at close range that you truly appreciate its rich detail. What appears to be ancient gnarled bark is in fact hundreds of carvings depicting all manner of wildlife, each integrated seamlessly into the trunk, roots, and limbs of the tree. A stunning symbol of the interdependence of all living things, the Tree of Life is the most visually compelling structure to be found in any Disney park.

In sharp contrast to the grandeur of the tree is the subject of the attraction housed within its trunk. Called *It's Tough to Be a Bug!*, this humorous 3-D film is about the difficulties of being a very small creature. *It's Tough to Be a Bug!* also contrasts with the relatively serious tone of the Animal Kingdom in general, standing virtually alone in providing some much needed levity and whimsy. *It's Tough To Be A Bug!* is similar to *Honey, I Shrunk the Audience* at Epcot in that it combines a 3-D film with an arsenal of tactile and visual special effects. In our view, the special effects are a bit overdone and the film slightly anemic. Even so, we rate the bugs as not to be missed.

Touring Tips   Because it's situated in the most eye-popping structure in the park, and also because there aren't that many attractions anyway, you can expect *It's Tough to Be a Bug!* to be mobbed most of the day. We recommend going in the morning after Kilimanjaro Safaris, Kali River Rapids, and Dinosaur. If you miss the bugs in the morning, try again in the late afternoon or use FASTPASS.

Be advised that *It's Tough to Be a Bug!* is very intense and that the special effects will do a number on young children as well as anyone who is squeamish about insects. A mother of two from Mobile shared this experience:

It's Tough to Be a Bug! was too intense for any kids. Our boys are five and seven and they were scared to death. They love bugs, and they hated this movie. All of the kids in the theater were screaming and crying. I felt like a terrible mother for taking them into this movie. It is billed as a bug movie for kids, but nothing about it is for kids.

But a Williamsville, New York, woman had it even worse:

We went [to the Animal Kingdom] our very first day and almost lost the girls to any further Disney magic due to the 3-D movie It's Tough to Be a Bug! It was their first Disney experience, and almost their last. The story line was nebulous and difficult to follow—all they were aware of was the torture of sitting in a darkened theater being overrun with bugs. Total chaos, the likes of which I've never experienced, was breaking out around us. A constant stream of parents headed to the exits with terrorized children. Those that were left behind were screaming and crying as well. The 11-year-old refused to talk for 20 minutes after the fiasco, and the three-and-a-half-year-old wanted to go home—not back to the hotel, but home.

Most readers, however, loved the bugs, including this mom from Brentwood, Tennessee:

Comments from your readers make [It's Tough to Be a] Bug! sound worse than Alien Encounter. It's not. It's intense like Honey, I Shrunk the Audience but mostly funny. The bugs are cartoonlike instead of realistic and icky, so I can't understand what all the fuss is about. Disney has conditioned us to think of rodents as cute, so kids think nothing of walking up to a mouse the size of a porta-john, but go nuts over some cartoon bugs. Get a grip!

Camp Minnie-Mickey

This land is designed to be the Disney characters' Animal Kingdom headquarters. A small land, Camp Minnie-Mickey is about the size of Mickey's Toontown Fair but has a rustic and woodsy theme like a summer camp. In addition to a character meeting and greeting area, Camp Minnie-Mickey is home to two live stage productions featuring Disney characters.

Situated in a cul-de-sac, Camp Minnie-Mickey is a pedestrian nightmare. Lines for the two stage shows and from the character greeting areas spill out into the congested walkways, making movement almost impossible. To compound the problem, hundreds of parked strollers clog the paths, squeezing the flow of traffic to a trickle. Meanwhile, hordes of guests trying to enter Camp Minnie-Mickey collide with guests trying to exit on the bridge connecting the camp to Discovery Island. To make matters worse, Disney positions vendor carts on the approaches to the bridge. It's a planning error of the first order, one that seems totally avoidable in a theme park with as much usable acreage as the Animal Kingdom.

Character Trails

Description and Comments   Characters can be found at the end of each of several "character trails" named Jungle, Forest, or some such, and Mickey and Minnie. Each trail has its own private reception area and, of course, its own queue. Jungle Characters features characters from *The Lion King* and *The Jungle Book,* while Forest Characters generally offers characters from *Winnie the Pooh.* The Minnie trail leads to Minnie and the Mickey trail to Mickey. Two characters are present in the Forest and Jungle greeting areas, while Minnie and Mickey each work solo. Sometimes other characters such as Goofy or Daisy work solo in place of the Jungle and Forest characters.

Touring Tips Waiting in line to see the characters can be very time-consuming. We recommend visiting early in the morning or late in the afternoon. Because there are fewer attractions at the Animal Kingdom than at the other parks, expect to find a disproportionate number of guests in Camp Minnie-Mickey. If the place is really mobbed, you may want to consider meeting the characters in one of the other parks. Ditto for the stage shows.

Festival of the Lion King

What It Is Theater-in-the-round stage show
Scope & Scale Major attraction
When to Go Before 11 a.m. or after 4 p.m.
Special Comments Performance times are listed in the handout park map
Author's Rating Upbeat and spectacular; ★★★★
Appeal by Age Group
  Pre-school ★★★★   Grade School ★★★★½ Teens ★★★★
  Young Adults ★★★★   Over 30 ★★★★   Senior Citizens ★★★★
Duration of Presentation 25 minutes
Preshow Entertainment None
Probable Waiting Time 20–35 minutes

Description and Comments This energetic production, inspired by Disney's *Lion King* feature, is part stage show, part parade, and part circus. Guests are seated in four sets of bleachers surrounding the stage and organized into separate cheering sections, which are called on to make elephant, warthog, giraffe, and lion noises. There is a great deal of parading around, some acrobatics, and a lot of singing and dancing. By our count, every tune from *The Lion King* (plus a couple of others) is belted out and reprised several times. No joke—if you don't know the words to all the songs by the end of the show, you must have been asleep.

Unofficial Guide readers have been almost unanimous in their praise of *Festival of the Lion King*. This letter from a Naples, Florida, mom is typical:

Festival of the Lion King *is a spectacular show with singers, dancers, fire twirlers, acrobats, robotics, and great set design. My whole family agreed this was the best thing we experienced at Animal Kingdom.*

Touring Tips This show is both popular and difficult to see. Your best bet is to go to the first show in the morning or to one of the last two performances in the evening. To see the show during the more crowded middle of the day, you'll need to queue up at least 35 minutes before show time. There are four separate lines, one for each set of bleachers. The queues fill from left to right and are seated in the same order. To minimize standing in the hot sun, refrain from hopping in line until the Disney people begin directing guests to the far-right queue. If you have small children or short adults in your party, sit higher up in the bleachers. The first five rows in particular have very little rise, making it difficult for those in rows two through five to see. Though the theater is covered and air is circulated by fans, there is no air-conditioning.

Pocahontas and Her Forest Friends

What It Is Conservation-theme stage show
Scope & Scale Major attraction
When to Go Before 11 a.m. or after 4 p.m.
Special Comments Performance times are listed in the daily entertainment schedule.
Author's Rating A little sappy; ★★½
Appeal by Age Group

| Pre-school ★★★½ | Grade School ★★★½ | Teens ★★★ |
| Young Adults ★★★½ | Over 30 ★★★ | Senior Citizens ★★★ |

Duration of Presentation 15 minutes
Preshow Entertainment None
Probable Waiting Time 20–30 minutes

Description and Comments This show featuring Pocahontas addresses the role of man in protecting the natural world. Various live creatures of the forest, including a raccoon, a snake, and a turkey, as well as a couple of audio-animatronic trees (Grandmother Willow and Twig), assist Pocahontas in making the point. The presentation is gushy and overacted but has its moments nonetheless.

However, as a Michigan reader reports, *Pocahontas* is not in the same league as *Festival of the Lion King:*

> Festival of the Lion King *was a wonderful show. Unfortunately, we saw it just before seeing the Pocahontas show. It put Pocahontas to shame. Instead of being moved by the show's message, I wondered how much kindling Grandmother Willow would make.*

Touring Tips Because the theater is relatively small, and because Camp Minnie-Mickey stays so mobbed, the Pocahontas show is hard to get into. Among other problems, its queuing area adjoins that of *Festival of the Lion King* next door. If you approach when a lot of guests are waiting, which is almost always, it's hard to figure out which show you're lining up for. To avoid the hassle, try to catch the show before 11 a.m. or after 3 p.m. Regardless of time of day, arrive at least 20 minutes before show time and ask a Disney cast member to steer you to the correct line.

Africa

Africa is the largest of the Animal Kingdom's lands, and guests enter through Harambe, Disney's idealized and immensely sanitized version of a modern, rural African town. There is a market (with modern cash registers), and counter-service food is available. What distinguishes Harambe is its understatement. Far from the stereotypical great-white-hunter image of an African town, Harambe is definitely (and realistically) not exotic. The buildings, while interesting, are quite plain and architecturally simple. Though certainly better maintained and more aseptic than the real McCoy, Disney's Harambe would be a lot more at home in Kenya than the Magic Kingdom's Main Street would be in Missouri.

Harambe serves as the gateway to the African veldt habitat, the Animal Kingdom's largest and most ambitious zoological exhibit. Access to the veldt is via the Kilimanjaro Safaris attraction, located at the end of Harambe's main drag near the fat-trunked baobab tree. Harambe is also the departure point for the train to Rafiki's Planet Watch and Conservation Station, the park's veterinary headquarters.

Kilimanjaro Safaris (FASTPASS)

What It Is Truck ride through an African wildlife reservation
Scope & Scale Super headliner

When to Go As soon as the park opens or in the two hours before closing
Author's Rating Truly exceptional; ★★★★★
Appeal by Age Group
  Pre-school ★★★★   Grade School ★★★★★ Teens ★★★★½
  Young Adults ★★★★½ Over 30 ★★★★½   Senior Citizens ★★★★★
Duration of Ride About 20 minutes
Average Wait in Line per 100 People ahead of You 4 minutes
Assumes Full-capacity operation with 18-second dispatch interval
Loading Speed Fast

Description and Comments The park's premier zoological attraction, Kilimanjaro Safaris offers an exceptionally realistic, albeit brief, imitation of an actual African photo safari. Thirty-two guests at a time board tall, open safari vehicles and are dispatched into a simulated African veldt habitat. Animals such as zebra, wildebeest, impala, Thomson's gazelle, giraffe, and even rhinos roam apparently free, while predators such as lions, as well as potentially dangerous large animals like hippos, are separated from both prey and guests by all-but-invisible, natural-appearing barriers. Although the animals have more than 100 acres of savanna, woodland, streams, and rocky hills to call home, careful placement of water holes, forage, and salt licks ensure that the critters are hanging out by the road when safari vehicles roll by.

A scripted narration provides a story line about finding Big Red and Little Red, a mother elephant and her baby, while an on-board guide points out and identifies the various animals encountered. Toward the end of the ride, the safari chases poachers who have just wounded Big Red. As the vehicle approaches the safari's terminating point, the poachers are seen being taken into custody.

Having traveled in Kenya and Tanzania, I will tell you that Disney has done an amazing job of replicating the sub-Saharan east African landscape. The main difference that an east African would notice is that Disney's version is greener and (generally speaking) less barren. Like on a real African safari, what animals you see (and how many) is pretty much a matter of luck. We tried Disney's safari upwards of a dozen times and had a different experience on each trip.

If the attraction has a shortcoming, it is the rather strident story line about the poachers and Big Red, which while thought-provoking, is somewhat distracting when you are trying to spot and enjoy the wildlife. Also, because the story is repeated on every trip, it really gets on your nerves after the first couple of times.

Touring Tips Kilimanjaro Safaris is the Animal Kingdom's top draw. In fact, we've not seen an attraction in any Disney park that so completely channels guest traffic. While Space Mountain, Test Track, and Tower of Terror attract throngs of early-morning guests, there remain a substantial number of additional guests who head for other attractions. At the Animal Kingdom, however, as many as 90% of those on hand at opening head straight for the safari, and later-arriving guests do exactly the same thing. Over the first couple of years, Disney tried any number of ploys to lure guests elsewhere, but to no avail. So, if you want to see Kilimanjaro Safaris without a long wait, be one of the first through the turnstiles and make a beeline for Africa. If you are held up en route by a rope barrier or by cast members, stay put until you are permitted to continue on to the attraction.

As a couple from Laureldale, Pennsylvania, explains, beating the crowd is not the only reason to race to Kilimanjaro Safaris first thing in the morning:

When I showed my Animal Kingdom photos to a coworker who had recently been to WDW, she remarked how "lucky" I was to see so many animals (she had been disappointed). I promptly told her that "luck" had nothing to do with it! We were willing to sacrifice sleep and breakfast to get there as soon as the gates opened and sprinted (which is no easy feat for two mid-dle-aged, out-of-shape people) to the Safari where we rode twice without waiting. We were rewarded with so many groups of animals it was hard to take pictures of all of them. Twice our truck stopped to let animals cross the road, and even the lions and cheetahs were up and around. If you want to see animals you must get your ample butts there early—it's worth it!

Waits for the Kilimanjaro Safaris diminish in late afternoon, sometimes as early 3:30, but more commonly around 5 or 5:30 p.m. As noted above, Kilimanjaro Safaris is a FASTPASS Attraction. If the wait exceeds 30 minutes when you arrive, by all means use FASTPASS. The downside to FASTPASS, and the reason we prefer that you ride as soon as the park opens, is that there aren't many other attractions in Africa to occupy attention while you wait for your FASTPASS return time. This means you will probably be touring somewhere far removed when it's time to backtrack to Safaris. The best way to avoid this disruption is to see the attraction first thing in the morning.

If you want to take photos on your safari, be advised that the vehicle doesn't stop very often, so be prepared to snap while under way. Also, don't worry about the ride itself: it really isn't very rough. Finally, the only thing that a young child might find intim-idating is crossing an "old bridge" that pretends to collapse under your truck.

Pangani Forest Exploration Trail

What It Is Walk-through zoological exhibit
Scope & Scale Major attraction
When to Go Before 10 a.m. or after 3:30 p.m.
Author's Rating ★★★
Appeal by Age Group

Pre-school ★★½	Grade School ★★★	Teens ★★½
Young Adults ★★★	Over 30 ★★★	Senior Citizens ★★★

Duration of Tour About 20–25 minutes

Description and Comments Because guests disembark from the safari at the entrance to the Pangani Forest Exploration Trail, most guests try the trail immediately after the safari. Winding between the domain of two troops of lowland gorillas, it's hard to see what, if anything, separates you from the primates. Also on the trail are a hippo pool with an underwater viewing area, a naked mole rat exhibit (I promise I'm not mak-ing this up), and some hyenas. A highlight of the trail is an exotic bird aviary so craftily designed that you can barely tell you're in an enclosure.

Touring Tips The Pangani Forest Exploration Trail is lush, beautiful, and jammed to the gills with people most of the time. Guests exiting the safari can choose between returning to Harambe or walking the Pangani Forest Exploration Trail. Not unexpect-edly, many opt for the trail. Thus, when the safari is operating at full tilt, it spews hun-dreds of guests every couple of minutes onto the Exploration Trail. The one-way trail in turn becomes so clogged that nobody can move or see much of anything. After a minute or two, however, you catch the feel of the mob moving forward in small lurches. From then on you shift, elbow, grunt, and wriggle your way along, every so often coming to an animal exhibit. Here you endeavor to work your way close to the rail but are opposed by people trapped against the rail who are trying to rejoin the surging crowd. The animals, as well as their natural-habitat enclosures, are pretty nifty if you can fight close enough to see them.

Clearly this attraction is either badly designed, misplaced, or both. Your only real chance for enjoying it is to walk through before 10 a.m. (i.e., before the safari hits full stride) or after 3:30 p.m.

Rafiki's Planet Watch

Rafiki's Planet Watch showed up on park maps in 2001. It's not a "land" and not really an attraction either. Our best guess is that Disney is using the name as an umbrella for Conservation Station, the petting zoo, and the environmental exhibits accessible from Harambe via the Wildlife Express train. Presumably, Disney hopes that invoking Rafiki (a beloved character from *The Lion King*) will stimulate guests to make the effort to check out things. As for your kids seeing Rafiki, don't bet on it. The closest likeness we've seen here is a two-dimensional wooden cutout.

Wildlife Express

What It Is Scenic railroad ride to Rafiki's Planet Watch and Conservation Station
Scope & Scale Minor attraction
When to Go Before 11 a.m. or after 3 p.m.
Special Comments Opens an hour after the rest of the park
Author's Rating Ho hum; ★★
Appeal by Age Group

Pre-school ★★★	Grade School ★★★	Teens ★½
Young Adults ★★½	Over 30 ★★½	Senior Citizens ★★½

Duration of Ride About 5–7 minutes one way
Average Wait in Line per 100 People ahead of You 9 minutes
Loading Speed Moderate

Description and Comments A transportation ride that snakes behind the African wildlife reserve as it makes its loop connecting Harambe to Rafiki's Planet Watch and Conservation Station. En route, you see the nighttime enclosures for the animals that populate the Kilimanjaro Safaris. Similarly, returning to Harambe, you see the backstage areas of Asia. Regardless which direction you're heading, the sights are not especially interesting.

Touring Tips Most guests will embark for Rafiki's Planet Watch and Conservation Station after experiencing the Kilimanjaro Safaris and the Pangani Forest Exploration Trail. Thus, the train begins to get crowded between 10 and 11 a.m. Though you may catch a glimpse of several species from the train, it can't compare to Kilimanjaro Safaris for seeing the animals.

Conservation Station

What It Is Behind-the-scenes walk-through educational exhibit
Scope & Scale Minor attraction

When to Go Any time
Special Comments Opens an hour after the rest of the park
Author's Rating Evolving; ★★★
Appeal by Age Group

Pre-school ★★½	Grade School ★★	Teens ★½
Young Adults ★★½	Over 30 ★★½	Senior Citizens ★★½

Probable Waiting Time None

Description and Comments Conservation Station is the Animal Kingdom's veterinary and conservation headquarters. Located on the perimeter of the African section of the park, Conservation Station is, strictly speaking, a backstage, working facility. Here guests can meet wildlife experts, observe some of the Station's ongoing projects, and learn about the behind-the-scenes operations of the park. The Station includes, among other things, a rehabilitation area for injured animals and a nursery for recently born (or hatched) critters. Vets and other experts are on hand to answer questions.

While there are several permanent exhibits, including an animal petting area, what you see at Conservation Station will largely depend on what's going on when you arrive. On the days we visited, there wasn't enough happening to warrant waiting in line twice (coming and going) for the train. Hopefully, Conservation Station will improve with age. Ditto for the train ride.

Most of our readers comment that Conservation Station is not worth the hassle of the train ride. A Tinley Park, Illinois, mom writes:

Skip Conservation Station at the Animal Kingdom. Between the train ride to get to it and being there, we wasted a precious one and a half hours!

A mother of one from Austin, Texas, had a better experience:

Best thing at Conservation Station was the wildlife experts presenting one animal at a time—live, with info—very interesting.

And a reader from Kent in the United Kingdom was amused by both the goings-on and the other guests:

The most memorable part of the Animal Kingdom for me was watching a veterinary surgeon and his team [at Conservation Station] perform an operation on a rat snake that had inadvertently swallowed a golf ball! Presumably believing it to be an egg. This operation took about an hour and caused at least one onlooker to pass out.

You can access Conservation Station by taking the Wildlife Express train directly from Harambe. To return to the center of the park, continue the loop from Conservation Station back to Harambe.

Touring Tips Conservation Station is interesting, but you have to invest a little effort and it helps to be inquisitive. Because it's on the far-flung border of the park, you'll never bump into Conservation Station unless you take the train.

Asia

Crossing the Asia Bridge from Discovery Island, you enter Asia through the village of Anandapur, a veritable collage of Asian themes inspired by the architecture and ruins of India, Thailand, Indonesia, and Nepal. Situated near the bank of the Chakranadi River (translation: the river that runs in circles) and surrounded by lush vegetation, Anandapur provides access to a gibbon exhibit and to Asia's two feature attractions, the Kali River Rapids whitewater raft ride and the Maharajah Jungle Trek. Also in Asia is *Flights of Wonder,* an educational production about birds.

Kali River Rapids (FASTPASS)

What It Is Whitewater raft ride

Scope & Scale Headliner

When to Go Before 10 a.m., after 4:30 p.m., or use FASTPASS

Special Comments You are guaranteed to get wet. Opens an hour after the rest of the park.

Author's Rating Short but scenic; ★★★½

Appeal by Age Group

Pre-school ★★★★   Grade School ★★★★   Teens ★★★★

Young Adults ★★★½   Over 30 ★★★½   Senior Citizens ★★★

Duration of Ride About 5 minutes

Average Wait in Line per 100 People ahead of You 5 minutes

Loading Speed Moderate

Description and Comments Whitewater raft rides have been a hot-weather favorite of theme-park patrons for almost 20 years. The ride itself consists of an unguided trip down a man-made river in a circular rubber raft with a platform seating 12 persons mounted on top. The raft essentially floats free in the current and is washed downstream through rapids and waves. Because the river is fairly wide with numerous currents, eddies, and obstacles, there is no telling exactly where the raft will go. Thus, each trip is different and exciting. At the end of the ride, a conveyor belt hauls the raft up to be unloaded and prepared for the next group of guests.

What distinguishes Kali River Rapids from other theme-park raft rides is Disney's trademark attention to visual detail. Where many raft rides essentially plunge down a concrete ditch, Kali River Rapids flows through a dense rain forest, past waterfalls, temple ruins, and bamboo thickets, emerging into a cleared area where greedy loggers have ravaged the forest, and finally drifting back under the tropical canopy as the river cycles back to Anandapur. Along the way, your raft runs a gauntlet of raging cataracts, log jams, and other dangers.

Disney has done a great job with the visuals on this attraction. The queuing area, which winds through an ancient southeast Asian temple, is one of the most striking and visually interesting settings of any Disney attraction. And though the sights on the raft trip itself are also first class, the attraction is marginal in two important respects. First, it's only about three and a half minutes on the water, and second, well . . . it's a weenie ride. Sure, you get wet, but otherwise the drops and rapids are not all that exciting. And how wet do you get? A reader from Plymouth, Michigan, has the answer:

The new whitewater rafting ride is great fun but beware!! Rather than just
getting a little wet, like Splash Mountain, we were soaked to the skin after

this ride. It was beyond "fun getting wet," literally drenching you with buckets of water. Poncho sales were brisk the day we were there.

You can use FASTPASS to ride later in the day when it's a little warmer. A family from Humble, Texas, rode early in the morning on a cool day, sharing this experience:

Our plan hit a definite wall upon experiencing Kali River Rapids as number two on the schedule. We did not read about the precautions for this ride in your book until after riding. The six-year-old and mom were COMPLETELY drenched—so much so that we actually had to leave the park and go back to our room at [Port Orleans] to change clothes. Since the temperature was around 60° that morning, we were pretty miserable by the time we got back to our room. Needless to say, our schedule was shot by that time. We would not recommend Kali River Rapids so early in the morning when the weather is chilly.

A couple from Spring, Texas, rode during warmer weather, reporting:

Kali River Rapids gives new meaning to the term "You May Get Wet." More like drenched to the bone! Splash Mountain is nothing close. Four hours of touring later I was only beginning to feel dry. Obviously, Disney needs to lessen the aquatic experience here. This unwelcome bath has resulted in an interesting and undesirable psychological reaction for both of us. [My companion] refused to go on any ride or even into any theater where there was a chance of getting wet. As for me, every time I've been unexpectedly sprayed by water, even after leaving Disney, I withdraw and shudder with fear.

But two self-described "single babes" admonish our soggy readers to "get over it":

If you're going to ride Kali River Rapids, tough it out and get wet. Don't wrap yourself in plastic. Wet butts dry fast and keep you cool in the meantime!

Touring Tips   This attraction is hugely popular, especially on hot summer days. Ride Kali River Rapids before 10 a.m., after 4:30 p.m., or use FASTPASS. You can expect to get wet and possibly drenched on this ride. Our recommendation is to wear shorts to the park and bring along a jumbo size trash bag as well as a smaller plastic bag. Before boarding the raft, take off your socks and punch holes in your jumbo bag for your head. Though you can also cut holes for your arms, you will probably stay dryer with your arms inside the bag. Use the smaller plastic bag to wrap around your shoes. If you are worried about mussing your hairdo, bring a third bag for your head. There's also a water-resistant compartment in the middle of the raft for stowing small items.

A Shaker Heights, Ohio, family who adopted our garbage bag attire, however, discovered that staying dry on the Kali River Rapids is not without social consequences:

I must tell you that the Disney cast members and the other people in our raft looked at us like we had just beamed down from Mars. Plus, we didn't cut arm holes in our trash bags because we thought we'd stay drier. Only problem was once we sat down we couldn't fasten our seat belts. The Disney person was quite put out and asked sarcastically whether we needed wetsuits and snorkels. After a lot of wiggling and adjusting and helping each other we finally got belted in and off we went looking like sacks of fertilizer with little heads perched on top. It was very embarrassing, but I must admit that we stayed nice and dry.

Maharaja Jungle Trek

What It Is Walk-through zoological exhibit
Scope & Scale Headliner
When to Go Anytime
Special Comments Opens an hour after the rest of the park
Author's Rating A standard-setter for natural habitat design; ★★★★
Appeal by Age Group
Pre-school ★★★　　Grade School ★★★½　Teens ★★★
Young Adults ★★★½　Over 30 ★★★★　　Senior Citizens ★★★★
Duration of Tour About 20–30 minutes

Description and Comments　The Maharaja Jungle Trek is a zoological nature walk similar to the Pangani Forest Exploration Trail, but with an Asian setting and Asian animals. You start with Komodo dragons and then work up to Malayan tapirs. Next is a cave with fruit bats. Ruins of the maharaja's palace provide the setting for Bengal tigers. From the top of a parapet in the palace you can view a herd of blackbuck antelope and Asian deer. The trek concludes with an aviary.

Labyrinthine, overgrown, and elaborately detailed, the temple ruin would be a compelling attraction even without the animals. Throw in a few bats, bucks, and Bengals and you're in for a treat.

Most readers agree. From a Tolland, Connecticut, woman:

We went to AK last year and must say—what a difference a year makes! We saw more animals in the first hour this visit than we did the whole day last year. The Bengal tigers were especially exciting—they look so close to where you are in the "ruins." The staff there was so helpful. You truly get the feeling they love their jobs. The kids especially liked the bat exhibit.

And a Washington, D.C. couple chipped in with this:

We went on the Maharaja Jungle Trek, which was absolutely amazing. We were able to see all the animals, which were awake by that time (9:30 a.m.), including the elusive tigers. The part of the jungle with the birds was fabulous. If you looked, you could spot hundreds of birds, some of which were eating on the ground a mere three feet away from me. Recommend to future visitors to take their time walking through the jungle, since most of the animals are not obvious to the breezing eye and you must look for them. It is worth the extra time to see such an unusual exhibit.

Touring Tips　The Jungle Trek does not get as jammed up as the Pangani Forest Exploration Trail and is a good choice for midday touring when most other attractions are crowded. The downside, of course, is that the exhibit showcases tigers, tapirs, and other creatures that might not be as active in the heat of the day as the proverbial mad dogs and Englishmen.

Flights of Wonder *at the Caravan Stage*

What It Is Stadium show about birds
Scope & Scale Major attraction
When to Go Anytime
Special Comments Performance times are listed in the handout park map
Author's Rating Unique; ★★★★
Appeal by Age Group
Pre-school ★★★★ Grade School ★★★★ Teens ★★★½
Young Adults ★★★★ Over 30 ★★★★ Senior Citizens ★★★★
Duration of Presentation 30 minutes
Preshow Entertainment None
Probable Waiting Time 20 minutes

Description and Comments Both interesting and fun, *Flights of Wonder* is well paced and showcases a surprising number of different bird species. The show has been rescripted, abandoning an improbable plot for a more straightforward educational presentation. The focus of *Flights of Wonder* is on the natural talents and characteristics of the various species, so don't expect to see any parrots riding bicycles. The natural behaviors, however, far surpass any tricks learned from humans. Overall, the presentation is fascinating and exceeds most guests' expectations. A Brattleboro, Vermont, reader found *Flights of Wonder* especially compelling, writing:

In our opinion the highlight of the Animal Kingdom is Flights of Wonder. *The ornithologist guide is not only a wealth of information but a talented, comedic entertainer. The birds are thrilling, and we especially appreciated the fact that their antics, although fascinating to behold, were not the results of training against the grain but actual survival techniques the birds use in the wild.*

Touring Tips *Flights of Wonder* plays at the stadium located near the Asia Bridge on the walkway into Asia. Though the stadium is covered, it's not air- conditioned, thus, early-morning and late-afternoon performances are more comfortable. Though we did not have any problem getting a seat for *Flights of Wonder*, the show's attendance has picked up since the rest of Asia opened. To play it safe, arrive about 10–15 minutes before show time.

DinoLand U.S.A.

This most typically Disney of the Animal Kingdom's lands is a cross between an anthropological dig and a quirky roadside attraction. Accessible via the bridge from Discovery Island, DinoLand U.S.A. is home to a children's play area, a nature trail, a 1,500-seat amphitheater, a couple of natural history exhibits, and Dinosaur, one of the Animal Kingdom's two thrill rides.

Dinosaur (FASTPASS)

What It Is Motion-simulator dark ride
Scope & Scale Super headliner
When to Go Before 10 a.m. or in the hour before closing
Special Comments Must be 40" tall to ride. Switching off option provided (see pages 254–257).
Author's Rating Really improved; ★★★★½
Appeal by Age Group

Pre-school †	Grade School ★★★★½	Teens ★★★★½
Young Adults ★★★★½	Over 30 ★★★★½	Senior Citizens ★★★½

† Sample size too small for an accurate rating.

Duration of Ride 3⅓ minutes
Average Wait in Line per 100 People ahead of You 3 minutes
Assumes Full-capacity operation with 18-second dispatch interval
Loading Speed Fast

Description and Comments Dinosaur, formerly known as Countdown to Extinction, is a combination track ride and motion simulator. In addition to moving along a cleverly hidden track, the ride vehicle also bucks and pitches (the simulator part) in sync with the visuals and special effects encountered. The plot has you traveling back in time on a mission of rescue and conservation. Your objective, believe it or not, is to haul back a living dinosaur before the species becomes extinct. Whoever is operating the clock, however, cuts it a little close, and you arrive on the prehistoric scene just as a giant asteroid is hurling toward Earth. General mayhem ensues as you evade carnivorous predators, catch Barney, and make your escape before the asteroid hits.

Dinosaur is a technological clone of the Indiana Jones ride at Disneyland. A good effort, though not as visually interesting as Indiana Jones, Dinosaur serves up nonstop action from beginning to end with brilliant visual effects. Elaborate even by Disney standards, the attraction provides a tense, frenetic ride embellished by the entire Imagineering arsenal of high-tech gimmickry. Although the ride is jerky, it's not too rough for seniors. The menacing dinosaurs, however, along with the intensity of the experience, make Dinosaur a no-go for younger children.

Dinosaur, to our surprise and joy, had been refined and cranked up a couple of notches on the intensity scale after its first year of operation. The latest version is darker, more interesting, and much zippier. A mother from Kansasville, Wisconsin, liked it a lot, commenting:

Dinosaur is the best ride at WDW. Our group of ten, ranging in age from 65 (grandma) to 8 (grandson), immediately—and unanimously!—got back in line immediately after finishing.

A 20-something guy from Muncie, Indiana, however, wasn't so sure:

The Dinosaur attraction was the scariest ride I have ever been on. I'm 24 and love thrill rides, but I didn't open my eyes for half of the ride. I can't believe younger children are permitted to ride.

A man from Irving, Texas, didn't mind the dinosaurs but got more than he bargained for in the lurching ride vehicle:

One attraction I think you missed the boat on was Dinosaur. I'm 38 and have ridden many roller coasters. I have never ridden anything that tossed me back and forth so far and so quickly as Dinosaur. The preshow was well done, but the ride itself was far too violent. I don't mind that it tossed and tilted me in one direction; my problem is that half a second later, it tossed and tilted me in other directions and kept tossing me back and forth. Aside from the welcome seat belts it was like a bucking bronco. You mentioned that it wasn't too bad for seniors—HA! Talk to my parents or to another couple I overheard disembarking. The violence (of the ride vehicle) was very gratuitous.

And speaking of younger children, we got plenty of feedback about their reactions: First, from a Michigan family:

Beware Dinosaur. My seven-year-old son withstood every ride Disney threw at him, from Body Wars to Space Mountain to Tower of Terror. Dinosaur, however, did him in. By the end of the ride, he was riding with his head down, scared to look around. It is intense, combining scary visual dinosaur effects with some demanding roller coaster–like simulation.

Next from a mother of two from Westford, Massachusetts:

My six-year-old felt the Dinosaur ride was far scarier than Alien Encounter or any other ride at Disney. It is very dark (like Alien), but the dinosaurs pop out at you very quickly—I witnessed several adults who were quite shaken by it as well.

Finally, from a Florida mom:

This is definitely not for the faint-hearted, and small children should not go on it unless they have nerves of steel!

Touring Tips   Disney situated Dinosaur in such a remote corner of the park that it takes guests awhile to find it. This, in conjunction with the overwhelming popularity of Kilimanjaro Safaris, left Dinosaur operating at less than capacity. To bump its numbers up, Disney even tried opening the attraction before the rest of the park, providing access to DinoLand through a backstage gate. By the time we went to press, Dinosaur was doing better but not attracting crowds comparable to Indiana Jones at Disneyland. Despite the slow start, we expect Dinosaur to turn into a big draw. Thus we continue to recommend that you ride early after experiencing Kilimanjaro Safaris. If you bump into a long line, use FASTPASS.

TriceraTop Spin

What It Is   Hub-and-spoke midway ride

Scope & Scale   Minor attraction

When to Go   First 90 minutes the park is open and in the hour before park closing

Author's Rating   Dumbo's prehistoric forebear; ★★

Appeal by Age Group

Pre-school ★★★★	Grade School ★★★	Teens ★★
Young Adults ★★	Over 30 ★★	Senior Citizens ★★

Duration of Ride   1½ minutes

Average Wait in Line per 100 People ahead of You 10 minutes
Loading Speed Slow

Description and Comments   Another Dumbo-like ride. Here you spin around a central hub until a dinosaur pops out of the top of the hub. You'd think with the collective imagination of the Walt Disney Company they'd come up with something a little more creative.

Touring Tips   An attraction for the children, except they won't appreciate the long wait for this slow-loading ride.

Primeval Whirl (FASTPASS)

What It Is Small coaster
Scope & Scale Minor attraction
When to Go During the first 60 minutes the park is open or in the hour before park closing
Special Comments 48" minimum height. Switching off option provided (see pages 254–257).
Author's Rating Wild Mouse on steriods; ★★★
Appeal by Age Group

Pre-school ★★★	Grade School ★★★½	Teens ★★★½
Young Adults ★★★	Over 30 ★★★	Senior Citizens ★★

Duration of Ride Almost 2½ minutes
Average Wait in Line per 100 People ahead of You 4½ minutes
Loading Speed Slow

Description and Comments   Primeval Whirl is a small coaster with short drops and curves, and it runs through the jaws of a dinosaur among other things. What makes this coaster different is that the cars also spin. Because guests cannot control the spinning, the cars spin and stop spinning according to how the ride is programmed. Sometimes the spin is braked to a jarring halt after half a revolution, and sometimes it's allowed to make one or two complete spins. The complete spins are fun, but the screeching-stop half-spins are almost painful. If you subtract the time it takes to rachet up the first hill, the actual ride time is about 90 seconds.

Touring Tips   Like Space Mountain, the ride is duplicated side by side, but with only one queue. When running smoothly, about 700 people per side can whirl in an hour; a goodly number for this type of attraction, but not enough to preclude long waits on busy-to-moderate days. If you want to ride, try to get on before 11 a.m. or use FASTPASS.

Theater in the Wild

What It Is Open-air venue for live stage shows
Scope & Scale Major attraction
When to Go Anytime
Special Comments Performance times are listed in the handout park map
Author's Rating Tarzan lays an egg; ★★½

Appeal by Age Group

Pre-school ★★★	Grade School ★★★★	Teens ★★★
Young Adults ★★★	Over 30 ★★★	Senior Citizens ★★★

Duration of Presentation 25–35 minutes

Preshow Entertainment None

Probable Waiting Time 20–30 minutes

Description and Comments The Theater in the Wild is a 1,500-seat covered amphitheater. The largest stage production facility in the Animal Kingdom, the theater can host just about any type of stage show. In the summer of 1999, the Theater in the Wild unveiled a rock musical production based on Disney's animated *Tarzan* movie. Called *Tarzan Rocks!*, the show features aerial acts as well as acrobatic stunts, including extreme skating. The musical score is by Phil Collins and drawn from the soundtrack of the film. If this sounds like a hodgepodge, you're right. Although the performers are both talented and enthusiastic, attempting to attach such disparate elements to the *Tarzan* plot (in a musical context yet!) produces a lumbering, uneven, and hugely redundant affair. Simply put, the whole equals significantly less than the sum of its parts. By way of analogy, *Tarzan Rocks!* reminds us of preparations in pretentious restaurants where the chef tries to combine every imaginable delicacy in one fancy dish (seared filet of beef topped with lump crabmeat au gratin and stuffed with goose pâté and venison medallions—you get the idea). We like parts of the presentation taken individually, but every time the show comes close to taking off, it fumbles into an awkward transition and loses its momentum. And unlike *Festival of the Lion King* in Camp Minnie-Mickey, there's not one single tune that sticks with you when the show's over.

A couple from Dix Hills, New York, concurs:

> *Tarzan Rocks has got to go. Aside from the roller stunts, all in our party were bored to tears. A big problem is that the songs from the movie are unmemorable, even when Phil Collins sings them, even more so when the cast members sing them.*

Touring Tips To get a seat, show up 20–25 minutes in advance for morning and late-afternoon shows, and 30–35 minutes in advance for shows scheduled between noon and 4:30 p.m. Access to the theater is via a relatively narrow pedestrian path. If you arrive as the previous show is letting out, you will feel like a salmon swimming upstream.

The Boneyard

What It Is Elaborate playground

Scope & Scale Diversion

When to Go Anytime

Special Comments Opens an hour after the rest of the park

Author's Rating Stimulating fun for children; ★★★½

Appeal by Age Group

Pre-school ★★★★½	Grade School ★★★★½	Teens —
Young Adults —	Over 30 —	Senior Citizens —

Duration of Visit Varies

Waiting Time None

Description and Comments This attraction is an elaborate playground, particularly appealing to kids age ten and younger, but visually appealing to all ages. Arranged in the form of a rambling open-air dig site, The Boneyard offers plenty of opportunity for exploration and letting off steam. Playground equipment consists of the skeletons of Triceratops, *Tyrannosaurus rex*, Brachiosaurus, and the like, on which children can swing, slide, and climb. In addition, there are sand pits where little ones can scrounge around for bones and fossils.

Touring Tips Not the cleanest Disney attraction, but certainly one where younger children will want to spend some time. Aside from getting dirty, or at least sandy, be aware that The Boneyard gets mighty hot in the Florida sun. Keep your kids well hydrated and drag them into the shade from time to time. If your children will let you, save the playground until after you have experienced the main attractions. Because The Boneyard is situated so close to the center of the park, it's easy to stop in whenever your kids get itchy. While the little ones clamber around on giant femurs and ribs, you can sip a tall cool one in the shade (still keeping an eye on them, of course).

As a Michigan family attests, kids love the Boneyard:

The highlight for our kids was the Boneyard, especially the dig site. They just kept digging and digging to uncover the bones of the wooly mammoth. It was also in the shade, and there were places for parents to sit, making it a wonderful resting place.

A Woodridge, Illinois, dad thinks maybe children love it too much, warning:

Beware parents, my kid is eight years old, and in Dinoland all he wanted to do was dig up the dino bones in the huge sand box. I saw time and time again parents trying unsuccessfully to drag their kids away from here so they could visit another attraction. This sand box is best left toward the end of the day when you just want to sit and relax while the kids let off energy.

Be aware that The Boneyard rambles over about a half-acre and is multi-storied. It's pretty easy to lose sight of a small child in the playground. Fortunately, there's only one entrance and exit. A mother of two from Stillwater, Minnesota, found the playground too large for her liking:

If you are a parent who likes to have your eyes on your kids at all times, The Boneyard is very scary for adults. Kids climb to the top [of the slides], and you can't see them at the top and you don't know what chute they will be exiting. It made me VERY nervous because I could not see them at all times. We left immediately!!

Live Entertainment in the Animal Kingdom

Stage Shows Stage shows are performed daily at the Theater in the Wild in DinoLand U.S.A., at Grandmother Willow's Grove and at the Lion King Theater in Camp Minnie-Mickey, and at the stadium in Asia. Presentations at Camp Minnie-Mickey and DinoLand U.S.A. feature the Disney characters.

Street Performers Street performers can be found most of the time at Discovery Island, at Harambe in Africa, at Anandapur in Asia, and in DinoLand U.S.A.

Afternoon Parade There has never been a parade in the Animal Kingdom comparable to the parades at the other parks. Until recently that is. Kicked off in the fall of 2001, Mickey's Jammin' Jungle Parade is complete with floats, Disney characters (especially those from *The Lion King, Jungle Book, Tarzan,* and *Pocahontas*), skaters, acrobats, and stilt walkers.

Though subject to change, the parade starts in Africa, crosses the bridge to Discovery Island, proceeds counterclockwise around the island, and then crosses the bridge to Asia. In Asia the parade turns left and follows the walkway paralleling the river back to Africa.

Kid's Discovery Club Informal, creative activity stations offer kids ages 4–8 a structured learning experience as they tour the Animal Kingdom. Set up along walkways in six theme areas, Discovery Club stations are manned by cast members who supervise a different activity at each station. A souvenir logbook, available free, is stamped at each station when the child completes the craft or exercise. Children enjoy collecting the stamps and noodling the puzzles in the logbook while in attraction lines.

Animal Encounters Throughout the day, knowledgeable Disney staff conduct impromptu short lectures on specific animals at the park. Look for a cast member in safari garb holding a bird, reptile, or small mammal.

Goodwill Ambassadors A number of Asian and African natives are on-hand throughout the park. Both gracious and knowledgeable, they are delighted to discuss their country and its wildlife. Look for them in Harambe and along the Pangani Forest Exploration Trail in Africa, and in Anandapur and along the Maharaja Jungle Trek in Asia. They can also be found near the main entrance and at The Oasis.

Traffic Patterns in the Animal Kingdom

For starters, because the Animal Kingdom is still pretty new, expect huge crowds for the foreseeable future, even during the off-season. The four crowd magnets are *It's Tough to Be a Bug!* in the Tree of Life, Kilimanjaro Safaris in Africa, Dinosaur in DinoLand U.S.A., and Kali River Rapids in Asia.

Because the park hosts large crowds with only a relative handful of attractions, expect for all the attractions to be extremely busy, and for Kilimanjaro Safaris to be mobbed. Most guests arrive in the morning, with a sizable number on hand prior to opening and a larger wave arriving before 10 a.m. Guests continue to stream in through the late morning and into the early afternoon, with the crowds peaking at around 2 p.m. From about 2:30 p.m. on, departing guests outnumber arriving guests by a wide margin, as guests who arrived early complete their tour and leave. Crowds thin appreciably by late afternoon and continue to decline into the early evening.

Because the number of attractions, including theater presentations, are limited, most guests complete a fairly comprehensive tour in two-thirds of a day if they arrive early. Thus, generally speaking, your best bet for easy touring is either to be on-hand when the park opens or to arrive at about 3 p.m. (if the part stays open until 7 or 8 p.m.), when the early birds are heading for the exits. If you decide to visit during the late afternoon, you might have to return on another afternoon to see everything.

How guests tour the Animal Kingdom depends on their prior knowledge of the park and its attractions. Guests arriving without much prior knowledge make their way to Discovery Island and depend on their handout park map to decide what to do next. Most are drawn to Africa and Kilimanjaro Safaris. A smaller number visit DinoLand U.S.A. first. Those guests who have boned up on the Animal Kingdom make straight for Kilimanjaro Safaris in Africa and Dinosaur in DinoLand U.S.A. Kali River Rapids in Asia and *It's Tough to Be a Bug!* in the Tree of Life are also early-morning favorites.

At the Magic Kingdom, you can tour clockwise or counterclockwise without returning to the central hub. To go from land to land at the Animal Kingdom, however, you usually have to pass through Discovery Island. Discovery Island and its attractions thus draw crowds earlier than the other lands and remain inundated throughout the day. Africa, likewise, draws heavy attendance but is set up to move crowds through in a controlled sequence. Attractions in DinoLand U.S.A., with the exception of Dinosaur, Primeval Whirl, and TriceraTop Spin, will be easily accessible most of the day. Camp Minnie-Mickey is congested from 9:30 a.m. until about 4 p.m., more because of poor traffic design than popularity.

Animal Kingdom Touring Plan

Animal Kingdom One-Day Touring Plan

Touring the Animal Kingdom is not as complicated as touring the other parks because it offers a smaller number of attractions. Also, most Animal Kingdom rides, shows, and zoological exhibits are oriented to the entire family, thus eliminating differences of opinion regarding how to spend the day. At the Animal Kingdom, the whole family can pretty much see and enjoy everything together.

Since there are fewer attractions than at the other parks, expect the crowds at the Animal Kingdom to be more concentrated. If a line seems unusually long, ask an Animal Kingdom cast member what the estimated wait is. If the wait exceeds your tolerance, try the same attraction again after 3 p.m., while a show is in progress at the Theater in the Wild in DinoLand U.S.A., or while some special event is going on.

The Animal Kingdom One-Day Touring Plan assumes a willingness to experience all major rides and shows. Be forewarned that Dinosaur, Primeval Whirl, and Kali River Rapids are sometimes frightening to children under age eight. Similarly, the theater attraction at the Tree of Life might be too intense for some preschoolers. When following the touring plan, simply skip any attraction you do not wish to experience.

Before You Go

1. Call (407) 824-4321 before you go to learn the park's hours of operation.

2. Purchase your admission prior to arrival.

At the Animal Kingdom

1. Arrive at the park one hour before the official opening time during summer and holiday periods, and 40 minutes before the official opening time the rest of the year. At the entrance plaza, pick up a park map and daily entertainment schedule. Wait at the entrance turnstiles to be admitted.

2. When admitted through the turnstiles, move quickly through The Oasis without stopping and cross the bridge into Discovery Island. Turn left after the bridge and walk clockwise around the Tree of Life until you reach the bridge to Africa. Cross the bridge and continue straight ahead to the entrance of Kilimanjaro Safaris. Experience Kilimanjaro Safaris. Unless the wait exceeds 30 minutes, do not use FASTPASS.

3. After the safari, head back toward the Africa bridge to Discovery Island, but turn left before crossing. Follow the walkway along the river to Asia. In Asia, ride Kali River Rapids.

   As a cost-cutting measure in 2001, Disney delayed the opening of Asia until one hour after the rest of the park. If Asia is not yet open when you arrive or if the weather is cool (or you just don't feel like getting wet), proceed to Steps 4–6. Return to Kali River Rapids after seeing *It's Tough to Be a Bug!* (Step 6). If the wait is more than 30 minutes for the raft ride when you return, use FASTPASS.

4. Following the raft trip, return to the entrance of Asia and turn left over the Asia bridge into Discovery Island. Pass the Beastly Bazaar and Flame Tree Barbeque and then turn left and cross the bridge into DinoLand U.S.A. After passing beneath the brontosaurus skeleton angle left to Primeval Whirl. Ride. *Note:* If you have children ages eight and younger in your party, they will want to ride TriceraTop Spin (a children's ride straight and to the left) after entering Dinoland. Ride TriceraTop Spin first, then Primeval Whirl.

5. Follow the signs to Dinosaur. Ride.

6. Next, retrace your steps to Discovery Island, bearing left after you cross the DinoLand bridge. See *It's Tough to Be a Bug!* in the Tree of Life. If the wait exceeds 30 minutes, use FASTPASS.

7. By now you will have most of the Animal Kingdom's potential bottlenecks behind you. Check your daily entertainment schedule for shows at the Theater in the Wild in DinoLand U.S.A., for *Flights of Wonder* in Asia, and for *Festival of the Lion King* and *Pocahontas* in Camp Minnie-Mickey. Plan the next part of your day around eating lunch and seeing these four shows. Before 11 a.m., arrive about 15–20 minutes prior to show time. During the middle of the day (11 a.m.–4 p.m.), you will need to queue up as follows:

For the Theater in the Wild:	30 minutes before show time
For the Caravan Stage	15 minutes before show time
For Pocahontas	25–30 minutes before show time
For the Lion King Theater	25–35 minutes before show time

8. Between shows, check out The Boneyard in DinoLand U.S.A. and the zoological exhibits around the Tree of Life and in The Oasis. The best time to meet the characters at Camp Minnie-Mickey is while performances are underway at the two Camp Minnie-Mickey amphitheaters.

9. Return to Asia and take the Maharajah Jungle Trek.

10. Return to Africa and take the Wildlife Express train to Rafiki's Planet Watch and Conservation Station. Tour the exhibits. If you want to experience Kilimanjaro Safaris again, obtain a FASTPASS before boarding the train.

11. Depart Rafiki's Planet Watch and Conservation Station and catch the train back to Harambe.

12. In Harambe, walk the Pangani Forest Exploration Trail.

13. Shop, snack, or repeat any attractions you especially enjoyed.

14. This concludes the touring plan. Be sure to allocate some time to visit the zoological exhibits in The Oasis on your way out of the park.

Part Thirteen

Disney-MGM Studios, Universal Orlando, and SeaWorld

Disney-MGM Studios vs. Universal Studios Florida

Disney-MGM Studios and Universal Studios Florida are direct competitors. Because both are large and expensive and require at least one day to see, some guests must choose one park over the other. To help you decide, we present a head-to-head comparison of the two parks, followed by a description of each in detail. In the summer of 1999, Universal launched its second major theme park, Universal's Islands of Adventure, which competes directly with Disney's Magic Kingdom. The new park is discussed in detail later in this section. (Universal Studios Florida, Islands of Adventure, the three Universal hotels, and the CityWalk complex are collectively known as Universal Orlando.) Lastly, a summary profile of SeaWorld concludes Part Thirteen.

Both Disney-MGM Studios and Universal Studios Florida draw their theme and inspiration from film and television. Both offer movie- and TV-themed rides and shows, some of which are just for fun, while others provide an educational, behind-the-scenes introduction to the cinematic arts. Both parks include working film and television production studios.

Nearly half of Disney-MGM Studios is off-limits to guests except by guided tour, while most all of Universal Studios Florida is open to exploration. Unlike Disney-MGM, Universal Orlando's open area includes the entire backlot, where guests can walk at leisure among movie sets.

Universal hammers on the point that it's first a working motion-picture and television studio, and only incidentally a tourist attraction. Whether this assertion is a point of pride with Universal or an explanation to the tourist is unclear. It's true, however, that guests are more likely to see movie or television production in progress at Universal Orlando than at Disney-MGM. On any day, production crews will be shooting on the Universal backlot in full view of guests who care to watch.

Universal Studios Florida is about twice as large as Disney-MGM, and because almost all of it is open to the public, most of the crowding and congestion so familiar in the streets and plazas of Disney-MGM is eliminated. Universal Studios Florida has plenty of elbow room.

Attractions are excellent at both parks, though Disney-MGM attractions are on average engineered to move people more efficiently. Each park offers stellar attractions that break new ground, transcending in power, originality, and technology any prior standard for theme-park entertainment. Universal offers *Terminator 2: 3-D,* which we consider the most extraordinary theater attraction in any American theme park, and Men in Black Alien Attack, an interactive high-tech ride where guests' actions determine the ending of the story. Disney-MGM Studios features *The Twilight Zone* Tower of Terror, our pick for Disney's best attraction. The next-best attractions in each park are also well matched: Back to the Future at Universal is in a dead heat with Star Tours at Disney-MGM.

Though Universal Studios must be credited with pioneering a number of innovative and technologically advanced rides, we must also point out that Universal's attractions break down more often than Disney-MGM's. Jaws and Kongfrontation, in particular, are notorious for their frequent breakdowns.

A Detroit woman who visited Universal Studios on a particularly bad day writes:

> Kongfrontation was broken, Earthquake was broken (with us in it for 30 minutes), and E.T. was broken (with us in line for 20 minutes). We got VIP passes for Earthquake, to come later without waiting ... It was finally online at about 6:45 p.m., and when we were just about to get on, it broke again. The rides at this park are really stupendous—very different from WDW, but I think they've bit off more than they can chew.

But a family from Baltimore, Ohio, reports a totally positive experience:

> I won't categorize Universal [Studios] except to say that it was the best. We centered our trip around WDW, but Universal [Studios] puts Disney to shame. It was not very crowded, the shows are excellent, and the rides are the best we've ever been on as far as entertainment value. We all agreed we could spend two to three days at Universal [Studios] and not get bored.

Amazingly, and to the visitor's advantage, each park offers a completely different product mix, so there is little or no redundancy for a person who visits both. Disney-MGM and Universal Studios Florida each provide good exposure to the cinematic arts, though Universal's presentations are generally more informative and comprehensive. Disney-MGM had a distinct edge in educational content until recently, when it turned several of its better tours into infomercials for Disney films. At Universal, you can still learn about post-production, sound-stages, set creation, special effects, directing, and cinematography without being bludgeoned by promotional hype.

Stunt shows are similar at both parks. Disney's *Indiana Jones Epic Stunt Spectacular* and Universal's *The Wild, Wild, Wild West Stunt Show* are both staged in 2,000-seat stadiums that allow a good view of the action. Both shows have their moments and are fairly informative.

We recommend you try one of the studios. If you enjoy one, you probably will enjoy the other. If you have to choose between them, consider:

1. Touring Time If you tour efficiently, it takes about seven to eight hours to see Disney-MGM Studios (including a lunch break). Because Universal Studios Florida is larger and contains more rides and shows, touring, including one meal, takes about 9–11 hours. One reader laments:

There is a lot more "standing" at Universal Studios, and it isn't as organized as [Disney-MGM]. Many of the attractions don't open until 10 a.m., and many shows seem to be going at the same time. We were not able to see nearly as many attractions at Universal as we were at [Disney-MGM] during the same amount of time. The one plus here is that there seems to be more property, and things are spaced out better so you have more elbow room.

As the reader observes, many Universal Studios attractions do not open until 10 a.m. or later. During our latest research visit, only a third of the major attractions were up and running when the park opened, and most theater attractions didn't schedule performances until 11 a.m. or after. This means that early in the day all park guests are concentrated among the relatively few attractions in operation. The number of attractions operating at opening varies according to season, at both parks. This is a departure for Disney-MGM Studios, where all rides used to operate at opening year-round and where 9 out of 11 theater attractions scheduled shows before 11 a.m. As a postscript, you will not have to worry about any of this if you tour either park using our touring plan. We'll keep you one jump ahead of the crowd and make sure that any given attraction is running by the time you get there.

2. Convenience If you're lodging along International Drive, I-4's northeast corridor, the Orange Blossom Trail (US 441), or in Orlando, Universal Studios Florida is closer. If you're lodging along US 27 or FL 192 or in Kissimmee or Walt Disney World, Disney-MGM Studios is more convenient.

3. Endurance Universal Studios Florida is larger and requires more walking than Disney-MGM, but it is also much less congested, so the walking is easier. Both parks offer wheelchairs and disabled access.

4. Cost   Both parks cost about the same for one-day admission, food, and incidentals. All attractions are included in the admission price.

5. Best Days to Go   In order, Tuesdays, Mondays, Thursdays, and Wednesdays are best to visit Universal Studios Florida. At Disney-MGM Studios, visit on Monday or Friday during the summer and on Monday and Tuesday during the off-season.

6. When to Arrive   For Disney-MGM, arrive with your ticket in hand 40 minutes before official opening time. For Universal Studios, arrive with your admission already purchased about 50 minutes before official opening time.

7. Young Children   Both Disney-MGM Studios and Universal Studios Florida are relatively adult entertainment offerings. By our reckoning, half the rides and shows at Disney-MGM and about two-thirds at Universal Studios have a significant potential for frightening young children.

8. Food   Food is generally much better at Universal Studios.

9. FASTPASS vs. Universal Express   Both Disney's FASTPASS and Universal's Universal Express allow guests to "schedule" a time window to ride crowded attractions; such guests are shunted into shorter lines that substantially reduce wait times. However, there are differences between the two programs. Disney's FASTPASS allows you to have only one pass at a time. At Universal, however, guests can get up to three passes at once for the Universal Express lines, depending on how many days of park admission they purchase. In addition, guests at Universal hotels can access the Universal Express lines all day long simply by flashing their hotel keys. That last perk can be especially valuable during peak season—with both FASTPASS and Universal Express, large mobs of guests can gobble up an entire day's worth of passes before noon. But if you're staying at a Universal property, you can keep using the Express line even when all the passes are gone.

Disney-MGM Studios

Disney-MGM Studios was hatched from a corporate rivalry and a wild, twisted plot. At a time when the Disney Company was weak and fighting off greenmail—hostile takeover bids—Universal's parent company at the time, MCA, announced they were going to build an Orlando clone of their wildly successful Universal Studios Hollywood theme park. Behind the scenes, MCA was courting the real-estate rich Bass brothers of Texas, hoping to secure the brothers' investment in the project. The Bass brothers, however, defected to the Disney camp, helped Disney squelch the hostile takeovers, and were front and center when Michael Eisner suddenly announced that Disney would also build a movie theme park in

Florida. A construction race ensued, with Universal and Disney each intent on opening first. Universal, however, was midprocess in the development of a host of new attraction technologies and was no match for Disney, who could import proven concepts and attractions from their other parks. In the end, Disney-MGM Studios opened almost two years before Universal Studios Florida.

The MGM Connection

To broaden the appeal and to lend additional historical impact, Disney obtained the rights to use the MGM (Metro-Goldwyn-Mayer) name, film library, motion-picture and television titles, excerpts, costumes, music, sets, and even Leo, the MGM lion. Probably the two most recognized names in motion pictures, Disney and MGM represent almost a century of movie history.

Comparing Disney-MGM Studios to the Magic Kingdom and Epcot

The Magic Kingdom entertains, modeling its attractions on Disney movies and TV. Epcot educates, pioneering exhibits and rides that teach. Disney-MGM does both. All three parks rely heavily on Disney special effects and audio-animatronics (robotics) in their entertainment mix.

Disney-MGM Studios is about the size of the Magic Kingdom and about half as large as the sprawling Epcot. Unlike the other parks, Disney-MGM is a working motion-picture and television production facility. This means, among other things, that about half of it has controlled access, with guests permitted only on guided tours or observation walkways.

When Epcot opened in 1982, Disney patrons expected a futuristic version of the Magic Kingdom. What they got was humanistic inspiration and a creative educational experience. Since then, Disney has tried to inject more magic, excitement, and surprise into Epcot. Remembering the occasional disappointment of those early Epcot guests, Disney fortified the Studios with megadoses of action, suspense, surprise, and, of course, special effects. The formula has proved so successful that it was trotted out again at the new Animal Kingdom theme park. If you want to learn about the history and technology of movies and television, Disney-MGM Studios will teach you plenty. If you just want to be entertained, you won't leave disappointed.

Self-Promotion Run Amok

While it's true that Disney-MGM Studios educates and entertains, what it does best is promote. Self-promotion of Disney films and products was once subtle and in context. It is now blatant, inescapable, and detracting. Although most visitors are willing to forgive Disney its excesses, Studios

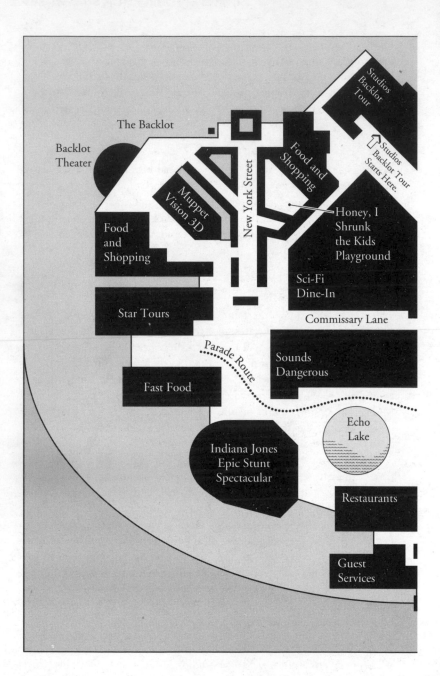

The Backlot

Backlot
Theater

Muppet
Vision 3D

Food
and
Shopping

Star Tours

New York Street

Food and
Shopping

Studios
Backlot
Tour

Studios
Backlot Tour
Starts Here.

Honey, I
Shrunk
the Kids
Playground

Sci-Fi
Dine-In

Commissary Lane

Parade Route

Fast Food

Sounds
Dangerous

Echo
Lake

Indiana Jones
Epic Stunt
Spectacular

Restaurants

Guest
Services

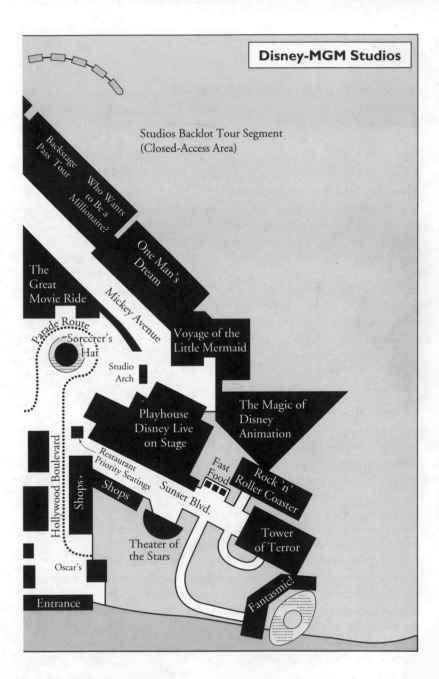

veterans will lament the changes and remember how good it was when education was the goal instead of the medium.

NOT TO BE MISSED AT DISNEY-MGM STUDIOS

Star Tours	*Fantasmic!*
Disney-MGM Studios Backlot Tour	*Voyage of the Little Mermaid*
Indiana Jones Epic Stunt Spectacular	*The Twilight Zone* Tower of Terror
Jim Henson's MuppetVision 3D	Rock 'n' Roller Coaster

How Much Time to Allocate

It's impossible to see all of Epcot or the Magic Kingdom in one day. Disney-MGM Studios, however, is more manageable. There's much less ground to cover by foot. Trams carry guests through much of the backlot and working areas, and attractions in the open-access parts are concentrated in an area about the size of Main Street, Tomorrowland, and Frontierland combined. Someday, no doubt, as Disney-MGM develops and grows, you'll need more than a day to see everything. For now, the Studios is a nice one-day outing.

Because Disney-MGM is smaller, however, it's more affected by large crowds. Our touring plans will help you stay a step ahead of the mob and minimize waiting in line. Even when the park is crowded, however, you can see almost everything in a day.

Disney-MGM Studios in the Evening

Because Disney-MGM Studios can be seen in three-fourths of a day, many guests who arrive early in the morning run out of things to do by 3:30 or 4 p.m. and leave the park. Their departure greatly thins the crowd and makes the Studios ideal for evening touring. Lines for most attractions are manageable, and the park is cooler and more comfortable. The *Indiana Jones Epic Stunt Spectacular* and productions at other outdoor theaters are infinitely more enjoyable during the evening than in the sweltering heat of the day.

One drawback to touring the Studios at night is that there won't be much activity on the production soundstages or in the Animation Building. Another is that you might get stuck eating dinner at the Studios. (If you must eat there, try Mama Melrose's or The Hollywood Brown Derby full-service dining.)

98, the Studios launched *Fantasmic!* (see pages 595–598), most spectacular nighttime entertainment event in the Disd nightly (weather permitting) in its own theater Terror, *Fantasmic!* is rated as "not to be missed." ng crowds have increased substantially at the studios because of *Fantasmic!* Some guests stay longer at Disney-MGM and others arrive after dinner from other parks expressly to see the show. Although crowds thin in the late afternoon, they build again as performance time approaches, making *Fantasmic!* a challenge to get into. Also adversely affected are the Tower of Terror and the Rock 'n' Roller Coaster, both situated near the entrance to *Fantasmic!*. Crowd levels throughout the remainder of the park, however, are generally light.

Arriving at Disney-MGM Studios

Disney-MGM Studios has its own pay parking lot and is served by the Disney transportation system. Most larger hotels outside the World shuttle guests to the Studios. If you drive, Disney's ubiquitous trams will transport you to the ticketing area and entrance gate.

Getting Oriented at Disney-MGM Studios

Guest Relations, on your left as you enter, serves as the park headquarters and information center, similar to City Hall in the Magic Kingdom and Guest Relations at Epcot and the Animal Kingdom. Go there for a schedule of live performances, lost persons, Package Pick-up, lost and found (on the right side of the entrance), general information, or in an emergency. If you haven't received a map of the Studios, get one here. To the right of the entrance are locker, stroller, and wheelchair rentals.

About one-half of the complex is set up as a theme park. As at the Magic Kingdom, you enter the park and pass down a main street. Only, this time it's Hollywood Boulevard of the 1920s and 1930s. At the end of Hollywood Boulevard is a replica of Hollywood's famous Chinese Theater. Lording over the plaza in front of the theater is a 122-foot-tall replica of the sorcerer hat Mickey Mouse wore in the animated classic *Fantasia*. Besides providing photo ops, the hat is the park's most central landmark, making it a good meeting place if your group becomes separated. In case you're wondering, Mickey would have to be 350 feet tall to wear the hat.

Though modest in size, the open-access areas of the Studios are confusingly arranged (a product of the park's hurried expansion in the early 1990s). As you face the hat, two guest areas—Sunset Boulevard and the Animation Courtyard—branch off Hollywood Boulevard to the right. Branching left off Hollywood Boulevard is the Echo Lake area. The open-access backlot wraps around the back of Echo Lake, the Chinese Theater, and the Animation Courtyard. You can experience all attractions here and in the other open-access sections of the park according to your tastes and time. Still farther to the rear is the limited-access backlot, consisting of the working soundstages, technical facilities, wardrobe shops, administrative offices, animation studios, and backlot sets. These are accessible to visitors on a guided tour by tram and foot.

HOLLYWOOD BOULEVARD SERVICES

Most of the park's service facilities are on Hollywood Boulevard, including:

Wheelchair & Stroller Rental Service	Right of the entrance at Oscar's
Banking Services	An ATM is outside the park to the right of the turnstiles.
Storage Lockers	Rental lockers are right of the main entrance, on the left of Oscar's.
Lost & Found	At Package Pick-up, right of the entrance
Live Entertainment/ Parade Information/ Character Information	Available free at Guest Relations and elsewhere in the park
Lost Persons	Report lost persons at Guest Relations
Walt Disney World & Local Attraction Information	At Guest Relations
First Aid	At Guest Relations
Baby Center/ Baby-Care Needs	At Guest Relations. Oscar's sells baby food and other necessities.
Film	At The Darkroom on the right side of Hollywood Boulevard, just beyond Oscar's

What to See

Try everything. As we have with the Magic Kingdom, Animal Kingdom, and Epcot, we identify attractions as "not to be missed." But Disney rides and shows usually exceed your expectations and always surprise.

Display Waiting Times

At the corner of Hollywood and Sunset Boulevards is a large display listing current waiting times for all Disney-MGM Studios attractions. It's updated continuously throughout the day. We've found the waiting times listed to be slightly overstated. If the display says the wait for Star Tours is 45 minutes, for example, you probably will have to wait about 35–40 minutes.

Disney-MGM Studios Attractions

Hollywood Boulevard

Hollywood Boulevard is a palm-lined re-creation of Hollywood's main drag during the city's golden age. Architecture is streamlined *moderne* with art deco embellishments. Most service facilities are here, interspersed with eateries and shops. Merchandise includes Disney trademark items, Hollywood and movie-related souvenirs, and one-of-a-kind collectibles obtained from studio auctions and estate sales.

Hollywood characters and roving performers entertain on the boulevard, and daily parades and other happenings pass this way.

Sunset Boulevard

Sunset Boulevard, evoking the 1940s, is a major addition to Disney-MGM Studios. The first right off Hollywood Boulevard, Sunset Boulevard provides another venue for dining, shopping, and street entertainment.

The Twilight Zone Tower of Terror (FASTPASS)

What It Is Sci-fi-theme indoor thrill ride
Scope & Scale Super headliner
When to Go Before 9:30 a.m. and after 6 p.m.
Special Comments Must be 40" tall to ride
Author's Rating Walt Disney World's best attraction; not to be missed; ★★★★★
Appeal by Age Group
  Pre-school ★★★   Grade School ★★★★★   Teens ★★★★★
  Young Adults ★★★★★   Over 30 ★★★★★   Senior Citizens ★★★★½
Duration of Ride About 4 minutes plus preshow
Average Wait in Line per 100 People ahead of You 4 minutes
Assumes All elevators operating
Loading Speed Moderate

Description and Comments The Tower of Terror is a new species of Disney thrill ride, though it borrows elements of The Haunted Mansion at the Magic Kingdom. The story is that you're touring a once-famous Hollywood hotel gone to ruin. As at Star Tours, the queuing area integrates guests into the adventure as they pass through the hotel's once-opulent public rooms. From the lobby, guests are escorted into the hotel's library, where Rod Serling, speaking on an old black-and-white television, greets the guests and introduces the plot.

The Tower of Terror is a whopper, 13-plus-stories tall. Breaking tradition in terms of visually isolating themed areas, you can see the entire Studios from atop the tower, but you have to look quick.

The ride vehicle, one of the hotel's service elevators, takes guests to see the haunted hostelry. The tour begins innocuously, but about the fifth floor things get pretty weird. You have entered the Twilight Zone. Guests are subjected to a full range of special effects as they encounter unexpected horrors and optical illusions. The climax of the adventure occurs when the elevator reaches the top floor (the 13th, of course) and the cable snaps.

The Tower of Terror is an experience to savor. Though the final plunges are calculated to thrill, the meat of the attraction is its extraordinary visual and audio effects. There's richness and subtlety here, enough to keep the ride fresh and stimulating after many repetitions.

A senior from the United Kingdom tried the Tower of Terror and liked it very much, writing:

I was thankful I had read your review of the Tower of Terror, or I would certainly have avoided it. As you say, it is so full of magnificent detail that it is worth riding, even if you don't fancy the drops involved.

The Tower has great potential for terrifying young children and rattling more mature visitors. If you have teenagers in your party, use them as experimental probes. If they report back that they really, really liked the Tower of Terror, run as fast as you can in the opposite direction.

Touring Tips   This one ride is worth your admission to Disney-MGM Studios. Because of its height, the Tower is a veritable beacon, visible from outside the park and luring curious guests as soon as they enter. Because of its popularity with school kids, teens, and young adults, you can count on a foot race to the attraction, as well as to the nearby Rock 'n' Roller Coaster, when the park opens. For the foreseeable future, expect the Tower to be mobbed most of the day. Experience it first thing in the morning, in the evening before the park closes, or use FASTPASS.

If you're on hand when the park opens and want to ride Tower of Terror first, position yourself on the far right side of Sunset Boulevard as close to the rope barrier as possible. Once in position, wait for the rope drop. When the park opens, cast members will walk the rope up the street toward Rock 'n' Roller Coaster and Tower of Terror. Just stay on the far right sidewalk and you'll be among the first to make the right turn to the entrance of the tower. Usually the Disney people get out of the way and allow you to run the last 100 feet or so. Also, be aware that about 65% of the folks waiting for the rope walk will head for Rock 'n' Roller Coaster. If you are not positioned on the far right, it will be almost impossible to move through the throng of coaster enthusiasts to make a right turn into Tower of Terror.

To save time, when you enter the library waiting area, stand in the far back corner across from the door where you entered and at the opposite end of the room from the TV. When the doors to the loading area open, you'll be one of the first admitted.

If you have young children (or anyone) who are apprehensive about this attraction, ask the attendant about switching off (pages 254–257).

A good strategy for riding both Tower of Terror and Rock 'n' Roller Coaster with minimum waits is to rush first thing after opening to Rock 'n' Roller Coaster and obtain FAST-PASSes, then line up for the Tower of Terror. Most days, by the time you finish experiencing the Tower of Terror it will be time to use your FASTPASS for Rock 'n' Roller Coaster.

Rock 'n' Roller Coaster (FASTPASS)

Motion Sickness

WARNING!

What It Is   Rock music–themed roller coaster
Scope & Scale   Headliner
When to Go   Before 10 a.m. or in the hour before closing
Special Comments   Must be 48" tall to ride; children younger than age 7 must ride with an adult. Switching off option provided (pages 254–257).
Author's Rating   Disney's wildest American coaster; not to be missed; ★★★★
Appeal by Age Group

Pre-school ★★★	Grade School ★★★★	Teens ★★★★
Young Adults ★★★★	Over 30 ★★★★	Senior Citizens ★★★

Duration of Ride Almost 1½ minutes
Average Wait in Line per 100 People ahead of You 2½ minutes
Assumes All trains operating
Loading Speed Moderate to fast

Description and Comments This is Disney's answer to the roller coaster prolif-
eration at Universal's Islands of Adventure and Busch Gardens theme parks. Exponentially wilder than Space Mountain or Big Thunder Mountain in the Magic Kingdom, the
Rock 'n' Roller Coaster is an attraction for fans of cutting-edge thrill rides. Although
the rock icons and synchronized music add measurably to the experience, the ride
itself, as opposed to sights and sounds along the way, is the focus here. The Rock 'n'
Roller Coaster offers loops, corkscrews, and drops that make Space Mountain seem
like the Jungle Cruise. What really makes this metal coaster unusual, however, is that
first, it's in the dark (like Space Mountain, only with Southern California nighttime
scenes instead of space), and second, you're launched up the first hill like a jet off a carrier deck. By the time you crest the hill, you'll have gone from 0 to 57 miles per hour in
less than three seconds. When you enter the first loop, you'll be pulling five g's. By comparison, that's two more g's than astronauts experience at lift-off on a space shuttle.

Reader opinions of Rock 'n' Roller Coaster have been predictably mixed, colored
invariably by how the reader feels about roller coasters. These comments are typical.
First from a mother of two from High Mills, New York:

*You can't warn people enough about Rock 'n' Roller Coaster. My daughter and
I refused to go on it at all. My nine-year-old son who had no problems with
any ride, including Tower of Terror, went on with my husband first thing in
the morning. My son came off so shaken he was "done for" the rest of the
day and never fully recuperated. My husband just closed his eyes and
hoped for the best.*

And from a Longmont, Colorado dad:

*Rock 'n' Roller Coaster: The first 15 seconds of this ride are spectacular. I've
never experienced anything like the initial take-off.*

From an Australian couple who traveled a long way to ride a coaster:

My wife and I are definitely not *roller coaster people. However, we found Rock
'n' Roller Coaster quite exhilarating—and because it's dark, we didn't
always realize that we were being thrown upside down. We rode it twice!*

Is Rock 'n' Roller the baddest coaster in Florida? Hard to say. Rock 'n' Roller has
the fastest launch acceleration by far, and, as we've discussed, it's a themed ride in the
dark, but the Incredible Hulk Coaster at Universal's Islands of Adventure and Kraken at
SeaWorld are both higher and offer more inversions (i.e., vertical loops, corkscrews,
barrel rolls, etc.). Also, Hulk and Kraken are much longer coasters. The Disney entry
offers the best visuals, but the view from Hulk and Kraken (for those with their eyes
open) is pretty spectacular. Finally, Rock 'n' Roller is the only one of the three with a
soundtrack synchronized throughout the entire ride.

Touring Tips This ride is not for everyone. If Space Mountain or Big Thunder push
your limits, stay away from the Rock 'n' Roller Coaster.

It's new, it's eye-catching, and it's definitely a zippy, albeit deafening, ride. Expect long
lines except in the first hour after opening and during the late-evening performance of

Fantasmic!. Ride first thing in the morning or use FASTPASS.

If you're on hand when the park opens, position yourself on the far left side of Sunset Boulevard as close to the rope barrier as possible. If there's already a crowd at the rope, you can usually work yourself forward by snaking along the wall of the Beverly Sunset Shop. Once in position, wait for the rope drop. When the park opens, cast members will walk the rope up the street toward Rock 'n' Roller Coaster and Tower of Terror. Stay on the far left sidewalk and you'll be among the first to make the left turn to the entrance of the coaster. Usually the Disney people get out of the way and allow you to run the last 100 feet or so.

A good strategy for riding both Tower of Terror and Rock 'n' Roller Coaster with minimum waits is to rush first thing after opening to Rock 'n' Roller Coaster and obtain FASTPASSes, then line up for the Tower of Terror. Most days, by the time you finish experiencing the Tower of Terror it will be time to use your FASTPASS for Rock 'n' Roller Coaster.

The Great Movie Ride

What It Is Movie-history indoor adventure ride
Scope & Scale Headliner
When to Go Before 10 a.m. and after 5 p.m.
Special Comments Elaborate, with several surprises
Author's Rating Unique; ★★★½
Appeal by Age Group

Pre-school ★★½	Grade School ★★★½	Teens ★★★½
Young Adults ★★★★	Over 30 ★★★★	Senior Citizens ★★★

Duration of Ride About 19 minutes
Average Wait in Line per 100 People ahead of You 2 minutes
Assumes All trains operating
Loading Speed Fast

Description and Comments Entering through a re-creation of Hollywood's Chinese Theater, guests board vehicles for a fast-paced tour through soundstage sets from classic films including *Casablanca, Tarzan, The Wizard of Oz, Aliens,* and *Raiders of the Lost Ark.* Each set is populated with new-generation Disney audio-animatronic (robot) characters, as well as an occasional human, all augmented by sound and lighting effects. One of Disney's larger and more ambitious dark rides, The Great Movie Ride encompasses 95,000 square feet and showcases some of the most famous scenes in filmmaking. Life-sized audio-animatronic sculptures of stars, including Gene Kelly, John Wayne, James Cagney, Julie Andrews, and Harrison Ford, inhabit some of the largest sets ever constructed for a Disney ride.

Plans to either modernize The Great Movie Ride or replace it altogether with a new attraction have been delayed by the recession and the downturn in travel following 9/11.

Touring Tips The Great Movie Ride draws large crowds (and lines) from the moment the park opens. As an interval-loading, high-capacity ride, lines disappear quickly. Even so, waits can exceed an hour after midmorning. (Actual waits usually run about one-third shorter than the time posted . If the chalkboard indicates an hour's wait, your actual time will be around 40 minutes.)

Star Tours (FASTPASS)

Motion Sickness

WARNING!

What It Is Indoor space flight–simulation ride
Scope & Scale Headliner
When to Go First hour and a half the park is open
Special Comments Expectant mothers and anyone prone to motion sickness are advised against riding. Too intense for many children younger than age 8. Must be 40" tall to ride.
Author's Rating Not to be missed; ★★★★
Appeal by Age Group

Pre-school ★★★★   Grade School ★★★★   Teens ★★★★
Young Adults ★★★★   Over 30 ★★★★   Senior Citizens ★★★★

Duration of Ride About 7 minutes
Average Wait in Line per 100 People ahead of You 5 minutes
Assumes All simulators operating
Loading Speed Moderate to fast

Description and Comments Based on the *Star Wars* movie series, this attraction is so much fun that it just makes you grin and giggle. Guests ride in a flight simulator modeled after those used for training pilots and astronauts. You're supposedly on a vacation outing in space, piloted by a droid (android, a.k.a. humanoid, a.k.a. robot) on his first flight with real passengers. Mayhem ensues almost immediately. Scenery flashes by, and the simulator bucks and pitches. You could swear you were moving at the speed of light. After several minutes of this, the droid somehow lands the spacecraft, and you discover you're about three times happier than you were when you boarded.

Touring Tips Star Tours hasn't been as popular at Disney-MGM Studios as it has been at Disneyland in California. Except on unusually busy days, waits rarely exceed 35–45 minutes. For the first couple of hours the park is open, expect a wait of 25 minutes or less. Even so, see Star Tours before 11 a.m. or use FASTPASS. If you have young children (or anyone) who are apprehensive about this attraction, ask the attendant about switching off (pages 254–257).

Star Tours is near the exit of the 2,000-seat stadium that houses *Indiana Jones*. When an *Indiana Jones* performance lets out, Star Tours is temporarily inundated. Ditto for *MuppetVision 3D* nearby. If you arrive in the midst of this mayhem, come back later.

Sounds Dangerous

What It Is Show demonstrating sound effects
Scope & Scale Minor attraction
When to Go Before 11 a.m. or after 5 p.m.
Author's Rating Funny and informative; ★★★
Appeal by Age Group

Pre-school ★★½   Grade School ★★★½   Teens ★★★
Young Adults ★★★   Over 30 ★★★   Senior Citizens ★★★★

Duration of Presentation 12 minutes
Preshow Entertainment Video introduction to sound effects
Probable Waiting Time 15–30 minutes

Description and Comments *Sounds Dangerous,* a film presentation starring Drew Carey as a blundering detective, is the vehicle for a crash course on movie and TV sound effects. Funny, educational, well paced, and (for once) not hawking some Disney flick or product, *Sounds Dangerous* is both entertaining and worthwhile. Earphones worn throughout the show make the various sounds seem very real, indeed . . . perhaps too real for some younger children during a part of the show when the theater is plunged into darkness. Overall, *Sounds Dangerous* is a winner and a vast improvement over the production it replaced.

Touring Tips Because the theater is relatively small, long waits (partially in the hot sun) are common here. Another thing: *Sounds Dangerous* is periodically inundated by guests coming from a just-concluded performance of the *Indiana Jones Epic Stunt Spectacular.* This is not the time to get in line. Wait at least 30 minutes and try again.

A reader from Israel suggests that a good time to catch *Sounds Dangerous* is just before the afternoon parade. If the parade starts on Hollywood Boulevard, it takes about 15–18 minutes to wind over to the theater—just long enough to catch the show and pop out right in time for the parade.

Indiana Jones Epic Stunt Spectacular (FASTPASS)

What It Is Movie-stunt demonstration and action show
Scope & Scale Headliner
When to Go First three morning shows or last evening show
Special Comments Performance times posted on a sign at the entrance to the theater
Author's Rating Done on a grand scale; ★★★★
Appeal by Age Group

Pre-school ★★★	Grade School ★★★★	Teens ★★★★
Young Adults ★★★★	Over 30 ★★★★	Senior Citizens ★★★★

Duration of Presentation 30 minutes
Preshow Entertainment Selection of "extras" from audience
Probable Waiting Time None

Description and Comments Coherent and educational, though somewhat unevenly paced, the popular production showcases professional stunt men and women who demonstrate dangerous stunts with a behind-the-scenes look at how it's done. Sets, props, and special effects are very elaborate.

While most live shows at Walt Disney World are revised from time to time, the *Stunt Spectacular,* as a Hamden, Connecticut, man laments, has not changed for years:

> Another bust was the Indy Jones show. The show is the same as it has been since it opened, but the acting grows tired. This is due for a restaging. Its counterpart at Universal, The Wild [Wild, Wild] West Stunt Show, was deemed superior by my group.

Indiana Jones was closed for renovation for several months in 2000. Though the sets and props have been refurbished and the special effects modernized, the content of the show remains essentially the same.

Touring Tips The Stunt Theater holds 2,000 people; capacity audiences are common. The first performance is always the easiest to see. If the first show is at 9:30 a.m.

or earlier, you can usually walk in, even if you arrive five minutes late. If the first show is scheduled for 9:45 a.m. or later, arrive 20 or so minutes early. For the second performance, show up about 20–35 minutes ahead of time. For the third and subsequent shows, arrive 30–45 minutes early. If you plan to tour during late afternoon and evening, attend the last scheduled performance. If you want to beat the crowd out of the stadium, sit on the far right (as you face the staging area) and near the top.

To be chosen from the audience to be an "extra" in the stunt show, arrive early, sit down front, and display unmitigated enthusiasm. A woman from Richmond, Virginia, explains:

Indiana Jones *was far and away the best show—we saw it twice on two different days. After the first performance, I realized the best way to get picked was to stand up, wave my arms, and shout when the "casting director" called for volunteers—sheer enthusiasm wins every time, and sitting towards the front helps, too. We stayed afterwards for autographs of the performers in the obligatory Mickey Mouse autograph book.*

Theater of the Stars

What It Is Live Hollywood-style musical, usually featuring Disney characters; performed in an open-air theater
Scope & Scale Major attraction
When to Go In the evening
Special Comments Performances are listed in the daily entertainment schedule
Author's Rating Excellent; ★★★★
Appeal by Age Group
  Pre-school ★★★★   Grade School ★★★★   Teens ★★★
  Young Adults ★★★   Over 30 ★★★★   Senior Citizens ★★★★
Duration of Presentation 25 minutes
Preshow Entertainment None
Probable Waiting Time 20–30 minutes

Description and Comments The *Theater of the Stars* combines Disney characters with singers and dancers in upbeat and humorous Hollywood musicals. The *Beauty and the Beast* show, in particular, is outstanding. The theater, which has been in three locations in the park over the years, seems finally to have found a permanent home on Sunset Boulevard. Vastly improved, it now offers a clear field of vision from almost every seat. Best, a canopy protects the audience from the Florida sun (or rain). The theater still gets mighty hot in the summer, but you can make it through a performance now without succumbing to heatstroke.

Touring Tips Unless you visit during the cooler months, see this show in the late afternoon or the evening. The production is so popular that you should show up 20–50 minutes early to get a seat.

Fantasmic!

What It Is Mixed-media nighttime spectacular
Scope & Scale Super headliner
When to Go Only staged in the evening

Special Comments Disney's best nighttime event
Author's Rating Not to be missed; ★★★★★
Appeal by Age Group
  Pre-school ★★★★   Grade School ★★★★★ Teens ★★★★½
  Young Adults ★★★★½ Over 30 ★★★★½   Senior Citizens ★★★★½
Duration of Presentation 25 minutes
Probable Waiting Time 50–60 minutes for a seat; 30 minutes for standing room
Description and Comments *Fantasmic!* is a mixed-media show presented one or more times each evening when the park is open late. Located off Sunset Boulevard behind the Tower of Terror, *Fantasmic!* is staged on a newly created lagoon and island opposite a 6,900-seat amphitheater. By far the largest theater facility ever created by Disney, the amphitheater can accommodate an additional 3,000 standing guests for a total audience of nearly 10,000.

    Fantasmic! is far and away the most extraordinary and ambitious outdoor spectacle ever attempted in any theme park. Starring Mickey Mouse in his role as the Sorcerer's Apprentice from *Fantasia,* the production uses lasers, images projected on a shroud of mist, fireworks, lighting effects, and music in combinations so stunning you can scarcely believe what you have seen. The plot is simple: good versus evil. The story gets lost in all the special effects at times, but no matter, it is the spectacle, not the story line, that is so overpowering. While beautiful, stunning, and powerful are words that immediately come to mind, they fail to convey the uniqueness of this presentation. It could be argued, with some validity, that *Fantasmic!* alone is worth the price of the Disney-MGM Studios admission.

    Readers, like this Amheart, Massachusetts, woman agree:

Fantasmic! was absolutely the best show any of us had ever seen. It is worth the 90-minute wait to see it. Disney Magic at its best!

    From a 30-year-old mother of one from Wake Forest, North Carolina:

Fantasmic! was the high point of the entire trip. We've never seen such an incredible show. It took us three nights to finally get in to it, and it was well worth it.

    A Queensbury, New York, dad offers this advice:

Don't see *Fantasmic!* at MGM before you see the laser/fireworks show at Epcot. *Fantasmic!* is the most entertaining show we've ever seen, and the technology is beyond belief. It really takes the shine off the other shows, which were truly wonderful.

    A Texas reader enjoyed *Fantasmic!* but had some problems with arriving over an hour before the show:

I liked *Fantasmic!*; the kids around me loved it. They shouted out every character's name as they appeared. But, it wasn't worth the wait. I had to arrive at 8:10 for a 9:30 showing. Nothing is worth an 80-minute wait. The only entertainment in the interim was a couple of cheerleaders urging the crowd to do the wave.

    A reader from Down Under found *Fantasmic!* a bit too sentimental:

We were disappointed by this show. While it features boats, characters, water, and light, it was a bit too nostalgic of Disney films. If this is what Mickey thinks about when he dreams, Minnie would be a little disappointed!

A mother of four from Virginia gives the show its due but offers this warning to parents with easily frightened children:

I was very disappointed with the Fantasmic! show. Yes, it was bright and spectacular, but it was so heavy on villains, evil, and horror that I simply could not believe I was in Disney World. There was far too much heavy emphasis, loud scary music, and evil scenes from movies thrown in our faces that I wanted to leave in the middle of it. If you have small children, do not go see this show. It is terrifying. Yes, of course, it ends with Mickey Mouse being a hero, but my God, you have to sit through every villain Disney has ever imagined endlessly coming at you, laughing at your fears, and scaring you with a musical score to go along with it. Even an eight-year-old girl next to us was hiding, terrified, at her parent's feet. I am warning every parent—boycott it!

Although the reader is dead on about the rogue gallery of Disney villains, most kids really do take Fantasmic! in stride. It is, however, a bit overwhelming for preschoolers. If you have kids ages seven or younger, you should prepare them for what they will see. Also, you can mitigate the fright factor somewhat by sitting back a bit.

Touring Tips Fantasmic! provides a whole new dimension to nighttime at Disney-MGM Studios. As a day-capping event, it is to the Studios what IllumiNations is to Epcot. While it's hard to imagine running out of space in a 10,000-person stadium, it happens almost every day. On evenings when there are two performances, the second show will always be less crowded. If you attend the first (or only) scheduled performance, show up at least an hour in advance. If you opt for the second show, arrive 50 minutes early. Readers underscore the importance of queuing up early:

From a Yorktown, Virginia, mom:

I think you seriously underestimated the time when people should arrive to see Fantasmic! if they want to get a seat. The stadium was already full when we arrived 45 minutes before the show was scheduled to start, and the remaining seats filled up quickly. Keep in mind this was during the off-season on one of the slower days of the week at Disney-MGM Studios.

A Richmond, Vermont, reader seconds the recommendation, writing:

Cast members at Disney-MGM Studios warned us to get to Fantasmic! at least one hour early. This will only get you the last, far-flung seats. If you want good seats, you'll need to arrive 90 minutes early.

Another reader complains about the treatment of standing guests but also discovered an "upside":

Our only criticism [of Fantasmic!] was that we were in the standing-room-only section where participants were treated like the great unwashed. Employees kept sniping at people to stay in the area, stay away from the fence, stay out of the bushes, etc. etc. The other spectators were great, but the employees really were tough on us. Since the show was [only] 25 minutes, *the standing part wasn't so bad. The upside was that it made for a really easy exit from the show.*

A father of three from Clarksburg, West Virginia, found that staying for the late performance worked best (note that late shows are offered only during busier times of the year):

Fantasmic! was fantastic. The 9:15 p.m. show was jammed all the time. We chose the 11 p.m. show (three times). The 11 p.m. show was never full. The second and third times we saw the show, we waited until 10:45 and walked right in and sat down. It's a must see!!

Disney offers reserved seats at *Fantasmic!* for dinner patrons of Mama Melrose's Ristorante, Hollywood & Vine, and the Hollywood Brown Derby. If you plan to eat at the restaurant anyway, this is a good way to avoid queuing up 90 minutes early. However, as a Pennsylvania woman cautions, don't expect good seats:

The only complaint we had was this voucher system for MGM's Fantasmic! show. They got you to eat at an expensive restaurant, and the reserved section [for Fantasmic!] was way on an end. We were glad we got there early enough to get good seating without the need of the voucher.

A New England reader agrees:

The reserved seats for the new priority seating dinner/guaranteed Fantasmic! entry program were on the far, far right—not a good deal.

A Cross Junction, Virginia, woman offers an alternative:

If planning to go to MGM's Fantasmic!, it's a good idea to buy deli sandwiches outside the park, pack them with snacks and water in your backpack, and get a seat early. Then you can sit and eat your dinner as you wait for a great show. This worked so well.

A mom from Virginia offers a warning about sitting too close to the action:

Avoid sitting near the front. We were stuck in the fourth row and despite no detectable wind, we were constantly sprayed by the fountains during the show. That might feel good after a hot summer day, but it was very unpleasant on a cool fall evening.

Rain and wind conditions sometimes cause *Fantasmic!* to be cancelled. Unfortunately, Disney officials usually do not make a final decision about whether to proceed or cancel until just before show time. We have seen guests wait stoically for over an hour with no assurance that their patience and sacrifice would be rewarded. We do not recommend arriving more than a few minutes before show time on rainy or especially windy nights. On nights like these, pursue your own agenda until ten minutes or so before show time and then head to the stadium to see what happens.

Finally, a mom from Pearland, Texas, found *Fantasmic!* too intense for her young child, writing:

Fantasmic! should come with a warning label. The show features a multitude of characters in various vignettes interspersed with water and laser light interludes as Mickey Mouse begins his lighthearted and fanciful dream. Unfortunately for the impressionable and tender-of-mind, the dream

*becomes a nightmare as the evil villains take over Mickey's imagination.
The combination of actual characters, their larger-than-life laser visages,
ominous unbearably loud music, and thundering explosions with blinding
flashes of light, fire, and sparks (which went on for a seemingly interminable length of time) sent hordes of parents with screaming children
fleeing for the exits. Naturally, good does eventually prevail over evil and
the finale returns to the beautiful, magical Disney style, but not soon
enough. Please, please warn parents not to take young children to this
show. (For adults and teenagers, it is truly spectacular.)*

Though we do not receive many reports of young children being terrified by *Fantasmic!*, the reader's point is well taken. We suggest you spend a little time preparing
your younger children for what they will see. Also, make sure to hang on to your children after *Fantasmic!* and to give them explicit instructions for regrouping in the event
you are separated.

Voyage of the Little Mermaid (FASTPASS)

What It Is Musical stage show featuring characters from the Disney movie *The Little
Mermaid*

Scope & Scale Major attraction

When to Go Before 9:45 a.m. or just before closing

Author's Rating Romantic, lovable, and humorous In the best Disney tradition; not
to be missed; ★★★★

Appeal by Age Group

Pre-school ★★★★	Grade School ★★★★	Teens ★★★½
Young Adults ★★★★	Over 30 ★★★★	Senior Citizens ★★★★

Duration of Presentation 15 minutes

Preshow Entertainment Taped ramblings about the decor in the preshow holding
area

Probable Waiting Time Before 9:30 a.m., 10–30 minutes; after 9:30 a.m., 35–70
minutes

Description and Comments *Voyage of the Little Mermaid* is a winner, appealing to
every age. Cute without being silly or saccharine, and infinitely lovable, the *Little Mermaid* show is the most tender and romantic entertainment offered anywhere in Walt
Disney World. The story is simple and engaging, the special effects impressive, and the
Disney characters memorable.

We receive a lot of mail from Europeans who complain about the "soppy sentimentality" of Americans in general and of Disney attractions in particular. These comments of a man from Bristol, England, are typical:

*Americans have an ability to think as a child and so enjoy the soppiness of the
Little Mermaid. English cynicism made it hard for us at times to see Disney stories as anything other than gushing, namby-pamby, and full of
stereotypes. Other Brits might also find the sentimentality cloying. Maybe
you should prepare them for the need to rethink their wry outlook on life
temporarily.*

Touring Tips   Because it's well done and located at a busy pedestrian intersection, *Voyage of the Little Mermaid* plays to capacity crowds all day. FASTPASS has helped redistribute crowds at *Voyage of the Little Mermaid.* At least 40–50% of each audience is drawn from the standby line. As a rough approximation, guests in the front third of the queuing area will usually make it into the next performance, and quite often folks in the front half of the queuing area will be admitted. Those in the back half of the queuing area will probably have to wait through two showings before being admitted.

When you enter the preshow lobby, stand near the doors to the theater. When they open, go inside, pick a row of seats, and let six to ten people enter the row ahead of you. The strategy is twofold: to obtain a good seat and be near the exit.

Finally, a Charlotte, North Carolina, mom took exception to our Fright Potential Rating for *Voyage of the Little Mermaid:*

> The guide let me down on the Little Mermaid show at MGM—the huge sea witch portrayed in laser lights, cartoon, and live action TERRIFIED my three-year-old. The description of the show led me to believe it was all sweetness and romance with no scariness.

Jim Henson's MuppetVision 3D (FASTPASS)

What It Is   3-D movie starring the Muppets
Scope & Scale   Major attraction
When to Go   Before 11 a.m. and after 4 p.m.
Author's Rating   Uproarious; not to be missed; ★★★★½
Appeal by Age Group
   Pre-school ★★★★½   Grade School ★★★★★   Teens ★★★★½
   Young Adults ★★★★½   Over 30 ★★★★½   Senior Citizens ★★★★½
Duration of Presentation   17 minutes
Preshow Entertainment   Muppets on television
Probable Waiting Time   12 minutes

Description and Comments   *MuppetVision 3D* provides a total sensory experience, with wild 3-D action augmented by auditory, visual, and tactile special effects. If you're tired and hot, this zany presentation will make you feel brand new.

Touring Tips   This production is very popular. Before noon, waits are about 20 minutes. Also, watch for throngs arriving from just-concluded performances of the *Indiana Jones Epic Stunt Spectacular.* If you encounter a long line, try again later. This is another attraction where FASTPASS has evened out the distribution of arriving guests. Bottom line, you can usually get in within 25 minutes without using FASTPASS.

Honey, I Shrunk the Kids Movie Set Adventure

What It Is   Small but elaborate playground
Scope & Scale   Diversion
When to Go   Before 11 a.m. or after dark
Author's Rating   Great for young children, optional for adults; ★★½

Appeal by Age Group
Pre-school ★★★★½   Grade School ★★★½   Teens ★★
Young Adults ★★½   Over 30 ★★★   Senior Citizens ★★½
Duration of Presentation Varies
Average Wait in Line per 100 People ahead of You 20 minutes

Description and Comments   This elaborate playground appeals particularly to kids age 11 and younger. The story is that you have been "miniaturized" and have to make your way through a yard full of 20-foot-tall blades of grass, giant ants, lawn sprinklers, and other oversized features.

Touring Tips   This imaginative playground has tunnels, slides, rope ladders, and a variety of oversized props. All surface areas are padded, and Disney personnel are on-hand to help keep children in some semblance of control.

While this Movie Set Adventure undoubtedly looked good on paper, the actual attraction has problems that are hard to "miniaturize." First, it isn't nearly large enough to accommodate the children who would like to play. Only 240 people are allowed "on the set" at a time, and many of these are supervising parents or curious adults who hopped in line without knowing what they were waiting for. Frequently by 10:30 or 11 a.m., the playground is full, with dozens waiting outside (some impatiently).

Also, there's no provision for getting people to leave. Kids play as long as parents allow. This creates uneven traffic flow and unpredictable waits. If it weren't for the third flaw, that the attraction is poorly ventilated (as hot and sticky as an Everglades swamp), there's no telling when anyone would leave.

A mom from Shawnee Mission, Kansas, however, disagrees:

Some of the things your book said to skip were our favorites (at least for the kids). We all thought the playground from Honey, I Shrunk the Kids was great—definitely worth seeing.

A mom from Tolland, Connecticut, however, found the playgound exasperating:

We let the kids hang out at [Honey, I Shrunk the Kids] because we thought it would be relaxing: NOT! You have three choices here: (1) Let your kids go anywhere and hope if they try to get out without your permission someone will stop them. Also hope that someone else will help your kids if they get caught up in the exhibit. (2) Go everywhere with your kids—this takes a lot of stamina and some athleticism. If you care about appearances this could be a problem because you look pretty stupid coming down those slides. But then again, there are women with bright red sailor hats that say "Minnie" and have a yellow flower in the middle of them, so how stupid could you look in comparison? (3) Try to visually keep track of your kids. This is impossible, so you will be either on the edge of or in the middle of an anxiety attack the whole time you are there.

If you visit during warmer months and want your children to experience the playground, get them in and out before 11 a.m. By late morning, this attraction is way too hot and crowded for anyone to enjoy. Reach the playground via the New York Backlot, or through the Studio Catering Company fast-food area.

To save time, a couple from Grand Rapids, Michigan, suggests:

We staked out a seat at the [fast-food] plaza near the exit of [Honey, I Shrunk the Kids playground] with our children. They then went in to play while I got their snacks and beverages. Meanwhile, we had an opportunity to rest and determine our next game plan. When they emerged, they were parched and tired, so the refreshment break was well timed.

New York Street Backlot

What It Is Walk-through backlot movie set
Scope & Scale Diversion
When to Go Anytime
Author's Rating Interesting, with great detail; ★★★
Appeal by Age Group

Pre-school ★½	Grade School ★★★	Teens ★★★
Young Adults ★★★	Over 30 ★★★	Senior Citizens ★★★

Duration of Presentation Varies
Average Wait in Line per 100 People ahead of You No waiting

Description and Comments This part of the Studios' backlot was previously accessible only on the tram segment of the Backlot Tour. Now guests can stroll the elaborate New York Street set and appreciate its rich detail. Opening this area to pedestrians also relieves some of the congestion in the Hollywood Boulevard and Echo Lake areas.

Touring Tips There's never a wait to enjoy the New York Street Backlot; save it until you've seen those attractions that develop long lines. Mickey Mouse signs autographs and poses for photos on the steps of the hotel in the middle of the block. It has no sign or visible name, but it has flags above the entrance. Consult the daily entertainment schedule for sessions.

Who Wants to Be a Millionaire (FASTPASS)

What It Is Look-alike version of the TV game show
Scope & Scale Major attraction
When to Go Before 11 a.m. or after 5 p.m.
Special Comments Contestants play for points, not dollars
Author's Rating No Regis, but good fun; ★★★★
Appeal by Age Group

Pre-school ★★	Grade School ★★★★	Teens ★★★★
Young Adults ★★★★	Over 30 ★★★★	Senior Citizens ★★★★

Duration of Presentation 25 minutes
Preshow Entertainment Video of Regis
Probable Waiting Time 20 minutes

Description and Comments It's the familiar ABC television game show sans Regis played on a replica of the real set, including all the snazzy lighting and creepy sound effects. Contestants are selected from among the audience and play for points and prizes. The 600-seat studio is located in Soundstages 2 and 3 on Mickey Avenue. To get there, go to the end of Hollywood Boulevard and turn right through the Studios Arch, then immediately left alongside *Voyage of the Little Mermaid.* The soundstages are about 80 yards down on the right.

Touring Tips Each member of the audience has a small electronic display and keypad to use for recording answers. The keypad has a key for each letter (A, B, C, and D), with each letter representing one of the four multiple choice answers to a given question. When the keypad lights up, typically just as the last choice (D) is revealed, that's your cue to enter your answer. The faster you enter the answer, the better your score. Most people hold their fingers ready and push the letter key designating their answer as fast as humanly possible. You can't change your answer, so once you push the key you're committed. Getting an answer right but taking longer is better than registering a wrong answer. Your score is tabulated electronically, with points awarded for being both fast and right.

If there is no one from a previous round continuing, the game will start with a "fastest finger" round, where the audience member who posts the fastest correct answer goes to the hot seat as a contestant. If the contestant wins the ultimate goal of one million points, decides to leave, or loses, the audience member with the highest score at that time will be the next contestant. Audience scores are displayed from time to time as the contestant reaches plateaus of 1,000 and 32,000 points. Unlike the real version where Regis gives contestants almost unlimited time to answer, you must answer in less than 30 seconds in the theme-park version. As a contestant you get three "life lines." You can consult the audience or have two wrong choices deleted as in the real game, or phone someone. In the Disney version the person on the other end of the line will be a stranger, someone else in the park. Prizes include pins, hats, polo shirts, and the like.

The first ten questions are fairly easy, with a number of the questions being Disney related. If the show ends while you are a contestant, you may or may not be invited to continue during the next show. Disney has experimented with both options.

Unofficial Guide friend Susan Turner was on hand for a number of shows. Here's her advice for putting yourself in the hot seat:

1. Answer correctly. *If you blow a question you can pretty much forget it.*

2. Answer quickly. *This is a very close second to answering correctly. If you don't have quick reflexes, it doesn't matter if you answer everything correctly. For the first questions (at least up until the 1,000-point question), this is most critical, as most of the audience will also be answering correctly.*

3. How to answer quickly. *The keypad consists of four buttons in a row marked "A, B, C, and D," with lights above each one. This panel will remain unlit until the D answer is put on the screen. This means you really must have the answer figured out before knowing the D answer. I quickly learned to avert my eyes from the screen to the answer panel when they were reading the C answer. By this time I had chosen my answer and had my finger on the correct button. In this way, I could watch for the panel to light and hit the button immediately. If you wait until they finish reading the D answer, or even watch for the D answer to show up on the screen, it's too late. This also means that if the answer is D, you need to figure this out by eliminating A–C. I found (and had this corroborated by others' experi-*

ences)' that I scored higher when there was a question with D as the answer, perhaps because most guests aren't ready to answer until the correct answer is read. In some ways the game is a bit more difficult as an audience member than as the one in the hot seat. Obviously, you don't have the three lifelines, but also you really don't have time to think through the answers. At the two point plateaus (i.e. 1,000 and 32,000) they pause and show the top ten guest scores, using the seat number for identification. The top ten scores are also shown when they need to refill the hot seat and at the end of a game. I found if I employed this strategy (i.e., immediate and correct answer), I was in the top ten about half of the time when they showed the 1,000-point level, and maybe three-fourths of the time at the 32,000-point level. If you are not in the top ten, you will not know your score. I wish they had little LEDs by each of the answer panels so you could keep up with your scores.

4. **Go to an early (or maybe late) show.** The earliest show was reported to be less than half full. I imagine [Millionaire] will be a very popular show and will be full at most if not all shows, but if there is a show that isn't at capacity, it will probably be the [first show of the day]. Fewer people raises your probability of getting in. Unfortunately this didn't occur to me until after I left WDW! If it had, I would most definitely have been at the first show.

5. **A note about the fastest fingers question.** This will only occur at the start of a game if no one returns from the last game. At the end of the game, if a contestant is in the hot seat and answers the last question correctly, they have the opportunity to return for the next show. For the fastest finger questions, they read the question and put it on the screen, then all four answers will appear at once. The problem I had with this the first time I played was having to recheck to see if B was to the right of or below A. I saw a couple of kids win this, and I'm not sure if they were just quick and smart, or if they just pushed buttons rapidly and randomly. There is a one-sixteenth chance of answering correctly, so with enough people employing this strategy someone is bound to get it right. Here again speed is very important. Some of these questions were Disney related (i.e., "Put these Epcot pavilions in the order that they appear starting with the entrance: Spaceship Earth, Innoventions, Imagination, American Pavilion"), while others were not (i.e., "Put these members of the whale family in order of size starting with the smallest: bottlenose dolphin, killer whale, gray whale, blue whale.")

6. **One final note about seating.** It does not matter where you sit—all seats are equipped with an answer pad. Because the studio is a near-replica of the TV studio, they include the ten "fastest fingers" seats on the floor (the ones with the screens). Guests sitting at these seats have no real advantage over guests in the stands. Also, there is a section of seats on the floor that is largely used as disabled seating. I wondered at first if they had answer keypads as well, and I found that indeed they do, though in the front row you

have to hold the keypad (in the stands the keypads are on the back of the chair in front of you).

We recommend catching a *Millionaire* show after you've experienced all of the park's rides. If waits are intolerable, use FASTPASS. For the record, more than 50% of the audience for each show, come from the standby line.

One Man's Dream

What It Is Tribute to Walt Disney
Scope & Scale Minor attraction
When to Go Anytime
Author's Rating Excellent! . . . and about time; ★★★★
Appeal by Age Group
  Pre-school ★   Grade School ★★½   Teens ★★★
  Young Adults ★★★½   Over 30 ★★★★   Senior Citizens ★★★★
Duration of Presentation 25 minutes
Preshow Entertainment Disney memorabilia
Probable Waiting Time (for film) 10 minutes

Description and Comments *One Man's Dream* is a long-overdue tribute to Walt Disney. Launched in 2001 to celebrate the 100th anniversary of Walt Disney's birthday, the attraction consists of an exhibit area showcasing Disney memorabilia and recordings, followed by a film documenting Disney's life. The exhibits chronicle Walt Disney's life and business. On display are a replication of Walt's California office, various innovations in animation developed by Disney, and early models and working plans for Walt Disney World as well as for various Disney theme parks around the world. The film provides a personal glimpse of Disney and offers insights regarding both Disney's successes and failures.

Touring Tips Give yourself some time here. Every minute spent among these extraordinary artifacts will enhance your visit to Walt Disney World, taking you back to a time when the creativity and vision that created Walt Disney World were personified by one struggling entrepreneur. Located to the right of *Millionaire* on Mickey Avenue, *One Man's Dream* will not be difficult to see. Try it during the hot, crowded middle part of the day.

Backlot Theater

What It Is Live Hollywood-style musical, usually based on a Disney film, and performed in an open-air theater
Scope & Scale Major attraction
When to Go First show in the morning or in the evening
Special Comments Performance times are listed in the daily entertainment schedule
Author's Rating Excellent; ★★★★
Appeal by Age Group
  Pre-school ★★★   Grade School ★★★½   Teens ★★★
  Young Adults ★★★★   Over 30 ★★★★   Senior Citizens ★★★★
Duration of Presentation 25–35 minutes

Preshow Entertainment None
Probable Waiting Time 20–30 minutes

Description and Comments The *Backlot Theater*, like *Theater of the Stars*, is an open-air venue for musical theater and concerts. Most productions are based on Disney films or animated features. An excellent show inspired by *The Hunchback of Notre Dame* played through most of 2001. The theater, on the far back side of New York Street, is generally well designed but has several obtrusive support columns. Though protected from the weather, the theater gets terribly hot during warmer months.

A Pennsylvania mom who stumbled onto the *Backlot Theater* says:

The greatest suprise was The Hunchback of Notre Dame *performance. I loved the staging, lighting, music, and costuming. It was excellent—a real highlight of our Disney experience.*

Touring Tips Unless you visit during cooler times, see the first morning show or the last evening show. To get to the *Backlot Theater*, walk down New York Street toward the Washington Square monument. At the square, turn left for a short block. Even though the theater's location is obscure, enough guests find it to fill the seats. Arrive early by 25 minutes or more to avoid sitting behind the columns.

Playhouse Disney Live on Stage

What It Is Live show for children
Scope & Scale Minor attraction
When to Go Per the daily entertainment schedule
Author's Rating A must for families with preschoolers; ★★★
Appeal by Age Group

| Pre-school ★★★★★ | Grade School ★★★½ | Teens ★★ |
| Young Adults ★★ | Over 30 ★★ | Senior Citizens ★★ |

Duration of Presentation 20 minutes
Special Comments Audience sits on the floor
Probable Waiting Time 10 minutes

Description and Comments The show features characters from the Disney Channel's *Rolie Polie Olie, The Book of Pooh, Bear in the Big Blue House*, and *Stanley*. A simple plot serves as the platform for singing, dancing, some great puppetry, and a great deal of audience participation. The characters, who ooze love and goodness, rally throngs of tots and preschoolers to sing and dance along with them. All the jumping, squirming, and high-stepping is facilitated by having the audience sit on the floor so that kids can spontaneously erupt into motion when the mood strikes. Even for adults without children, it's a treat to watch the tikes rev up. If you have a younger child in your party, all the better: just stand back and let the video roll.

For preschoolers, *Playhouse Disney* will be the highlight of their day, as a Thomasville, North Carolina, mom attests:

Playhouse Disney at MGM was fantastic! My three-year-old loved it. The children danced, sang, and had a great time.

Touring Tips The show is headquartered in what was formerly the Soundstage Restaurant located to the immediate right of the Animation Tour. Because the tykes just can't get enough, it has become the toughest ticket at the Studios. Show up at least 30 minutes before showtime. Once inside, pick a spot on the floor and take a breather until the performance begins.

The Magic of Disney Animation

What It Is Walking tour of the Disney Animation Studio
Scope & Scale Major attraction
When to Go Before 11 a.m. and after 5 p.m.
Author's Rating Not as good as previous renditions; ★★★½
Appeal by Age Group

Pre-school ★★★	Grade School ★★★	Teens ★★★
Young Adults ★★★★	Over 30 ★★★★	Senior Citizens ★★★★

Duration of Presentation 36 minutes
Preshow Entertainment Gallery of animation art in waiting area
Average Wait in Line per 100 People ahead of You 7 minutes

Description and Comments The public, for the first time, sees Disney artists at work. Since Disneyland opened in 1955, fans have petitioned Walt Disney Productions to offer an animation studio tour. Finally, after an interminable wait, an admiring public may watch artists create Disney characters.

Disney continues to fiddle with sequencing of this tour. During our last visit in 2001, we thought the new sequence disrupted the flow of the tour. After entering the Animation Building, you see an eight-and-a-half minute introductory film on animation. Starring Walter Cronkite and Robin Williams as your tour hosts, it's an absolute delight. After the film, an artist demonstrates cartooning technique.

Next you enter the studio and watch artists and technicians through large windows. Formerly you'd start with story and character development and work sequentially through animation (characters are brought to life in rough art); to clean up (rough art is refined to finished line drawings); to effects and backgrounds (backgrounds for the characters are developed); and to photocopying, where drawings are transferred from paper to plastic sheets, called cels, before being finished with ink and paint. Now, unfortunately, you are rushed through the viewing area. Nobody explains what the cartoonists are doing, and there's no sense of process. Finally, you are herded into a theater for a retrospective look at Disney animation over the years. In the final analysis, the only really coherent segments of the tour are the canned ones (i.e., the films at the beginning, the cartoonist demonstration, and the retrospective at the end). Watching real artists at work is almost an after-thought, and a darn brief one at that. For most guests, the experience is wholly satisfactory—but oh, if they could have taken the tour back when it was really top-notch.

Touring Tips Some days, the animation tour doesn't open until 11 a.m., by which time the park is pretty full. Check the entertainment schedule for tour hours, and try to go before noon. The tour is a relatively small-volume attraction, and lines begin to build on busy days by mid- to late morning.

Disney-MGM Studios Backlot Tour

What It Is Combination tram and walking tour of modern film and video production

Scope & Scale Headliner

When to Go Anytime

Author's Rating Educational and fun; not to be missed; ★★★★

Appeal by Age Group

Pre-school ★★★   Grade School ★★★★   Teens ★★★★

Young Adults ★★★★   Over 30 ★★★★   Senior Citizens ★★★★

Duration of Presentation About 35 minutes

Special Comments Use the restroom before getting in line.

Preshow Entertainment A video before the special effects segment and another video in the tram boarding area

Description and Comments About two-thirds of Disney-MGM Studios is a working film and television facility, where actors, artists, and technicians work on productions year-round. Everything from TV commercials, specials, and game shows to feature motion pictures are produced. Visitors to Disney-MGM can take the backstage studio tour to learn production methods and technologies.

Disney periodically changes the name of this tour. At press time, it was called the Disney-MGM Studios Backlot Tour.

The tour begins on the edge of the backlot with the special effects walking segment, which was revamped in 2002, then continues with the tram segment. To reach the Disney-MGM Studios Backlot Tour, turn right off Hollywood Boulevard through the Studio Arch into the Animation Courtyard. Bear left at the corner where *Voyage of the Little Mermaid* is situated. Follow the street until you see a red brick warehouse on your right. Go through the door and up the ramp.

The first stop is a special effects water tank where technicians explain the mechanical and optical tricks that "turn the seemingly impossible into on-screen reality." Included are rain effects and a naval battle. The waiting area for this part of the tour displays miniature naval vessels used in filming famous war movies.

A prop room separates the special effects tank and the tram tour. Trams depart about once every four minutes on busy days, winding among production and shop buildings before stopping at the wardrobe and crafts shops. Here, costumes, sets, and props are designed, created, and stored. Still seated on the tram, you look through large windows to see craftsmen at work.

The tour continues through the backlot, where western desert canyons and New York City brownstones exist side by side with suburban residential streets. The tour's highlight is Catastrophe Canyon, an elaborate special-effects movie set where a thunderstorm, earthquake, oil-field fire, and flash flood are simulated. The tour's tram portion ends at Backstage Plaza, where you can avail yourself of rest rooms, food, and drink. To reach the start of the soundstage tour, most recently called Backstage Pass, head back past the entrance of the special effects/tram tour toward the *Little Mermaid*.

Touring Tips Because the Backlot Tour is one of Disney's most efficient attractions, you will rarely wait more than 15 minutes (usually less than ten). Take the tour at your convenience, but preferably before 5 p.m., when the workday ends for the various workshops.

Live Entertainment at Disney-MGM Studios

When the Studios opened, live entertainment, parades, and special events weren't as fully developed or elaborate as those at the Magic Kingdom or Epcot. With the introduction of an afternoon parade and elaborate shows at *Theater of the Stars,* the Studios joined the big leagues. These outstanding performances, coupled with the Sorcery in the Sky fireworks spectacular, gave Disney-MGM live entertainment every bit as compelling as that in the other parks. In the fall of 1998, Disney-MGM launched a new edition of *Fantasmic!,* a water, fireworks, and laser show that draws rave reviews. *Fantasmic!,* staged in its own specially designed 10,000-person amphitheater, makes the Studios the park of choice for spectacular nighttime entertainment. *Fantasmic!* is profiled in detail on pages 595–598.

Afternoon Parade   Staged one or more times a day, the parade begins near the park's entrance, continues down Hollywood Boulevard, and circles in front of the giant hat. From there, it passes in front of *Sounds Dangerous* and ends by Star Tours. An alternate route begins at the far end of Sunset Boulevard and turns right onto Hollywood Boulevard.

The parade features floats and characters from Disney's animated features. Excellent parades based on *Mulan, Aladdin, Toy Story,* and *Hercules,* among others, have been produced. The current parade showcases Disney characters in vintage autos. Colorful, creative, and totally upbeat, the afternoon parade is great. It does, however, bring pedestrian traffic to a standstill along its route and hampers crossing the park. If you're anywhere on the parade route when the parade begins, your best bet is to stay put and enjoy it. Our favorite vantage point is the steps of the theater next to *Sounds Dangerous.*

Theater of the Stars   This covered amphitheater on Sunset Boulevard is the stage for production reviews, usually featuring music from Disney movies and starring Disney characters. Performances are posted in front of the theater and are listed in the daily entertainment schedule in the handout guidemap.

Backlot Theater   This stage is home to musical productions featuring Disney characters and/or based on Disney films. A stage adaptation of *Pocahontas* preceded a musical drawn from *The Hunchback of Notre Dame.* The Backlot Theater is roughly behind the Muppets theater. Walk down New York Street toward the back of the park. At the end of the street, turn left.

Many readers, including this woman from East Lansing, Michigan, are surprised by the quality of the Disney-MGM Studios stage shows:

What I loved most about MGM, though, were the shows, and especially The Hunchback of Notre Dame *show. These shows were nearly Broadway caliber and had actors who were very talented singers and dancers. I think the shows are the best-kept secrets at Disney World. I expected some cute little show and was truly amazed by the quality of the performances, costumes, and sets.*

Disney Characters Find characters at the *Theater of the Stars* and Backlot Theater, in parades, on New York Street, in the Animation Courtyard, by Al's Toy Barn, in Backstage Plaza, and along Mickey Avenue. Mickey sometimes appears for autographs and photos on Sunset Boulevard. A breakfast or lunch with characters is offered most days at the Hollywood and Vine Cafeteria.

Street Entertainment Jugglers and other roving performers appear on Hollywood and Sunset boulevards. The Studios' modest marching band and a brass quartet play Hollywood Boulevard, Sunset Boulevard, Studio Courtyard, and the Echo Lake area. Not exactly street entertainment, a piano player performs daily at The Hollywood Brown Derby.

Disney-MGM Studios Touring Plan

Disney-MGM Studios One-Day Touring Plan

Because Disney-MGM offers fewer attractions, touring isn't as complicated as at the Magic Kingdom or Epcot. Most Disney-MGM rides and shows are oriented to the entire family, eliminating disagreements on how to spend the day. Whereas in the Magic Kingdom Mom and Dad want to see *The Hall of Presidents,* Big Sis is revved to ride Space Mountain, and the preschool twins are clamoring for Dumbo the Flying Elephant, at Disney-MGM Studios the whole family can pretty much tour together.

Since there are fewer attractions, crowds are more concentrated at Disney-MGM. If a line seems unusually long, ask an attendant what the estimated wait is. If it exceeds your tolerance, retry the attraction while *Indiana Jones* is in progress or during a parade or special event. These draw people away from the lines.

Our touring plan assumes a willingness to experience all major rides and shows. Be aware that the Rock 'n' Roller Coaster, Star Tours, The Great Movie Ride, *The Twilight Zone* Tower of Terror, and the Catastrophe Canyon segment of the tram tour sometimes frighten children younger than eight. Further, Star Tours and the Rock 'n' Roller Coaster can upset anyone prone to motion sickness. When following the plan, skip any attraction you don't wish to experience.

Before You Go

1. Call (407) 824-4321 to verify the park's hours.

2. Buy your admission before arriving.

3. Make lunch and dinner priority seatings (if desired) before you arrive by calling (407) WDW-DINE.

4. The schedule of live entertainment changes from month to month and even from day to day. Review the handout daily entertainment schedule to get a fairly clear picture of your options.

Touring Plan

By way of introduction, we didn't believe it when our new touring plan software (see pages 73–78) spit out this plan. It requires a fair amount of backtracking and postpones several big attractions until later in the day. Field testing, however, confirmed that it saves about 40 minutes over other plans.

1. Arrive at the park, admission in hand, 40 minutes before official opening time.

2. When you're admitted, grab a park map and a daily entertainment schedule from the little round shop straight ahead and just inside the turnstiles. Then blow down Hollywood Boulevard and turn right onto Sunset Boulevard. Stay to the right side of the street and proceed to the Tower of Terror. Ride. If your route is blocked by a rope barrier, position yourself as near the rope as possible and on the right side of the street. When you are allowed to proceed, go directly to the Tower of Terror.

3. After exiting the Tower of Terror, bear right to Rock 'n Roller Coaster. Obtain FASTPASSes for the Rock 'n' Roller Coaster.

4. After obtaining FASTPASSes, backtrack down Sunset Boulevard and turn right on Hollywood Boulevard. On the far side of the giant hat is The Great Movie Ride. Enjoy.

5. Exit the Great Movie Ride and bear left through the Studios Arch. Just inside the arch and to the left is *Voyage of the Little Mermaid*. See the show.

6. Return to Rock 'n Roller Coaster and ride using your FASTPASSes.

7. Backtrack to the Studio Arch. On your right after passing through, take the Magic of Disney Animation Tour.

8. Exit the Animation Tour and take a right at the *Little Mermaid* corner onto Mickey Avenue. About 40 yards down on your right, take in a show of *Who Wants to Be a Millionaire*. Use FASTPASS if you are unlikely to be admitted to the next scheduled show.

9. Check the daily entertainment schedule for performances of the *Indiana Jones Epic Stunt Spectacular* (FASTPASS), as well as shows at the *Theater of the Stars* and the Backlot Theater. If you have pre-schoolers in your party, also include *Playhouse Disney*. Work these shows in at your convenience as you continue the touring plan.

10. See *Sounds Dangerous*, which faces Echo Lake near *Indiana Jones*.

11. Take the Backlot Tour. The entrance is down Mickey Avenue from *Who Wants to Be a Millionaire*.

12. Exit to the left after the Backlot Tour and head up Mickey Avenue towards the *Little Mermaid*. Just past *Who Wants to Be a Millionaire*, see *One Man's Dream*.

13. Return back down Mickey Avenue and pass through the Studio Catering Company counter service restaurant, exiting on New York Street. Go left on New York Street and then right at the fake tall buildings. See *MuppetVision 3D*.

14. Head in the direction of the Echo Lake. Ride Star Tours.

15. Explore the New York Street Set if you didn't see enough enroute to the Muppets.

16. Tour Hollywood and Sunset Boulevards. Enjoy *Fantasmic!*.

17. This concludes the touring plan. Eat, shop, enjoy live entertainment, or revisit your favorite attractions.

Universal Orlando

Universal Orlando is close to completion in the expansion project that has transformed the facility into a destination resort with two theme parks; a shopping, dining, and entertainment complex; and three hotels. The second theme park, Islands of Adventure (described later in this section), opened in 1999 with five theme areas.

A new system of roads and two multistory parking facilities are connected by moving sidewalks to CityWalk, a shopping, dining, and night-time entertainment complex that also serves as a gateway to both the Universal Studios Florida and Islands of Adventure theme parks. City-Walk includes the world's largest Hard Rock Cafe, complete with its own concert facility; an Emeril's restaurant; a NASCAR Cafe, with an auto-racing theme; a Pat O'Brien's New Orleans nightclub, with dueling pianos; a Motown Cafe; a Bob Marley restaurant and museum; a multi-faceted Jazz Center; an E! Entertainment production studio; Jimmy Buffett's Margaritaville; and a 16-screen cinema complex.

The Portofino Bay Hotel opened in 1999 with 750 rooms, followed by the 650-room Hard Rock Hotel in late 2000. The third hotel, the Royal Pacific Resort, opened in 2002 with 1,000 rooms.

Arriving at Universal Orlando

The Universal Orlando complex can be accessed directly from I-4. Once on-site, you will be directed to park in one of two multitiered parking garages. Parking runs $6 for cars and $8 for RVs. Be sure to write down the location of your car before heading for the parks. From the garages, moving sidewalks deliver you to the Universal CityWalk dining, shopping, and entertainment venue described above. From CityWalk, you can access the main entrances of both Universal Studios Florida and Islands of Adventure theme parks. Even with the moving walkways, it takes about 10–12 minutes to commute from the garages to the entrances of the theme parks.

Universal offers One-Day, Two-Day, Three-Day, and Annual Passes. Multiday passes allow you to visit both Universal theme parks on the same day, and unused days are good forever. Multiday passes also allow for early entry on select days. Passes can be obtained in advance on the phone with your credit card at (800) 711-0080. All prices are the same whether you buy your admission at the gate or in advance. Prices shown below include tax.

	Adults	Children (3–9)
One-Day, One Park Pass	$51	$40
Two-Day Escape Pass	$91	$75
Three-Day Escape Pass (sold at gate)	$106	$90
Two-Park Annual Pass	$175	$175

If you want to visit more than one park on a given day, have your park pass and hand stamped when exiting your first park. At the second park use the readmission turnstile, showing your stamped pass and hand.

Combination passes are available: A four-park, seven-day pass allows unlimited entry to Universal Studios, Universal's Islands of Adventure, SeaWorld, and Wet 'n Wild and costs about $170 for adults and $136 for children (ages three to nine). A five-park, ten-day pass provides unlimited entry to Universal Studios, Universal's Islands of Adventure, SeaWorld, Wet 'n Wild, and Busch Gardens and costs about $209 for adults and $168 for children.

The main Universal Orlando information number is (407) 363-8000. Reach Guest Services at (407) 224-6035, schedule a character lunch at (407) 224-6339, and order tickets by mail at (800) 224-3838.

Early Entry and Universal Express

Universal is continually experimenting with a complicated scheme of early entry and line-breaking privileges. Call before you make plans, but this is how it looked as we went to press.

Early theme-park admission is available to multiday pass holders and guests at Universal hotels. These visitors can enter either Universal Studios Florida (Sunday and Thursday) or Islands of Adventure (Monday and Wednesday) one hour before official opening. Only select attractions are operating during the early-entry period, and sometimes even these

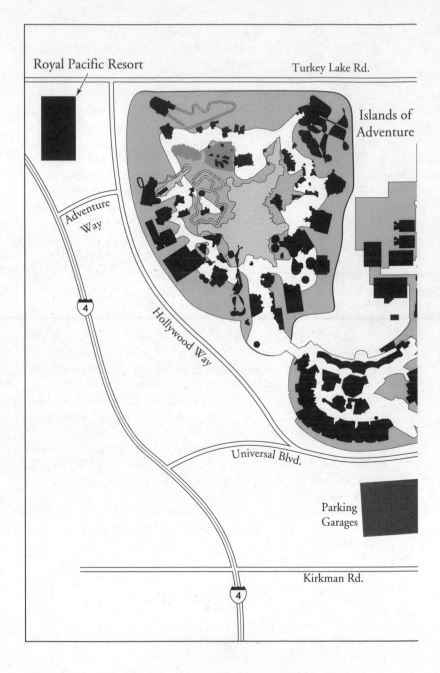

Royal Pacific Resort

Turkey Lake Rd.

Islands of
Adventure

Adventure
Way

4

Hollywood Way

Universal Blvd.

Parking
Garages

Kirkman Rd.

4

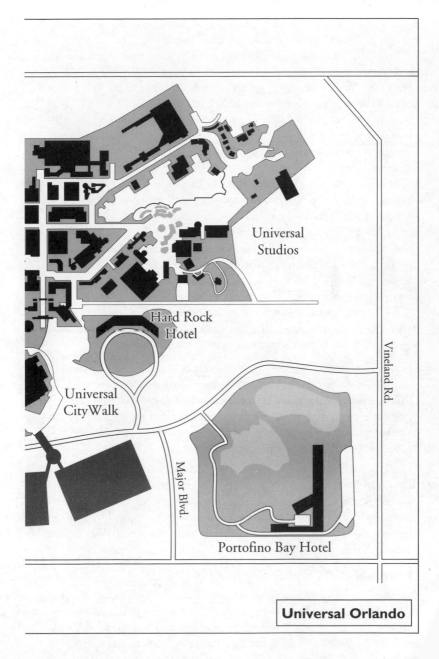

Universal Studios

Hard Rock Hotel

Universal CityWalk

Vineland Rd.

Major Blvd.

Portofino Bay Hotel

Universal Orlando

may be temporarily closed. Call ahead to make sure the early-entry attractions are up and running on the day of your visit.

The Universal Express program has gone through multiple revisions, but it seems to have stabilized in its current form. Much like with Disney's FASTPASS, theme park guests are issued Universal Express return tickets at kiosks set near the entrances of popular attractions. These return tickets have a 15-minute time window printed on them, good for admission later in the day to the Express queue at a particular attraction. This special queue bypasses much of the main line, and those waiting in it generally have priority over the proles stuck in the regular queue.

The main difference between Universal Express and FASTPASS is that Universal multiday ticket holders can get up to three return tickets at once, allowing them to hit several attractions in succession. Single-day pass holders can only have one return ticket at a time, just like FAST-PASS. Moreover, guests at Universal hotels can enter the Express line all day long, merely by flashing their Universal hotel keycard—a perk that can be invaluable during peak season, when large crowds will have already captured the entire day's worth of passes by noon.

This system dramatically affects crowd movement (and touring plans) in the Universal parks, since all guests can access the Express line to some degree. A woman from Yorktown, Virginia, writes:

> People in the [Express] line were let in at a rate of about ten to one over the regular line folks. This created bottlenecks and long waits for people who didn't have the express privilege at the very times when it is supposed to be easier to get around! The fallout from this was that we just kind of poked around until noon, then found basically no wait for ANYTHING (even Spider-Man) in the afternoon.

And there's yet another option: the singles line. Several attractions have this special line for guests riding alone. As Universal employees will tell you, this line is often even faster than the Express line. We strongly recommend you use this line or the Express line whenever possible, as it will decrease your overall wait and leave more time for repeat rides or just bumming around the parks.

Universal, Kids, and Scary Stuff

Although there's plenty for younger children to enjoy at the Universal parks, the majority of the major attractions have the potential for wig-
ᵍ out kids under eight years of age. At Universal Studios Florida, for-
ʳister, Kongfrontation, Earthquake, Jaws, Men in Black, Back to
ᵉ, and *Terminator 2: 3-D*. Most young children take the stunt
ᵈe, though there are gunfire and explosions involved. E.T. is a
ˢt part of the ride is a little intense for a few preschoolers,

but the end is all happiness and harmony. Interestingly, very few families report problems with *Beetlejuice's Rock 'n Roll Graveyard Revue* or *The Gory Gruesome & Grotesque Horror Make-up Show*. Anything not listed is pretty benign.

At Universal's Islands of Adventure, watch out for The Incredible Hulk Coaster, Dr. Doom's Fearfall, The Adventures of Spider-Man, the Jurassic Park River Adventure, Dueling Dragons, and *Poseidon's Fury*. Popeye & Bluto's Bilge-Rat Barges is wet and wild, but most younger children handle it well. Dudley Do-Right's Ripsaw Falls is a toss-up, to be considered only if your kids liked water-flume rides. The Sinbad stunt show includes some explosions and startling special effects, but once again, children tolerate it well. Nothing else should pose a problem.

Lodging at Universal Orlando

Universal currently has three operating resort hotels. The 750-room Portofino Bay Hotel is a gorgeous property set on an artificial bay and themed like an Italian coastal town. The 650-room Hard Rock Hotel is an ultra-cool "Hotel California" replica, with slick contemporary design and a hip, friendly attitude. The 1,000-room, Polynesian-themed Royal Pacific Resort is the most inexpensive of the three, but it's still sumptuously decorated and richly appointed. All three are excellent hotels; the Portofino and the Hard Rock are on the pricey side.

Like Disney, Universal offers a number of incentives to stay at their hotels. Perks available that mirror those offered by the Mouse include free parking, delivery to your room of purchases made in the parks, tickets and reservation information from hotel concierges, priority dining reservations at Universal restaurants, and the ability to charge purchases to your room account.

Otherwise, Universal offers complimentary transportation by bus or water taxi to Universal Studios, Islands of Adventure, CityWalk, Sea-World, and Wet n' Wild. Hotel guests are eligible for early admission to the theme parks, and they may use the Universal Express program with impunity all day long (see "Early Entry and Universal Express" above). Universal lodging guests are also eligible for "next available" table privileges at CityWalk restaurants and similar priority admission to Universal Orlando theme park shows.

Universal Studios Florida

Universal City Studios Inc. has run a studios tour and movie-theme tourist attraction for more than 29 years, predating all Disney parks except Disneyland. In the early 1980s, Universal announced plans to build a new theme-park complex in Florida. But while Universal labored over its new project, Disney jumped into high gear and rushed its own studios/theme park onto the market, beating Universal by a year and a half. Universal Studios Florida opened in June 1990. At that time, it was almost four times the size of Disney-MGM Studios (Disney-MGM has since expanded somewhat), with much more of the facility accessible to visitors. Like its sister facility in Hollywood, Universal Studios Florida is spacious, beautifully landscaped, meticulously clean, and delightfully varied in its entertainment. Rides are exciting and innovative and, as with many Disney rides, focus on familiar and/or beloved movie characters or situations.

On Universal Studios Florida's E.T. ride, you escape the authorities on a flying bike and leave Earth to visit E.T.'s home planet. In Kongfrontation, King Kong tears up a city with you in it. In Jaws, the persistent great white shark makes heart-stopping assaults on your small boat, and in Earthquake—The Big One, special effects create the most realistic earthquake simulation ever produced. Guests also ride in a Delorean-cum-time machine in yet another chase, this one based on the film *Back to the Future,* and fight alien bugs with zapper guns in Men in Black. Two new attractions opening in spring 2003 (based on the *Jimmy Neutron* and *Shrek* movies) promise to raise the entertainment stakes even higher.

While these rides incorporate state-of-the-art technology and live up to their billing in terms of excitement, creativity, uniqueness, and special effects, some lack the capacity to handle the number of guests who frequent major Florida tourist destinations. If a ride has great appeal but can accommodate only a small number of guests per ride or per hour, long lines form. It isn't unusual for the wait to exceed an hour and a quarter for the E.T. ride.

Happily, most shows and theater performances at Universal Studios Florida are in theaters that accommodate large numbers of people. Since many shows run continuously, waits usually don't exceed twice the show's performance time (40–50 minutes). At several shows, the audience moves to three or more staging areas as the presentation unfolds.

Universal Studios Florida is laid out in an upside-down L configuration. Beyond the main entrance, a wide boulevard stretches past several shows and rides to a New York City backlot set. Branching off this pedestrian thoroughfare to the right are five streets that access other areas of the studios and intersect a promenade circling a large lake.

The park is divided into five sections: the Front Lot/Production Central, New York, Hollywood, San Francisco/Amity, and Expo Center. Where one section begins and another ends is blurry, but no matter. Guests orient themselves by the major rides, sets, and landmarks and refer, for instance, to "New York," "the waterfront," "over by E.T.," or "by Mel's Diner." The area of Universal Studios Florida open to visitors is about the size of Epcot.

The park offers all standard services and amenities, including stroller and wheelchair rental, lockers, diaper-changing and infant-nursing facilities, car assistance, and foreign-language assistance. Most of the park is accessible to disabled guests, and TDDs are available for the hearing impaired. Almost all services are in the Front Lot, just inside the main entrance.

Universal Studios offers character meals on Tuesdays and Thursdays during slow season, and Monday–Friday during high season. Meals are hosted by at least four Hanna-Barbera characters at the International Food Bazaar, just inside the park on the right. The cost is $13.50 for adults and $8.75 for children ages three to nine for an all-you-can-eat cafeteria-style breakfast.

NOT TO BE MISSED AT UNIVERSAL STUDIOS FLORIDA

Back to the Future	Terminator 2: 3-D
Earthquake—The Big One	The Wild, Wild, Wild West Stunt Show
Jaws	Men in Black Alien Attack

Universal Studios Florida Attractions

Terminator 2: 3-D

What It Is 3-D thriller mixed-media presentation
Scope & Scale Super headliner
When to Go After 3:30 p.m.
Special Comments The nation's best theme-park theater attraction; very intense for some preschoolers and grade-schoolers
Author's Rating Furiously paced high-tech experience; not to be missed; ★★★★★
Appeal by Age Group

Pre-school ★★★	Grade School ★★★★	Teens ★★★★★
Young Adults ★★★★★	Over 30 ★★★★★	Senior Citizens ★★★★

uration of Presentation 20 minutes, including an 8-minute preshow
Probable Waiting Time 20–40 minutes

Description and Comments The Terminator "cop" from *Terminator 2* morphs to life and battles Arnold Schwarzenegger's T-100 cyborg character. If you missed the *Terminator* flicks, here's the plot: A bad robot arrives from the future to kill a nice boy. Another bad robot (who has been reprogrammed to be good) pops up at the same time to save the boy. The bad robot chases the boy and the rehabilitated robot, menacing the audience in the process.

The attraction, like the films, is all action, and you really don't need to understand much. What's interesting is that it uses 3-D film and a theater full of sophisticated technology to integrate the real with the imaginary. Images seem to move in and out of the film, not only in the manner of traditional 3-D, but also in actuality. Remove your 3-D glasses momentarily and you'll see that the guy on the motorcycle is actually onstage.

We've watched this type of presentation evolve, pioneered by Disney's *Captain EO, Honey, I Shrunk the Audience,* and *MuppetVision 3D. Term-inator 2: 3-D,* however, goes way

Universal Studios Florida

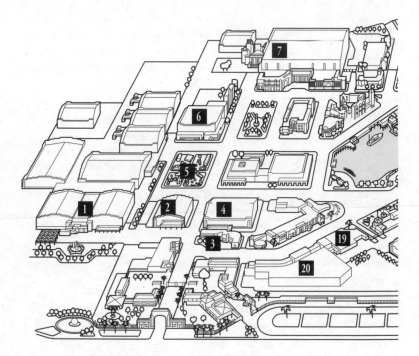

EXIT TO VINELAND RD. →

beyond lasers, with moving theater seats, blasts of hot air, and spraying mist. It creates a multidimensional space that blurs the boundary between entertainment and reality. Is it seamless? Not quite, but it's close. We rank *Terminator 2: 3-D* as not to be missed and consider it the absolute best theme-park attraction in the United States. If *Terminator 2: 3-D* is the only attraction you see at Universal Studios Florida, you'll have received your money's worth.

Touring Tips The 700-seat theater changes audiences about every 19 minutes. Even so, because the show is new and hot, expect to wait about 30–45 minutes. The attraction, on Hollywood Boulevard near the park's entrance, receives huge traffic during morning and early afternoon. By about 3 p.m., however, lines diminish somewhat. Though you'll still wait, we recommend holding off on *Terminator 2: 3-D* until then. If you can't stay until late afternoon, see the show first thing in the morning. Families with young children should know that the violence characteristic of the *Terminator* movies is largely absent from the attraction. There's suspense and action but not much blood and guts.

Jimmy Neutron Attraction (opens spring 2003)

What It Is Cartoon science demonstration and simulation ride
Scope & Scale Major attraction
When to Go The first hour after park opening or the last hour before park closing
Author's Rating Not open at press time
Appeal by Age Group Not open at press time

Description and Comments This as-yet-unnamed attraction, based on the Nickelodeon movie *Jimmy Neutron: Boy Genius,* replaces The Funtastic World of Hanna-Barbera. In addition to Jimmy, the attraction will also feature a mob of other characters from Nickelodeon, including SpongeBob SquarePants, the Rugrats, the Fairly Odd Parents, and the Wild Thornberrys. The story, insamuch as we can understand it, takes place in two parts. At first, guests are invited to participate in a demonstration of Jimmy's newest invention, which apparently allows one to spy on what's currently happening outside the attraction (no wonder he's a genius!). After that, an alien plot is revealed, and guests are strapped into motion-simulator vehicles (similar to those from the Hanna-Barbera ride) in order to help Jimmy defend the Earth. These "Rocket Pods" will move and react in synch with a movie projected onto a huge screen.

Touring Tips As this new attraction will no doubt be popular, we advise seeing it at the very beginning or end of park hours. The situation is complicated by the fact that the other new attraction at Universal Studios Florida—this one based on the movie *Shrek*—will be going up at about the same time and right next door to Jimmy. If both Jimmy Neutron and Shrek are up and running, get a Universal Express pass for Shrek, experience Jimmy Neutron, then come back to Shrek to hit your Express time window.

Shrek Attraction (opens spring 2003)

What It Is 3-D "OgreVision" theater show with additional sensory stimuli
Scope & Scale Headliner
When to Go The first hour the park is open or after 4 p.m.
Author's Rating Not open at press time

Appeal by Age Group Not open at press time

Description and Comments Another new attraction without a final name at press time, this one (which replaces "Alfred Hitchcock: The Art of Making Movies") is based on characters from the hit movie *Shrek*. A preshow presents the villain from the movie, Lord Farquaad, as he appears on various screens to describe his posthumous plan to haunt the good ogre Shrek and his companions. The plan is posthumous since Lord Farquaad ostensibly died in the movie, and it's his ghost making the plans, but never mind. Guests then move into the main theater, don their 3-D glasses, and recline in seats equipped with "tactile transducers" and "pneumatic air propulsion and water spray nodules capable of both vertical and horizontal motion." As the 3-D film plays, guests will also be subjected to smells relevant to the on-screen action (oh boy). Given the enormous success Universal had with *Terminator 2: 3-D*, this could well be the next step in the evolution of this kind of presentation. Incidentally, the Shrek attraction will also be the first to debut simultaneously at both the Orlando and Hollywood parks.

Touring Tips Since it supposedly will involve remaking the staid facade of the Alfred Hitchcock attraction into a scary castle (Hitchcock would probably have approved), the new Shrek show would draw crowds even if it wasn't a new top-shelf afffair. Combine that with the new Jimmy Neutron attraction going up right next door and opening at the same time, and this corner of Universal Studios will liven up considerably. On the plus side, Universal claims that they'll be able to move 2,400 guests an hour through Shrek, so if true, that will speed things up considerably. If both Shrek and Jimmy Neutron are up and running, get a Universal Express pass for Shrek, experience Jimmy Neutron, then come back to Shrek to hit your Express time window.

Nickelodeon Studios Walking Tour

What It Is Behind-the-scenes guided tour

Scope & Scale Minor attraction

When to Go When Nickelodeon shows are in production (usually weekdays)

Author's Rating ★★★

Appeal by Age Group

Pre-school ★★½	Grade School ★★★★	Teens ★★★
Young Adults ★★★	Over 30 ★★★	Senior Citizens ★★★

Duration of Tour 36 minutes

Probable Waiting Time 30–45 minutes

Description and Comments The tour examines set construction, soundstages, wardrobe, props, lighting, video production, and special effects. Much of this information is presented more creatively in the "Alfred Hitchcock" and *Horror Make-Up Show* productions, but the Nickelodeon tour is tailored for kids. They're made to feel supremely important; their opinions are used to shape future Nickelodeon programming.

The Game Lab, where guests preview strange games being tested for possible inclusion on Nickelodeon, adds some much-needed zip. It ends with a lucky child getting "slimed." If you don't understand, consult your children.

Touring Tips While grade-schoolers, especially, enjoy this tour, it's expendable for everyone else. Go on a second day or second visit at Universal. If Nickelodeon isn't in production, forget it.

Twister

What It Is Theater presentation featuring special effects from the movie *Twister*
Scope & Scale Major attraction
When to Go Should be your first show after experiencing all rides
Special Comments High potential for frightening young children
Author's Rating Gusty; ★★★½
Appeal by Age Group

Pre-school ★★   Grade School ★★★★   Teens ★★★★
Young Adults ★★★★   Over 30 ★★★★   Senior Citizens ★★★★

Duration of Presentation 15 minutes
Probable Waiting Time 26 minutes

Description and Comments Replacing the *Ghostbusters* attraction in 1998, *Twister* combines an elaborate set and special effects, climaxing with a five-story-tall simulated tornado created by circulating more than 2 million cubic feet of air per minute.

Touring Tips The wind, pounding rain, and freight-train sound of the tornado are deafening, and the entire presentation is exceptionally intense. School children are mightily impressed, while younger children are terrified and overwhelmed. Unless you want the kids hopping in your bed whenever they hear thunder, try this attraction yourself before taking your kids.

Kongfrontation

What It Is Indoor adventure ride featuring King Kong
Scope & Scale Major attraction
When to Go Before 11 a.m.
Special Comments May frighten young children
Author's Rating ★★★★
Appeal by Age Group

Pre-school ★★★½   Grade School ★★★★   Teens ★★★½
Young Adults ★★★½   Over 30 ★★★   Senior Citizens ★★★

Duration of Ride 4½ minutes
Loading Speed Moderate

Description and Comments Guests board an aerial tram to ride from Manhattan to Roosevelt Island. En route, they hear the giant ape has escaped. The tram passes evidence of Kong's path of destruction and encounters the monster himself. In the course of the journey, King Kong demolishes buildings, uproots utility poles, swats helicopters, and hurls your tram car to the ground.

Touring Tips A lot of fun when it works. Ride in the morning after Men in Black, Back to the Future, E.T. Adventure, and Jaws.

The Gory Gruesome & Grotesque Horror Make-Up Show

What It Is Theater presentation on the art of make-up
Scope & Scale Major attraction

When to Go After you have experienced all rides

Special Comments May frighten young children

Author's Rating A gory knee-slapper; ★★★½

Appeal by Age Group

Pre-school ★★★	Grade School ★★★½	Teens ★★★½
Young Adults ★★★½	Over 30 ★★★½	Senior Citizens ★★★½

Duration of Presentation 25 minutes

Probable Waiting Time 20 minutes

Description and Comments Lively, well-paced look at how make-up artists create film monsters, realistic wounds, severed limbs, and other unmentionables. Funnier and more upbeat than many Universal Studios presentations, the show also presents a wealth of fascinating information. It's excellent and enlightening, if somewhat gory.

Touring Tips Exceeding most guests' expectations, the *Horror Make-Up Show* is the sleeper attraction at Universal. Its humor and tongue-in-cheek style transcend the gruesome effects, and most folks (including preschoolers) take the blood and guts in stride. It usually isn't too hard to get into.

Earthquake—The Big One

What It Is Combination theater presentation and adventure ride

Scope & Scale Major attraction

When to Go In the morning, after Kongfrontation

Special Comments May frighten young children

Author's Rating Not to be missed; ★★★★

Appeal by Age Group

Pre-school ★★★	Grade School ★★★★	Teens ★★★★
Young Adults ★★★★	Over 30 ★★★★	Senior Citizens ★★★★

Duration of Presentation 20 minutes

Loading Speed Moderate

Description and Comments Film shows how miniatures are used to create special effects in earthquake movies, followed by a demonstration of how miniatures, blue screen, and matte painting are integrated with live-action stunt sequences (starring audience volunteers) to create a realistic final product. Afterward, guests board a subway from Oakland to San Francisco and experience an earthquake—the big one. Special effects range from fires and runaway trains to exploding tanker trucks and tidal waves. This is Universal's answer to Disney-MGM's Catastrophe Canyon. The special effects are comparable, but the field of vision is better at Catastrophe Canyon. Nonetheless, Earthquake is one of Universal's more compelling efforts.

Touring Tips Experience Earthquake in the morning, after you ride Men in Black, Back to the Future, E.T., Jaws, and Kongfrontation.

Jaws

What It Is Adventure boat ride

Scope & Scale Headliner

When to Go Before 11 a.m.

Special Comments Will frighten young children

Author's Rating Not to be missed; ★★★★

Appeal by Age Group

Pre-school ★★½	Grade School ★★★★	Teens ★★★★
Young Adults ★★★★	Over 30 ★★★★	Senior Citizens ★★★★

Duration of Ride 5 minutes

Loading Speed Fast

Probable Waiting Time Per 100 People Ahead of You 3 minutes

Assumes All 8 boats are running

Description and Comments Jaws delivers five minutes of nonstop action, with the huge shark repeatedly attacking. A West Virginia woman, fresh from the Magic Kingdom, told us the shark is "about as pesky as that witch in Snow White." While the story is entirely predictable, the shark is realistic and as big as Rush Limbaugh.

What makes the ride unique is its sense of journey. Jaws builds an amazing degree of suspense. It isn't just a cruise into the middle of a pond where a rubber fish assaults the boat interminably. Add inventive sets and powerful special effects, and you have a first-rate attraction.

A variable at Jaws is the enthusiasm and acting ability of your boat guide. Throughout the ride, the guide must set the tone, elaborate the plot, drive the boat, and fight the shark. Most guides are quite good. They may overact a bit, but you can't fault them for lack of enthusiasm. Consider also that each guide repeats this wrenching ordeal every eight minutes.

Touring Tips Jaws is as well designed to handle crowds as any theme-park attraction in Florida. People on the boat's left side tend to get splashed more. If you have young children, consider switching off (pages 254–257).

A mother of two from Williamsville, New York, who believes our warning about getting wet should be more strongly emphasized, has this to say:

Your warning about the "Jaws" attraction . . . is woefully understated. Please warn your readers—we were seated on the first row of the boat. My nine-year-old sat at the end of the boat (first person on the far left), and I was seated next to him. We were wary of these seats as I had read your warning, but I felt prepared. NOT!!!! At "that" moment the water came flooding over the left front side of the boat, thoroughly drenching the two of us and filling our sneakers with water. Unfortunately for us, this was only our third attraction of the day (9:30 a.m.) and we still had a long day ahead of us. It was a rather chilly and windy 62° day. We went to the rest rooms, removed our shorts, and squeezed out as much water as we could, but we were very cold and uncomfortable all day. This will be our most vivid and lasting memory of our day at Universal Studios!!!

A dad from Seattle suggests that getting wet takes a backseat to being terrified:

Our eight-year-old was so frightened by Jaws that we scrapped the rest of the Universal tour and went back to E.T. An employee said she wouldn't recommend it to anyone under ten. Maybe you should change "may frighten small children" to "definitely will scare the pants off most children."

Men in Black Alien Attack

What It Is Interactive dark thrill ride
Scope & Scale Super headliner
When to Go First thing in the morning
Special Comments May induce motion sickness. Must be 42" tall to ride. Switching off available (pages 254–257).
Author's Rating Buzz Lightyear on steroids; not to be missed; ★★★★½
Appeal by Age Group

Pre-school †   Grade School ★★★★½ Teens ★★★★★
Young Adults ★★★★★ Over 30 ★★★★★   Senior Citizens ★★★★
  † Sample size too small for an accurate rating

Duration of Ride 2½ minutes
Loading Speed Moderate to Fast

Description and Comments   Based on the movie of the same name, Men in Black brings together actors Will Smith and Rip Torn (as Agent J and MIB Director Zed) for an interactive sequel to the hit film. The story line has you volunteering as a Men in Black (MIB) trainee. After an introduction warning that aliens "live among us" and articulating MIB's mission to round them up, Zed expands on the finer points of alien spotting and familiarizes you with your training vehicle and your weapon, an alien "zapper." Following this, you load up and are dispatched on an innocuous training mission that immediately deteriorates into a situation where only you are in a position to prevent aliens from taking over the universe. Now, if you saw the movie you understand that the aliens are mostly giant, exotic bugs and cockroaches and that zapping the aliens involves exploding them into myriad, gooey body parts. Thus, the meat of the ride (no pun intended) consists of careening around Manhattan in your MIB vehicle and shooting aliens. The technology at work is similar to that used in the Spider-Man attraction at Universal's Islands of Adventure, which is to say that it's both a wild ride and one where movies, sets, robotics, and your vehicle are all integrated into a fairly seamless package.

Men in Black is interactive in that your marksmanship and ability to blast yourself out of some tricky situations will determine how the story ends. Also, you are awarded a personal score (like Disney's Buzz Lightyear Space Ranger Spin) and a score for your car. There are about three dozen possible outcomes and literally thousands of different ride experiences determined by your pluck, performance, and in the final challenge your intestinal fortitude.

Touring Tips   Each of the 120 or so alien figures has sensors that activate special effects and respond to your zapper. Aim for the eyes and keep shooting until the aliens' eyes turn red. Also, many of the aliens shoot back, causing your vehicle to veer or spin. In the mayhem, you might fail to notice that another vehicle of guests runs along beside you on a dual track. This was included to instill a spirit of competition for anyone who finds blowing up bugs and saving the universe less than stimulating. Note that after a certain point, you can shoot the flashing "vent" on top of this other car and make them spin around. Of course, they can do the same to you . . .

Although there are many possible endings, the long lines at this headliner attraction will probably dissuade you from experiencing all but one or two. To avoid a long wait, hotfoot it to MIB as soon as the park opens.

Back to the Future — The Ride

What It Is Flight-simulator thrill ride
Scope & Scale Super headliner
When to Go First thing in the morning after Men in Black
Special Comments Very rough ride; may induce motion sickness.
Must be 40" tall to ride. Switching off available (pages 254–257).
Author's Rating Not to be missed, if you have a strong
stomach; ★★★★★

Motion
Sickness

WARNING!

Appeal by Age Group

Pre-school †   Grade School ★★★★★   Teens ★★★★★
Young Adults ★★★★★   Over 30 ★★★★   Senior Citizens ★★½
† Sample size too small for an accurate rating

Duration of Ride 4½ minutes
Loading Speed Moderate

Description and Comments This attraction is to Universal Studios Florida what
Space Mountain is to the Magic Kingdom: the most popular thrill ride in the park. Guests
in Doc Brown's lab get caught up in a high-speed chase through time that spans a million
years. An extremely intense simulator ride, Back to the Future is similar to Star Tours
and Body Wars at Walt Disney World but is much rougher and more jerky. Though the
story doesn't make much sense, the visual effects are wild and powerful. The vehicles
(Delorean time machines) in Back to the Future are much smaller than those of Star
Tours and Body Wars, so the ride feels more personal and less like a group experience.

Touring Tips As soon the park opens, guests stampede to Men in Black and Back to
the Future. Our recommendation: Be there when the park opens, and join the rush. If
you don't ride before 10 a.m., your wait may be exceptionally long. *Note:* Sitting in the
rear seat of the car makes the ride more realistic.

E.T. Adventure

What It Is Indoor adventure ride based on the *E.T.* movie
Scope & Scale Major attraction
When to Go Before 10 a.m.

Author's Rating ★★★★
Appeal by Age Group

Pre-school ★★★★   Grade School ★★★★   Teens ★★★½
Young Adults ★★★½   Over 30 ★★★½   Senior Citizens ★★★½

Duration of Ride 4½ minutes
Loading Speed Moderate

Description and Comments Guests aboard a bicycle-like conveyance escape with
E.T. from earthly law enforcement officials and then journey to E.T.'s home planet. The
attraction is similar to Peter Pan's Flight at the Magic Kingdom but is longer and has
more elaborate special effects and a wilder ride.

Touring Tips Most preschoolers and grade-school children love E.T. We think it
worth a 20- to 30-minute wait, but nothing longer. Lines build quickly after 9:45 a.m.,
and waits can be more than two hours on busy days. Ride in the morning, right after

Men in Black and Back to the Future. Guests who balk at sitting on the bicycle can ride in a comfortable gondola.

A mother from Columbus, Ohio, writes about horrendous lines at E.T.:

The line for E.T. took two hours! The rest of the family waiting outside thought that we had gone to E.T.'s planet for real.

A woman from Richmond, Virginia, objects to how Universal represented the waiting time:

We got into E.T. without much wait, but the line is very deceptive. When you see a lot of people waiting outside and the sign says "ten-minute wait from this point," it means ten minutes until you are inside the building. But there's a very long wait inside [before] you get to the moving vehicles.

Woody Woodpecker's KidZone

What It Is Interactive playground and kid's roller coaster

Scope & Scale Minor attraction

When to Go Anytime

Author's Rating A good place to let off steam; ★★★

Appeal by Age Group

Pre-school ★★★★	Grade School ★★★	Teens —
Young Adults —	Over 30 —	Senior Citizens —

Description and Comments Rounding out the selection of other nearby kid-friendly attractions, the KidZone consists of Woody Woodpecker's Nuthouse Coaster and an interactive playground called Curious George Goes to Town. The child-sized roller coaster is small enough for kids to enjoy but sturdy enough for adults, though its moderate speed might unnerve some smaller children (the minimum age to ride is three years old). The Curious George playground exemplifies the Universal obsession with wet stuff; in addition to innumerable spigots, pipes, and spray guns, two giant roof-mounted buckets periodically dump a thousand gallons of water on unsuspecting visitors below. Kids who want to stay dry can mess around in the foam-ball playground, also equipped with chutes, tubes, and ball-blasters.

Touring Tips After its unveiling, Universal employees dubbed this area "Peckerland." Visit the playground after you've experienced all the major attractions.

Animal Planet Live!

What It Is Animal tricks and comedy show based on the popular network's programs

Scope & Scale Major attraction

When to Go After you have experienced all rides

Author's Rating Cute lil' critters; ★★★

Appeal by Age Group

Pre-school ★★★★	Grade School ★★★★★	Teens ★★★
Young Adults ★★★	Over 30 ★★★	Senior Citizens ★★★½

Duration of Presentation 20 minutes

Probable Waiting Time 25 minutes

Description and Comments This show aims to build on the popularity of the TV channel Animal Planet's various programs and characters, integrating video segments from the TV shows with live sketches, jokes, and animal tricks performed onstage. The idea is to create eco-friendly family entertainment that mirrors the themes of Animal Planet programming. Several of the animal thespians are veterans of television and movies, and many were rescued from shelters. Audience members can participate as well; where else will you get the chance to hold an eight-foot albino reticulated python in your lap?

Touring Tips Check the entertainment schedule for show times.

The Wild, Wild, Wild West Stunt Show

What It Is Stunt show with a western theme
Scope & Scale Major attraction
When to Go After you've experienced all rides
Author's Rating Solid and exciting; ★★★★
Appeal by Age Group

| Pre-school ★★★★½ | Grade School ★★★★ | Teens ★★★★ |
| Young Adults ★★★★ | Over 30 ★★★★ | Senior Citizens ★★★★ |

Duration of Presentation 16 minutes
Probable Waiting Time None

Description and Comments The *Wild West* stunt show has shootouts, fistfights, horse tricks, and high falls, all exciting and well executed. The fast-paced show is staged about ten times daily in a 2,000-seat, covered stadium. Unlike the stunt show on the lagoon, the action is easy to follow.

Touring Tips Show times are listed in the daily entertainment guide; go at your convenience. In summer, the stadium is more comfortable after dusk.

Fievel's Playland

What It Is Children's play area with water slide
Scope & Scale Minor attraction
When to Go Anytime
Author's Rating A much-needed attraction for preschoolers; ★★★★
Appeal by Age Group

| Pre-school ★★★★ | Grade School ★★★★ | Teens ★★★ |
| Young Adults ★★★ | Over 30 ★★★ | Senior Citizens ★★★ |

Probable Waiting Time 20–30 minutes for the water slide; otherwise, no waiting

Description and Comments Imaginative playground features ordinary household items reproduced on a giant scale, as a mouse would experience them. Pre-schoolers and grade-schoolers can climb nets, walk through a huge boot, splash in a sardine-can fountain, seesaw on huge spoons, and climb onto a cow skull. Most of the playground is reserved for pre-schoolers, but a water slide/raft ride is open to all ages.

Touring Tips Walk into Fievel's Playland without waiting, and stay as long as you want. Younger children love the oversized items, and there's enough to keep teens and adults busy while little ones let off steam. The water slide/raft ride is open to everyone but is extremely slow-loading and carries only 300 riders per hour. With an average wait of 20–30 minutes, we don't think the 16-second ride is worth the trouble. Also, you're highly likely to get soaked.

Lack of shade is a major shortcoming of the entire attraction. Don't go during the heat of the day.

Beetlejuice's Rock 'n Roll Graveyard Revue

What It Is Rock-and-roll stage show
Scope & Scale Minor attraction
When to Go At your convenience
Author's Rating Outrageous; ★★★½
Appeal by Age Group

| Pre-school ★★★★ | Grade School ★★★★ | Teens ★★★★ |
| Young Adults ★★★½ | Over 30 ★★★½ | Senior Citizens ★★★½ |

Duration of Presentation 18 minutes
Probable Waiting Time None

Description and Comments High-powered rock-and-roll stage show stars Beetlejuice, Frankenstein, the Bride of Frankenstein, Wolfman, Dracula, and the Phantom of the Opera. In addition to fine vintage rock, the show features some of the most exuberant choreography found anywhere, plus impressive sets and special effects.

Touring Tips Mercifully, this attraction has been moved under cover.

A Day in the Park with Barney

What It Is Live character stage show
Scope & Scale Major children's attraction
When to Go Anytime
Author's Rating A great hit with preschoolers; ★★★★
Appeal by Age Group

| Pre-school ★★★★½ | Grade School ★★★ | Teens ★★ |
| Young Adults ★★½ | Over 30 ★★★ | Senior Citizens ★★★ |

Duration of Presentation 12 minutes plus character greeting
Probable Waiting Time 15 minutes

Description and Comments Barney, the purple dinosaur of Public Television fame, leads a sing-along with the help of the audience and sidekicks Baby Bop and BJ. A short preshow gets the kids lathered up before they enter the theater, Barney's Park. Interesting theatrical effects include wind, falling leaves, clouds and stars in the simulated sky, and snow. After the show, Barney exits momentarily to allow parents and children to gather along the stage. He then thunders back and moves from child to child, hugging each and posing for photos.

Touring Tips If your child likes Barney, this show is a must. It's happy and upbeat, and the character greeting that follows is the best organized we've seen in any theme park. There's no line and no fighting for Barney's attention. Just relax by the rail and await your hug. There's also a great indoor play area nearby, designed especially for wee tykes.

Lucy, a Tribute

What It Is Walk-through tribute to Lucille Ball
Scope & Scale Diversion
When to Go Anytime
Author's Rating A touching remembrance; ★★★
Appeal by Age Group

Pre-school ★	Grade School ★★	Teens ★★
Young Adults ★★★	Over 30 ★★★	Senior Citizens ★★★

Probable Waiting Time None

Description and Comments The life and career of comedienne Lucille Ball are spotlighted, with emphasis on her role as Lucy Ricardo in the long-running television series *I Love Lucy*. Well designed and informative, the exhibit succeeds admirably in recalling the talent and temperament of the beloved redhead.

Touring Tips See Lucy during the hot, crowded midafternoon, or on your way out of the park. Adults could easily stay 15–30 minutes. Children, however, get restless after a couple of minutes.

Street Scenes

What It Is Elaborate outdoor sets for making films
Scope & Scale Diversion
When to Go Anytime
Special Comments You'll see most sets without special effort as you tour the park
Author's Rating One of the park's great assets; ★★★★★
Appeal by Age Group

Pre-school ★★★	Grade School ★★★★½	Teens ★★★★½
Young Adults ★★★★½	Over 30 ★★★★★	Senior Citizens ★★★★★

Probable Waiting Time No waiting

Description and Comments Unlike at Disney-MGM Studios, all Universal Studios Florida's backlot sets are accessible for guest inspection. They include New York City streets, San Francisco's waterfront, a New England coastal town, Rodeo Drive and Hollywood Boulevard, and a Louisiana bayou.

Touring Tips You'll see most as you walk through the park.

Universal Studios Florida Touring Plan

Universal Studios Florida One-Day Touring Plan

This plan is for all visitors. If a ride or show is listed that you don't want to experience, skip that step and proceed to the next. Move quickly from attraction to attraction and, if possible, don't stop for lunch until after Step 10.

Buying Admission to Universal Studios Florida

One of our big gripes about Universal Studios is that there never are enough ticket windows open in the morning to accommodate the crowd. You can arrive 45 minutes before official opening time and still be in line to buy your admission when the park opens. Therefore, we strongly recommend you buy your admission in advance. Passes are available by mail from Universal Studios at (800) 224-3838. They are also sold at the concierge desk or attractions box office of many Orlando-area hotels. If your hotel doesn't offer tickets, try Guest Services at the Radisson Twin Towers (407) 351-1000, at the intersection of Major Boulevard and Kirkman Avenue.

Many hotels that sell Universal admissions don't issue actual passes. Instead, the purchaser gets a voucher that can be redeemed for a pass at the theme park. Fortunately, the voucher-redemption window is separate from the park's ticket sales operation. You can quickly exchange your voucher for a pass and be on your way with little or no wait.

Touring Plan

As we went to press, two major new attractions (based on the movies *Jimmy Neutron: Boy Genius* and *Shrek,* respectively) were in the works for Universal Studios Florida. When these two open in the spring of 2003, they will dramatically change guest traffic patterns. This is because they are on the opposite side of the park from the former two top draws, Men in Black Alien Attack and Back to the Future. Any plan to see all the attractions at Universal Studios will require some hotfooting across the park between these two pairs of attractions. However, it also means that guest traffic will be more evenly distributed (and lines shold be shorter overall). As these new patterns emerge, feel free to opportunistically jump into short lines and make liberal use of Universal Express.

1. Call (407) 363-8000 the day before your visit for the official opening time.

2. On the day of your visit, eat breakfast and arrive at Universal Studios Florida 50 minutes before opening time with your admission pass or an admission voucher in hand. If you have a voucher, exchange it for a pass at the voucher-redemption window. Pick up a map and the daily entertainment schedule.

3. Line up at the turnstile. Ask any attendant whether any rides or shows are closed that day. Adjust the touring plan accordingly.

4. When the park opens, go straight down the Plaza of the Stars. Pass Rodeo Drive on your right. When you reach Nickelodeon Way on your left, you should be standing between the Jimmy Neutron attraction on your left and the Shrek attraction on your right. If both are up and running, try to get a

Universal Express pass for Shrek usable later in the day (around lunchtime if possible). If you can't get a Shrek pass for that time period, don't sweat it; Shrekwill have a large enough capacity to keep lines moving even on crowded days. After you've gotten your Universal Express pass for Shrek (or not), see Jimmy Neutron. If neither Shrek nor Jimmy Neutron are operating yet, skip head to Step 5 and Men in Black.

5. Exit Jimmy Neutron, take a left on Rodeo Drive to Hollywood Boulevard, pass Mel's Diner (on your left), and (keeping the lagoon on your left) go directly to Men in Black. Ride.

6. After Men in Black, backtrack to Back to the Future and ride.

7. Exit left and pass the International Food Bazaar. Continue bearing left past *Animal Planet Live!* and go to the E.T. Adventure. Ride.

8. Retrace your steps toward Back to the Future. Keeping the lagoon on your left, cross the bridge to Amity. Ride Jaws.

9. Exit and turn left down The Embarcadero. Postpone Earthquake and head directly to Kongfrontation in the New York set. Go ape.

10. Return to San Francisco. Ride Earthquake—The Big One.

11. Work your way back toward the main entrance. Is it time for your Universal Express window for Shrek yet? If so, see Shrek. If not, take a breather and have lunch. Unless your Shrek time window is a long way off, see that show before moving on to Step 12.

12. If you're still intact after various alien assaults, a bike ride to another galaxy, a shark attack, an earthquake, and an encounter with King Kong, take on a tornado. Return to the New York set and see Twister. The line will appear long but should move quickly as guests are admitted inside.

13. If you haven't already eaten, do so now. Work in your Shrek visit if that hasn't come along yet.

14. At this point you have five major attractions yet to see:
Terminator 2: 3-D
The Gory Gruesome & Grotesque Horror Make-Up Show
Animal Planet Live!
The Wild, Wild, Wild West Stunt Show
Beetlejuice's Rock 'n Roll Graveyard Revue

   Animal Planet Live!, the *Beetlejuice* show, and the stunt shows are performed several times daily, as listed in the entertainment schedule. Plan the remainder of your itinerary according to the next listed shows for these presentations. *The Horror Make-Up Show* (across from Mel's Diner) runs pretty much continuously and can be worked in as time permits. Try to see *Terminator 2: 3-D* after 3:30 p.m., but whatever you do, don't miss it.

15. Our touring plan doesn't include the Nickelodeon Studios Tour, Woody Woodpecker's KidZone, or *A Day in the Park with Barney.* If you have school-age children in your party, consider taking the Nickelodeon tour in late afternoon or on a second day at the park. If you're touring with preschoolers, see Barney after you ride E.T., and then head for KidZone.

16. This concludes the touring plan. Spend the remainder of your day revisiting your favorite attractions or inspecting sets and street scenes you may have missed. Also, check your daily entertainment schedule for live performances that interest you.

Universal's Islands of Adventure

When Universal's Islands of Adventure theme park opened in 1999, it provided Universal with enough critical mass to actually compete with Disney. Universal finally has on-site hotels, a shopping and entertainment complex, and two major theme parks. Doubly interesting is that the new Universal park is pretty much just for fun—in other words, a direct competitor to Disney's Magic Kingdom, the most visited theme park in the world. How direct a competitor is it? Check out the box on page 638 for a direct comparison.

And though it may take central Florida tourists awhile to make the connection, here's what will dawn on them when they finally do: Universal's Islands of Adventure is a brand-new, state-of-the-art park competing with a Disney park that is more than 25 years old and has not added a major new attraction for many years.

Of course, that's only how it looks on paper. The reality, as they say, is still blowing in the wind. The Magic Kingdom, after all, is graceful in its maturity and much beloved. And then there was the question on everyone's mind: could Universal really pull it off? Recalling the disastrous first year that the Universal Studios Florida park experienced, we held our breath to see if Islands of Adventure's innovative, high-tech attractions would work. Well, not only did they work, they were up and running almost two months ahead of schedule. Thus, the clash of the titans is once again hot. Universal is coming on strong with the potential of sucking up three days of a tourist's week (more, if you include Universal's strategic relationship with SeaWorld and Busch Gardens). And that's more time than anyone has spent off the Disney campus for a long, long time.

Through it all, Disney and Universal spokesmen downplayed their fierce competition, pointing out that any new theme park makes central Florida a more marketable destination. Behind closed doors, however, it's a Pepsi/Coke–type rivalry that will undoubtedly keep both companies working hard to gain a competitive edge. The good news, of course, is that this competition translates into better and better attractions for you to enjoy.

Beware of the Wet and Wild

Although we have described Universal's Islands of Adventure as a direct competitor to the Magic Kingdom, there is one major qualification you should be aware of. Whereas most Magic Kingdom attractions are designed to be enjoyed by guests of any age, attractions at Islands of

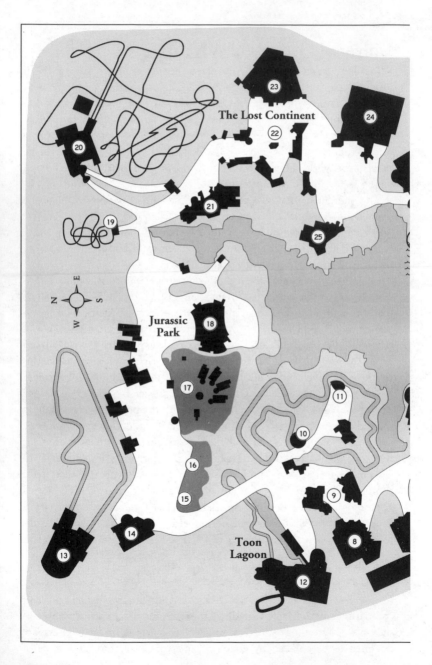

Islands of Adventure

Port of Entry
1. Island Skipper Tours
2. Confisco's Grill

Marvel Super Hero Island
3. Incredible Hulk Coaster
4. Storm Force
5. Cafe 4
6. Dr. Doom's Fearfall
7. The Amazing Adventure of Spider-Man

Toon Lagoon
8. Comic Strip Café
9. Comic Strip Lane
10. Popeye & Bluto's Bilge-Rat Barges
11. Me Ship, *The Olive*
12. Dudley Do-Right's Ripsaw Falls

Jurassic Park
13. Jurassic Park River Adventure
14. Thunder Falls Terrace
15. Camp Jurassic
16. Pteranodon Flyers
17. Triceratops Encounter
18. Jurassic Park Discovery Center

The Lost Continent
19. The Flying Unicorn
20. Dueling Dragons
21. The Enchanted Oak Tavern (and Alchemy Bar)
22. Sinbad's Village
23. *The Eighth Voyage of Sinbad*
24. *Poseidon's Fury!: Escape from the Lost City*
25. Mythos Restaurant

Seuss Landing
26. Sylvester McMonkey McBean
27. If I Ran the Zoo
28. Caro-Seuss-El
29. The Once-ler's House
30. Circus McGurkus Cafe Stoo-pendous
31. One Fish Two Fish Red Fish Blue Fish
32. The Cat in the Hat

Adventure are largely created for an under-40 population. The roller coasters at Universal are serious with a capital "S," making Space Mountain and Big Thunder Mountain look about as tough as Dumbo. In fact, seven out of the nine top attractions at Islands are thrill rides, and of these, there are three that not only scare the bejeezus out of you but also drench you with water.

In addition to thrill seekers, families with young children will find a lot to do at Islands of Adventure. There are three interactive playgrounds for little ones, as well as six rides that young children will enjoy. Of the thrill rides, only the two in Toon Lagoon (described later) are marginally appropriate for young children, and even on these rides your child needs to be fairly stalwart.

ISLANDS OF ADVENTURE VS. THE MAGIC KINGDOM

Islands of Adventure	Magic Kingdom
Six Islands (includes Port of Entry)	Seven Lands (includes Main Street)
Two adult roller coaster attractions	Two adult roller coaster attractions
A Dumbo-type ride	Dumbo
One flume ride	One flume ride
Toon Lagoon character area	Mickey's Toontown Fair character area

Getting Oriented at Islands of Adventure

Both Universal theme parks are accessed via the Universal CityWalk entertainment complex. Crossing CityWalk from the parking garages, you can bear right to Universal Studios Florida or left to Universal's Islands of Adventure.

Universal's Islands of Adventure is arranged much like the World Showcase section of Epcot, in a large circle surrounding a lake. Unlike Epcot, however, the Islands of Adventure theme areas evidence the sort of thematic continuity pioneered by Disneyland and the Magic Kingdom. Each land, or island in this case, is self-contained and visually consistent in its theme, though you can see parts of the other islands across the lake.

Passing through the turnstiles, you first encounter the Moroccan-style Port of Entry, where you will find Guest Services, lockers, stroller and wheelchair rentals, ATM banking, lost and found, and, of course, shopping. From the Port of Entry, moving clockwise around the lake, you can access Marvel Super Hero Island, Toon Lagoon, Jurassic Park, the Lost Continent, and Seuss Landing. You can crisscross the lake on small boats, but otherwise there is no in-park transportation.

NOT TO BE MISSED AT ISLANDS OF ADVENTURE

The Incredible Hulk Coaster	Dueling Dragons
The Adventures of Spider-Man	*Poseidon's Fury!*
Jurassic Park River Adventure	

Islands of Adventure Attractions

Marvel Super Hero Island

This island, with its futuristic and retro-future design and comic book signage, offers shopping and attractions based on Marvel Comics characters.

The Adventures of Spider-Man

What It Is Indoor adventure simulator ride based on Spider-Man

Scope & Scale Super headliner

When to Go Before 10 a.m.

Special Comments Must be 40" tall to ride

Author's Rating Our choice for the best attraction in the park; ★★★★★

Appeal by Age Group

Pre-school ★★★	Grade School ★★★★★	Teens ★★★★★
Young Adults ★★★★★	Over 30 ★★★★★	Senior Citizens ★★★★

Duration of Ride 4½ minutes

Loading Speed Fast

Description and Comments Covering 1½ acres and combining moving ride vehicles, 3-D film, and live action, Spider-Man is frenetic, fluid, and astounding. The visuals are rich and the ride is wild, but not jerky. Although the attractions are not directly comparable, Spider-Man is technologically on a par with Disney-MGM's Tower of Terror, which is to say that it will leave you in awe. As a personal aside, we love both and would be hard-pressed to choose one over the other.

The storyline is that you are a reporter for the *Daily Bugle* newspaper (where Peter Parker, a.k.a. Spider-Man, works as a mild-mannered photographer), when it's discovered that evil villains have stolen (I promise I'm not making this up) the Statue of Liberty. You are drafted on the spot by your cantankerous editor to go get the story. After speeding around and being thrust into "a battle between good and evil," you experience a 400-foot "sensory drop" from a skyscraper roof all the way to the pavement. Because the ride is so wild and the action so continuous, it's hard to understand the plot, but you're so thoroughly entertained that you don't really care. Plus, you'll want to ride again and again. Eventually, with repetition, the story line will begin to make sense.

Touring Tips Ride first thing in the morning after The Incredible Hulk Coaster or in the hour before closing.

The Incredible Hulk Coaster

What It Is Roller coaster

Scope & Scale Super headliner

When to Go Before 9:30 a.m.

Special Comments Must be 54" tall to ride

Author's Rating A coaster lover's coaster; ★★★★½

Appeal by Age Group

Pre-school ½	Grade School ★★★★★	Teens ★★★★★
Young Adults ★★★★★	Over 30 ★★★★	Senior Citizens ★★½

Duration of Ride 1½ minutes

Loading Speed Moderate

Description and Comments There is as always a story line, but for this attraction it's of no importance whatsoever. What you need to know about this attraction is simple. You will be launched like a cannonball shot from 0 to 40 miles per hour in two seconds, and then you will be flung upside down 100 feet off the ground, which will, of course, induce weightlessness. From there it's a mere seven rollovers punctuated by two plunges into holes in the ground before you're allowed to get out and throw up.

Seriously, the Hulk is a great roller coaster, perhaps the best in Florida, providing a ride comparable to Montu (Busch Gardens) with the added thrill of an accelerated launch (instead of the more typical uphill crank). Plus, like Montu, the ride is smooth. You won't be jarred and whiplashed on the Incredible Hulk.

Touring Tips The Hulk gives Spider-Man a run as the park's most popular attraction. Ride first thing in the morning. Universal provides electronic lockers near the entrance of the Hulk to deposit any items that might depart your person during the Hulk's seven inversions. Program the number of your locker into the terminal and follow the instructions. You'll receive a slip of paper with a code you can enter when you return to retrieve your stuff. The locker is free if you only use it for a short time. If you leave things in the locker for a couple of hours, however, you'll have to pay a modest rental charge. When you reach the boarding area, note that there is a separate line for those who want to ride in the first row.

Dr. Doom's Fearfall

What It Is Lunch liberator

Scope & Scale Headliner

When to Go Before 9:15 a.m.

Special Comments Must be 52" tall to ride

Author's Rating More bark than bite; ★★★

Appeal by Age Group

Pre-school —	Grade School ★★★	Teens ★★★★
Young Adults ★★★½	Over 30 ★★★	Senior Citizens —

Duration of Ride 40 seconds

Loading Speed Slow

Description and Comments Here you are (again) strapped into a seat with your feet dangling and blasted 200 feet up in the air and then allowed to partially free-fall back down. If you are having trouble forming a mental image of this attraction, picture the midway game where a macho guy swings a sledgehammer, propelling a metal sphere up a vertical shaft. At the top of the shaft is a bell. If the macho man drives the sphere high enough ⌐o ring the bell, he wins a prize. Got the idea? OK, on this ride you are the metal sphere.

The good news is this ride looks much worse than it actually is. The scariest part by far is the apprehension that builds as you sit, strapped in, waiting for the thing to launch. The blasting up and free-falling down parts are really very pleasant.

Touring Tips   We've seen glaciers that move faster than the line to Dr. Doom. If you want to ride without investing half a day, be one of the first in the park to ride. Fortunately, if you're on hand at opening time, being among the first isn't too difficult (mainly because the nearby Hulk and Spider-Man attractions are bigger draws).

Storm Force Accelatron

Motion Sickness

WARNING!

What It Is   Indoor spinning ride

Scope & Scale   Minor attraction

Special Comments   May induce motion sickness

When to Go   Before 10:30 a.m.

Author's Rating   Teacups in the dark; ★★★

Appeal by Age Group

Pre-school ★★★½   Grade School ★★★   Teens ★★★

Young Adults ★★★   Over 30 ★★★   Senior Citizens ★★★

Duration of Ride   1½ minutes

Loading Speed   Slow

Description and Comments   Storm Force is a spiffed-up indoor version of Disney's nausea-inducing Mad Tea Party. Here you spin to the accompaniment of a simulated thunderstorm and swirling sound and light. There's a story line that loosely ties this midway-type ride to the Marvel Super Hero theme area, but it's largely irrelevant and offers no advice on keeping your lunch down.

Touring Tips   Ride early or late to avoid long lines. If you're prone to motion sickness, keep your distance.

Toon Lagoon

Toon Lagoon is cartoon art translated into real buildings and settings. Whimsical and gaily colored, with rounded and exaggerated lines, Toon Lagoon is Universal's answer to Mickey's Toontown Fair in the Magic Kingdom. The main difference between the two toon lands is that (as you will see) you have about a 60% chance of going into hypothermia at Universal's version.

Dudley Do-Right's Ripsaw Falls

What It Is   Flume ride

Scope & Scale   Headliner

When to Go   Before 11 a.m.

Special Comments   Must be 48" tall to ride

Author's Rating   A minimalist Splash Mountain; ★★★½

Appeal by Age Group

Pre-school ★★½   Grade School ★★★★   Teens ★★★½

Young Adults ★★★   Over 30 ★★★½   Senior Citizens ★★½

Duration of Ride 5 minutes
Loading Speed Moderate

Description and Comments Inspired by the *Rocky and Bullwinkle* cartoon series, this ride features Canadian Mountie Dudley Do-Right as he attempts to save Nell from evil Snidely Whiplash. Story line aside, it's a flume ride, with the inevitable big drop at the end. Universal claims this is the first flume ride to "send riders plummeting 15 feet below the surface of the water." No need to bring diving gear—in reality you're just plummeting into a tunnel.

The only problem with this attraction is that everyone inevitably compares it to Splash Mountain at the Magic Kingdom. The flume is as good as Splash Mountain's, and the final drop is a whopper, but the theming and the visuals aren't even in the same league. The art, sets, audio, and jokes at Dudley Do-Right are minimalist at best; it's Dudley Do-Right's two-dimensional approach versus Splash Mountain's three-dimensional presentation. Taken on its own terms, however, Dudley Do-Right is a darn good flume ride.

Touring Tips This ride will get you wet, but on average not as wet as you might expect (it looks worse than it is). If you want to stay dry, however, arrive prepared with a poncho or at least a big garbage bag with holes cut out for your head and arms. After riding, take a moment to gauge the timing of the water cannons that go off along the exit walk. This is where you can really get drenched. While younger children are often intimidated by the big drop, those who ride generally enjoy themselves. Ride first thing in the morning after experiencing the Marvel Super Hero rides.

Popeye & Bluto's Bilge-Rat Barges

What It Is Whitewater raft ride
Scope & Scale Headliner
When to Go Before 10:30 a.m.
Special Comments Must be 48" tall to ride
Author's Rating Bring your own soap; ★★★★
Appeal by Age Group

Pre-school ★★★ Grade School ★★★★½ Teens ★★★★
Young Adults ★★★★ Over 30 ★★★½ Senior Citizens ★★½

Duration of Ride 4½ minutes
Loading Speed Moderate

Description and Comments This sweetly named attraction is a whitewater raft ride that includes an encounter with an 18-foot-tall octopus. Engineered to ensure that everyone gets drenched, the ride even provides water cannons for highly intelligent nonparticipants ashore to fire at those aboard. The rapids are rougher and more interesting, and the ride longer, than the Animal Kingdom's Kali River Rapids. But nobody surpasses Disney for visuals and theming, though the settings of these two attractions (cartoon set and Asian jungle river, respectively) are hardly comparable.

Touring Tips If you didn't drown on Dudley Do-Right, here's a second chance. You'll get a lot wetter from the knees down on this ride, so use your poncho or garbage bag and ride barefoot with your britches rolled up. In terms of beating the crowds, ride the barges in the morning after experiencing the Marvel Super Hero attractions and Dudley Do-Right. If you are lacking foul weather gear or forgot your trash bag, you might want to put off riding until last thing before leaving the park. Most preschoolers enjoy the raft ride. Those who are frightened react more to the way the rapids look as opposed to the roughness of the ride.

Me Ship, The Olive

What It Is Interactive playground
Scope & Scale Minor attraction
When to Go Anytime
Author's Rating Colorful and appealing for kids; ★★★
Appeal by Age Group

Pre-school ★★★★	Grade School ★★★½	Teens ½
Young Adults ½	Over 30 ½	Senior Citizens —

Description and Comments The Olive is Popeye's three-story boat come to life as an interactive playground. Younger children can scramble around in Swee' Pea's Playpen, while older sibs shoot water cannons at riders trying to survive the adjacent Bilge-Rat raft ride.

Touring Tips If you're into the big rides, save this for later in the day.

Comic Strip Lane

What It Is Walk-through exhibit and shopping/dining venue
Scope & Scale Diversion
When to Go Anytime

Description and Comments This is the main street of Toon Lagoon. Here you can visit the domains of Beetle Bailey, Hagar the Horrible, Krazy Kat, the Family Circus, and Blondie and Dagwood, among others. Shops and eateries tie into the cartoon strip theme.

Touring Tips This is a great place for photo ops with cartoon characters in their own environment. It's also a great place to drop a few bucks in the diners and shops, but you probably already figured that out.

Jurassic Park

Jurassic Park (for anyone who's been asleep for 20 years) is a Steven Spielberg film franchise about a fictitious theme park with real dinosaurs. Jurassic Park at Universal's Islands of Adventure is a real theme park (or at least a section of one) with fictitious dinosaurs.

Jurassic Park River Adventure

What It Is Indoor/outdoor adventure ride based on the Jurassic Park movies
Scope & Scale Super headliner
When to Go Before 11 a.m.
Special Comments Must be 42" tall to ride
Author's Rating Better than its Hollywood cousin; ★★★★
Appeal by Age Group

Pre-school ★★★	Grade School ★★★★½	Teens ★★★★
Young Adults ★★★★	Over 30 ★★★★	Senior Citizens ★★★½

Duration of Ride 6½ minutes
Loading Speed Fast

Description and Comments   Guests board boats for a water tour of Jurassic Park. Everything is tranquil as the tour begins, and the boat floats among large herbivorous dinosaurs such as brontosaurus and stegosaurus. Then, as word is received that some of the carnivores have escaped their enclosure, the tour boat is accidentally diverted into Jurassic Park's maintenance facilities. Here, the boat and its riders are menaced by an assortment of hungry meat eaters led by the ubiquitous T-Rex. At the climactic moment, the boat and its passengers escape by plummeting over an 85-foot drop billed as the "longest, fastest, steepest water descent ever built" (did anyone other than me notice the omission of the word wettest?).

Touring Tips   Though the boats make a huge splash at the bottom of the 85-foot drop, you don't get all that wet. Unfortunately, before the boat leaves the dock, you must sit in the puddles left by previous riders. Once underway there's a little splashing, but nothing major until the big drop at the end of the ride. When you hit the bottom, however, enough water will cascade into the air to extinguish a three-alarm fire. Fortunately, not all that much lands in the boat.

Young children must endure a double whammy on this ride. First, they are stalked by giant, salivating (sometimes spitting) reptiles, and then they're sent catapulting over the falls. Unless your children are fairly stalwart, wait a year or two before you spring the River Adventure on them.

Triceratops Encounter

What It Is Prehistoric petting zoo
Scope & Scale Minor attraction
When to Go Before 11:30 a.m.
Author's Rating Well executed; ★★★
Appeal by Age Group

Pre-school ★★★★	Grade School ★★★★	Teens ★★★½
Young Adults ★★★½	Over 30 ★★★½	Senior Citizens ★★★½

Duration of Show 5 minutes
Probable Waiting Time 15–25 minutes

Description and Comments   Guests are ushered in groups into a "feed and control station," where they can view and pet a 24-foot-long, animatronic triceratops dinosaur. While the trainer lectures about the creature's behaviors, habits, and lifestyle, the triceratops breathes, blinks, chews, and flinches at the touch of the guests.

Touring Tips   Nothing is certain, but this may be the only attraction in the park where you won't get wet. Just to be sure, however, stand near the middle of the dinosaur. Though not a major attraction, Triceratops Encounter is popular and develops long lines. Make it your first show/exhibit after experiencing the rides.

Discovery Center

What It Is Interactive natural history exhibit
Scope & Scale Minor attraction
When to Go Anytime

Author's Rating ★★★
Appeal by Age Group

Pre-school ★★½	Grade School ★★★½	Teens ★★★
Young Adults ★★★	Over 30 ★★★	Senior Citizens ★★★

Description and Comments The Discovery Center is an interactive, educational exhibit that mixes fiction from the movie, such as using fossil DNA to bring dinosaurs to life, with various skeletal remains and other paleontological displays. One exhibit allows guests to watch an animatronic raptor being hatched. Another allows you to digitally "fuse" your DNA with a dinosaur to see what the resultant creature would look like. Other exhibits include dinosaur egg scanning and identification and a quiz called "You Bet Jurassic."

Touring Tips Cycle back after experiencing all the rides or on a second day. Most folks can digest this exhibit in 10–15 minutes.

Pteranodon Flyers

What It Is Dinosaur version of Dumbo the Flying Elephant
Scope & Scale Minor attraction
When to Go When there's no line
Author's Rating All sizzle, no steak; ½
Appeal by Age Group

Pre-school ★★★	Grade School ★★	Teens ★
Young Adults ★½	Over 30 ★	Senior Citizens ★½

Duration of Ride 1¼ minutes
Loading Speed Slower than anyone thought possible

Description and Comments This attraction is Islands of Adventure's biggest blunder. Engineered to accommodate only 170 persons per hour (about half the hourly capacity of Dumbo!), the ride swings you along a track that passes over a small part of Jurassic Park. We recommend that you skip this one. Why? Because the Jurassic period will probably end before you reach the front of the line! And your reward for all that waiting? A one minute and fifteen second ride. Plus, the attraction has a name that nobody over 12 years old can pronounce.

Touring Tips Photograph the pteranodon as it flies overhead. You're probably looking at something that will someday be extinct.

Camp Jurassic

What It Is Interactive play area
Scope & Scale Minor attraction
When to Go Anytime
Author's Rating Creative playground, confusing layout; ★★★
Appeal by Age Group

Pre-school ★★★	Grade School ★★★	Teens —
Young Adults —	Over 30 —	Senior Citizens —

Description and Comments Camp Jurassic is a great place for children to let off steam. Sort of a Jurassic version of Tom Sawyer Island, kids can explore lava pits, caves, mines, and a rain forest.

Touring Tips   Camp Jurassic will fire the imaginations of the under-13 set. If you don't impose a time limit on the exploration, you could be here awhile. The layout of the play area is confusing and intersects the queuing area for the Pteranodon Flyers. If your child accidentally lines up for the Pteranodons, he'll be college age before you see him again.

The Lost Continent

This area is an exotic mix of Silk Road bazaar and ancient ruins, with Greco-Moroccan accents. And you thought your decorator was nuts. Anyway, this is the land of mythical gods, fabled beasts, and expensive souvenirs.

Poseidon's Fury! Escape from the Lost City

What It Is   High-tech theater attraction
Scope & Scale   Headliner
When to Go   After experiencing all the rides
Special Comments   Audience stands throughout
Author's Rating   Packs a punch; ★★★★
Appeal by Age Group

Pre-school ★★	Grade School ★★★★	Teens ★★★★
Young Adults ★★★★	Over 30 ★★★★	Senior Citizens ★★★★

Duration of Presentation   17 minutes including preshow
Probable Waiting Time   25 minutes

Description and Comments   In the first incarnation of this story, the Greek gods Poseidon and Zeus duked it out, with Poseidon as the heavy. Poseidon fought with water, and Zeus fought with fire, though both sometimes resorted to laser beams and smoke machines. In the new version, the rehabilitated Poseidon now tussles with an evil wizardish guy, and everybody uses fire, water, lasers, smoke machines, and angry lemurs (note: lemurs not actually used). As you might have inferred, the new story is, if anything, even more incoherent than the previous version. Regardless, most of the special effects are still amazing, and the theming of the preshow areas is quite imposing. The plot unravels in installments as you pass through a couple of these areas and finally into the main theater. Though the production is a little slow and plodding at first, it wraps up with quite an impressive flourish. There's some great technology at work here. *Poseidon* is by far and away the best of the Islands of Adventure theater attractions.

Touring Tips   If you are still wet from Dudley Do-Right, the Bilge-Rat Barges, and the Jurassic Park River Adventure, you might be tempted to cheer the evil wizard's flame jets in hopes of finally drying out. Our money, however, is on Poseidon. It's legal in Florida for theme parks to get you wet, but setting you on fire is somewhat frowned upon.

Frequent explosions and noise may frighten younger children, so exercise caution with pre-schoolers. Shows run continuously if the technology isn't on the blink. We recommend catching *Poseidon* after experiencing your fill of the rides.

Dueling Dragons

What It Is   Roller coaster
Scope & Scale   Headliner
When to Go   Before 10:30 a.m.

Special Comments Must be 54" tall to ride
Author's Rating Almost as good as The Hulk Coaster; ★★★★
Appeal by Age Group

Pre-school —	Grade School ★★★★	Teens ★★★★
Young Adults ★★★★	Over 30 ★★★★	Senior Citizens ★★

Duration of Ride A minute and 45 seconds
Loading Speed Moderate

Description and Comments This high-tech coaster launches two trains (Fire and Ice) at the same time on tracks that are closely intertwined. Each track, however, is differently configured so that you get a different experience on each. Several times, a collision with the other train seems imminent, a catastrophe that seems all the more real because the coasters are inverted (i.e., suspended from above so that you sit with your feet dangling). At times, the two trains and their passengers are separated by a mere 12 inches.

Because this is an inverted coaster, your view of the action is limited unless you are sitting in the front row. This means that most passengers miss seeing all these near collisions. But don't worry; regardless of where you sit, there's plenty to keep you busy. Dueling Dragons is the highest coaster in the park and also claims the longest drop at 115 feet, not to mention five inversions. And like the Hulk, it's a nice smooth ride all the way.

Coaster cadets are already arguing about which seat on which train provides the wildest ride. We prefer the front row on either train, but coaster loonies hype the front row of Fire and the last row of Ice.

Touring Tips The good news about this ride is that you won't get wet unless you wet yourself. The bad news is that wetting yourself comes pretty naturally. The other bad news is that the queuing area for Dueling Dragons is the longest, most convoluted affair we've ever seen, winding endlessly through a maze of subterranean passages. After what feels like a comprehensive tour of Mammoth Cave, you finally emerge at the loading area where you must choose between riding Fire or Ice. Of course, at this critical juncture, you're as blind as a mole rat from being in the dark for so long. Our advice is to follow the person in front of you until your eyes adjust to the light. Try to ride during the first 90 minutes the park is open. Warn anyone waiting for you that you might be a while. Even if there is no line to speak of, it takes 10–12 minutes just to navigate the caverns and not much less time to exit the attraction after riding. However, if lines are low, park employees will open special doors marked "Re-entry to Fire" or "Re-entry to Ice" (depending on what coaster you just rode) that allow you to get right back to the head of the queue and ride again. Finally, if you don't have time to ride both Fire and Ice, be advised that the *Unofficial* crew unanimously prefers Fire to Ice.

The Eighth Voyage of Sinbad

What It Is Theater stunt show
Scope & Scale Major attraction
When to Go Anytime as per the daily entertainment schedule
Author's Rating Not inspiring; ★★
Appeal by Age Group

Pre-school ★★★	Grade School ★★★½	Teens ★★½
Young Adults ★★★	Over 30 ★★★	Senior Citizens ★★½

Duration of Presentation 17 minutes
Probable Waiting Time 15 minutes

Description and Comments A story about Sinbad the Sailor is the glue that (loosely) binds this stunt show featuring water explosions, ten-foot-tall circles of flame, and various other daunting eruptions. The show reminds us of those action genre movies that substitute a mind-numbing succession of explosions, crashes, and special effects for plot and character development. Concerning Sinbad, even if you bear in mind that it's billed as a stunt show, the production is so vacuous and redundant that it's hard to get into the action. Fans of the *Hercules* and *Xena* TV shows might appreciate the humor more than the average showgoer.

Touring Tips See Sinbad after you've experienced the rides and the better-rated shows. The theater seats 1,700; performance times are listed in the daily entertainment schedule.

The Flying Unicorn

What It Is Children's roller coaster
Scope & Scale Minor attraction
When to Go Before 11 a.m.
Author's Rating A good beginner's coaster; ★★★
Appeal by Age Group

Pre-school ★★★★	Grade School ★★★½	Teens ★★
Young Adults ★★	Over 30 ★	Senior Citizens ★

Duration of Ride 1 minute
Loading Speed Slow

Description and Comments A child-sized roller coaster through a forest setting, the Flying Unicorn provides a nonthreatening way to introduce young children to the genre.

Touring Tips This one loads very slowly. Ride before 11 a.m.

Seuss Landing

A ten-acre theme area based on Dr. Seuss's famous children's books. Like at Mickey's Toontown in the Magic Kingdom, all of the buildings and attractions replicate a whimsical, brightly colored cartoon style with exaggerated features and rounded lines.

The Cat in the Hat

What It Is Indoor adventure ride
Scope & Scale Major attraction
When to Go Before 11:30 a.m.
Author's Rating Seuss would be proud; ★★★½
Appeal by Age Group

Pre-school ★★★★	Grade School ★★★★	Teens ★★★
Young Adults ★★★½	Over 30 ★★★½	Senior Citizens ★★★½

Duration of Ride 3½ minutes

Loading Speed Moderate

Description and Comments Guests ride on "couches" through 18 different sets inhabited by animatronic Seuss characters, including The Cat in the Hat, "Thing 1," "Thing 2," and the beleaguered goldfish who tries to maintain order in the midst of mayhem. Well done overall, with nothing that should frighten younger children.

Touring Tips This is fun for all ages. Try to ride early.

One Fish, Two Fish, Red Fish, Blue Fish

What It Is Wet version of Dumbo the Flying Elephant
Scope & Scale Minor attraction
When to Go Before 10 a.m.
Author's Rating Who says you can't teach an old ride new tricks?; ★★★½
Appeal by Age Group
Pre-school ★★★★   Grade School ★★★★   Teens ★★★
Young Adults ★★★   Over 30 ★★★   Senior Citizens ★★★
Duration of Ride 2 minutes
Loading Speed Slow

Description and Comments Imagine Dumbo with Seuss-style fish instead of elephants and you've got half the story. The other half of the story involves yet another opportunity to drown. Guests steer their fish up or down 15 feet in the air while traveling in circles. At the same time, they try to avoid streams of water projected from "squirt posts." A catchy song provides clues for avoiding the squirting.

Though ostensibly a children's ride, the song and the challenge of steering your fish away from the water jets make this attraction fun for all ages.

Touring Tips We don't know what it is about this theme park and water, but you'll get wetter than at a full-immersion baptism.

Caro-Seuss-El

What It Is Merry-go-round
Scope & Scale Minor attraction
When to Go Before 10:30 a.m.
Author's Rating Wonderfully unique; ★★★½
Appeal by Age Group
Pre-school ★★★★   Grade School ★★★★   Teens —
Young Adults —   Over 30 —   Senior Citizens —
Duration of Ride 2 minutes
Loading Speed Slow

Description and Comments Totally outrageous, the Caro-Seuss-El is a full-scale, 56-mount merry-go-round made up exclusively of Dr. Seuss characters.

Touring Tips Even if you are too old or don't want to ride, this attraction is worth an inspection. Whatever your age, chances are good you'll see some old friends. If you are touring with young children, try to get them on early in the morning.

Sylvester McMonkey McBean's Very Unusual Driving Machines

What It Is Indoor/outdoor track ride
Scope & Scale Major attraction
When to Go Before 10:30 a.m.
Author's Rating Not open at press time
Appeal by Age Group Not open at press time
Duration of Ride 5 minutes
Loading Speed Slow

Description and Comments This long-titled ride offers a tour of Seuss Landing on an elevated track, passing in and out of various attractions, shops, and restaurants. The inspiration, a Seuss book about discrimination, is sort of lost in the translation. Also lost is whatever it takes to get the ride up and running. As the park entered its fourth year, the attraction still was not operational.

Touring Tips Visually appealing. You can cover the same territory on foot.

If I Ran the Zoo

What It Is Interactive playground
Scope & Scale Minor attraction
When to Go Anytime
Author's Rating Eye-catching; ★★★
Appeal by Age Group

Pre-school ★★★★	Grade School ★★★	Teens —
Young Adults —	Over 3 —	Senior Citizens —

Description and Comments Based on Dr. Seuss's *If I Ran the Zoo,* this playground is divided into three distinct areas—Hedges, Water, and the New Zoo. Each area features various interactive elements, including, of course, another opportunity for a good soaking.

Touring Tips Visit this playground after you've experienced all the major attractions.

Islands of Adventure Touring Plan

Islands of Adventure One-Day Touring Plan

Be aware that there are an inordinate number of attractions in this park that will get you wet. If you want to experience them, come armed with ponchos, large plastic garbage bags, or some other protective covering. Failure to follow this prescription will make for a potentially squishy, sodden day.

This plan is for groups of all sizes and ages and includes thrill rides that may induce motion sickness or get you wet. If the plan calls for you to experience an attraction that does not interest you, simply skip that attraction and proceed to the next step. Be aware that the plan calls for some back-tracking. If you have young children in your party, customize the plan to fit their needs and take advantage of switching off at thrill rides.

1. Call (407) 363-8000, the main information number, the day before your visit for the official opening time. Try to purchase your admission sometime prior to the day you intend to tour.

2. On the day of your visit, eat breakfast and arrive at Universal Orlando 50 minutes before opening time. Park, buy your admission (if you did not purchase it in advance), and wait at the turnstiles to be admitted.

3. While at the turnstile, ask an attendant whether any rides or shows are closed that day. Adjust the touring plan accordingly.

4. When the park opens, go straight through the Port of Entry and take a left, crossing the bridge into Marvel Super Hero Island. At Super Hero Island, bear left to The Incredible Hulk Coaster.

5. Ride Incredible Hulk.

6. Exiting Hulk, hustle immediately to The Adventures of Spider-Man, also in Marvel Super Hero Island.

7. Dr. Doom's Fearfall, to the left of Spider-Man, is sort of a poor man's Tower of Terror. What's more, it loads about as fast as molasses on a shingle. We suggest you skip it. However, if you're bound and determined to ride, now's the time. *Note:* Steps 8–10 involve attractions where you will get wet. If you're not up for a soaking this early in the morning, skip ahead to Step 11, but be advised that you may have a bit of a wait at the Toon Lagoon attractions later in the day.

8. Continuing clockwise around the lake, depart Super Hero Island and cross into Toon Lagoon.

9. In Toon Lagoon, ride Dudley Do-Right's Ripsaw Falls.

10. Also in Toon Lagoon, subject yourself to Popeye & Bluto's Bilge-Rat Barges.

11. After the barge ride, continue your clockwise circuit around the lake, passing through Jurassic Park without stopping. Continue to the Lost Continent.

12. At the Lost Continent, ride both tracks of Dueling Dragons.

13. While at the Lost Continent, experience *Poseidon's Fury! Escape from the Lost City.*

14. Depart the Lost Continent, moving counterclockwise around the lake, and enter Jurassic Park.

15. In Jurassic Park, try the Jurassic Park River Adventure.

16. Also in Jurassic Park, check out Triceratops Encounter.

17. Return to the Lost Continent. Check the daily entertainment schedule for the next performance of *The Eighth Voyage of Sinbad* stunt show. If a show is

scheduled to begin within 30 minutes or so, go ahead and check it out. Otherwise, skip ahead to Step 18 and work *Sinbad* in later.

18. From the Lost Continent, move clockwise around the lake to Seuss Landing. Ride The Cat in the Hat.

19. While in Seuss Landing, ride Sylvester McMonkey McBean if it's operating.

20. At this point, you will have done all the big stuff. Spend the rest of your day experiencing attractions you bypassed earlier or repeating ones you especially enjoyed.

About SeaWorld

Many dozens of readers have written to extol the virtues of SeaWorld. The following are representative. An English family writes:

> The best organized park [is] SeaWorld. The computer printout we got on arrival had a very useful show schedule, told us which areas were temporarily closed due to construction, and had a readily understandable map. Best of all, there was almost no queuing. Overall, we rated this day so highly that it is the park we would most like to visit again.

A woman in Alberta, Canada, gives her opinion:

> We chose SeaWorld as our fifth day at "The World." What a pleasant surprise! It was every bit as good (and in some ways better) than WDW itself. Well worth the admission, an excellent entertainment value, educational, well run, and better value for the dollar in food services. Perhaps expand your coverage to give them their due!

A father of two from Winnipeg, Manitoba, gives SeaWorld's nighttime laser show top marks, commenting:

> But the absolute topper is the closing laser show, which beats out IllumiNations at Epcot for extravaganza. The SeaWorld show combines fireworks, lasers, and moving holographic images back-projected on a curtain of water. In the word of our older daughter: awesome! And you watch the whole thing seated in the lakeside arena, instead of jostling for a standing view around the Epcot lagoon.

A reader from Sylvania, Georgia, believes Disney could learn a thing or two from SeaWorld:

> Disney ought to take a look at how well this place is run. I know they don't have the same crowds or the exciting rides, but there is still a lot of entertainment here and never a wait. This allows you to set your pace without worrying about what you'll have to miss. You'll see it all no matter how you do it, you'll come away feeling you got better value for your dollars, you won't feel as

tired as a Disney day, and you will probably learn more, too. Only downside is you'll probably be hungry. Food is not one of the park's assets.

Okay, here's what you need to know (for additional information, call (407) 363-2613). SeaWorld is a world-class marine-life theme park near the intersection of I-4 and the Bee Line Expressway. Open daily from 9 a.m. to 10 p.m., SeaWorld charges about $46 admission (plus tax) for adults and $37 (plus tax) for children (ages three to nine). Combination passes, which include admission to SeaWorld, Universal Studios, Islands of Adventure, Wet 'n Wild, and Busch Gardens, are also available. Parking is $6 per car, $7 per RV or camper. Discount coupons for SeaWorld admission are available in the free visitor magazine found in most (but not Disney) hotel lobbies. Figure six to nine hours to see everything, but only five or so if you stick to the big deals.

SeaWorld is about the size of the Magic Kingdom and requires about the same amount of walking. Most attractions are accessible to nonambulatory disabled persons. In terms of size, quality, and creativity, SeaWorld is unequivocally on a par with Disney's major theme parks. Unlike Walt Disney World, however, SeaWorld primarily features stadium shows or walk-through exhibits. This means that you will spend about 90% less time waiting in line during eight hours at SeaWorld than you would for the same-length visit at a Disney park.

Because lines, with one or two exceptions, aren't much of a problem at SeaWorld, you can tour at almost any time of day. We recommend you start about 3:30 or 4 p.m. (when the park is open until 9 p.m. or later). Many of the day's early guests will have left by this hour, and you'll be able to enjoy the outdoor attractions in the relative cool of late afternoon and evening. If you visit in the morning, arrive early or late. Midmorning arrivals tend to create long waits at the ticket windows.

A daily entertainment schedule is printed conveniently on a placemat-sized map of the park. The four featured shows are:

- Shamu Killer Whale Show
- Sea Lion and Otter Show
- Atlantis Water Ski Show
- Whale and Dolphin Discovery Show

When you arrive, build your itinerary around these shows. You'll notice immediately as you check the performance times that they're scheduled in a way that makes it almost impossible to see them back to back. The Shamu show, for example, might run from 5 to 5:25 p.m. Ideally, you'd like to bop over to the Sea Lion and Otter Show, which begins at 5:30 p.m. Unfortunately, five minutes isn't enough time to exit Shamu

Stadium and cross the park to the Sea Lion & Otter Stadium. SeaWorld, of course, planned it this way so you would stay longer.

It is possible to catch the Shamu show and the Sea Lion and Otter Show in succession by sitting near an exit at Shamu Stadium and leaving a minute or two early (while the performers are taking their bows). Getting a couple of minutes' head start on the crowd and hurrying directly to the Sea Lion & Otter Stadium will get you seated just as the show is beginning. While this strategy allows you to see more in a short time, it makes for a somewhat frenetic and less relaxing tour.

If you're going to a show in Shamu Stadium or at the Atlantis Water Ski Stadium, don't worry about arriving late. Both stadiums are huge, so you almost certainly will get a seat. Plus, there isn't much in the first few minutes of either show that you can't afford to miss. The same goes for the Whale and Dolphin Discovery Show. The beginning of the Sea Lion and Otter Show, however, is really good; try to be on time.

Kraken and Journey to Atlantis are SeaWorld's entries into the theme-park super-attraction competition. Occupying the equivalent of six football fields, Journey to Atlantis is the world's first attraction to combine elements of a high-speed water ride and a roller coaster. By the way, you'll get soaked. Kraken is the newest, longest, tallest, and fastest roller coaster in Orlando. There's some debate about the smoothness of its ride, though. Catch both rides just after the park opens or be prepared to wait.

Stand-alone exhibits feature dolphins, stingrays, pelicans, spoonbills, flamingos, and the Anheuser-Busch Clydesdale horses, plus a tidal pool and tropical rain forest.

STAR RATINGS FOR SEAWORLD ATTRACTIONS

★★★★½	Kraken (roller coaster)
★★★★½	Terrors of the Deep (shark and eel exhibit)
★★★★½	Penguin Encounter (penguin and puffin exhibit)
★★★★	Manatees: The Last Generation (manatee exhibit)
★★★★	Wild Arctic (simulation ride and Arctic wildlife polar bears)
★★★★	Shamu Killer Whale Show
★★★★	Sea Lion and Otter Show
★★★★	Atlantis Water Ski Show
★★★★	Journey to Atlantis
★★★★	Pacific Point Preserve (sea lion exhibit)
★★★★	Shamu's Happy Harbor (children's play area)
★★★★	Whale and Dolphin Discovery Show
★★★½	Tropical Reef (reef-fish aquarium exhibit)

★★★	Hawaiian Rhythms (Polynesian dance and music)
★★½	Mermaids, Myths, & Monsters (fireworks and lasers; nights only)
★★½	SeaWorld Theater (SeaWorld propaganda and dancing fountains)
★★	Nautilus Theatre (musical revue)

Discovery Cove

SeaWorld's intimate new park, Discovery Cove, is a welcome departure from the hustle and bustle of other Orlando parks; the slower pace of this park could be the over-stimulated family's ticket back to mental health. With a focus on personal guest service and one-on-one animal encounters, Discovery Cove admits only 1,000 guests per day.

The main draw at Discovery Cove is the chance to swim with their troupe of 25 Atlantic bottlenose dolphins. The 90-minute dolphin swim experience is open to visitors ages six and up who are comfortable in the water. The experience begins with an orientation led by trainers and an opportunity for participants to ask questions. Next, small groups wade into shallow water for an introduction to the dolphins in their habitat. The experience culminates with two to three guests and a trainer swimming into deeper water for closer interaction with the dolphins. Afterward, swimmers are invited to discuss their experiences with the trainers and, of course, purchase photographs of themselves with the dolphins.

Other exhibits at Discovery Cove include the Coral Reef and the Aviary. You can snorkel or swim in the Coral Reef, which houses thousands of exotic fish as well as an underwater shipwreck and hidden grottos. In the Aviary, you can touch and feed gorgeous tropical birds. The park is threaded by a "tropical river," in which you can float or swim, and dotted with beaches, which serve as pathways to the attractions.

All guests are required to wear flotation vests when swimming, and lifeguards are omnipresent. You'll your bathing suit, pool shoes, and a cover-up. On rare days when it's too cold to swim in Orlando, guests are provided with free wet suits. Discovery Cove also provides fish-friendly sunscreen samples; guests may not use their own sunscreen.

Discovery Cove is open 9 a.m.–5:30 p.m. every day of the year. Since admission is limited to 1,000 guests per day, you should purchase tickets well in advance by calling (877) 4-DISCOVERY or visiting **www. discoverycove.com.** Admission is $199 per person (there is no children's discount) and includes the dolphin swim, self parking, one meal, and use of beach umbrellas, lounge chairs, towels, lockers, and swim and snorkel gear. Discovery Cove admission also includes a seven-day pass to SeaWorld. If you're not interested in the dolphin swim, you can visit Discovery Cove for $109 per person for the day.

Part Fourteen

The Water Theme Parks

Disney has three swimming theme parks, and two more independent water parks are in the area. At Disney World, River Country is the oldest and smallest park. Typhoon Lagoon is the most diverse Disney splash pad, while Blizzard Beach takes the prize for the most slides and most bizarre theme. Outside the World, find Wet 'n Wild and Water Mania.

At all Disney water parks, the following rules and prices apply: one cooler per family or group is allowed, but no glass and no alcoholic beverages; towels $1, locker $5 (plus $2 deposit for lockers), life jacket $25 refundable deposit.

Blizzard Beach

Blizzard Beach is Disney's most exotic water adventure park and, like Typhoon Lagoon, it arrived with its own legend. This time, the story goes, an entrepreneur tried to open a ski resort in Florida during a particularly savage winter. Alas, the snow melted; the palm trees grew back; and all that remained of the ski resort was its Alpine lodge, the ski lifts, and, of course, the mountain. Plunging off the mountain are ski slopes and bobsled runs transformed into water slides. Visitors to Blizzard Beach catch the thaw: icicles drip and patches of snow remain. The melting snow has formed a lagoon (the wave pool), fed by gushing mountain streams.

Like Typhoon Lagoon, Blizzard Beach is distinguished by its landscaping and the attention paid to executing its theme. As you enter Blizzard Beach, you face the mountain. Coming off the highest peak and bisecting the area at the mountain's base are two long slides. To the left of the slides is the wave pool. To the right are the children's swimming area and the ski lift. Surrounding the layout like a moat is a tranquil stream for floating in tubes. Picnic areas are scattered around the park, as are pleasant places for sunbathing.

On either side of the highest peak are tube, raft, and body slides. Including the two slides coming off the peak, Blizzard Beach has 17 slides. Among them is Summit Plummet, Disney World's longest speed slide, which begins with a 120-foot free-fall, and the Teamboat Springs water bobsled run, 1,200 feet long.

For our money, the most exciting and interesting slides are the Slusher Gusher and Teamboat Springs on the front right of the mountain, and Run-Off Rapids on the back side of the mountain. Slusher Gusher is an undulating speed slide that we consider as exciting as the more vertical Summit Plummet without being as bone-jarring. On Teamboat Springs, you ride in a raft that looks like a round, children's blow-up wading pool. The more people you load into the raft, the faster it goes. If you have only a couple in it, the slide is kind of a snore.

Run-Off Rapids is accessible from a path that winds around the far left bottom of the mountain. The Rapids consists of three corkscrew tube slides, one of which is enclosed and dark. As at Teamboat Springs, you'll go much faster on a two- or three-person tube than on a one-person tube. If you lean so that you enter curves high and come out low, you'll really fly. Because we like to steer the tube and go fast, we much prefer the open slides (where we can see) to the dark, enclosed tube. We thought crashing through the pitch-dark tube felt disturbingly like being flushed down a toilet.

The Snow Stormer's mat slides on the front of the mountain are fun but not as fast or interesting as Run-Off Rapids. The Toboggan Racers at front and center on the mountain consists of eight parallel slides where riders are dispatched in heats to race to the bottom. The ride itself is no big deal, and the time needed to get everybody lined up ensures that you'll wait extra long to ride. On one visit, as an added annoyance, we had to line up once to get a mat and again to actually ride.

A ski lift carries guests to the mountaintop (you can also walk up), where they can choose from Summit Plummet, Slusher Gusher, or Teamboat Springs. For all other slides at Blizzard Beach, the only way to reach the top is on foot. If you're among the first in the park and don't have to wait to ride, the ski lift is fun and provides a bird's-eye view of the park. After riding once to satisfy your curiosity, however, you're better off taking the stairs to the top.

The wave pool, called Melt-Away Bay, has gentle, bobbing waves. The float creek, Cross Country Creek, circles the park, passing through the mountain. The children's areas, Tike's Peak and Ski Patrol Training Camp, are creatively designed, nicely isolated, and, like the rest of the park, visually interesting.

Like Typhoon Lagoon, Blizzard Beach is a bit convoluted in its layout. With slides on both the front and back of the mountain, it isn't always easy to find a path leading to where you want to go.

At the ski resort's now-converted base area are shops; counter-service food; rest rooms; and tube, towel, and locker rentals. Blizzard Beach has its own parking lot but offers no lodging, though Disney's All-Star and Coronado Springs Resorts are almost within walking distance. Disney resort and campground guests can commute to the park aboard Disney buses.

Because it's novel and has popular slides, Blizzard Beach fills early during hotter months. To stake out a nice sunning spot and to enjoy the slides without long waits, arrive at least 35 minutes before the official opening time. Admission is about $32 per day for adults and $26 per day for children ages three to nine. Children younger than three are admitted free. If you're going primarily for the slides, you'll have about two hours in the early morning to enjoy them before the waiting becomes intolerable.

Typhoon Lagoon

Typhoon Lagoon is comparable in size to Blizzard Beach and about four times larger than River Country. Ten water slides and streams, some as long as 400 feet, drop from the top of a 100-foot-tall, man-made mountain. Landscaping and an "aftermath-of-a-typhoon" theme add adventure to the wet rides.

Entry to Typhoon Lagoon is through a misty rain forest that emerges in a ramshackle tropical town, where concessions and services are situated. Special sets make every ride an odyssey as swimmers encounter bat caves, lagoons and pools, spinning rocks, formations of dinosaur bones, and many other imponderables.

Typhoon Lagoon has its own parking lot but no lodging. Disney resort and campground guests can commute to the park on Disney buses.

Like Blizzard Beach, Typhoon Lagoon is expensive: about $32 a day for adults and $26 a day for children ages three to nine. Children younger than three are admitted free. If you indulge in all features of Typhoon Lagoon, admission is a fair value. If you go primarily for the slides, you will have only two early-morning hours to enjoy them before the wait becomes prohibitive.

Typhoon Lagoon provides water adventure for all ages. Activity pools for young children and families feature geysers, tame slides, bubble jets, and fountains. For the older and more adventurous are two speed slides, four corkscrew body slides, and three tube rapids rides (plus one children's rapids ride) plopping off Mount Mayday. Slower metabolisms will like the scenic, meandering, 2,100-foot-long stream that floats tubers through a hidden grotto and rain forest. And, of course, the sedentary will usually find plenty of sun to sleep in. Typhoon Lagoon's surf pool and Shark Reef are unique, and the wave pool is the world's largest inland surf facility, with waves up to six feet high (enough, so Disney says, to "encompass an oceanliner"). Shark Reef is a saltwater snorkeling pool where guests can swim among real fish.

Shark Reef

Fins, mask, snorkel, and wet-suit vest are provided free in the wooden building beside the diving pool. After you obtain the proper equipment (no forms or money involved), you shower and then report to a snorkeling instructor. After a brief lesson, you swim about 60 feet to the other side of the pool. You aren't allowed to paddle aimlessly, but must traverse the pool more or less directly.

The reef is fun in early morning. Equipment collection, shower, instruction, and the quick swim can be accomplished without much hassle. Also, because few guests are present, attendants are more flexible about your lingering in the pool or making minor departures from the charted course.

Later, as crowds build, it becomes increasingly difficult and time-consuming to provide the necessary instruction. The result is platoons of would-be frogmen restlessly awaiting their snorkeling lesson. Guests are grouped in impromptu classes with the entire class briefed and then launched together. What takes four or five minutes shortly after opening can take more than an hour by 11 a.m.

By far the most prevalent species in the pool are the dual-finned Homo sapiens. Other denizens include small, colorful tropical fish, some diminutive rays, and a few very small leopard and hammerhead sharks. In terms of numbers, it would be unusual to cross the pool and not see some fish. On the other hand, you aren't exactly bumping into them.

It's very important to fit your diving mask on your face so that it seals around the edges. Brush your hair from your forehead and sniff a couple of times once the mask is in place, to create a vacuum. Mustaches often prevent the mask from sealing properly. The first indication that your mask isn't correctly fitted will be saltwater in your nose.

If you don't want to swim with fish early in the morning or fight crowds later in the day, visit the underwater viewing chamber, accessible anytime without waiting, special equipment, showers, instruction, or water in your nose.

Typhoon Lagoon Surf Pool

While Blizzard Beach, Wet 'n Wild, and Water Mania have wave pools, Typhoon Lagoon has a *surf pool*. Most people will encounter larger waves here than they have in the ocean. The surf machine puts out a wave about every 90 seconds (just about how long it takes to get back in position if you caught the previous wave). Perfectly formed and ideal for riding, each wave is about five to six feet from trough to crest. Before you join the fray, watch two or three waves from shore. Since each wave breaks in almost the same spot, you can get a feel for position and timing. Observing other surfers is also helpful.

The best way to ride the waves is to swim about three-fourths of the way to the wall at the wave-machine end of the surf pool. When the wave comes (you will both feel and hear it), swim vigorously toward the beach, attempting to position yourself one-half to three-fourths of a body length below the breaking crest. The waves are so perfectly engineered that they will either carry you forward or bypass you. Unlike an ocean wave, they won't slam you down.

A teenage girl from Urbana, Illinois, notes that the primary hazard in the surf pool is colliding with other surfers and swimmers:

The surf pool was nice except that I kept landing on really hairy fat guys whenever the big waves came.

The best way to avoid collisions while surfing is to paddle out far enough that you will be at the top of the wave as it breaks. This tactic eliminates the possibility of anyone landing on you from above and assures maximum forward visibility. A corollary to this: The worst place to swim is where the wave actually breaks. You will look up to see a six-foot wall of water carrying eight dozen screaming surfers bearing down on you. This is the time to remember every submarine movie you've ever seen . . . Dive! Dive! Dive!

Tuesday mornings 6:30–9 a.m. (before the park opens), you can take surfing lessons (with a surfboard) from Craig Carroll's Cocoa Beach Surf School. Practice waves range from three to six feet tall. Most of the school's students are first timers. Cost is $125 per person, and equipment is provided. For reservations and more information, call (407) WDW-PLAY.

A final warning: The surf pool has a knack for loosening watchbands, stripping jewelry, and sucking stuff out of your pockets. Don't take anything out there except your swimsuit (and hold on to it).

River Country

The oldest of the Disney swimming parks, River Country was closed during 2002 as a consequence of the soft travel market. Although there has been no word regarding permanent closure, its future for the moment is cloudy.

River Country is among the most aesthetically pleasing of the water theme parks—it's beautifully landscaped and immaculately manicured, with rocky canyons and waterfalls skillfully blending with white-sand beaches. The park is even positioned to take advantage of the breeze off Bay Lake. The least expensive of Disney's water parks, River Country costs about $17 a day for adults and $14 a day for children ($14 adults, $11 children for Fort Wilderness guests).

For pure and simple swimming and splashing, River Country gets high marks. Its slides, however, don't begin to compete with its big brothers or nearby competitors. Whereas Blizzard Beach and Wet 'n Wild feature more than 16 major slides and tube rides, River Country has 1 tube ride and 2 corkscrew slides. Few slides and many swimmers add up to long lines. If slides are your thing, go elsewhere. Many readers, including this Reader, Coventry, Rhode Island family prefer River Country, writing:

We liked River Country best! For low tech swimming and old fashioned fun! Nice break from lines, etc.

What River Country has going for it, however, is that it's always less crowded than the other water parks and it's easily accessible from the Magic Kingdom. We have a number of readers who stow their bathing suits in a locker when they arrive at the Magic Kingdom. When the park gets hot and crowded, they retrieve their suits and take the boat from the Magic Kingdom to River Country. This option is especially attractive (and more affordable) if you are a Disney resort guest using a Park-Hopper Plus or Ultimate Park-Hopper pass.

Sunbathers will enjoy River Country, particularly if they lie near the lakefront to take advantage of the cooling breezes. Most chaise lounges are basically flat, with the head slightly elevated, and don't have adjustable backs. They leave a great deal to be desired for a comfortable reading position or for lying on your stomach.

Reaching River Country by car is a hassle. You're directed to a parking lot, where you leave your car, gather your belongings, and wait for a Disney bus to take you to the park. The ride is rather lengthy, and pity the poor soul who left his bathing suit in the car (a round trip to retrieve it will take about 30 minutes). In the morning, the bus from the parking lot to River Country is very crowded. We suggest catching the bus to Pioneer Hall (which loads at the same place in the parking lot), then walking to River Country from there. Another option is to access River Country by boat from the Magic Kingdom or one of the Magic Kingdom resorts. Of these, the most direct route is to park at the Wilderness Lodge and catch a boat from there to River Country.

There's no lodging at River Country, but it's within walking distance of much of Fort Wilderness Campground. Food is available, or you can pack a lunch to eat in the park's picturesque, shaded, lakeside picnic area. Access is by bus from the Transportation and Ticket Center (junction and transfer point for the Epcot and Magic Kingdom monorails) or from the River Country parking lot at the entrance of Fort Wilderness Campground.

Disney vs. Wet 'n Wild and
Water Mania Swimming Theme Parks

Wet 'n Wild, on International Drive in Orlando, is on a par with Blizzard Beach and beats Typhoon Lagoon, River Country, and Water Mania for slides. The headliners at Wet 'n Wild are the Black Hole, the Surge, and the Fuji Flyer. At the Black Hole, guests descend on a two-person tube down a totally enclosed corkscrew slide, sort of a wet version of Space Mountain—only much darker. Our researchers think this is the most exciting slide at any Florida swimming theme park (Water Mania, Typhoon Lagoon, and Blizzard Beach have similar slides). The Surge launches groups of five down a 580-foot twisting, turning course. The Fuji Flyer is a 450-foot water-toboggan course. Another Wet 'n Wild thrill slide is Bomb Bay, which drops guests from a compartment resembling a bomb bay down a chute angled at 79°.

Water Mania, on US 192 south of I-4, edges out Typhoon Lagoon for slides and is less crowded than its competitors. In addition, it's the only water park to offer a stationary surfing wave.

What sets Disney water parks apart is not so much their slides and individual attractions but the Disney attention to detail in creating an integrated adventure environment. Both eye and body are deluged with the strange, the exotic, the humorous, and the beautiful. Wilder slides and rapids rides can be found elsewhere, but other water parks can't compete with Disney in diversity, variety, adventure, and total impact. Water Mania is nicely landscaped, but it doesn't have a theme. Wet 'n Wild, though attractive and clean, is cluttered and not especially appealing to the eye.

In the surf and wave pool department, Typhoon Lagoon wins hands down, with Wet 'n Wild taking second place. All of the parks have an outstanding water activity area for young children, and all except River Country feature unique attractions. Wet 'n Wild has a ride in which guests kneel on water skis, and Blizzard Beach has a 1,200-foot water bobsled. At Typhoon Lagoon, guests can snorkel among live fish, and Water Mania has a surfing wave.

Prices for one-day admission are about the same at Wet 'n Wild, Blizzard Beach, and Typhoon Lagoon, and slightly less at Water Mania. River Country is the least expensive of the water parks. Discount coupons are often available in local visitor magazines for Water Mania and Wet 'n Wild.

Wet 'n Wild is open until 11 p.m. during summer; the Disney swimming parks and Water Mania generally close between 5 and 8 p.m. The late closing is a huge plus for Wet 'n Wild. Warm Florida nights are great for enjoying a water theme park. There's less waiting for slides, and the pavement is cooler under your feet. To top it off, Wet 'n Wild features live music in the evening at its Wave Pool Stage and sells half-price tickets after 4 p.m. on days when the park is open late.

If your primary interest is sunning and swimming, you can't beat River Country. It's beautiful and usually has a nice breeze blowing off Bay Lake. If you're into slides, Blizzard Beach is tops among the Disney water parks, with Wet 'n Wild leading the independents. Typhoon Lagoon offers enough slides to keep most folks happy, has its signature surf pool, and provides the most variety. If you like slides but not crowds and are willing to sacrifice exotic surroundings for more elbow room, Water Mania is a good and cheaper choice. For evening and nighttime swimming fun, Wet 'n Wild is the only game in town.

Typhoon Lagoon vs. Blizzard Beach

Many Walt Disney World guests aren't interested in leaving the World. For them, the question is which is better, Typhoon Lagoon or Blizzard Beach? Our readers answer.

A mother of four from Winchester, Virginia, gives her opinion:

> At Blizzard Beach the family raft ride is great, [but] the kids' area is poorly designed. As a parent, when you walk your child to the top of a slide or the tube ride, they are lost to your vision as they go down because of the fake snow drifts. There are no direct ways down to the end of the slides, so little ones are left standing unsupervised [while] parents scramble down from the top. The Typhoon Lagoon kids' area is far superior in design.

A couple from Woodridge, Illinois, writes:

> We liked Blizzard Beach much more. It seems like they took everything from Typhoon Lagoon and made it better and faster. Summit Plummet was awesome—a total rush. Worth the half-hour wait. Toboggan and bobsled rides were really exciting—bobsled really throws you around. Family tube ride was really good—much better and much longer than at Typhoon Lagoon. Tube rides were great, especially in enclosed tube. If you only have time to go to one water park, go to Blizzard Beach.

A New England couple agrees:

> The slides at Blizzard Beach were longer and [there were] more of them, decreasing wait time. We had planned on spending a day at Typhoon Lagoon but were very bored and disappointed—having to wait in long lines for measly, short rides. We definitely recommend Blizzard Beach over Typhoon Lagoon!

A Waynesboro, Pennsylvania, family recommends both parks:

We got to two of the water parks, Blizzard Beach and Typhoon Lagoon. Both are spectacular, although BB definitely has much better slides, and its family raft ride is easily twice as long. Still, Shark Reef [at Typhoon Lagoon] is an experience not to be missed, as are the waves. Both creeks with tubes were my personal faves. What utter slothdom!

But a hungry reader from Aberdeen, New Jersey, complains:

At Blizzard Beach, there is only one main place to get food (most of the other spots are more for snacks). At lunchtime, it took almost 45 minutes to get some sandwiches and drinks.

A couple from Bowie, Maryland, didn't enjoy Summit Plummet:

The tallest and fastest slide at Blizzard Beach gave me a bunch of bruises. Even my husband hurt for a few days. It wasn't a fun ride, and we both agree that it wasn't worth waiting in line for. Basically, you drop until you hit the slide and that is why everyone comes off rubbing their butts. They say you go 60 mph on a 120-foot drop. I'll never do it again.

A man from Lexington, Massachusetts, who felt like a "hen egg in a skillet" reports:

Blizzard Beach is not well thought out. No shade from the Florida sun and way too much hot concrete.

Typhoon Lagoon won over a Texas family:

The water parks were great! Our favorite for the whole family was Typhoon Lagoon. There was a lot of shade if you wanted, the river around was better [than at Blizzard Beach], and the surf pool was great.

When to Go

The best way to avoid standing in lines is to visit the water parks when they're less crowded. Because the parks are popular among locals, weekends can be tough. We recommend going on a Monday or Tuesday, when most other tourists will be visiting the Magic Kingdom, Epcot, the Animal Kingdom, or Disney-MGM Studios and locals will be at work or school. Fridays are good because people traveling by car commonly use this day to start home. Sunday morning also has lighter crowds. During summer and holiday periods, Typhoon Lagoon and Blizzard Beach fill to capacity and close their gates before 11 a.m.

A Newbury Park, California, reader gives an idea of what "crowded" means:

The only disappointment we had at WDW was Typhoon Lagoon. While WDW was quite uncrowded, Typhoon Lagoon seemed choked with people. I'd hate to see it on a really crowded day. Even the small slides had lines greater than 30 minutes. They weren't worth half the wait. Castaway Creek might have been relaxing, but I found it to be a continuous traffic jam. I [also] would have enjoyed the snorkeling area except we were forced to go through at warp speed. After half a day we returned to the Yacht Club, where Stormalong Bay provided much more pleasant water recreation.

A mom from Manlius, New York, writes:

Because we had the 5-Day Park-Hopper Plus pass, we also visited Typhoon Lagoon, arriving before opening so we could stake out a shady spot. The kids loved it until the lines got long (11 a.m. to noon), but I hated it. It made Coney Island seem like a deserted island in the Bahamas. Floating on Castaway Creek was really unpleasant. Whirling around in a chlorinated, concrete ditch with some stranger's feet in my face, periodically getting squirted by waterguns, passing under cascades of cold water, and getting hung up by the crowd is not at all relaxing for me. My husband and I then decided to "bob" in the surf pool. After about ten minutes of being tossed around like corks in boiling water, he turned a little green around the gills and we sought the peace of our shady little territory which, in our absence, had become much, much smaller. We sat and read our books, elbow to elbow with other pleasure-seekers, until the kids had their fill. They, however, loved the body slides and the surf waves, commenting on how useful your "coach's tip" was.

A visitor from Middletown, New York, had a somewhat better experience at Typhoon Lagoon:

On our second trip [to Typhoon Lagoon], we dispensed with the locker rental (having planned to stay for only the morning when it was least crowded), and at park's opening just took right off for the Storm Slides before the masses arrived—it was perfect! We must have ridden the slides at least five times before any kind of line built up, and then we were also able to ride the tube and raft rides (Keelhaul and Mayday Falls) in a similar uncrowded, quick fashion because everyone else was busy getting their lockers! We also experienced the Shark Reef snorkeling three times with minimal crowds that day, because, I think, most people overlook this attraction. Shark Reef is lots of fun and a great way to cool off since their water temp is well below the wave pool's.

If your schedule is flexible, a good time to visit the swimming parks is midafternoon to late in the day when the weather has cleared after a storm. The parks usually close during bad weather. If the storm is prolonged, most guests leave for their hotels. When Typhoon Lagoon, Blizzard Beach, or River Country reopen after inclement weather has passed, you almost have a whole park to yourself.

Planning Your Day at Disney Water Parks

Disney swimming theme parks are almost as large and elaborate as the major theme parks. You must be prepared for a lot of walking, exercise, sun, and jostling crowds. If your group really loves the water, schedule your visit early in your vacation. For many families, a visit to a water park is the highlight of their trip. If you go at the beginning of your stay, you'll have more flexibility if you want to return.

To have a great day and beat the crowd at any Disney water park, consider:

1. Getting Information. Call (407) 824-4321 the night before you go to ask when your chosen park opens.

2. To Picnic or Not to Picnic. Decide whether you want to carry a picnic lunch. Guests are permitted to take lunches and beverage coolers into the parks. No alcoholic beverages are allowed. Glass containers of any kind (including mayonnaise, mustard, peanut butter, and pickle jars) are likewise forbidden.

3. Getting Started. If you are going to Blizzard Beach or Typhoon Lagoon, get up early, have breakfast, and arrive at the park 40 minutes before opening. If you have a car, drive instead of taking a Disney bus. If you're going to River Country, you don't have to get there so early.

4. Attire. Wear your bathing suit under shorts and a T-shirt so you don't need to use lockers or dressing rooms. Regarding women's bathing suits, be advised that it is extremely common for women of all ages to part company with the top of their two-piece suit on the slides. Wear shoes. Paths are relatively easy on bare feet, but there's a lot of ground to cover. If you have tender feet, wear your shoes as you move around the park, removing them when you raft, slide, or go into the water. Shops in the parks sell sandals, "Reef Runners," and other protective footwear that can be worn in and out of the water.

5. What to Bring. You will need a towel, suntan lotion, and money. Since wallets and purses get in the way, lock them in your car's trunk or leave them at your hotel. Carry enough money for the day and your Disney resort I.D. (if you have one) in a plastic bag or Tupperware container. Though nowhere is completely safe, we felt very comfortable hiding our plastic money bags in our cooler. Nobody disturbed our stuff, and our cash was much easier to reach than if we'd stashed it in a locker across the park. If you're carrying a wad or you worry about money anyway, rent the locker.

A Canadian reader offers another option if you don't feel comfortable stashing your valuables

As our admission was from a Park Hopper Plus ticket, I was concerned about our multiday passes being stolen or lost, yet I didn't want the hassle of a locker. Once inside, I noticed several guests wearing small plastic boxes on strings around their necks, and was pleased to find these for sale in the gift shop. They are waterproof and available in two sizes for around $5, with the smallest being just big enough for passes/credit cards and a bit of money. I would have spent nearly as much on locker rental, so I was able to enjoy the rest of the day with peace of mind and also have it for future days at water parks or the community pool at home.

6. What Not to Bring. Personal swim gear (fins, masks, rafts, etc.) aren't allowed. Everything you need is either provided or available to rent. If you forget your towel, you can rent one (cheap!). If you forget your swimsuit or lotion, they're for sale. Personal flotation devices (life jackets) are available free of charge, but you must leave a credit card number or a driver's license as a deposit (held until the equipment is returned).

7. Admissions. Purchase your admission in advance or about 45 minutes before official opening time. If you're staying at a Disney property, you may be entitled to an admission discount; bring your hotel or campground I.D. Guests staying five or more days should consider the Park-Hopper Plus or Ultimate Park Hopper Passes, which include admission to all Disney swimming parks.

8. Lockers. Rental lockers are $5 per day, of which $2 is refunded when you return your key. Lockers are roomy enough for one person or a couple, but are a stretch for an entire family. Though you can access your locker freely all day, not all lockers are conveniently located.

Getting a locker at Blizzard Beach or Typhoon Lagoon is truly competitive. When the gates open, guests race to the locker rental desk. Once there, the rental procedure is somewhat slow. If you aren't among the first in line, you can waste a lot of time waiting to be served. We recommend you skip the locker. Carry only as much cash as you will need for the day in a watertight container you can stash in your cooler. Ditto for personal items including watches and eyeglasses. With planning, you can manage nicely without the locker and save time and hassle in the bargain.

9. Tubes. Tubes for bobbing on the waves, floating in the creeks, and riding the tube slides are available for free.

10. Getting Settled. Establish your base for the day. There are many beautiful sunning and lounging spots scattered throughout all Disney swimming parks. Arrive early, and you can almost have your pick. The breeze is best along the beaches of the surf pools at Blizzard Beach and Typhoon Lagoon. At River Country, pick a spot that fronts Bay Lake. At Typhoon Lagoon, if there are children younger than six in your party, choose an area to the left of Mount Mayday (ship on top) near the children's swimming area.

Available are flat lounges (unadjustable) and chairs (better for reading), shelters for guests who prefer shade, picnic tables, and a few hammocks.

The best spectator sport at Typhoon Lagoon is the bodysurfing in the surf pool. It's second only to being out there yourself. With this in mind, position yourself to have an unobstructed view of the waves.

11. A Word about the Slides. Water slides come in many shapes and sizes. Some are steep and vertical, some long and undulating. Some resemble corkscrews; others imitate the pool-and-drop nature of whitewater streams. Depending on which slide, swimmers ride mats, inner tubes, or rafts. On body slides, swimmers slosh to the bottom on the seat of their pants.

Modern traffic engineering bows to old-fashioned queuing. At water slides, it's one person, one raft (or tube) at a time, and the swimmer on deck can't go until the person preceding him is safely out of the way. Thus, the slide's hourly capacity is limited compared to the continuously loading rides in the major theme parks. Because a certain interval between swimmers is required for safety, the only way to increase capacity is to increase the number of slides and rapids rides.

Though Typhoon Lagoon and Blizzard Beach are huge parks with many slides, they're overwhelmed almost daily by armies of guests. If your main reason for going to Typhoon Lagoon or Blizzard Beach is the slides and you hate long lines, be among the first guests to enter the park. Go directly to the slides and ride as many times as you can before the park fills. When lines for the slides become intolerable, head for the surf or wave pool, or the tube-floating streams.

For maximum speed on a body slide, cross your legs at the ankles and cross your arms over your chest. When you take off, arch your back so almost all of your weight is on your shoulder blades and heels (the less contact with the surface, the less resistance). Steer by shifting most of your upper-body weight onto one shoulder blade. For top speed on turns, weight the shoulder blade on the outside of each curve. If you want to go slow (what's the point?), distribute your weight equally as if you were lying on your back in bed. For curving slides, maximize speed by hitting the entrance to each curve high and exiting the curve low.

Some slides and rapids have a minimum height requirement. Riders for Humunga Kowabunga at Typhoon Lagoon and for Slush Gusher and

Summit Plummet at Blizzard Beach, for example, must be four feet tall. Pregnant women and persons with back problems or other health difficulties shouldn't ride.

12. Floating Streams. Disney's Blizzard Beach and Typhoon Lagoon and the independent Water Mania and Wet 'n Wild offer mellow floating streams. A great idea, the floating streams are long, tranquil, inner-tube rides that give you the illusion that you're doing something though you're being sedentary. For wimps, wussies, and exhausted people of all ages, floating streams are an answered prayer.

Disney's streams flow ever so slowly around the entire park, through caves and beneath waterfalls, past gardens, and under bridges. They offer a relaxing alternative to touring a park on foot.

Floating streams can be reached from several put-in and take-out points. There are never lines; just wade into the creek and plop into one of the inner tubes floating by. Ride the gentle current all the way around or get out at any exit. If you lie back and go with the flow, it will take 30–35 minutes to float the full circuit.

Predictably, there will be guests on whom the subtlety of floating streams is lost. They will be racing, screaming, and splashing. Let them pass, stopping a few moments, if necessary, to distance yourself from them.

13. Lunch. If you didn't bring a picnic, you can buy food. Portions are adequate to generous; quality is comparable to fast-food chains; and prices (as you would expect) are a bit high.

14. More Options. If you really are a water puppy, consider returning to your hotel for a heat-of-the-day nap and coming back to the water park for some early-evening swimming. Special lighting after dusk makes Typhoon Lagoon and Blizzard Beach enchanting. Crowds tend to be lighter in the evening. If you leave the park and want to return, be sure to keep your admission ticket and have your hand stamped. If you're staying in a hotel served by Disney buses, older children can return on their own to the water parks, giving Mom and Dad a little private quiet time.

15. Bad Weather. Thunderstorms are common in Florida. During summer afternoons, such storms can be a daily occurrence. Swimming parks close during a storm. Most storms, however, are short lived, allowing the swimming park to resume normal operations. If a storm is severe and prolonged, it can cause a great deal of inconvenience. In addition to the park's closing, guests compete aggressively for shelter, and Disney resort guests may have to compete for seats on a bus back to the hotel.

We recommend you monitor the local weather forecast the day before you go, checking again in the morning before leaving for the swimming park. Scattered thundershowers are to be expected, but moving storm fronts are to be avoided. Because Florida is so flat, approaching weather can be seen from atop the slide platforms at the swimming parks. Particularly if you're dependent on Disney buses, leave the park earlier, rather than later, when you see a storm moving in.

16. Endurance. The water parks are large and require almost as much walking as one of the theme parks. Add to this wave surfing, swimming, and all the climbing required to reach the slides, and you'll be pooped by day's end. Unless you spend your hours like a lizard on a rock, don't expect to return to the hotel with a lot of energy. Consider something low-key for the evening. You probably will want to hit the hay early.

17. Lost Children and Lost Adults. It's as easy to lose a child or become separated from your party at one of the water parks as it is at a major theme park. Upon arrival, pick a very specific place to meet in the event you are separated. If you split up on purpose, set times for checking in. Lost-children stations at the water parks are so out of the way that neither you nor your lost child will find them without help from a Disney employee. Explain to your children how to recognize a Disney employee (by their distinctive name tags) and how to ask for help.

Part Fifteen

Beyond the Parks

Downtown Disney

Downtown Disney is a shopping, dining, and entertainment development strung out along the banks of the Buena Vista Lagoon. On the far right is the Downtown Disney Marketplace (formerly known as the Disney Village Marketplace). In the middle is the gated (admission-required) Pleasure Island nighttime entertainment, and on the far left is Disney's West Side.

Downtown Disney Marketplace

Although the Marketplace offers interactive fountains, a couple of playgrounds, a Lagoon-side amphitheater, and watercraft rentals, it is primarily a shopping and dining venue. The centerpiece of shopping is the World of Disney, the largest Disney trademark merchandise store in the world. If you can't find what you are looking for in this 38,000-square-foot Noah's Ark of Disney stuff, it probably doesn't exist. Another noteworthy retailer is the LEGO Imagination Center, showcasing a number of huge and unbelievable sculptures made entirely of LEGO "bricks." Almost worthy of a special trip, spaceships, sea serpents, sleeping tourists, and dinosaurs are just a few of the sculptures on display. The latest addition is Pooh Corner, an entire store full of Winnie the Pooh merchandise. Rounding out the selection are stores specializing in resort wear, athletic attire and gear, Christmas decorations, Barbie dolls, Disney art and collectibles, and handmade craft items. Also located in the Marketplace is Studio M, where guests can have a professional photograph taken with Mickey. Most retail establishments are open from 9:30 a.m. until 11:30 p.m.

Rainforest Cafe is the headliner restaurant at the Marketplace. There is also Cap'n Jack's Oyster Bar, Wolfgang Puck pizza kitchen, a soda fountain, a deli and bakery, and a McDonald's. Full-service restaurants are profiled in Part Nine: Dining in and around Walt Disney World.

Pleasure Island

Pleasure Island is a nighttime entertainment complex. Though admission is charged after 7 p.m., shops and restaurants are open with no admission required during the day. Detailed coverage of the nightspots is provided in Part Seventeen: Nightlife in and out of Walt Disney World. Pleasure Island's shops offer more Disney art, casual fashions, Disney character merchandise, movie collectibles, and music memorabilia. Superstar Studios is a recording studio where you can make your own music video. There are several full-service restaurants at Pleasure Island. Fulton's Crab House and the Portobello Yacht Club can be accessed at any time without paying admission to Pleasure Island. The Pleasure Island Jazz Company is within the gated part of Pleasure Island.

Disney's West Side

The West Side is the newest addition to Downtown Disney and offers a broad range of entertainment, dining, and shopping. Restaurants include the House of Blues, which serves Cajun specialties; Planet Hollywood, offering movie memorabilia and basic American fare; Bongo's Cuban Cafe, serving Cuban favorites; and Wolfgang Puck Cafe, featuring California cuisine. All four West Side restaurants are profiled in Part Nine: Dining in and around Walt Disney World.

West Side shopping is some of the most interesting in WDW. For starters, there's a Virgin (records and books) Megastore. Across the street is the Guitar Gallery by George's Music, specializing in custom, collector, rare, and unique guitars. Other specialty shops include a cigar shop, a rock-and-roll and movie memorabilia store, and a western apparel boutique.

In the entertainment department, there is DisneyQuest, an interactive theme park contained in a building; the House of Blues, a concert and dining venue; and a 24-screen AMC movie theater. The West Side is also home to *Cirque du Soleil,* a not-to-be-missed production show with a cast of almost 100 performers and musicians. The House of Blues concert hall and *Cirque du Soleil* are described in Part Seventeen: Nightlife in and out of Walt Disney World. DisneyQuest is described in detail below.

DisneyQuest

For more than a decade, major theme parks have experimented with attractions based on motion-simulation and virtual reality technologies. Among other things, these technologies have allowed thrill rides with the punch of a roller coaster to be engineered and operated in spaces as small as a one-car garage. Analogous to the computer industry, where the power of a bulky mainframe is now available in a laptop, Disney is pioneering the concept of a theme park in a box, or in the case of DisneyQuest, a modest five-story building.

Opened in the summer of 1998 in the West Side area of Downtown Disney, DisneyQuest contains all the elements of the larger Disney theme parks. There is an entrance area that facilitates your transition into the park environment and leads to the gateways of four distinct themed lands, here referred to as zones. As at other Disney parks, almost everything is included in the price of your admission.

It takes about two to four hours to experience DisneyQuest, once you get in, depending on the crowd. Disney claims that it limits the number of guests admitted to ensure that each person has a positive experience. Right, so does the Super Bowl, and that's about how big the crowd feels much of the time at DisneyQuest. Once DisneyQuest hits capacity, newly arriving guests are lined up outside to wait until departing guests make some room. Weekday mornings are the least crowded times to visit.

DisneyQuest, in concept and attraction mix, is aimed at a youthful audience, say 8–35 years of age, though younger and older patrons will enjoy much of what it offers. The feel is dynamic, bustling, and noisy. Those who haunt the electronic games arcades at shopping malls will feel most at home at DisneyQuest. And like most malls, when late afternoon turns to evening, the median age at DisneyQuest rises toward adolescents and teens who have been released from parental supervision for awhile.

You begin your experience in the Departure Lobby, adjacent to admission sales. From the Departure Lobby you enter a "Cyberlator," a sort of "transitional attraction" (read elevator) hosted by the genie from *Aladdin*, that delivers you to an entrance plaza called Ventureport. From here you can enter the four zones. Like in the larger parks, each zone is distinctively themed. Some zones cover more than one floor, so, looking around, you can see things going on both above and below you. The four zones, in no particular order, are Explore Zone, Score Zone, Create Zone, and Replay Zone. In addition to the zones, DisneyQuest offers two restaurants and the inevitable gift shop.

Though most kids and adolescents aren't going to care, the zone layout at DisneyQuest may confuse adults trying to orient themselves. Don't count on trapping certain kids in certain zones either, or planning a rendezvous inside one without designating a specific location. Each zone spreads out over multiple levels, with stairways, elevators, slides, and walkways linking them in a variety of ways. Still, as we said, the labyrinthine design of the place won't bother most youngsters, who are usually happy just to wander (or dash madly) between games and rides.

Explore Zone

The gateway to Explore Zone is the tiger's-head cave from *Aladdin*. You can descend to the attractions area on a 150-foot corkscrew slide or use more traditional means like elevators or ramps. The headline attraction in Explore Zone is the Virtual Jungle Cruise, where you paddle a six-person raft. The raft is a motion simulator perched on top of blue air bags that replicate the motion of water. Responding to the film of the river projected before you, you can choose among several routes through the rapids. The motion simulator responds to sensors on your paddle, so the ride you experience simulates the course you choose. As if navigating the river isn't enough, man-eating dinosaurs and a cataclysmic comet are tossed in for good measure. Another Explore Zone attraction, Aladdin's Magic Carpet Ride, is a virtual reality trip through the streets of Agrabah.

Score Zone

Here you pass through a slash in a giant comic book to enter a theme area based on comic book characters and competition. The big deal here are enlarged, high-tech versions of electronic and video games where you pit your skill and reflexes against other players. The headliner is Mighty Ducks Pinball Slam, where you stand atop a mammoth hockey puck. By manipulating a joystick, you control the motion of your puck as it bounces around a virtual reality pinball machine. In Ride the Comix, you once again don virtual reality headgear to ride off into comic book scenes and do battle with archvillains.

Create Zone

A digital artist's palette serves as the entrance to Create Zone. Featured here is CyberSpace Mountain, an attraction where you can design your own roller coaster—including 360° loops—and then go for a virtual reality–motion simulator ride on your creation. Also in the Create Zone are Animation Academy, a sort of crash tutorial on Disney animation, and Magic Mirror, where you can perform virtual plastic surgery on yourself. Other creative attractions include virtual beauty salon makeovers and painting on an electronic canvas.

Replay Zone

Replay Zone draws its theme from a 1950s view of the future. Basically, it's three levels of classic midway games with a few futuristic twists. The balls on the Skeeball games, for example, glow in the dark. Winners of the various games earn redemption tickets, which can be redeemed for midway-type prizes. The pièce de résistance of Replay Zone is Buzz Lightyear's Astro Blasters, a fancy version of bumper cars. Here guests pilot two-person bumper-bubbles that suck up grapefruit-sized balls from the floor and fire them from an air cannon at other vehicles. Direct hits cause the other vehicles to spin momentarily out of control.

Reader response to DisneyQuest is very mixed, as evidenced by the following comments.

From a Kendall Park, New Jersey, mother of two:

DisneyQuest was a huge letdown. There were tremendous waits inside and outside.

And from a Pennsylvania family with kids ages 11 and 13:

Our only really big disappointment was DisneyQuest. What a rip-off! My husband and daughters paid $26.50 to get in because the guy at the window told us that fee covered nearly all the experiences. Once inside, they found that at least half the stuff they wanted to do cost mega-extra-bucks. Also, my youngest child, at 50", was one inch too short for the two rides she most wanted to try. Nowhere outside is any of this explained. It's truly an offensive deal for people who have already spent scads in their darned parks. I plan to write and let them know what I think of such tactics.

A Virginia mother of two teens sounded a more positive note:

DisneyQuest was a big hit with our 13-year-old son. The food at DisneyQuest (the Cheesecake Factory) was excellent.

For a family of five from Cleveland, Ohio, DisneyQuest was a slam dunk:

Your description and reader feedback had us a little skeptical. But with another cold day on hand, we gave it a shot. If you have right brain (creative) kids, you can't miss. Your book said two to three hours for DQ. We had dinner reservations that forced a cutoff at seven hours, otherwise we could have pulled an all-nighter with them! Forget the arcade stuff; our kids focused on the Create Zone. The interactive stuff was fascinating. I think DQ provides parents the best chance to see their kids' brains and personalities in action since it's so interactive.

Finally, a family from Columbia, Maryland, offers this advice to parents with babies and toddlers:

Alert your readers to bring a baby carrier/backpack to DisneyQuest. You're there for several hours, and absolutely no strollers are allowed in the entire building.

Disney's Wide World of Sports

Disney's Wide World of Sports complex is a 200-acre, state-of-the-art competition and training complex consisting of a 7,500-seat ballpark, a fieldhouse, and dedicated venues for baseball, softball, tennis, track and field, beach volleyball, and 27 other sports. From Little League Baseball to rugby to beach volleyball, the complex hosts a mind-boggling calendar of professional and amateur competitions, with one or more events scheduled nearly every day.

During late winter and early spring, the complex is the spring training home of the Atlanta Braves. In August of 2002, the Wide World of Sports hosted the Tampa Bay Bucs' NFL Training camp. The Braves are a fixture in the spring, but the status of the Bucs' camp beyond 2002 has not been announced. Although Disney guests are welcome at the sports complex as paid spectators (prices vary according to event), none of the facilities are available for guests' use unless they are participants in a scheduled organized competition. To learn what events are scheduled during your visit, call (407) 828-3267.

In addition to scheduled competitive events, a program called the NFL Experience is operated daily from 11 a.m. until about 5 p.m. Appealing primarily to school-age boys, the NFL Experience is a supervised activity that allows kids to kick field goals, catch and throw passes, catch punts, and run through a small obstacle course, among other things. Though the NFL Experience is sometimes the only thing going on at the Wide World of Sports complex, Disney nevertheless charges full admission. Our advice is to pass on the Wide World of Sports unless there is a specific event you want to see. Call the sports complex directly to confirm event times and venues (as opposed to trusting Disney guest relations personnel at the theme parks or hotels).

Counter-service and full-service dining are available at the sports complex, but there's no on-site lodging. Disney's Wide World of Sports is off Osceola Parkway, between World Drive and where the parkway crosses I-4 (no interstate access). The complex has its own parking lot and is accessible via the Disney Transportation System.

The Disney Wilderness Preserve

Located about 40–60 minutes south of Walt Disney World is the Disney Wilderness Preserve, a real wetlands restoration area operated by the Nature Conservancy in partnership with Disney. At 12,000 acres, this is as real as Disney gets. There are hiking trails, an interpretive center, and guided outings on weekends. Trails wind through grassy savannas, beneath ancient cypress trees, and along the banks of pristine Lake Russell. It's open daily from 9 a.m. to 5 p.m., and general admission is $2 for adults and $1 for children ages 6–17. Guided trail walks are offered on Saturday at no extra cost, and "buggy" rides are available on Sunday afternoon. The buggy in question is a mammoth amphibious contraption, and the rides last a few hours. The buggy ride is $7 for adults and $5 for children ages 6–17; reservations are highly recommended. *Note:* Disney information doesn't know anything about the wilderness preserve, including the fact that it exists. For information and directions call the preserve directly at (407) 935-0002. Finally, we *Unofficials* love the place: it's a delightful change of pace from the artificiality of the theme parks. And as for the buggy ride, it could possibly be the high point of your Disney vacation.

Walt Disney World Speedway

Adjacent to the Transportation and Ticket Center parking lot, the one-mile tri-oval course is host to several races each year. Between competitions, it's home to the Richard Petty Driving Experience, where you can ride in a two-seater stock car for $89 or learn to drive one. Courses are by reservation only and cost between $349 (8 laps), $749 (18 laps), and $1,199 (30 laps). You must be age 18 or older, have a valid driver's license, and know how to drive a stick shift to take a course. For information, call (800) 237-3889.

Walt Disney World Recreation

Most Walt Disney World guests never make it beyond the theme parks, the water parks, and Downtown Disney. Those who do, however, discover an extraordinary selection of recreational opportunities ranging from guided fishing expeditions and water skiing outings to hayrides, horseback riding, fitness center workouts, and miniature golf. If it's something you can do at a resort, it's probably available at Walt Disney World.

Boat, bike, and fishing equipment rentals are handled on an hourly basis. Just show up at the rental office during operating hours and they'll fix you up. The same goes for various fitness centers in the resort hotels. Golf, tennis, fishing expeditions, water ski excursions, hayrides, trail rides, and most spa services must be scheduled in advance. Though every resort features an extensive selection of recreational options, those resorts located on a navigable body of water offer the greatest variety. Also, the more upscale a resort, the more likely it is to have such amenities as a fitness center and spa. In addition, you can rent boats and other recreational equipment at the Marketplace in Downtown Disney.

Walt Disney World Golf

Walt Disney World has six golf courses, all expertly designed and meticulously maintained. The Magnolia, the Palm, and the Oak Trail are across Floridian Way from the Polynesian Resort. They envelop the Shades of Green recreational complex, and the pro shops and support facilities adjoin the Shades of Green hotel (for military personnel and retirees only). Lake Buena Vista Golf Course is at the Disney Institute, near Walt Disney World Village and across the lake from Pleasure Island. The Osprey Ridge and Eagle Pines courses are part of the Bonnet Creek Golf

Club near the Fort Wilderness Campground. In addition to the golf courses, there are driving ranges and putting greens at each location.

Oak Trail is a nine-hole course for beginners. The other five courses are designed for the mid-handicap player and, while interesting, are quite forgiving. All courses are popular, with morning tee times at a premium, especially January–April. To avoid the crowds, play on a Monday, Tuesday, or Wednesday, and sign up for a late-afternoon tee time.

Peak season for all courses is September–April; off-season is May–August. Off-season and afternoon twilight rates are available. Carts are required (except at Oak Trail) and are included in the greens fee. Tee times may be reserved 60 days in advance by Disney resort guests, 30 days in advance for day guests with a credit card, and 7 days in advance without guarantee. Proper golf attire is required: collared shirt and Bermuda-length shorts or slacks.

Besides the ability to book tee times further in advance, guests of Walt Disney World–owned resorts get several other useful benefits that may sway a golfer's lodging decision. These include discounted greens fees, charge privileges, and the shipping of your clubs between facilities, if, say, you are playing the Lake Buena Vista course one day and a course at one of the other two golf facilities the next. The single most important, and least known, benefit is the provision of free roundtrip taxi transportation between the golf courses and your hotel, which lets you avoid moving your car or dragging your clubs on Disney buses. The cabs, which make access to the courses much simpler, are paid by vouchers happily supplied to hotel guests.

Palm Golf Course ★★★★

1950 West Magnolia/Palm Drive, Lake Buena Vista, FL 32830; (407) WDW-GOLF

Established 1970 **Designer** Joe Lee **Status** Resort
Fees Seasonal; call for current rates
Facilities Pro shop, driving range, practice green, locker rooms, snack bar, beverage cart, and club and shoe rentals
Tees   Blue   6,957 yards, par 72, USGA 73.0, slope 133
White 6,461 yards, par 72, USGA 70.7, slope 129
Gold   6,029 yards, par 72, USGA 68.7, slope 124
Red   5,311 yards, par 72, USGA 70.4, slope 124

Comments   The Palm is Disney's best course, with lesser-known architect Joe Lee showing up the marquee designers that headline the Bonnet Creek Golf Club. Home to the Disney/Oldsmobile Classic PGA Tour event, it has numerous lakes coming into play on nine holes, and sand everywhere, with 94 hazards. The highlight, however, is a set of excellent greens, a real surprise, given the heavy volume of play. The defining characteristic is a set of holes where water separates tees from landing areas and landing areas from greens, a wet take on desert-style target golf. The signature 18th, with its island green, caps a fine set of finishing holes and has been ranked as high as fourth in difficulty among all holes on the PGA Tour's many venues. But four sets of well-spaced tees make the course playable for all abilities, and along with its sister course Magnolia, the facility boasts a multi-level natural grass practice range that is among the largest in the nation.

Magnolia Golf Course ★★★½

1950 West Magnolia/Palm Drive, Lake Buena Vista, FL 32830; (407) WDW-GOLF

Established 1970 **Designer** Joe Lee **Status** Resort
Fees Seasonal; call for current rates
Facilities: Pro shop, driving range, practice green, locker rooms, sports bar, beverage cart, and club and shoe rentals
Tees   *Blue* 7,190 yards, par 72, USGA 73.9, slope 133
         White 6,642 yards, par 72, USGA 71.6, slope 128
         Gold 6,091 yards, par 72, USGA 69.1, slope 123
         Red 5,253 yards, par 72, USGA 70.5, slope 123

Comments   Another fine Joe Lee creation, Magnolia shares its best traits with the Palm, including excellent greens, practice facilities, a dramatic finishing sequence, and plenty of water. From the back tees it is Disney's longest course and features a whopping 97 bunkers, including the famous one in the shape of Mickey Mouse's head. But the layout is slightly less challenging than the Palm, with no water on most of the par-3s. Like the Palm, this course hosts the Disney/Oldsmobile Classic.

Osprey Ridge Golf Course ★★★½

3451 Golf View Drive, Lake Buena Vista, FL 32830; (407) WDW-GOLF

Established 1992 **Designer** Tom Fazio **Status** Resort
Fees Seasonal; call for current rates
Facilities Pro shop, driving range, practice green, locker rooms, Sand Trap Bar and Grill, beverage cart, and club and shoe rentals
Tees   *Black* 7,101 yards, par 72, USGA 73.9, slope 135
         Silver 6,680 yards, par 72, USGA 71.8, slope 128
         Gold 6,103 yards, par 72, USGA 68.9, slope 121
         Red 5,402 yards, par 72, USGA 70.5, slope 122

Comments   This Tom Fazio layout is a thoroughly modern course that included a large amount of earth moving in its construction. Its main characteristics are large rolling mounds and elevated tees and greens. The greens are huge, almost to the point of bizarre, making them easy to hit but leaving approaches at four-putt distances where you almost cannot hit the ball hard enough to get it to the hole.

Eagle Pines Golf Course ★★★½

3451 Golf View Drive, Lake Buena Vista, FL 32830; (407) WDW-GOLF

Established 1992 **Designer** Pete Dye **Status** Resort

Fees Seasonal; call for current rates

Facilities Pro shop, driving range, practice green, locker rooms, Sand Trap Bar and Grill, beverage cart, banquet facilities, and club and shoe rentals

Tees *Black* 6,722 yards, par 72, USGA 72.3, slope 131

Silver 6,309 yards, par 72, USGA 69.9, slope 125

Gold 5,520 yards, par 72, USGA 66.3, slope 115

Red 4,838 yards, par 72, USGA 68, slope 111

Comments In contrast to neighboring Osprey Ridge, Pete Dye crafted a course reminiscent of the Carolina Sandhills, with fairways lined with native grasses and flanked by waste areas of straw and sand. Dish-shaped greens are at or below the levels of the fairway, emphasizing well-struck approach shots to hold the putting surfaces. Water is in play on nearly every hole, and aesthetically, this is the most impressive of the Disney courses with the mix of sand, straw, lush green fairways, and blue lakes. It is also forgiving for a Dye course, since the waste areas act as buffers to stop errant shots before they reach the water.

Lake Buena Vista Golf Course ★★★

2200 Club Lake Drive, Lake Buena Vista, FL 32830; (407) WDW-GOLF

Established 1971 **Designer** Joe Lee **Status** Resort

Fees Seasonal; call for current rates

Facilities Pro shop, driving range, practice green, locker rooms, snack bar, beverage cart, and club and shoe rentals

Tees *Blue* 6,819 yards, par 72, USGA 72.7, slope 128

White 6,268 yards, par 72, USGA 70.1, slope 123

Gold 5,919 yards, par 72, USGA 68.2, slope 120

Red 5,194 yards, par 73, USGA 69.4, slope 120

Comments As with the other Joe Lee courses, there are several memorable holes here, and the greens are in fine shape. But this layout is the only one at Disney with housing on it, a lot of housing, which detracts from the golf experience. The course is geographically unique among the other layouts, tucked behind the Disney Institute, and has a swampy feel reminiscent of the area's pre-Disney everglades with trees dripping Spanish moss. Narrow fairways and small greens emphasize accuracy over length.

Oak Trail Golf Course ★★½

1950 West Magnolia/Palm Drive, Lake Buena Vista, FL 32830; (407) WDW-GOLF

Established 1980 **Designer** Ron Garl **Status** Resort

Fees Adult, $32; child, $20. Includes use of a pull cart (course is walking only). To replay the course costs an additional $16 for adults and $10 for children.

Facilities Pro shop, driving range, practice green, locker rooms, sports bar, beverage cart, and club and shoe rentals

Tees *White* 2,913 yards, par 36

Red 2,532 yards, par 36

Comments   This Ron Garl nine-holer is a "real" course, not an executive par-3 like many nine-hole designs. Geared towards introducing children to the game, it also makes a good quick-fix or warm-up before a round, and the walking-only layout is the only walkable routing at Walt Disney World.

Golf beyond Walt Disney World

The greater Orlando area has enough high-quality courses to rival better known golfing Meccas such as Scottsdale and Palm Springs, but unlike these destinations with their endless private country clubs, Orlando is unique because almost all its courses are open for some sort of public play. Because of its easy airport access, wonderful climate, and good golf facilities (along with Florida's lack of a personal income tax) Orlando is the single most popular residence for PGA Tour players, including Tiger Woods, Mark O'Meara, Lee Janzen, Nick Faldo, and Ernie Els.

Of the many golf courses and resorts in the area, one stands head and shoulders above the rest, especially because it actually abuts Walt Disney World. Not only the location of this course is excellent: the sprawling 1500-acre Hyatt Regency Grand Cypress is superb in every way, with top-notch golf, lodging, dining, grounds, and an enormous fantasy pool complex. One of the world's largest free form pools, it includes waterfalls, caves, waterslides, and a swim-up grotto bar. The resort also hides a world-class equestrian center with riding and instruction for all abilities. But the standout feature is the golf, which would be worth a trip regardless where the resort was located. The facilities are first rate, from the luxurious clubhouse with its free shoe shines, to the computerized GPS systems on the carts. The golf club is also home to an excellent instructional facility, the Grand Cypress Academy of Golf. Because of the many amenities and the wonderful location, the Hyatt is one of the priciest resorts in Orlando, but since only guests can play the courses, consider making the investment.

Grand Cypress Golf Club,   ★★★★½
North/East/South Courses

One North Jacaranda, Orlando, FL 32836; (800) 835-7377 or (407) 239-1904

Established 1984 **Designer** Jack Nicklaus **Status** Resort (guests only)
Fees $150 ($100 in summer)
Facilities Pro shop, driving range, practice greens, locker rooms, restaurant, beverage cart, carts equipped with Global Positioning Systems, and club and shoe rentals.
Tees North/South Tees
    Gold 6,993 yards, par 72, USGA 73.9, slope 130
    Blue 6,335 yards, par 72, USGA 70.7, slope 123

White 5,823 yards, par 72, USGA 68.5, slope 121
Red 5,332 yards, par 72, USGA 71.1, slope 119

North/East Tees
Gold 6,955 yards, par 72, USGA 73.9, slope 130
Blue 6,294 yards, par 72, USGA 70.9, slope 124
White 5,790 yards, par 72, USGA 68.6, slope 121
Red 5,056 yards, par 72, USGA 69.1, slope 114

South/East Tees
Gold 6,906 yards, par 72, USGA 74.4, slope 132
Blue 6,363 yards, par 72, USGA 71.6, slope 126
White 5,789 yards, par 72, USGA 69.3, slope 123
Red 5,130 yards, par 72, USGA 70.2, slope 123

Comments While the unique Scottish aspect of the New Course and its position as the resort's marquee course make it more popular, the three Nicklaus Nines are actually better. This course can be played in three different 18-hole combinations, but the South is the very best nine at the resort, so try to book either North/South or South/East. The North/South combination hosted the LPGA Tournament of Champions from 1994 to 1996, as well as the PGA Tour Skills Challenge and the Shark Shootout. This course is one of the most beautiful in Orlando, and water is found on 13 of the holes, creating additional peril. There are many unique and interesting holes, several with true risk/reward choices such as shortcuts over lakes. The undulating greens are guarded by pot bunkers and grass depressions and are kept in superb shape. Unlike the New Course, you will have very few opportunities to bump and run the ball onto the green and will have to land the ball on the green with your approach.

Grand Cypress Golf Club, New Course ★★★★

One North Jacaranda, Orlando, FL 32836; (800) 835-7377 or (407) 239-1904

Established 1988 **Designer** Jack Nicklaus **Status** Resort (guests only)
Fees $180 ($100 in summer)
Facilities Pro shop, driving range, practice greens, locker rooms, restaurant, beverage cart, carts equipped with Global Positioning Systems, and club and shoe rentals.
Tees *Black* 6,773 yards, par 72, USGA 72.1, slope 126
   White 6,181 yards, par 72, USGA 69.4, slope 117
   Red 5,314 yards, par 72, USGA 69.8, slope 117

Comments The New Course is Jack Nicklaus' homage to the famous Old Course at St. Andrews, Scotland, the birthplace of golf. The first and last two holes are replicas of those at the Old Course, and other features such as the famous Swilcan Bridge and some of the huge bunkers are recreated here. In between are Nicklaus's original holes, done in a links style, with double greens, pot bunkers, tall rough, and wide, hard fairways. As on most Scottish links courses, there are no trees, and with nothing to deflect the wind, it will play havoc with your shots when it is blowing. If you've never had a chance to play Scottish courses, the New is a very reasonable facsimile that captures both the spirit and history of the sport's earliest form.

Other Standout Courses in Orlando

Among the many public courses throughout the area, a handful stand out and are worth leaving Walt Disney World to play. Although there are good-quality golf resorts such as Grenelefe and Mission Hills well outside Orlando, these are all quite convenient to the theme parks:

Championsgate

Three miles from Walt Disney World, and close to Celebration, lies the city's newest golf resort, so new that the lodging, including an Omni hotel, won't open until at least mid-2003. But the centerpiece of the $800 million, 1,400-acre facility are the two Greg Norman–designed courses, which are open and worth a visit.

Championsgate International Course ★★★★

1400 Masters Boulevard, Championsgate, FL 33837; (888) 558-9301 or (407) 787-4653

Established 2001 **Designer** Greg Norman **Status** Public
Fees $185 ($68 in summer)
Facilities Pro shop, driving range, practice greens, locker rooms, restaurant, beverage cart, and club and shoe rentals.
Tees *Trophy* 7,363 yards, par 72, USGA 76.3, slope 143
 Legends 6,792 yards, par 72, USGA 73.7, slope 137
 Champions 6,239 yards, par 72, USGA 71.2, slope 132
 Heritage 5,518 yards, par 72, USGA 72.3, slope 117

Comments   The tougher and more highly ranked of the two layouts, the International lives up to its name by recreating the feel of the championship courses of the British Isles. Laid out in a links style, the course has carpet-like fairways framed by the stark unfinished look of brown dunes, mounds, and severe pot bunkers. From the tips, it is one of the state's most challenging courses, with Florida's highest USGA rating at 76.3.

Championsgate National Course ★★★½

1400 Masters Boulevard, Championsgate, FL 33837; (888) 558-9301 or (407) 787-4653

Established 2001 **Designer** Greg Norman **Status** Public
Fees $185 ($68 in summer)
Facilities Pro shop, driving range, practice greens, locker rooms, restaurant, beverage cart, and club and shoe rentals.
Tees *Trophy* 7,128 yards, par 70, USGA 75.1, slope 133
 Legends 6,427 yards, par 70, USGA 72.0, slope 126
 Champions 5,937 yards, par 70, USGA 70.9, slope 124
 Heritage 5,150 yards, par 70, USGA 69.8, slope 111

Comments: The kinder, gentler course at Championsgate, the National is a resort-style layout, which ambles through 200-acres of citrus groves in a traditional parkland routing with far less water than the International. Deep greens welcome bump and run shots, and the length is manageable from every set of tees.

Orange County National

Five miles south of Disney in Winter Garden lies Orlando's premier daily-fee public facility, winner of numerous industry awards and consistently named among the nation's top public golf clubs by most golf publications. The 45-holes and one of the country's best practice facilities occupy nearly 1,000 verdant acres, with no homes or other distractions, just pure golf. It is also easily the region's best value, and onsite lodging packages run just $110 a night in peak season, including lodging, a round of golf and free play on the 9-hole course. The par-29 executive Tooth Course is well maintained and has a surprising variety of holes and water hazards for a short course, offering a very satisfying golf fix for those in a hurry.

Panther Lake   ★★★★½

16301 Phil Ritson Way, Winter Garden, FL 34787; (888) 727-3672 or (407) 656-2626

Established 1997 **Designer** Phil Ritson and David Harmon **Status** Public
Fees $60–$80 (including lunch)
Facilities Lodging, pro shop, driving range, practice greens, locker rooms, restaurant, beverage cart, and club and shoe rentals.
Tees *Tour* 7,295 yards, par 72, USGA 75.7, slope 137
   Championship 6,816 yards, par 72, USGA 73.2, slope 132
   Member/Guest 6,298 yards, par 72, USGA 70.7, slope 128
   Forward 5,073 yards, par 72, USGA 71.5, slope 125

Comments Panther Lake was the nation's first course designed to showcase 18 signature holes, and no expense was spared to make the course beautiful, just as none is spared to keep it in excellent condition. The front nine is carved from Florida wetlands with water at every turn, while the much different back has a Carolinas-like style with surprising elevation changes, stands of pines and oaks, and hard to hold greens emphasizing accuracy. While both courses here are excellent, the sheer beauty makes Panther Lake the first choice for those without time to play both.

Crooked Cat   ★★★★

16301 Phil Ritson Way, Winter Garden, FL 34787; (888) 727-3672 or (407) 656-2626

Established 1997 **Designer** Phil Ritson and David Harmon **Status** Public
Fees $50–$70 (including lunch)
Facilities Lodging, pro shop, driving range, practice greens, locker rooms, restaurant, beverage cart, and club and shoe rentals.
Tees *Tour* 7,277 yards, par 72, USGA 75.4, slope 140
   Championship 6,748 yards, par 72, USGA 72.9, slope 134
   Member/Guest 6,035 yards, par 72, USGA 69.3, slope 121
   Forward 5,5236 yards, par 72, USGA 70.3, slope 120

Comments Variety is the spice of life, and this partner to the very modern Panther Lake is a throwback to Scottish-style links courses, with few trees, wide fairways, and heather mixed in the rough. Large sloped greens welcome bump and run shots, but are protected by deep bunkers of both grass and sand. It is as well maintained as its sibling.

The Best of the Rest

Arnold Palmer's Bay Hill Club & Lodge ★★★★

9000 Bay Hill Boulevard, Orlando, FL 32819; (888) 422-9445 or (407) 876-2429

Established 1961 **Designer** Dick Wilson **Status** Resort
Fees $195 (resort guests only)
Facilities Lodging, pro shop, driving range, practice greens, locker rooms, restaurant, beverage cart, and club and shoe rentals.
Tees *Palmer* 7,114 yards, par 72, USGA 74.6, slope 141

      Championship 6,586 yards, par-72, USGA 71.8, slope 127

      Men's 6,198 yards, par 72, USGA 70.2, slope 124

      Ladies 5,192 yards, par 72, USGA 72.3, slope 133

Comments Bay Hill is famous in the golf world as the home club of the King, Arnold Palmer, and is the site of his Bay Hill Invitational each year, a tournament that Tiger Woods has dominated in recent years. The irony is that Palmer's club was built 40 years ago, before Palmer himself became a brand-name golf course designer, yet the Dick Wilson layout remains equal to or better than anything Palmer has managed on his own. When he is in town, which is most of the time, Palmer makes a point of stopping by the clubhouse daily, and half the attraction of staying and playing here is to see him. The other half is the course. It is comprised of three 9s, but it is the Challenger and Champion combination that is the most popular and the one on which the PGA Tour event is played. This combo starts off with a roar, featuring the toughest opening hole on the PGA Tour, a 414-yard par-4 uphill, dogleg left that is heavily bunkered, both in the fairway and around the green. The course ends in similar fashion with one of the toughest closers around, but in between are lots of gentler birdie opportunities. Variety, class, and tradition are the mainstays of Bay Hill.

Metrowest Country Club ★★★½

2100 S. Hiawassee Road, Orlando, FL 32835; (407) 299-1099

Established 1987 **Designer** Robert Trent Jones, Jr. **Status** Public
Fees $105
Facilities Pro shop, driving range, practice greens, locker rooms, restaurant, beverage cart, and club and shoe rentals.
Tee *Blue* 7,051 yards, par 72, USGA 71.7, slope 127

      White 6,467 yards, par 72, USGA 70.3, slope 122

      Red 5,978yards, par 72, USGA 68.2, slope 117

      Ladies 5,325 yards, par 72, USGA 71.1, slope 110

Comments Fans of Robert Trent Jones, Jr. will recognize the use of water hazards to make holes more dramatic, such as on approaches to peninsula greens. But there is less water than he usually uses, and far less than on most Florida courses. The result is a less penal test, with a lower slope and rating than most upscale area layouts. The strength of the course, which is a local favorite, is its variety, mixing doglegs, elevation changes, and interesting green complexes with the wide fairways that make it fun to play.

Miniature Golf

A couple of years ago, the Disney Intelligence Patrol (DIP) noticed that as many as 113 guests a day were sneaking out of Walt Disney World to play Goofy Golf. Applying the logic of the boy who jammed his finger in the dike, Disney feared a hemorrhage of patrons from the theme parks. The thought of those truant guests making instant millionaires of miniature golf entrepreneurs on International Drive was enough to give a fat mouse ulcers.

The response to this assault on Disney's market share was Fantasia Gardens Miniature Golf, an 11-acre complex with two 18-hole dink-and-putt golf courses. One course is an "adventure" course, themed after Disney's animated film *Fantasia*. The other course, geared more toward older children and adults, is an innovative approach-and-putt course with sand traps and water hazards.

Fantasia Gardens is beautifully landscaped and creatively executed. There are fountains, animated statues, topiaries, flower beds, and a multitude of other imponderables that you're unlikely to find at most putt-putt courses.

Fantasia Gardens is on Epcot Resort Boulevard, across the street from the Walt Disney World Swan. To reach Fantasia Gardens via Disney transportation, take a bus or boat to the Swan resort.

The cost to putt at this course is $9.25 for adults and $7.50 for children. If you arrive hungry or naked, Fantasia Gardens has a snack bar and gift shop. For more information, call (407) 560-8760.

In 1999, Disney opened Winter Summerland, a second miniature golf facility located next to the Blizzard Beach water park. Winter Summerland offers two 18-hole courses—one has a blizzard in Florida theme, while the other sports a tropical holiday theme. The Winter Summerland courses are much easier than the Fantasia courses, making them a better choice for families with preteen children. It's open daily, 10 a.m.–11 p.m., and the cost is the same as for Fantasia Gardens.

Part Sixteen

Shopping in and out
of Walt Disney World

The *Unofficial Guide* aims to help you see as much as possible, not buy as much as possible. But we acknowledge that for many, a vacation is an extended shopping spree. If you're among these shoppers, you'll love exploring the stores at and around Walt Disney World. You'll notice that our touring plans keep you on-track to see attractions, dissuading you somewhat from shopping. However, to give you a notion of what it means to an enthusiast, we share this letter from a Los Angeles couple:

> We would like to point out that, although your book discourages it, the shopping is a divine experience at WDW for those who like to shop. One does not shop in WDW for bargains (that's what flea markets, garage sales, and Target are for), but Disney buyers obtain a large selection of above-average to excellent quality merchandise, much of it not available anywhere else (not even a Disney Store or catalog), and arrange it attractively and imaginatively (at the exit of almost every attraction). They are marketing geniuses! Not even the largest shops have all the merchandise they have to offer, hence, a shopper can make little discoveries in almost every shop—even the smallest hotel gift shops. That, coupled with congenial, helpful Disney staff and services like complimentary hotel delivery, make shopping its own attraction at WDW.

And a woman from, Suffolk, Virginia, offers this:

> Let readers know if they are into shopping to allot at least six hours for Disney Marketplace and West Side.

Central Florida is a shopper's mecca. With more than 44 million square feet of retail space, Orlando is the fastest growing retail market in the United States, according to the Orlando–Orange County Convention and Visitors Bureau, and millions of visitors from around the globe have retailers scrambling to keep up with demand.

Beyond the ubiquitous mouse ears and T-shirts, avid shoppers can find a wide array of items, from hard-to-find imports from Epcot's World Showcase to unbelievable bargains from hundreds of off-price outlets. Since we figure you are not in Orlando *just* for the shopping, we'll whittle down our lists to the best of the best. We will take a look at all four Disney theme parks, the Disney resorts, and Downtown Disney, then head for the other shopping hot spots around central Florida.

There are too many shops to mention every single one, but we'll tell you what's special and point out the smart buys—and the overpriced merchandise. We'll tell you where to locate hard-to-find goods. If a shop has a special, not-to-be-missed quality, we have marked it with a ★.

Shopping in Walt Disney World

Tips for Disney Shopping

After exhaustive research in all four Disney theme parks, water parks, and resorts, we can assure you that the Disney brand merchandise is pretty much the same wherever you go. The only big differences are items with logos for specific resorts or theme parks. So if you are short on time, save your shopping spree for one favorite theme park or for the World of Disney shop in Downtown Disney Marketplace, the largest Disney shop in the world. Browsers will quickly begin to note the sameness in merchandise.

Merchandise costs do not differ across Disney property. A beach towel, for instance, was the same price at every location we checked. Ditto for sale merchandise: if it's on sale at one store, it's on sale in all stores (though you may not be able to find it at all locations).

You pay top dollar for merchandise in Disney stores. However, there are often sales (though almost never at World of Disney, the premier Disney store), generally half-price markdowns. For bathing suits, clothing, and jewelry, you'll pay full retail in every shop—not unlike shopping at any resort anywhere in the world.

If you are staying in a Disney hotel, you can have all of your packages delivered to the front entrance of any of the four Disney parks—Magic Kingdom, Epcot, Disney-MGM Studios, or the Animal Kingdom—to avoid carrying them around. For a nominal charge, you can ship them by FedEx to your home.

If you are a member of The Disney Club, ask if a discount is offered before making a purchase. A one-year family membership is about $40. For information, call (800) 49-DISNEY or check www.disneyclub.com.

Some shops at Downtown Disney Marketplace and Pleasure Island give a 15% discount to Disney resort guests for purchases of at least $50 if they pay with an American Express card. Just ask. And you must show your resort I.D. card.

If you remember on your flight home that you forgot to buy mouse ears for your nephew, call the Walt Disney Attractions Mail Order Department on weekdays at (407) 363-6200 or the catalog department at (800) 237-5751. Most trademark merchandise sold at Walt Disney World is available.

I Need ...

Where at Disney World is the best selection of a particular item? Here are a few recommendations:

Bathing Suits

Atlantic Wear and Wardrobe Emporium, Disney's Beach Club Resort
Calypso Straw Market, Disney's Caribbean Beach Resort
Polynesian Princess, Disney's Polynesian Resort

Men's Clothing

Bally at Disney's Grand Floridian Resort & Spa
Commander Porter's at Disney's Grand Floridian Resort & Spa
The Contemporary Man, Disney's Contemporary Resort
Harrington Bay Clothiers, Downtown Disney Marketplace

Women's Clothing

Commander Porter's, Disney's Grand Floridian
The Contemporary Woman, Disney's Contemporary Resort
Harrington Bay Clothiers, Downtown Disney Marketplace

Sportswear

Bonnet Creek Pro Shop, Bonnet Creek Golf Club
Contemporary Racquet Club, Disney's Contemporary Resort
ESPN Club, Disney's BoardWalk
Team Mickey's Athletic Club, Downtown Disney Marketplace

Jewelry

Kingdom Jewels Ltd., Disney's Contemporary Resort
Mitsukoshi Department Store (pearls and watches), the Japan pavilion in Epcot
    World Showcase
Uptown Jewelers, Magic Kingdom
World of Disney (Disney-themed jewelry), Downtown Disney Marketplace

---

10 CHEAP (BUT COOL) SOUVENIRS AT WDW FOR UNDER $10

Kid socks with Mickey Mouse logo	$5
A Disney autograph book	$5.50
Disney luggage tags	$5
A Mickey Mouse key chain with light	$5

10 CHEAP (BUT COOL) SOUVENIRS AT WDW FOR UNDER $10 *(cont.)*	
Disney "beanie babies"	$6
Mickey Mouse cup	$4.50
Bouquet of five Pooh lollipops	$3.50
Mickey hair clips	$0.80
Mickey Mouse spoon-straw	$3
Embroidered Mickey Mouse hat	$6.36

Downtown Disney

If shopping is an essential part of your Disney vacation, we recommend your first stop be Downtown Disney, with three shopping areas, each with its own special feel: the Marketplace, Pleasure Island, and West Side. If you have time constraints and need to limit your shopping spree to a single stop, this is it. Except for specialty items, like a Stetson hat from a little shop in the Magic Kingdom's Frontierland or silk rugs from the Japan pavilion at Epcot, you can find a little bit of everything at Downtown Disney.

Downtown Disney stretches along the shore of Buena Vista Lagoon at the intersection of Buena Vista Drive and Hotel Plaza Boulevard. It's a pleasant walk from the Marketplace on the east end to the West Side, with Pleasure Island situated between the two areas. The West Side has smaller shops with trendy merchandise; the Marketplace is loaded with Disney merchandise and a smattering of non-Disney products; Pleasure Island is really a nighttime entertainment district, but there are a few shops worth considering. So, what you're shopping for determines the best place to park—free parking on a surface lot spreads from one end to the other.

The Marketplace

The Marketplace is open Sunday–Thursday, 9:30 a.m.–11 p.m.; Friday and Saturday, 9:30 a.m.–11:30 p.m. There are 16 shops and 7 places to eat, including Rainforest Cafe. Wheelchair and stroller rental are available at Guest Services, located on the waterfront a considerable distance from the parking area. It's a comfortable place to stroll and people-watch. Near the central area is a carousel that runs daily from 9:30 a.m. to 11 p.m.; it's decorated with hand-painted renderings of the Marketplace shops, and cost is a steep $2 per ride. If you don't mind the kids getting wet, check out the free "Fun Fountains" throughout the Marketplace— streams of water that intermittently squirt out of the spongy sidewalk, soaking energetic youngsters on hot summer days. The Marketplace is accessible by Disney bus or boat. Lockers are available for 50 cents on the dock by the steps. Coins must be inserted each time the locker is opened.

In recent years, longtime Marketplace shoppers have complained that the merchandise is "too Disney" and that the unusual shops (a great linen shop, for instance) have all disappeared and been replaced with Disney shops. You'll still find non-Disney merchandise (bathing suits, clothes, etc.), just not in the abundance of the old Marketplace.

Top Shops at the Marketplace

2R's Reading and Riting   This small shop has a decent selection of best-sellers, hardbacks, paperbacks, children's books, CD-ROMs, and gift stationery. No bargains but plenty of choices for poolside reading.

Art of Disney   Next door to 2R's, Art of Disney sells limited-edition animation cels and pricey Disney creations, from pottery to crystal. You'll pay dearly for any of the merchandise.

★ **World of Disney**   It's a Disney superstore with 12 rooms—50,000 square feet—stacked with Disney merchandise, from underwear to clocks to Cinderella dresses. Pick up a basket as you walk in, shop throughout, and check out at any cash register in the store. It's decidedly less crowded and frenetic than theme-park shops except on evenings when the parks close early.

★ **Disney's Day of Christmas**   This shop is just plain fun, with hundreds of holiday decorations and a two-story tree decorated with Disney characters. We especially like the back room of non-Disney baubles, from elegant ornaments to a Lladro nativity. Plenty of ornaments under $5 here make great souvenirs. A hot seller in all of the Christmas shops is the Disney monorail train with tracks to put around the Christmas tree like an old-fashioned train (also carried in some toy stores).

Disney at Home   If you want to sleep on expensive Pooh sheets, light expensive Disney candles, or eat on expensive Mickey Mouse plates, you'll find something for every room in the house. It may be a little too cute for anyone but a true Disneyphile.

Gourmet Pantry   The stock includes a lot of groceries—cookies, canned goods, and a small deli—but you're better off heading for a local supermarket. However, we do recommend a stop at the bakery or candy corner for one of the gargantuan, gooey Rice Krispies bars. Part of the store carries Disney kitchenware and cookbooks, with everything from Mickey salt and pepper shakers to dinner plates designed by architect Michael Graves.

★ **LEGO Imagination Center**   This is the perfect rest stop for parents, and you don't even have to go in the store. A 3,000-square-foot outdoor, hands-on play area has bins of LEGOS where kids can go crazy while parents take a break. Inside is all the latest LEGO paraphernalia. Check out the life-size human family made entirely of LEGOs, including a snoring grandpa asleep on a bench.

EUROSPAIN Not the place to take rambunctious kids—there's beautiful glassware and full-lead crystal at every turn. This expensive shop has been a part of the Marketplace for more than 20 years, and you can still watch artisans at work blowing glass, carving monograms on crystal, and practicing the art of Damascene (inlaying gold and silver into specially forged steel).

Ghirardelli Soda Fountain & Chocolate Shop You can smell the chocolate when you walk in for a free sample. There are plenty of chocolate souvenirs, but treat yourself to their "world-famous" hot-fudge sundae, with the decadent hot fudge made daily at the shop. The line for ice cream usually winds out the door.

Harrington Bay Clothiers Another longtime Marketplace tenant, this clothing shop used to carry only men's clothing but now has a section for women. Brands include Ralph Lauren, Tommy Hilfiger, and Tommy Bahama. Great sales on occasion, but otherwise no bargains.

Generation BeneFits Junior clothing for young men and women with brands such as Tommy Hilfiger, Calvin Klein, Roxy, Quicksilver, and Hana.

Pooh Corner Winnie the Pooh merchandise, with everything from housewares to clothing, stationery, mugs, and more—all Pooh.

Team Mickey's Athletic Club From soccer to basketball to golf, this shop features sports apparel. Much of it sports Mickey Mouse and Goofy logos, but there's a decent selection of Nike sportswear and tennis shoes as well.

Pleasure Island

It's best known for its nightclubs, but the shops are open daily from 10:30 a.m. to 2 a.m. We don't recommend stopping to shop; the half dozen or so small stores carry mostly Disney and Pleasure Island logo merchandise or ordinary goods. After 7 p.m. you must pay a cover charge to enter because of the nightclubs and street entertainment. One mildly interesting shop is **Reel Finds,** with autographed prints of film and TV stars: a Brad Pitt photo goes for $310, while a signed photo of Oprah Winfrey is just $195.

Disney's West Side

The West Side is open every day, 11 a.m.–1 a.m. This is the hip new extension of the Marketplace and Pleasure Island, with shops that are full of fun chotchkes for compulsive buyers. Virgin Megastore towers above the smaller shops that line the walkway between Pleasure Island and the West Side.

Top Shops on Disney's West Side

★ **Virgin Megastore** The biggest hit is this giant record/CD/video/book store, with more than 150,000 music titles on CD and cassette and 300 listening stations for previewing CDs. A separate classical room features more than 20,000 titles. Music and movie titles on video, laserdisc, and DVD number 20,000, including new releases, classics, international films, and documentaries.

Candy Cauldron   Watch them make gooey treats in the open kitchen. You can buy everything from jellybeans to caramel apples and cotton candy—more than 200 sweets are on the shelves.

Celebrity Eyeworks   You'll find trendy sunglasses, designer eyeglasses, and displays that show the film and TV stars who wear them at this shop. A solid selection—Revo, Oakely, Gucci, Calvin Klein, Donna Karan, Harley Davidson—but you pay top price, up to $1,000 for a pair of Boucherons.

★ **Guitar Gallery**   More than 150 custom, collector, and rare guitars and accessories line the walls in this tiny shop tucked between the giant Virgin Megastore and the AMC 24 Theatres. Prices range from $199 for a beginner electric guitar to $25,000 for a Jimmie Rodger Limited Edition. The guitar-shaped checkout counter is inlaid with mother of pearl.

★ **Hoypoloi**   Not a set of mouse ears in sight but one of our favorite shops, with one-of-a-kind pieces of art from various regions of the United States—Zen water fountains, contemporary art glass, and wooden boxes. To give you a better sense of the merchandise, one of their signature items is a red incense coil from an eighteenth-century Japanese incense maker.

Magnetron   You've got to see this place to believe the funky collection of 20,000 magnets lining the steel walls—magnets that talk, sing, ring, beep, light up, and glow in the dark. Kids love it, and souvenirs are pretty cheap.

Sosa Family Cigars   They hand roll 'em here and feature great imports, including Arturo Fuente, Cuesta Rey, Diamond Crown, La Gloria Cubana, Macanudo, Puros Indios, Padron, Partagas, and Sosa. A walk-in humidor stores the top brands.

THEME PARK SHOPS WITH THE BEST DISNEY STUFF

Magic Kingdom

Main Street	Emporium (largest selection at Magic Kingdom)
Tomorrowland	Mickey's Star Traders

Epcot

Future World	Mouse Gear (largest selection at Epcot)
World Showcase	Disney Traders (left side of Showcase Plaza)

Disney-MGM Studios

Hollywood Boulevard	Mickey's of Hollywood

THEME PARK SHOPS WITH THE BEST DISNEY STUFF (continued)

Disney-MGM Studios *(continued)*

Sunset Boulevard	Once Upon a Time
Studio Courtyard	Animation Gallery

Animal Kingdom

Safari Village	Island Mercantile
	Wonders of the Wild

Epcot

We enjoy wandering in and out of the shops in the 11 World Showcase pavilions, looking for unusual finds and bargains. Often you will see sale items, especially in the shops in France and Italy, but most of the imported merchandise is relatively expensive. However, the Epcot shops may be the only place in the United States that carries some lines of merchandise.

Aside from the World Showcase, two stores in Future World are worth a mention: **Mouse Gear** (the old Centorium) on the east side of Future World is the biggest Disney shop in any of the four theme parks. You can find almost any Disney merchandise here, and there is a substantial selection of adult and children's clothing. Prices are the same as at other Disney merchandise shops. On the other side of Future World is **The Art of Disney Epcot Gallery,** featuring animation production cels, hand-painted cels, character models, and more.

Walking clockwise around the World Showcase, here's what you'll find:

★ **Mexico** Let your eyes adjust to the dim light in the **Plaza De Los Amigos,** a lovely re-creation of a charming Mexican city at dusk, where a live mariachi band often entertains passersby. Carts are piled with blankets, sombreros, paper flowers, tambourines, and straw bags. Sure, the merchandise may be cheaper south of the border, but these prices aren't bad: piñatas are wildly popular at $8–$10; kids' straw hats are $4.50; and straw bags cost $12, while blankets are $18–$30. Around the perimeter, smaller shops offer higher-priced merchandise, including clay pots, margarita glasses, and elegant silver frames, all imported.

★ **Norway** **The Puffin's Roost** is a series of small shopping galleries with popular imports such as an entire room of trolls (from $20) and wooden Christmas ornaments (the tiny straw ones are just $2.50). Other hard-to-find imports include Laila perfume and body lotion and Helly Hansen outerwear. And the Norway pavilion is the exclusive U.S. importer of Dale of Norway clothing, including thick woolen sweaters (around $240) and pricey but everlasting toboggans. You'll also find pewter, glass, porcelain, and a limited selection of LEGOs.

★ **China** China features one of our favorite shops, piled with imports from real silk kimonos to cloisonné and thick silk rugs. **Yong Feng Shangdian** is more like a rambling department store than a shop. You'll find everything here from silk fans to $4,000 jade sculptures to antique furniture. The silk dresses and robes are competitively priced in the $100 range. Darling handbags are $25, and slippers are $10. We always admire the handwoven pure silk carpets, starting at a reasonable $240 for a two-by-four-foot rug and topping out around $2,500 for an eight-by-ten-foot rug. Carpet prices are comparable to what you would pay in a retail shop—if you could find one that imports them. Kids love rummaging through the toy bins in the covered outdoor area, where you also can get your name written in Chinese on a fan for about $4.

Village Traders, a shop between China and Germany, sells Kenyan woodcarvings for about the same price you would pay at the carving center in Mombasa where they're made.

★ **Germany** Eight small shops interconnect on both sides of the cobblestone central plaza and provide an impressive collection of imports. The tiny **Das Kaufhaus** stocks hundreds of limited-edition steins and glassware. Next door is **Volkskunst,** where the walls are covered with Schneider cuckoo clocks—one of the largest collections in the United States. Prices start at $28, and the largest floor model in stock was a whopping $6,000. Next is **Der Teddybär,** with lifelike dolls, including Engel Puppe dolls (create your own and watch it made for $120), imported porcelain dolls, and Steiff plush toys. Across the plaza, **Kunstarbeit in Kristall** carries a fabulous collection of Swarovski, including pins, earrings, necklaces, bracelets, and a $400 tiara. Next is **Süssigkeiten,** full of imported sweets from Gummy Bears to spicy *Lebkuchen* (crisp German Christmas cookies). The **Weinkeller** adjoins Süssigkeiten, with nearly 300 varieties of German wine from the vineyards of H. Schmitt Söhne. You can purchase a bottle of the hard-to-find *Eiswein,* at $48 the most expensive bottle in the shop. Step through the door to **Die Weihnachts Ecke,** where Christmas ornaments and handmade nutcrackers are on display year-round. The beautiful nutcrackers start at $14 and go all the way to $250 for an elaborate set called The Three Kings. Last stop is **Glas Und Porzellan,** showcasing Goebel glass and porcelain objects. You'll often find a German artist painting the delicate M.I. Hummel figurines, which start at $68 for a tiny version and range up to $24,000 for a giant "Apple Tree Girl and Apple Tree Boy" creation.

★ **Italy** **Il Bel Cristallo** showcases Venetian glass and porcelain figurines and recently added Giuseppe Armani figurines from Florence, including the limited-edition Nativity for $1,100. In the front of the shop is a beautiful collection of handbags in the $150 range, handmade silk ties for a reasonable $29, and silk scarves for $44. Across the walkway is **Delizie Italiane,** a gourmet shop with Perugina chocolates, and **La Cucina Italiana,** with gourmet foods, cookware, and wine. Nothing spectacular, but a solid selection of imports.

American Adventure   The **Heritage Manor Gifts** shop is a huge disappointment, with hand-crafted souvenirs and lots of American flag–inspired clothing. They have a small collection of books on American history, but it's not worth the footsteps.

★ **Japan**   A U.S. branch of Japan's 300-year-old **Mitsukoshi Department Store** stretches along one entire side of the pavilion. They had just one silk kimono in stock when we visited ($255) but a vast array of polyester robes ($59). We preferred the 100% cotton version for $69. You'll find Shiseido soaps and body lotions, a sizable collection of Pokemon paraphernalia, sushi and tea sets, and bonsai. At the back of the store is a fabulous case of pricey Mikimoto pearls (rings, necklaces, bracelets, and earrings), Seiko watches, and trendy G-Shock watches. No bargains here, but cool stuff. And tourists line up to pay for any oyster guaranteed to have a pearl in its belly. The saleswoman opens the bi-valve and polishes your pearl for a mere $14.15 (plus tax).

★ **Morocco**   How about an imported two-by-four-foot rug for just $25? That's the asking price in **Casablanca Carpets,** where Berber carpets, colorful Rabat carpets, prayer rugs, and throw pillows are piled in the tiny gallery. The $25 version is machine made; you'll pay $300–$500 for the real deal, handwoven. Across the street, three shops wend through the pavilion: **Tangier Traders** offers woven belts, leather sandals, purses, and fezzes; **Marketplace in the Median** has straw hats, sheepskin wallets, and bags; and **The Brass Bazaar** features brass, of course, and inexpensive ceramic kitchenware (not dishwasher safe). We like the bottles of refreshing rosewater for $7.

★ **France**   A longtime favorite. We always find a few moments to browse in **Plume et Palette,** now a perfume shop with more than 100 imports and the exclusive U.S. importer of St. Dupont Paris. You'll also find Chanel, Christian Dior, Jean Patou, and Cabotine de Grès. Take a minute to admire the sweet collection of fabulous Limoges boxes, all in the $200 range. Across the shaded walkway is **La Signature,** the Guerlain cosmetics and fragrance shop, with a wide selection of lipsticks, makeup, and perfumes. Cross over to **Les Vins de France** and **L'Esprit de la Provence,** two stores in one, with a wine room and a broad selection of Provençal goods. The wine is Barton and Guestier; you won't find any bargains, but they carry Chef Roger Verge's 1998 rosé Provence vintage (the wine he serves in his restaurant in the south of France) for just $11.95. In

La Provence, the hand-painted Santon dolls are a bargain at $35. Beautiful candles, dishes, cookbooks, vinegars, mustards, and more all come from Provence. You'll pay top price, but the indulgence is worth it.

★ **United Kingdom** A handful of interesting imports are scattered throughout a half dozen small shops. Breeze through the **Toy Soldier,** where the selection is pretty much limited to uninteresting Winnie the Pooh merchandise, but stop in **The Crown & Crest** to look up your family name in the coat of arms book—they will create your family's insignia on paper. You'll also find dart boards, limited-edition chess sets, and Locharron of Scotland wool tartans, including the Princess Di memorial tartan for $40. Next is **Pringle of Scotland,** but you won't find sweaters on the shelves anymore; according to the Irish saleswoman, Pringle is no longer making lamb's wool and cashmere sweaters, socks, hats, ties, and mittens. Instead, the shop carries exclusive and costly Wimbledon togs.

Across the street, **The Queen's Table** once carried a large collection of china but is now limited to perfumes, soaps, and powders from Woods of Windsor, Taylor of London, and Bronnley. Next door is **The Magic of Wales,** a quaint shop with exquisite tea sets, including Scottish thistle ($30 per cup and saucer), and the English dog rose. **The Tea Caddy** stocks English tea, including Fortnum & Mason and Twinings, and biscuits and candies.

★ **Canada** There's not much shopping here, but the popular new **Roots** boutique in **Northwest Mercantile** has a wide selection of merchandise, including caps, jackets, T-shirts, boots, clogs, and backpacks. There are just 12 Roots stores in the United States, and this is the only one on the East Coast. And we like the pure maple syrup, just $2.95 for a small bottle (enough for one serving of pancakes). Bigger bottles, up to $25, are stocked, too.

Beyond Epcot, shopping is hit-or-miss in the other three theme parks. You'll find the same basic Disney merchandise everywhere, with specialty items for each park tossed in. However, there are still some unusual shops amid all the Disney goods.

Disney-MGM Studios

On Hollywood Boulevard just to the left of the park entrance is a California mission–style house called ★ **Sid Cahuenga's One-of-a-Kind,** which is loosely inspired by junk shops in southern California, the land of movie stars. You'll find plenty of autographed photos of film and TV stars, old movie posters, even Elvis Presley's silver tie tack for $1,100. Nothing is cheap.

Other fun shops on the right side of the street include: **Celebrity 5 & 10,** with Disney-MGM Studios merchandise (lots of inexpensive souvenirs); **The Darkroom,** for Kodak cameras, including disposable ones, film, and accessories; and **L.A. Cinema Storage,** full of kid's clothing, PJ's, and items inspired by recent Disney film releases. Across the boulevard, **Keystone Clothiers** carries an array of Disney clothes for grown-ups, while the adjacent **Mickey's of Hollywood** carries plush toys, watches, more T-shirts, hats, sunglasses, and more—virtually nothing without a Disney logo. There's plenty to look at but not much to recommend.

On Sunset Boulevard, you'll find more Disney logos in **Legends of Hollywood,** a Winnie the Pooh–themed store and the best stop at Disney-MGM for Pooh collectors, and **Mouse about Town,** with men's apparel, including golf-themed accessories. **Villains in Vogue** features merchandise themed to the villains of Disney films, like Cruella de Vil and Malificent (who buys this stuff?). Disney-themed housewares and gifts are in **Once Upon a Time,** next to the **Planet Hollywood Superstore.** In **Sunset Club Couture** there's a sizable stock of Disney jewelry and scads of watches, as well as an artist on standby to personalize character watches—you choose the face you want from a selection of art and they create it in miniature.

Elsewhere in the park: ★ **Animation Gallery** in the Animation Building has an impressive collection of cels and other collectibles. You'll pay the same price here as in all the other Disney art galleries. **It's a Wonderful Shop,** near Jim Henson's MuppetVision 3D theater, features Christmas decoration year-round; it's the same merchandise on a smaller scale that's found in the Christmas shops throughout Disney World. You can pick up a decent leather hat ($48) just like Harrison Ford's at the **Indiana Jones Adventure Outpost** outside the amphitheater. **In Character,** next to *Voyage of the Little Mermaid,* is the best spot in this park for Disney dress-up clothes for little ones.

Disney's Animal Kingdom

Though Disney merchandise again dominates, the newest Disney theme park has a fair array of animal-themed items. Most shops are in the centrally located Discovery Island: **Beastly Bazaar** features cute straw safari hats with Mickey, Pluto, or Winnie the Pooh ears, stuffed Disney toys in safari garb, and Animal Kingdom watches; **Wonders of the Wild** has men's and women's clothes and jewelry and popular Tree of Life souvenirs; and **Island Mercantile** offers more (yawn) Disney character merchandise. **Creature Comforts** is the stop for children's clothing and toys

In Africa ★ **Mombasa Marketplace** showcases reasonably priced African-themed pottery, musical instruments, and masks. Often you'll find an artisan from Kenya carving walking sticks on the front porch. From there, if you catch the train to Conservation Station, stop just outside the exit at **Out of the Wild,** featuring an array of conservation-themed souvenirs—books, toys, hats, and more.

The newest land at Animal Kingdom, Asia, has only open-air kiosks, where we found beautiful Bridge to Bali sarongs in one-of-a-kind batik patterns for just $20. Also for sale were incense burners, bamboo wind chimes, and paper lamp covers, nicely themed but all easy to pass by.

Our hands-down favorite at the Animal Kingdom is ★ **Chester & Hester's Dinosaur Treasures** in DinoLand U.S.A., inspired by kitschy roadside attractions from the 1950s and 1960s. It's worth a look just to check out the amusing architecture. Chances are you'll find an appropriate Animal Kingdom souvenir—hand-puppet dinosaurs, T-shirts, you name it.

The Magic Kingdom

Bypass the Magic Kingdom shops if you're on a one-day visit. If you have two or more days, browse the shops in early afternoon when many of the attractions are crowded. Store your purchases in lockers at the Main Street rail station while you tour or have them forwarded from shops to Parcel Pick-up and retrieve them when you leave the park.

Much of the non-Disney merchandise that was once available in the Magic Kingdom has disappeared from the shelves. For instance, longtime visitors may remember Liberty Square's Olde World Antiques with unique brass, silver, and pewter, but today it's a shop full of Disney Christmas ornaments. Or remember when the Yankee Trader stocked soufflé dishes and escargot holders? Now it's all Mickey Mouse kitchenware.

Main Street, U.S.A.   Since Main Street, U.S.A., stays open one hour after official park closing, you could save your shopping time until the end of the day. Sixteen shops line the street, but only two are of note: If you want a monogrammed mouse ears hat, ★ **The Chapeau** on Main Street is the only place at Walt Disney World to purchase it (there is a hat shop at the Studios, but there you pay extra for the monogramming); at the **Emporium,** the Disney superstore, you can basically count on one-stop shopping if time is of the essence.

Fun for browsing are the **Main Street Market House,** featuring kitchenware; **Crystal Arts,** where the glassblower entertains and the glass and crystal merchandise is similar to that at EUROSPAIN at Downtown Disney Marketplace; and the **Main Street Confectionary,** which occupies prime real estate on the corner of Town Square and is the biggest candy shop in all four theme parks, with every sweet imaginable and employees making fudge and candy apples. For clothes, try **Disney & Co., Main Street Athletic Club,** and **Disney Clothiers,** offering Disney apparel for all ages. For expensive baubles and watches, check out **Uptown Jewelers.** Fans of *101 Dalmatians* might want to check out **The Firehouse Gift Station** next to Town Hall for souvenirs inspired by the film. For animation cels and Disney collectibles, try the **Main Street Gallery.**

For interactive spending, let the artist at **The Shadow Box** snip your silhouette out of black paper or stop in the **Harmony Barber Shop** for a trim—it's open daily 9 a.m.–5 p.m. no reservations necessary. Lots of parents bring babies here for their first haircut.

Adventureland The new **Agrabah Bazaar,** across from Aladdin's Magic Carpet Ride, was not open at press time but will feature Middle Eastern clothes and costumes. Near Pirates of the Caribbean, **House of Treasure** carries replicas of famous ships, ships to build in a bottle, and pirate costumes. The adjoining **Plaza Del Sol Caribe Bazaar** has an ample selection of women's sundresses, straw hats, and bags (to us, it's a somewhat odd place to sell women's clothing).

Frontierland Children gravitate to the cowboy hats, feathered head-dresses, moccasins, sheriff's badges, and other play stuff in the **Frontier Trading Post.** The Trading Post also stocks authentic white Stetson hats for $85.

Liberty Square ★ **Heritage House** has a collection of framed photos and autographs worth checking out—Ronald Reagan ($685), Dwight D. Eisenhower ($1,200), and Abraham Lincoln ($14,000). Or you can buy a flag from all 50 states for just $1.95. **Ye Old Christmas Shoppe** is a repeat of the holiday shops in all the other Disney parks. **Yankee Trader,** before an interesting kitchen shop full of gadgets and gizmos, now carries Mickey Mouse–themed kitchenware. Cute, but it's the same everywhere.

Fantasyland Shops are themed to the attractions, like **Pooh's Thotful Shop** at The Many Adventures of Winnie the Pooh and **Seven Dwarfs Mine** near Snow White's Adventures. A favorite for little girls is ★ **Tinker Bell's Treasures,** with a large selection of frilly costumes—Belle, Snow White, Cinderella, and others. **The King's Gallery** in Cinderella Castle offers an odd assortment of knight-wear, swords, and shields; it's one of the old-time shops that has not changed much over the years.

Mickey's Toontown Fair **County Bounty** is a good place to load up on kid souvenirs.

Tomorrowland The sci-fi stock in **Merchant of Venus** has been significantly reduced, but they still carry some campy items like glitter lava lamps. However, it's mostly a Tomorrowland souvenir shop, along with adjacent **Mickey's Star Traders,** and both are usually packed with teenagers. Neither is worth a stop unless you're killing time.

Walt Disney World Resorts

Every Disney hotel has gift shops and themed shopping, with specially created Disney merchandise. The Grand Floridian, for instance, sells the thick terrycloth robes you find in the rooms, and Wilderness Lodge and Villas has a line of Wilderness Lodge clothing. The general Disney merchandise is the same at all hotels, and prices do not vary.

Following are some shops worth a stop. We have not mentioned every shop in every resort, only those with something unusual to offer beyond the standard Disney merchandise.

Disney's Grand Floridian Resort & Spa   The best shoe store at Disney is high-priced ★ **Bally of Switzerland** on the second floor. **Commander Porter's** shop for men and women carries Polo Ralph Lauren, Tommy Hilfiger, golf wear, and even cigars and lighters.

Disney's Polynesian Resort   If you're looking for swimwear or casual clothes, there are two high-quality shops here: **Robinson Crusoe Esq.** for men, with Nautica and Reyn Spooner lines, and the **Polynesian Princess** for women, featuring Liz Claiborne designs among others.

Disney's BoardWalk Resort   Shopping could be better here; there's nothing out of the ordinary—Disney souvenirs, a handful of bathing suits. One shop worth a stop is **Wyland Galleries,** featuring environmental art that depicts marine animals in their natural setting. The graceful sculptures of dolphins are breathtaking.

Disney's Contemporary Resort   The fourth floor is a good one-stop shopping destination. For souvenirs, **Fantasia** carries a solid selection, including children's clothing and toys. Across the concourse, **Contemporary Woman** and **Contemporary Man** shops adjoin, with a surprisingly good choice of styles, including plenty of women's bathing suits. You'll often find good sales on clothing here. And the nearby **Kingdom Jewels Ltd.** carries high-end trinkets, both Disney and non-Disney items.

Disney's Wilderness Lodge and Villas Resort   **Wilderness Lodge Mercantile** is a general catch-all shop, with sundries, souvenirs, and even a substantial line of Wilderness Lodge outdoor clothing. But we always find something fun in the little corner devoted to non-Disney items— scented pine cones for the fireplace, hand-rolled candles, and such. Merchandise changes frequently.

Disney's Yacht & Beach Club Resort   The Yacht Club has **Fittings & Fairings Clothes and Notions,** offering souvenirs and a limited selection of casual men's and women's clothing. At the Beach Club, **Atlantic Wear and Wardrobe Emporium** carries more casual clothing and racks of bathing suits. Both are expensive.

Disney's Caribbean Beach Resort   We're not sure we'd make the trip to shop here, but the spacious **Calypso Straw Market** has fun casual wear for women and plenty of bathing suits.

Walt Disney World Dolphin   Cartier watches and other expensive gems are showcased in **Brittany Jewels.** A small clothing store, **Statements of Fashion,** carries high-end clothing for men and women.

Disney Water Parks

All three water parks—Typhoon Lagoon, Blizzard Beach, and River Country—have shops for sunning essentials like bathing suits, hats, towels, sunscreen, sandals, beach chairs, sunglasses, and film. Nothing is cheap.

Disney Outlet Stores

On International Drive at Belz Factory Outlet Mall and on State Route 535 in the Lake Buena Vista Factory Stores, you can find marked down Disney goods, but the selection is limited. Disney Beanies, for instance, were just $1.99 ($5.95 at Disney), but the selection was Sneezy, the Genie from *Aladdin,* and Pete's Dragon—none of the prized Disney characters. T-shirts were in the $7 range, and sweatshirts cost around $13. And in between the markdowns was full-priced merchandise, so beware. If you're not picky, you can round up a fair number of souvenirs. Both stores are owned by one company, so stock is comparable. The Belz store is slightly larger, but when we visited the shop at the Lake Buena Vista Factory Stores had supplemented space with a giant outdoor tent sale, which they often do.

A Kentucky family had a hard time getting to the Belz Outlet, warning:

> *Avoid International Drive between the BeeLine Expressway and Oak Ridge Road. After crawling for what seemed like an hour, we reached the Belz Outlet Stores. We were grinding our teeth at the congestion. Take Interstate 4 directly to the Oak Ridge Road exit. It's much faster. PS: Belz Outlet Stores had some great buys on Disney stuff. Worth the trip.*

Shopping beyond Walt Disney World

Celebration

The "town that Disney built" near Walt Disney World on US 192 gets its fair share of tourists who like to stroll in this town that is home to about 600 people. No one shop is worth going out of the way for, but there are three good restaurants (Italian, Cuban, and American), a two-screen theater, and a handful of shops. Because Celebration is an upscale community with homes that cost upwards of $150,000, the shops are all high-end.

You can purchase fresh coffee beans at **Barnie's Coffee & Tea,** where Celebration residents often gather on the patio for a freshly brewed cup. Specialty stores include: **Chambers Jewelers; Downeast Orvis; Market Street Gallery,** with greeting cards, candles, and gifts for the home; **Soft as a Grape,** with casual clothing for the whole family; **Village Mercantile,** with men's and women's clothing; **White's Books & Gifts,** with a solid selection of hardbacks and paperbacks as well as newspapers, magazines, and gifts; **Jerard's,** with gifts and home accessories; and **Wyland Galleries,** with the art of Wyland, a noted marine-life artist, including prints, sculpture, glass, and furniture (similar to the gallery at Disney's BoardWalk Resort).

Most shops are open Monday–Saturday, 10 a.m.–9 p.m. Also on Main Street is a **Gooding's** grocery store that is much smaller than most of their other central Florida stores. Even Celebration residents don't do their regular shopping here but rather use it for impulse buying or lunch items from the deli.

CityWalk

While Downtown Disney is 120 acres (with a strolling area equivalent to about ten city blocks), CityWalk is 30 acres in a relatively compact area between the two Universal theme parks. Downtown Disney has about 32 shops, and CityWalk features 13.

At both destinations, the shopping complements the restaurants and clubs. Without question, Disneyphiles will prefer Downtown Disney where at least a third of the shops are Disney themed. CityWalk is most comparable to the West Side at Downtown Disney, and though the 66-acre West Side is more than twice the size, there are actually a few more shops at CityWalk, covering a broader spectrum of merchandise than the West Side. Nearly all of the CityWalk shops are clustered in front of the Universal Cineplex.

Shop hours at CityWalk are 11 a.m.–11 p.m. Parking is plentiful in the Universal Studios' garage; it's a steep $7 before 6 p.m. but free in the evening.

CityWalk shops are fun for browsing and impulse buys. Our favorites include: **Dapy** and **Glow!** for trendy gifts; **Endangered Species,** with merchandise from T-shirts to jewelry to housewares designed to "raise awareness of the plight of endangered species, ecosystems, and cultures worldwide"; **Fresh Produce Sportswear** for colorfully designed clothes for men, women, and children; **Cigarz at CityWalk,** with hand-rolled cigars, cordials, malt scotches, and coffees; **Quiet Flight** for cool customized surfboards and beachwear; **Captain Crackers,** a favorite for kids with moving animals and funny toys; and **All Star Collectibles,** where sports fans can find team collectibles, videos, and other sports-related merchandise.

For jewelry, **Fossil** has a notable collection of Fossil brand watches (also sunglasses and leather goods), **Silver** showcases silver jewelry for men and women, and **Elegant Illusions** sells reasonably priced imitations of expensive designer jewelry.

The **Universal Studios Store** offers one-stop shopping for all theme-park merchandise, from Woody Woodpecker to *Jurassic Park.*

International Drive

"I Drive" is the heart of central Florida's tourist district, jammed with hotels, motels, discount stores, and cheap restaurants. Locals generally avoid the area except for the outlet malls (which we will discuss separately). Two shopping malls on the newer, more refined south end of the street are worth a look if you're staying on International Drive or nearby.

The Mercado at 8445 International Drive has 60 specialty shops, including 6 apparel shops, 6 jewelry and collectibles stores, and 20 specialty shops, selling candles, kites, toys, electronics, cigars, and coffee. It's a pleasant walk from many I-Drive hotels. And there are nine restaurants and the *Titanic* Ship of Dreams attraction that tells the story of the famous ship. Merchandise is mostly costly trinkets, so it's not worth a drive out of your way (unless you're a *Titanic* fan). Open seven days a week, 10 a.m.–10 p.m.

Also on the south end of the street at 9101 International Drive is **Pointe*Orlando,** with more than 60 stores. This 17-acre center gets a lot of its business from the convention center, located less than a mile away, rather than from the locals. Hours are Sunday–Thursday, 10 a.m.–10 p.m.; Friday and Saturday, 10 a.m.–11 p.m.

Clothing stores at Pointe*Orlando include: **Tommy Jeans; Boardwalk Surf & Sport,** carrying Billabong, No Fear, O'Neill, Rip Curl, and Quicksilver; **Abercrombie & Fitch; Everthing But Water,** with an excellent selection of bathing suits; **Banana Republic; A/X Armani Exchange; Disney Worldport; Gap; Speedo; Players Golf,** with Tommy Hilfiger, Greg Norman, Bobby Jones, and Tommy Bahama fashions; and **Victoria's Secret.**

Among specialty shops are **FAO Schwarz** toy store; **Eyetems,** featuring Cartier, Hilfiger, and Calvin Klein frames; **Art's Original Cigar Factory; Dapy;** and **Bath and Body Works.** Pointe*Orlando prices are full retail, but there are always sales.

Outlets

Like every major tourist destination in the United States, central Florida has hundreds of factory outlets, and most are near major attractions. We spent many hours checking prices and merchandise and can generally conclude that in most of the stores you will save about 20% on desirable merchandise and up to 75% on last-season (or older) stock. Some stores in the outlet malls are full retail or sell a few brands at a 20% discount and the rest at full price. If you're picky, you often can do just as well or better at a major department store's end-of-season sales.

The granddaddy of outlet shopping in Orlando is still one of the best: **Belz Factory Outlet World** and **Belz Designer Outlet Centre,** both just off the north end of International Drive. The two comprise the largest of the outlet centers—160 name-brand stores. This is where the locals head for bargains.

★ **Belz Factory Outlet World,** the largest center of its kind in the United States, is at 5401 West Oakridge Road and includes 185 stores in two separate malls and four annexes. Hours are Monday–Saturday, 10 a.m.–9 p.m.; Sunday, 10 a.m.–6 p.m. Major stores include **Anne Klein, Bugle Boy, Danskin, Etienne Aigner, The Gap, Guess, Jockey, Levi's, Mikasa, Nike, Oneida, Olga Warner,** and **Reebok.** Again, shop carefully. We found some great buys on current merchandise in The Gap, but meager reductions on the top-of-the-line Nike shoes.

Just around the corner is ★ **Belz Designer Outlet Center** at 5401 West Oakridge Road. Hours are Monday–Saturday, 10 a.m.–9 p.m.; Sunday, 11 a.m.–6 p.m. If you only have time to shop one outlet center, this is the one we prefer, mainly for the great buys at **Off 5th**—the Saks Fifth Avenue outlet. If you're lucky enough to be in town during a sale, the overstuffed racks in the big store offer some great bargains, with designer togs and shoes for up to 75% off. Also in this center are **Coach, Donna Karan, Jones New York, Ann Taylor Loft, Cole Haan, Kenneth Cole,** and **Waterford/Wedgwood.**

The Belz folks are planning to open a third center, **Festival Bay,** nearby on International Drive. The mall will have 1.1 million square feet of shops, but at press time only **Bass Pro Shops Outdoor World** was open.

Another popular outlet is **Lake Buena Vista Factory Stores** on State Route 535 near Disney World (take Exit 68 off I-4, then go two miles south on SR 535). Hours are Monday–Saturday, 10 a.m.–9 p.m.; Sunday, 10 a.m.–6 p.m. We were a little disappointed in the inventory, and the discounts were in the 10–20% range. (We can find scads of markdowns in retail stores that are comparable.) This center has one of the discount Disney merchandise shops, **Character Corner,** but you can't be too choosy about souvenirs if you shop here. Other key tenants include **Adidas, Gap, Liz Claiborne, Nine West, Oshkosh B'Gosh Superstore,** and **Reebok.**

Newcomer ★ **Orlando Premium Outlets** is setting new standards for outlet shopping, with 110 shops at Vineland Avenue off I-4 at Exit 68 near Lake Buena Vista (open Monday–Saturday, 10 a.m.–11 p.m.; Sunday, 10 a.m.–9 p.m.). An impressive array of shops includes **Banana**

Republic, Barneys New York, Brooks Brothers, DKNY, Escada, Fubu, Giorgio Armani, Louis Feraud, Nautica, Nike, Polo Ralph Lauren, TSE, and **Versace.** You'll also find **Disney's Character Premiere,** with plenty of Disney merchandise, and a food court with numerous fast-food options.

Stand-alone outlet stores we like: **Dansk Factory Outlet** at 5247 International Drive (open Monday–Saturday, 10 a.m.–9 p.m.; Sunday, 11 a.m.–6 p.m.), with Dansk's distinguished dinnerware, teakwood, glassware, and gifts; **Edwin Watts Golf Shop** at 7024 International Drive (open Monday–Friday, 9:30 a.m.–8 p.m.; Saturday, 9:30 a.m.–6 p.m.; Sunday, noon–5 p.m.); **Lenox Factory Store** at 5265 International Drive (open Monday–Saturday, 10 a.m.–9 p.m.; Sunday, 10 a.m.–6 p.m.), with savings on discontinued china and crystal; and the **Great Western Boot Outlet** at 5597 International Drive, carrying Nocona, Stetson, Wrangler, and other brands.

Traditional Shopping

We're told that next to Disney World, more tourists visit ★ **Florida Mall** than any other central Florida destination—one of the reasons it offers currency exchange and foreign language assistance. It's the biggest mall in the area with 200 shops, so it's best to go early in the morning and park near one of the major department stores you want to check out.

It's located at 8001 South Orange Blossom Trail (at the corner of Sand Lake Road, SR 482, and South Orange Blossom Trail, US 441), and hours are Monday–Saturday, 10 a.m.–9:30 p.m.; Sunday, 11 a.m.–6 p.m.

The biggest news was the addition of a new wing in the late 1990s with **Saks Fifth Avenue.** Since then, the expansion has continued with new space for **Restoration Hardware, Brooks Brothers, J. Crew,** and **Pottery Barn. Nordstrom's** recently announced it will open a store there by 2002. The mall is anchored by **Saks, Burdines, Gayfers, Parisian, JC Penney, Dillard's,** and **Sears.**

Another not-to-be-missed shopping destination in central Florida is ★ **Park Avenue** in Winter Park, a small town just north of Orlando. The street, anchored by Rollins College on the south end, is lovely for strolling, window-shopping, and dining, and has a mix of high-end shops. Favorites include **Restoration Hardware, Tuni's** (chic women's apparel), **Be Be's** (trendy children's wear), **Williams-Sonoma, Gap, Jacobson's** (a local department store), **Talbot's, Caswell-Massey, Crabtree & Evelyn, L'Occitane** (French imports), **Timothy's Gallery** (exquisite one-of-a-kind jewelry), and **Birkenstock.** Prices are high, but there are terrific sidewalk sales a few times a year.

If time permits, the **Charles Hosmer Morse Museum of American Art** on the north end of the shopping district has the world's largest collection of Tiffany glass and a wonderful little gift shop.

Most stores open at 10 a.m. but close early, generally by 6 p.m., including weekends. Traffic on the two-lane brick street can be a bear, so avoid driving down Park Avenue; instead, take a side street and search for on-street parking a block or two off the main drag. We also recommend using the new parking garage on the south end of the street.

To get to Park Avenue from the International Drive–WDW–Universal area, take Interstate 4 north, exit at Fairbanks Avenue, and head east. Park Avenue is approximately five miles.

Part Seventeen

Nightlife in and out of Walt Disney World

Walt Disney World at Night

Disney so cleverly contrives to exhaust you during the day that the thought of night activity sends most visitors into shock. Walt Disney World, however, offers much for the hearty and the nocturnal to do in the evenings.

In the Parks

Epcot's major evening event is *IllumiNations,* a laser and fireworks show at World Showcase Lagoon. Show time is listed in the daily entertainment schedule.

In the Magic Kingdom are the popular evening parade(s) and *Fantasy in the Sky* fireworks. Consult the daily entertainment schedule for performances.

On nights when the park is open late, Disney-MGM Studios features a fireworks presentation called Sorcery in the Sky and *Fantasmic!,* a laser, special effects, and water spectacular. The daily entertainment schedule lists times.

At present there is no nighttime entertainment at the Animal Kingdom.

At the Hotels

The Floating Electrical Pageant is a sort of Main Street Electrical Parade on barges. Starring King Neptune and creatures of the sea, the nightly pageant (backed by Handel played on a doozie of a synthesizer), is one of our favorite Disney productions. The first performance of the short but captivating show is at 9 p.m. off the Polynesian Resort docks. From there, it circles around and repeats at the Grand Floridian at 9:15 p.m., heading afterward to Fort Wilderness Campground, Wilderness Lodge and Villas, and the Contemporary Resort.

For something more elaborate, consider a dinner theater. If you want to go honky-tonkin', many lodgings at the Disney Village Hotel Plaza have lively bars.

At Fort Wilderness Campground

The nightly campfire program at Fort Wilderness Campground begins with a sing-along led by Disney characters Chip 'n' Dale and progresses to cartoons and a Disney movie. Only Disney lodging guests may attend. There's no charge.

At Disney's BoardWalk

Jellyrolls at the BoardWalk features dueling pianos and sing-alongs in the image of New Orleans' Pat O' Brien's. The BoardWalk has Disney's first and only brew pub. A sports bar, an upscale dance club, and several restaurants complete the BoardWalk's entertainment mix. Access is by foot from Epcot, by launch from Disney-MGM Studios, and by bus from other Disney World locations.

Taste varies, of course, but the *Unofficial Guide* research team rates Jellyrolls as their personal favorite of all the Disney nightspots, including the clubs at Pleasure Island. It's raucous, upbeat, frequently hilarious, and positively rejuvenating. The piano players are outstanding, and they play nonstop with never a break. Best of all, it's strictly adult.

At Downtown Disney

Pleasure Island   Pleasure Island, Walt Disney World's nighttime entertainment complex, offers eight nightclubs for one admission price. Dance to rock, soul, or country; take in a comedy show; or listen to some jazz. Pleasure Island is in Downtown Disney next to Downtown Disney Marketplace and is accessible from the theme parks and the Transportation and Ticket Center by shuttle bus. For details on Pleasure Island and a touring plan, see pages 719–725.

Downtown Disney Marketplace   It's flog your wallet each night at the Marketplace with shops open until 11:30 p.m.

Disney's West Side   Disney's West Side is a 70-acre shopping, restaurant, and nightlife complex situated to the left of Pleasure Island. Not to be confused with the West End Stage at nearby Pleasure Island, this latest addition to Downtown Disney features a 24-screen AMC movie complex, Disney Quest pay-for-play indoor theme park (see pages 674–677), a permanent showplace for the extraordinary *Cirque du Soleil,* and a 2,000-capacity House of Blues concert hall. Dining options include Planet Holly wood, a 450-seat Cajun restaurant at House of Blues, Wolfgang Puck Cafe (serving gourmet pizza and California fare), and Bongo's (Cuban cuisine), owned by Gloria and Emilio Estefan. The complex can be accessed via Disney buses from most Disney World locations.

House of Blues

Type of Show Live concerts with an emphasis on rock and blues
Tickets and Information (407) 934-2222
Admission Cost with Taxes $8–50, depending on who is performing
Nights of Lowest Attendance Monday and Tuesday
Usual Show Times Monday–Thursday, 8:30; Friday and Saturday, 9:30 **Dark** Sunday

Description and Comments The House of Blues, developed by original Blues Brother Dan Aykroyd, features a restaurant and Blues Bar, as well as the concert hall. The restaurant serves from 11 a.m. until 2 a.m., making it one of the few late-night dining options in Walt Disney World. Live music cranks up every night at 11 p.m. in the restaurant/Blues Bar, but even before then, the joint is way beyond ten decibels. The Music Hall next door features concerts by an eclectic array of musicians and groups. During our last visit, the showbill listed gospel, blues, funk, ska, dance, salsa, rap, zydeco, hard rock, groove rock, and reggae groups over a two-week period.

Touring Tips Prices vary from night to night according to the fame and drawing power of the featured band. Tickets ranged from $7–35 during our visits but go higher when a really big name is scheduled.

The Music Hall is set up like a nightclub, with tables and bar stools for only about 150 people and standing room for a whopping 1,850 people. Folks dance when there's room and sometimes when there isn't. The tables and stools are first-come, first-served, with doors opening an hour before show time on weekdays and 90 minutes before show time on weekends. Acoustics are good, and the showroom is small enough to provide a relatively intimate concert experience. All shows are all ages unless otherwise indicated.

Cirque du Soleil

Type of Show Circus as theater
Tickets and Information (407) 939-7600
Admission Cost with Taxes $71; $41 ages 3–9
Cast Size 72
Night of Lowest Attendance Thursday
Usual Show Times Thursday–Monday, 6 p.m. and 9 p.m.
Smoking Allowed No
Author's Rating ★★★★★
Appeal by Age Group
   Under 21 ★★★★ | 21–37 ★★★★★ | 38–50 ★★★★★ | 51 and up ★★★★½
Duration of Presentation An hour and a half (no intermission)

Description and Comments Cirque du Soleil is a far cry from a traditional circus but retains all the fun and excitement. It is whimsical, mystical, and sophisticated, yet pleasing to all ages. The action takes place on an elaborate stage that incorporates almost every part of the theater. The original musical score is exotic, like the show.

Note: In the following paragraph, we get into how the show *feels* and why it's special. If you don't care how it feels, or if you are not up to slogging through a boxcar of adjectives, the bottom line is simple: *Cirque du Soleil* is great. See it.

Cirque du Soleil is a most difficult show to describe. To categorize it as a circus does not begin to cover its depth, though its performers could perform with distinction in any circus on earth. *Cirque du Soleil* is more, much more than a circus. It combines elements of Classical Greek theater, mime, the English morality play, Dali surrealism, Fellini characterization, and Chaplin comedy. *Cirque du Soleil* is at once an odyssey, a symphony, and an exploration of human emotions. The show pivots on its humor, which is sometimes black, and engages the audience with its unforgettable characters. Though light and uplifting, it is also poignant and dark. Simple in its presentation, it is at the same time extraordinarily intricate, always operating on multiple levels of meaning. As you laugh and watch the amazingly talented cast, you become aware that your mind has entered a dimension seldom encountered in a waking state. The presentation begins to register in your consciousness more as a seamless dream than as a stage production. You are moved, lulled, and soothed as well as excited and entertained. The sensitive, the imaginative, the literate, and those who love good theater and art will find nothing in all of Walt Disney World that compares with *Cirque du Soleil*.

Thus far, as the following comments suggest, we have not received one negative comment about *Cirque du Soleil*.

From a 40-year-old mother of two from Waynesboro, Pennsylvania:

> *Outside the parks, the only thing we did was explore Downtown Disney and go to* Cirque du Soleil *one night. We'd made reservations months in advance. It was absolutely incredible, and I'd recommend it to anyone who doesn't mind the extra $$ outlay.*

From an Iowa City, Iowa, couple:

> *In terms of shows and attractions,* Cirque du Soleil *was absolutely wonderful and anyone with the time should make an attempt to go. I could go on and on about it, but I think just "GO!" is enough.*

From a 40-something mom from Chester, New Hampshire:

> Cirque du Soleil *was spectacular—plan to arrive a half hour early for the preshow.*

From a mother of three from Stafford, Washington:

> Cirque du Soleil *is fantastic. If you go to Disney World and your kids are older than ten you should definitely do this. If it means giving up a day at the park due to the expense,* Cirque du Soleil *is worth it.*

From an Andover, Massachusetts, mother:

> *One of the true highlights of the trip was seeing* Cirque du Soleil. *The ticket prices were a bit steep and I debated doing it. But I thought it might be enjoyable for my non-Disney-loving husband and decided it was no more expensive than the rest of the trip. In fact, we all loved it, and it was the best money we spent.*

Finally, from a Vermont family:

Thank you for singing the praises of Cirque du Soleil. I almost didn't buy tickets, thinking we'd have plenty to do and that there was no need to spend the extra money, but you were right in placing it on a plane of its own. It must be seen to be believed, and our family will never forget it.

Touring Tips   Be forewarned that the audience is an integral part of *Cirque du Soleil* and that at almost any time you might be plucked from your seat to participate. Our advice is to loosen up and roll with it. If you are too rigid, repressed, hungover, or whatever to get involved, politely but firmly decline to be conscripted. Then fix a death grip on the arms of your chair. Tickets for reserved seats can be purchased in advance at the *Cirque's* box office or over the phone using your credit card. Oh yeah, don't wait until the last minute; book well in advance from home.

Walt Disney World Dinner Theaters

Several dinner theater shows play each night at Walt Disney World, and unlike other Disney dining venues, they make hard reservations instead of priority seatings. You must guarantee advance dinner-show reservations with a credit card. You will receive a confirmation number and be told to pick up your tickets at a Disney hotel Guest Services desk. Unless you cancel your tickets at least 48 hours before your reservation time, your credit card will still be charged the full amount. Dinner-show reservations can be made up to two years in advance; call (407) 939-3463. While getting reservations for the *Polynesian Luau* isn't too tough, booking the *Hoop-Dee-Doo Revue* is a trick of the first order. Call as soon as you're certain of the dates of your visit. The earlier you call, the better your seats will be.

A couple from Bismarck, North Dakota, explains:

I'm glad we made our reservations so early (a year in advance). I was able to reserve space for us at the Luau at the Polynesian and the Hoop-Dee-Doo Revue. At both of these, they seat you according to when you made your reservation. At the Hoop-Dee-Doo Revue, we had a front center table. We were so close to the stage, we could see how many cavities the performers had!

If you can't get reservations and want to see one of the shows:

1. Call (407) 939-3463 at 9 a.m. each morning while you're at Disney World to make a same-day reservation. There are three performances each night, and for all three combined, only 3 to 24 people total will be admitted with same-day reservations.

2. Arrive at the show of your choice 45 minutes before show time (early and late shows are your best bets) and put your name on the standby list. If someone with reservations fails to show, you may be admitted.

Hoop-Dee-Doo Revue

Pioneer Hall, Fort Wilderness Campground; (407) 939-3463

Show Times 5, 7:15, and 9:30 p.m. nightly **Cost** $47; $24 ages 3–11.
Discounts Seasonal; American Express discount at 9:30 show only
Type of Seating Tables of various sizes to fit the number in each party, set in an Old West–style dance hall
Menu All-you-can-eat barbecue ribs, fried chicken, corn-on-the-cob, and strawberry shortcake
Vegetarian Alternative On request (at least 24 hours in advance)
Beverages Unlimited beer, wine, sangria, and soft drinks

Description and Comments   Six Wild West performers arrive by stagecoach (sound effects only) to entertain the crowd inside Pioneer Hall. There isn't much plot, just corny jokes interspersed with song or dance.

Given Disney's technical resources and its pool of talented entertainers, the *Hoop-Dee-Doo Revue* is rather amateurish, with decidedly low entertainment value. Jokes are lame and tend to dwell on puns. One marathon of puns using the word "bear" even prompted a six-year-old sitting nearby to shout in exasperation, "Stop saying 'bear.'" Audience participation includes sing-alongs, hand-clapping, and a finale that uses volunteers to play parts onstage. Performers are accompanied by a banjo player and pianist who provide quiet accompaniment while the food is being served.

The fried chicken and corn-on-the-cob are good, but the ribs are a bit tough. With the all-you-can-eat policy, at least you can get your money's worth by stuffing yourself silly. There isn't much value in the show.

While the *Hoop-Dee-Doo Revue* is far from being the best dinner show in the Disney World/Orlando area, traveling to Fort Wilderness and absorbing the rustic atmosphere of Pioneer Hall augments the adventure. For repeat Disney World visitors, an annual visit to the revue is a tradition of sorts. Plus, good or not, the revue is all Disney, and for some folks that's enough. The fact that performances sell out far in advance give the experience a special (if undeserved) aura.

Most of our readers enjoy the *Hoop-Dee-Doo Revue*, but not all. The thoughts of a Texas family are typical:

What is all the hoop-dee-doo with the Hoop-Dee-Doo Revue? *The food was okay, if "gut-busting" fare is your idea of a fine night out, and the entertainment was pleasant. As a dinner theater, however, our family of three found it unexceptional in every respect but its cost. Had your review of the* Revue *tempered its enthusiasm (much as you present its Polynesian counterpart), we probably would have canceled our reservation, pocketed the $100 and spent the evening joyously stunned by another glorious light-and-fireworks spectacle.*

An alternative to the *Hoop-Dee-Doo Revue* is the Fort Liberty show, a non-Disney attraction on FL 192.

If you go to the *Hoop-Dee-Doo Revue*, allow plenty of time to get there. The experience of a reader from Houston, Texas, makes the point:

We had 7:30 p.m. reservations for the Hoop-Dee-Doo Revue, so we left
[Disney-]MGM just before 7 and drove directly to Fort Wilderness. Two
important things to note: First, the road direction signs at WDW are terrible. I would recommend a daylight orientation drive upon arrival, except
that there are so many ways to get confused that one might be lulled into
a false sense of security. Second, when we got to Fort Wilderness, we had
great difficulty determining where Pioneer Hall was and how to get there. I
accosted several people and found a man who could tell us where we were
on the map, and that a bus was the only way to get to Pioneer Hall. I
would recommend leaving for Pioneer Hall one hour before your show
reservations. Boredom is not nearly so painful as anxiety (reservations are
held until 15 minutes after the stated time).

A California dad suggests:

To go to the Hoop-Dee-Doo Revue at Fort Wilderness, take the boat from
the Magic Kingdom rather than any bus. This [is] contrary to the "official"
directions. The boat dock is a short walk from Pioneer Hall [in Fort Wilder-
ness], while the bus goes to the [main] Fort Wilderness parking lot where
one has to transfer to another bus to Pioneer Hall.

Polynesian Luau

Disney's Polynesian Resort; (407) 939-3463

Show Times Tuesday–Saturday, 5:15 and 8 p.m. **Cost** $47; $24 ages 3–11
Discounts Seasonal; American Express discount for all shows
Type of Seating Long rows of tables, with some separation between individual par-
ties. The show is performed on an outdoor stage, but all seating is covered. Ceiling
fans provide some air movement, but it can get warm, especially at the early show.
Menu Tropical fruit, roasted chicken, island pork ribs, shrimp, mixed vegetables, rice,
and pineapple cake; chicken tenders, mini–corn dogs, and mac and cheese are also
available for children
Vegetarian Alternative On request
Beverages Beer, wine, and soft drinks

Description and Comments South Sea–island native dancing follows a
"Polynesian-style," all-you-can-eat meal. The dancing is interesting and largely authentic,
and dancers are attractive though definitely PG in the Disney tradition. We think the
show has its moments and the meal is adequate, but neither is particularly special.

The Polynesian Luau suffers from excruciatingly slow pacing, with long periods with
nothing but recorded background music. After a long intermission, there is a demonstration of island dances preceding a performance by a dancer twirling flaming batons.
All the dancers perform well, but this show becomes a snoozer really early. The show
has more value as a history lesson and is about as interesting. Audience participation
includes learning the hula and yelling "a-LOHHH-ha" a lot.

A well-traveled, married couple from Fond du Lac, Wisconsin, comments:

The Polynesian [Luau] *was a beautiful presentation, better than some shows we have seen in Hawaii! The food, however, lacked in all areas. Better food has come out of Disney kitchens. During our visit, the fruit platter was chintzy, the honey-roasted chicken was a bit fatty, and the pineapple cake was dry.*

Mickey's Backyard Barbecue

Near River Country, Fort Wilderness Campground; (407) 939-3463

Show Times Tuesday and Thursday: 6:30 p.m.   **Cost** $38; $25 ages 3–11
Special Comment Operates from early March through late November
Type of Seating Picnic tables
Menu Baked chicken, barbecued pork ribs, burgers, hotdogs, corn, beans, vegetables, salads and slaw, bread, and watermelon and marble cake for dessert
Vegetarian Alternatives On request
Beverages Unlimited beer, wine, lemonade, and iced tea

Description and Comments   Situated along Bay Lake and held in a covered pavilion next to the River Country swimming park, *Mickey's Backyard Barbecue* features Mickey, Minnie, Chip 'n' Dale, and Goofy, along with a live country band and line dancing. Though the pavilion gets some breeze off Bay Lake, we recommend going during the spring or fall if possible. The food is pretty good, as is, fortunately, the insect control.

Because the barbecue is seasonal, dates are usually not entered into the WDW-DINE reservations system until late February or early March. Once the dates are in the system you can make priority seatings for anytime during the dinner show's nine-month season.

The easiest way to get to the barbecue is to drive and park in the River Country lot. A second alternative is to take a boat from the Magic Kingdom or from one of the resorts on the Magic Kingdom monorail. Though getting to the barbecue is not nearly as effortful as commuting to the *Hoop-Dee-Doo Revue*, give yourself at least 45 minutes if you plan to arrive by boat.

Other Area Dinner Theaters

Central Florida probably has more dinner attractions than anywhere else on earth. The name dinner attraction is something of a misnomer, because dinner is rarely the attraction. These are audience-participation shows or events with food served along the way. They range from extravagant productions where guests sit in arenas at long tables, to intimate settings at individual tables. Don't expect terrific food, but if you're looking for something entertaining outside Walt Disney World, consider one of these.

If you decide to try a non-Disney dinner show, scavenge local tourist magazines from brochure racks and hotel desks outside the World. These free publications usually have discount coupons for area shows.

Pleasure Island

Pleasure Island is a six-acre nighttime entertainment complex on a man-made island in Downtown Disney. It consists of eight nightclubs, restaurants, and shops. A few of the restaurants and shops are open during the day, but the nightclubs don't start opening until 7 p.m. Some of the clubs may not open until 8 p.m. or later, and Pleasure Island doesn't fully come alive until after 9 or even 10 p.m.

Admission Options   One admission (about $20) entitles a guest to enjoy all eight nightclubs. Guests younger than 18 must be accompanied by a parent after 7 p.m. Unlimited eight-day admission to Pleasure Island is included in All-in-One passes.

Alcoholic Beverages   Guests not recognizably older than 21 must provide proof of their age if they wish to buy alcoholic beverages. To avoid repeated checking as the patron club-hops, a color-coded wristband indicates eligibility. All nightclubs serve alcohol. Those under 21, while allowed in all clubs except Mannequins and the BET Soundstage Club, aren't allowed to buy alcoholic beverages. Finally, and gratefully, you don't have to order drinks at all. You can enjoy the entertainment at any club and never buy that first beer. No server will hassle you.

Dress Code   Casual is in, but shirts and shoes are required.

New Variations on an Old Theme   The single-admission nightclub complex was originated in Florida at Orlando's Church Street Station in historic downtown Orlando. Starting fresh, Disney eliminated some problems that haunted Church Street Station and other nightspots over the years.

Good News for the Early-to-Bed Crowd   If you aren't nocturnal or you're tired from a long day in the theme parks, you don't have to wait until midnight for Pleasure Island to hit its stride. All bands, dancers, comedians, and showmen come on like gangbusters early in the evening. Later in the evening as the crowd builds and becomes more lubricated, Pleasure Island assumes the character of a real adult nightspot. During the transition (i.e., after dinner), however, it is not unusual to see a lot of kids in the clubs.

It's Possible to Visit All the Clubs in One Night   Whereas performances in nightclubs elsewhere might be an hour or more in duration, at Pleasure Island shows are shorter but more frequent. This allows guests to move among clubs without missing much. Since you can catch the essence of a club pretty quickly, there's no need to hang around for two or three drinks to see what's going on. This format enables guests to have a complete and satisfying experience in a brief time, then move to another club if they want.

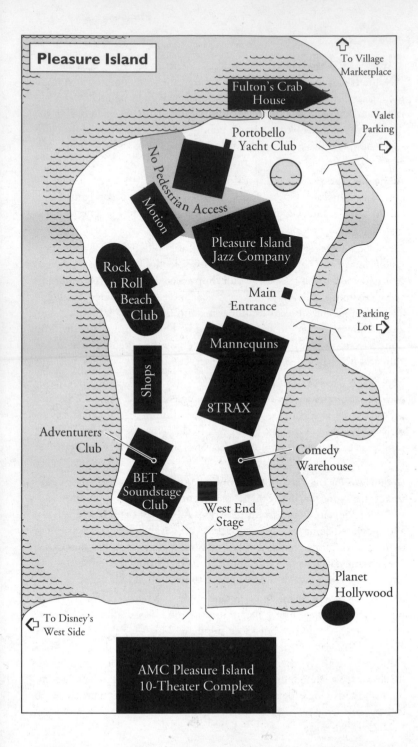

Pleasure Island

To Village Marketplace

Valet Parking

Fulton's Crab House

Portobello Yacht Club

No Pedestrian Access

Motion

Pleasure Island Jazz Company

Rock n Roll Beach Club

Main Entrance

Parking Lot

Mannequins

Shops

8TRAX

Adventurers Club

Comedy Warehouse

BET Soundstage Club

West End Stage

Planet Hollywood

To Disney's West Side

AMC Pleasure Island 10-Theater Complex

The music clubs (Rock n Roll Beach Club, 8TRAX, Motion, BET Soundstage Club, Mannequins Dance Palace, and the Pleasure Island Jazz Company) go nonstop. Sometimes, there are special performances within the ongoing club entertainment. The Adventurers Club and the Comedy Warehouse offer scheduled shows.

We are very high on Pleasure Island. The cover is a little pricey and the drinks aren't cheap, but the entertainment is absolutely top-notch. And if you arrive before 9 p.m., you'll have time to sample all of the clubs, albeit briefly.

A reader reminds us that "sampling" the clubs, as we suggest, isn't the same as spending some time and really appreciating them:

Pleasure Island clubs take much more time to appreciate than you allow. We spent two evenings and only got to four places.

We get considerable mail from couples in their 30s and 40s arguing Pleasure Island's merits (or lack thereof). These quotes are representative.

A reader from Bettendorf, Iowa, writes:

I would not spend the money to go to Pleasure Island again. It is quite obvious that Disney is interested in the 21- to 30-year-old crowd here. There were many people our age (38) and older looking for something to do and not finding it. The Adventurers Club is the only real Disney creation on the island. Walt Disney World crosses all age brackets, and I expected the same from Pleasure Island. What a disappointment! I think you need to go back to the drawing board on your evaluation of Pleasure Island (and so does Disney).

A central Texas couple disagrees:

Your description, even with the statement that you are high on Pleasure Island, didn't prepare my wife and me for what a great place it is. Perhaps our expectations were moderate, but we thought it was an absolute blast, and we are neither under 40 nor club hounds.

For a Duluth, Georgia, man, Pleasure Island was a real eye-opener (at least according to his wife):

My husband couldn't believe the girls in the middle of the road selling Jell-O shooters! (I don't think we're in Disney anymore, Toto!)

Sorry, Invited Guests Only   Occasionally, particularly before 9 p.m., certain Pleasure Island clubs are reserved for private parties and are declared temporarily off-limits to paying guests.

Parking Is a Hassle   Pleasure Island's parking lot often fills up. On the bright side, the lot is now well marked. If you jot down the location of your space, you'll be able to find your car when it's time to leave. A good strategy is to park in the lot adjacent to the movie theaters and Disney's West Side and enter via the bridge connecting the West Side to Pleasure Island. Because there's an admission booth at the bridge, there's no need to enter through Pleasure Island's main gate.

Pleasure Island Touring Plan

Pleasure Island First-Timers' Touring Plan

This itinerary is for first-timers at Pleasure Island who want to visit all of the clubs in one night. It provides a taste of each venue. If you settle someplace that you really enjoy, you probably won't complete the circuit.

1. Arrive by 6 p.m. if you intend to eat at a Pleasure Island restaurant. If you eat before you go, arrive at about 7:30 or 8 p.m.

2. Buy your admission.

3. **Comedy Warehouse**   Go left from the admission windows at the main entrance to the Comedy Warehouse. This is Pleasure Island's toughest ticket. There are normally five shows nightly, with the two earlier shows (usually 7:30 and 8:25 p.m.) easiest to get into. If a show begins within 30 minutes, hop in line. If show time is more than 30 minutes away, check out the Rock n Roll Beach Club down the street. Use your judgment about whether you have time to buy a drink. Return to the Comedy Warehouse 30 minutes before show time. If you don't arrive at Pleasure Island in time to catch either of the first two shows, plan to queue at least 35 minutes before show time for subsequent performances.

4. **Motion**   Motion is the newest of the Pleasure Island clubs, replacing the country-western Wildhorse Saloon in 2001 (and leaving the complex without a country-music venue for the first time in its history). Disney says the club features everything from "Top 40 to alternative," which basically means they are going to hedge their bet and try different formats until they find one that catches on. Our under-30 Unofficials are betting that Motion will ultimately offer house or techno music (i.e., lots of synthesizers and 120 beats per minute).

5. **Pleasure Island Jazz Company**   Turn left from Motion and hit the Pleasure Island Jazz Company next door. The club features live jazz and blues and hosts jam sessions with local musicians. The crowd, more diverse in age and appearance than at other clubs, sits at tables flanking the stage on three sides.

6. **Adventurers Club**   When you're done at the Jazz Company, walk left and back to the Comedy Warehouse side of the island, and enter the Adventurers Club. Patterned after a stuffy English gentlemen's club, the Adventurers Club is a two-story, turn-of-the-century affair with big armchairs, walls covered with animal heads (some of which talk), and other artifacts.

Many guests will stroll through the club, inspect the ridiculous decor, and leave, not realizing they missed the main attraction: a show in the club's library downstairs. About once every 30 or 40 minutes, all guests will be ushered into the library for a performance. Nobody tells guests a show is upcoming; they must either hang around long enough to be invited in or intuit that, with Disney, what you see isn't what you get.

When you arrive at the Adventurers Club, ask an attendant when the next show in the library will begin. If it's in 20 minutes or less, go in and have a drink. If it's a long while, the BET Soundstage Club is next door.

7. **BET Soundstage Club**   Opened in partnership with Black Entertainment Television, this club features hip-hop, soul, and R&B. The dance floor is cool and showy, and the club gets packed as bands finish up at the West End Stage directly outside. The club is restricted to ages 21 and up, so there's a definite adult vibe.

8. **8TRAX**   When Pleasure Island opened, this was an under-21 club called Videopolis East. For various reasons (fights and teenage gang conflicts), it was closed and reopened as Cage, which targeted older (over-21) rockers but never achieved much of an identity. Now it's 8TRAX, a '70s disco featuring the music of K. C. and the Sunshine Band, the Bee Gees, and Donna Summer. Though the decor during our last visit was the same steel beams,

catwalks, and metal mesh that imbued the club's previous incarnations with such charm, it was clear that the '70s concept had taken root. The place was rocking.

9. **Mannequins Dance Palace** Backtrack toward Pleasure Island's front entrance to Mannequins, a ritzy, techno-pop, rock dance club with a revolving dance floor, incredible lighting, and wild special effects. The music is all DJ, but the sound system is superb (and very, very loud). There is often a line waiting to enter. This has less to do with the club's popularity than with the fact that Disney prefers guests to enter via an elevator to the second floor. The elevator helps distribute guests throughout the club, but there's a perfectly good entrance on the first floor. For some reason, cast members at the entrance will often invite 40-something (and older) guests to enter directly, without being subjected to the elevator. Patrons younger than 21 aren't allowed in Mannequins through either entrance.

10. **Rock n Roll Beach Club** Proceed to the Beach Club, featuring oldies and current rock. Bands here are always first-rate, and they raise the roof beginning early in the evening. Electronic games and pool are available for those who don't wish to dance.

11. **West End Stage** Continue to the West End Stage. It isn't a club, but it's the most happening place on Pleasure Island. Live rock bands perform under the stars in the plaza. The BET Soundstage Club and Adventurers Club are on one side, and Comedy Warehouse stands on the other. Bands are super, as are lighting and sound systems. The high stage provides excellent visibility. Performances usually occur four times each night, with a grand finale at 11:45 p.m., accompanied by fireworks, showers of confetti, and blazing searchlights. Street vendors sell drinks.

12. **Pleasure Island Restaurants** Though noisy, crowded, and expensive, restaurants here offer a variety of creative and well-prepared dishes. For detailed profiles of Pleasure Island restaurants, see Part Nine: Dining in and around Walt Disney World.

    Restaurants include Fulton's Crab House, on the Empress Lilly riverboat, specializing in shellfish and fresh Florida seafood, and the Portobello Yacht Club, serving seafood, pasta, and pizza. Casual yet stylish, the Portobello does a creditable job with its varied Italian fare.

    Another big player on Pleasure Island is Planet Hollywood, at the entrance to Disney's West Side. While the food is pretty good and the servings large, the main draw is the Hollywood memorabilia decorating the restaurant. Unless you eat at strange times, expect long waits for a table.

    Our researchers half-jokingly refer to Planet Hollywood as the restaurant with an attitude. A reader from Bartlesville, Oklahoma, agrees:

Planet Hollywood was NOT a pleasant experience. We arrived at 5 p.m. and still had to wait an hour [to be seated]. I had the feeling of being herded like cattle. I also felt the staff manipulated things so there was always a line (i.e., there were several tables that stayed empty during the time we were waiting). The hosts on duty were rude. Our waiter was friendly and the food was good, but by that time I was too stressed out to care. This was

*the only time at Disney World that we were treated rudely. I understand
Planet Hollywood is not owned or operated by Disney, and the contrast in
attitude was quite apparent.*

Priority seating is strongly recommended for all full-service restaurants. If
you don't have one, arrive by 6 p.m. or eat after 10 p.m. An alternative is to
eat sandwiches and snacks in the clubs. It isn't necessary to buy club admission to eat at the restaurants. Most are also open during the day.

If no Pleasure Island restaurant lights your candle, a number of themed
and nonthemed restaurants are within easy walking distance at the
Downtown Disney Marketplace and at Disney's West Side. Again, priority
seating is advised for the full-service restaurants.

13. **Pleasure Island Shopping**   Some shops on the Island are attractions in
themselves. At Cover Story, guests dress up before being photographed for
the mock cover of a major magazine. Want to see yourself on *Cosmo?*
Here's the place. Similarly, Superstar Studio lets you star in your own music
video. Props include keyboard, drums, and guitar. Video technicians record
your lipsyncing (or you can actually sing). Post-production adds realism to
your tape. Work alone or with a group of your friends. If you don't want
your own magazine cover or rock video, watch others make them. It's a
hoot!

It isn't necessary to pay admission to shop at Pleasure Island during
the day. In the evening, all of the Island except the restaurants is gated. For
more on shopping, see Part Sixteen: Shopping in and out of Walt Disney
World.

A Word about Universal CityWalk

CityWalk is Universal's version of Pleasure Island. In addition to a number of restaurants, you'll find a jazz club, a reggae club, a Pat O'Briens
dueling-pianos club, a Hard Rock Cafe and concert venue, a Motown
Cafe with live R&B, Jimmy Buffett's Margaritaville, and a dance club
called The Groove with high-tech lighting and visual effects. If you do
decide to dine at CityWalk, your options include Jimmy Buffett's Margaritaville, Emeril's Restaurant, Bob Marley—A Tribute to Freedom,
Latin Quarter, Pat O'Brien's, Hard Rock Cafe, NBA City, NASCAR
Cafe, Motown Cafe, and Pastamoré (for more information on CityWalk
restaurants, see pages 342–343). For dancing, try Motown Cafe, The
Groove, Latin Quarter, or Bob Marley—A Tribute to Freedom. And if
you're in the mood for live music, check out Motown Cafe, Pat
O'Brien's, Bob Marley—A Tribute to Freedom, Latin Quarter, CityJazz,
or Jimmy Buffett's Margaritaville.

There's no admission charge to enjoy the shops, restaurants, and street
entertainment. As concerns the clubs, you can buy a pass for about $8

that admits you to all the clubs (like at Pleasure Island), or if you prefer, you can pay a cover charge (usually about $5) at each club you visit. In addition to the clubs, shops, and restaurants, there's a 20-screen Cineplex movie theater.

CityWalk vs. Pleasure Island

Just as Universal's Islands of Adventure theme park allows for more direct competition with Disney's Magic Kingdom, CityWalk squares off with Pleasure Island in the field of nightlife entertainment.

As the underdog, CityWalk tries to catch the wave of the hottest fads in nightclubs and dining. Pleasure Island tends more toward themes and trends with long-established general appeal. Since Pleasure Island has the vast pool of Disney guests to draw from, CityWalk aggressively tries to attract locals in addition to tourists. Overall, Pleasure Island caters to guests who might like to indulge in a little clubbing on their vacation but normally don't make a habit of pub-crawling. CityWalk presents a flashy buffet of premiere nightclubs and restaurants that you might normally find scattered around a large metropolis.

One key difference is that the larger CityWalk is not as physically enclosed as Pleasure Island since it serves as a sort of open portal to the Universal parks. In addition, the CityWalk clubs don't have cover charges until about 9 p.m. So, if you're not interested in jumping around, arrive early, pick the club you like best, and settle in for the rest of the night. More than at Pleasure Island, several CityWalk establishments are both restaurants and clubs, allowing you to have dinner and dance the night away under the same roof. Both complexes have outdoor areas featuring frequent live music, festivals, and other events; both also have large multiscreen move theaters.

All that said, which entertainment complex you might prefer depends on individual tastes. Consult the chart below.

HOW CITYWALK AND PLEASURE ISLAND COMPARE

CityWalk	Pleasure Island
Adjacent to Universal's theme parks	Adjacent to Downtown Disney
Parking decks free after 6 p.m.	Parking is hectic; use Disney transport
About $8 for pass to all clubs	About $20 for admission to complex
Half local/half tourist; mostly adults ages 20–30	Mostly older teens or curious adults
Ten restaurants	Four restaurants
Four dance clubs	Five dance clubs
Six live music venues	Three live music venues
Upscale mall-fare shopping	Disney memorabilia; hipster clothing

Appendix

Readers' Questions to the Author

Following are questions and comments from *Unofficial Guide* readers. Some frequently asked questions are addressed in every edition of the *Unofficial Guide.*

Question:

When you do your research, are you admitted to the parks free? Do the Disney people know you are there?

Answer:

We pay the regular admission and usually the Disney people do not know we are on-site. Similarly, both in and out of Walt Disney World, we pay for our own meals and lodging.

Question:

How often is the Unofficial Guide *revised?*

Answer:

We publish a new edition once a year, but we make corrections every time we go to press, usually about three times a year.

Question:

Do you write each new edition from scratch?

Answer:

We do not. With a destination the size of Walt Disney World it's hard enough keeping up with what's new. Moreover, we put great effort into communicating the most salient, useful information in the clearest possible language. If an attraction or hotel has not changed, we are very reluctant to tinker with its coverage for the sake of freshening up the writing.

Question:

I have never read any other Unofficial Guides. *Are they all as negative and cynical as* The Unofficial Guide to Walt Disney World *or do you just resent Disney?*

Answer:

What some readers perceive as negative and cynical, we see as objective and constructive. And no, we don't resent anyone. Our job is to prepare you for both the best and worst of Walt Disney World. As it happens, some folks are very passionate about what one reader called "the inherent goodness of Disney." These folks might be more comfortable with press releases or the Official Guide than with the strong consumer orientation found in the *Unofficial Guide.* That having been said, we would like to point out that while some readers take us to task for being overly negative about Walt Disney World, others complain that we are too positive.

Question:

How are your age group ratings determined? I am 42 years old. During Star Tours, I was quite worried about hurting my back. If the senior citizens rating is determined only by those brave enough to ride, it will skew the results.

Answer:

The reader makes a good point. Unfortunately, it's impossible to develop a rating unless the guest (of whatever age group) has actually experienced the attraction. So yes, all age group ratings are derived exclusively from members of that age group who have experienced the attraction. Health problems, such as a bad back, however, can affect guests of any age, and Disney provides more than ample warnings on attractions that warrant such admonitions. But if you're in good health, our ratings will give you a sense of how much others in your age group enjoyed the attraction. Our hope, of course, is twofold: first, that you will be stimulated to be adventurous, and second, that a positive experience will help you be more open-minded.

Question:

I have an old edition of the Unofficial Guide. *How much of the information [in it] is still correct?*

Answer:

Veteran travel writers will acknowledge that 5–8% of the information in a guidebook is out of date by the time it comes off the press! Walt Disney World is always changing. If you are using an old edition of the *Unoffi-*

cial Guide, descriptions of attractions still existing should be generally accurate. However, many other things change with every edition, particularly the touring plans and the hotel and restaurant reviews. Finally, and obviously, older editions of the *Unofficial Guide* do not include new attractions or developments.

Question:

How many people have you surveyed for your "age group ratings" on the attractions?

Answer:

Since the publication of the first edition of the *Unofficial Guide* in 1985, we have interviewed or surveyed just over 24,500 Walt Disney World patrons. Even with such a large survey population, however, we continue to have difficulty with certain age groups. Specifically, we love to hear from seniors about their experiences with Splash Mountain, Big Thunder Mountain Railroad, Space Mountain, *Alien Encounter,* Star Tours, Tower of Terror, Rock 'n' Roller Coaster, Body Wars, Test Track, Kali River Rapids, and Dinosaur.

Question:

Do you stay in Walt Disney World? If not, where do you stay?

Answer:

We do stay at Walt Disney World lodging properties from time to time, usually when a new hotel opens. Since we began writing about Walt Disney World in 1982, we have stayed in over 61 different properties in various locations around Orlando, Lake Buena Vista, and Kissimmee.

Question:

What is your favorite Florida attraction?

Answer:

What attracts me (as opposed to my favorite attraction) is Juniper Springs, a stunningly beautiful stream about one and a half hours north of Orlando in the Ocala National Forest. Originating as a limestone aquifer, crystal clear water erupts from the ground and begins a ten-mile journey to the creek's mouth at Lake George. Winding through palm, cypress, and live oak, the stream is more exotic than the Jungle Cruise, and alive with birds, animals, turtles, and alligators. Put in at the Juniper Springs Recreation Area on FL 40, 36 miles east of Ocala. The seven-mile trip to the FL 19 bridge takes about four and a half hours. Canoe rentals and shuttle service are available at the recreation area. Phone (352) 625-2808 for information.

Readers' Comments

Readers love to share tips. Here's one from a St. Louis mom:

If dining at Downtown Disney, we found it best to arrive before 7 p.m. We ate
there twice and had no problem getting seated immediately, but after 7
everywhere was packed. They do not do priority seating at Downtown Disney.

From a Hammond, Indiana, dad:

The Osceola Parkway toll road parallels US 192 to the north and is a great
way to bypass those miles and miles of construction.

A lot of readers share tips about saving money. Here's a good one from
a Canadian reader:

I highly recommend the website of the Florida Travel and Tourist Bureau
(www.2000orlando-florida.com). As well as info on area attractions, it has
great deals on hotels and car rentals that you can't get elsewhere. I paid
$600 less for our hotel than the best price I could get through a travel
agent or directly from the hotel!

For auto club members, I highly recommend getting the free pass for AMA's
Diamond Lots at WDW (at your local AMA office before you leave home).
The Diamond Lots are usually right next to the park entrance (only the
handicapped parking is closer). You are close enough to walk to the park
entrance rather than having to wait for the shuttle. A time and hassle
saver!

And from an Ann Arbor, Michigan, mother of three:

Even though we stayed on Disney property, we stopped off on [US] 192 and
loaded up on the local freebie visitor magazines and coupon books. We
estimate they saved us over $200, mostly on food.

From an Annapolis, Maryland, reader:

Have your hotel fax you a confirmation of your reservation. If we had not
done this we would have found ourselves without a room over the Easter
holiday. Even with confirmation we spent an hour arguing with a totally
bone-headed hotel manager.

A Bastrop, Texas, reader shared a great discovery:

We found a really good and amazingly affordable Mexican restaurant that
you all missed. It's called Jalapeno's Grill & Cantina and is located on US
192 toward Kissimmee.

We tried it, and we agree—it's good.

From a Franklin, Tennessee, dad:

We always use the Florida Turnpike to get to WDW. Usually we exit at Clermont on US 27 and then turn onto US 192 for the rest of the way to Disney. This year we stayed on the Turnpike all the way to I-4 and then took I-4 over. It was faster and much easier on the nerves.

And from an Owensboro, Kentucky, reader:

I cannot express enough the need to bring plenty of film for your camera. I thought I had enough but ran out and had to buy some at the resort. Each 36-exposure roll averaged $9! Take extra rolls from home; you can always use them at Christmas if you don't at Disney.

Taking the long view helped a Texarkana, Texas, family:

I cannot emphasize the importance of realizing that you cannot see all [of WDW] in one trip. I realize that your guide is set up to help people try to accomplish just this for those who feel they can only afford one trip to WDW. But if people can in any way—even if it means staying at a cheaper hotel—get into the mindset that they will not be able to see it all in one trip and just focus on a few most important events/attractions on this trip and plan to come back again, it will save them stress and help make their trip more enjoyable.

An Iowa City, Iowa, couple offers this observation about being in touch with your feelings:

We didn't build rest breaks into our plans but were willing to say, "okay, I'm just not having fun right now; we should leave the park," and go on to something else (like a water park, hotel pool, or shopping trip to Downtown Disney). This is a skill I would like to see more people develop. I can't count the number of people or families who were obviously not having fun. People should remember that yelling at their kids in public ruins the fun for everyone else nearby.

When touring the theme parks, a Baltimore couple discovered that timing is everything:

Waiting time for attractions, food, or anything else, greatly depends on when you do things. For physical reasons my partner doesn't ride thrill rides, so we skipped some of the super headliners (the mountains, Tower of Terror, etc.). At Magic Kingdom opening time, when people are racing (and that's no exaggeration—I saw old ladies body checking teenagers) to Space Mountain, we went to Adventure, Liberty, and Frontier Lands and literally walked on rides we had planned to see (and some we didn't) until lunchtime. (Including Pirates, Jungle Cruise, Haunted Mansion, Country

Bears, Tiki Birds, and Tom Sawyer). This type of strategy worked with all of the parks, except for Animal Kingdom, where everyone wants to see the same four things. However, we got there super early and efficiently walked to Safari when the park opened and got right on (saw lots of animals, too). Overall, if hoards of people are sprinting to an attraction, it doesn't take a genius to figure out that you should do something else.

We receive a lot of mail, both pro and con, about our *Unofficial* approach to Walt Disney World. The following comments are representative. From a Des Moines, Iowa, mom:

My family called me the "Disney Nazi" because I made them get up early and keep moving to follow your plans. After we got home, they sent me flowers, thanking me for working so hard and calling it "The Vacation of a Lifetime!"

A mom from State College rendered a split decision:

The Unofficial Guide kept bumming me out, but I did appreciate its more realistic information.

And then there was the woman from Suwanee, Georgia, who offers a suggestion for the perfect Disney vacation:

Your book made our trip a much more successful one. It also frustrated our male adults, who erroneously believed this was a trip for their enjoyment. We followed your advice to get up early and see as much as possible before an early lunch. But the men refused to go back to the hotel for a nap and a meal outside the park, so we fought the crowds until 3 or 4 p.m., by which time everyone was exhausted and cranky. My mother and I decided our next trip will include your guidebook and the children, but no men!

Finally, this family from Jeanette, Pennsylvania, could teach us all a thing or two about rolling with the punches:

Except for the parks being closed when the terrorist attacks occurred, and the hurricane coming in at the end of the week, it was a wonderful time.

And so it goes.

Hotel Index

Restaurant Index

Subject Index

the Unofficial Guide®

Recommended Attraction Visitation Times & Pocket Outline Touring Plans

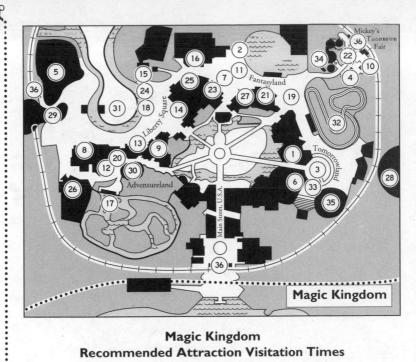

Magic Kingdom
Recommended Attraction Visitation Times

It is best to see attractions with visitation times listed as "anytime" during the more crowded middle part of the day (noon to 4 p.m.).

1. *Alien Encounter:* Before 10 a.m., during parades, or after 6 p.m.
2. Ariel's Grotto: Before 10 a.m./after 9 p.m.
3. Astro Orbiter: Before 11 a.m./after 5 p.m.
4. Barnstormer: Before 10:30 a.m., during events, or just before closing
5. Big Thunder Mountain Railroad: Before 10 a.m., hour before closing, or use FASTPASS
6. Buzz Lightyear's Space Ranger Spin: Before 10:30 a.m./after 6 p.m.
7. Cinderella's Golden Carrousel: Before 11 a.m./after 8 p.m.
8. *Country Bear Jamboree:* Before 11:30 a.m., during parades, or 2 hours before closing
9. *The Diamond Horseshoe Saloon Revue:* Per entertainment schedule
10. Donald's Boat: Anytime
11. Dumbo: Before 10 a.m./after 9 p.m.
12. *Enchanted Tiki Birds:* Before 11 a.m./after 3:30 p.m.
13. Frontierland Shootin' Arcade: Anytime
14. *The Hall of Presidents:* Anytime
15. The Haunted Mansion: Before 11:30 a.m./after 8 p.m.
16. It's a Small World: Anytime
17. Jungle Cruise: Before 10 a.m., 2 hours before closing, or use FASTPASS
18. *Liberty Belle* Riverboat: Anytime

—continued on other side—

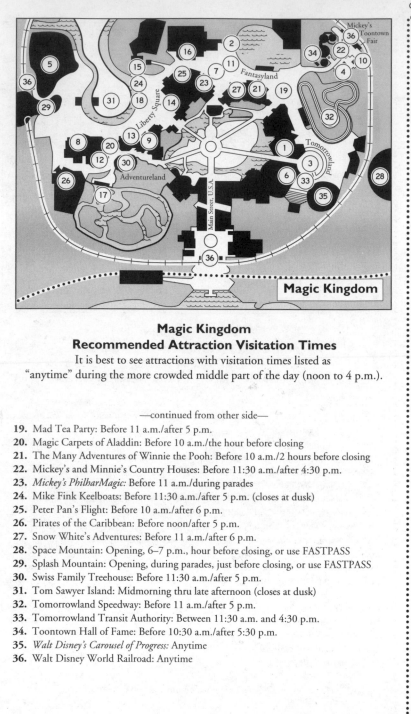

Magic Kingdom
Recommended Attraction Visitation Times

It is best to see attractions with visitation times listed as "anytime" during the more crowded middle part of the day (noon to 4 p.m.).

—continued from other side—

19. Mad Tea Party: Before 11 a.m./after 5 p.m.

20. Magic Carpets of Aladdin: Before 10 a.m./the hour before closing

21. The Many Adventures of Winnie the Pooh: Before 10 a.m./2 hours before closing

22. Mickey's and Minnie's Country Houses: Before 11:30 a.m./after 4:30 p.m.

23. *Mickey's PhilharMagic:* Before 11 a.m./during parades

24. Mike Fink Keelboats: Before 11:30 a.m./after 5 p.m. (closes at dusk)

25. Peter Pan's Flight: Before 10 a.m./after 6 p.m.

26. Pirates of the Caribbean: Before noon/after 5 p.m.

27. Snow White's Adventures: Before 11 a.m./after 6 p.m.

28. Space Mountain: Opening, 6–7 p.m., hour before closing, or use FASTPASS

29. Splash Mountain: Opening, during parades, just before closing, or use FASTPASS

30. Swiss Family Treehouse: Before 11:30 a.m./after 5 p.m.

31. Tom Sawyer Island: Midmorning thru late afternoon (closes at dusk)

32. Tomorrowland Speedway: Before 11 a.m./after 5 p.m.

33. Tomorrowland Transit Authority: Between 11:30 a.m. and 4:30 p.m.

34. Toontown Hall of Fame: Before 10:30 a.m./after 5:30 p.m.

35. *Walt Disney's Carousel of Progress:* Anytime

36. Walt Disney World Railroad: Anytime

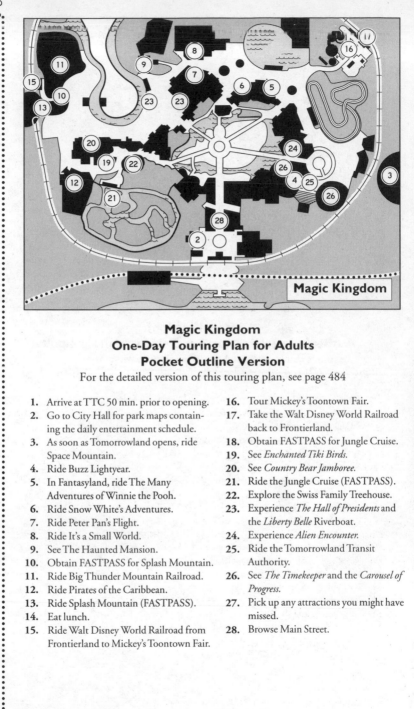

Magic Kingdom
One-Day Touring Plan for Adults
Pocket Outline Version
For the detailed version of this touring plan, see page 484

1. Arrive at TTC 50 min. prior to opening.
2. Go to City Hall for park maps containing the daily entertainment schedule.
3. As soon as Tomorrowland opens, ride Space Mountain.
4. Ride Buzz Lightyear.
5. In Fantasyland, ride The Many Adventures of Winnie the Pooh.
6. Ride Snow White's Adventures.
7. Ride Peter Pan's Flight.
8. Ride It's a Small World.
9. See The Haunted Mansion.
10. Obtain FASTPASS for Splash Mountain.
11. Ride Big Thunder Mountain Railroad.
12. Ride Pirates of the Caribbean.
13. Ride Splash Mountain (FASTPASS).
14. Eat lunch.
15. Ride Walt Disney World Railroad from Frontierland to Mickey's Toontown Fair.

16. Tour Mickey's Toontown Fair.
17. Take the Walt Disney World Railroad back to Frontierland.
18. Obtain FASTPASS for Jungle Cruise.
19. See *Enchanted Tiki Birds*.
20. See *Country Bear Jamboree*.
21. Ride the Jungle Cruise (FASTPASS).
22. Explore the Swiss Family Treehouse.
23. Experience *The Hall of Presidents* and the *Liberty Belle* Riverboat.
24. Experience *Alien Encounter*.
25. Ride the Tomorrowland Transit Authority.
26. See *The Timekeeper* and the *Carousel of Progress*.
27. Pick up any attractions you might have missed.
28. Browse Main Street.

Magic Kingdom
Author's Selective One-Day Touring Plan for Adults
Pocket Outline Version
For the detailed version of this touring plan, see page 486.

1. Arrive at TTC 50 min. prior to opening.
2. Go to City Hall for park maps containing the daily entertainment schedule.
3. As soon as Tomorrowland opens, ride Space Mountain.
4. Ride Buzz Lightyear.
5. Ride The Many Adventures of Winnie the Pooh.
6. Ride Peter Pan's Flight.
7. Ride It's a Small World.
8. See The Haunted Mansion.
9. Obtain FASTPASS for Splash Mountain.
10. Ride Big Thunder Mountain Railroad.
11. Ride Pirates of the Caribbean.
12. Ride Splash Mountain (FASTPASS).
13. Eat lunch.
14. Take Walt Disney World Railroad from Frontierland to Mickey's Toontown Fair.

15. Tour Mickey's Toontown Fair.
16. Take the Walt Disney World Railroad back to Frontierland.
17. Obtain FASTPASS for Jungle Cruise.
18. See *Enchanted Tiki Birds.*
19. See the *Country Bear Jamboree.*
20. Take the Jungle Cruise (FASTPASS).
21. Explore the Swiss Family Treehouse.
22. Experience the *Liberty Belle* Riverboat and *The Hall of Presidents.*
23. Experience *Alien Encounter.*
24. See *The Timekeeper* and *Walt Disney's Carousel of Progress* (open seasonally).
25. Pick up any attractions you might have missed.
26. Browse Main Street.

Magic Kingdom
One-Day Touring Plan for Parents with Young Children
Pocket Outline Version

For the detailed version of this touring plan, see page 488.
Review the Small Child Fright Potential Chart on pages 246–249.

1. Arrive at TTC 50 min. prior to opening.
2. Go to City Hall for park maps containing the daily entertainment schedule.
3. Rent strollers (if necessary).
4. Ride Dumbo the Flying Elephant.
5. Ride The Many Adventures of Winnie the Pooh.
6. Ride Peter Pan's Flight.
7. Ride It's a Small World.
8. See *Mickey's PhilharMagic*.
9. See The Haunted Mansion.
10. Ride the Jungle Cruise. If wait is longer than 30 minutes, obtain FASTPASS instead.
11. Visit Tom Sawyer Island in Frontierland.
12. If you have a FASTPASS for Jungle Cruise, ride now. If not, skip to Step 13.
13. Take Walt Disney World Railroad from Frontierland to Main Street, U.S.A. Return to hotel for lunch and a nap.
14. Return to the Magic Kingdom and proceed to Frontierland.
15. Obtain FASTPASS for Splash Mountain.
16. See the *Country Bear Jamboree*.
17. Ride Pirates of the Caribbean.
18. Explore the Swiss Family Treehouse.
19. Ride Splash Mountain (FASTPASS).
20. Obtain FASTPASS for Buzz Lightyear.
21. Ride the Tomorrowland Transit Authority.
22. Visit Mickey's Toontown Fair.
23. Ride Buzz Lightyear (FASTPASS).
24. Check the entertainment schedule for live performances, parades, fireworks, etc., or try any attractions you missed.

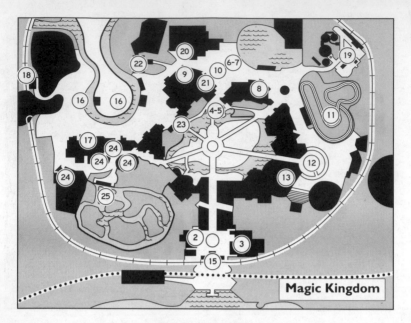

Magic Kingdom
Dumbo-or-Die-in-a-Day Touring Plan
for Parents with Young Children
Pocket Outline Version

For the detailed version of this touring plan, see page 491.
Review the Small Child Fright Potential Chart on pages 246–249.
(Interrupt the touring plan for lunch, rest, and dinner.)

1. Arrive at TTC 50 min. prior to opening.
2. Go to City Hall for park maps containing the daily entertainment schedule.
3. Rent a stroller (if needed).
4. Go to Cinderella's Castle.
5. Make dinner priority seating at the castle.
6. Ride Dumbo the Flying Elephant.
7. Ride Dumbo again.
8. Ride The Many Adventures of Winnie the Pooh.
9. Ride Peter Pan's Flight.
10. Ride Cinderella's Golden Carrousel.
11. Ride the Tomorrowland Speedway.
12. Ride the Astro Orbiter.
13. Ride Buzz Lightyear.
14. Return to the hotel for lunch and a nap.
15. Return to the Magic Kingdom. Take the WDW Railroad to Frontierland.
16. Go to Tom Sawyer Island.

18. Take the train to Mickey's Toontown Fair.
19. Walk through Mickey's and Minnie's Country Houses, play on Donald's Boat, and visit Toontown Hall of Fame.
20. If you have time before dinner, ride It's a Small World.
21. Eat, then see Mickey's *PhilharMagic.*
22. See the Haunted Mansion.
23. Watch the evening parade.
24. Obtain FASTPASS for the Jungle Cruise (if necessary), then experience *Enchanted Tiki Birds,* Magic Carpets of Aladdin, Swiss Family Treehouse, and possibly Pirates of the Caribbean.
25. Ride the Jungle Cruise (FASTPASS).
26. Repeat favorite attractions.
27. Depart Magic Kingdom.

Magic Kingdom
Two-Day Touring Plan
Pocket Outline Version
For the detailed version of this touring plan, see page 493.

Day One

1. Arrive at TTC 50 min. prior to opening.
2. Go to City Hall for park maps containing the daily entertainment schedule.
3. As soon as Tomorrowland opens, ride Space Mountain.
4. Ride The Many Adventures of Winnie the Pooh.
5. Ride Peter Pan's Flight.
6. See *Mickey's PhilharMagic*.
7. Ride It's a Small World.
8. Experience The Haunted Mansion.
9. Ride the *Liberty Belle* Riverboat.
10. Eat lunch.
11. See *The Hall of Presidents*.
12. See the *Country Bear Jamboree*.
13. In Frontierland, explore Tom Sawyer Island.
14. Go to Tomorrowland via the central hub.
15. Experience *Alien Encounter*.
16. Ride the Tomorrowland Transit Authority.
17. Enjoy the shops, see some live entertainment, or revisit favorite attractions.

Magic Kingdom

Magic Kingdom
Two-Day Touring Plan
Pocket Outline Version
For the detailed version of this touring plan, see page 000.
Day Two

1. Arrive at TTC 50 min. prior to opening.
2. Go to City Hall for park maps containing the daily entertainment schedule.
3. Ride Buzz Lightyear.
4. Ride Splash Mountain.
5. Ride Big Thunder Mountain Railroad.
6. In Adventureland, ride the Jungle Cruise (FASTPASS).
7. See *Enchanted Tiki Birds.*
8. Walk through the Swiss Family Treehouse.
9. Enjoy Pirates of the Caribbean.
10. Eat lunch.
11. Take the Walt Disney World Railroad to Mickey's Toontown Fair.
12. Tour Mickey's Toontown Fair.
13. Go to Tomorrowland.
14. If you haven't eaten yet, try Cosmic Ray's Starlight Cafe or the Plaza Pavilion.
15. See *Walt Disney's Carousel of Progress* (open seasonally).
16. See *The Timekeeper* (open seasonally).
17. Enjoy the shops, see some live entertainment, or revisit favorite attractions.

Epcot

Recommended Attraction Visitation Times

It is best to see attractions with visitation times listed as "anytime" during the more crowded middle part of the day (noon to 4 p.m.).

1. *The American Adventure:* Anytime
2. Body Wars (Wonders of Life): Before 10:45 a.m./after 5 p.m.
3. *Circle of Life Theater* (The Land): Before 11 a.m./after 2 p.m.
4. *Cranium Command* (Wonders of Life): Before 11 a.m./after 2 p.m.
5. El Río del Tiempo (Mexico): Before 11 a.m./after 3 p.m.
6. *Food Rocks* (The Land): Before 11 a.m./after 2 p.m.
7. *Honey, I Shrunk the Audience:* Before 11:30 a.m., after 6 p.m., or use FASTPASS
8. *Impressions de France* (France): Before noon/after 4 p.m.
9. Innoventions: Second day or after major attractions
10. Journey into Your Imagination: Before 11:30 a.m./after 6 p.m.
11. Living with the Land (The Land): Before 10:30 a.m., after 7:30 p.m., or use FASTPASS
12. The Living Seas: Before 11:30 a.m./after 3 p.m.
13. Maelstrom (Norway): Before noon, after 4:30 p.m., or use FASTPASS
14. *The Making of Me* (Wonders of Life): Early morning/after 4:30 p.m.
15. Mission: Space: First 30 minutes the park is open or use FASTPASS
16. *O Canada!* (Canada): Anytime
17. Spaceship Earth: Before 11 a.m./after 3 p.m.
18. Test Track: First 30 minutes the park is open, just before closing, or use FASTPASS
19. Universe of Energy: Before 11:15 a.m./after 4:30 p.m.
20. *Wonders of China* (China): Anytime

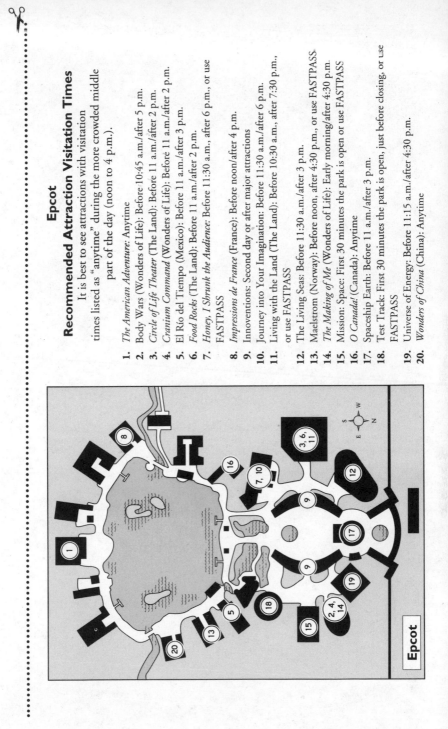

Epcot

Epcot
One-Day Touring Plan
Pocket Outline Version

For the detailed version of this touring plan, see page 536.
(Interrupt the touring plan for lunch, dinner, and *IllumiNations*.)

1. Arrive 40 minutes before official opening time.
2. Go to Guest Relations and make restaurant priority seatings, then ride Mission: Space if it's open.
3. Ride Test Track. If wait exceeds 30 minutes, obtain FASTPASS instead.
4. In the Wonders of Life pavilion, ride Body Wars.
5. Go to the Land pavilion.
6. Ride Living with the Land.
7. Take the Journey Into Your Imagination ride, then see *Honey, I Shrunk the Audience*.
8. Go back to the Land and see *Food Rocks* and *The Circle of Life*.
9. Experience The Living Seas.
10. Ride Spaceship Earth.
11. Visit the Universe of Energy.
12. See *Cranium Command*.
13. Go to the World Showcase.
14. At Canada, see the movie.
15. Visit the United Kingdom.
16. At France, see the movie.
17. Visit Morocco.
18. Tour Japan.
19. See *The American Adventure*.
20. Visit Italy.
21. Tour Germany.
22. See *Wonders of China*.
23. Ride Maelstrom in Norway.
24. Ride El Río del Tiempo in Mexico.
25. Depart Epcot.

Epcot

Epcot
Author's Selective One-Day Touring Plan
Pocket Outline Version

For the detailed version of this touring plan, see page 538. (Interrupt the touring plan for lunch, dinner, and *IllumiNations*.)

1. Arrive 40 minutes before official opening time.
2. Go to Guest Relations and make restaurant priority seatings, then ride Mission: Space if it's open.
3. Ride Test Track. If wait exceeds 30 minutes, obtain FASTPASS instead.
4. Ride Body Wars in the Wonders of Life pavilion.
5. Ride Living with the Land.
6. Take the Journey Into Your Imagination ride, then see *Honey, I Shrunk the Audience*.
7. See The Living Seas.
8. Ride Spaceship Earth.
9. Visit the Universe of Energy.
10. See *Cranium Command*.
11. Go to the World Showcase.
12. See the *American Adventure* and the films at France and China. Take the boat ride in Norway.
13. Enjoy *IllumiNations*, then depart Epcot.

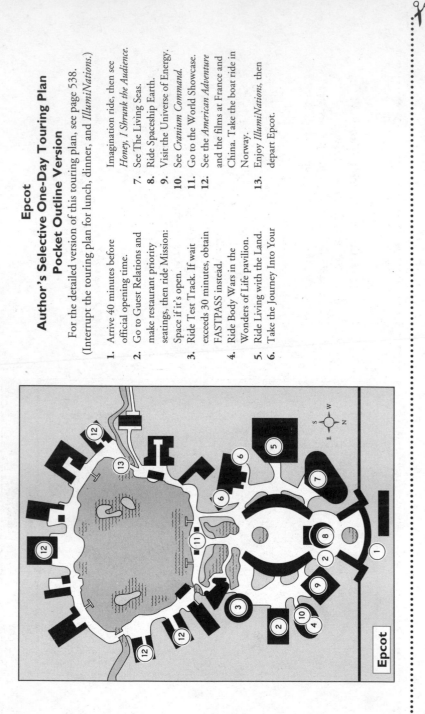

Epcot

Epcot
Two-Day Sunrise/Starlight Touring Plan
Pocket Outline Version

For the detailed version of this touring plan, see page 540.
(Interrupt the touring plan for lunch.)

Day One

1. Arrive 40 minutes before official opening time.
2. Go to Guest Relations and make priority seatings, then ride Mission: Space if it's open.
3. Ride Test Track. If wait exceeds 30 minutes, obtain FASTPASS instead.
4. Ride Body Wars.
5. Ride Living with the Land.
6. Take the Journey Into Your Imagination ride, then see *Honey, I Shrunk the Audience.*
7. Go to the World Showcase.
8. Ride El Río del Tiempo in Mexico.
9. Ride Maelstrom in Norway.
10. See *Wonders of China.*
11. Visit Germany and Italy.
12. See *The American Adventure.*
13. Visit Japan and Morocco.
14. Depart Epcot.

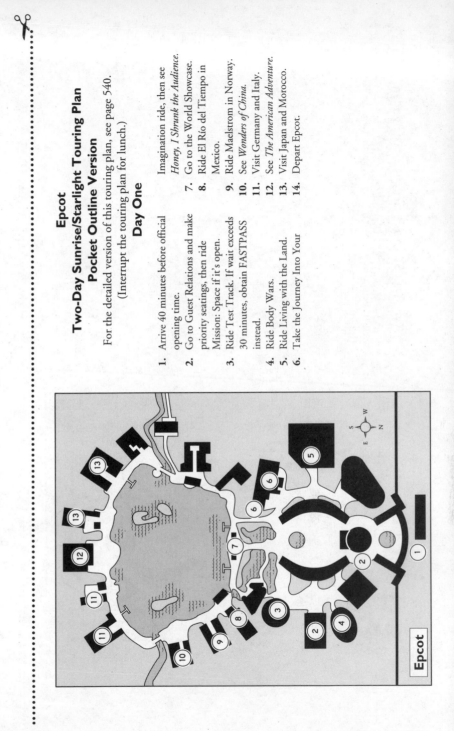

Epcot

777

Epcot
Two-Day Sunrise/Starlight Touring Plan
Pocket Outline Version

For the detailed version of this touring plan, see page 000.
(Interrupt the touring plan for dinner and *IllumiNations*.)

Day Two

1. Arrive at Epcot at 1 p.m. Pick up a park map containing the daily entertainment schedule at Guest Relations.
2. Make dinner priority seatings.
3. Ride Spaceship Earth.
4. See *Cranium Command*.
5. Visit the Universe of Energy.
6. Go to The Living Seas.
7. See *Food Rocks* and *The Circle of Life* at The Land.
8. See *O Canada!*
9. Visit the United Kingdom.
10. At France, see the movie.
11. Enjoy dinner and *IllumiNations*.
12. Depart Epcot.

Epcot

Epcot
Two-Day Early Riser Touring Plan
Pocket Outline Version

For the detailed version of this touring plan, see page 543.
Parents with young children should review the Small Child Fright
Potential Chart on pages 246–249.

Day One

1. Arrive 45 minutes before official opening time.
2. Ride Mission: Space if it's open.
3. Ride Body Wars at Wonders of Life.
4. See *Cranium Command.*
5. Experience the Universe of Energy.
6. Go to Guest Relations and make restaurant priority seatings.
7. Ride Spaceship Earth.
8. Visit the Living Seas.
9. Ride Living with the Land.
10. See *Food Rocks* and *The Circle of Life* in The Land.
11. See *O Canada!*
12. Visit the United Kingdom.
13. Explore Innoventions East and West.
14. Depart Epcot.

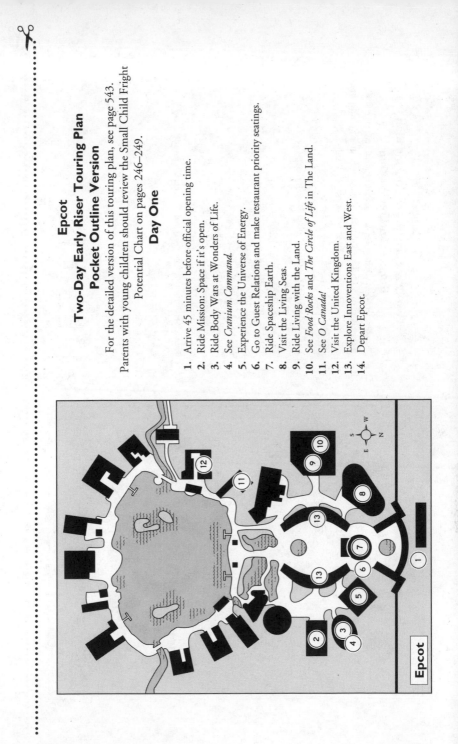

Epcot

Epcot
Two-Day Early Riser Touring Plan
Pocket Outline Version

For the detailed version of this touring plan, see page 000.
Parents with young children should review the Small Child Fright
Potential Chart on pages 000–000.

Day Two

1. Arrive 45 minutes before official opening time.
2. Go to Guest Relations and make priority seatings.
3. Walk through Innoventions East and head to Test Track.
4. Ride Test Track. If wait exceeds 30 minutes, use FASTPASS.
5. Ride Living With the Land if you missed it yesterday.
6. Take the Journey Into Your Imagination Ride, then see *Honey I Shrunk the Audience.*
7. Go to the World Showcase.
8. Ride El Río del Tiempo in Mexico.
9. Ride Maelstrom in Norway. If wait exceeds 20 minutes, use FASTPASS.
10. See *Wonders of China.*
11. Visit Germany and Italy.
12. See *The American Adventure.*
13. Visit Japan and Morocco.
14. See *Impressions de France.*
15. Visit the United Kingdom.
16. See *O Canada!*
17. Enjoy dinner and *IllumiNations.*
18. Depart Epcot.

Epcot

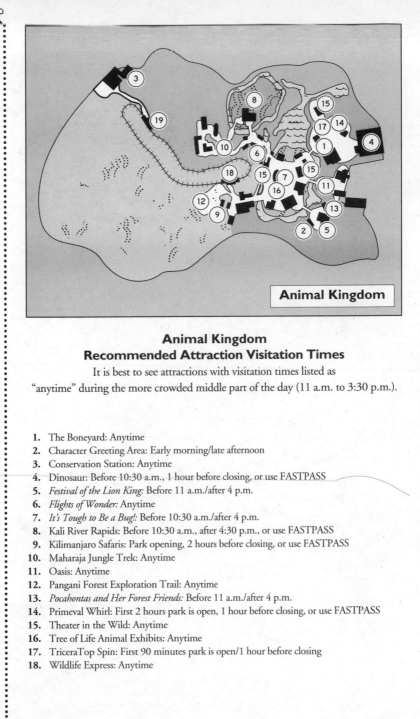

Animal Kingdom
Recommended Attraction Visitation Times

It is best to see attractions with visitation times listed as
"anytime" during the more crowded middle part of the day (11 a.m. to 3:30 p.m.).

1. The Boneyard: Anytime
2. Character Greeting Area: Early morning/late afternoon
3. Conservation Station: Anytime
4. Dinosaur: Before 10:30 a.m., 1 hour before closing, or use FASTPASS
5. *Festival of the Lion King:* Before 11 a.m./after 4 p.m.
6. *Flights of Wonder:* Anytime
7. *It's Tough to Be a Bug!:* Before 10:30 a.m./after 4 p.m.
8. Kali River Rapids: Before 10:30 a.m., after 4:30 p.m., or use FASTPASS
9. Kilimanjaro Safaris: Park opening, 2 hours before closing, or use FASTPASS
10. Maharaja Jungle Trek: Anytime
11. Oasis: Anytime
12. Pangani Forest Exploration Trail: Anytime
13. *Pocahontas and Her Forest Friends:* Before 11 a.m./after 4 p.m.
14. Primeval Whirl: First 2 hours park is open, 1 hour before closing, or use FASTPASS
15. Theater in the Wild: Anytime
16. Tree of Life Animal Exhibits: Anytime
17. TriceraTop Spin: First 90 minutes park is open/1 hour before closing
18. Wildlife Express: Anytime

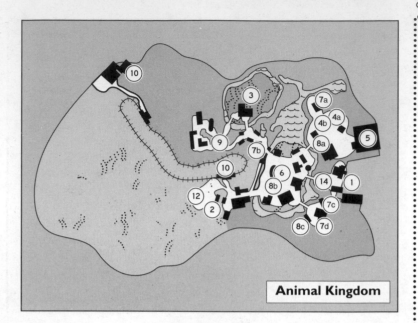

Animal Kingdom
One-Day Touring Plan
Pocket Outline Version

For the detailed version of this touring plan, see page 576.

1. Arrive 40 minutes prior to opening.
2. Experience the Kilimanjaro Safaris. If wait exceeds 30 minutes, use FASTPASS.
3. Ride Kali River Rapids. If wait exceeds 30 minutes, use FASTPASS.
4. Ride Primeval Whirl (4a) in Dino-Land U.S.A. If you have small children, ride TriceraTop Spin (4b) before Primeval Whirl.
5. Ride Dinosaur.
6. See *It's Tough to Be a Bug!* If wait exceeds 30 minutes, use FASTPASS.
7. Eat lunch and work in the following shows: Theater in the Wild (7a), *Flights of Wonder* (7b), *Pocahontas* (7c), and *Festival of the Lion King* (7d).

8. Check out The Boneyard (8a) and exhibits at the Tree of Life (8b). Also, meet the characters at Camp Minnie-Mickey (8c).
9. Walk the Maharaja Jungle Trek.
10. Return to Africa and take the train to Rafiki's Planet Watch and Conservation Station. Tour the exhibits.
11. Catch the train back to Harambe.
12. Walk the Pangani Forest Exploration Trail.
13. Shop, snack, or repeat any attractions you especially enjoyed.
14. Visit the zoological exhibits in The Oasis and exit the Animal Kingdom.

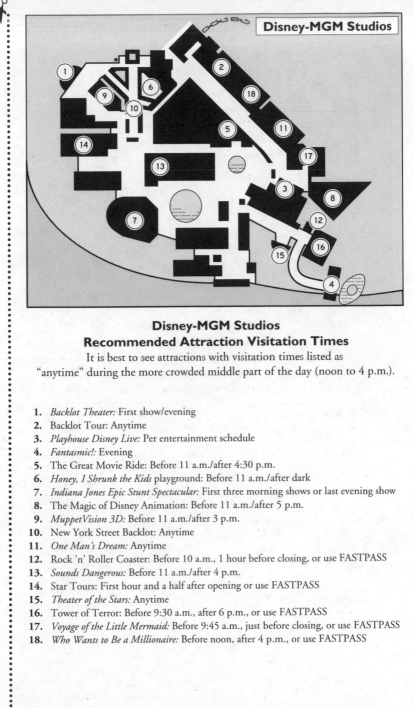

Disney-MGM Studios

Disney-MGM Studios
Recommended Attraction Visitation Times

It is best to see attractions with visitation times listed as
"anytime" during the more crowded middle part of the day (noon to 4 p.m.).

1. *Backlot Theater:* First show/evening
2. Backlot Tour: Anytime
3. *Playhouse Disney Live:* Per entertainment schedule
4. *Fantasmic!:* Evening
5. The Great Movie Ride: Before 11 a.m./after 4:30 p.m.
6. *Honey, I Shrunk the Kids* playground: Before 11 a.m./after dark
7. *Indiana Jones Epic Stunt Spectacular:* First three morning shows or last evening show
8. The Magic of Disney Animation: Before 11 a.m./after 5 p.m.
9. *MuppetVision 3D:* Before 11 a.m./after 3 p.m.
10. New York Street Backlot: Anytime
11. *One Man's Dream:* Anytime
12. Rock 'n' Roller Coaster: Before 10 a.m., 1 hour before closing, or use FASTPASS
13. *Sounds Dangerous:* Before 11 a.m./after 4 p.m.
14. Star Tours: First hour and a half after opening or use FASTPASS
15. *Theater of the Stars:* Anytime
16. Tower of Terror: Before 9:30 a.m., after 6 p.m., or use FASTPASS
17. *Voyage of the Little Mermaid:* Before 9:45 a.m., just before closing, or use FASTPASS
18. *Who Wants to Be a Millionaire:* Before noon, after 4 p.m., or use FASTPASS

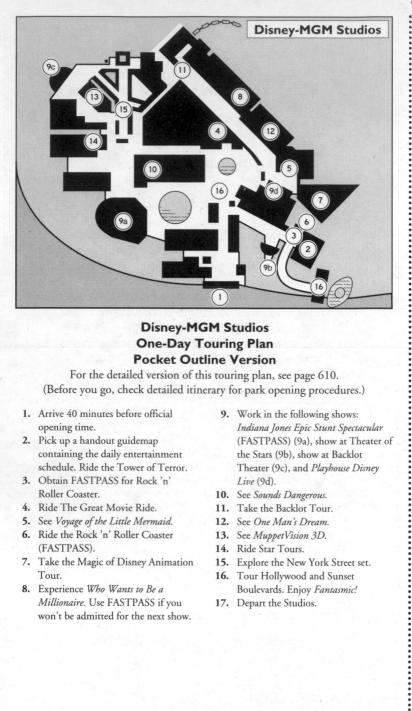

Disney-MGM Studios
One-Day Touring Plan
Pocket Outline Version

For the detailed version of this touring plan, see page 610.
(Before you go, check detailed itinerary for park opening procedures.)

1. Arrive 40 minutes before official opening time.
2. Pick up a handout guidemap containing the daily entertainment schedule. Ride the Tower of Terror.
3. Obtain FASTPASS for Rock 'n' Roller Coaster.
4. Ride The Great Movie Ride.
5. See *Voyage of the Little Mermaid*.
6. Ride the Rock 'n' Roller Coaster (FASTPASS).
7. Take the Magic of Disney Animation Tour.
8. Experience *Who Wants to Be a Millionaire*. Use FASTPASS if you won't be admitted for the next show.

9. Work in the following shows: *Indiana Jones Epic Stunt Spectacular* (FASTPASS) (9a), show at Theater of the Stars (9b), show at Backlot Theater (9c), and *Playhouse Disney Live* (9d).
10. See *Sounds Dangerous*.
11. Take the Backlot Tour.
12. See *One Man's Dream*.
13. See *MuppetVision 3D*.
14. Ride Star Tours.
15. Explore the New York Street set.
16. Tour Hollywood and Sunset Boulevards. Enjoy *Fantasmic!*
17. Depart the Studios.

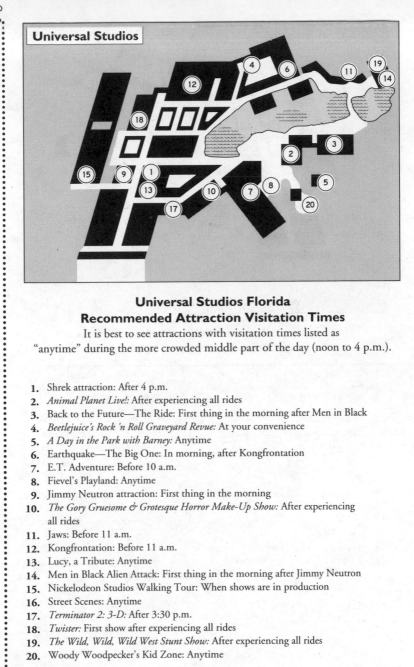

Universal Studios Florida
Recommended Attraction Visitation Times

It is best to see attractions with visitation times listed as "anytime" during the more crowded middle part of the day (noon to 4 p.m.).

1. Shrek attraction: After 4 p.m.
2. *Animal Planet Live!:* After experiencing all rides
3. Back to the Future—The Ride: First thing in the morning after Men in Black
4. *Beetlejuice's Rock 'n Roll Graveyard Revue:* At your convenience
5. *A Day in the Park with Barney:* Anytime
6. Earthquake—The Big One: In morning, after Kongfrontation
7. E.T. Adventure: Before 10 a.m.
8. Fievel's Playland: Anytime
9. Jimmy Neutron attraction: First thing in the morning
10. *The Gory Gruesome & Grotesque Horror Make-Up Show:* After experiencing all rides
11. Jaws: Before 11 a.m.
12. Kongfrontation: Before 11 a.m.
13. Lucy, a Tribute: Anytime
14. Men in Black Alien Attack: First thing in the morning after Jimmy Neutron
15. Nickelodeon Studios Walking Tour: When shows are in production
16. Street Scenes: Anytime
17. *Terminator 2: 3-D:* After 3:30 p.m.
18. *Twister:* First show after experiencing all rides
19. *The Wild, Wild, Wild West Stunt Show:* After experiencing all rides
20. Woody Woodpecker's Kid Zone: Anytime

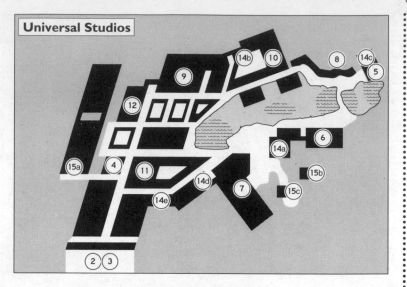

Universal Studios
One-Day Touring Plan
Pocket Outline Version
For the detailed version of this touring plan, see page 632.

1. Call (407) 363-8000 the day before your visit for the official opening time.
2. Arrive 50 minutes before opening and pick up a map and entertainment schedule.
3. Line up at the turnstile. Ask if any rides are closed and adjust touring plan.
4. Ride the Jimmy Neutron attraction (opens spring 2003). Right before or right after, get a lunchtime Universal Express pass for the adjacent Shrek attraction (11).
5. Ride Men in Black Alien Attack.
6. Ride Back to the Future.
7. Ride E.T. Adventure.
8. Ride Jaws.
9. Ride Kongfrontation.
10. Ride Earthquake—The Big One.
11. See the Shrek attraction (opens spring 2003), using Universal Express if needed.
12. See *Twister*.
13. This is a good time for lunch.
14. See *Animal Planet Live!* (14a), *Beetlejuice's Rock 'n Roll Graveyard Revue* (14b), and *The Wild, Wild, Wild West Stunt Show* (14c) as convenient, according to the daily entertainment schedule. As time permits, work *The Gory Gruesome & Grotesque Horror Make-Up Show* (14d), which runs continuously, into your schedule. See *Terminator 2: 3-D* (14e) after 3:30 p.m.
15. Take school-age children on the Nickelodeon tour (15a) in late afternoon and preschoolers to see Barney (15b) after riding E.T., and then head for Woody Woodpecker's KidZone (15c).
16. Revisit favorite rides and shows. See any live performances you may have missed.

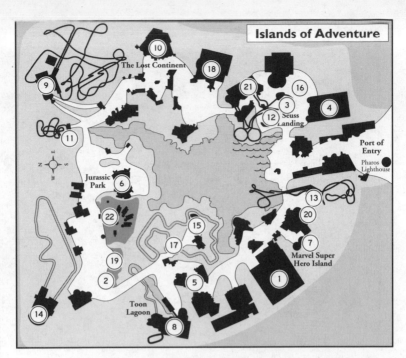

Universal's Islands of Adventure
Recommended Attraction Visitation Times

It is best to see attractions with visitation times listed as "anytime" during the more crowded middle part of the day (noon to 4 p.m.).

1. The Adventures of Spider-Man: Before 10 a.m.
2. Camp Jurassic: Anytime
3. Caro-Seuss-El: Before 10:30 a.m.
4. The Cat in the Hat: Before 11:30 a.m.
5. Comic Strip Lane: Anytime
6. Discovery Center: Anytime
7. Dr. Doom's FearFall: Before 9:15 a.m.
8. Dudley Do-Right's Ripsaw Falls: Before 11 a.m.
9. Dueling Dragons: Before 10:30 a.m.
10. *The Eighth Voyage of Sinbad:* Anytime per the entertainment schedule
11. The Flying Unicorn: Before 11 a.m.
12. If I Ran the Zoo: Anytime
13. The Incredible Hulk Coaster: Before 9:30 a.m.

—continued on other side—

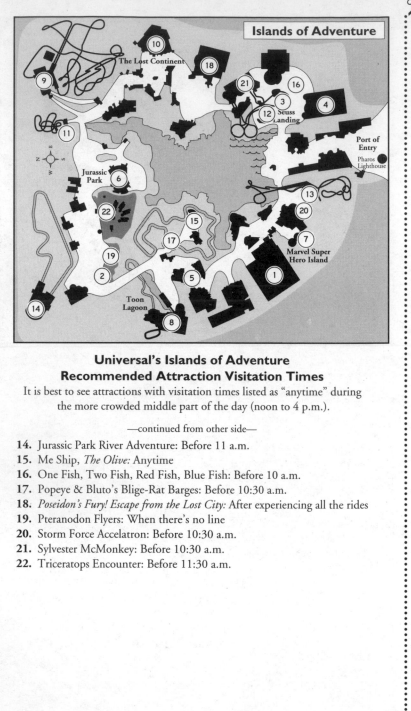

Universal's Islands of Adventure
Recommended Attraction Visitation Times

It is best to see attractions with visitation times listed as "anytime" during the more crowded middle part of the day (noon to 4 p.m.).

—continued from other side—

14. Jurassic Park River Adventure: Before 11 a.m.
15. Me Ship, *The Olive:* Anytime
16. One Fish, Two Fish, Red Fish, Blue Fish: Before 10 a.m.
17. Popeye & Bluto's Blige-Rat Barges: Before 10:30 a.m.
18. *Poseidon's Fury! Escape from the Lost City:* After experiencing all the rides
19. Pteranodon Flyers: When there's no line
20. Storm Force Accelatron: Before 10:30 a.m.
21. Sylvester McMonkey: Before 10:30 a.m.
22. Triceratops Encounter: Before 11:30 a.m.

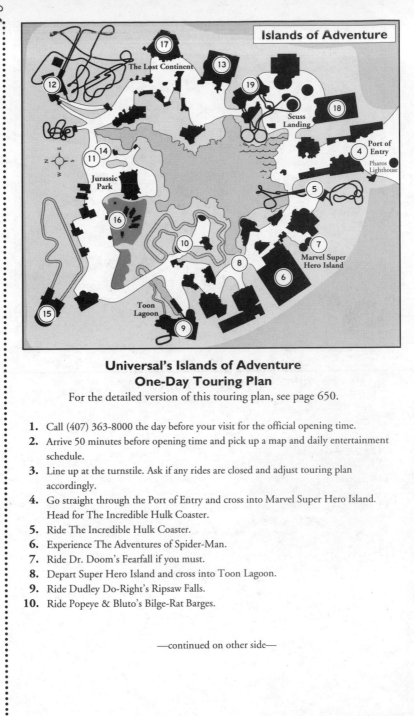

The Lost Continent

Seuss Landing

Port of Entry

Pharos Lighthouse

Jurassic Park

Marvel Super Hero Island

Toon Lagoon

Universal's Islands of Adventure
One-Day Touring Plan

For the detailed version of this touring plan, see page 650.

1. Call (407) 363-8000 the day before your visit for the official opening time.
2. Arrive 50 minutes before opening time and pick up a map and daily entertainment schedule.
3. Line up at the turnstile. Ask if any rides are closed and adjust touring plan accordingly.
4. Go straight through the Port of Entry and cross into Marvel Super Hero Island. Head for The Incredible Hulk Coaster.
5. Ride The Incredible Hulk Coaster.
6. Experience The Adventures of Spider-Man.
7. Ride Dr. Doom's Fearfall if you must.
8. Depart Super Hero Island and cross into Toon Lagoon.
9. Ride Dudley Do-Right's Ripsaw Falls.
10. Ride Popeye & Bluto's Bilge-Rat Barges.

—continued on other side—

789

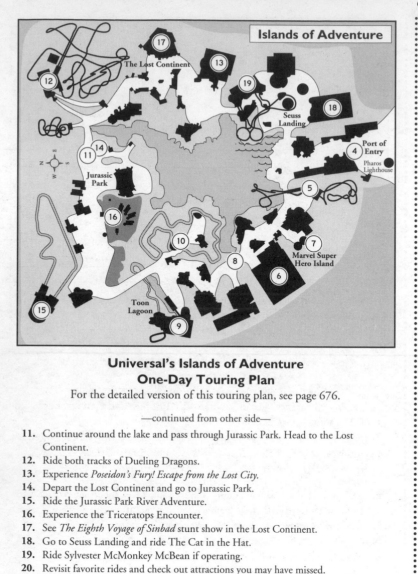

Universal's Islands of Adventure
One-Day Touring Plan

For the detailed version of this touring plan, see page 676.

—continued from other side—

11. Continue around the lake and pass through Jurassic Park. Head to the Lost Continent.
12. Ride both tracks of Dueling Dragons.
13. Experience *Poseidon's Fury! Escape from the Lost City*.
14. Depart the Lost Continent and go to Jurassic Park.
15. Ride the Jurassic Park River Adventure.
16. Experience the Triceratops Encounter.
17. See *The Eighth Voyage of Sinbad* stunt show in the Lost Continent.
18. Go to Seuss Landing and ride The Cat in the Hat.
19. Ride Sylvester McMonkey McBean if operating.
20. Revisit favorite rides and check out attractions you may have missed.

If you would like to express your opinion about Walt Disney World or this guidebook, complete the following survey and mail it to:

Unofficial Guide Reader Survey
P.O. Box 43673
Birmingham, AL 35243

Inclusive dates of your visit _____ Your Hometown _____
Your e-mail address _____

Members of your party:

	Person 1	Person 2	Person 3	Person 4	Person 5
Gender (M or F)					
Age					

How many times have you been to Walt Disney World? _____
On your most recent trip, where did you stay? _____

Concerning accommodations, on a scale with 100 best and 0 worst, how would you rate:

The quality of your room? _____ The value for the money? _____
The quietness of your room? _____ Check-in/checkout efficiency? _____
Shuttle service to the parks? _____ Swimming pool facilities? _____

Did you rent a car? _____ From whom? _____

Concerning your rental car, on a scale with 100 best and 0 worst, how would you rate:

Pickup processing efficiency? _____ Return processing efficiency? _____
Condition of the car? _____ Cleanliness of the car? _____
Airport shuttle efficiency? _____

Concerning your touring:

Who in your party was most responsible for planning the itinerary? _____
What time did you normally get started in the morning? _____
Did you usually arrive at the theme parks prior to opening? _____
Did you return to your hotel for rest during the day? _____
What time did you normally go to bed at night? _____

On a scale with 100 best and 0 worst, rate how the touring plans worked:

Park	Name of Plan	Rating
Magic Kingdom		
Epcot		
Animal Kingdom		
Disney-MGM		
Universal Studios		
Islds. of Adventure		

Concerning your dining experiences (also see WDW Restaurant Survey on following pages):

How many restaurant meals (including fast food) did you average per day? _____

How much (approximately) did your party spend on meals per day? _____

Favorite restaurant outside of Walt Disney World? _____

Did you buy this guide: Before leaving? _____ While on your trip? _____

How did you hear about this guide?

Loaned or recommended by a friend _____   Radio or TV _____

Newspaper or magazine _____   Bookstore salesperson _____

Just picked it out on my own _____   Library _____

Internet _____

What other guidebooks did you use on this trip? _____

_____

On the 100 best and 0 worst scale, how would you rate them? _____

_____

Using the same scale, how would you rate the *Unofficial Guide?* _____

Are *Unofficial Guides* readily available in bookstores in your area? _____

Have you used other *Unofficial Guides?* _____ Which one(s)? _____

Comments about your Walt Disney World vacation or about the *Unofficial Guide:* _____

_____

_____

_____

_____

_____

_____

_____

_____

_____

_____